TOWER OF THE WINDS
UNIVERSITY OF OXFORD IN TRANSITION

Works on paper by Weimin He

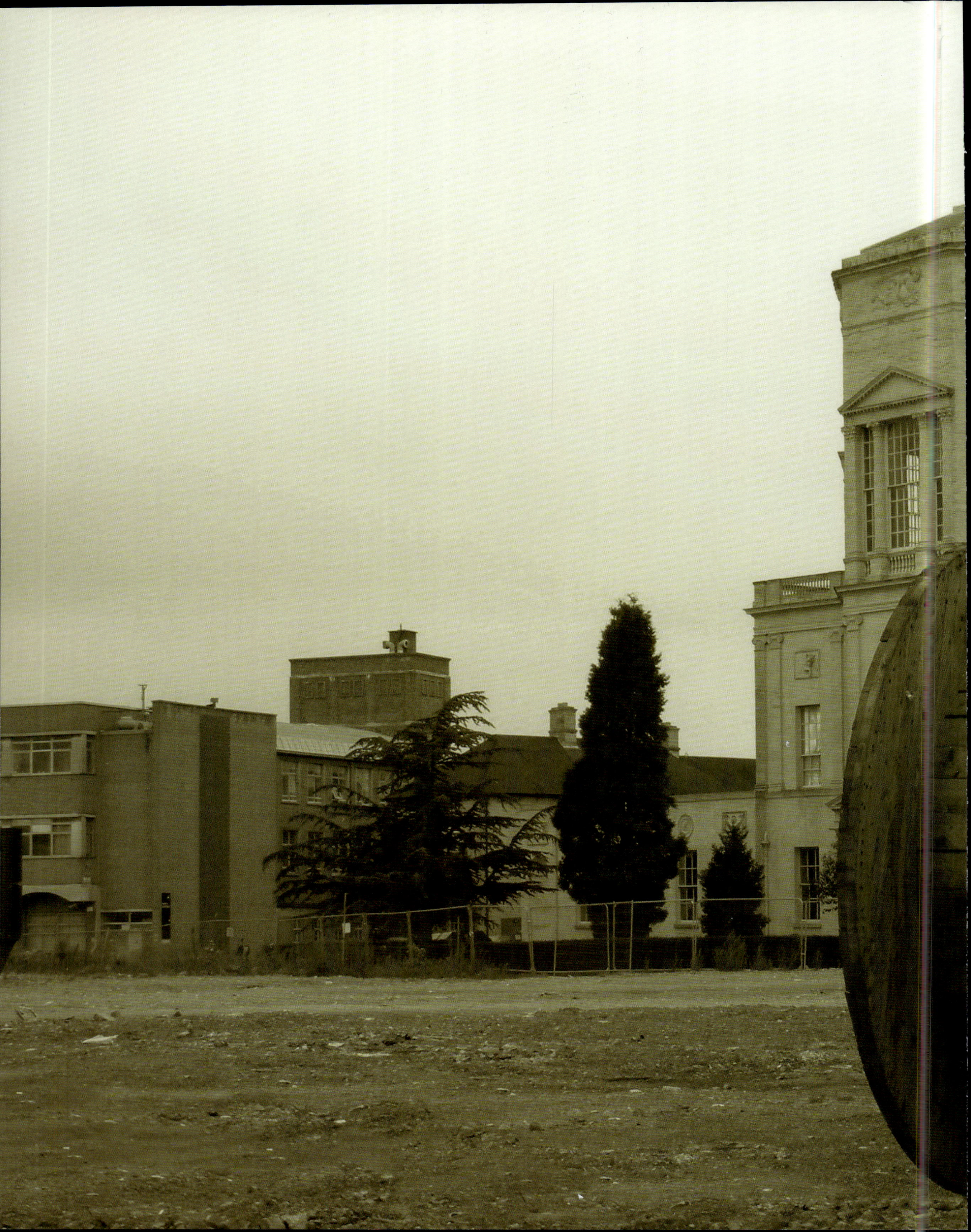

Tower of the Winds
University of Oxford in transition

Works on paper by Weimin He

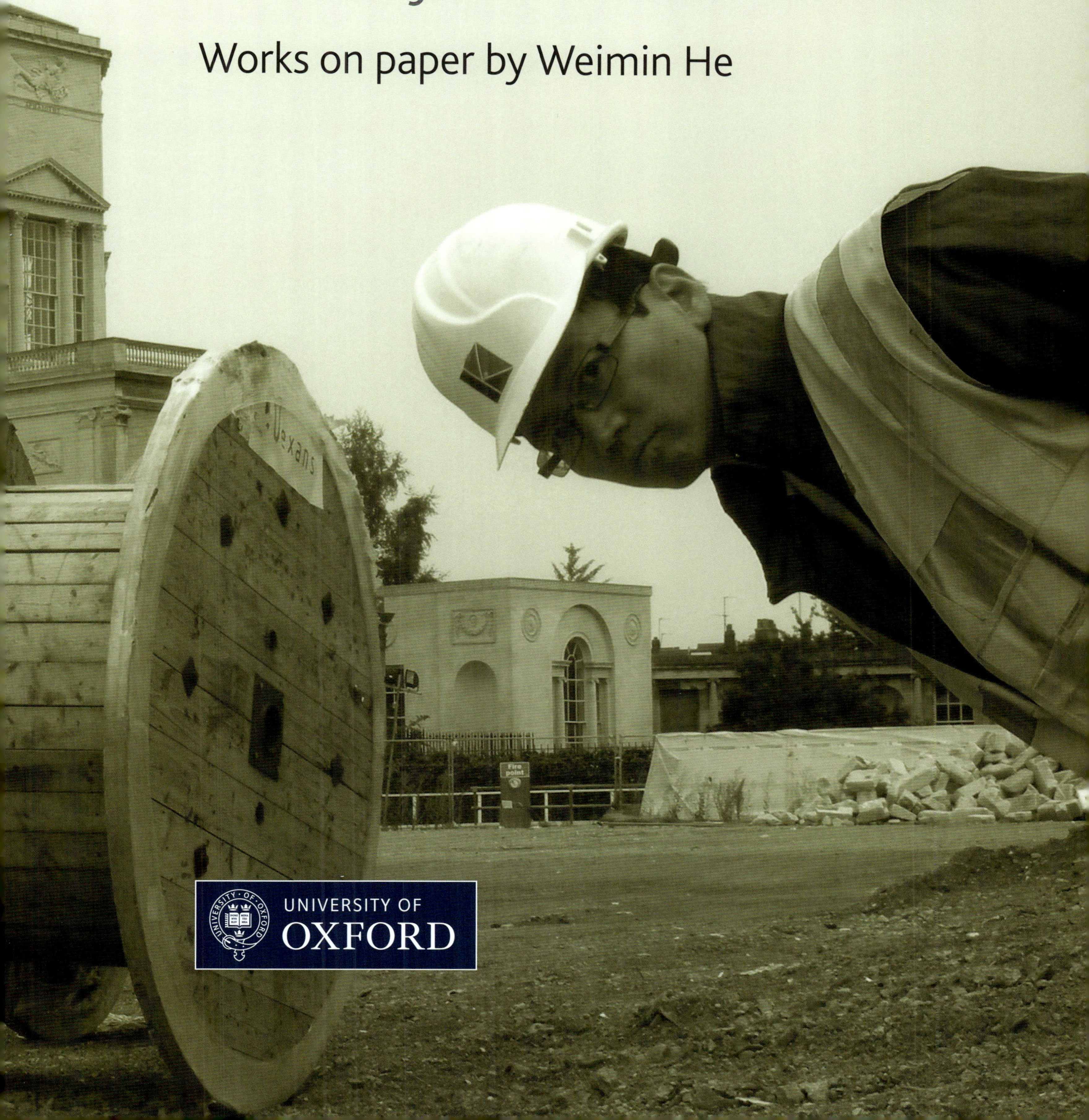

UNIVERSITY OF
OXFORD

TOWER OF THE WINDS
UNIVERSITY OF OXFORD IN TRANSITION
WORKS ON PAPER BY WEIMIN HE

British Library Cataloguing in Publications Data
A catalogue record for this book is available from the British Library
ISBN: 978-1-78926-952-9

Text editor: Catherine Bradley
Designer: Stephen Hebron
Photographer: Kinga Lubowiecka

Printed and bound in Malta by Gutenberg Press

UNIVERSITY OF OXFORD

AUTHOR'S NOTE

In this book, as in previous publications, my name is generally given in the Westernised style, as Weimin He. However, in her essay Anne Farrer refers to several Chinese artists, including myself, and has thus used the correct order for Chinese names, with the surname first: He Weimin.

To my parents

獻給我的父親母親

Weimin He

Weimin He (DPhil/RE) was born in Heilongjiang, Northeast China, in 1964. He studied art from an early age and worked as a professional artist in Heilongjiang Museum of Art before coming to the UK in 1999. He was awarded a DPhil at the University of Ulster in 2005. In the same year he moved to Oxford, where he worked as Christensen Fellow of Chinese Painting at the Ashmolean Museum until 2008 and then worked for eight months as artist-in-residence at the Museum. From 2009 to 2015 he worked as artist-in-residence at the Oxford University Estates Services. Weimin He is a Fellow of the Royal Society of Painter Printmakers, a member of the Chinese Artists' Association and a Trustee of the Muban Educational Trust. He is also a life drawing tutor at the Ruskin School of Art, Oxford University.

Contributors

REBECCA BAXTER is Head of Development and Alumni Relations at Kellogg College, University of Oxford.

ANNE FARRER is Senior Research Fellow at the Muban Educational Trust, and Consultant in Chinese Art at Sotheby's Institute of Art – London.

SIR JOHN HOOD was Vice-Chancellor of the University of Oxford from 2004 to 2009, and is Chairman of the Rhodes Trustees.

ISOBEL HUGHES is Director of Operations, Oxford University Estates Service.

RICHARD OVENDEN is Bodley's Librarian, University of Oxford.

Contents

Foreword

Sir John Hood

The University of Oxford's architectural heritage and built environment are magnificent. Created over the course of many centuries, they provide their own unique inspiration for all who live and work in them, as well as for the many people who visit and otherwise encounter them.

The University itself is a dynamic, international, scholarly institution, where research and teaching opportunities continue to grow and evolve. In their turn these have created demand for the renovation of existing facilities and the creation of new. During the past two decades that demand has become increasingly intense. In response new buildings have been built and others, many hidden away out of the sight of passers-by, have been refurbished – often with financial support from old members and friends of the University and its Colleges.

Construction of major academic facilities represents a significant challenge at the best of times. In an historic University and City, such challenges are magnified at every stage: design and planning, demolition, procurement, logistics, manpower, physical construction, fit-out and commissioning. It is a contractual, time constrained, risk-sharing operation between client and contractor. Both arcane and technologically advanced processes are involved. They can be messy and dangerous as well as highly complex, requiring advanced skills, deep experience and wise judgements. Ultimately, successful construction is the product of the people who make it happen, especially those who are 'on the job'.

This compelling book contains the artist Weimin He's visual record of the creation of recent buildings at the University, as well as one at Somerville College. A multi-award winning Chinese woodcut printmaker and ink painter, Weimin was a Christensen Fellow in Chinese Painting at the Ashmolean Museum from 2005 to 2008, its artist-in-residence from 2008 to 2009 and the University Estates Department's artist-in-residence from 2009 to 2015. Those tenures covered the renovation and extension of the Ashmolean, the first phase of the development of the Radcliffe Quadrant, Somerville College's abutting student accommodation building and the refurbishment of the New Bodleian Library, now renamed the Weston Library after its major benefactor.

Weimin has successfully set out to capture the essence of construction – the people and materials as well as the processes of demolishing, digging and building. He captures beautifully the tactile nature of construction work and the hard-wrought experience of its exponents. Many of the works are framed by the wider historic built environment. For instance, the Tower of the Winds is situated on the northern border of the Radcliffe Quadrant, within the estate of Green Templeton College. Prominent in a number of the works herein, the Tower gives its name to this book.

Tower of the Winds is an important and impressive record, the outcome of visionary partnership between an ancient, yet in many respects an intensely modern institution, and an exceptional artist. I commend it.

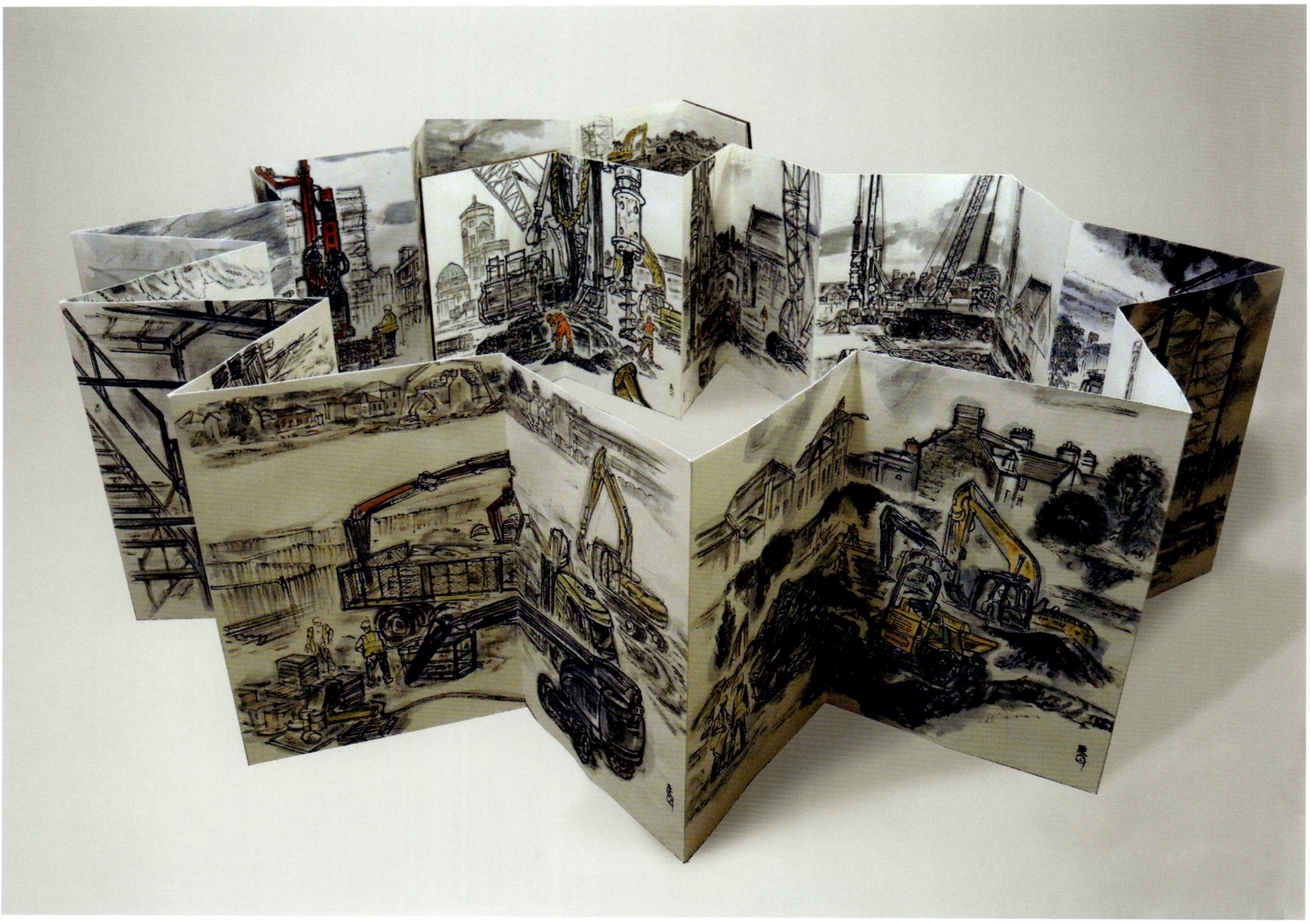

Transformation in Representation

Anne Farrer

Opposite: fig.1 He Weimin Somerville College student accommodation and Mathematical Institute albums. 2011. Brush and ink; colour added later to monochrome painting. Album leaves made of *xuan* paper.

This publication celebrates the creative record made by the artist He Weimin 何為民 (also written as Weimin He) during his six-year residency for the University of Oxford Estates Services from 2009 to 2015. The imaginative decision to appoint him as artist-in-residence to document important changes in Oxford's historic buildings has involved the artist in adapting his expressive and technical range for pictorial documentation of the buildings, machinery and individuals involved. The versatility of He Weimin's background in the creative arts, academic research and museum work will have greatly enhanced his approach to the task of documenting these major projects in Oxford.

Most important in equipping He Weimin for this project has been his fine art education in China. The systems of Chinese art academy education, founded on early twentieth-century European models, stress technical training in drawing and sketching as an integral part of fine art courses. Trained to draw models in the academy studio, sketching in the countryside and in the urban context, Chinese artists from Xu Beihong 徐悲鴻 (1895–1953) to Xu Bing 徐冰 (b.1955) have produced an impressive collection of drawings and sketches, now part of museum collections worldwide. The art academy environment that He Weimin entered in the 1980s was taught by professors who had followed socialist realist models in their creative work, portraying images of workers in industry and agriculture as well as national minority peoples. He Weimin and his contemporaries, studying in China in the 1980s and 1990s, gradually developed individual artistic voices, often relying on a re-examination of historical models and aspects of China's pre-modern culture. He Weimin's technical and artistic training has provided a valuable foundation for developing his creative vision in representational work for the current project.

Scenes in monochrome

He Weimin's work, carried out over the six-year period of his artist-in-residence, has resulted in more than one thousand images displaying a range of stylistic variation in the use of line and colour. The artist's initial drawings during this period consisted of line drawings with images using felt-tip pen, fine ink pen and the Chinese brush on Chinese *xuan* paper. They were made on both single sheets and in folded album form, and on European cartridge paper (fig.1).

The earliest works of He Weimin's residency document the demolition of the Radcliffe Infirmary buildings between January and July 2009. These drawings, made with felt-tip pen, represent the demolition site surrounded by the historic buildings of Oxford's city centre. Drawn with a black line of even thickness and density, the vistas are portrayed with minute attention to detail, with parallel lines and repeated forms (see cat.2, p.38). This set of drawings contrast black line against the white background of the paper, presenting a strongly graphic rhythm throughout the work. Many are signed by the artist with the characters *Weimin* in Chinese seal script. In later drawings of this series, produced in summer 2009, He Weimin gives a stronger visual focus to the central image, the giant piles of debris of the demolition site, by varying the use of straight line and linear patterns (see cat.25, p.50).

The majority of monochrome works made by He Weimin during his period of residency are executed with the Chinese brush and ink on paper. The complex techniques of handling the brush and the use of Chinese ink are learned from a young age, forming the basis of Chinese calligraphy and its related application in painting. The use of calligraphic brushwork for painting on paper first emerged in eleventh-century China. It became central to scholar-amateur painting from the thirteenth century, when the leading master Zhao Mengfu 趙孟頫 (1254–1322) described elements of landscape representation in terms of different calligraphic styles. Although painters of the scholar-amateur tradition did represent particular geographical locations and scenic spots in their work, they usually produced images with freehand brushwork in abbreviated style, accompanied by inscriptions containing literary or historical references. By contrast, descriptive representation in pre-modern Chinese painting was associated with the work of professional artists who painted on silk, often at the imperial court, recording architecture with the formal *jiehua* 界畫 (ruled-line painting) style. He Weimin's works combine the sensitivity and variety of strokes common to the scholar-amateur tradition with a high level of representational and narrative description previously associated with the technical paintings of Chinese professional artists.

He Weimin continues the use of soft linear brushwork that featured in work carried out during his Ashmolean Museum residency (2008–9). In a detailed painting showing the construction of the Andrew Wiles Building, occupied by the Mathematical Institute (see cat.143, p.127), He Weimin gives a view of the new multi-storey building in soft, highly controlled freehand brushwork. Behind the building site rises a crane, and the Radcliffe Observatory and distant landscape are shown in lighter ink in the background. The artist has added broad, quickly applied diagonal brushstrokes to the interior of the building and to the side of the newly constructed wall; he has used an expressive calligraphic technique known as *feibai* 飛白 (flying white) in which the hairs of the inked brush separate, leaving white spaces. Other simpler compositions within this series include a view of men operating a pile-driver in a sunken area of the Andrew Wiles Building construction site, with the ground level

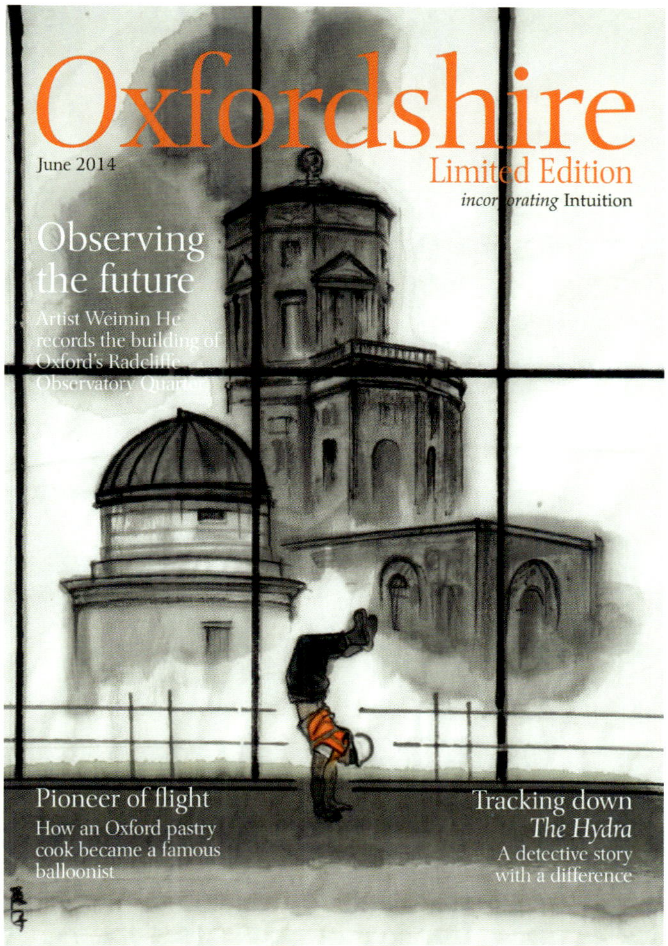

Fig.2 He Weimin. Job done. 2013. The work is shown here on the cover of the *Oxfordshire Limited Edition*, published by *Oxford Times*, June 2014.

here depicted at the top of the painting (see cat.137, p.121). This painting, like many others produced during He Weimin's residency, was initially painted in outline, the colour being applied at a later stage. He Weimin's keen observation of architectural structures is shown in the view of construction workers replacing old roof timbers with new ones as they refurbish the Radcliffe Infirmary building (see cat.133, p.118).

The majority of He Weimin's work during his period of residency records scenes of construction. Also included here, however, are more intimate views which made an impression on the artist as he wandered through the construction sites. A painting of the debris on the Radcliffe Observatory Quarter after demolition captures the sense of desolation, as building debris mixes with the remnants of former structures, inscribed with company names (see cat.84, p.77). In contrast a scene at the edge of the Radcliffe Observatory Quarter construction site depicts an oasis of plants and flowers close to the excavation equipment in the background (see cat.85, p.80). A figure of a construction worker, his safety tabard picked out in orange gouache, is observed doing a handstand in a moment of off-duty playfulness in the Andrew Wiles Building construction site (see cat.162, p.142); the action takes place in front of a large window with the Radcliffe Observatory in the background (fig.2). A view

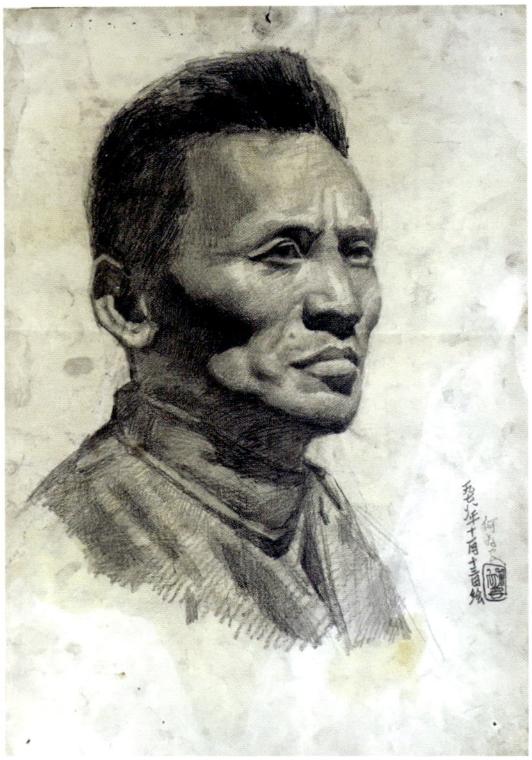

Fig. 3 He Weimin. He Jixing, father of the artist. 1978. Pencil on paper. Collection of the artist. Paper size: 39.2 × 27.3 cm.

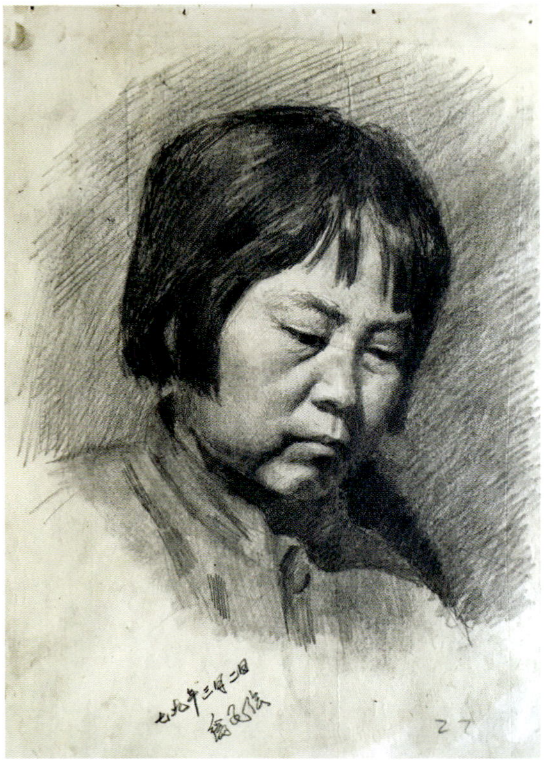

Fig.4 He Weimin. Lü Lilian, mother of the artist. 1979. Pencil on paper. Collection of the artist. Paper size: 29.5 × 22 cm.

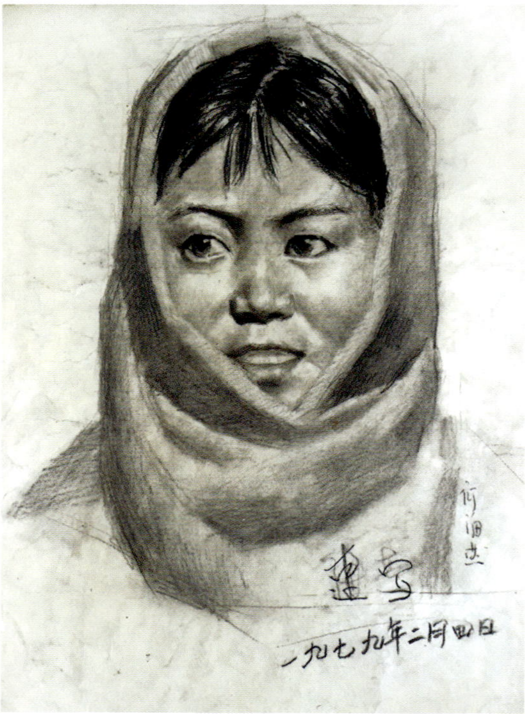

Fig.5 He Weimin. He Haiyan, elder sister of the artist. 1979. Charcoal pencil on paper. Collection of the artist. Paper size: 39.2 × 27.3 cm.

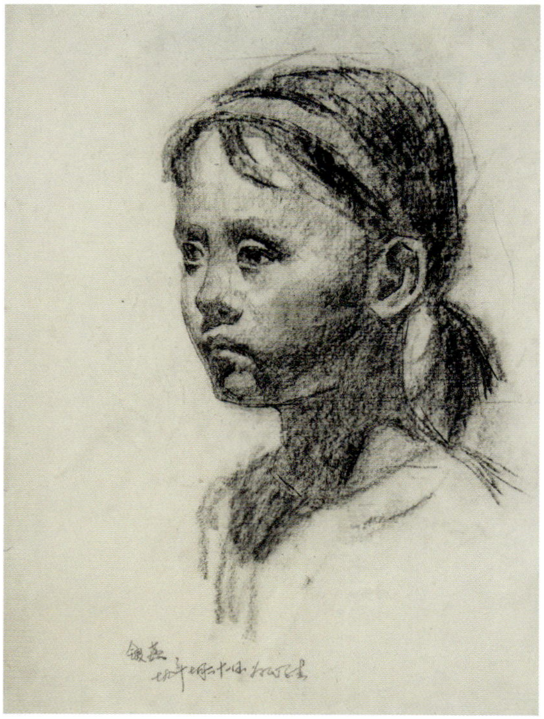

Fig.6 He Weimin. He Yinyan, younger sister of the artist. 1979. Charcoal pencil on paper. Collection of the artist. Paper size: 39.2 × 27.3 cm.

of the changing room of the Blavatnik School of Government construction site shows the outer garments of the builders hanging up and their boots and shoes discarded, all skilfully represented with He Weimin's angular brushwork (see cat.49, p.61).

Figure drawing and portraiture

He Weimin's artist-in-residence work included a large volume of figure drawings depicting portraits and figure groups. He Weimin's experience of figure drawing began in his childhood and teenage years, when he drew self-portraits in pencil, made sketches of political figures and copied propaganda posters (figs 3–8). During his undergraduate years at Harbin Normal University (1982–6), he studied life drawing as part of his principal studies in oil painting (fig.9). In 1989 the artist made a series of line drawings of individuals from farming communities in the distant northern Shaanxi province of northern China, known as the Shanbei 陕北 region (figs 10 and 11). He developed an interest in making sketches of city life in China in the early 1990s and continued to produce sketches following a move to Belfast in 1999.

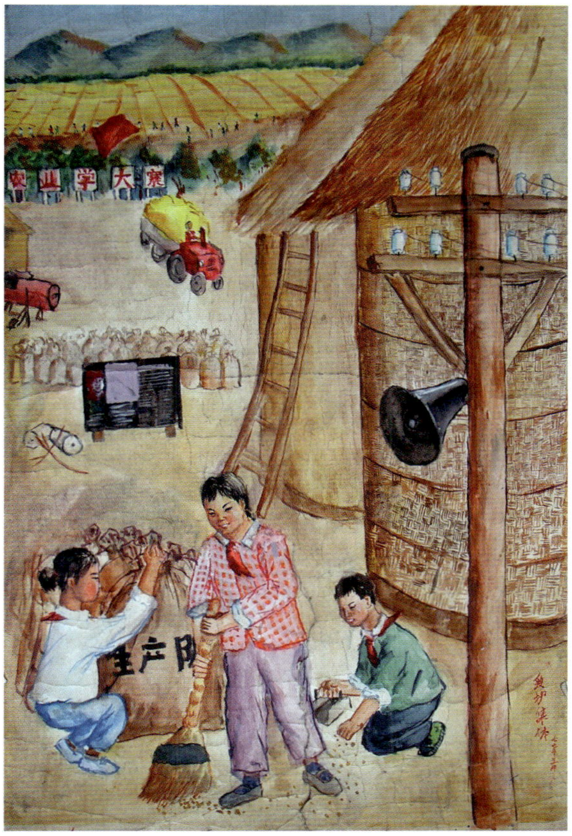

Fig.7 He Weimin. Treasure every grain. 1977. Watercolour on paper. Collection of the artist. Paper size: 43.9 × 30.8 cm.

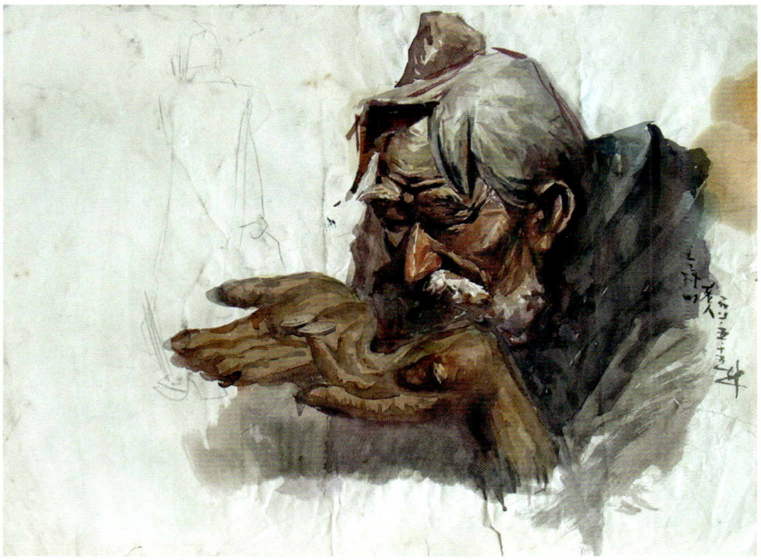

Fig.8 He Weimin. Begging elderly man. 1981. Watercolour on paper. Collection of the artist. Paper size: 27 × 39 cm.

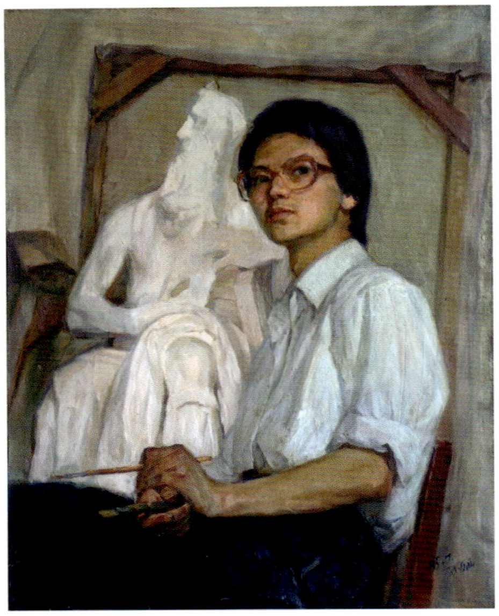

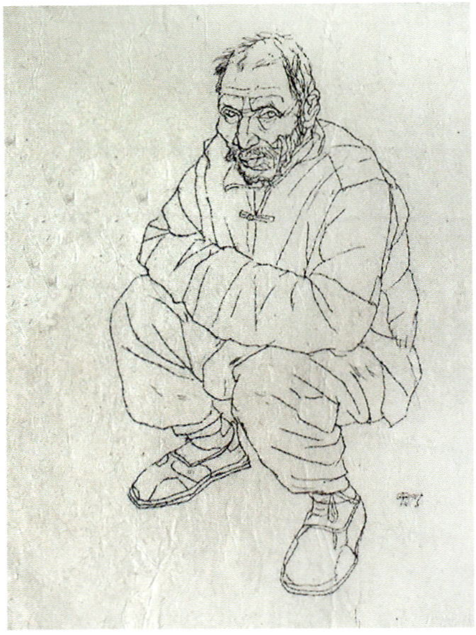

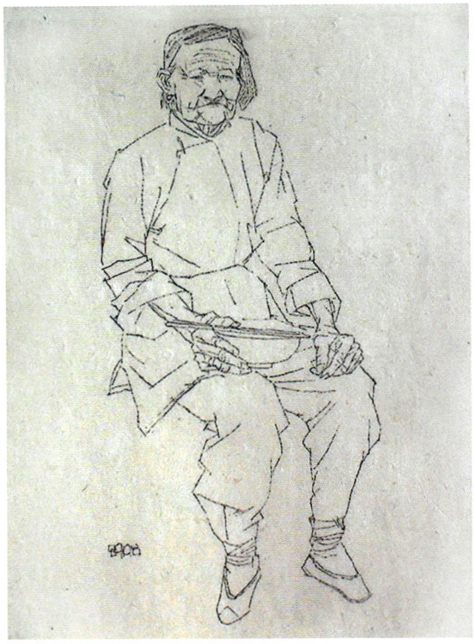

Fig.9 He Weimin. Self-portrait. 1985. Oil painting on canvas. Collection of the artist. Canvas size: 84 × 68 cm.

Figs 10 and 11 He Weimin. People from northern Shaanxi province. 1989. Pen and ink on hemp paper. Private collection.

This twenty-year experience in observing and recording details of daily life formed the basis of He Weimin's artist-in-residence work in Oxford. Here he had privileged access to sites associated with the rebuilding of the Ashmolean and the Radcliffe Observatory Quarter construction projects beginning in 2009. He attended project meetings, recording in pen and ink drawings the facial expressions and informal posture of figures seated round the table (see cat.29, p.52). Other more formal portraits, such as those of Project Leader Steve Hollard (see cat.231, p.180) and Project Director Mike Morris (see cat.230, p.180), both employed by the Laing O'Rourke Construction Company, are among the finest of He Weimin's brush and ink portraits in this project. Informal figure drawings in pen and ink include a drawing of the plasterer Elliott Carter (see cat.216, p.175). In other drawings of construction workers relaxing in the canteen, He Weimin makes use of an engaging, cartoon-like style of drawing (see cat.30, p.52).

The use of colour

From 2014 He Weimin returned to his earlier line drawings to add tone and colour. This process began by his addition of colour to drawings reproduced on the hoardings around the Radcliffe Observatory Quarter construction site (fig.12). He Weimin subsequently experimented with the use of colour to create different expressive effects. For a Chinese artist aware of his artistic heritage, the use of colour in painting would have evoked clear associations with specific categories of painting, including Buddhist painting and the court painting of pre-modern China, as well as socialist realist painting of the post-1950s. His earlier experience in the use of colour had been in in oil painting during his undergraduate studies, but he had also painted on silk, which involved an exacting technical approach. Prior to He Weimin's artist-in-residency projects in Oxford, he produced a set of ten small paintings on silk entitled *Belfast Diary* (2003–7); each was minutely painted in ink and colour and inspired by the detail and technical focus of Song dynasty (960–1279) court painting (fig.13). These paintings were time-consuming, each taking between one week and a year to finish. The exacting technique required the outline to be applied at least three times; the colour also required repeated applications to achieve

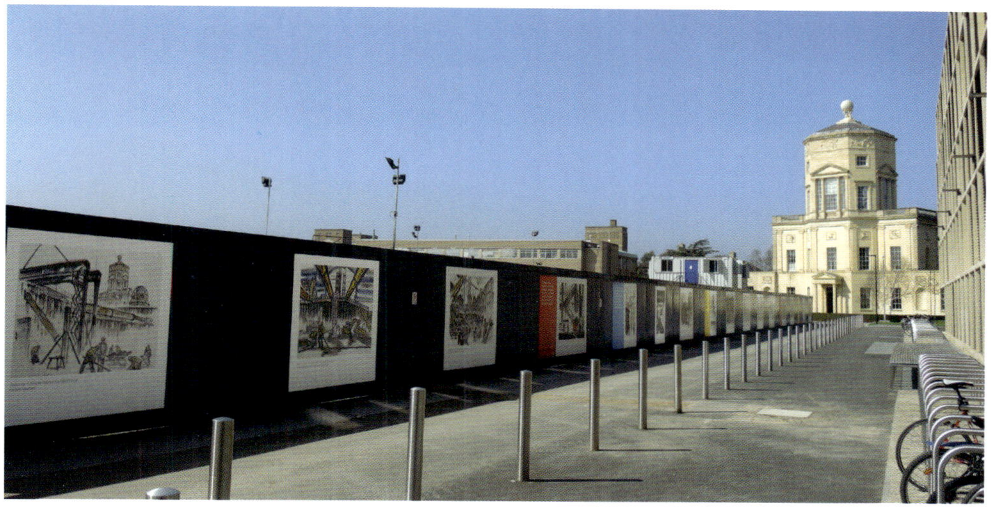

Fig.12 Hoardings around the construction site; the Radcliffe Observatory is in the background. 19 June 2015. Photograph by He Weimin.

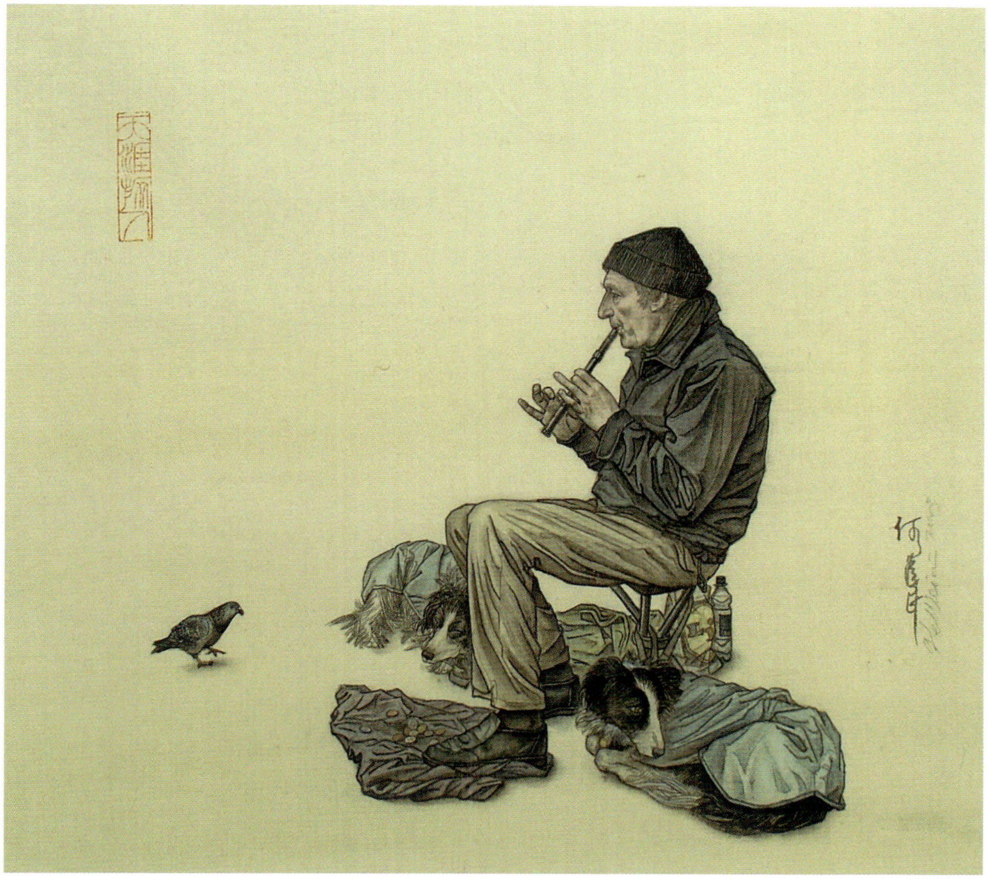

Fig.13 He Weimin. **Belfast Diary – Street Musician 1**. 2003. Ink and colour on sized silk. Private collection. Silk size: 21 × 29 cm.

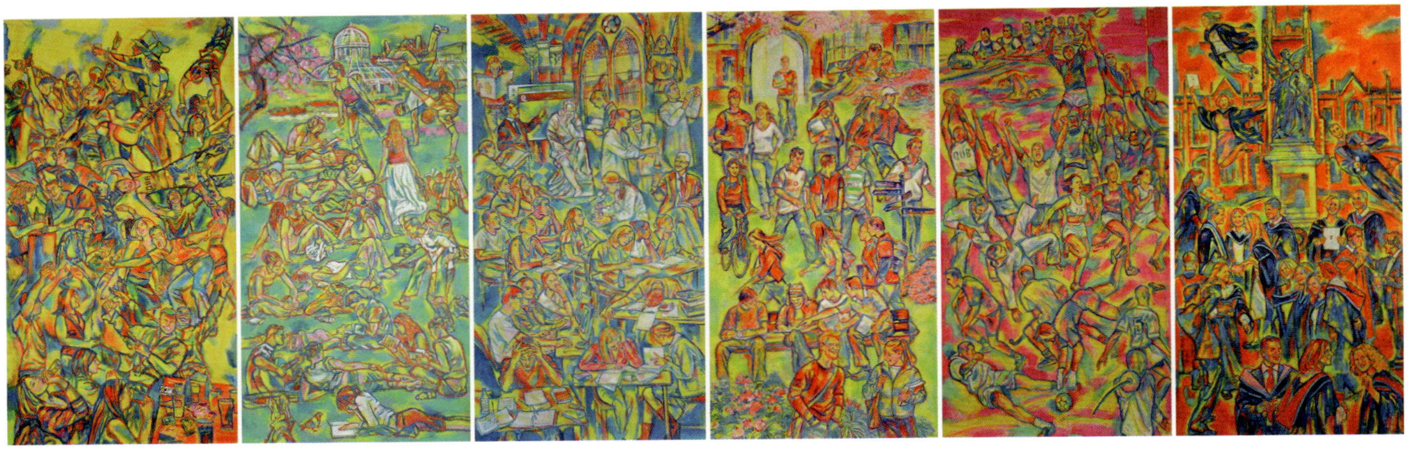

Fig.14 He Weimin. **University life.** 2004. Set of six paintings, Chinese mineral watercolour and gouache on *xuan* paper. Collection of the Queen's University, Belfast. Each painting: 180 × 82 cm.

the depth of tone. In 2004 Queen's University, Belfast commissioned a set of six paintings from He Weimin for the students' union building. In these paintings He Weimin uses vivid, contrasting colours in a modernist manner to give energy to the scenes of student life (fig.14). Experience of the varied approaches to colour in these and other paintings would have contributed to He Weimin's creative use of colour in his artist-in-residency paintings.

The challenge for He Weimin in adding colour to his drawings was to extend the use of colour in innovative ways to enhance his earlier line drawings. In many paintings He Weimin added small amounts of colour to scenes of construction sites, giving tone and realism to particular focal points. In a painting of the Andrew Wiles Building under construction, for instance, blue wash behind the image of the pile-driver gives it focus and emphasis, while yellow and red gouache, added to details of the construction workers' clothes and the bodywork of the machinery, serves to enhance the representational interest of the scene (see cat.137, p.121). Elsewhere He Weimin reworks earlier paintings by adding a substantial amount of colour. The appearance of a composition showing the Radcliffe Observatory Quarter after demolition, originally painted in 2010. is reworked four years later with the addition of a band of grey inkwash to darken the sky. Red and blue are added to the central mound of debris and the foreground is littered with coloured items of debris and building rubble. The reworked composition has the appearance of a mountain-top, surrounded by mist as if part of a landscape, and the scene has a gloomy and foreboding appearance (see cat.84, p.77).

He Weimin transforms his compositions by adding non-realistic colour, taking the paintings far beyond their original documentary function. He Weimin playfully represents an interior construction scene within the Andrew Wiles Building site with contrasting colours of blue, red and orange, representing the vertical, diagonal and horizontal members of the construction plant (see cat.160, p.140). This image is clear reference to a prize-winning woodblock print by Song Enhou 宋恩厚 (b.1936) entitled *Five Colours, Six Hues* (*Wuyan liuse* 五顏六色) (1984), which represents a schematised view of a factory interior using bright colours. In a further composition portraying the subterranean level of the Blavatnik School of Government, the artist uses patches of yellow, blue and red in a non-specific manner to brighten and lift the ambiance of the painting (see cat.173, p.152). In other paintings He Weimin gives his compositions a sense of dramatic contrast through the addition of bright colour and heavy inkwash. In a depiction of sunset at the Blavatnik School of Government, both the foreground and part of the sky are overpainted with dark inkwash, giving a gloomy view of approaching evening. This in turn is lightened and focused by an orange band of sky representing the brightness of the setting sun (see cat.168, p.147).

In a few of He Weimin's paintings produced in 2013, the artist uses a different technique known as 'boneless' (*mogu* 沒骨) painting, used in Chinese landscape and flower painting. In these works he defines the composition and elements of the paintings with colour-wash alone: there is no initial outline. In a composition showing cyclists passing the Weston Library site on a snowy day, the lack of linear detail and the pooled colour showing the stone face of the Weston Library intensify the emptiness and lack of clarity of the wintery scene (see cat.257, p.191).

The climax of the work of He Weimin's residency may be found in his group of paintings enhanced with layers of bright colour, all produced for the Weston Library project. Here the artist was inspired by the use of colour both in European painting and in Buddhist painting from Chinese Central Asia. He had observed the use of colour in works by postimpressionist artists, particularly those of Cézanne, which he had examined at the Ashmolean Museum. An additional source of inspiration was the mineral pigments and use of line in Buddhist wall-paintings of the Sui (581–618) and Tang (618–907) dynasties from the Caves of the Thousand Buddhas near Dunhuang. He Weimin's own paintings, made late in his residency, began with a fine outline drawing of the construction workers, together with a carefully defined structure of interior and exterior scenes. Layers of colour were then applied in distinct linear and rectangular dabs, bringing texture and movement to the painting and creating compositions of great vibrancy. In his work *On the Broad*, for example, initially painted in 2014 and completed in 2016, the fine portraits of the two off-duty construction workers on the right are shown looking towards the red excavator in the top left-hand side of the painting (see cat.272, p.203). Colour greatly enhances the realistic appearance of the two seated men, but elsewhere its use in patches of yellow, red and blue is imaginary rather than realistic: it has been applied to give focus and texture to the scene. The colour of the roadway passing in front of the seated figures is painted with linear strokes, giving movement through the painting.

Another painting belonging to this group, *Blue mist*, was similarly painted in 2013 and completed in 2016 (see cat.271, p.202). It shows a scaffolder lifting a pole high up on a scaffolding platform with a view of the Oxford city centre below. Exact colour carefully added to the image of the scaffolder gives the impression of near-photographic realism. The colour elsewhere in the painting is used for dramatic effect. He Weimin's use of blue in this painting is imaginary, but it greatly enhances the height of the foreground scene and the appearance of the distant roadway with traffic far below. The tones of orange represent the honey-coloured limestone of Oxford's buildings. In this painting the artist deliberately overstates the luminosity of the colours as a means of enhancing the height, depth and drama of the scene.

Woodcuts

The artist's print as a category of fine art in China owes its existence to the Modern Woodcut Movement, a modernist art movement that began in the late 1920s. It was inspired and led by the writer and intellectual Lu Xun 魯迅 (1881–1936) who, following ideas embodied in the early twentieth-century Japanese *Sōsaku-hanga* movement, introduced the concept of the 'creative [woodblock] print' (*chuangzuo muke* 創作木刻). In this concept all creative processes, including drawing, cutting, printing and finishing, were carried out by the artist.

Lu Xun encouraged the young print artists who joined this movement to use the block cutter's knife with freedom, enhancing the spontaneous nature of the printed image. He believed that the artist's print could provide a new art form, cheap to produce and able to represent imagery accessible to all levels of society. Lu Xun introduced a wide range of print models from abroad, including German expressionist prints and prints by artists from Soviet Russia,

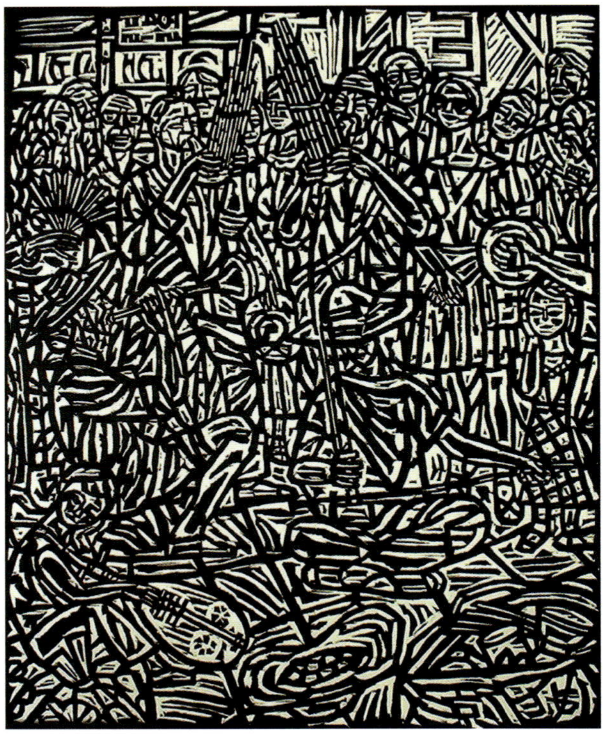

Fig.15 He Weimin. City Diary – Street musician. 1994. Woodcut printed with oil-based ink on *xuan* paper. Image size: 60 × 50 cm.

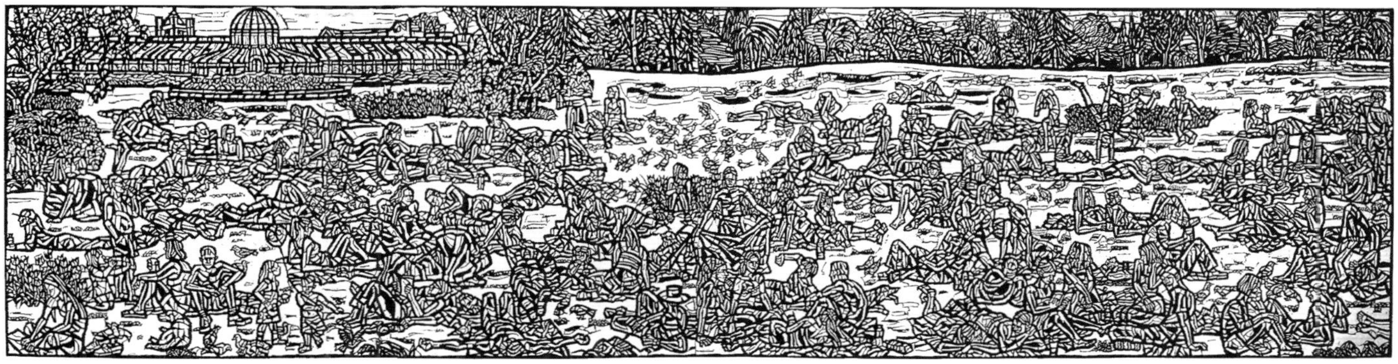

Fig.16 He Weimin. In the Sunshine. 2002. Woodcut printed with oil-based ink on *xuan* paper. Image size: 40 × 160 cm.

which resulted in images printed in black ink on paper – a category of prints that became known in China as *heibai muke* 黑白木刻 (black and white woodblock prints). The success of the 'creative print' in the 1930s and 1940s led to printmaking being nationally incorporated into the art academy curriculum from the 1950s. It was from these printmaking departments that the generations of print artists of the People's Republic of China have emerged.

He Weimin's interest in woodblock printing emerged gradually during his teenage years and in his twenties; it was independent of direct influence from the propagandist print movement associated with the Great Northern Wastes of his native Heilongjiang province. As a teenager He Weimin studied drawing with the print artist Li Ming 李明, often watching his teacher making woodcuts. He subsequently became interested in the vernacular woodblock prints he had seen in Jiangxi province and made a series of oil paintings based on the print images. In 1989, during a visit to northern Shaanxi, He Weimin became fascinated by the way in which images were represented with a series of connected lines in locally made papercuts. These inspired him to create drawings with interconnected lines, which he later developed into lithographs and woodcuts.

Printmaking became the specialism of He Weimin's Master's degree (1988–91) at the Lu Xun Academy of Fine Arts, in Shenyang, Liaoning province, where he studied under Lu Tan 路坦 (1934–89) and Quan Xianguang 全顯光 (b.1931). His woodcuts of the early to mid-1990s continued the representation of images within a network of lines. These were mostly black and white woodcuts printed in oil-based ink, with titles such as *City Diary – on the bus* (1993), *City Diary –Street Musician* (1994) and *City Diary – Tourists* (1994) (fig.15). He Weimin's doctoral studies at the University of Ulster in Belfast developed ideas of the relationship between the linear structure of seal impressions and woodblock printing. These ideas became the basis of the artist's personal woodcut style, in which relief images were represented within a network of broad and fine interconnected lines. One of He Weimin's major works made during this period was *In the Sunshine* (2002); it represented the joy of figures relaxing in the sun in the Belfast Botanical Gardens at a time when the political 'troubles' continued elsewhere in the city (fig.16).

Opposite:

Top left: fig.17 He Weimin. Sketch for *Tower of the Winds VII*. 2012. Pencil on cartridge paper. Image size: 36 × 26 cm; paper size: 42 × 29.7 cm.

Top right: fig.18 He Weimin. Preparation of the woodblock for *Tower of the Winds VII*. The pencil drawing was transferred to the woodblock, then drawn with brush and ink to create a clear image.

Bottom left: fig.19 He Weimin. Woodblock for *Tower of the Winds VII*: cutting in progress.

Bottom right: fig.20 He Weimin. Nearly completed woodblock for *Tower of the Winds VII*.

He Weimin made a series of seven woodcuts entitled *Tower of the Winds I–VII* between 2009 and 2012 as part of his artist-in-residency (see cats 282–290, pp.216–224). The title of the print series refers to the eighteenth-century Radcliffe Observatory, its form modelled on the famous octagonal 'Tower of the Winds' in Athens, built in 50 BC. This imposing landmark at the centre of the area of reconstruction in Oxford is the focal point of each print in He Weimin's 'Tower of the Winds' series. For He Weimin the woodcut is a significantly different process from that of the drawing or sketch in its technique and artistic expression. Whereas drawing is a relatively immediate means of recording, images represented in the woodcut medium develop gradually, through a process of deliberation, to devise the nature of the linear forms within the composition. The woodblock used for each print was a culmination of a number of stages, beginning with a soft pencil drawing and culminating in the strong graphic lines of the finished block, cut in plywood (figs 17–20). In He Weimin's 'Tower of the Winds' print series, each print presents an assembly of architectural and sculptural images juxtaposed with dynamic – and sometimes violent – scenes of the construction process. In *Tower of the Winds I* (2009), the distant Radcliffe Observatory shown in the top right-hand corner is balanced by the small figures of three construction workers in the bottom left-hand corner (see cat.282, p.216). The central area of the print is dominated by powerful angular lines filled with rough ink tone, representing the complex processes of change involved in the building project. He Weimin's bold treatment and emphatic contrast of black and white in this series are a departure from the more detailed linear structures of his earlier woodcuts; they present a new, semi-abstract mode of graphic expression.

The large oeuvre produced by He Weimin during the six-year period of his artist-in-residency in Oxford represents an impressive visual record of construction projects and a finely observed record of the personnel and activities involved. This project has provided He Weimin with an outstanding opportunity to develop his creative talent in different media. It has resulted in a compelling and evocative body of work that extends far beyond the boundaries of mere representation.

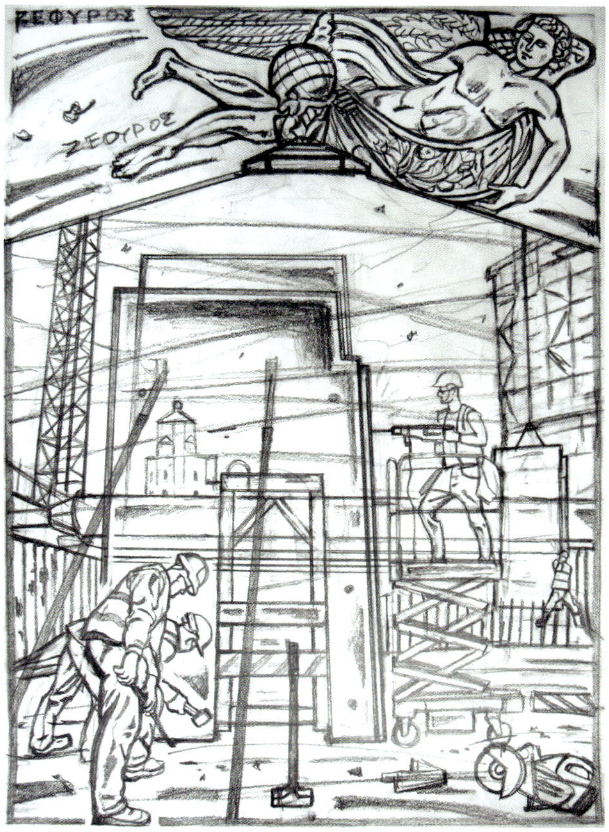
ΖΕΦΥΡΟΣ

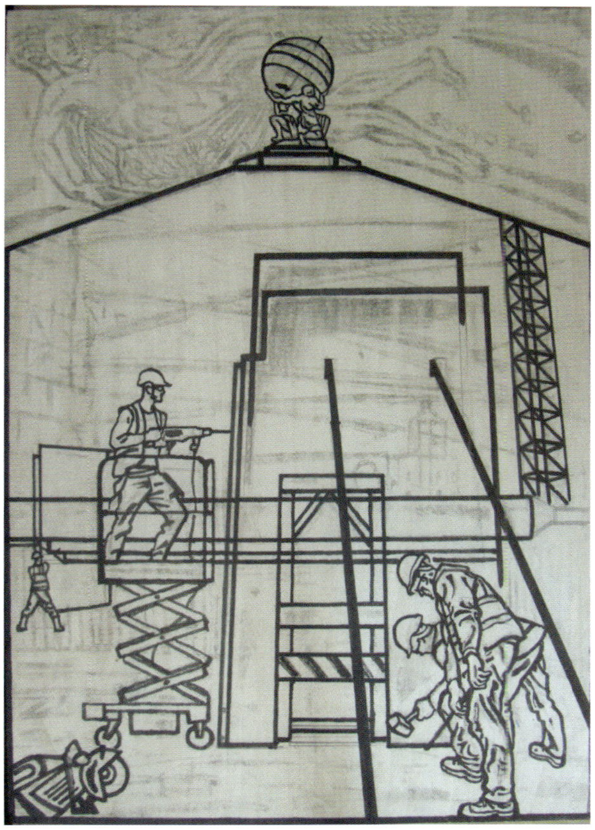

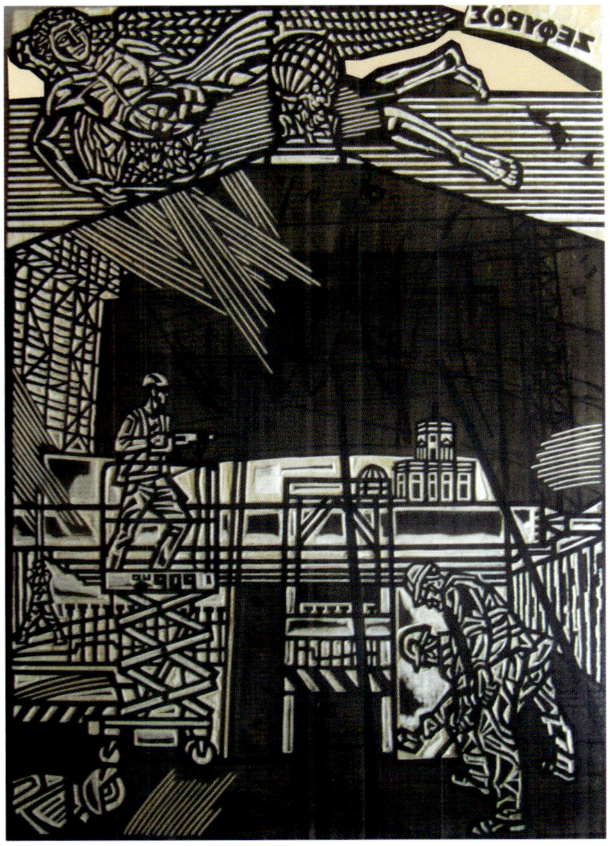

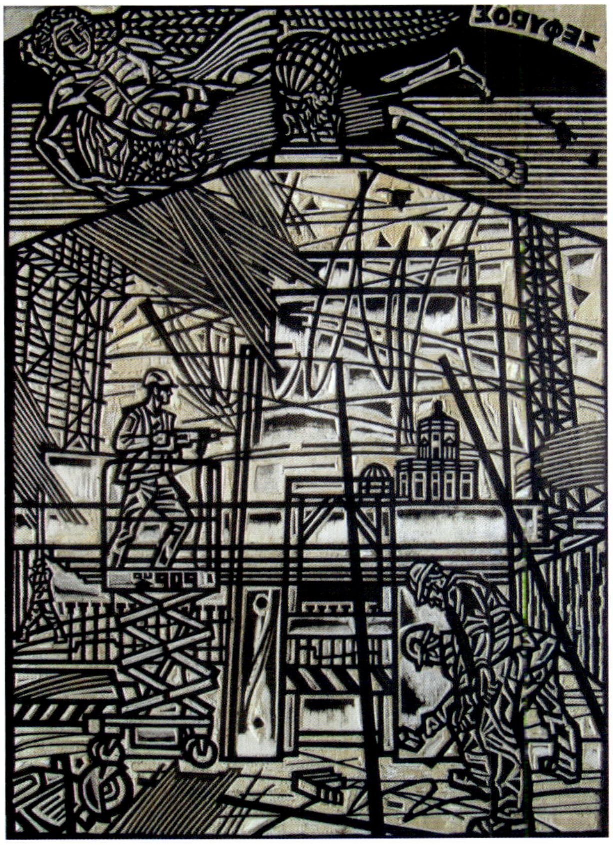

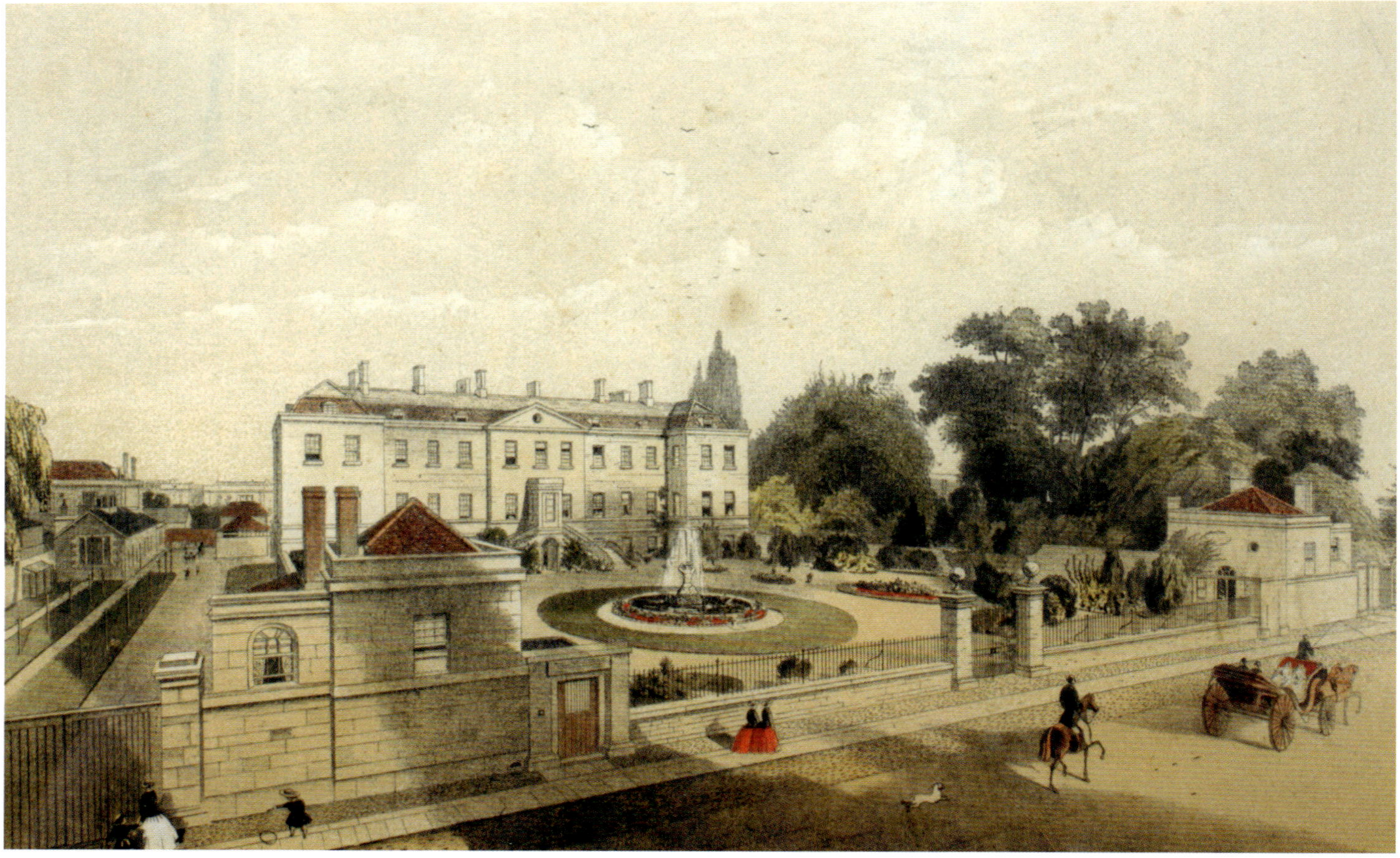

The Radcliffe Observatory Quarter site and the Weston Library

Isobel Hughes and Rebecca Baxter

Opposite: fig.21 The Radcliffe Infirmary from Woodstock Road, 1863/65. Hand-coloured print. Courtesy of Oxfordshire Health Archives.

Over the last 800 years the colleges and the University of Oxford have played a significant role in shaping the architecture and layout of the city.

Buildings such as the Bodleian Library and the Radcliffe Camera were built to complement the work of the colleges. It was not until the mid-nineteenth century, however, that the first large areas of University buildings began to spring up. In 1850 the establishment of the new Honours School of Natural Science led to the development of the Science Area and the Keble Triangle. The decision to build the New Bodleian Library in Broad Street in the 1930s demonstrated the University's commitment to the city centre. Over the course of the last 150 years the University estate has continued to expand within the city, following an increase in academic activities and administrative functions that could not be accommodated within the collegiate structure. As a consequence, much of the core University estate is located within central Oxford.

With the constraints of a compact city centre the Radcliffe Infirmary site on Woodstock Road was identified as a potential parcel of land. In March 2003 the NHS sold the site to the University.

A brief history of the Radcliffe Observatory Quarter site

Dr John Radcliffe played a pivotal role in the development of Oxford, albeit posthumously through a large bequest to the University. The son of an attorney, Radcliffe had acquired a fortune as a private London doctor; the rich and famous, including royalty, were among his patients. He always maintained that his success sprang from his Oxford education, and when he died in 1714 he made a number of bequests to the University, most notably £40,000 to create a new library, now known as the Radcliffe Camera. The residue of Radcliffe's estate was to be used by his trustees for 'such charitable objects as they in their discretion think best'. The first such charitable object in Oxford was the creation of the Radcliffe Infirmary, and the second the Radcliffe Observatory.

The Radcliffe Trustees released funds for the construction of the Infirmary, which commenced in 1759, and gave an annual grant towards its operation. The architect for the new building was Stiff Leadbetter, one of the most successful architect-builders of the 1750s–60s, who presented his plans to the Trustees on 8 March 1759. However, Leadbetter died before the work was finished and John Sanderson oversaw its completion. The project was plagued by delays and cost overruns, but the Infirmary eventually opened on 18 October 1770 (fig.21).

Developments over the first century of the Infirmary's existence were slow. In 1824 the original brewhouse was converted into the 'Hakewill Fever Ward', with the brewhouse and laundry moving to the south-east corner of the site. In 1834 the Trustees gave up a piece of land to the newly formed parish of St Paul's to allow the construction of the new church, which partially covered the old burial ground. In 1857 a new Outpatients' block was completed. In the same year, improvements were made to the front courtyard with the provision of the fountain, in the form of Triton and designed by James Bell, and the lowering of the high stone wall, to be replaced with railings. This was followed almost immediately in 1863 by the Accident Ward and the new mortuary, and then in 1865 by St Luke's Chapel, to the design of A. W. Blomsfield.

Development continued, albeit at a slower pace, for the rest of the nineteenth and early twentieth centuries. In 1911 the Outpatients' Building was demolished and the present building, designed by Edward Warren, opened in 1913 (fig.22). It was generally agreed that the Infirmary was poorly organised and short of space. With an eye on the future, the Trustees purchased

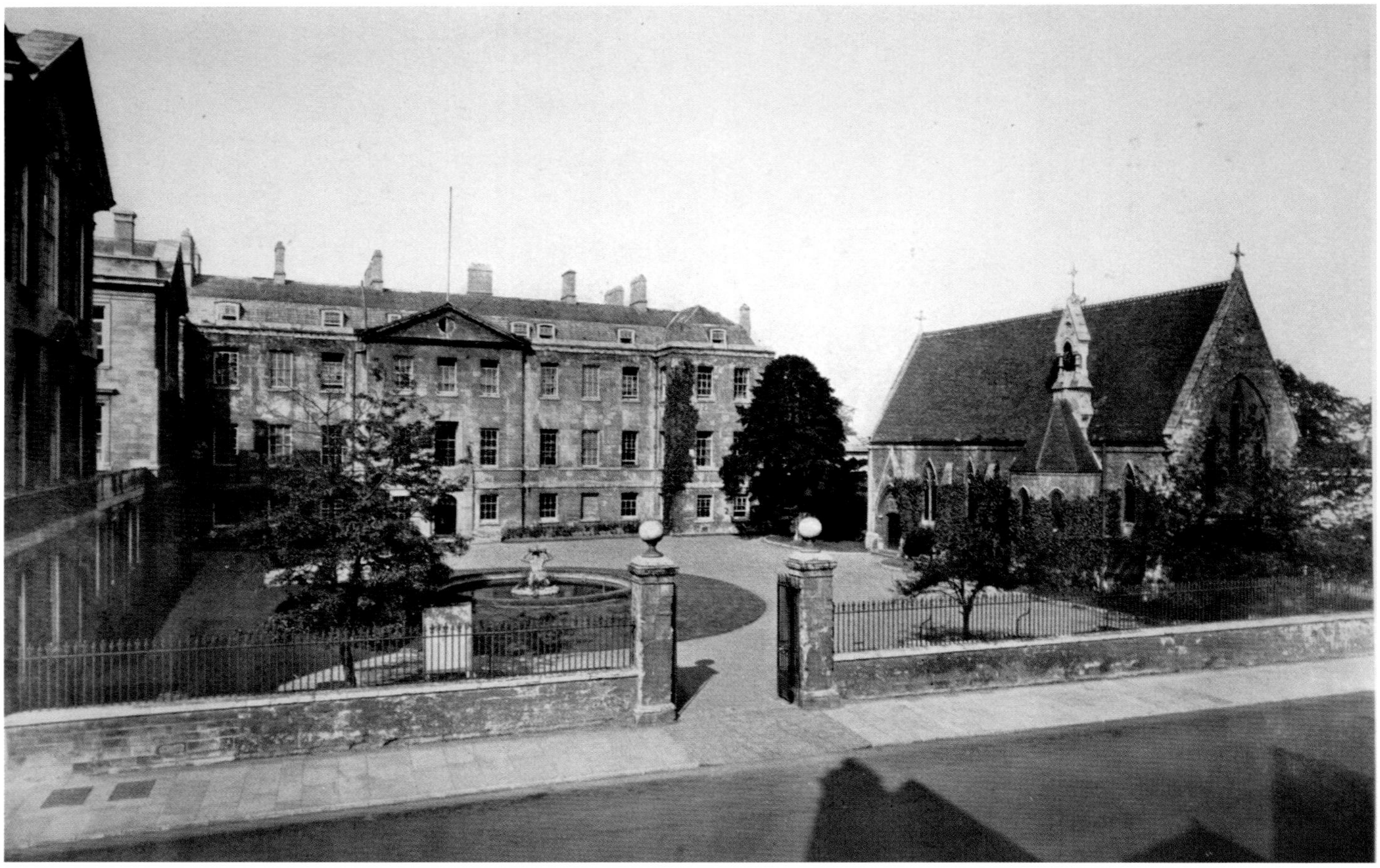

Fig.22 Photograph of the Radcliffe Infirmary Main Entrance, 1933. Courtesy of Oxfordshire Health Archives.

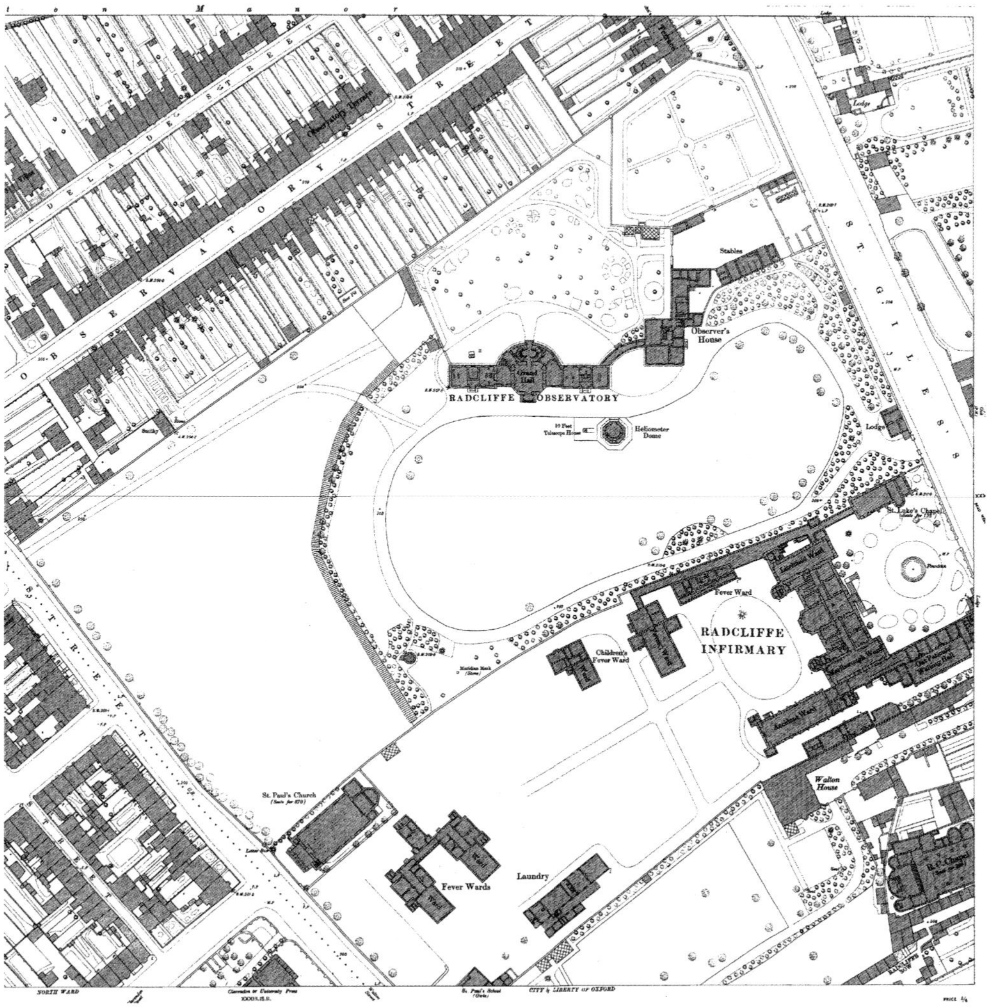

Fig.23 Map of the Radcliffe Infirmary site, Ordnance Survey map, 1874. Crown copyright.

the Manor House Estate in Headington, now the site of the John Radcliffe Hospital (fig.23).

The greatest expansion occurred in the interwar period. In 1924 William Morris (later to become Lord Nuffield) presented the Infirmary with £90,000, a gift that led to a new era. The major contribution Morris made to the Infirmary was the negotiation in 1929 of the purchase of the Observatory site, enabling the Infirmary to expand. Under Nuffield's leadership, and with his generous financial help, the next ten years saw significant development on the site. The transformation was remarkable: from being a competent county hospital, the Radcliffe Infirmary became a world leader in medical research.

After extensive development in the 1930s, the Board of Governors of the United Oxford Hospitals, appointed by the Ministry of Health, took over responsibility in 1948 for hospitals in the city. The Radcliffe Infirmary became a state hospital. In the 1970s new development ceased due to the opening of the new John Radcliffe Hospital in Headington. The Infirmary finally closed in 2007.

Early history of the Weston (New Bodleian) Library

The Weston Library (formerly the New Bodleian Library) is one part of the Bodleian Library complex – a group of buildings in Broad Street comprising the Weston, the Clarendon Building, the Old Bodleian and the Radcliffe Camera. These are also many other libraries across Oxford which are part of the Bodleian, such as the Radcliffe Science Library and the Bodleian Law Library.

The history of the library begins long before the Weston (New Bodleian) was constructed. The first University Library was established by Humphrey, Duke of Gloucester, and in 1488 a reading room was opened above the Divinity School. By the middle of the sixteenth century this had fallen into decline, and remained unused until Sir Thomas Bodley funded the reinstatement of the library in 1598. Located on the south side of Broad Street, the new building was opened in 1602 and called Bodley's Library.

It was not long before the Bodleian began to suffer from a lack of space. Extensions to the building were made in the seventeenth century in an attempt to provide more space, namely Arts End and Selden End of Duke Humphrey's Library, and further spaces in neighbouring buildings would be used in the years to come.

The Clarendon Building, constructed from 1712 to 1713, was designed for the use of the University Press. Between 1737 and 1748 the Radcliffe Library was constructed to the south of the Bodleian with funds from a bequest by the eminent physician Dr John Radcliffe (see above). Designed by James Gibbs, it was initially a separate entity from the Bodleian. By 1860 the two were integrated, however, and the Radcliffe Library became known as the Radcliffe Camera.

Lack of space remained a problem: by 1834 there were estimated to be around 220,000 books and 21,000 manuscripts in the library. More space was gained during the nineteenth century by removing some of the collection to the University Galleries (now the Ashmolean Museum) and through the integration of the Radcliffe Library. In 1909–12 an underground book store was installed beneath Radcliffe Square. After its construction the library was the largest in the world, and the first to feature modern compact shelving. This proved to be only a temporary solution, however, and during the early twentieth century the idea of a new, modern library was put forward.

Construction of the Weston (New Bodleian) Library 1936–46

In 1925 the Librarian of the Bodleian, Dr Arthur Ernest Cowley, warned the University that the Library would run out of space in ten years' time. He began to look at potential solutions, and it was decided that the construction of a new building within the city centre was the best course of action (fig.24).

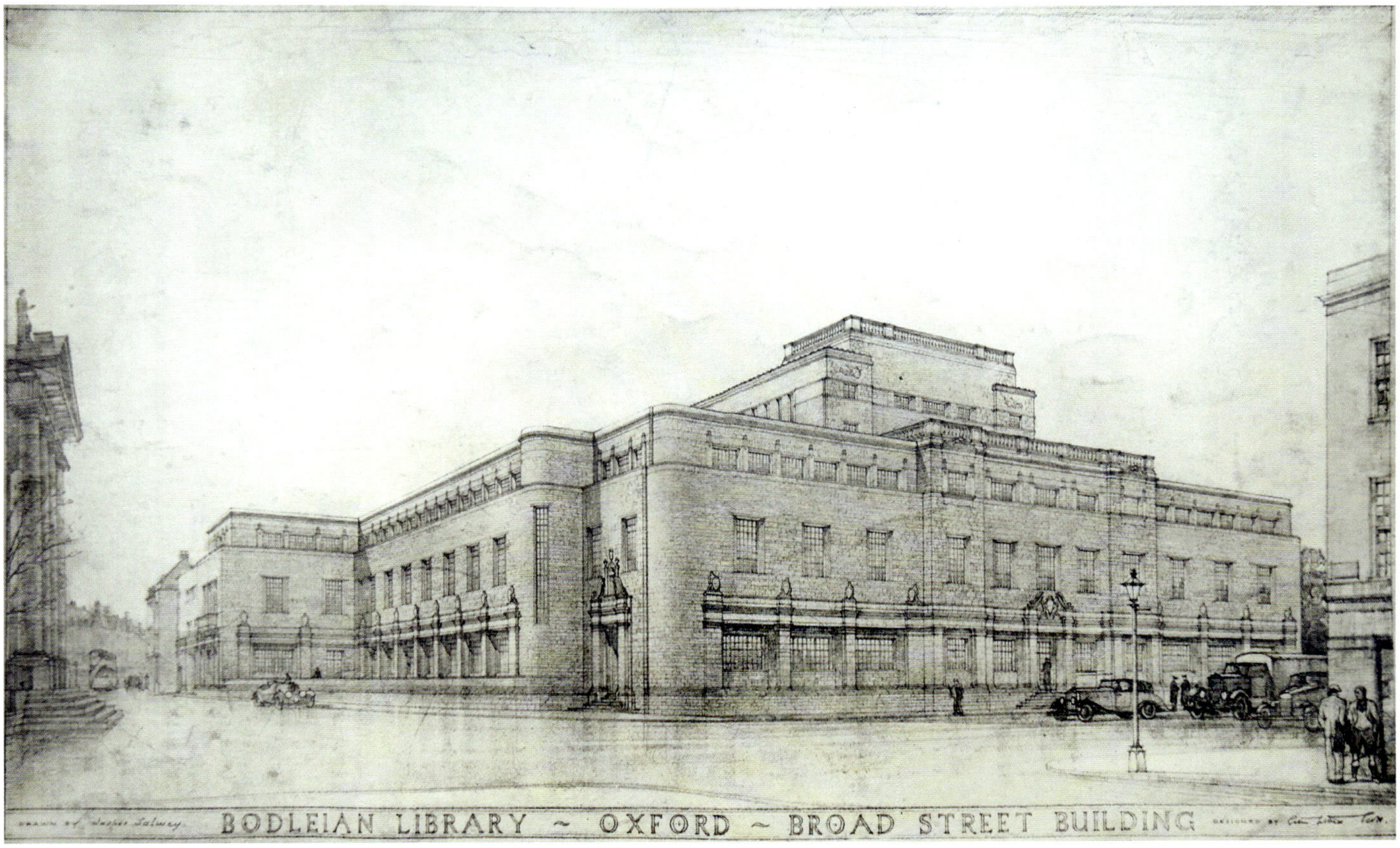

Fig.24 Drawing of the Broad Street building of the Bodleian Library by Sir Giles Gilbert Scott, 1934. Courtesy of the Bodleian Libraries, University of Oxford.

In 1926 the Rockefeller Foundation agreed to provide three-fifths of the cost of a new library, provided that the University would contribute the remainder. This was the catalyst for the creation of a Commission, under Sir Henry Miers, involving visits to modern University libraries in Europe and America with a view to informing designs for the New Library. In a report published in 1931, the Library Commission determined that the best option was to build a book stack rather than a library. The site chosen was opposite the Clarendon Building, on the north of Broad Street.

Following the appointment of Sir Giles Gilbert Scott as architect in June 1934, it was decided that the new building on the Broad Street site would be a book store and library extension capable of holding approximately five million books. It would be connected to the Old Bodleian via a mechanical conveyor belt and pneumatic tube system.

Construction of the library began in December 1936, with the building work being conducted by Benfield and Loxley of Oxford. Thirteen seventeenth-century terraced houses on the corner of Broad Street and Parks Road had to be demolished to make way for the building. Two other properties, nos. 48 and 49, were due to be retained to the west of the site, but became very unstable following demolition of adjacent properties; they were completely reconstructed in 1936. The foundation stone of the New Bodleian was laid by Queen Mary on 25 June 1937. Construction was completed three years later, in 1940, at a cost of £379, 000.

Due to the outbreak of the Second World War the library could not be opened, but this time was used to transfer 1.5 million books over from the old library. The basement of the building was also used for war work and partially converted into an air raid shelter (though the shelter was never actually put to use).

Following the end of the war, the New Bodleian Library was officially opened by George VI in a ceremony held in October 1946. The construction was described as being, 'an experiment in working a new library building into an old historic framework'; its architect, Sir Giles Gilbert Scott, drew on several influences to create a unique style, essentially an Art Deco/Art Moderne take on Classical Revivalism. The use of materials, styles, architectural features and design elements form a modern building in keeping with the style of its time, though touched rather heavily by the inspiration of surrounding buildings, from medieval timber frames to the ornate Classical Revivalism of the Sheldonian Theatre and Clarendon Building.

A library for the twenty-first century

The New Bodleian remained relatively unchanged until 2010, with only relatively minor alterations. A full refurbishment of the library was started in 2010 to a design by Wilkinson Eyre architects, and the Library was re-opened to the public in March 2015. The refurbishment dramatically changed the layout of the ground floor of the New Bodleian Library, renamed the Weston Library in recognition of a significant donation from the Garfield Weston Foundation. The central stacks and south perimeter offices were replaced with a new, publicly accessible area including a café, exhibition and events space. This space is connected to Broad Street by a colonnade, created by altering the original window openings to provide an arcaded front entrance. The entire structure of the central stack has been replaced to create a new book stack suitable for housing the Bodleian's world-class special collection of books and manuscripts.

Introduction to Weston Library Watercolours

Richard Ovenden

Oxford is a city where the stones engender an air of timelessness. The inventor of photography, William Henry Fox Talbot, described the city as 'the place of the genius of repose'. Look more closely and you will see that the appearance of solidity masks a reality of constant change and renewal in the buildings of the city and the university, and especially so with the Bodleian Library.

Weimin He captures just such a process with his beautiful watercolours of the Weston Library. The dramatic scenes of demolition and construction which he depicts are rendered with an eye to the contradictions that are ever-present in the university: his images perfectly convey the dynamism and the permanence of Oxford. Through the richness of his palette he shows us the beauty of these buildings' point of transition from one structure to another. In a city that has been the subject of a great many artists, Weimin He has achieved a near miracle: he has brought originality in both subject and approach, and accomplished it with a unique eye and with astounding beauty.

Artist's Notes

Since childhood art has been my all-consuming passion. Until I worked as artist-in-residence for eight months at the Ashmolean Museum in 2008, I had never been fond of portraying construction sites. When I first worked as artist-in-residence in the Ashmolean I was keen to draw the builders, and gradually became attracted by the ever-changing building sites themselves.

Compared to the Ashmolean site, the eleven-acre Radcliffe Observatory Quarter is vast. At the beginning I was fascinated by the demolition of the 1950s Radcliffe Infirmary buildings. Making sketches of demolition seemed to be a process of competition with the speed of the relentless excavators. The scattered debris and diffused dust of the site often stimulated me to 'interpret' the scene with a personal visual language. I was tempted to 'write' the images rather than 'drawing' them with a felt pen since I believe 'writing' directly carries one's psychological DNA. From gigantic twisted steel beams to small fragments of debris, all seemed to tell stories of the history of the ground, its glory or lamentation. The archaeological discovery of objects from 4,000 years ago through the Anglo-Saxon period, the Greek-style observatory, the chapel embodying the richness of culture – these elements also inspired me to create work centred on the theme 'Tower of the Winds'.

Starting with the Somerville College student accommodation project, I began to use Chinese brushes. These have long been regarded as the most flexible painting tools, producing sophisticated techniques over 2,000 years primarily for calligraphy or painting landscapes, flowers and birds. It was a challenge to depict urban cityscapes, especially construction sites with excavators, scaffolding and modern architecture. I feel the unalterable character of brushwork reveals the artist's inner self more effectively – like those of music notes, every stroke is a record of time, or of life.

The use of a leporello album means that no single album leaf can be removed or replaced if the artist makes a mistake. In fact my innumerable 'mistakes' forced me to find solutions; they therefore often gave me an opportunity to discover different possibilities, to turn them into advantages. The painting of album leaves taught me to embrace 'mistakes' rather than fear making them.

From the middle stage of the Andrew Wiles Building project, I started to use single sheets of Chinese *xuan* paper which allowed me to draw or paint on both sides. This technique extended to the painting of the Radcliffe Infirmary, the Outpatients building refurbishment and the Blavatnik School of Government projects. *Xuan* paper also enabled me to achieve subtle tones and rich layers to express myself more freely. The seemingly uncontrollable nature of ink and colour 'bleeding' on the paper transformed the use of *xuan* paper into an adventure.

To the viewer the construction site might be dusty and noisy, full of concrete, steel and dominated by motionless materials or machinery. After being on the construction site for a while, I gradually started to perceive it from a different perspective. The process itself is organic, dynamic and full of life; it shows human power when one witnesses a building grow and to me it became a privilege to observe the process so closely. In actual fact, every picture I drew or painted had to come from my direct observation of the site. I liked spending time on site sketching what happened in front of me, absorbing and capturing the energy of the site. My drawings are often a combination of events over a lengthy period of time, not just a record of one moment.

As a 'builder' on site, my constructions needed 'demolition' and 'reconstruction' too. For a certain period I worked at three different construction sites simultaneously, and it was very hard to follow the speed of the construction with brushes. So many of my paintings were completed afterwards, even after the period of my residency had ended. Some sketches were done within a few minutes, but others might take several hours or days. Some ink paintings could take a few months or years to finish – even longer than constructing an actual building.

Sometimes I felt lacking in inspiration; my brain went blank when faced with the vast construction site. Creating artwork as a job of work is not always possible – yet by keeping going and working through the darkness, light may shine suddenly as a reward (figs 25 and 26).

The Weston Library site is separate from the ROQ site, located at the heart of the University of Oxford and inspired by old masters such as J. M. W. Turner, whom I greatly admire. I decided to depict the scenes with watercolour, which

Fig.25 Poster for the exhibition *Drawings and prints of the ROQ site by Weimin He*, 14–20 May 2012.

Fig. 26
The purpose-built, temporary gallery for the exhibition *Drawings and prints of the ROQ site by Weimin He*, 14–20 May 2012. The exhibition was held in the former Radcliffe Infirmary Outpatients Building (now Radcliffe Primary Care Building). Photograph Weimin He.

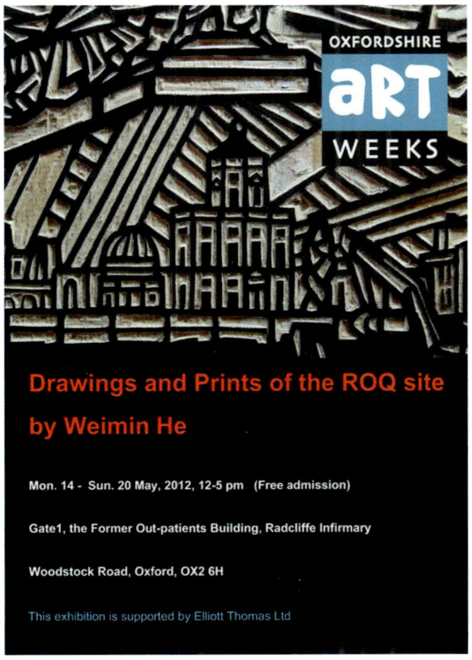

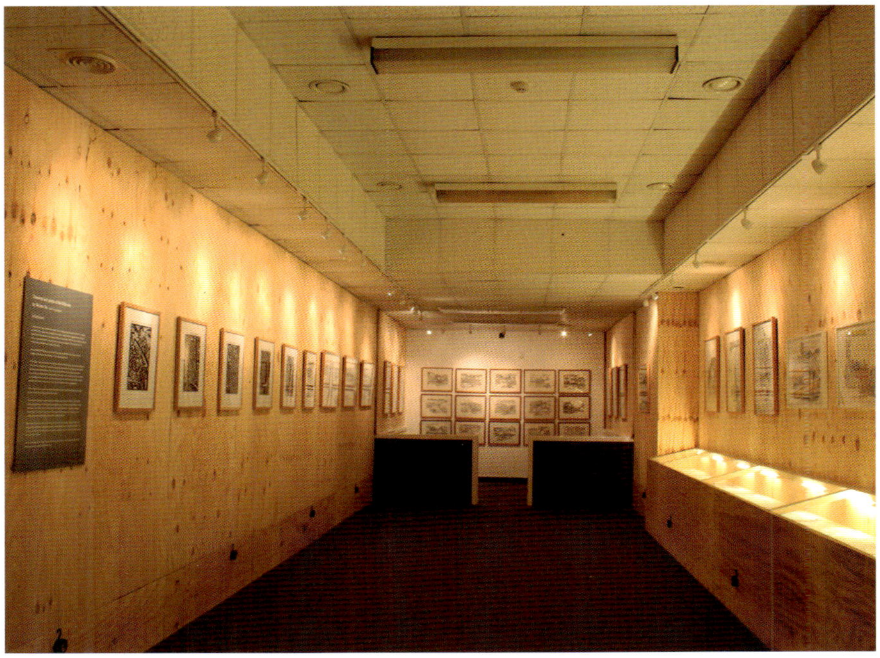

is a challenging medium, but I thought I might be able to create something different (figs 27 and 28).

Works presented in this publication are selected from a large quantity of sketches and ink paintings. Some works are in ink alone, and some are in colour, but I value the works in ink just as highly. For me art is more than a technical, intellectual or conceptual exercise: it comes from my instincts and reflects my true nature. I tried to express the images with my thoughts and sensibilities, extending them beyond what I had observed. I am not interested in following trends or fashions in art, but aim rather to discover the Dao of painting and life. Hence I realised the path to free expression has to go through discipline and constant hard work. It is a journey to find oneself and put one's heart into each work. I also believe that best works are produced out of God's assistance. God will not turn up until you have worked diligently and devoted your life to your work.

'The Tower of the Winds' witnessed the galaxies over the centuries. From an astronomer's point of view six years might be a million times quicker than a blink of eye, but it was a long and important period in my life. I have always been wary of the word 'record'. since to me this seems a phlegmatic activity; a superficial 'record' of construction scenes could easily be done by using modern devices in less than a second. However, I gradually came to accept it as I think these works are indeed my own 'record' of the historical transformation of the world-renowned University. They are also records of my life's trajectory, revealing struggle and joyfulness, confusion and determination. These six years were a journey in discovering myself, and the works from that time are records of my thinking and aesthetic endeavours which will take my life and art forward in a new direction.

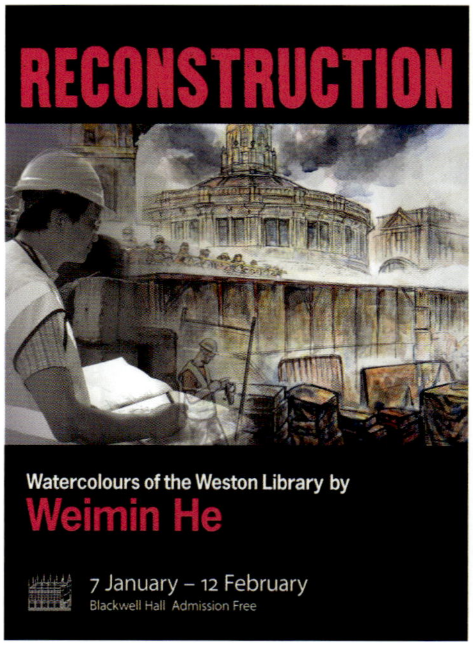

Fig. 27 Poster for the exhibition *Reconstruction – Watercolours of the Weston Library by Weimin He*, 7 January–12 February 2017. Courtesy of the Bodleian Libraries, University of Oxford.

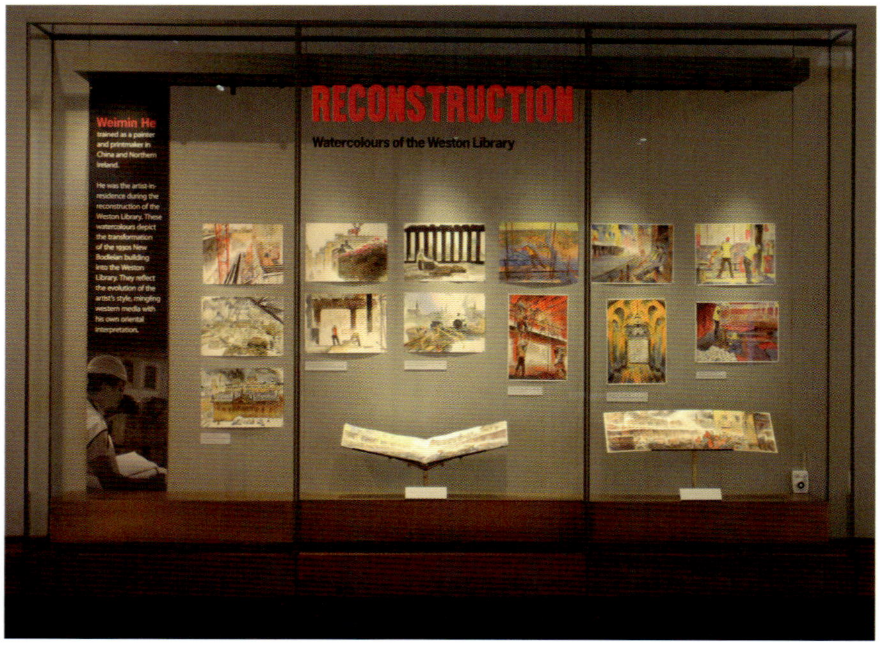

Fig. 28 The exhibition *Reconstruction – Watercolours of the Weston Library by Weimin He*. 7 January–12 Feburary 2017, held at the Weston Library, Oxford University. Photograph courtesy of the Bodleian Libraries, University of Oxford.

Acknowledgements

First and foremost I wish dedicate this book to my father He Jixing 何吉星 and especially to my beloved late mother Lü Lilian 呂麗蓮. I also wish to thank my sisters He Haiyan and He Yinyan: without my family's immeasurable support I would not have been able to complete this project.

I wish to express my gratitude to Sir John Hood, former Vice-Chancellor of the University of Oxford, for his constant support to the project. I feel greatly privileged to have his foreword in this book.

This project has been primarily funded and supported by the Oxford University Estates Services (OUES). I would like to express my gratitude to my former line manager Isobel Hughes, Director of Operations, for her constant support over the years. I also wish to express my gratitude to Paul Goffin, Director of the OUES, and Mike Wigg, former Head of Capital Projects, for their support of the project.

I wish to thank Richard Ovenden, Bodley's Librarian, for his support of the project and his beautifully written introduction to my Weston Library watercolours. I feel a great debt to the former Bodley Librarian, Sarah E. Thomas, and apologise for not having kept my promise to produce a satisfactory woodcut – but I will rectify this.

My gratitude also goes to Declan McCarthy, Head of Ashmolean Publishing and Licensing, for his enormous support for the publication of this book. I also wish to express my sincere thanks to Professor Christopher Brown, the former Director of the Ashmolean Museum.

I feel honoured to have had the help of Dr Anne Farrer, a renowned historian of Chinese painting and graphic art. She has supported my work over the years and has kindly written an article about my work for this publication, for which I am most grateful. I also wish to thank Professor David Barker, my DPhil supervisor; he has been my supervisor in research, artistic practice and in life for nearly two decades.

Sylvia Vetta, a very prolific writer and special friend, has voluntarily promoted the project through interviews, publications and organising events from its beginning. Her generous contribution to the project is immeasurable.

Gordon Aldrick is a very special friend of mine. I wish to express my gratitude for the vision and guidance he has given to the project, and for his friendship over the years.

I wish to thank Professor Andrew Hamilton, former Vice-Chancellor, for his crucial support during a difficult period of my life.

I wish to thank Catherine Bradley for meticulous attention to the task of copy-editing, and for her great patience. I also wish to thank designer Stephen

Hebron and artist and professional photographer Kinga Lubowiecka for their highly professional work.

I would also like to express my heartfelt gratitude to Florence Waters, writer, art journalist and artist. Her constructive views and selfless help in assisting me to select work have made a huge difference to this book.

During the six-year period and subsequently, I have been fortunate to benefit greatly from the assistance of many people at the University of Oxford, construction companies and elsewhere. I would like particularly to thank (in alphabetical order) Caroline Ashley, Stewart Basham, Rebecca Baxter, Anthony Cammell, Paul Chinn, Carolyne Culver, Annette Cunningham, John Elinger, Andrew Ffrench, Emma Flood, Sallyanne Gilchrist, Gao Xiaohong, Guy Graham, Jane Hayter-Hames, Huang Pingping, Li Pei, Liu Yan, Mike Morris, Sarah Ng, Caroline Reynolds, Philip Rust, Diane West, Joseph Winkelman, Xu Yanjiao, Spring Zhang, Zhang Yujie and Zhang Wenjing.

Last but by no means least, I wish to thank Professor Denise Lievesley CBE, Principal of Green Templeton College, and Timothy Clayden, archaeologist and Bursar of GTC, for offering me the wonderful opportunity to develop my project at Green Templeton College.

Weimin He
August 2018

Catalogue

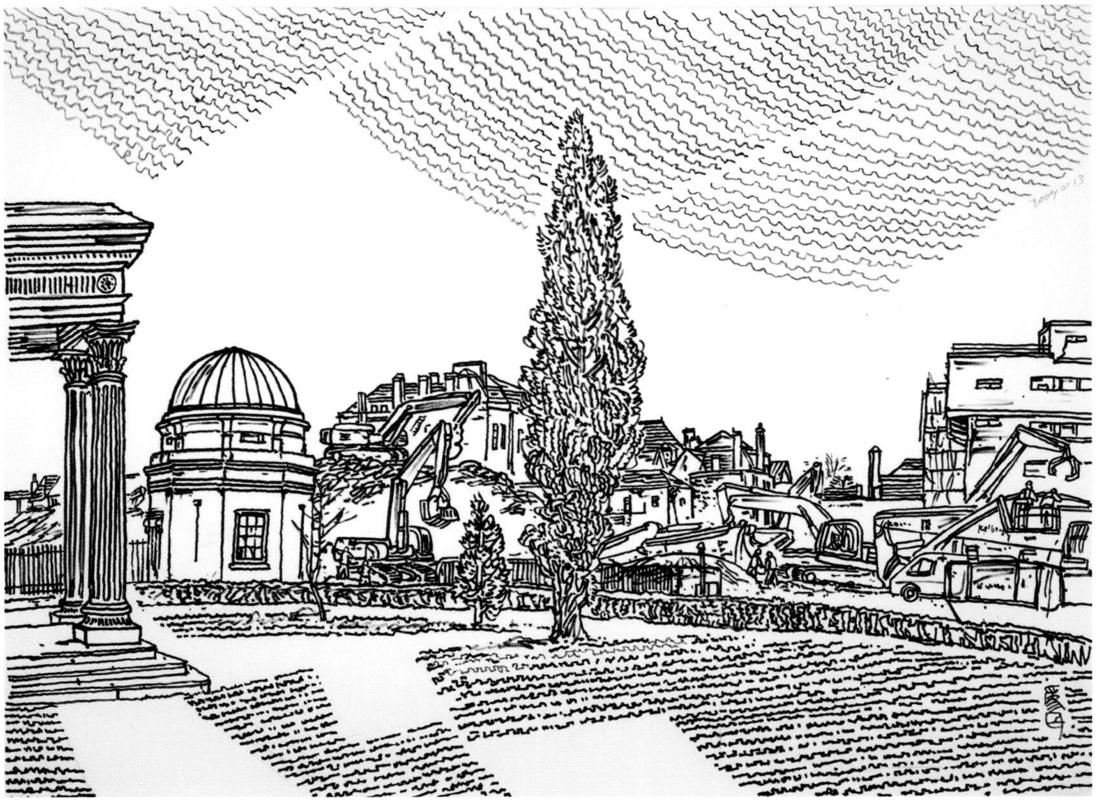

CAT.1
Solitary tree – demolition of the Radcliffe Infirmary buildings. 13 January 2009. Felt-tip pen on cartridge paper. Paper size: 42 × 59.4 cm

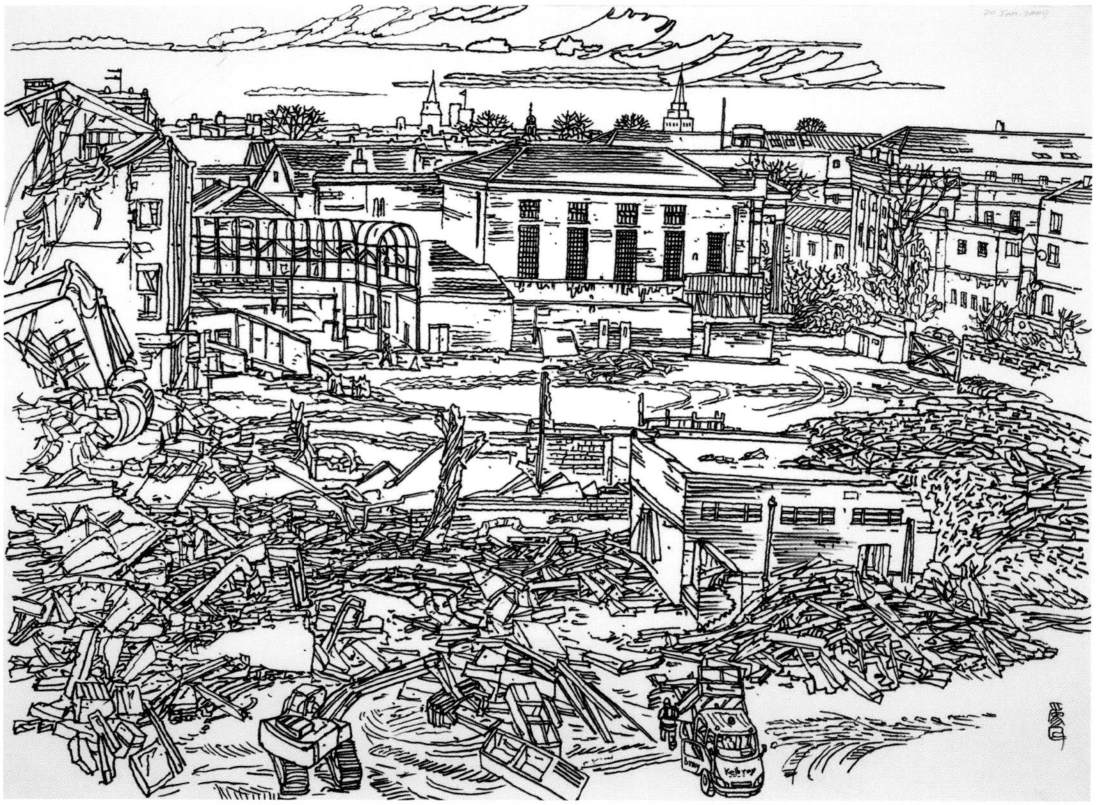

CAT.2
Let bygones be bygones. 20 January 2009. Felt-tip pen on cartridge paper. Paper size: 42 × 59.4 cm

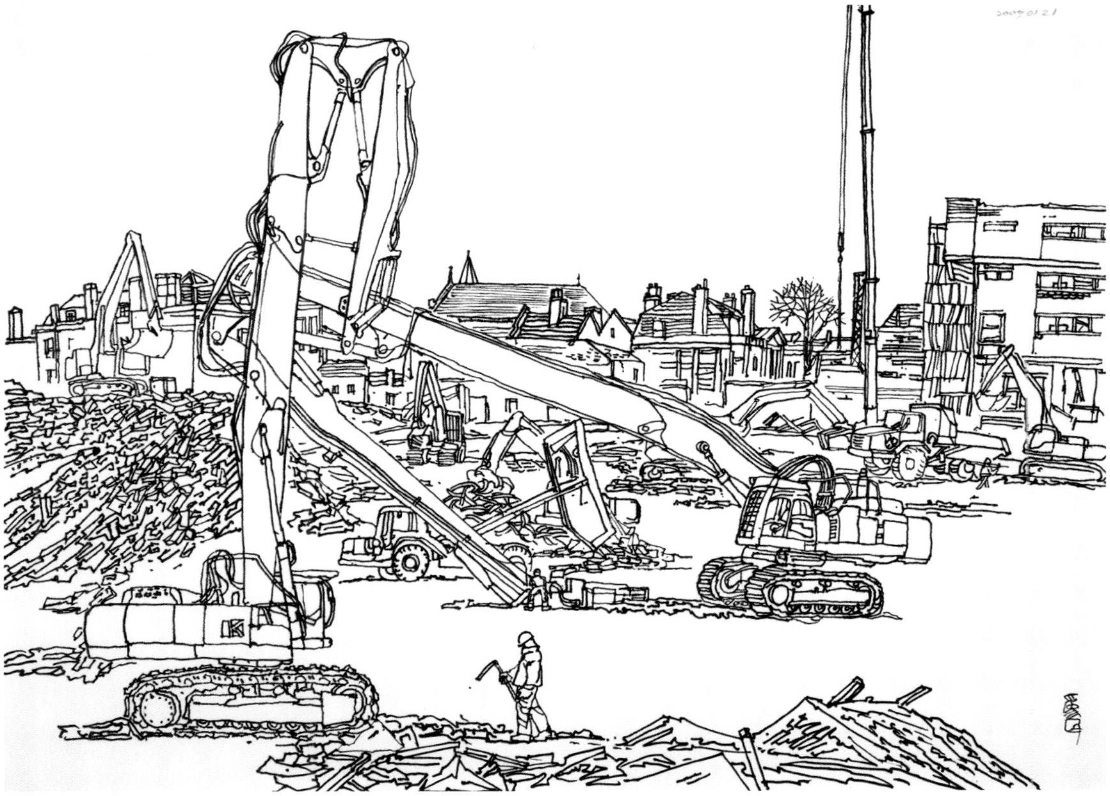

CAT.3
Wards once stood – Radcliffe Observatory Quarter site.
21 January 2009. Felt-tip pen on cartridge paper. Paper size: 42 × 59.4 cm

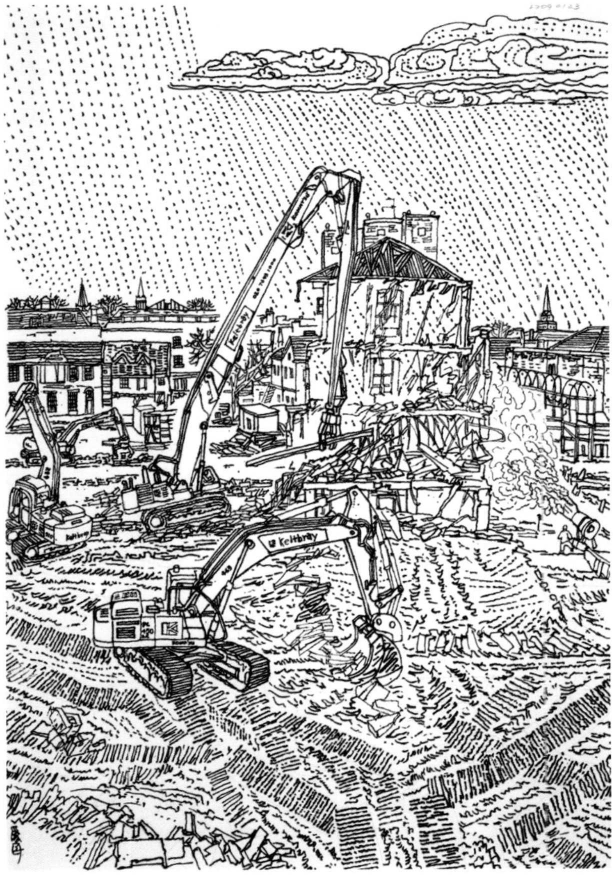

CAT.4
Patchy rain. 23 January 2009.
Felt-tip pen on cartridge paper.
Paper size: 59.4 × 42 cm

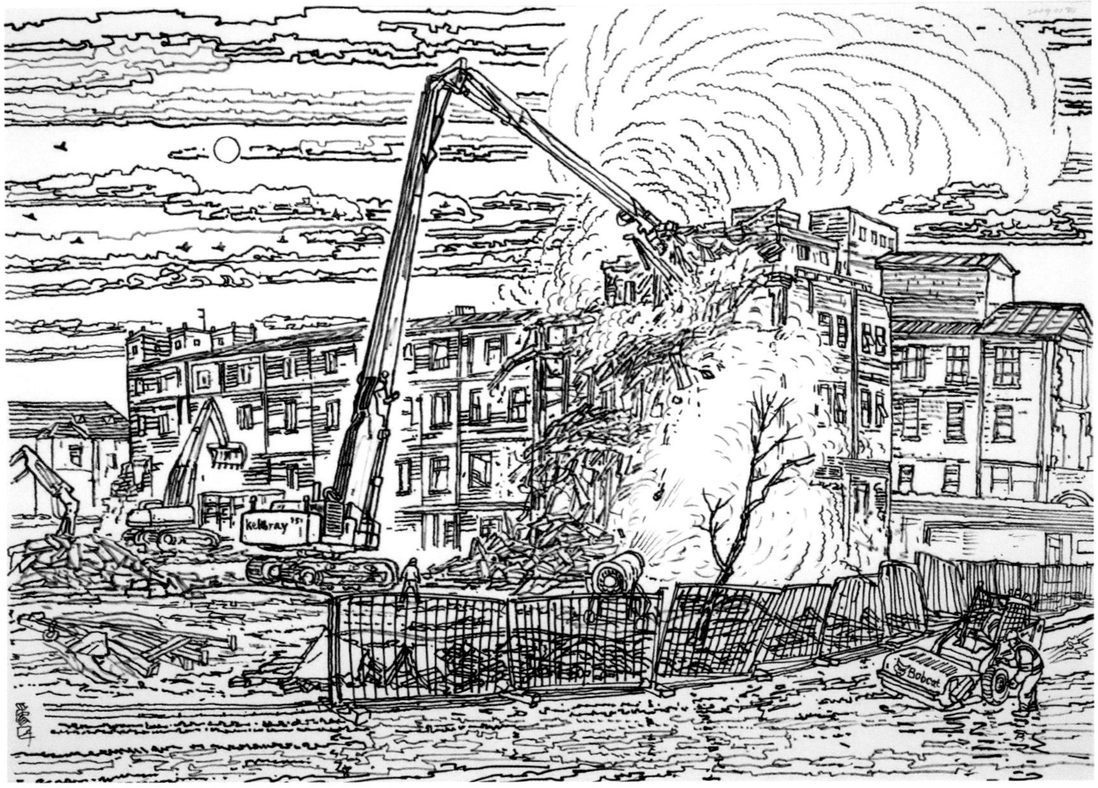

CAT.5
Eating away of the past.
24 January 2009. Felt-tip pen on cartridge paper. Paper size: 42 × 59.4 cm

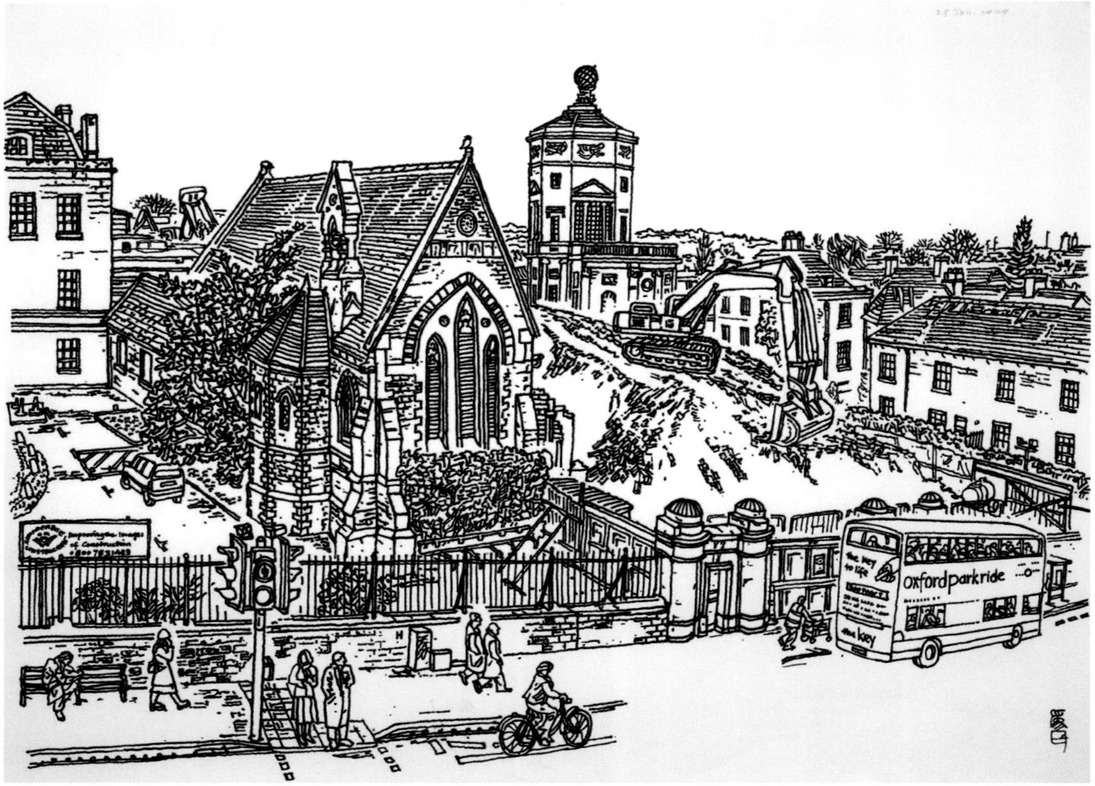

CAT.6
Transformation kicks off.
28 January 2009. Felt-tip pen on cartridge paper. Paper size: 42 × 59.4 cm

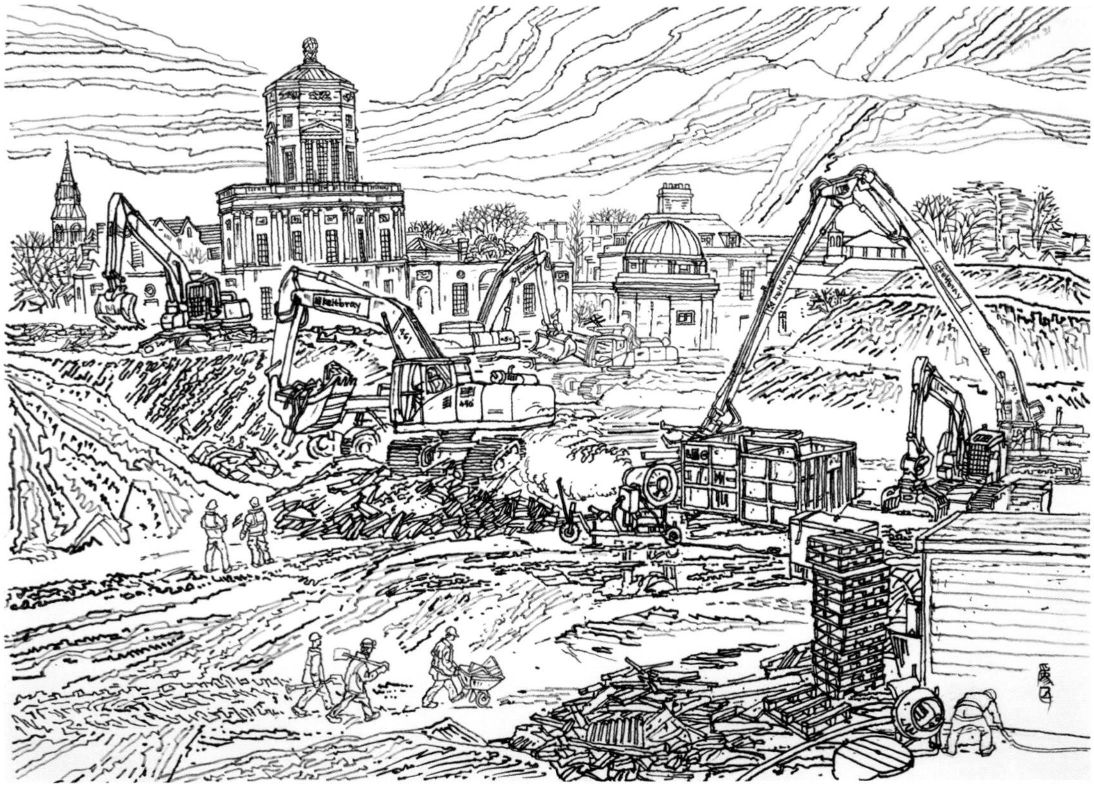

CAT.7
Waves of the site. 31 January 2009. Felt-tip pen on cartridge paper. Paper size: 42 × 59.4 cm

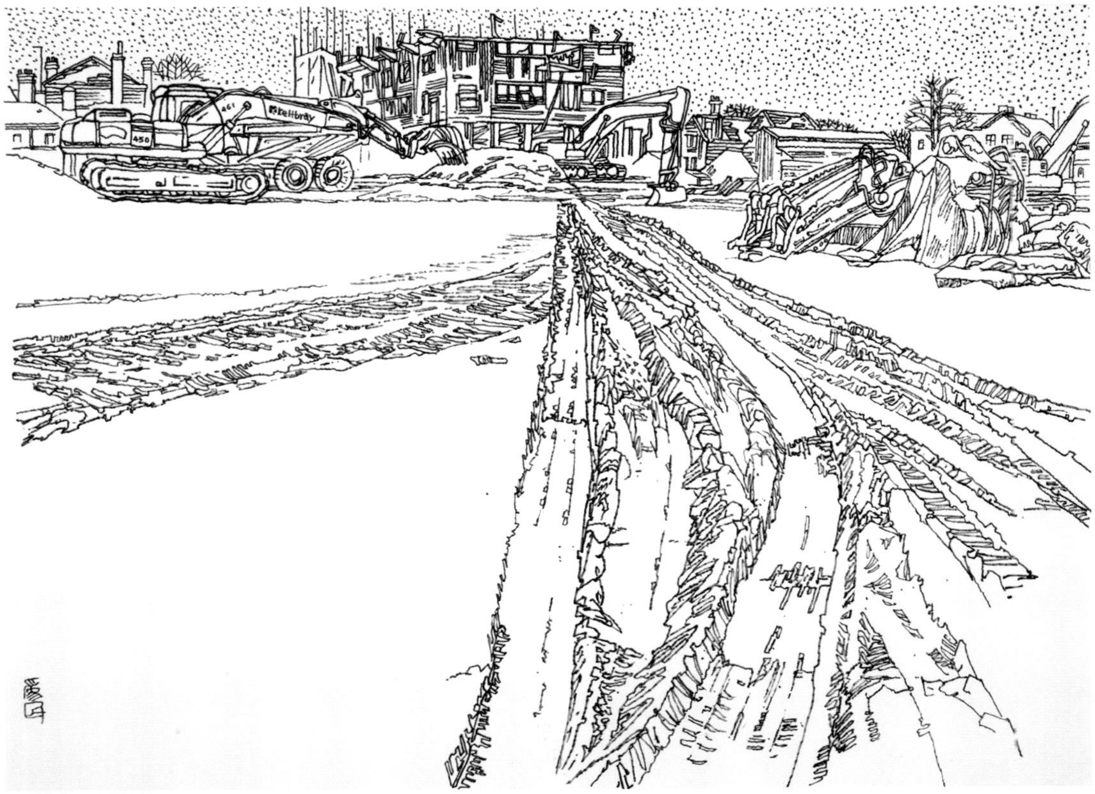

CAT.8
Silent snow. 3 February 2009. Felt-tip pen on cartridge paper. Paper size: 42 × 59.4 cm

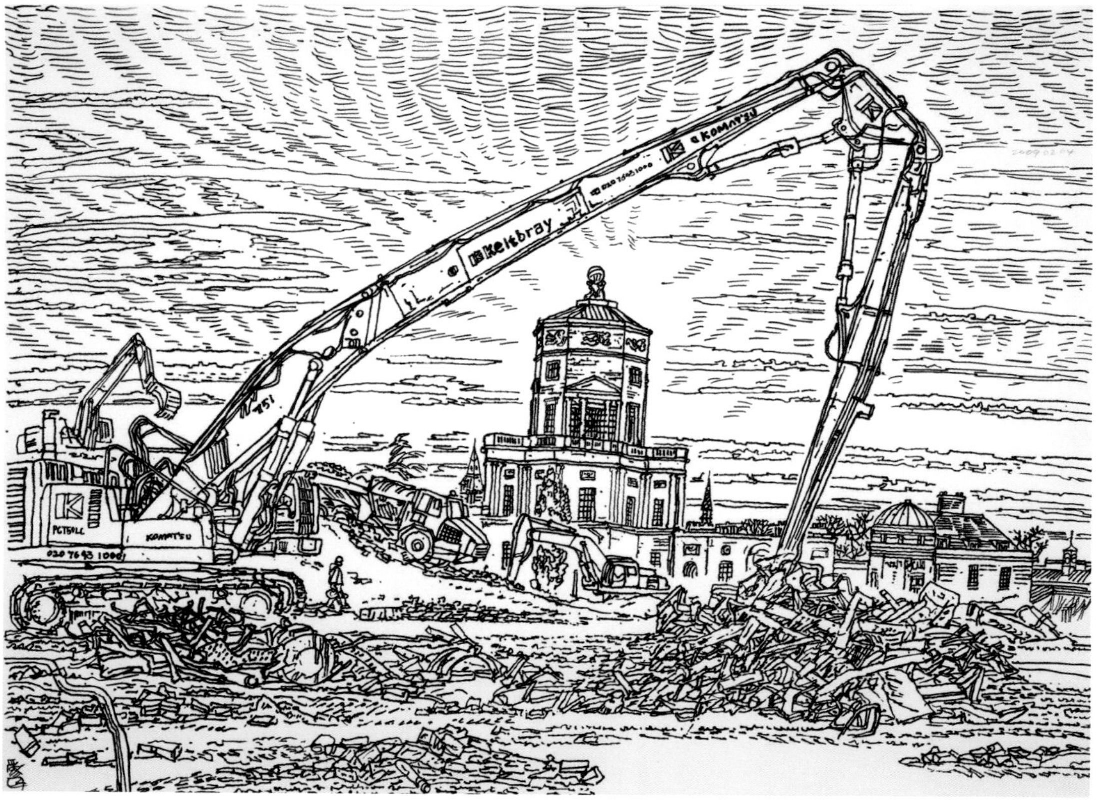

CAT.9
Triumphal arch. 4 February 2009. Felt-tip pen on cartridge paper. Paper size: 42 × 59.4 cm

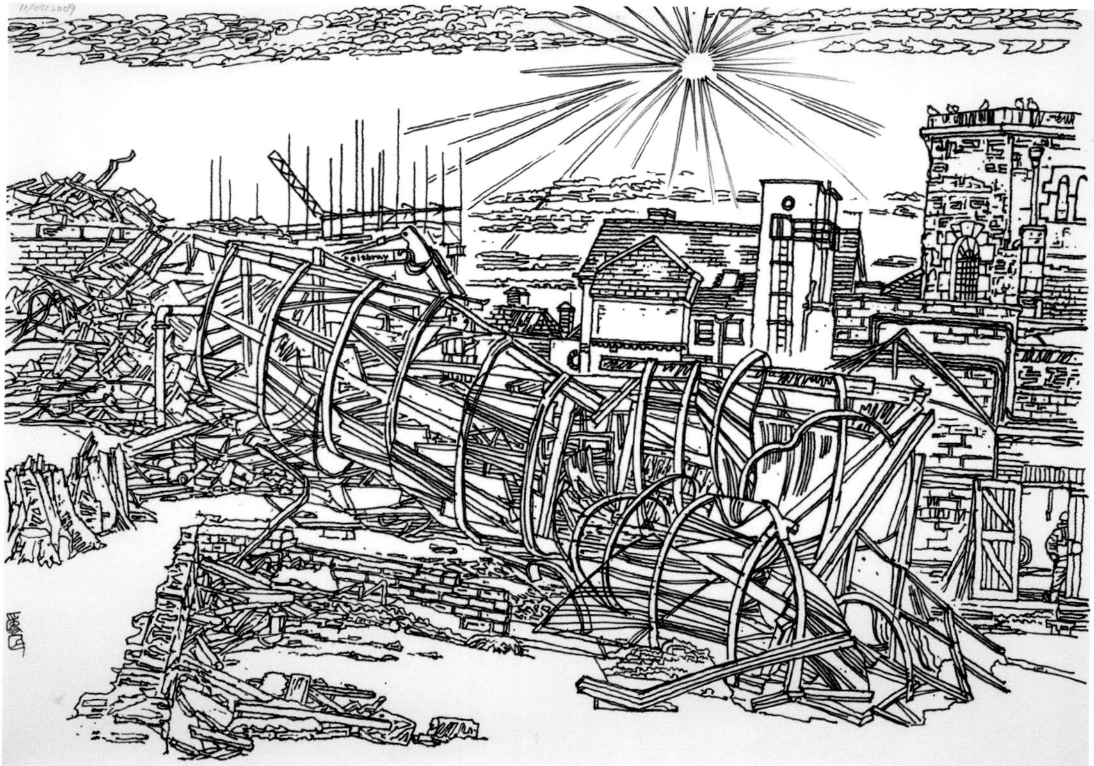

CAT.10
Fallen pathway. 11 February 2009. Felt-tip pen on cartridge paper. Paper size: 42 × 59.4 cm

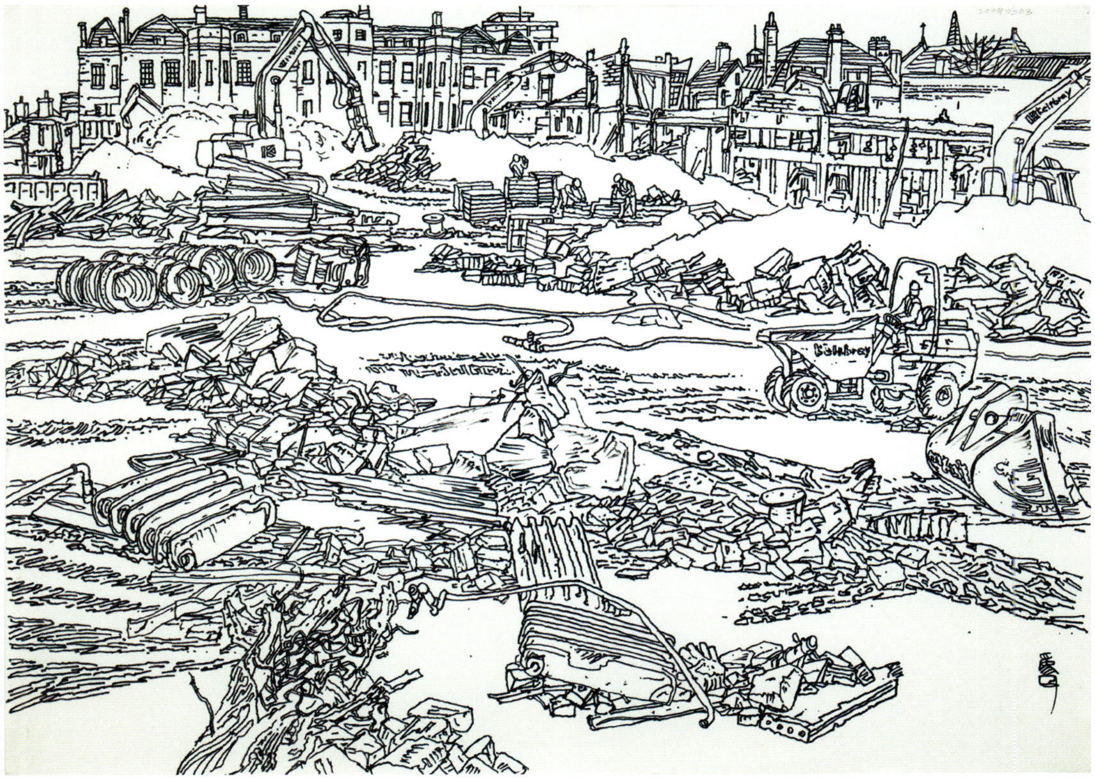

CAT.11
The shape of things to come.
3 March 2009. Felt-tip pen on cartridge paper. Paper size: 29.7 × 42 cm

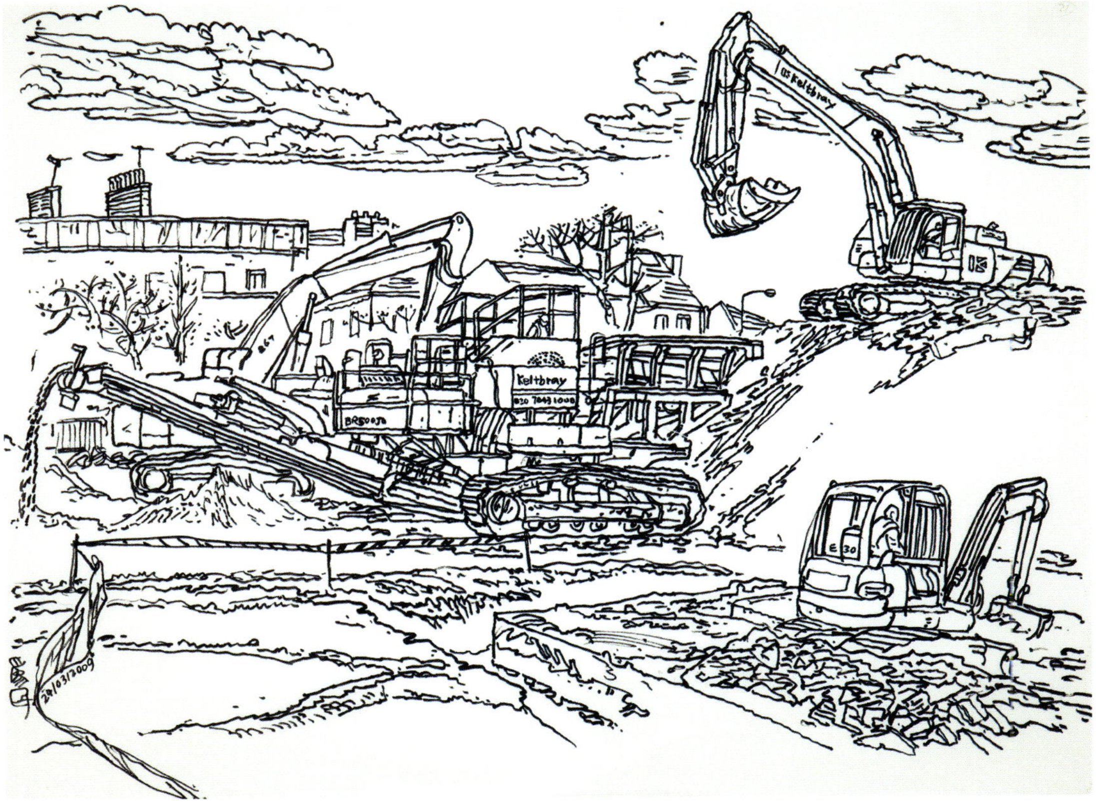

CAT.12
Stone breaking. 24 March 2009. Felt-tip pen on cartridge paper. Paper size: 29.7 × 42 cm

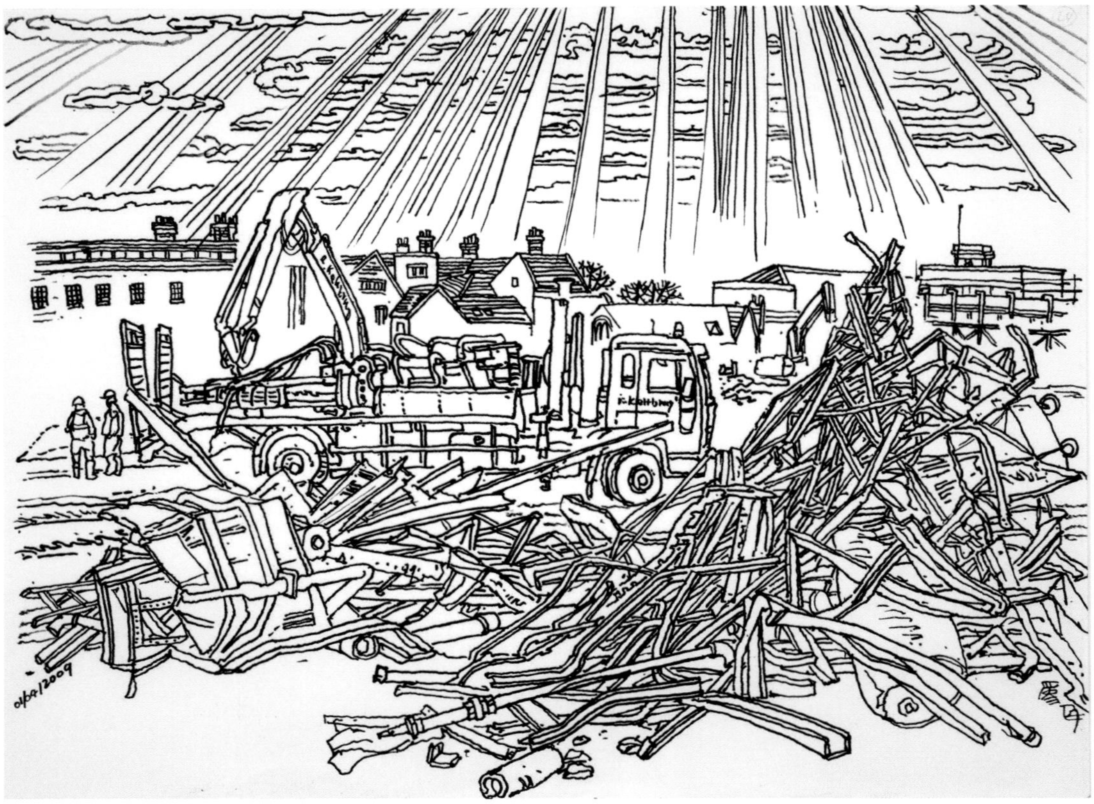

CAT.13
Shafts of sunlight. 1 April 2009. Felt-tip pen on cartridge paper. Paper size: 29.7 × 42 cm

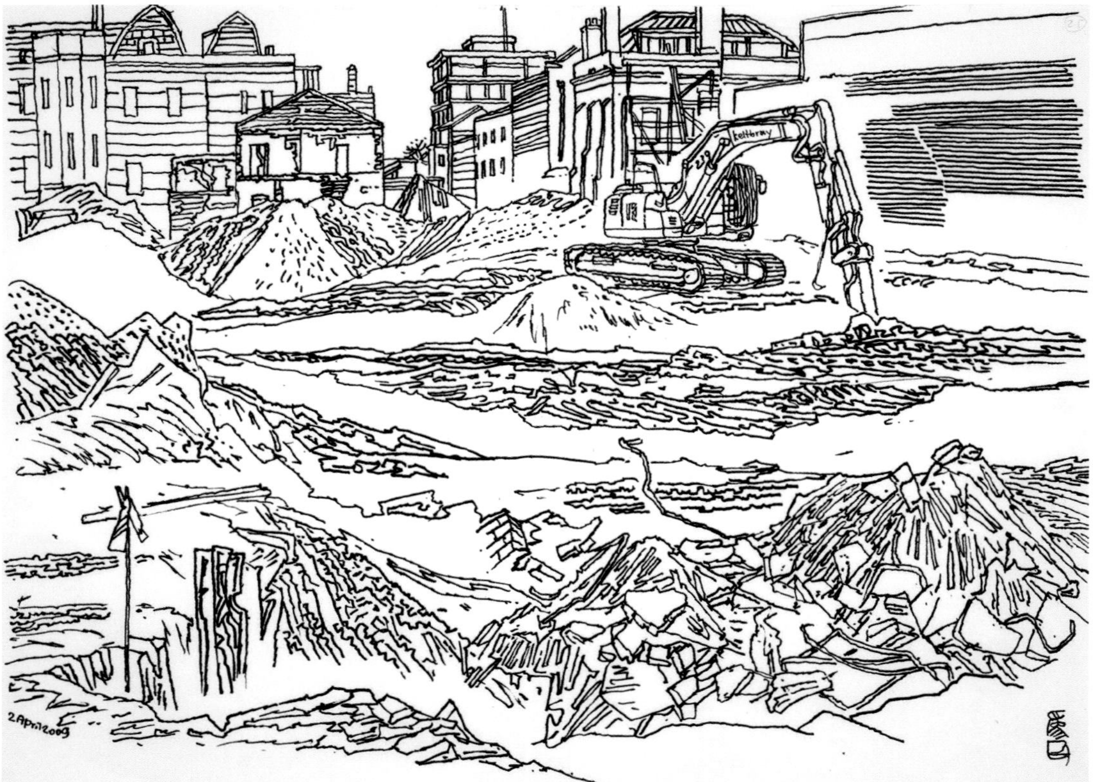

CAT.14
Digging the past – Somerville College student accommodation. 2 April 2009. Felt-tip pen on cartridge paper. Paper size: 29.7 × 42 cm

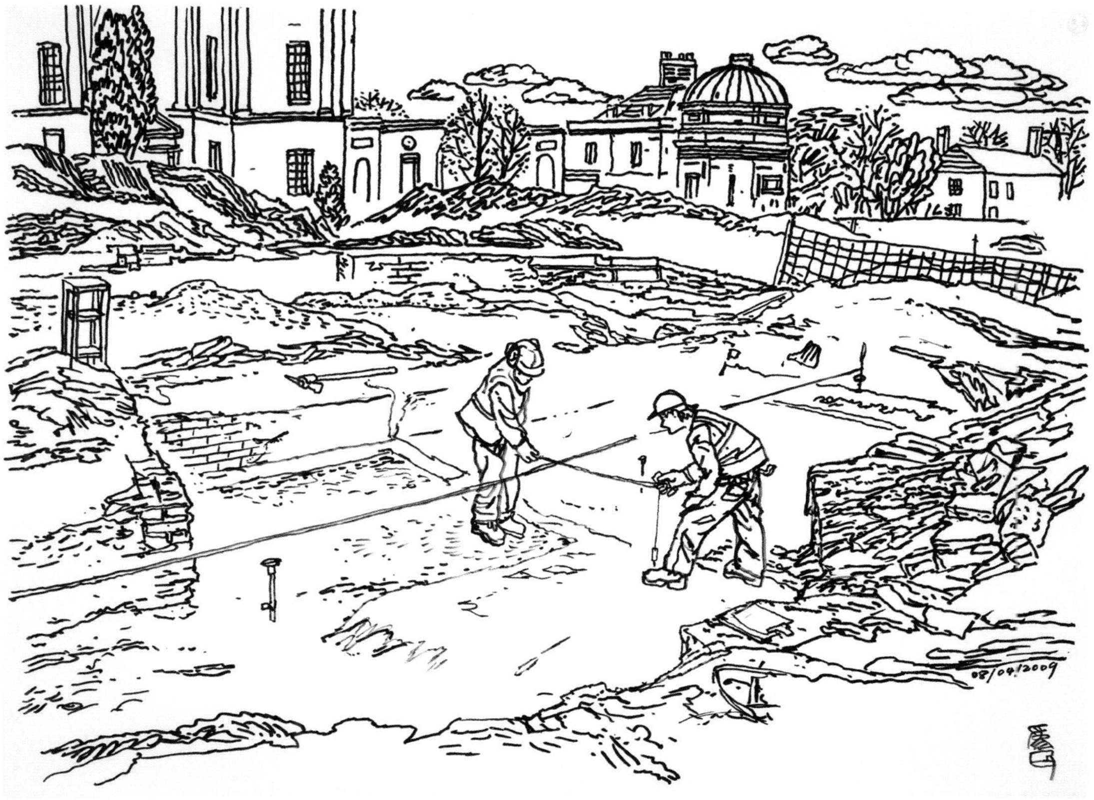

CAT.15
Measuring the past. 8 April 2009. Felt-tip pen on cartridge paper. Paper size: 29.7 × 42 cm

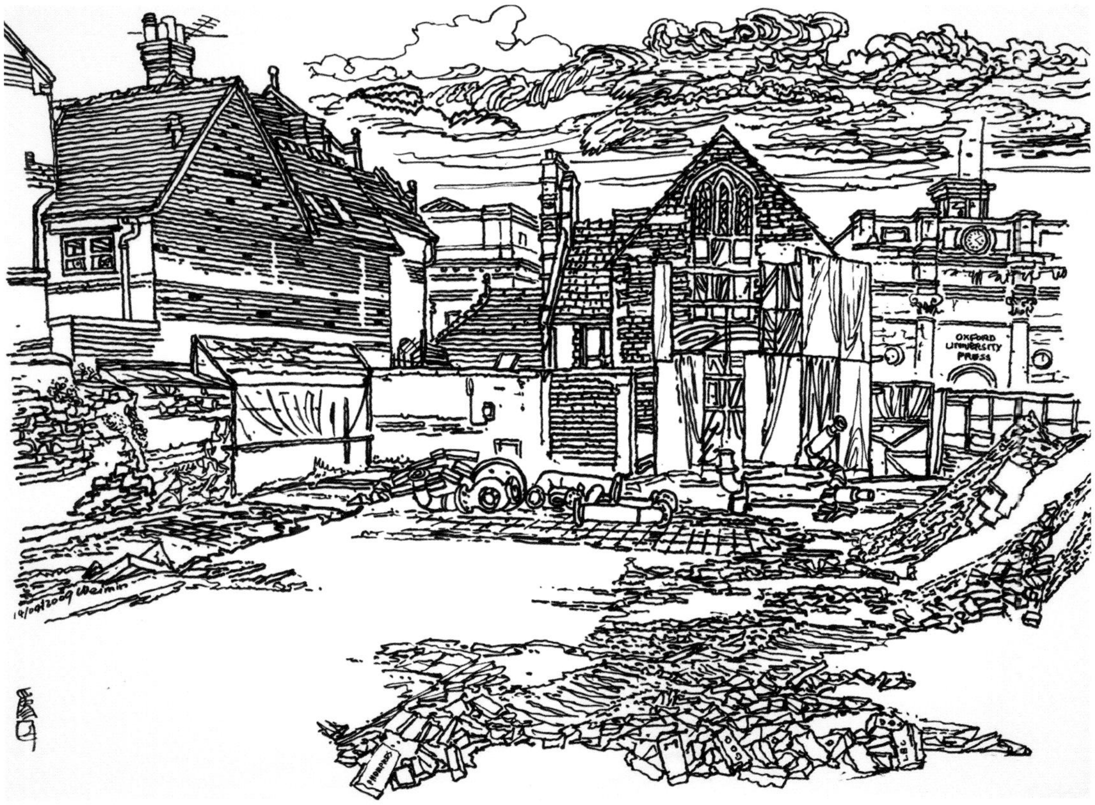

CAT.16
View toward Oxford University Press. 14 April 2009. Felt-tip pen on cartridge paper. Paper size: 29.7 × 42 cm

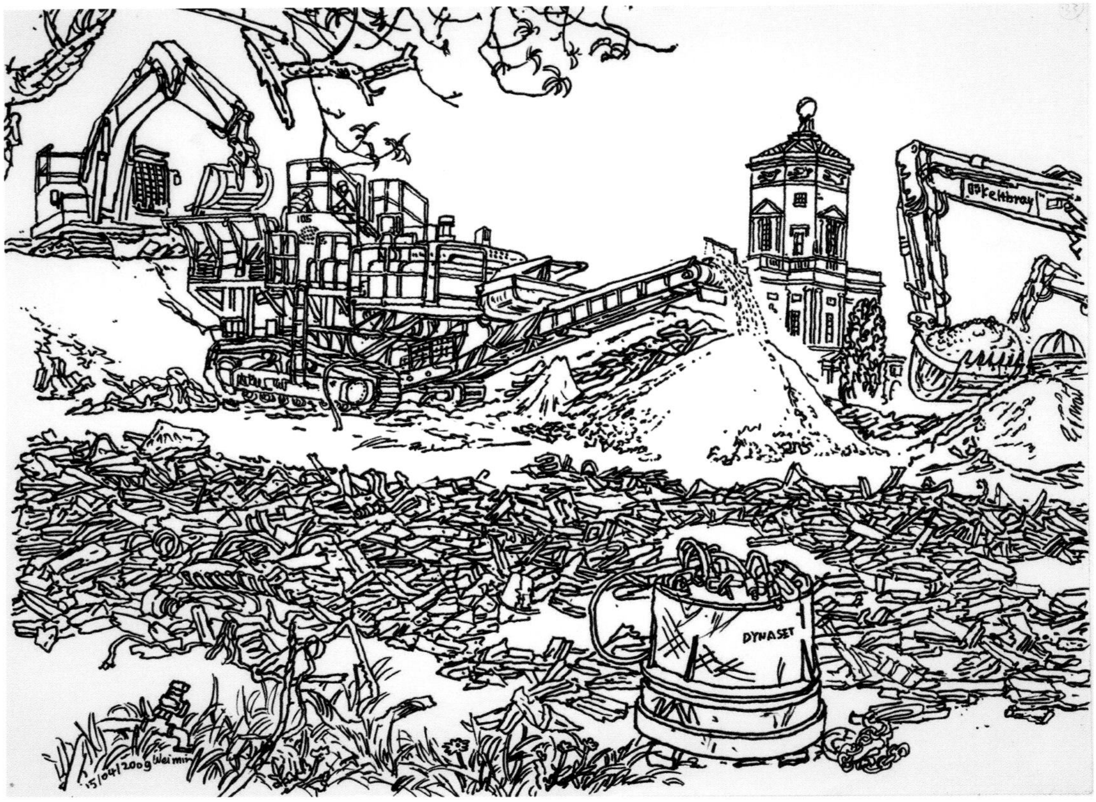

CAT.17
Breaking stones. 15 April 2009. Felt-tip pen on cartridge paper. Paper size: 29.7 × 42 cm

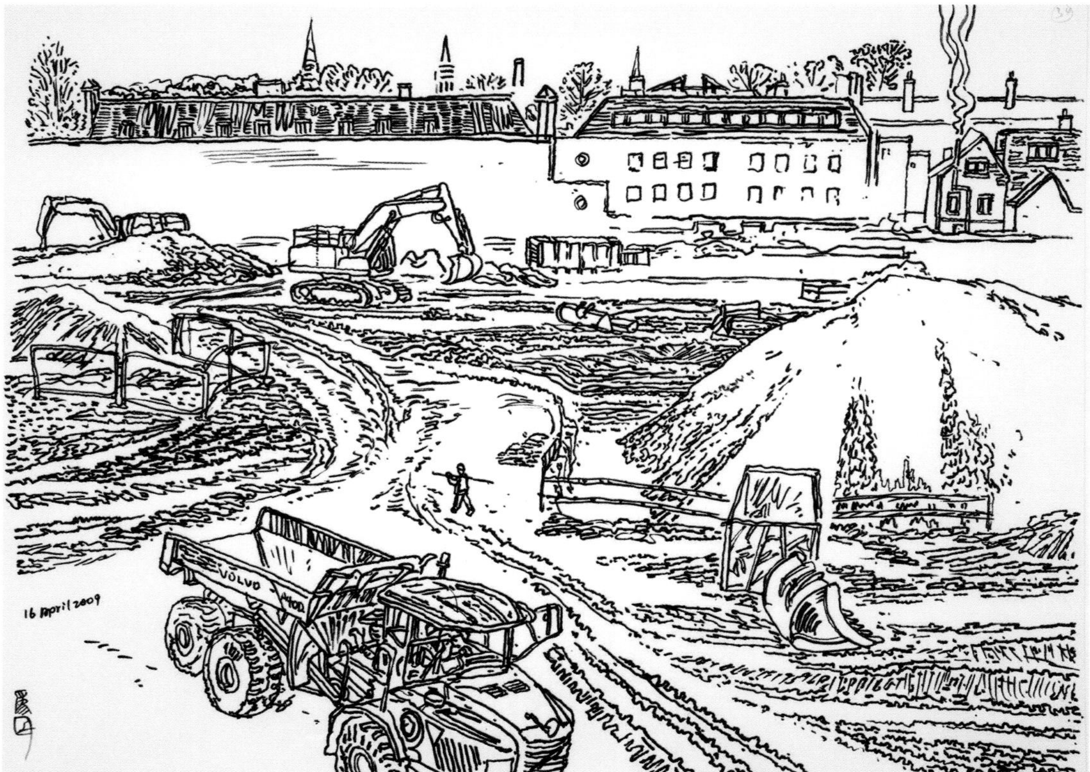

CAT.18
Tracks – view from the Gibson building. 16 April 2009. Felt-tip pen on cartridge paper. Paper size: 29.7 × 42 cm

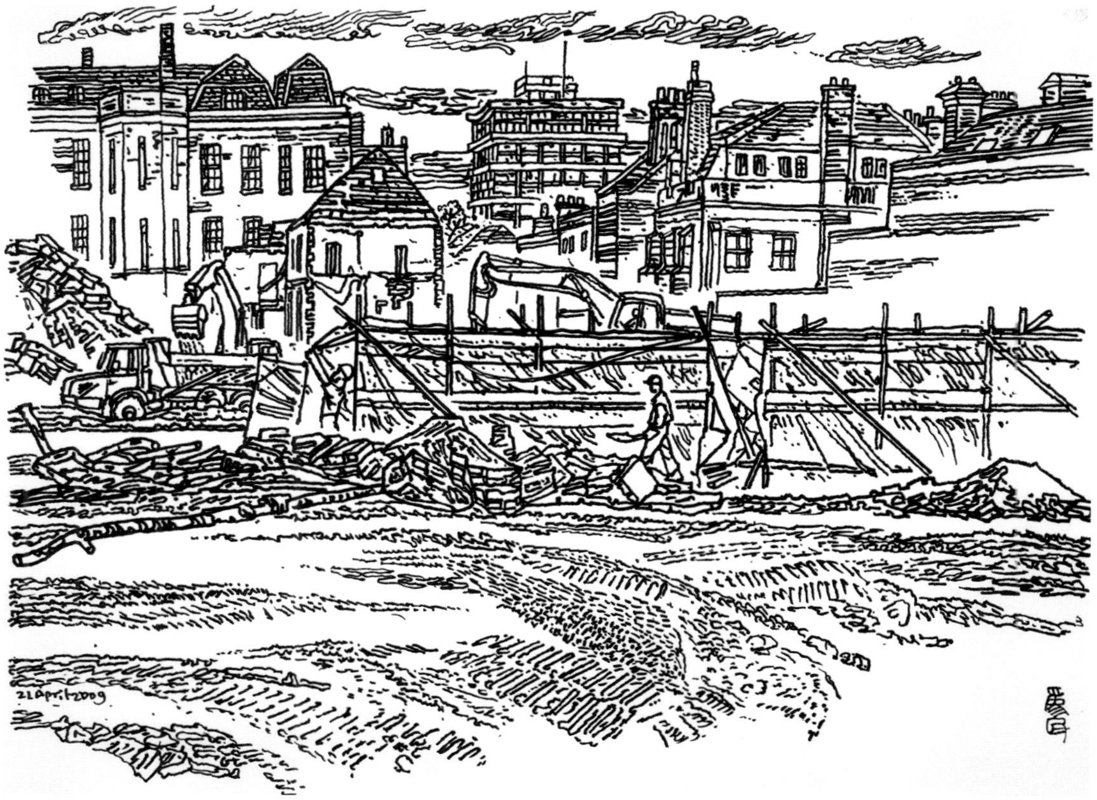

CAT.19
Covering a Neolithic square enclosed ditch – behind Somerville College. 21 April 2009. Felt-tip pen on cartridge paper. Paper size: 29.7 × 42 cm

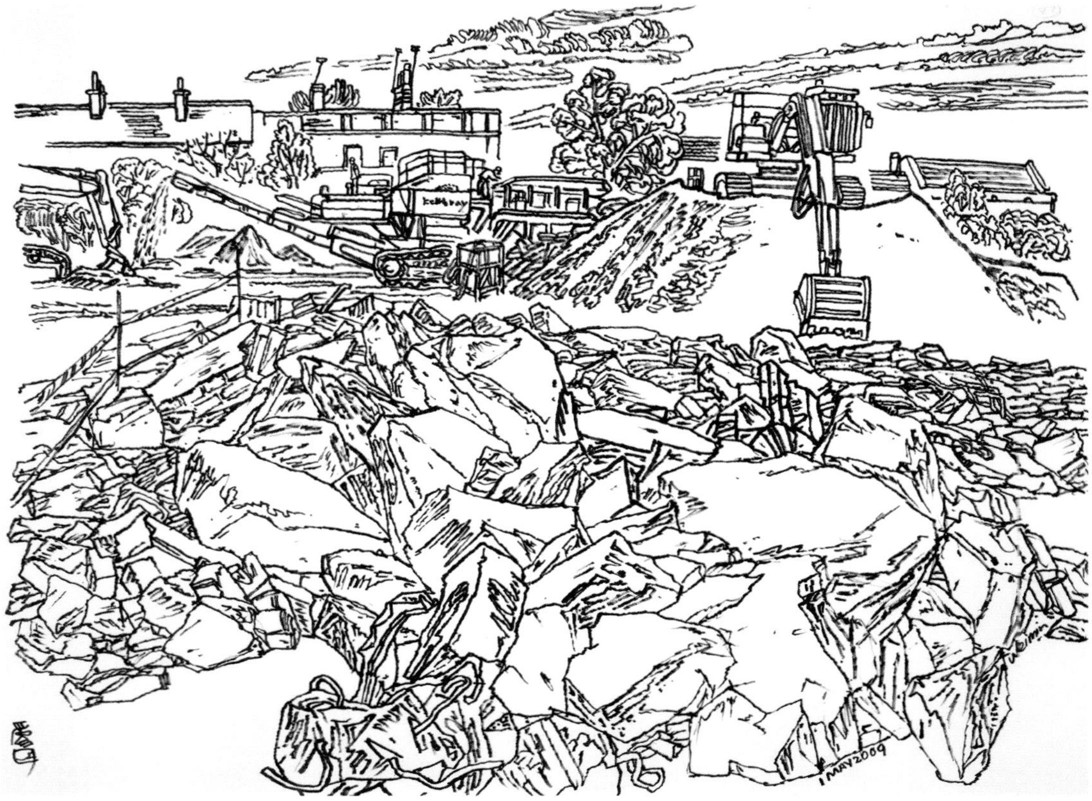

CAT.20
Boulders and bricks. 1 May 2009. Felt-tip pen on cartridge paper. Paper size: 29.7 × 42 cm

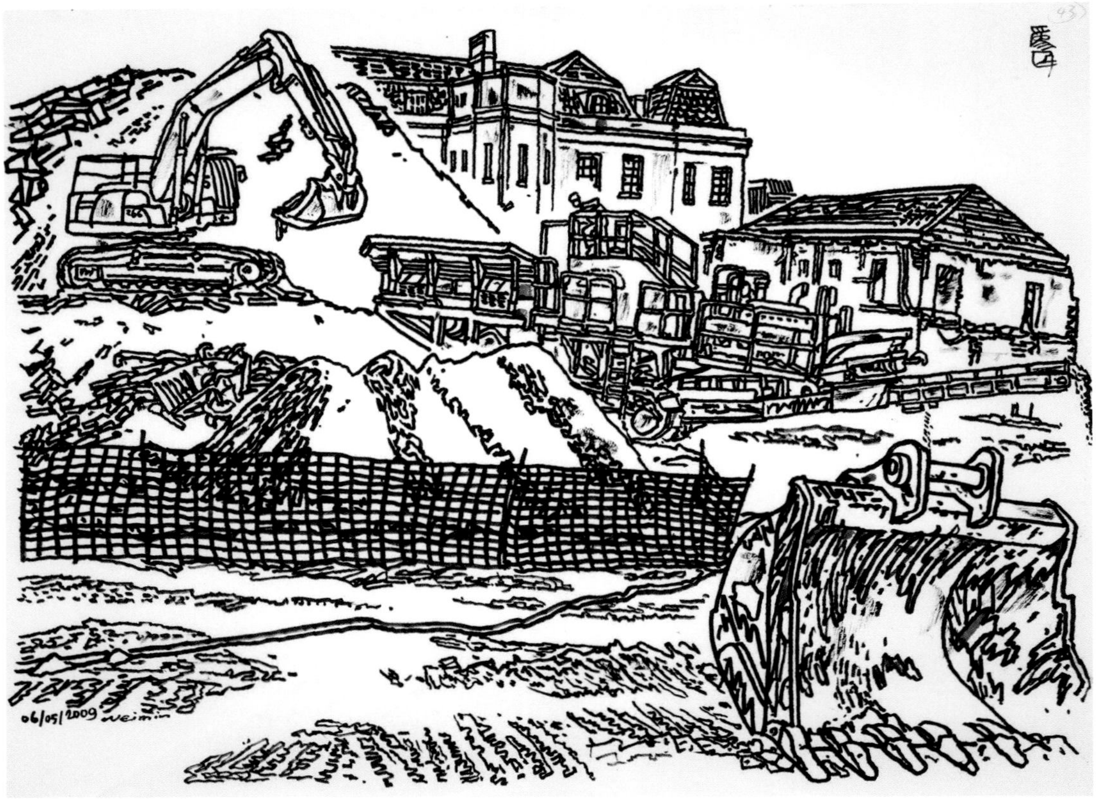

CAT.21
Turning past into dust. 6 May 2009. Felt-tip pen on cartridge paper. Paper size: 29.7 × 42 cm

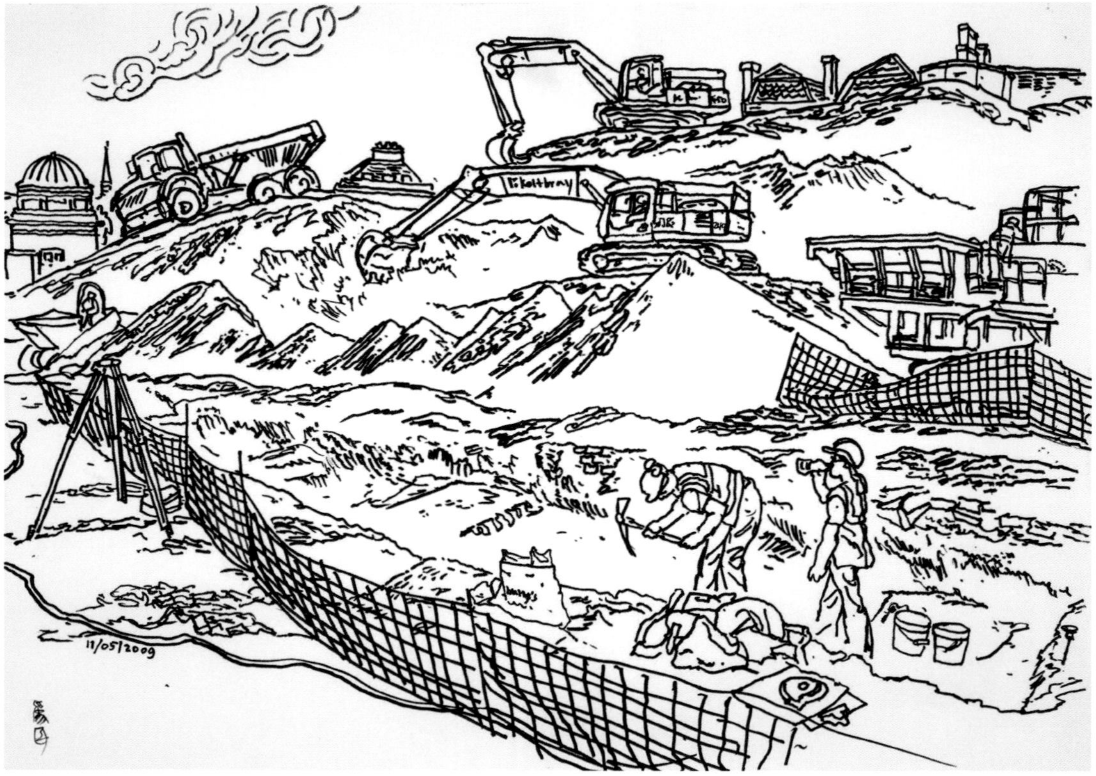

CAT.22
In search of a lost past. 11 May 2009. Felt-tip pen on cartridge paper. Paper size: 29.7 × 42 cm

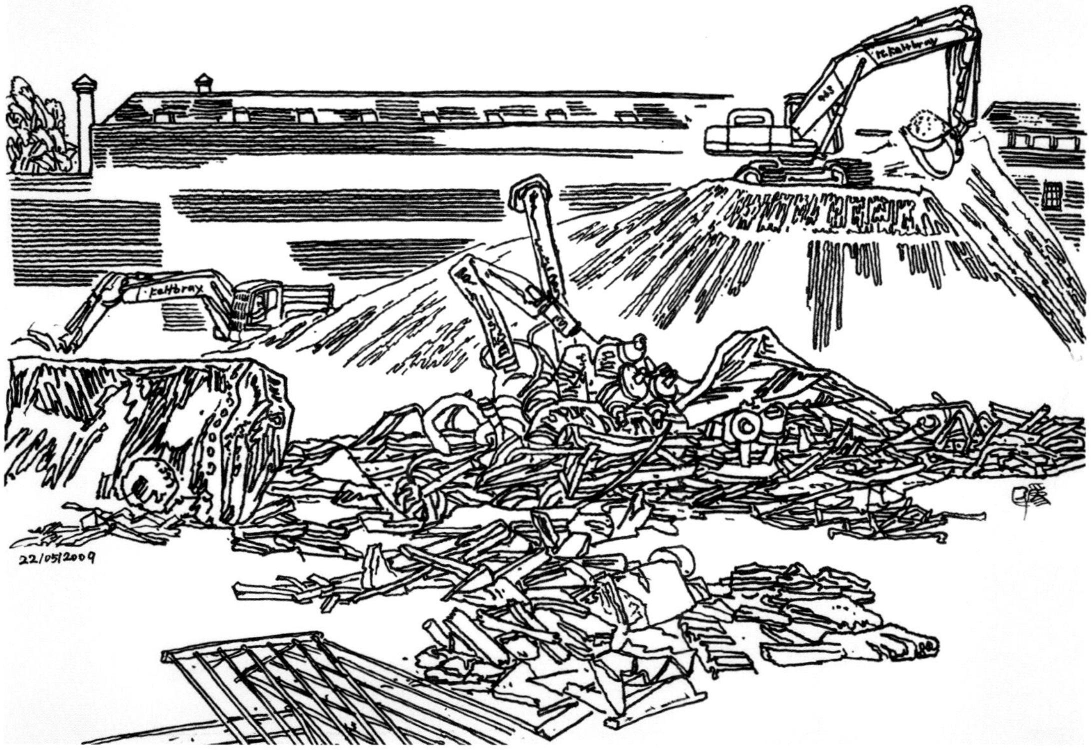

CAT.23
Mountains arising. 22 May 2009. Felt-tip pen on cartridge paper. Paper size: 29.7 × 42 cm

CAT.24
Unfinished. 1 June 2009. Brush on *xuan* paper. Paper size: 40 × 178 cm

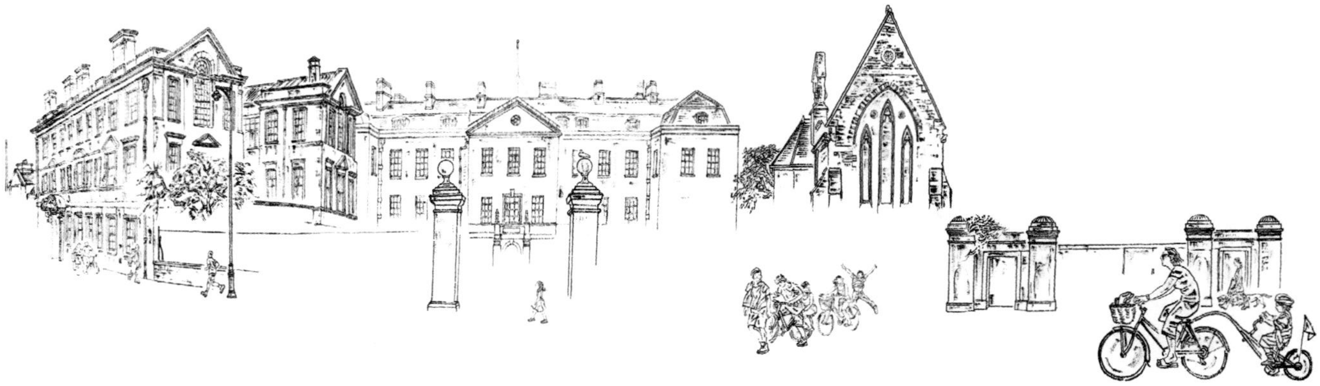

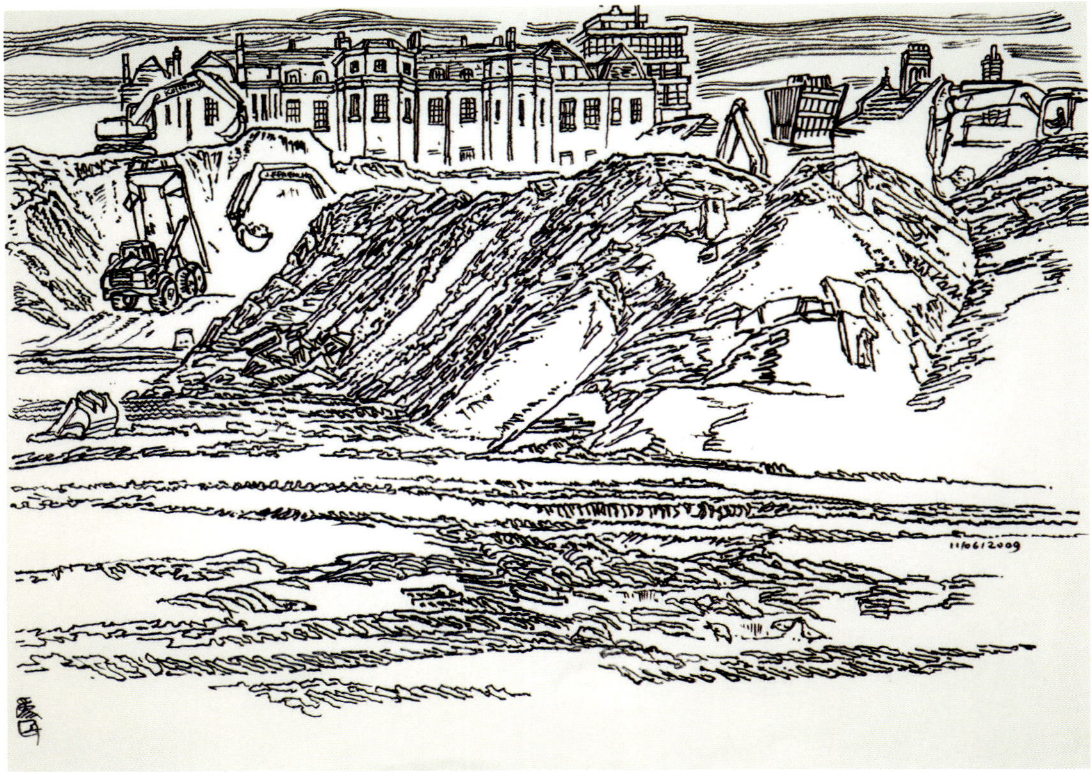

CAT.25
Moving mountains. 11 June 2009. Felt-tip pen on cartridge paper. Paper size: 29.7 × 42 cm

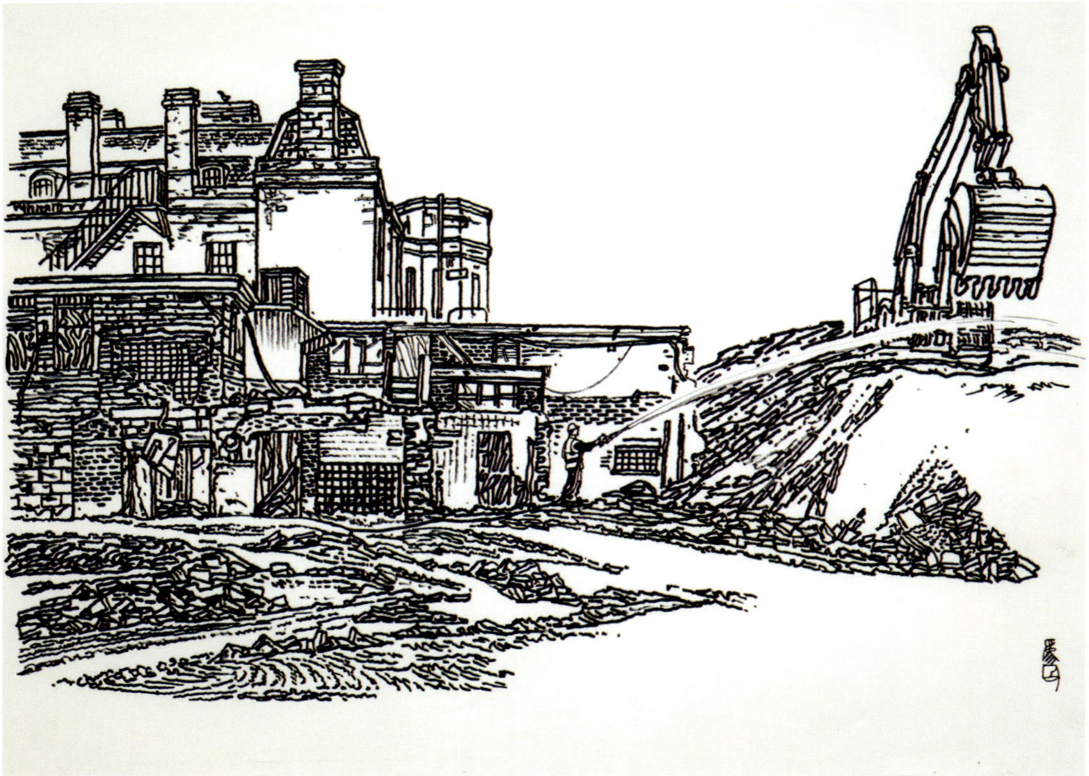

CAT.26
Damping down the past – beside the former Radcliffe Infirmary. 7 July 2009. Felt-tip pen on cartridge paper. Paper size: 29.7 × 42 cm

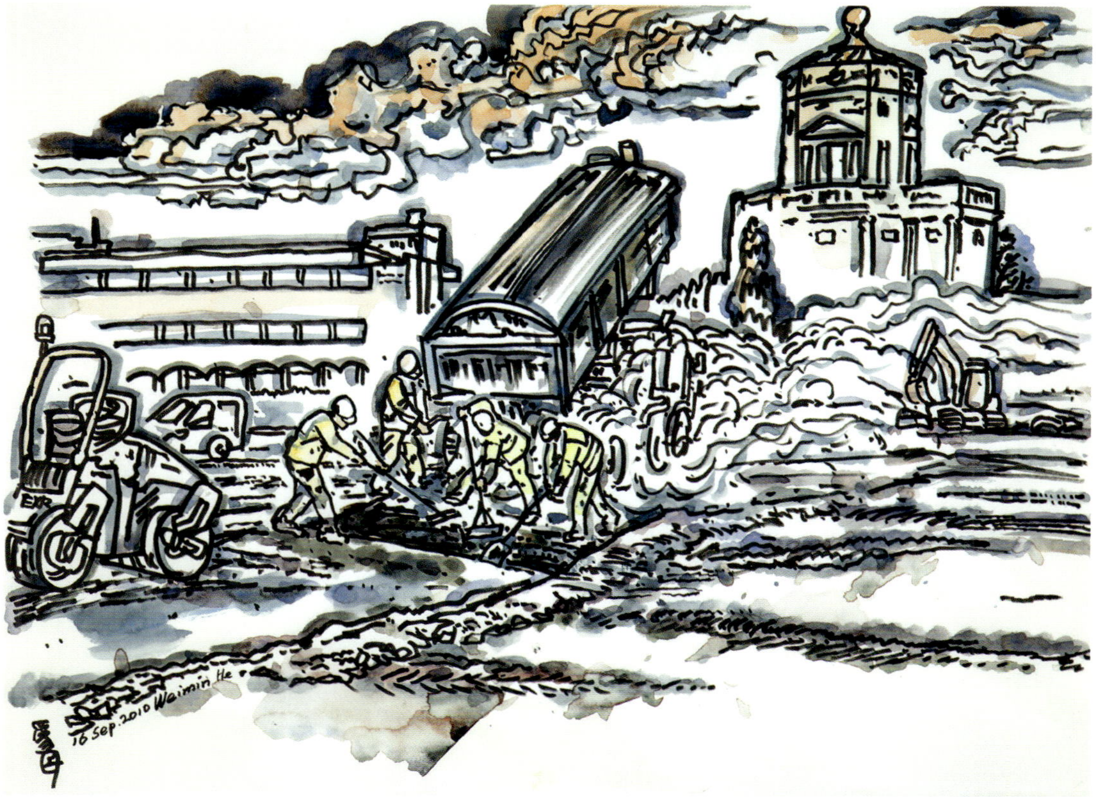

CAT.27
Heatwave. 16 September 2010. Felt-tip pen and watercolour on cartridge paper. Paper size: 29.7 × 42 cm

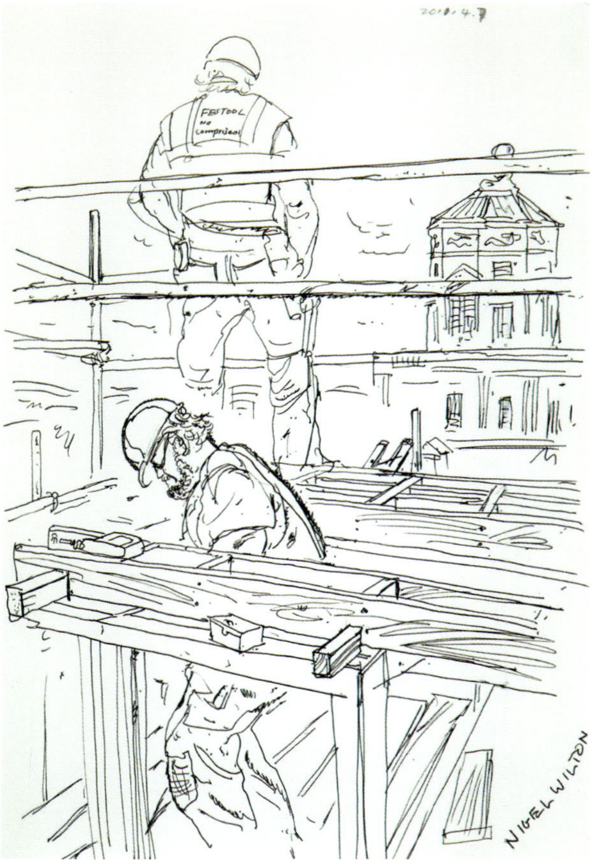

CAT.28
Carpenters – Somerville College student accommodation. 7 April 2011. Pen and ink on sketchbook made of cartridge paper. Paper size: 21 × 29.7 cm

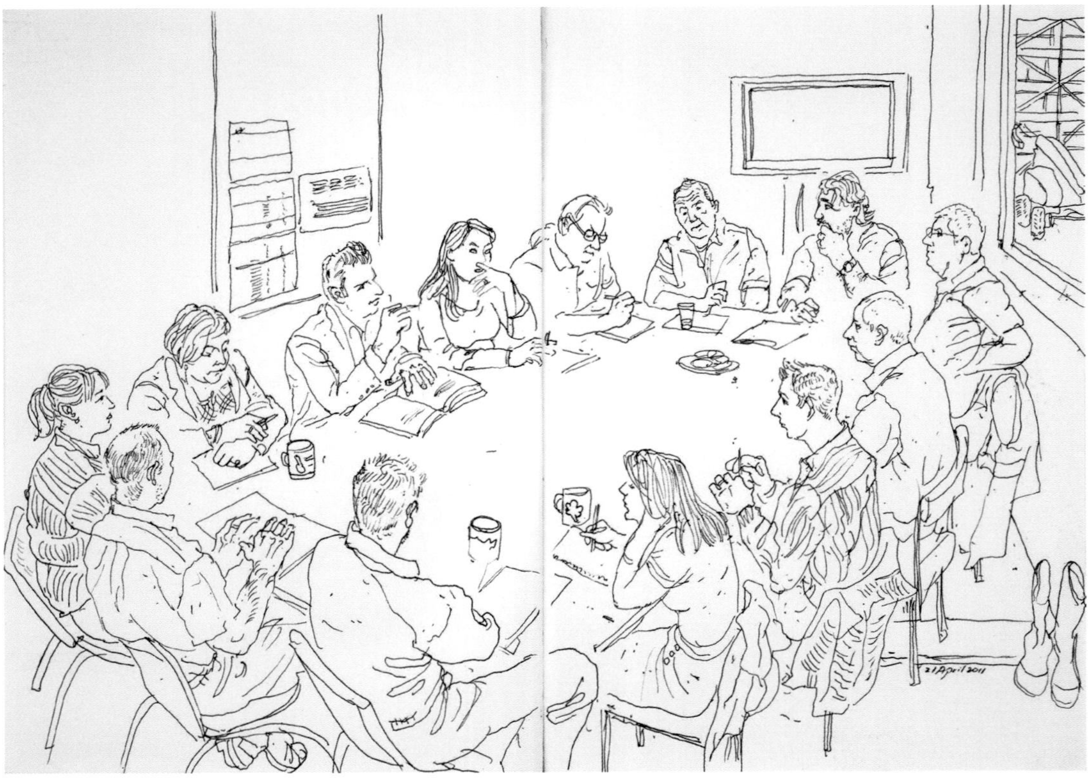

CAT.29

The meeting of the minds.
21 April 2011. Pen and ink on sketchbook made of cartridge paper. Paper size: 29.7 × 42 cm

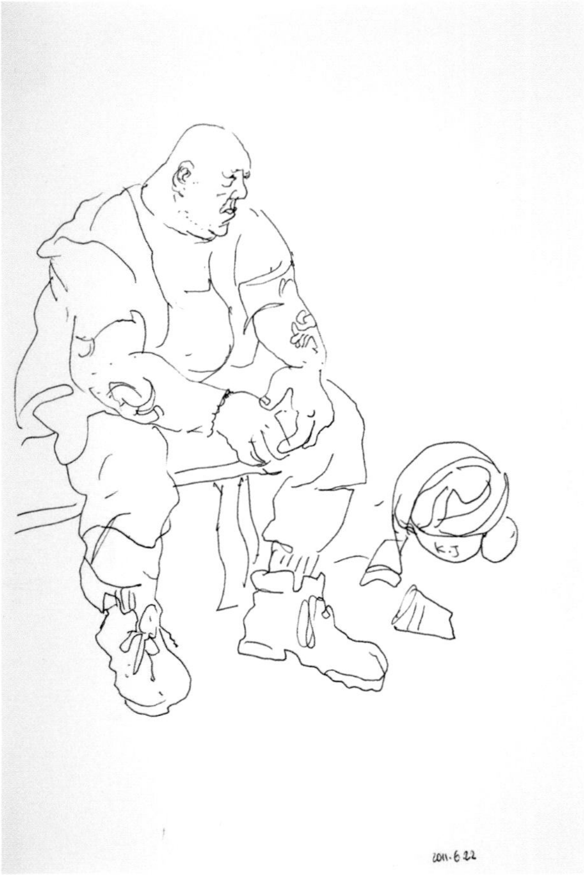

CAT.30

Daydreaming. 22 June 2012. Pen and ink on sketchbook made of cartridge paper. Paper size: 21 × 29.7 cm

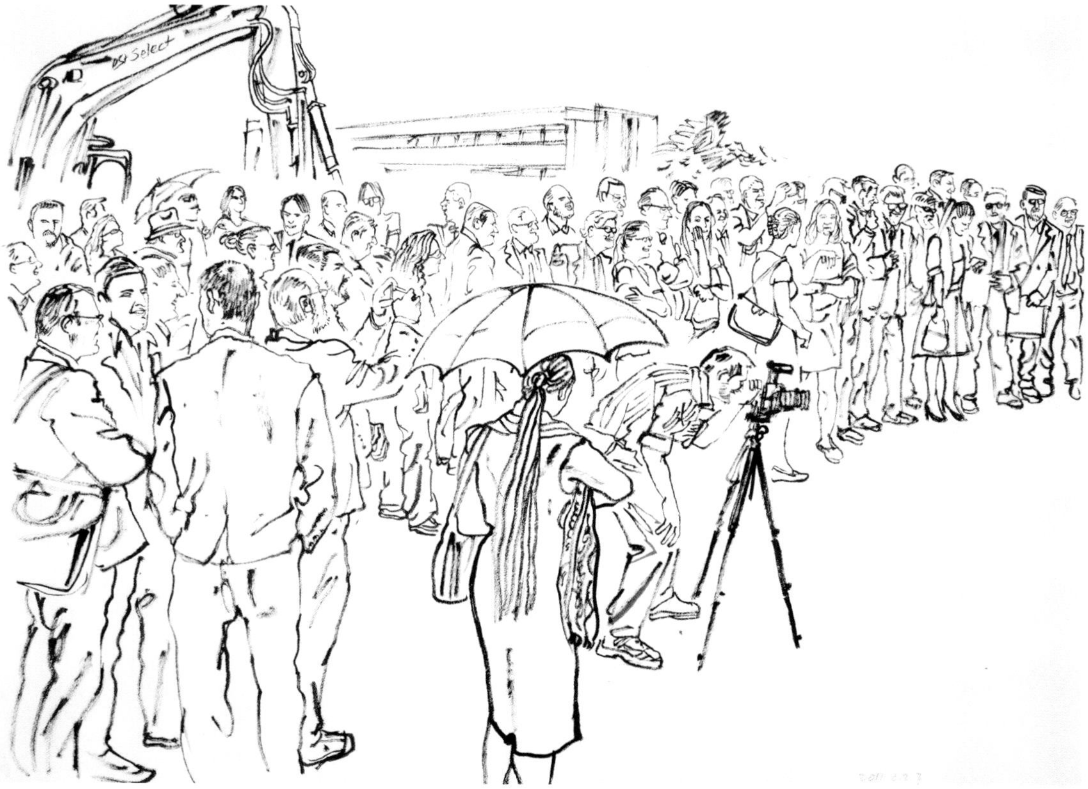

CAT.31
View through the lens – Mathematical Institute's topping out ceremony. 3 August 2011. Brush and ink on sketchbook made of cartridge paper. Paper size: 29.7 × 42 cm

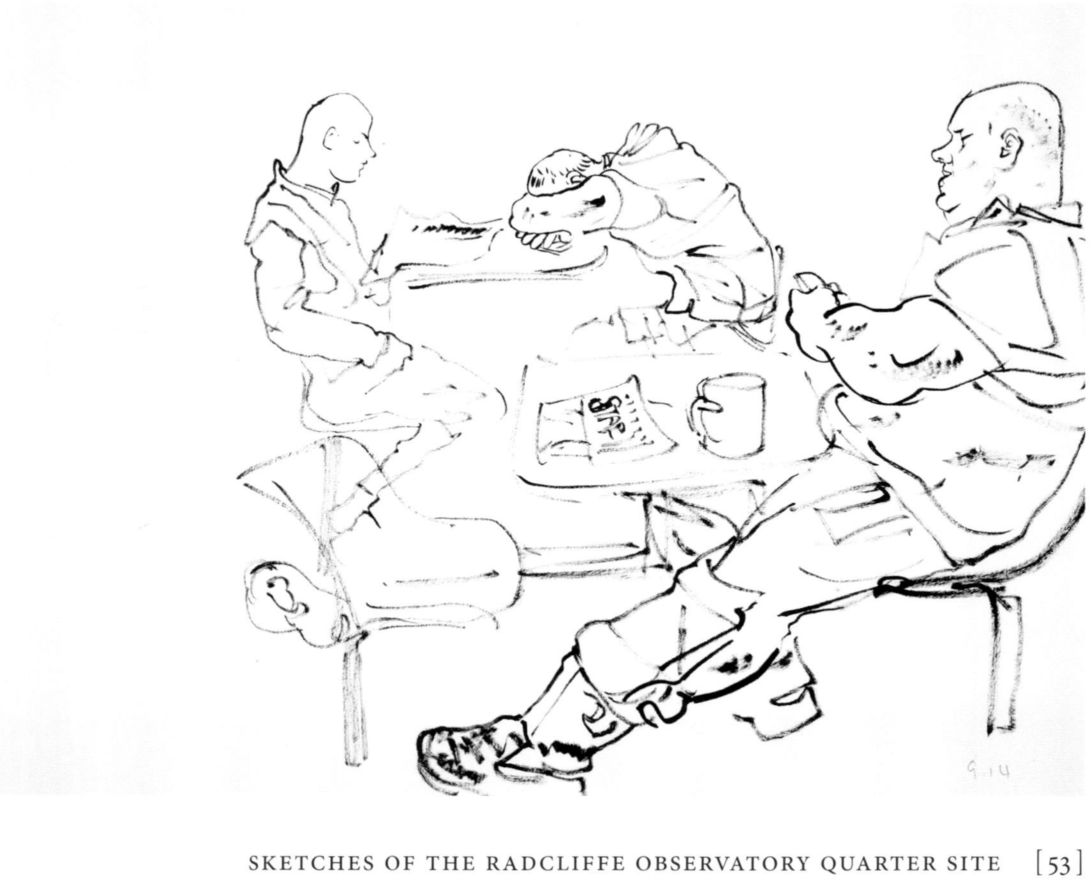

CAT.32
Builders in canteen.
14 September 2011. Brush and ink on sketchbook made of cartridge paper. Paper size: 29.7 × 42 cm

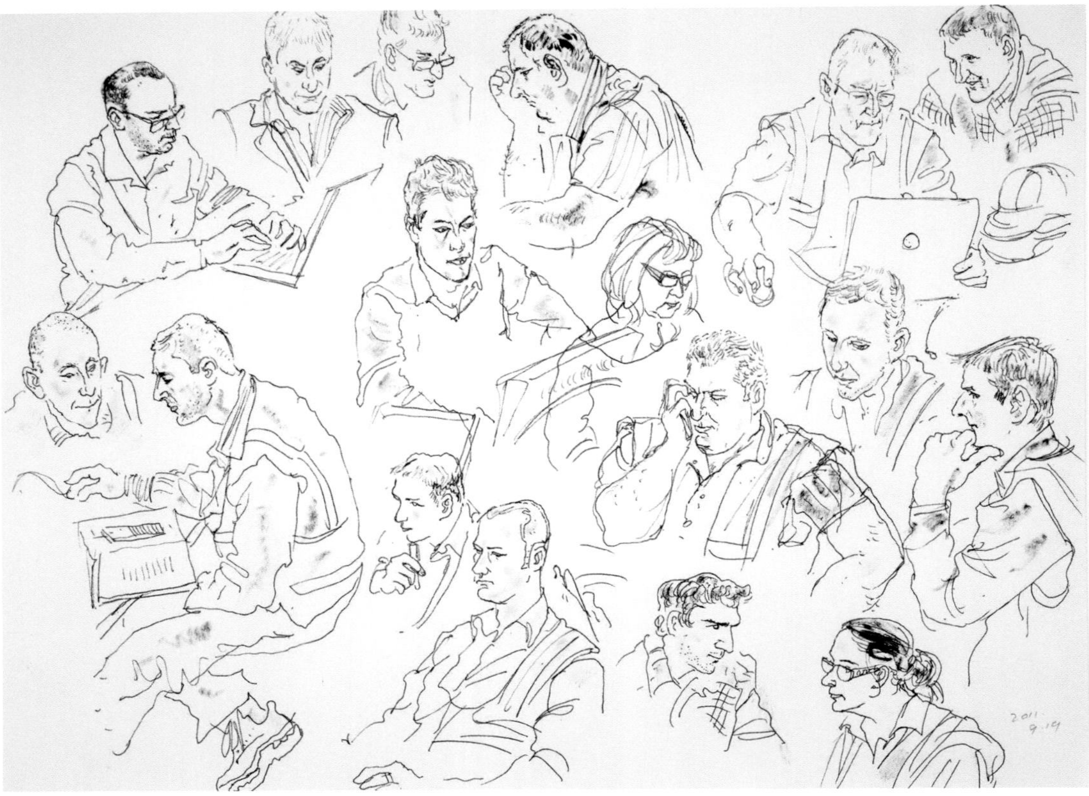

CAT.33
Managers at work. 19 September 2011. Pen and ink on sketchbook made of cartridge paper. Paper size: 29.7 × 42 cm

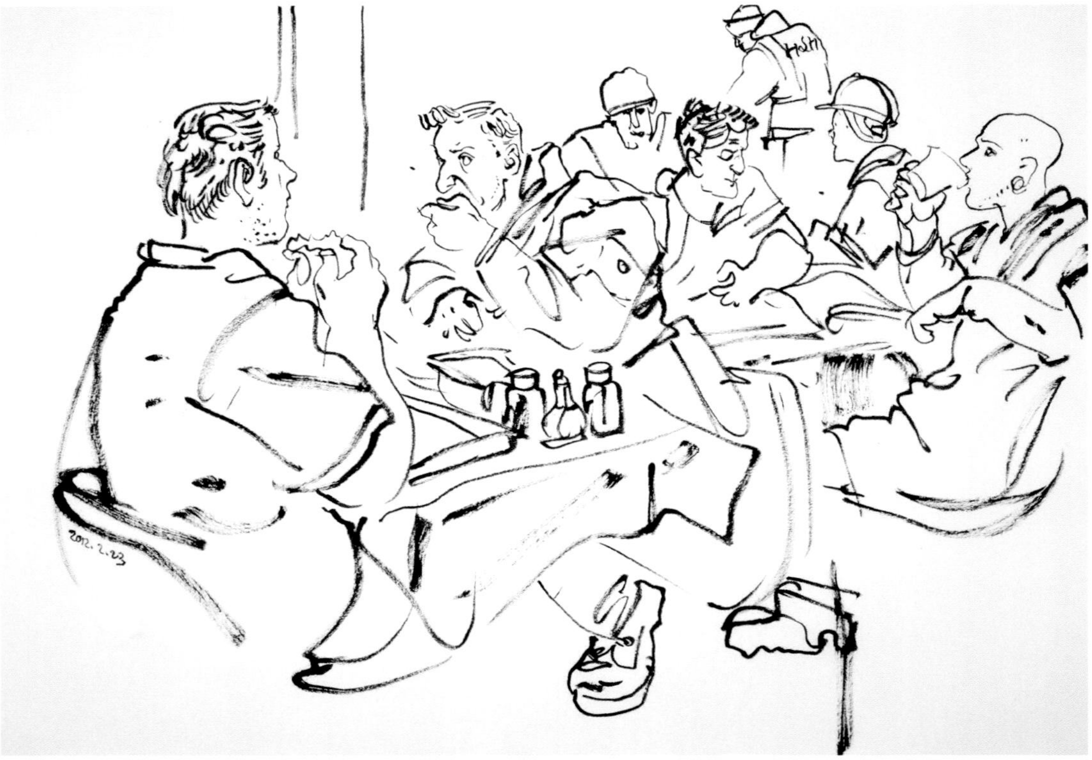

CAT.34
Tucking in. 23 February 2012. Brush and ink on sketchbook made of cartridge paper. Paper size: 29.7 × 42 cm

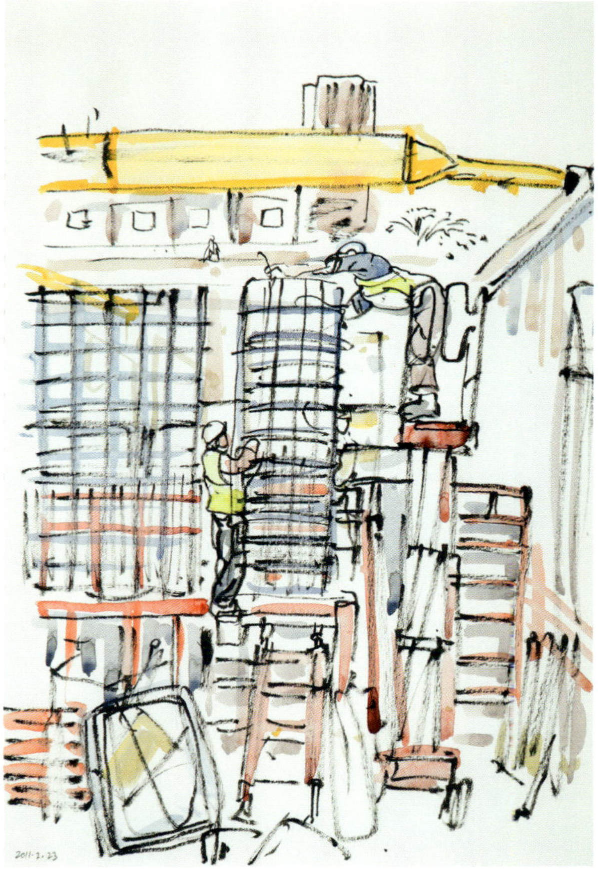

CAT.35
Base calculation – Mathematical Institute. 23 February 2012. Brush, ink and watercolour on sketchbook made of cartridge paper. Paper size: 42 × 29.7 cm

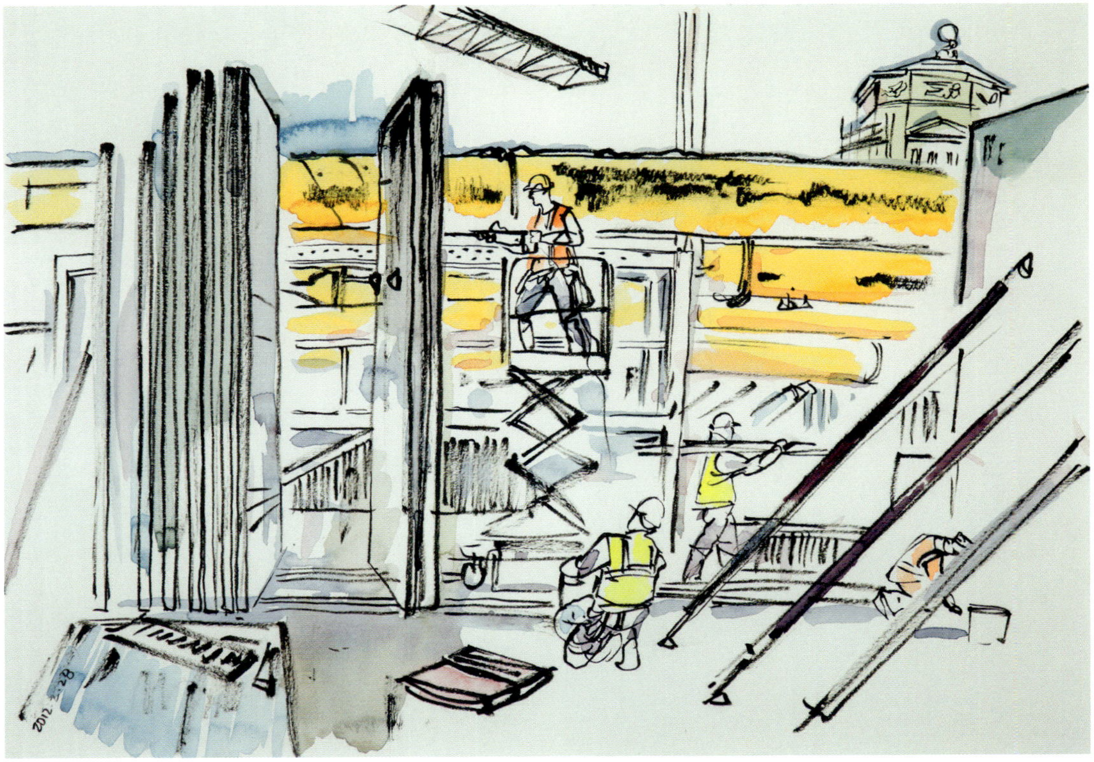

CAT.36
Shoring up the basement – Mathematical Institute.
28 February 2012. Brush, ink and watercolour on sketchbook made of cartridge paper. Paper size: 29.7 × 42 cm

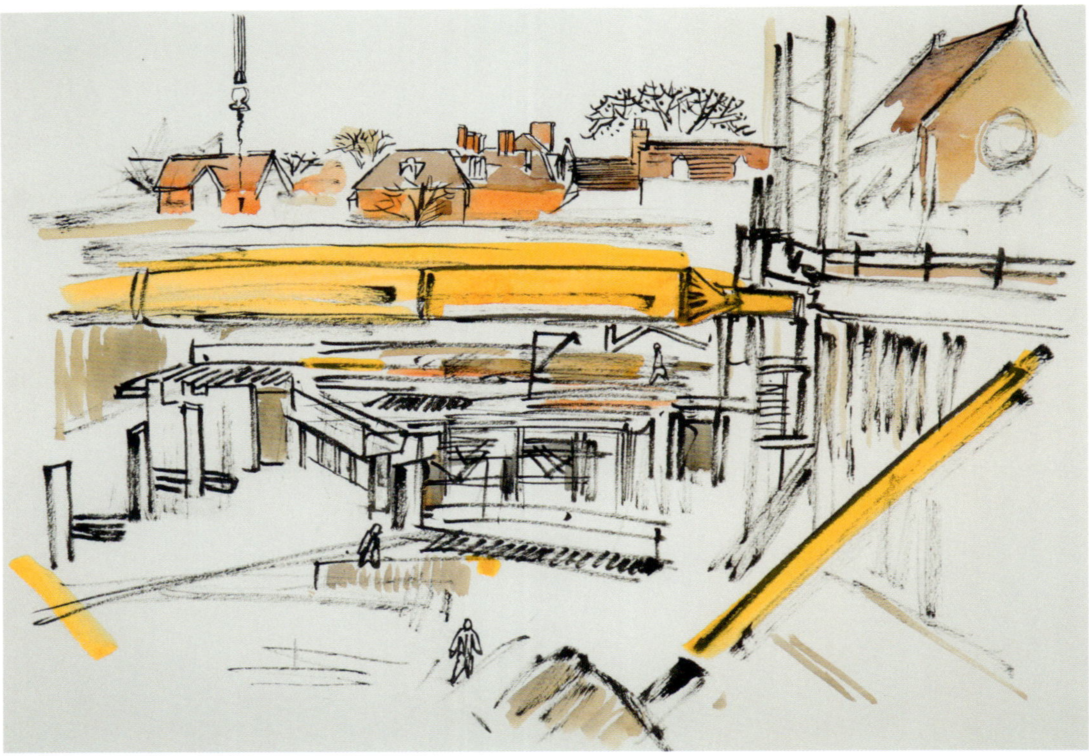

CAT.37 (left)
Core of strength – Mathematical Institute. 29 February 2012. Brush, ink and watercolour on sketchbook made of cartridge paper. Paper size: 29.7 × 42 cm

CAT.38 (bottom left)
Temporary support – Mathematical Institute. 9 March 2012. Brush, ink and watercolour on sketchbook made of cartridge paper. Paper size: 42 × 29.7 cm

CAT.39 (bottom right)
Tower. 4 January 2013. Brush, ink and watercolour on sketchbook made of cartridge paper. Paper size: 29.7 × 21cm

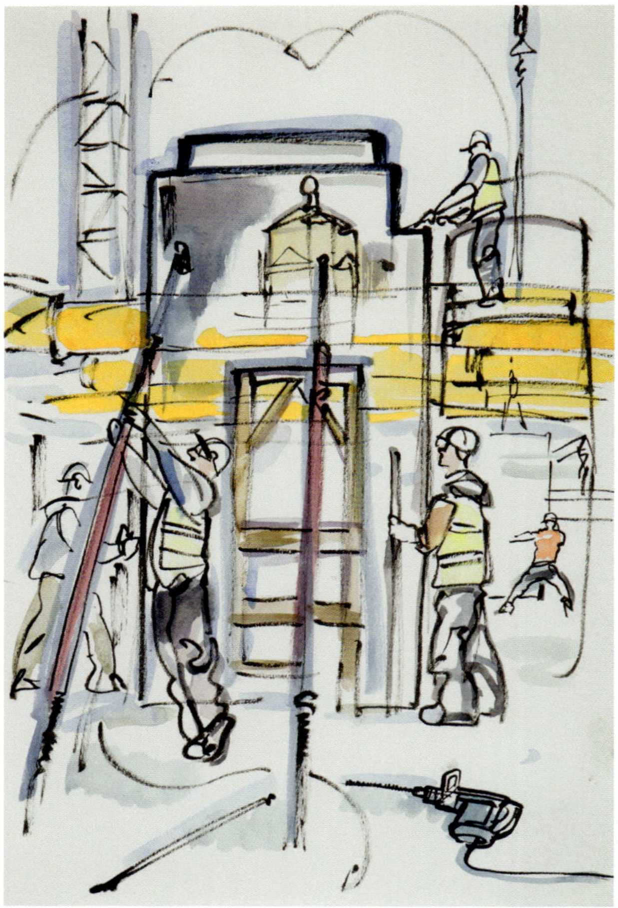

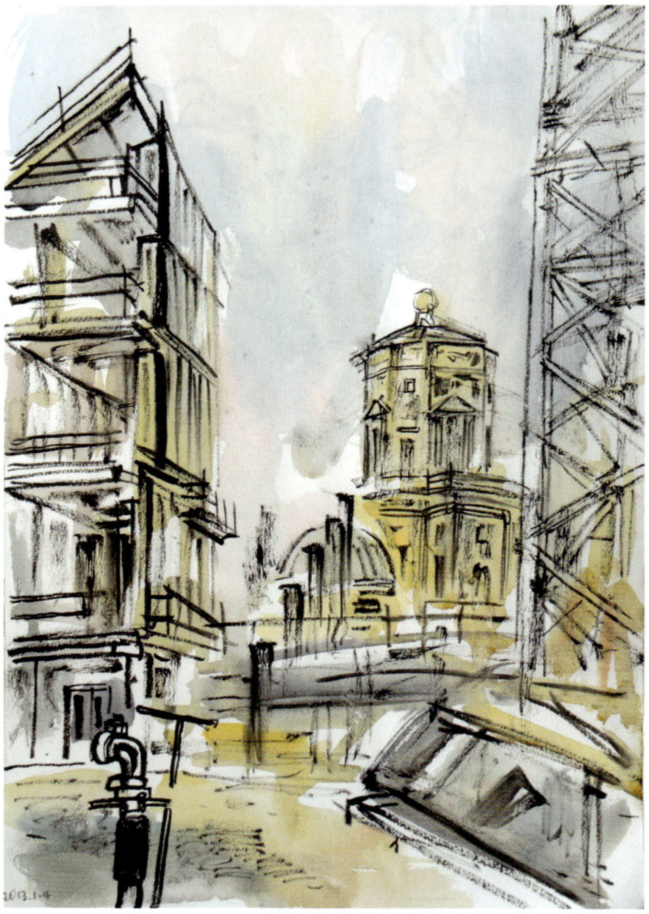

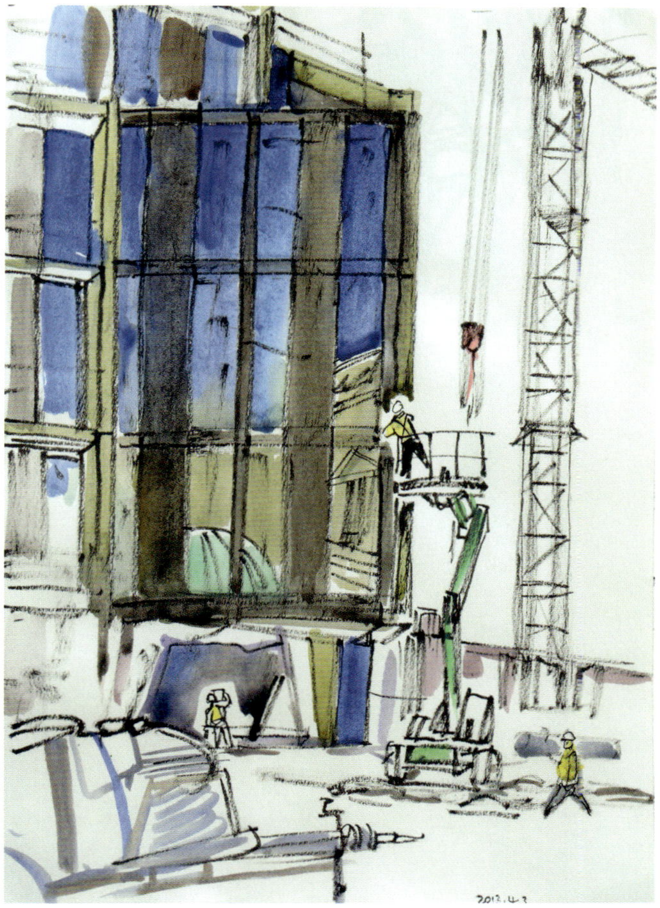

CAT.40
Blue reflections – Mathematical Institute. 3 April 2013. Brush, ink and watercolour on sketchbook made of cartridge paper. Paper size: 29.7 × 21cm

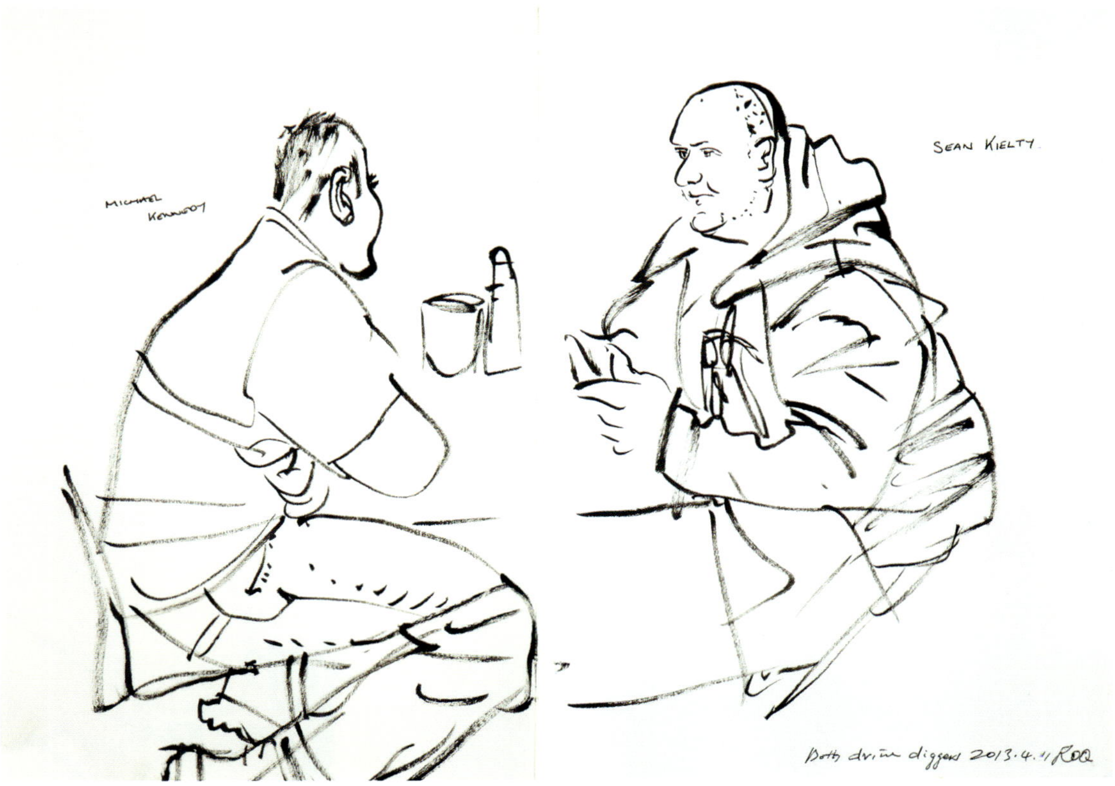

CAT.41
Digger drivers. 11 April 2013. Brush and ink on sketchbook made of cartridge paper. Paper size: 29.7 × 42cm

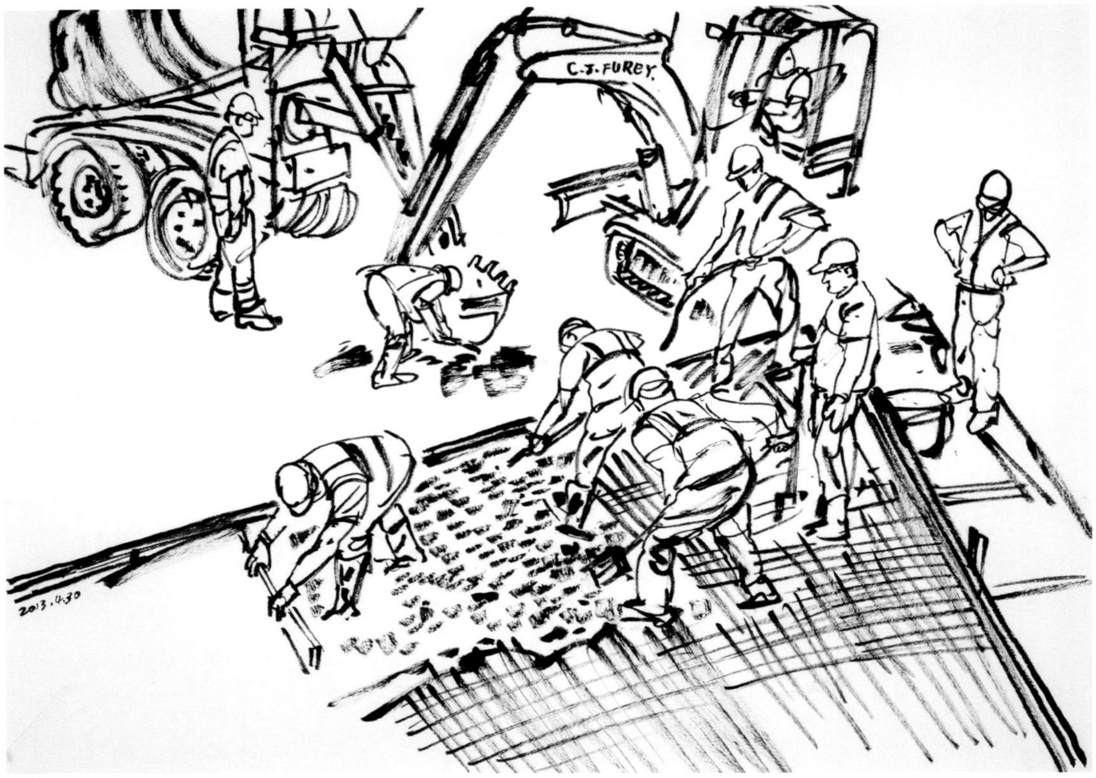

CAT.42
Smoothing concrete – Mathematical Institute.
30 April 2013. Brush and ink on sketchbook made of cartridge paper. Paper size: 29.7 × 42 cm

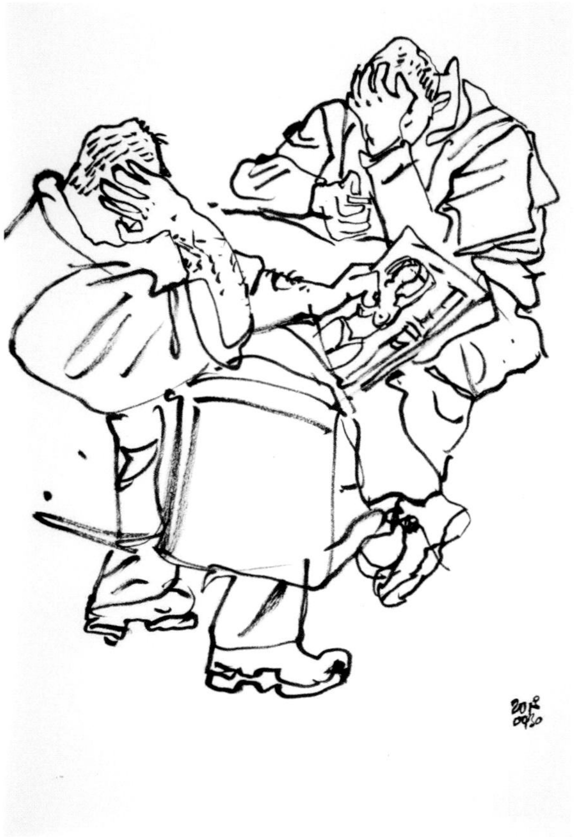

CAT.43
Engrossed – Radcliffe Observatory Quarter site canteen.
30 April 2013. Brush and ink on sketchbook made of cartridge paper. Paper size: 42 × 29.7cm

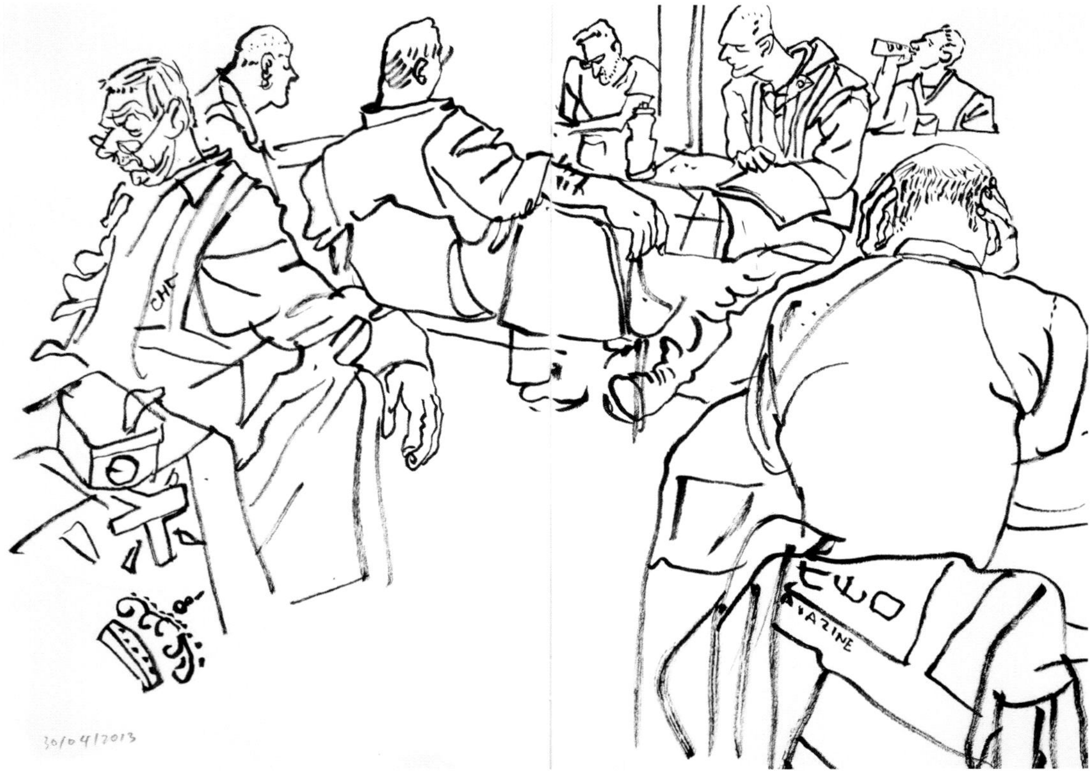

CAT.44
Knackered. 30 April 2013. Brush and ink on sketchbook made of cartridge paper. Paper size: 29.7 × 42cm

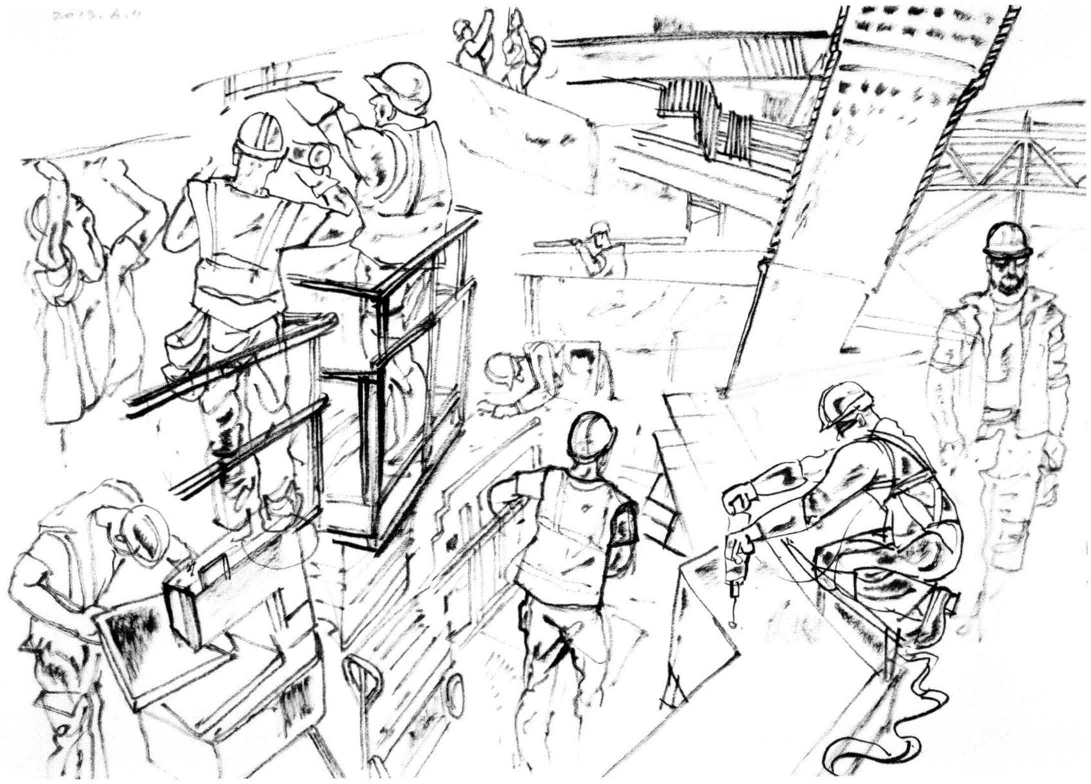

CAT.45
All trades on site – Mathematical Institute.
11 June 2013. Brush and ink on sketchbook made of cartridge paper. Paper size: 29.7 × 42 cm

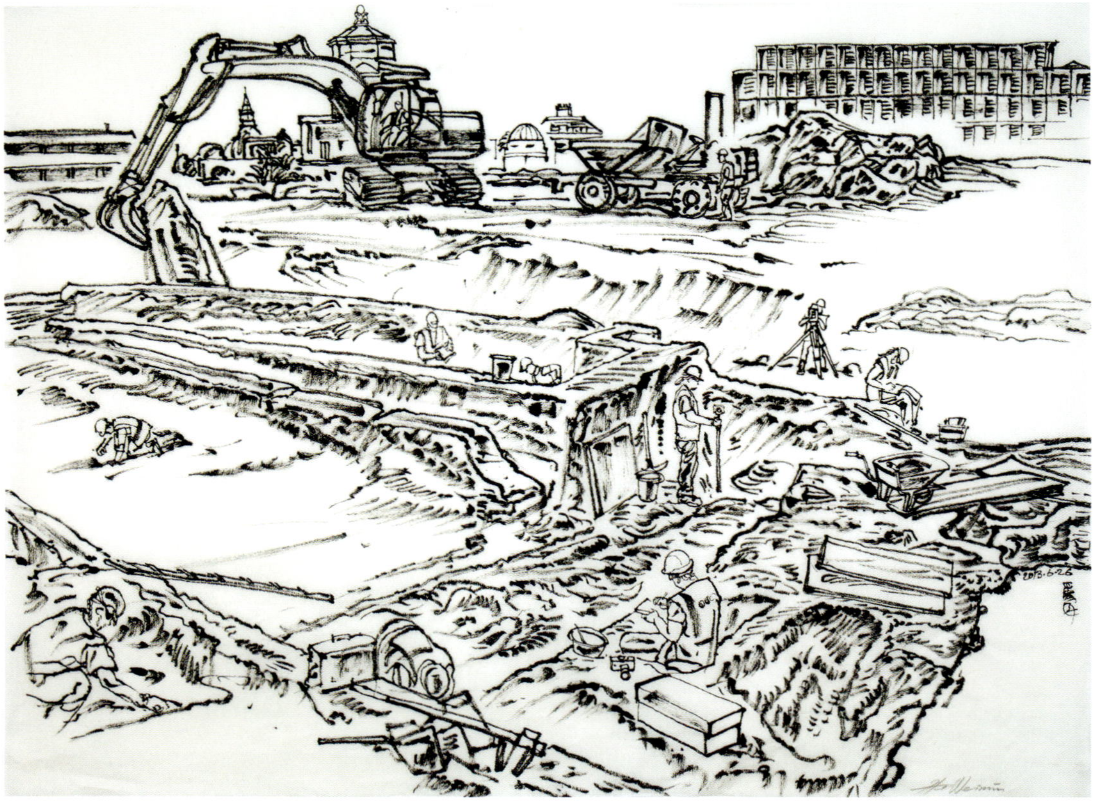

CAT.46
Uncovering the secret of the past – Blavatnik School of Government. 26 June 2013. Brush and ink on *xuan* paper. Paper size: 42 × 61 cm

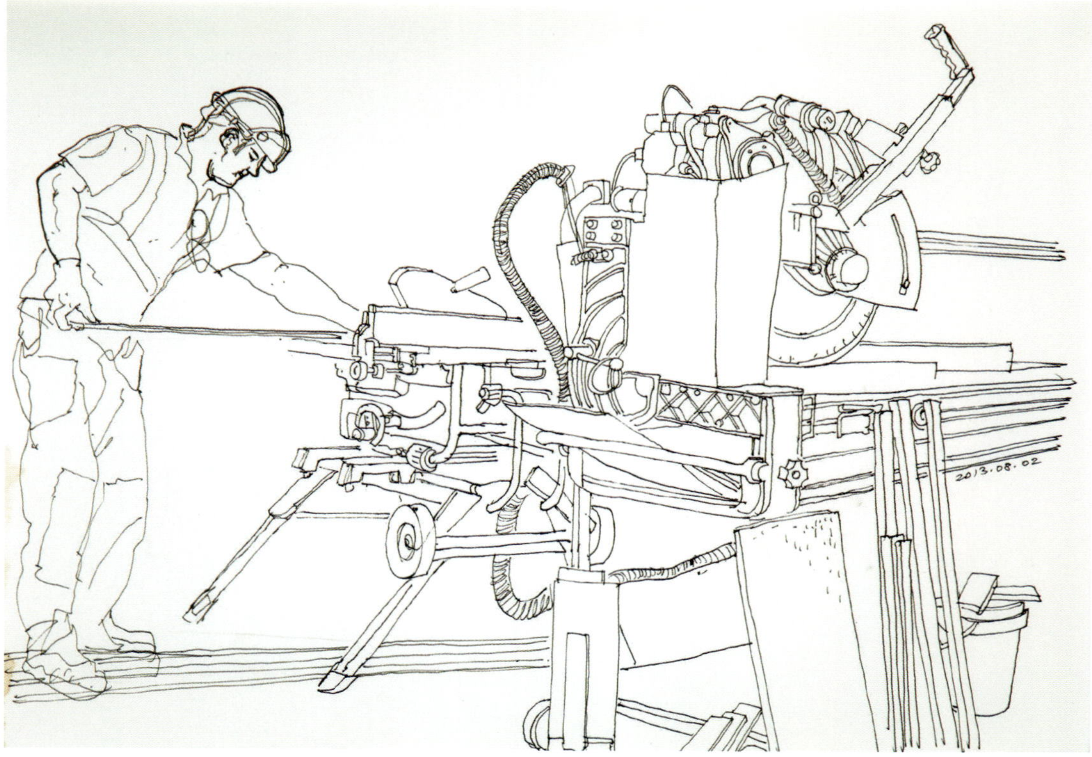

CAT.47
Slicing beam – Mathematical Institute. 2 August 2013. Pen and ink on sketchbook made of cartridge paper. Paper size: 21 × 29.7cm

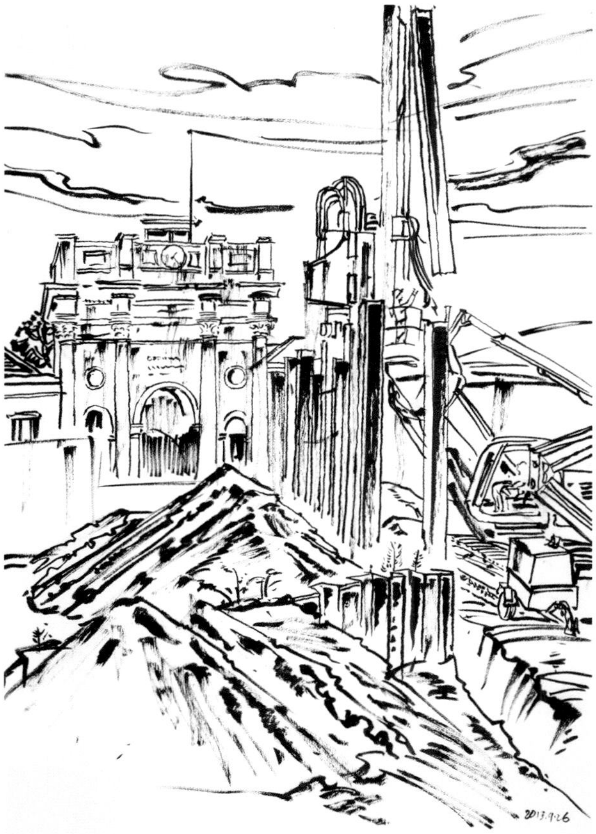

CAT.48 (left)
Steel and earth – Blavatnik School of Government. 26 September 2013. Brush and ink on sketchbook made of cartridge paper. Paper size: 29.7 × 42 cm

CAT.49 (bottom left)
Changing room – Radcliffe Observatory Quarter. 25 November 2013. Brush and ink on *xuan* paper. Paper size: 42 × 61 cm

CAT.50 (bottom right))
Basement work under way – Blavatnik School of Government. 9 January 2014. Brush and ink on sketchbook made of cartridge paper. Paper size: 42 × 29.7 cm

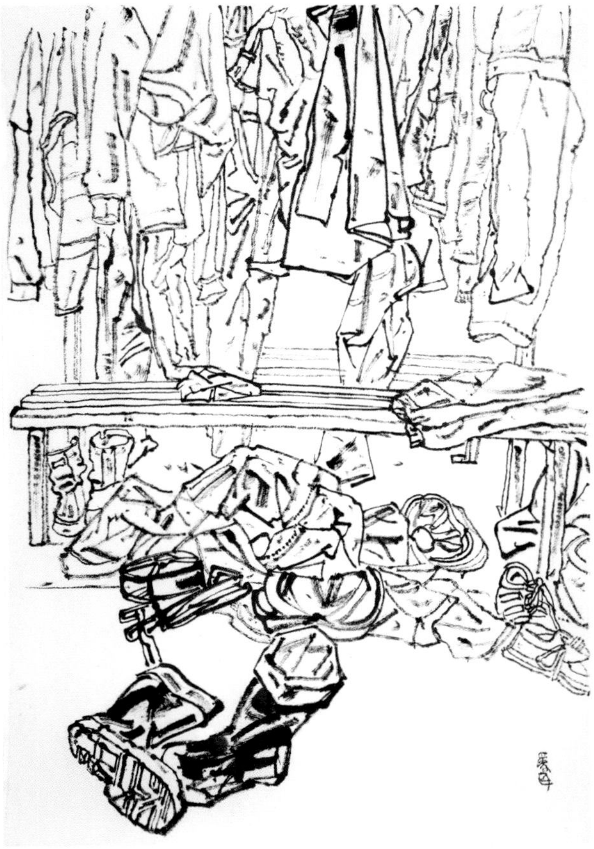

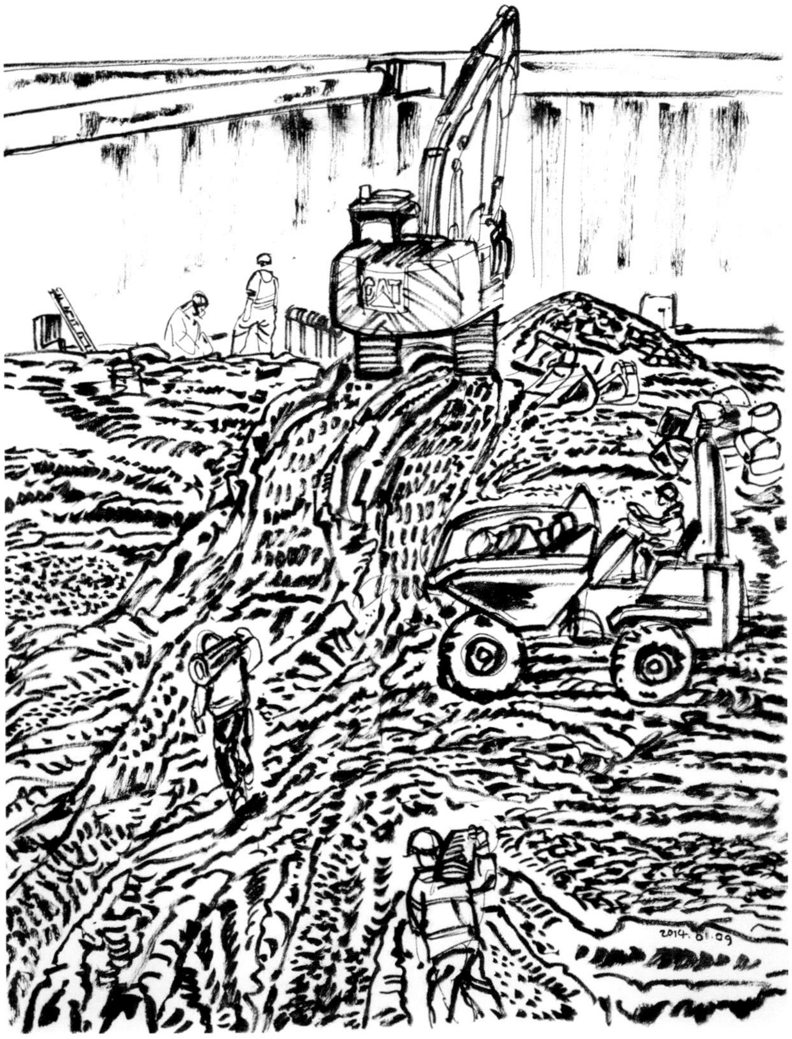

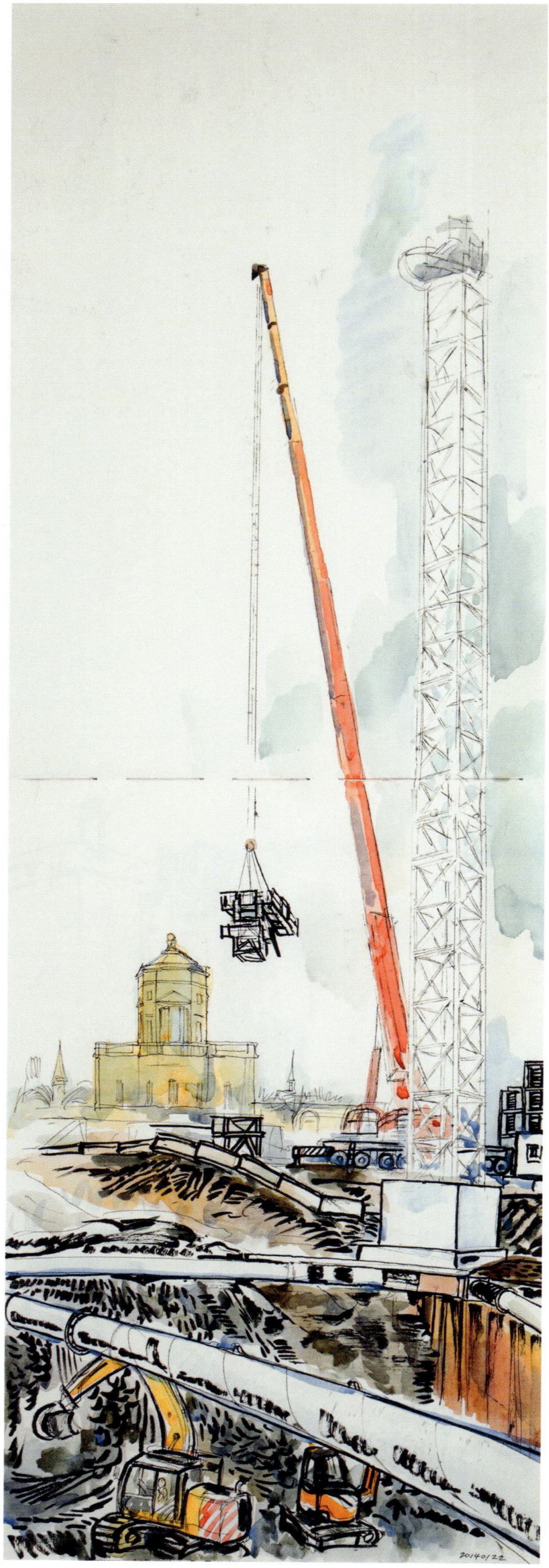

CAT.51
Dreaming spires – Blavatnik School of Government. 22 January 2014.
Pen, brush, ink and watercolour on sketchbook made of cartridge paper.
Paper size: 84 × 29.7 cm

CAT.52
Clearing the basement – Blavatnik School of Government. 22 January 2014.
Pen and watercolour on sketchbook made of cartridge paper. Paper size: 42 × 29.7 cm

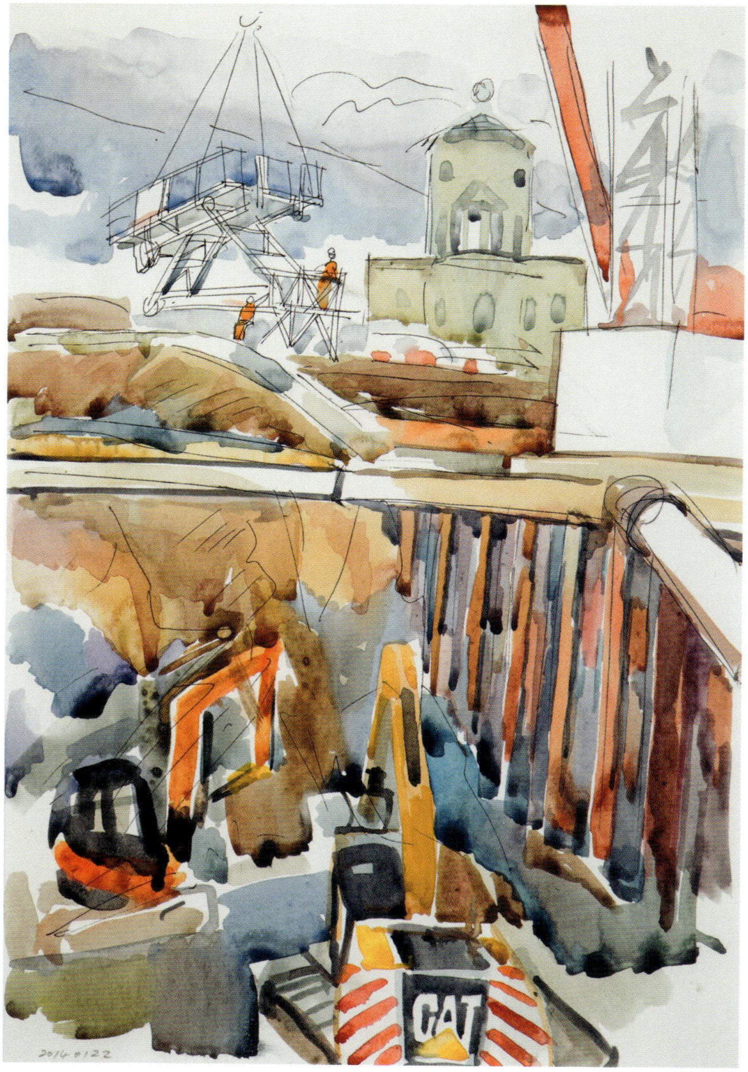

CAT.53 (right)
A delicate balance – Blavatnik School of Government.
13 February 2014. Pen and watercolour on sketchbook made of cartridge paper. Paper size: 29.7 × 42 cm

CAT.54 (bottom left)
Laying of the metal grid – Blavatnik School of Government basement.
19 February 2014. Brush and ink on sketchbook made of cartridge paper. Paper size: 42 × 29.7 cm

CAT.55 (bottom right)
Yellow excavator – Blavatnik School of Government basement with Andrew Wiles building. 26 February 2014. Brush, ink and watercolour on sketchbook made of cartridge paper. Paper size: 42 × 29.7 cm

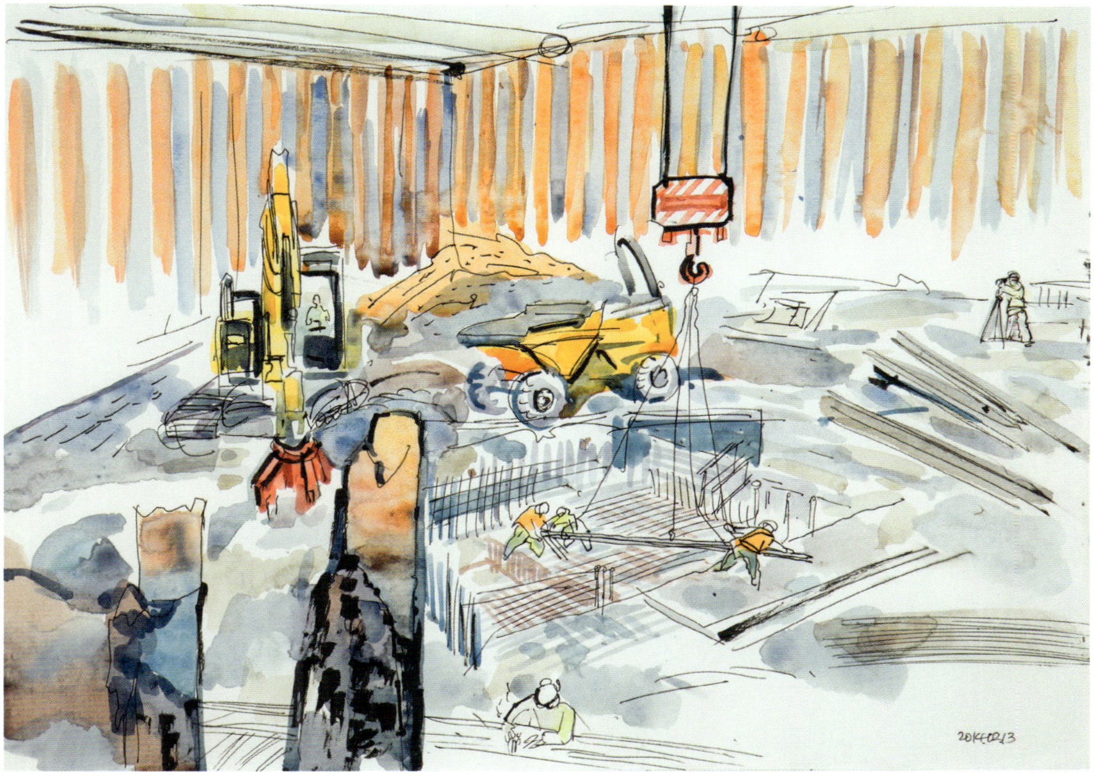

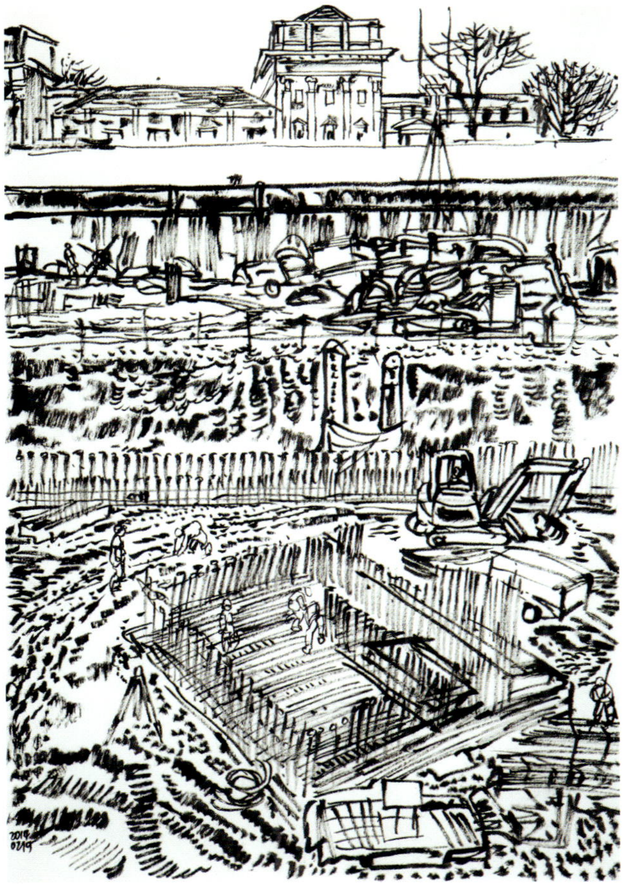

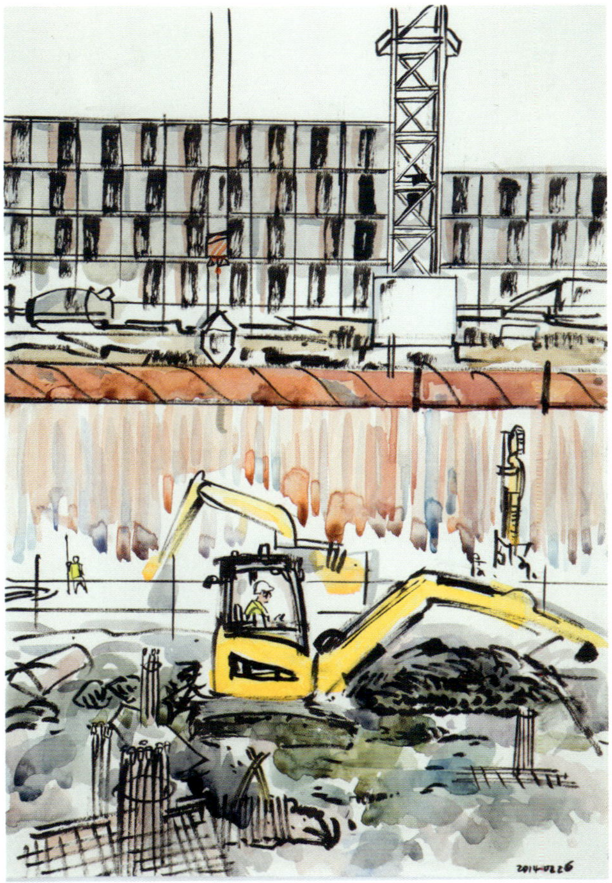

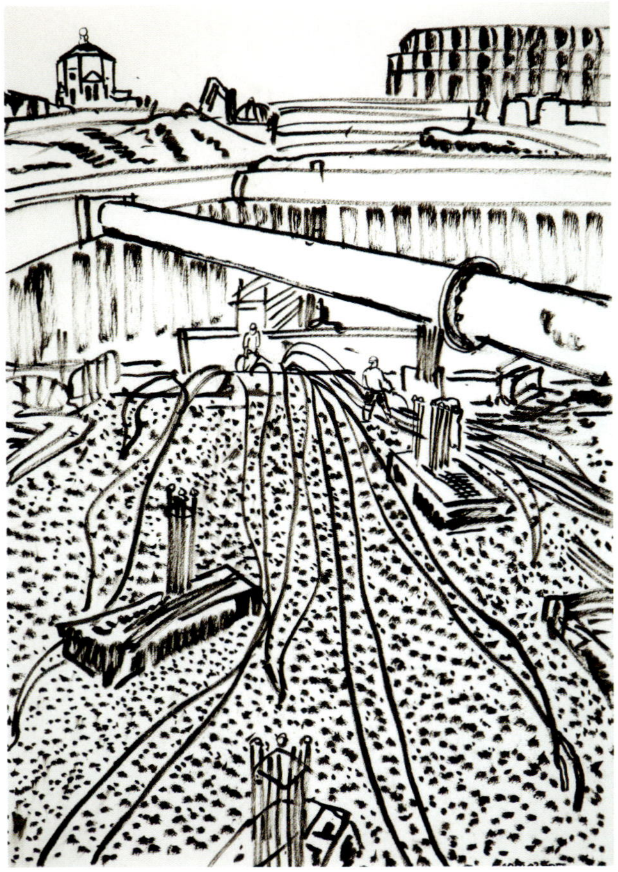

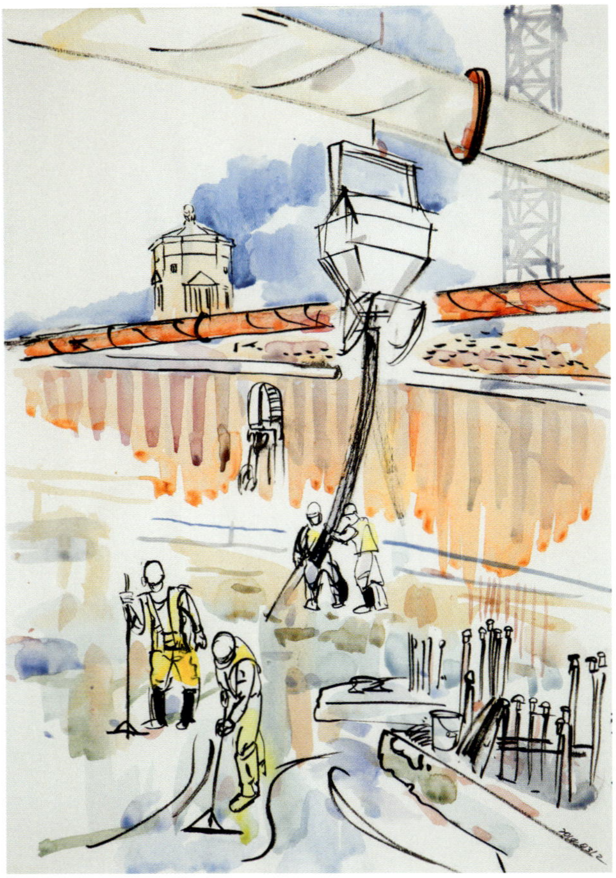

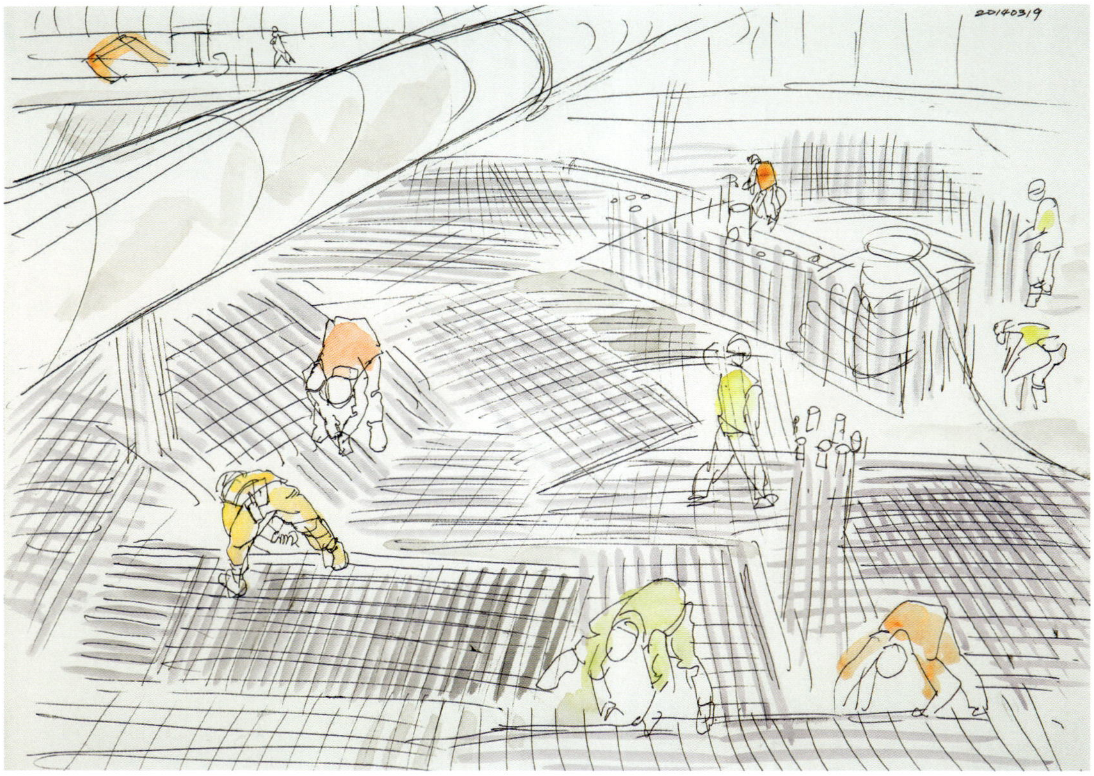

CAT.56 (top left)
Wiring – Blavatnik School of Government. 5 March 2014. Brush and ink on sketchbook made of cartridge paper. Paper size: 42 × 29.7 cm

CAT.57 (top right)
Red prop – Blavatnik School of Government. 12 March 2014. Brush, ink and watercolour on sketchbook made of cartridge paper. Paper size: 42 × 29.7 cm

CAT.58 (left)
Field of steel – Blavatnik School of Government. 19 March 2014. Pen and watercolour on sketchbook made of cartridge paper. Paper size: 29.7 × 42 cm

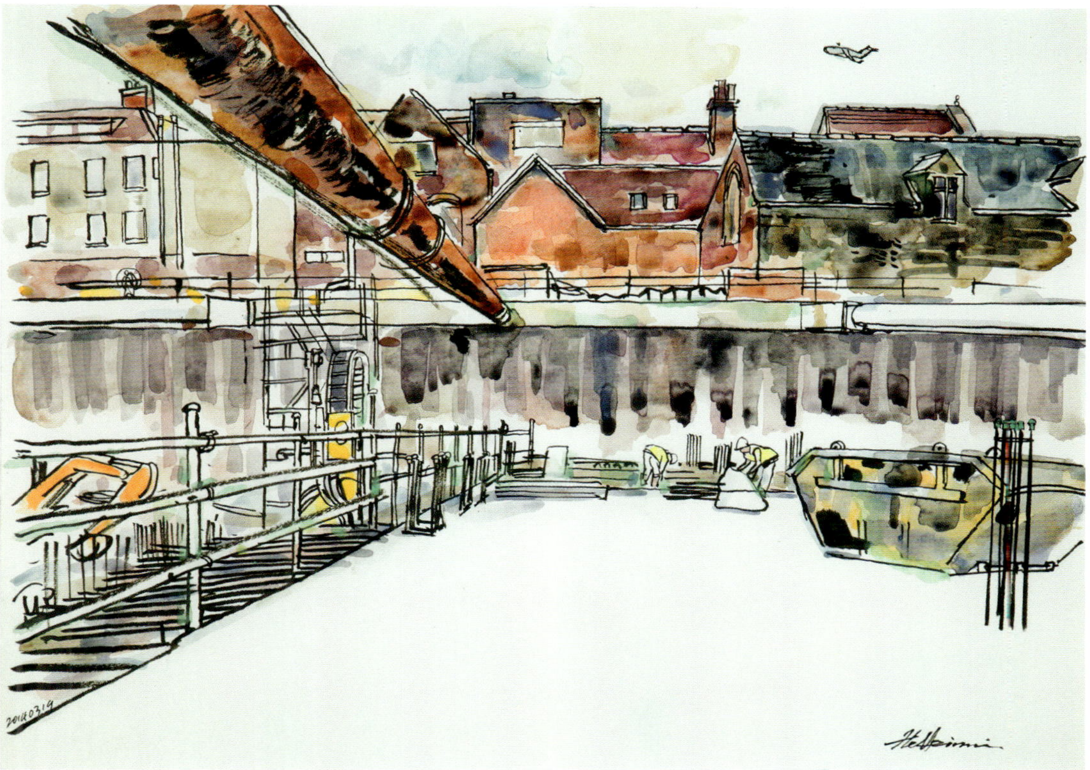

CAT.59
Passing aeroplane – Blavatnik School of Government.
19 March 2014. Brush, ink and watercolour on sketchbook made of cartridge paper. Paper size: 29.7 × 42 cm

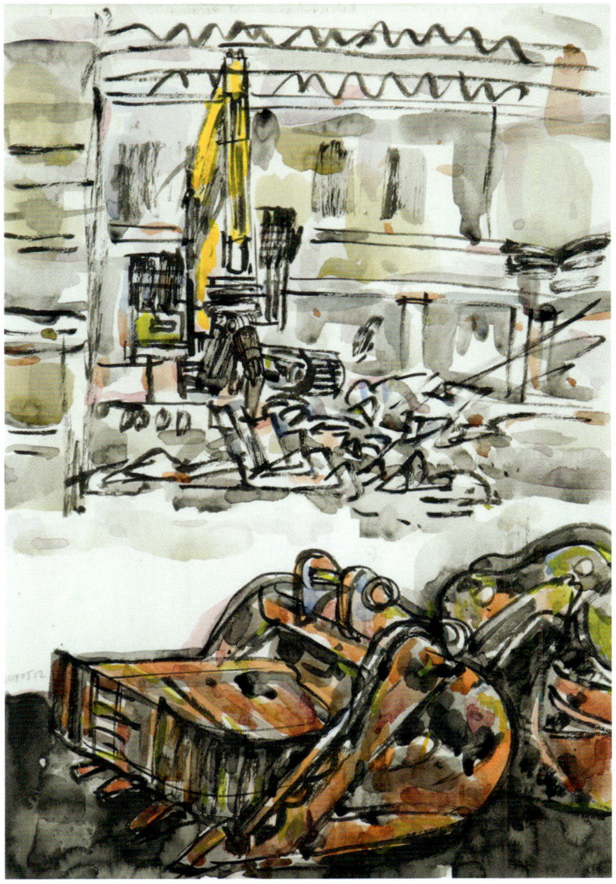

CAT.60
Sleeping giant – construction of Blavatnik School of Government basement. 12 May 2014. Brush, ink and watercolour on sketchbook made of cartridge paper. Paper size: 42 × 29.7 cm

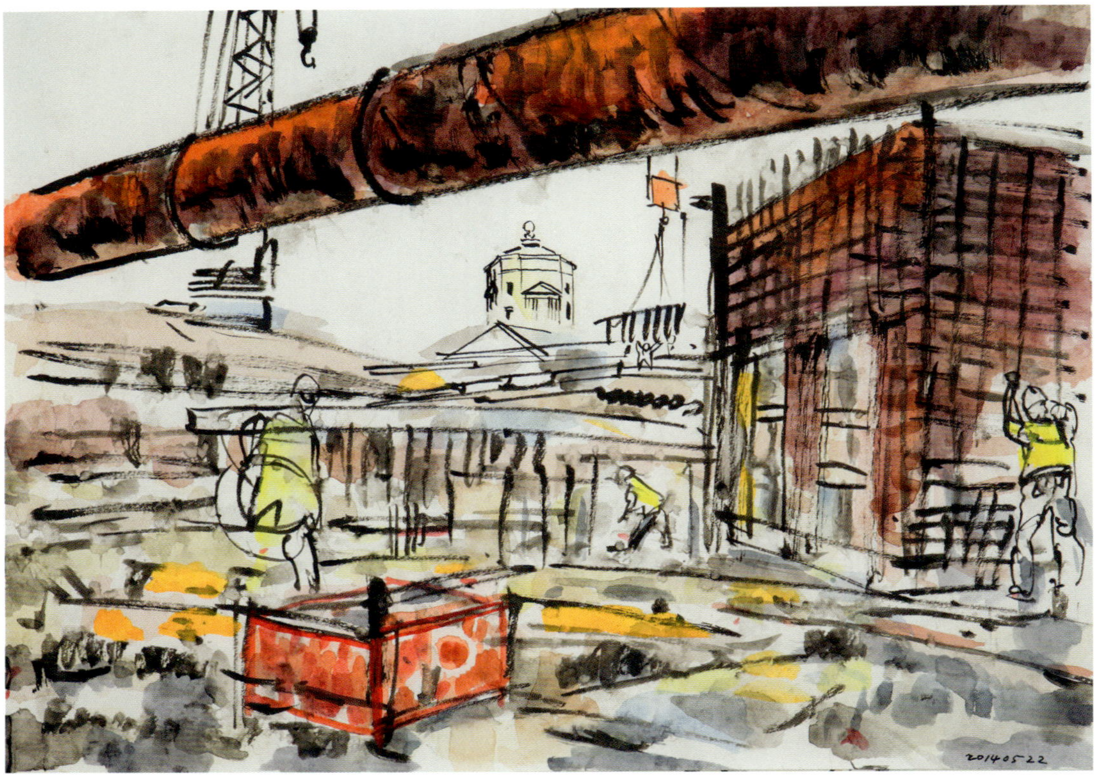

CAT.61
Pipeline in the rain – Blavatnik School of Government. 22 May 2014. Brush, ink and watercolour on sketchbook made of cartridge paper. Paper size: 29.7 × 42 cm

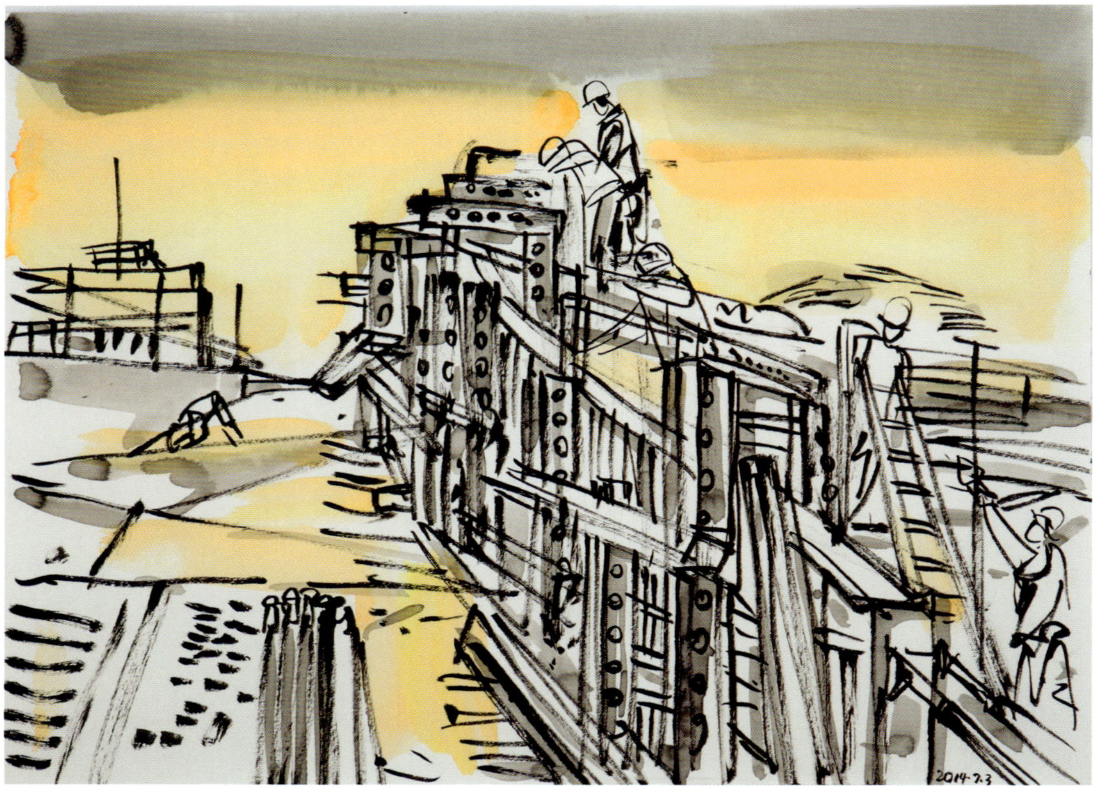

CAT.62
Spiral taking shape –Blavatnik School of Government. 3 July 2014. Brush, ink and watercolour on sketchbook made of cartridge paper. Paper size: 29.7 × 42 cm

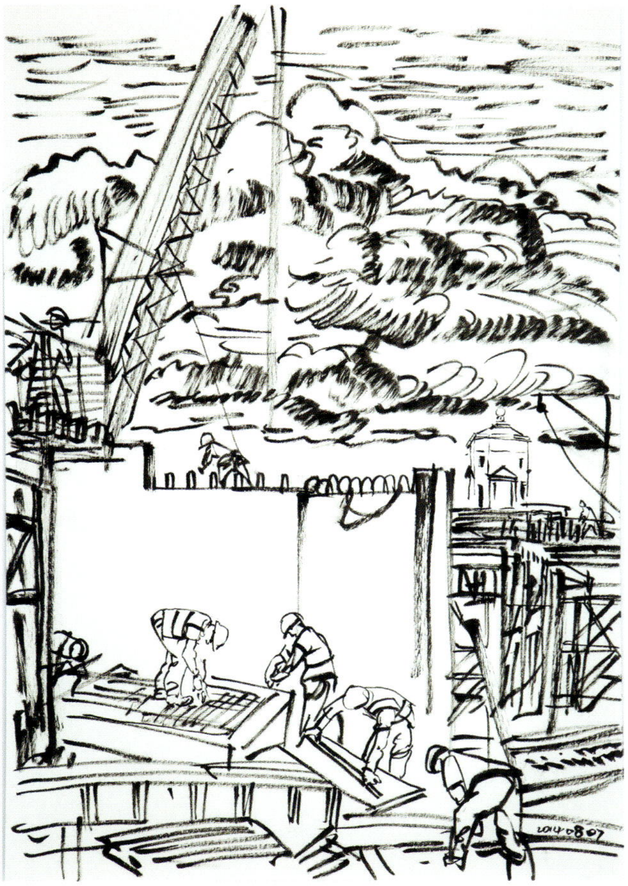

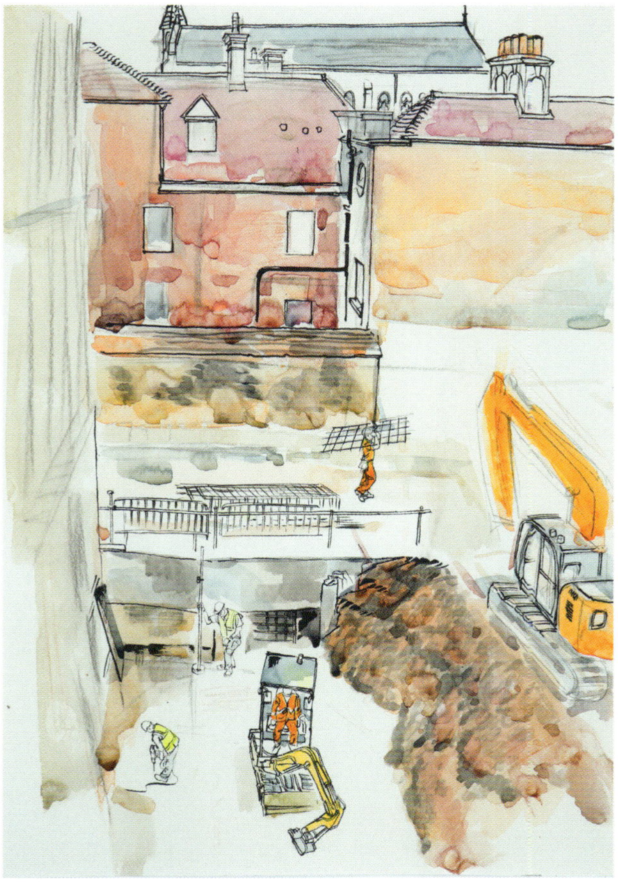

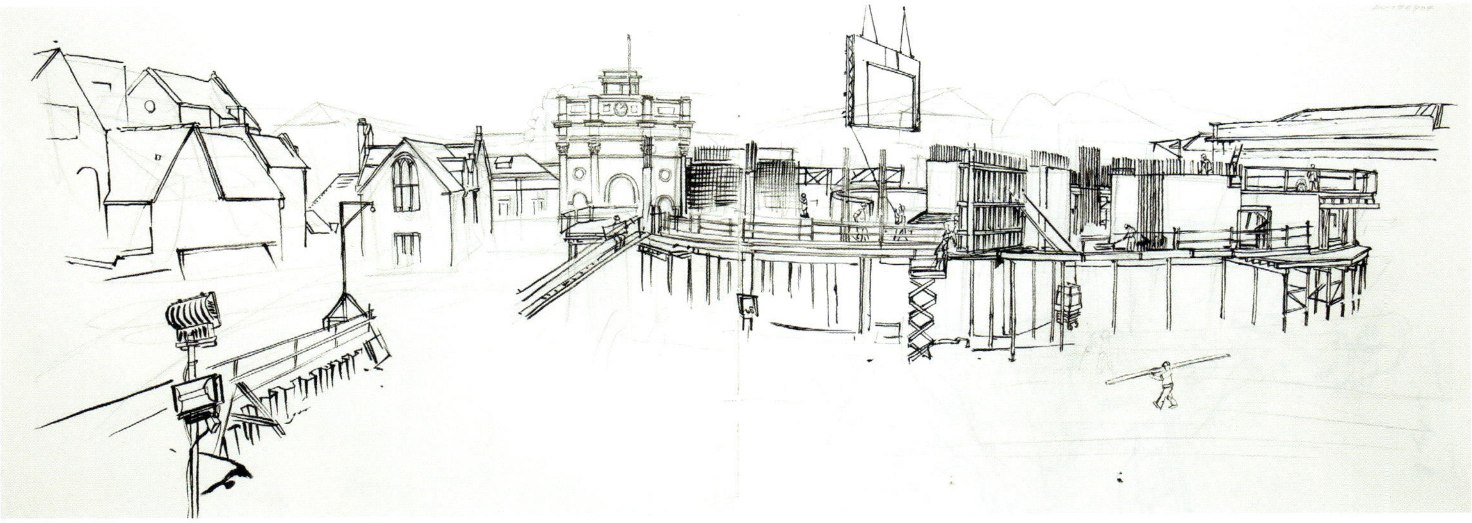

CAT.63 (top left)
Internal wall –Blavatnik School of Government. 7 August 2014. Brush and ink on sketchbook made of cartridge paper. Paper size: 29.7 × 42 cm

CAT.64 (top right)
Pink roofs – extension to the former Outpatients. 28 August 2014. Pen and watercolour on sketchbook made of cartridge paper. Paper size: 42 × 29.7 cm

CAT.65 (above)
Taking shape – Blavatnik School of Government. 4 September 2014. Brush and ink on sketchbook made of cartridge paper. Paper size: 29.7 × 84 cm

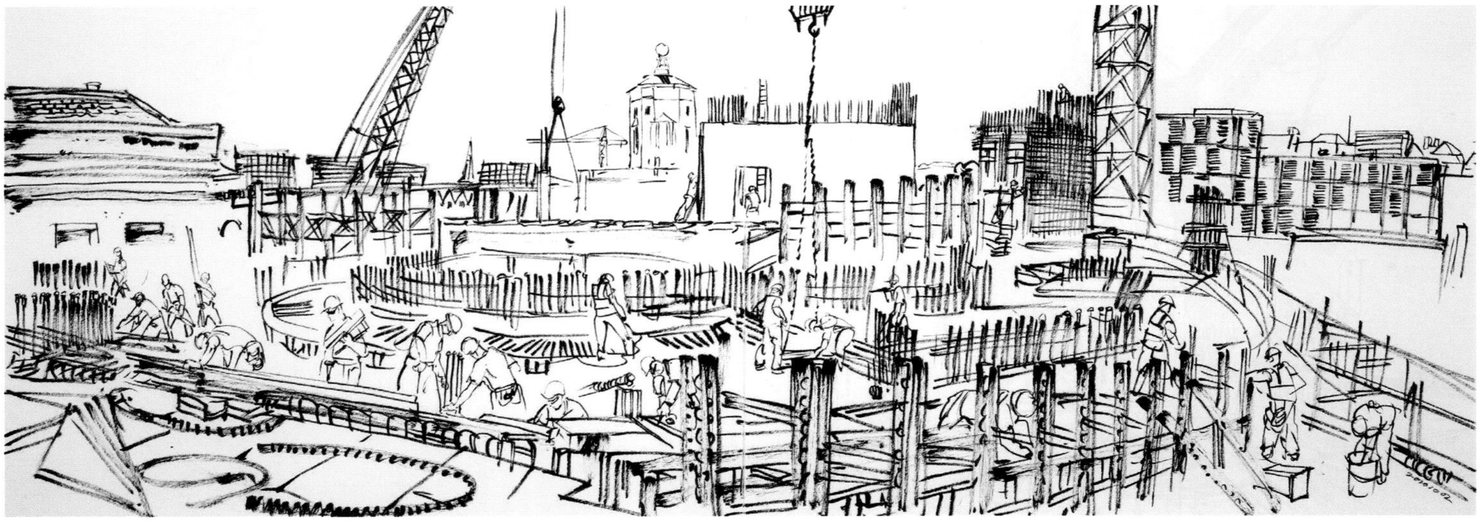

CAT.66
Growing circles – Blavatnik School of Government. 2 October 2014. Brush and ink on sketchbook made of cartridge paper. Paper size: 29.7 × 84 cm

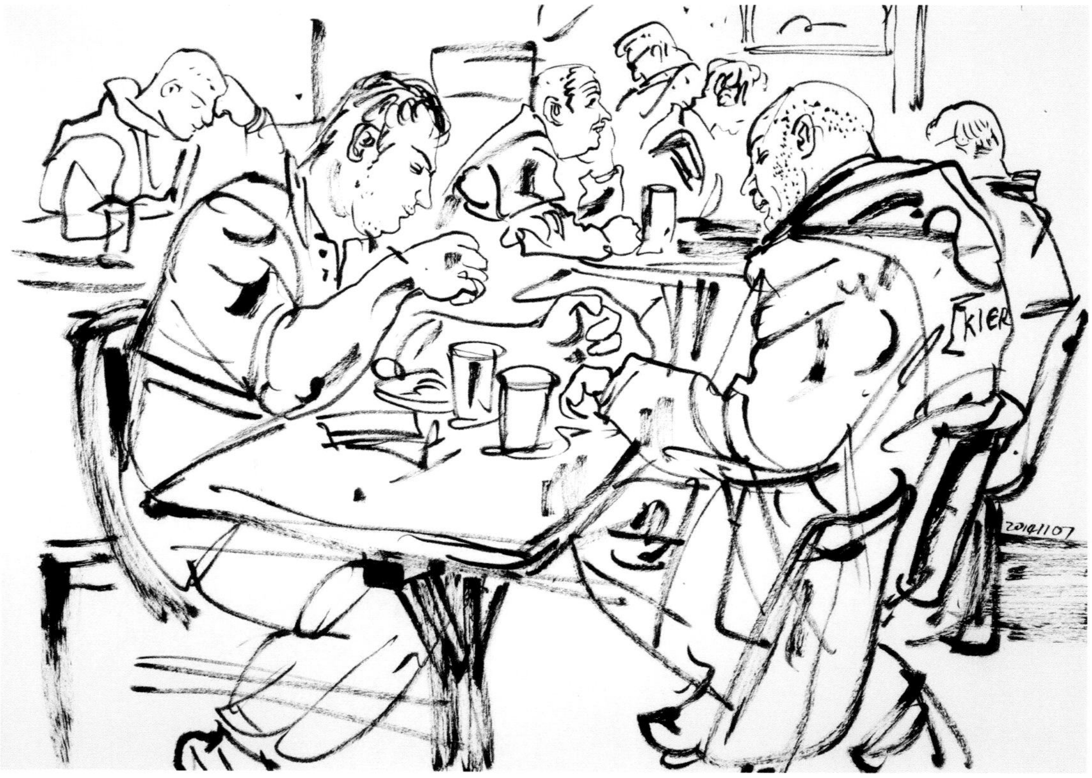

CAT.67
Builders in canteen. 7 November 2014. Brush and ink on sketch-book made of cartridge paper. Paper size: 29.7 × 42 cm

CAT.68 (right)
Pipefitter Giuseppe Geillo and his mates. 20 November 2014. Brush and ink on sketchbook made of cartridge paper. Paper size: 29.7 × 42 cm

CAT.69 (bottom left)
Grey day – refurbishment of the Outpatients building. 18 December 2014. Brush, ink and watercolour on sketchbook made of cartridge paper. Paper size: 59.4 × 42 cm

CAT.70 (bottom right)
Interior view – refurbishment of the Outpatients building. 9 January 2015. Brush, ink and watercolour on sketchbook made of cartridge paper. Paper size: 59.4 × 42 cm

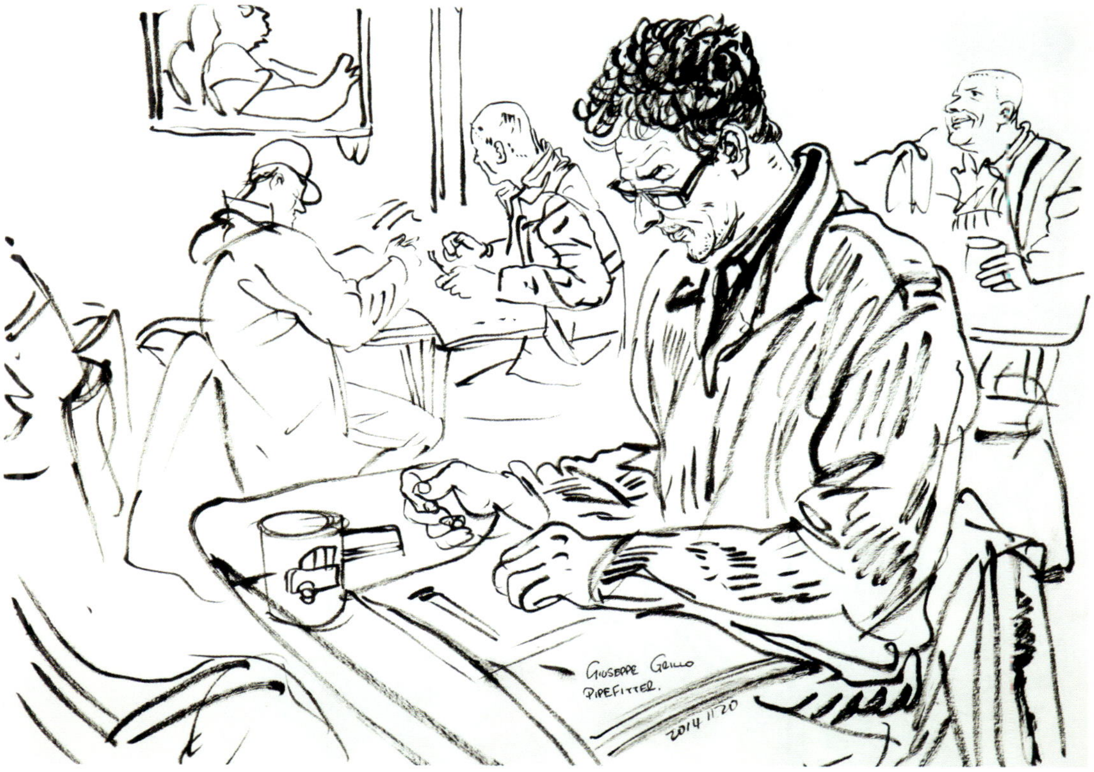

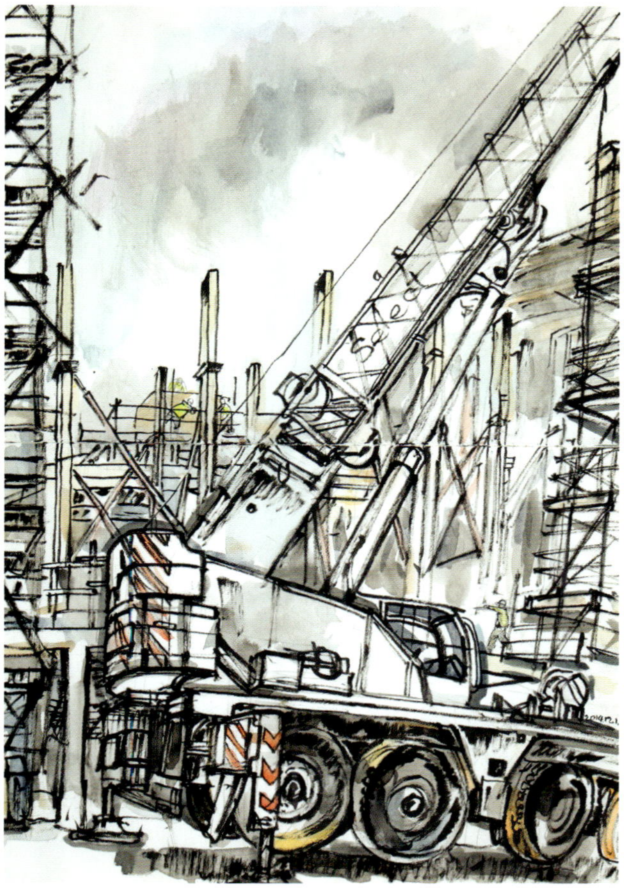

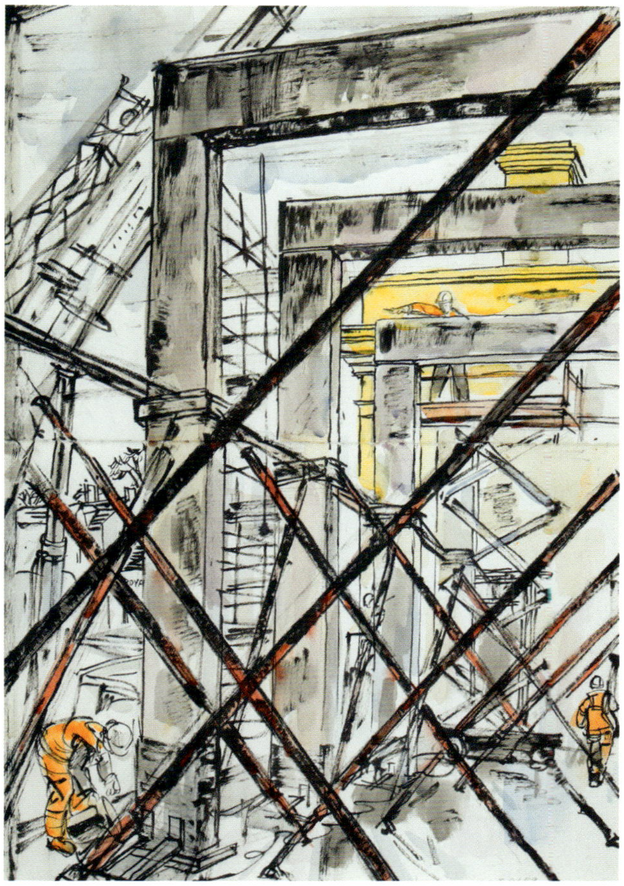

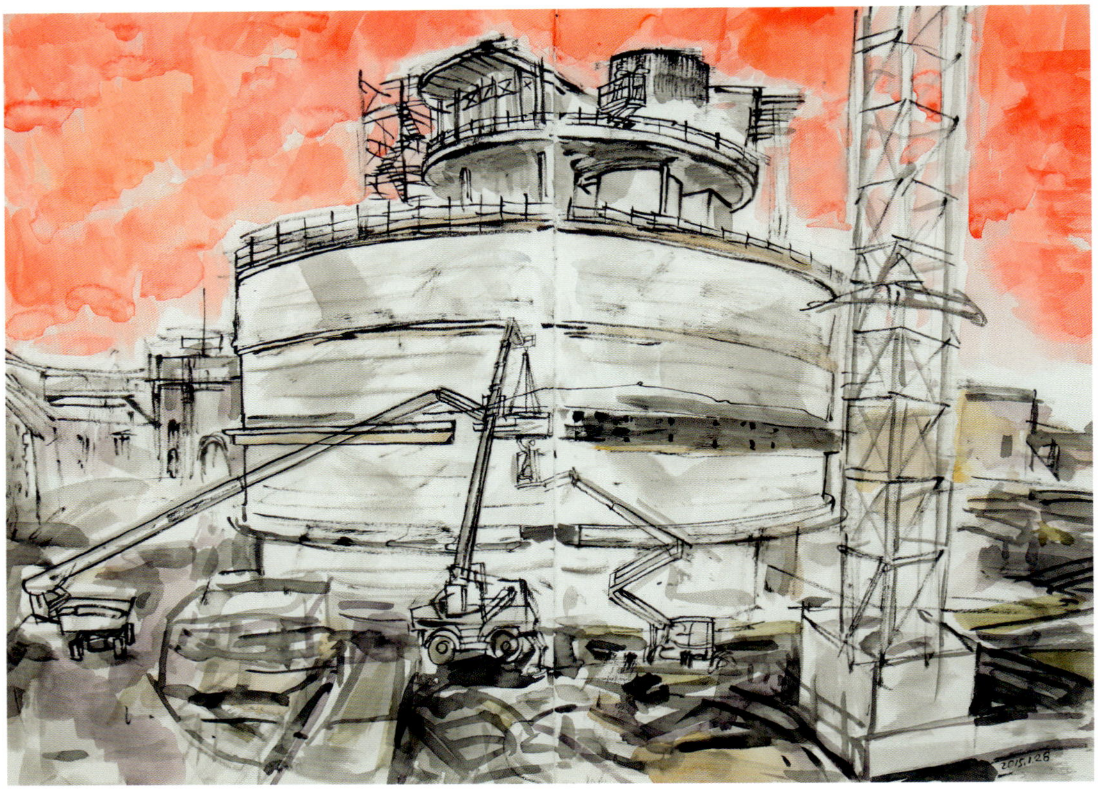

CAT.71
Red sky over the Blavatnik School of Government.
28 January 2015. Brush, ink and watercolour on sketchbook made of cartridge paper. Paper size: 42 × 59.4 cm

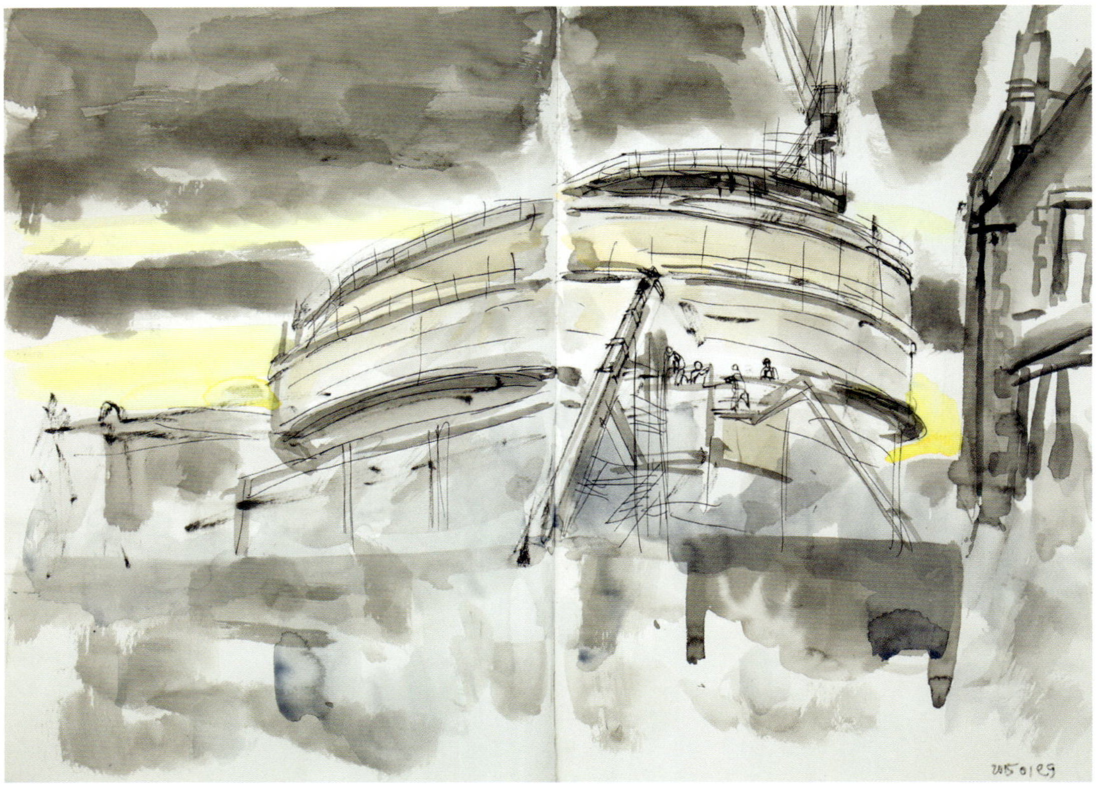

CAT.72
To be transformed – Blavatnik School of Government.
29 January 2015. Brush, ink and watercolour on sketchbook made of cartridge paper. Paper size: 42 × 59.4 cm

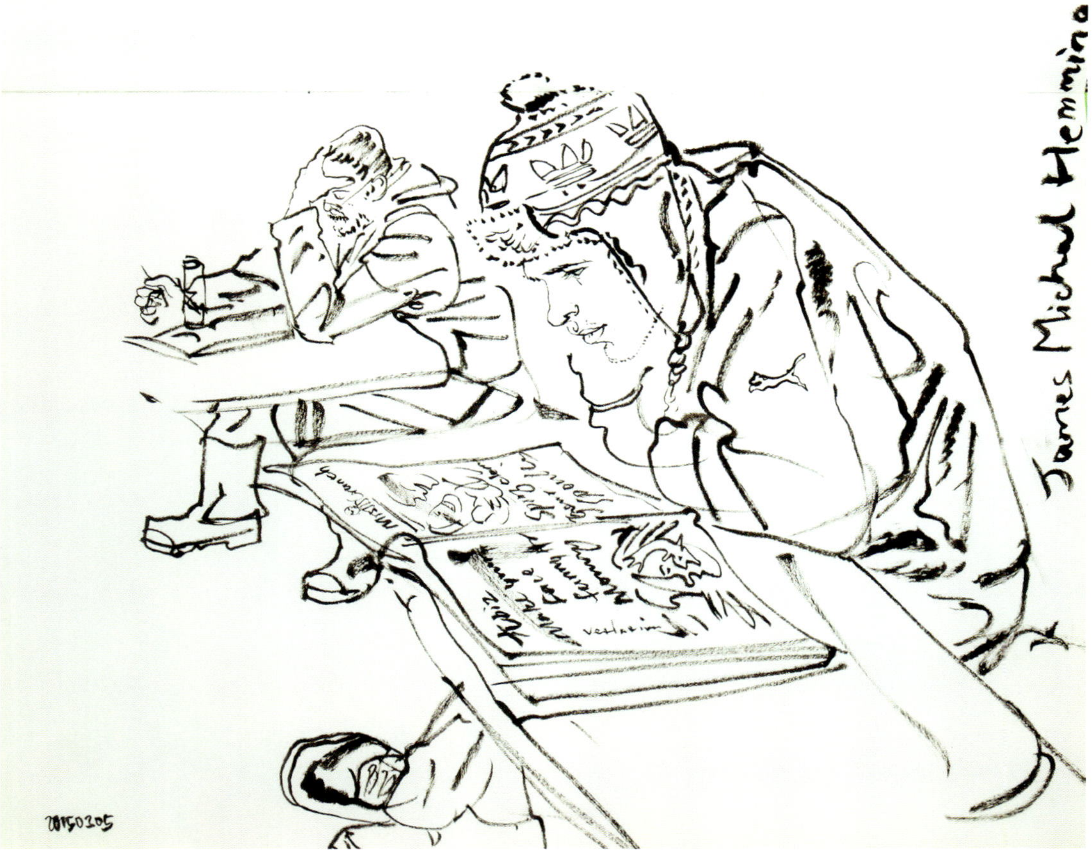

CAT.73
Cold day, warm hat. 5 March 2013. Brush and ink on sketchbook made of cartridge paper. Paper size: 29.7 × 42 cm

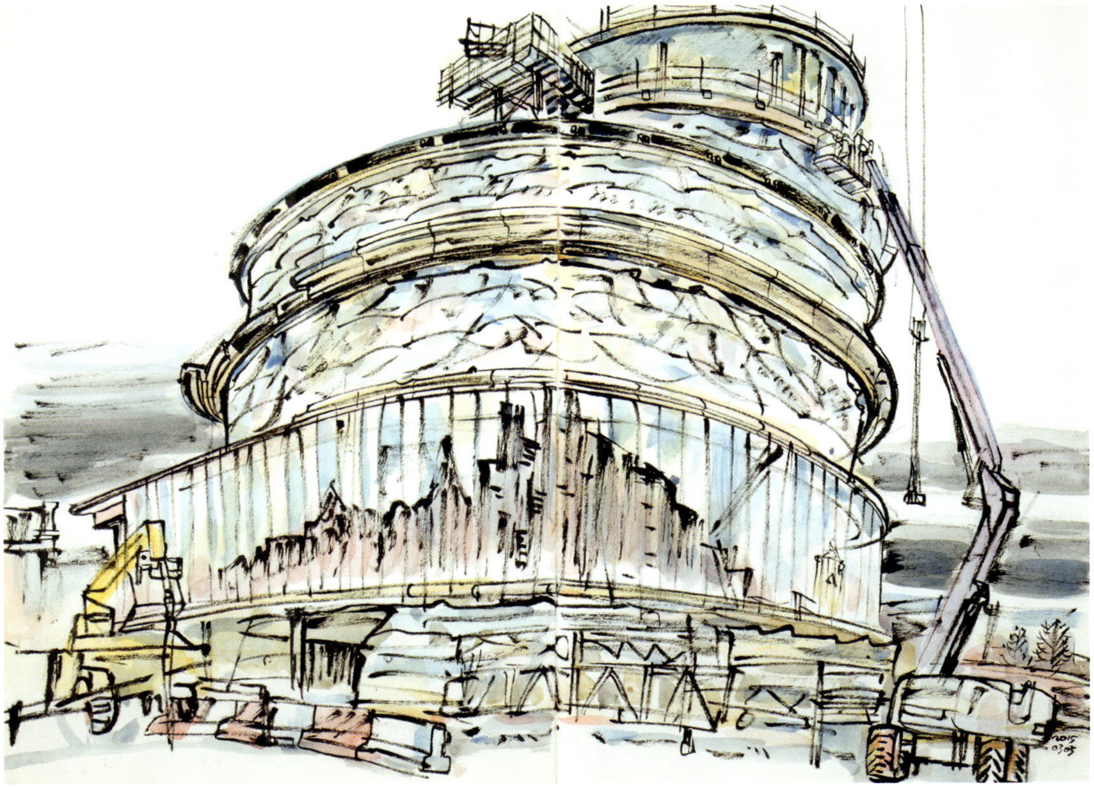

CAT.74
Oxford Tower of Babel – Blavatnik School of Government. 15 March 2015. Brush, ink and watercolour on sketchbook made of cartridge paper. Paper size: 42 × 59.4 cm

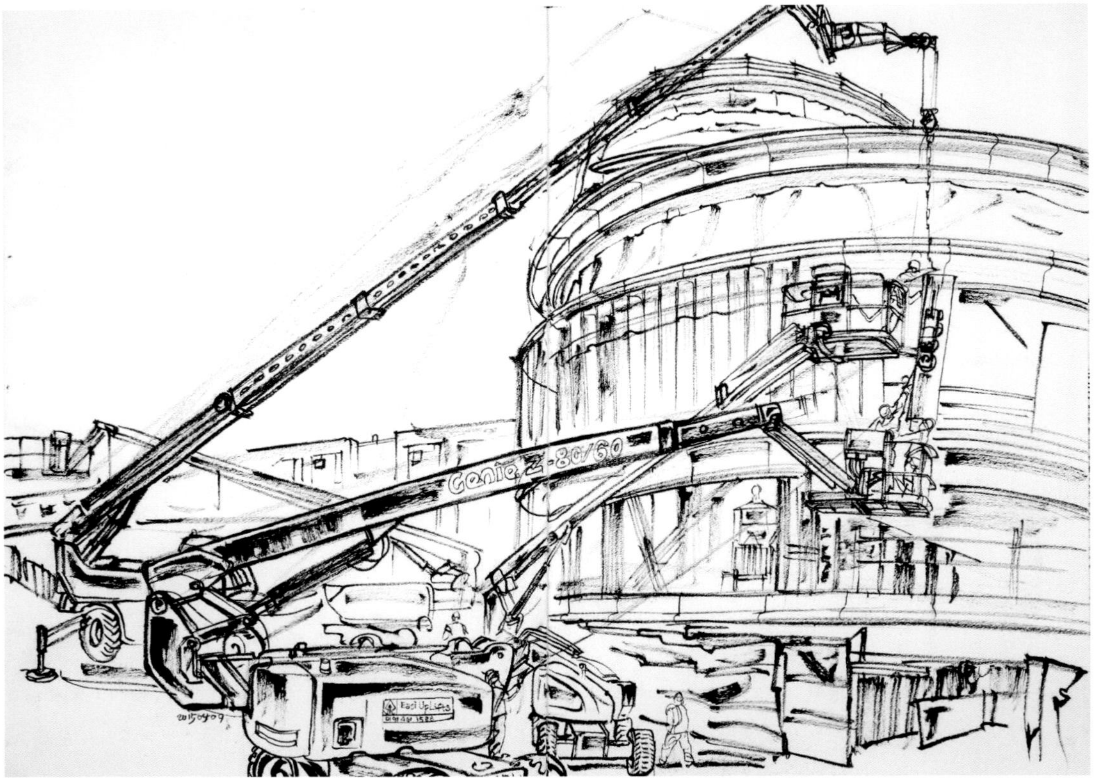

CAT.75
Tower in the tower – Blavatnik School of Government.
9 April 2015. Brush and ink on sketchbook made of cartridge paper. Paper size: 42 × 59.4 cm

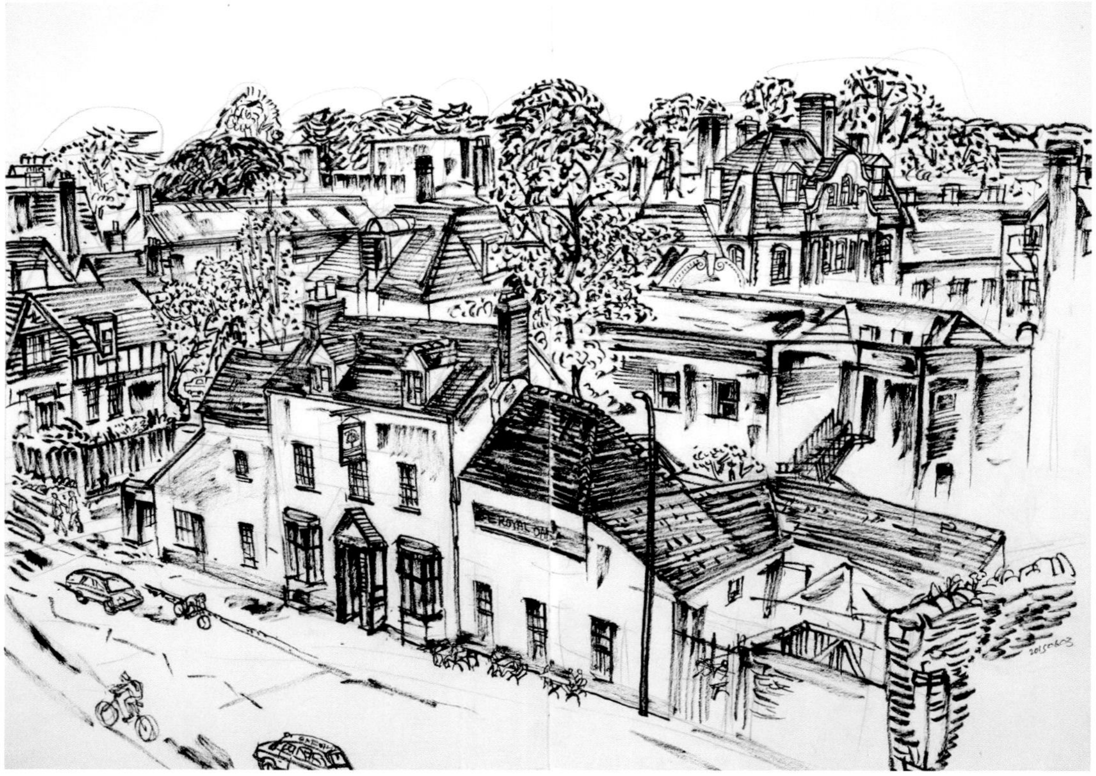

CAT.76
Royal Oak from the Outpatients building. 3 June 2015. Brush and ink on sketchbook made of cartridge paper. Paper size: 42 × 59.4 cm

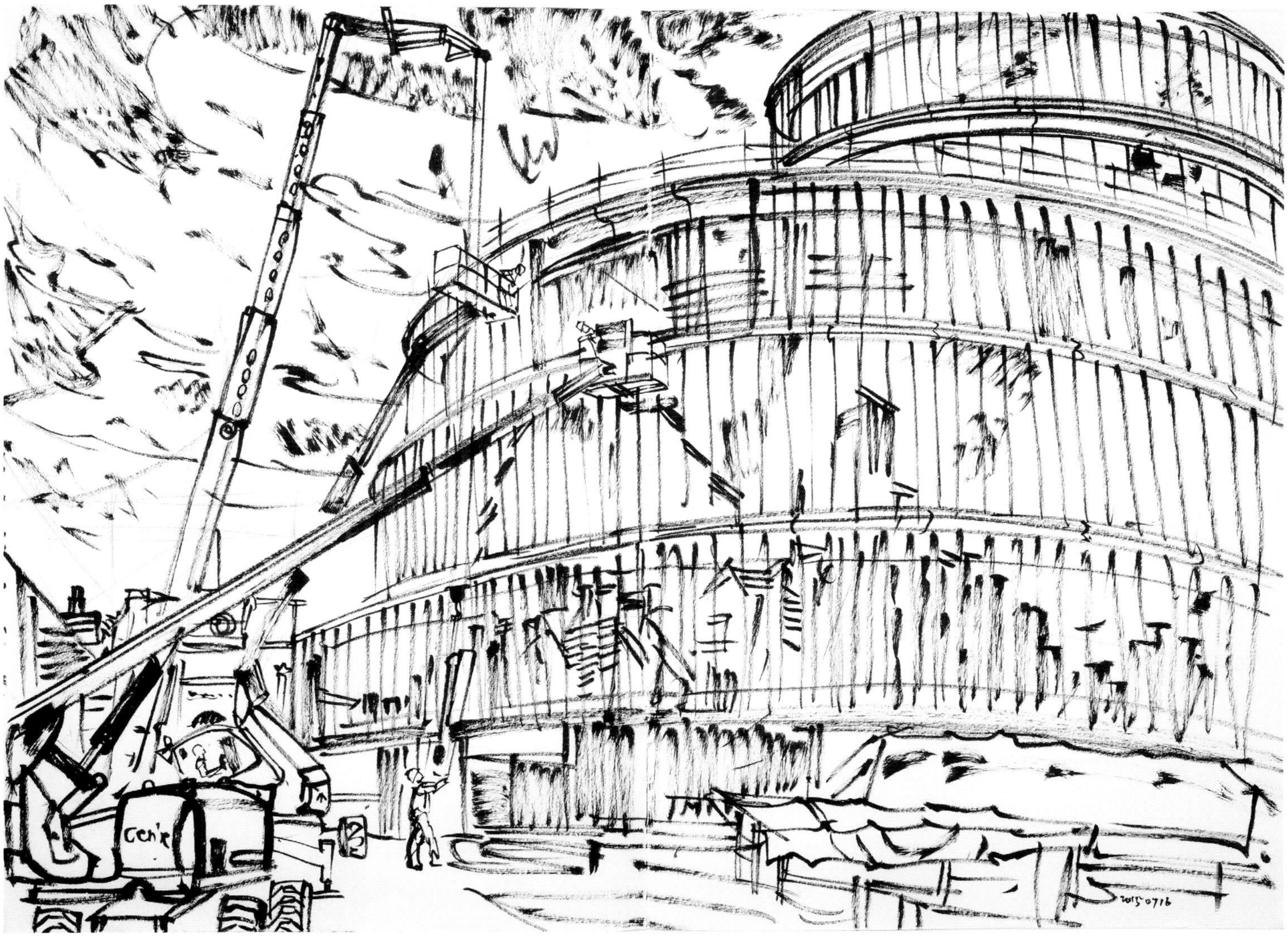

CAT.77

Brushing the past – Blavatnik School of Government. 16 July 2015. Brush and ink on sketchbook made of cartridge paper. Paper size: 42 × 59.4 cm

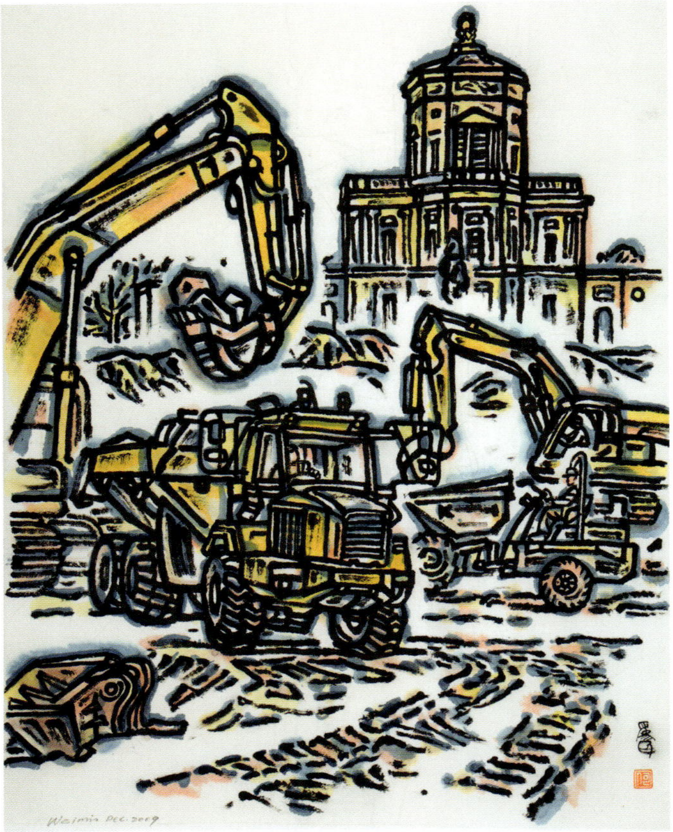

CAT.78 (left)
Steel arms in action. 1 December 2009. Brush, ink and watercolour on *xuan* paper. Paper size: 52.5 × 42.3 cm

CAT.79 (bottom left)
Resting graptor bucket. 2 December 2009. Brush, ink and watercolour on *xuan* paper. Paper size: 52.5 × 42.3 cm

CAT.80 (bottom right)
Triton and pigeon. 16 August 2010. Brush, ink and watercolour on *xuan* paper. Paper size: 50.5 × 34.5 cm

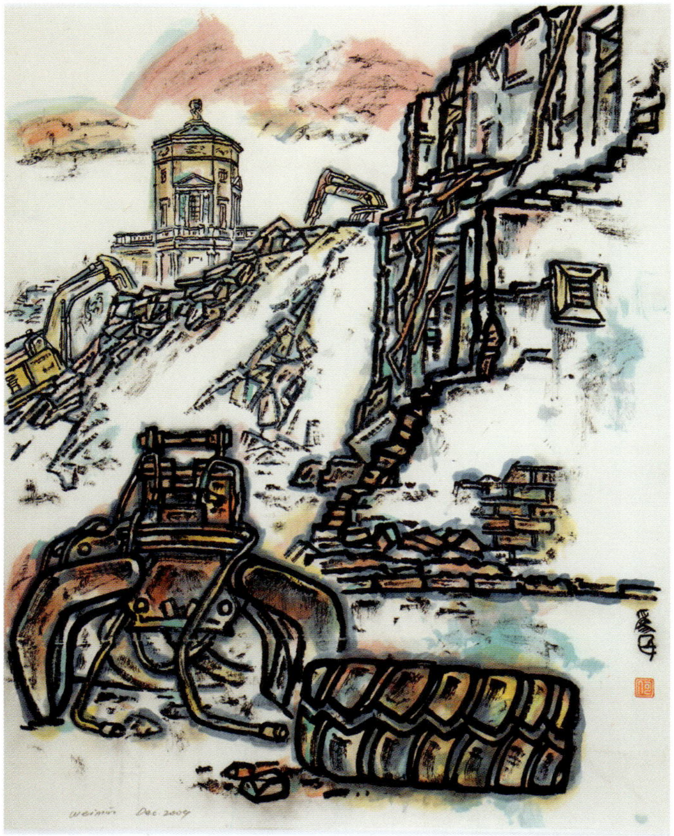

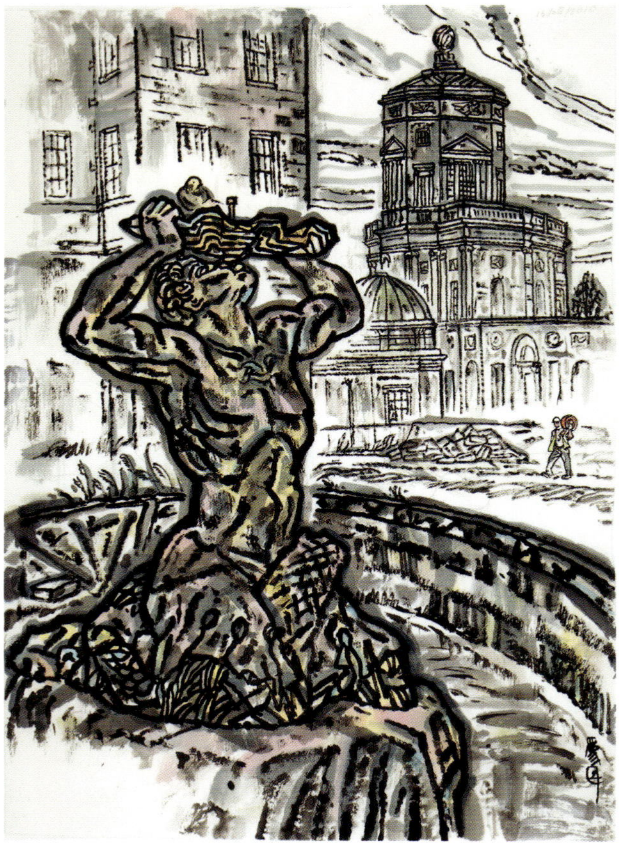

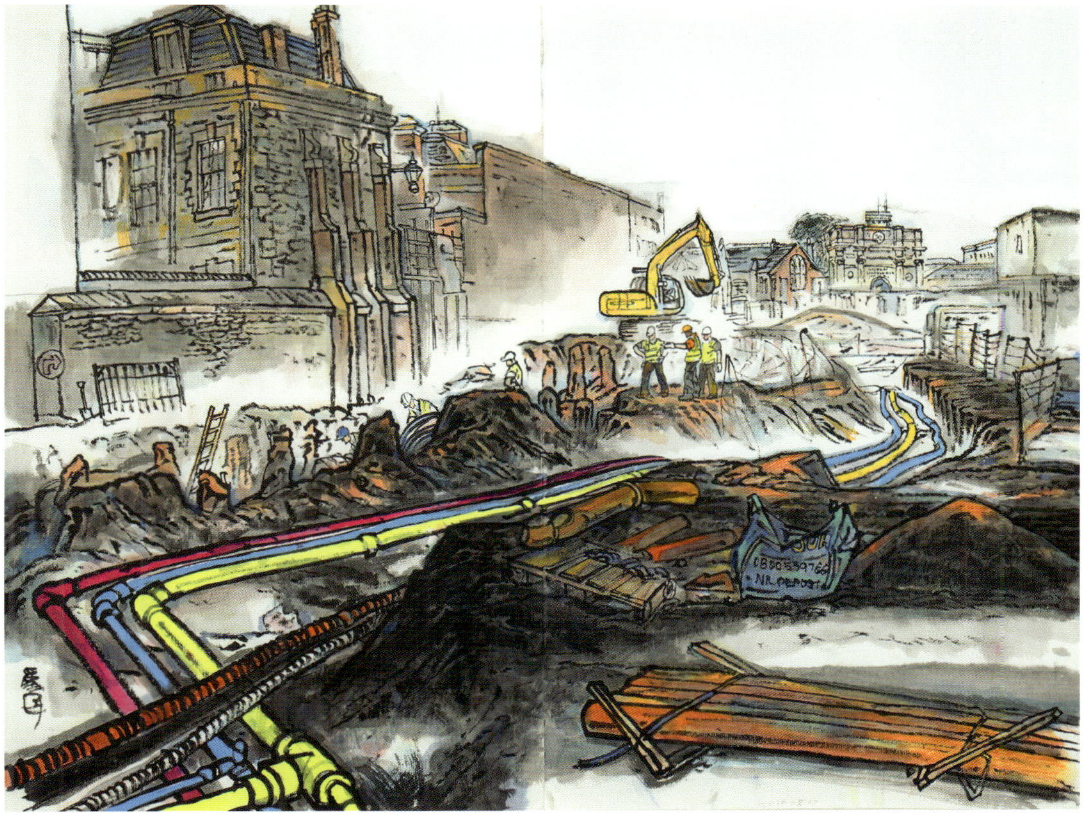

CAT.81
Bright pipes – Somerville College student accommodation.
17 August 2010. Brush, ink and watercolour on album leaves.
Paper size: 41.6 × 55.6 cm

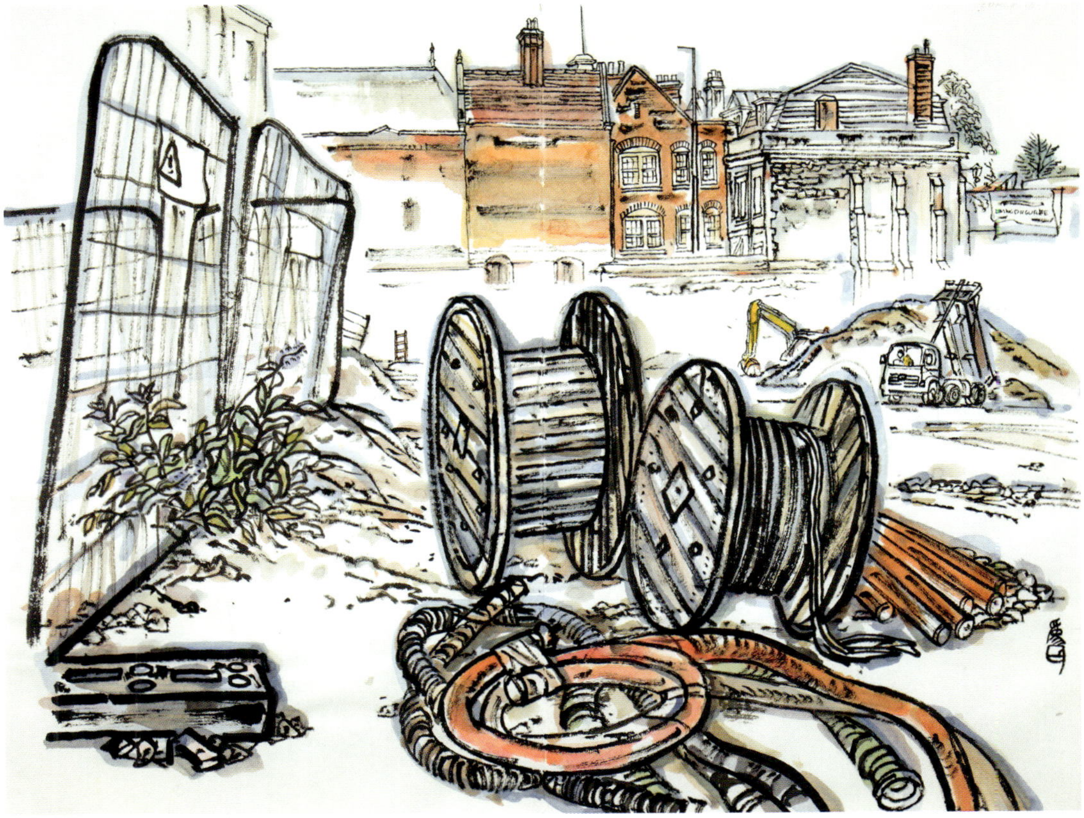

CAT.82
Fenced off – Somerville College student accommodation.
18 August 2010. Brush, ink and watercolour on album leaves.
Paper size: 41.6 × 55.6 cm

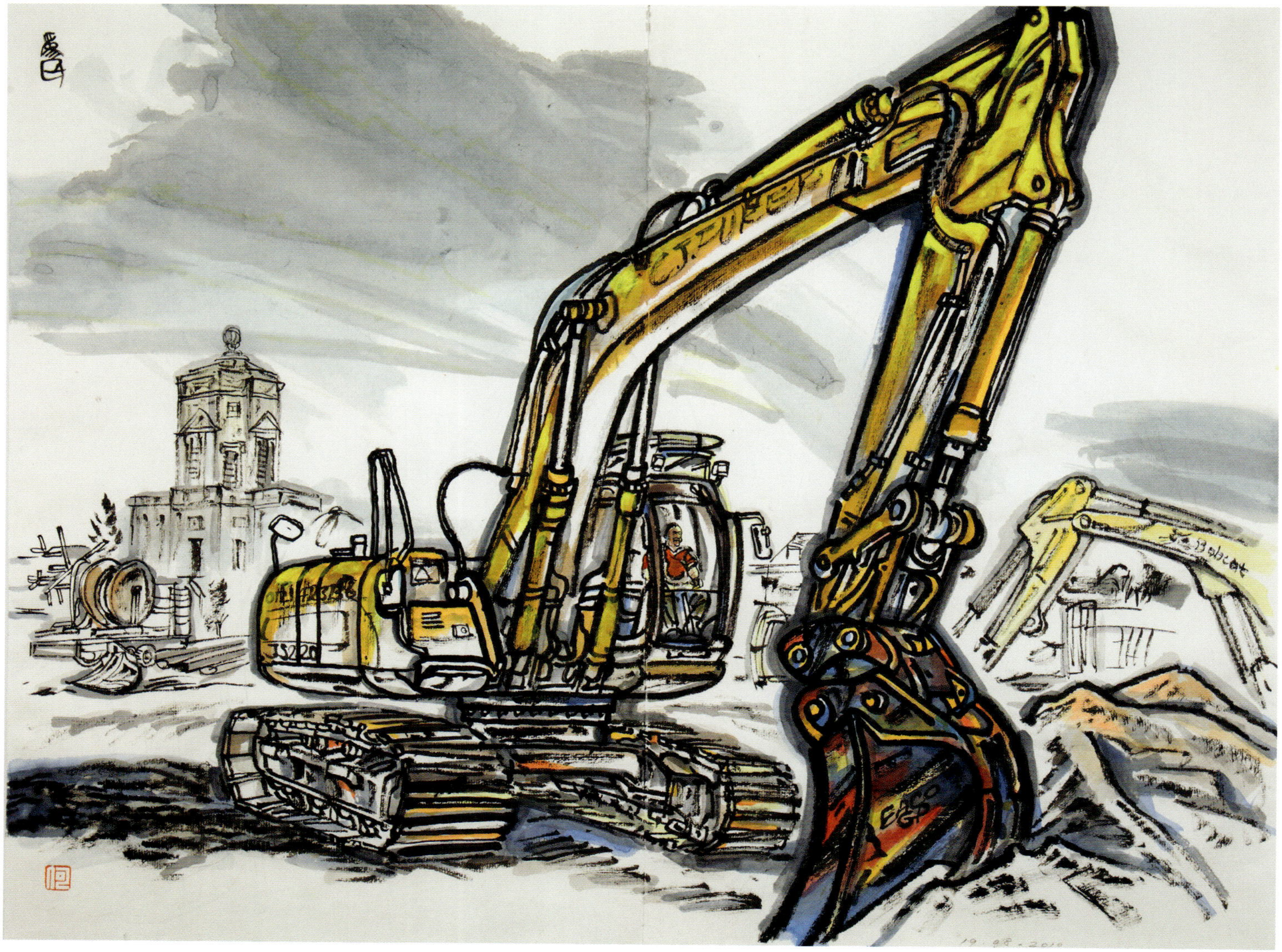

CAT.83

Steel claw yellow dragon – Somerville College student accommodation. 19 August 2010. Brush, ink and watercolour on album leaves. Paper size: 41.6 × 55.6 cm

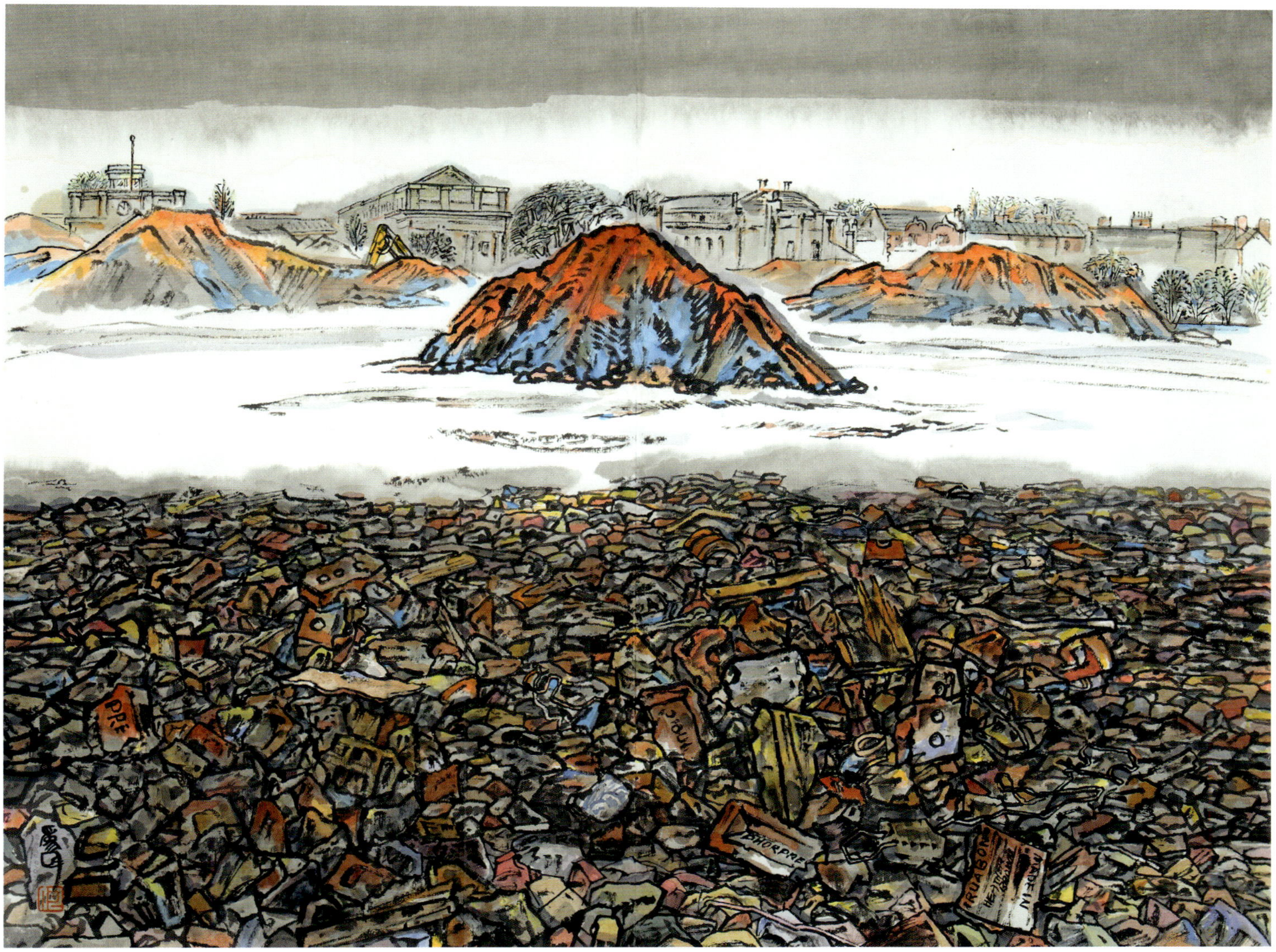

CAT.84
Past, present and future – Radcliffe Observatory Quarter. 20 August 2010.Brush, ink and watercolour on album leaves. Paper size: 41.6 × 55.6 cm

Detail overleaf

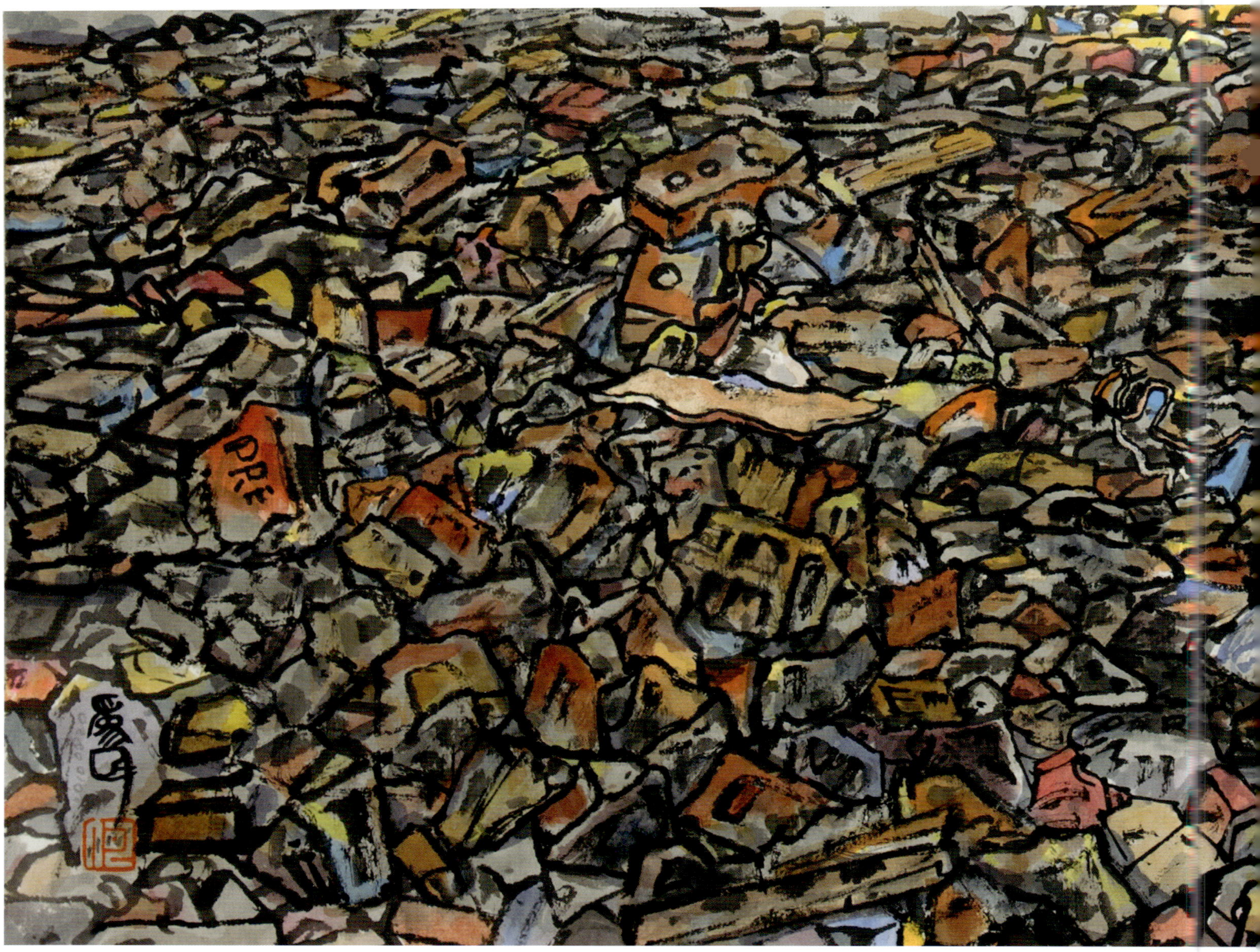

CAT.84 (detail)

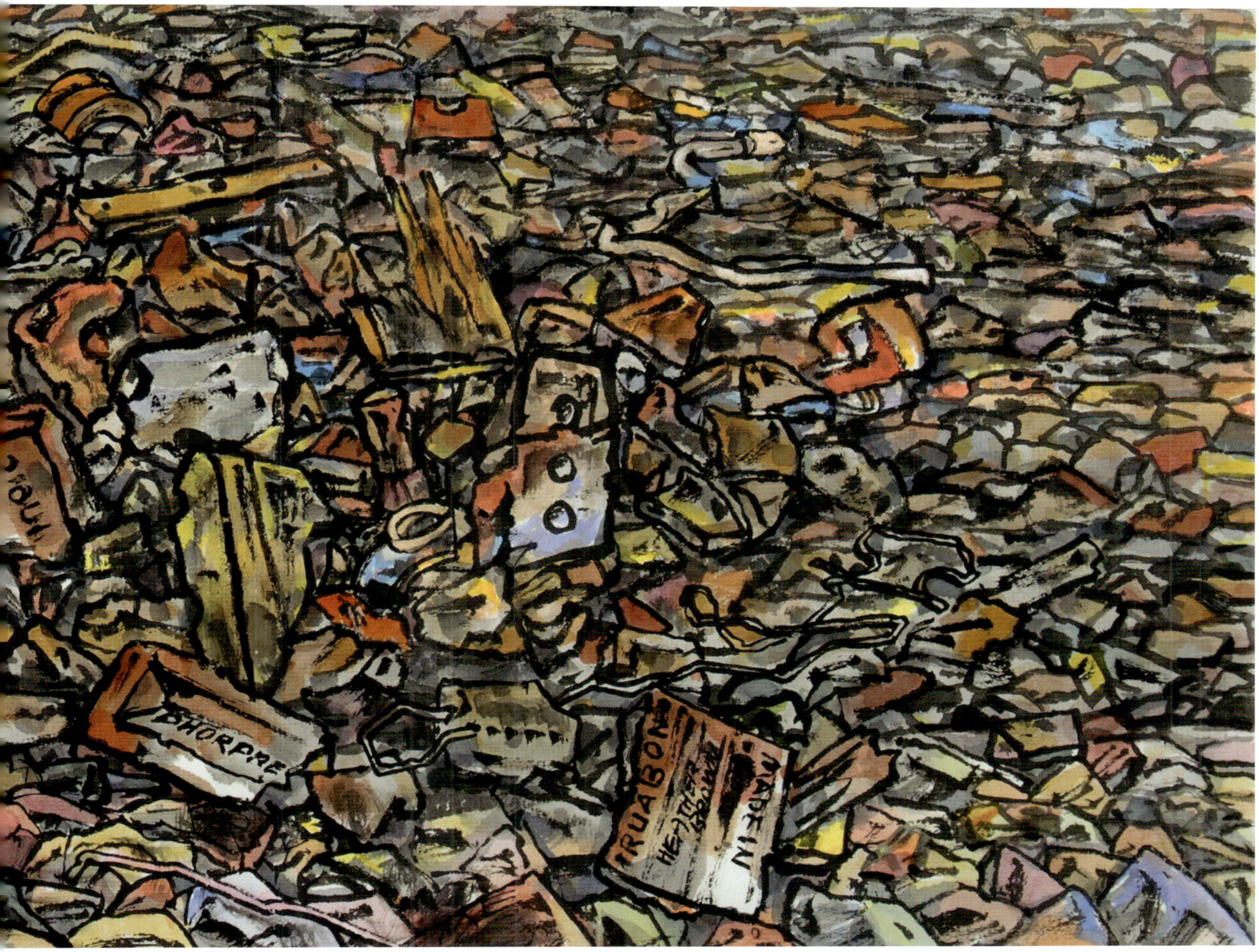
RUABON

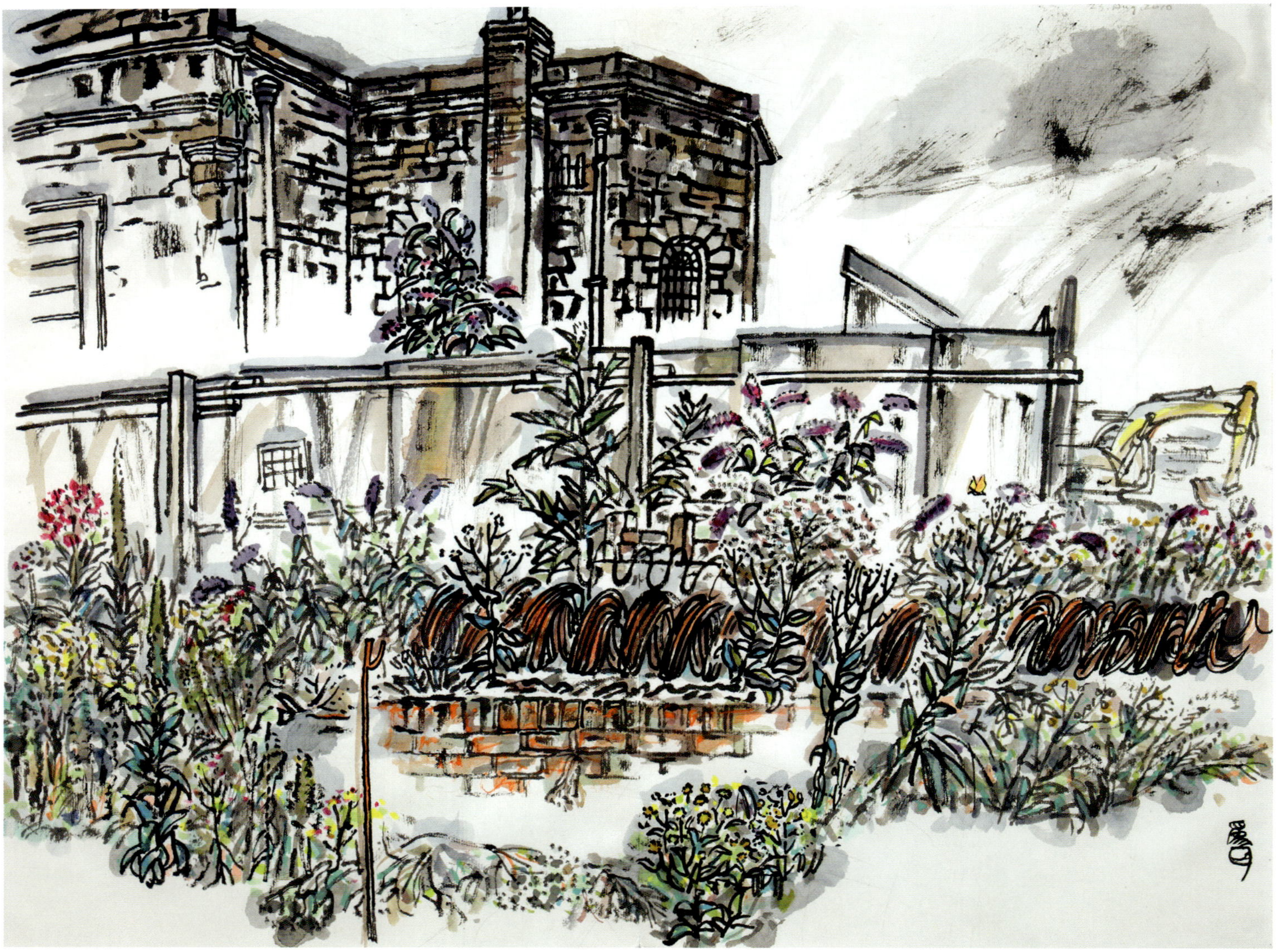

CAT.85
An unremarkable corner. 23 August 2010.
Brush, ink and watercolour on album leaves.
Paper size: 41.6 × 55.6 cm

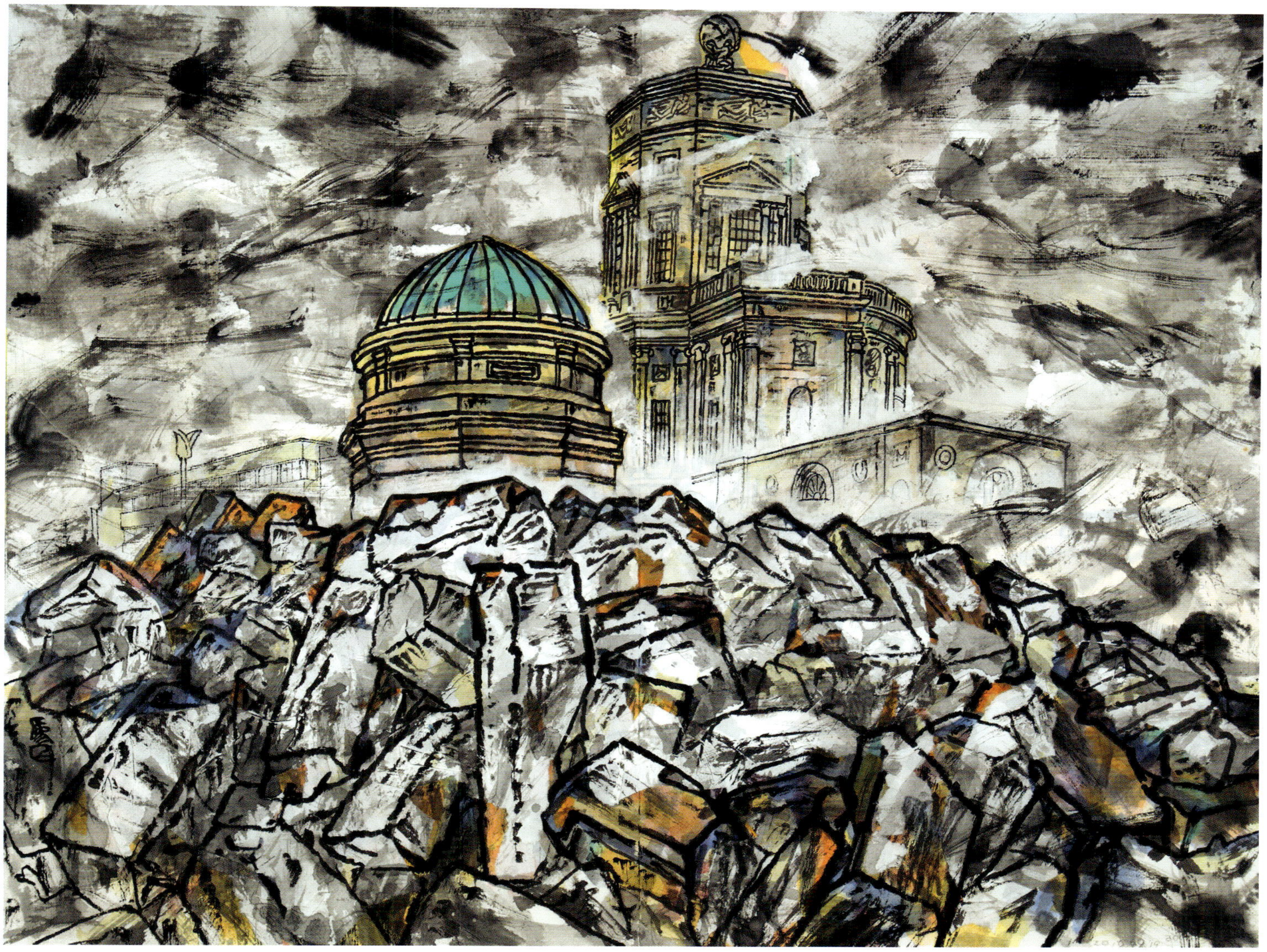

CAT.86
Winds come, winds go. 19 September 2010.
Brush, ink, watercolour and collage on album leaves. Paper size: 41.6 × 55.6 cm

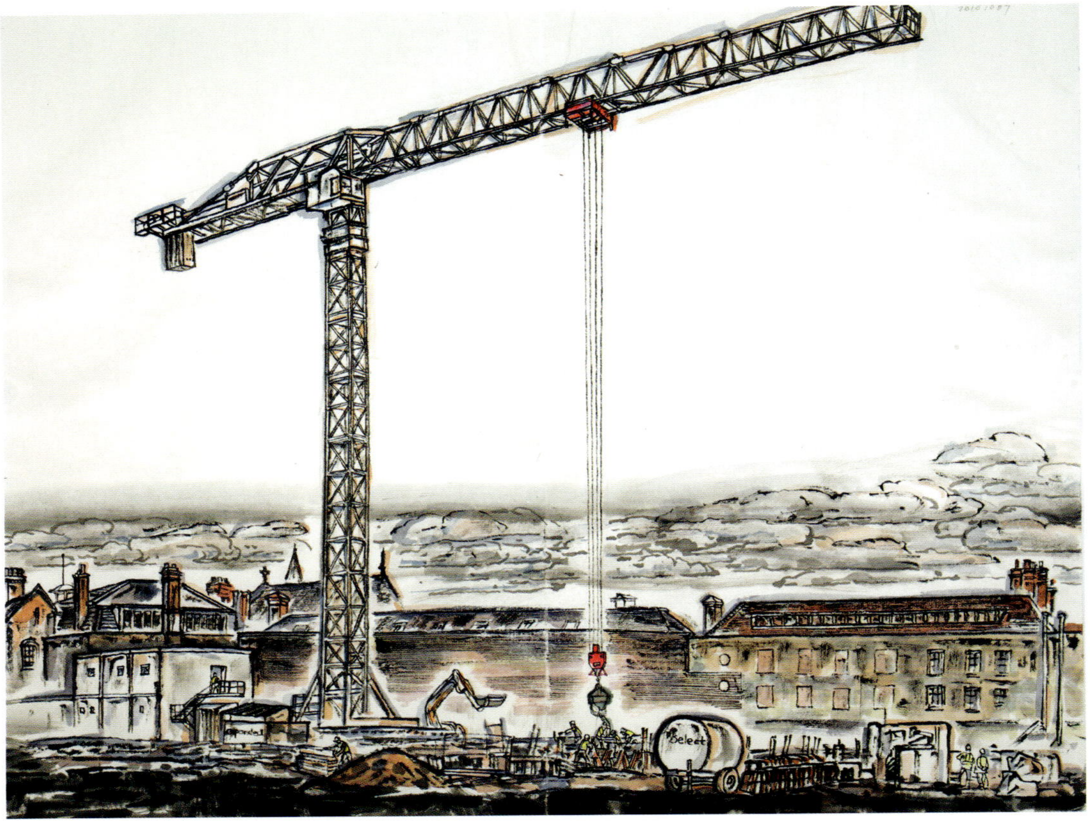

CAT.87
Sky high – Somerville College student accommodation.
7 October 2010. Brush, ink and watercolour on album leaves.
Paper size: 41.6 × 55.6 cm

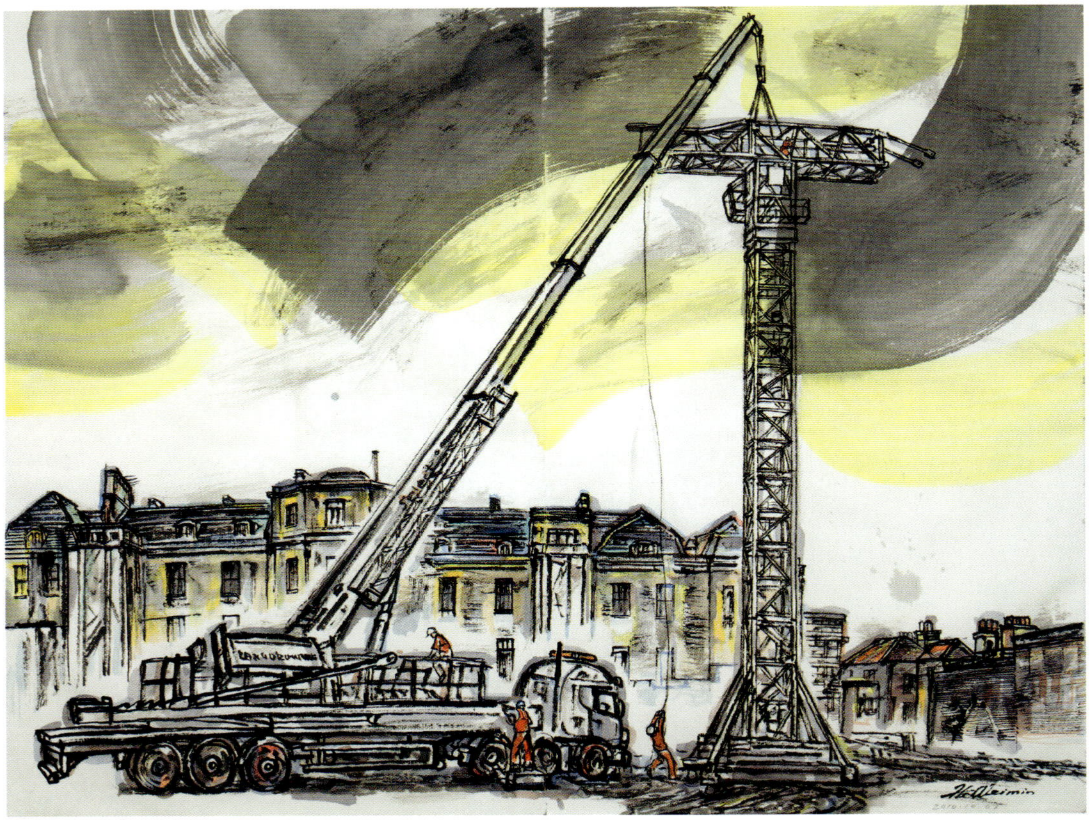

CAT.88
Brushing the sky – Somerville College student accommodation.
7 October 2010. Brush, ink and watercolour on album leaves.
Paper size: 41.6 × 55.6 cm

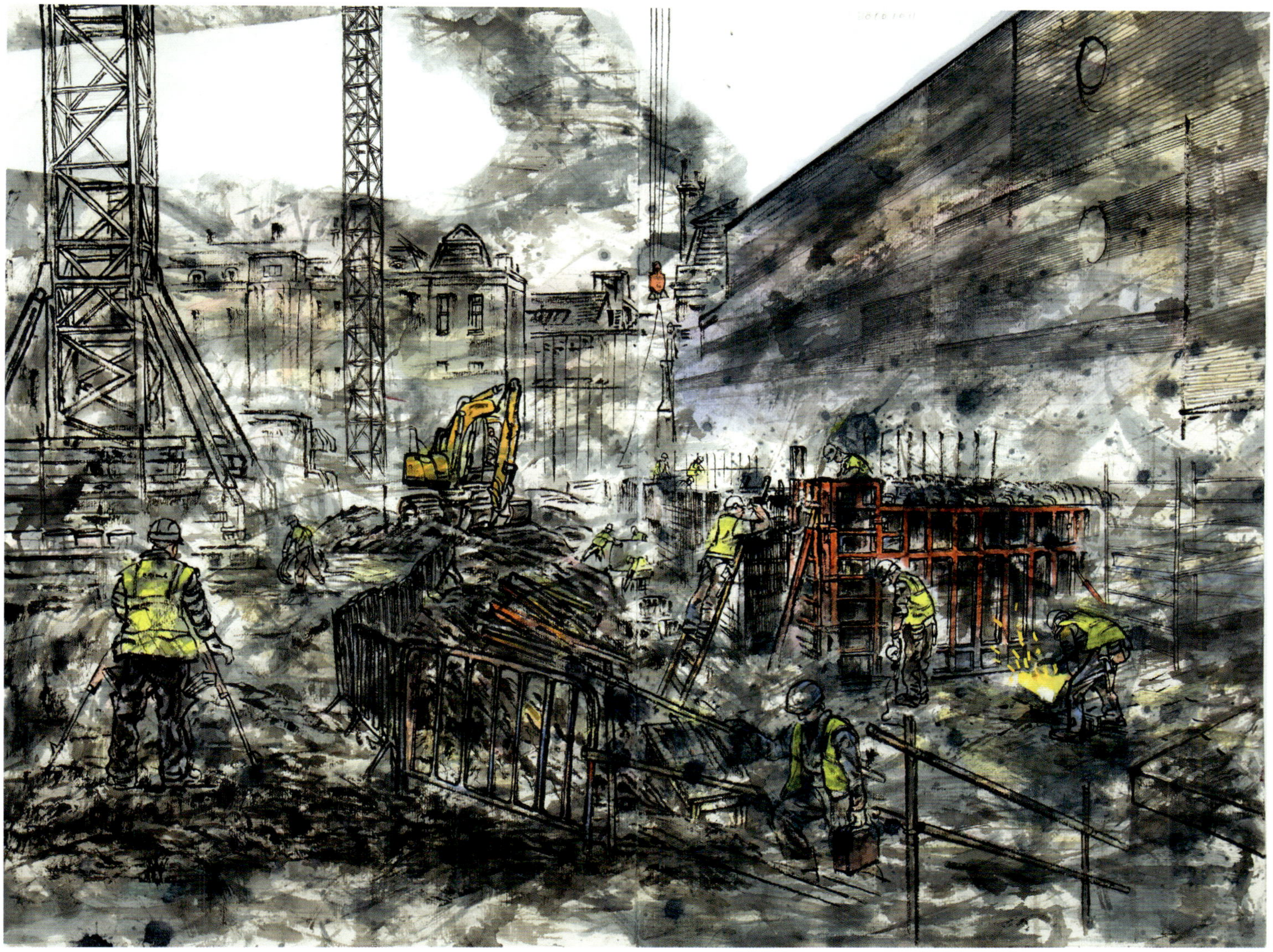

CAT.89
Cacophony – Somerville College student accommodation. 11 October 2010. Brush, ink, watercolour and collage on album leaves. Paper size: 41.6 × 55.6 cm

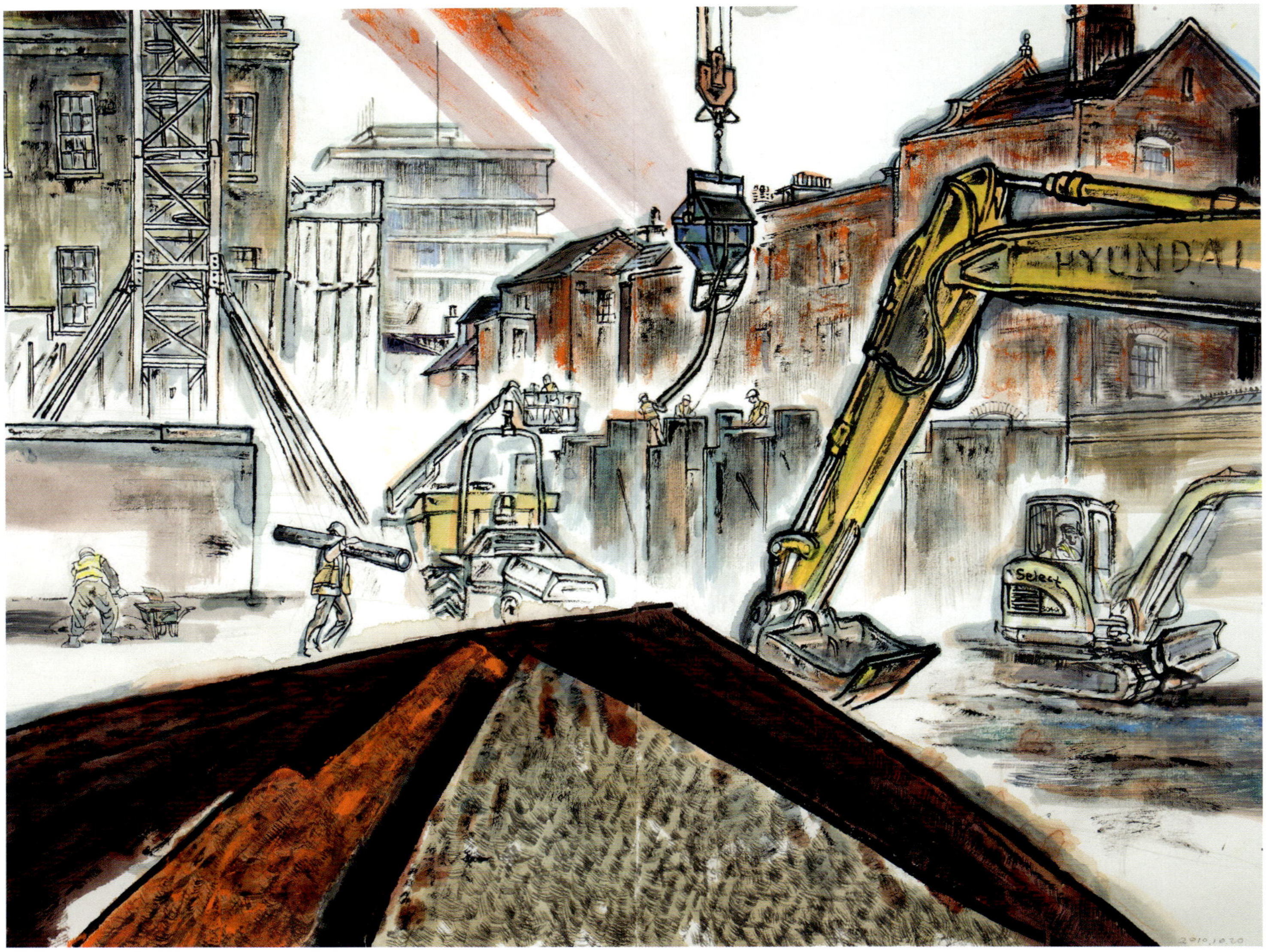

CAT.90
Shifts of light – Somerville College student accommodation. 20 October 2010. Brush, ink and watercolour on album leaves. Paper size: 41.6 × 55.6 cm

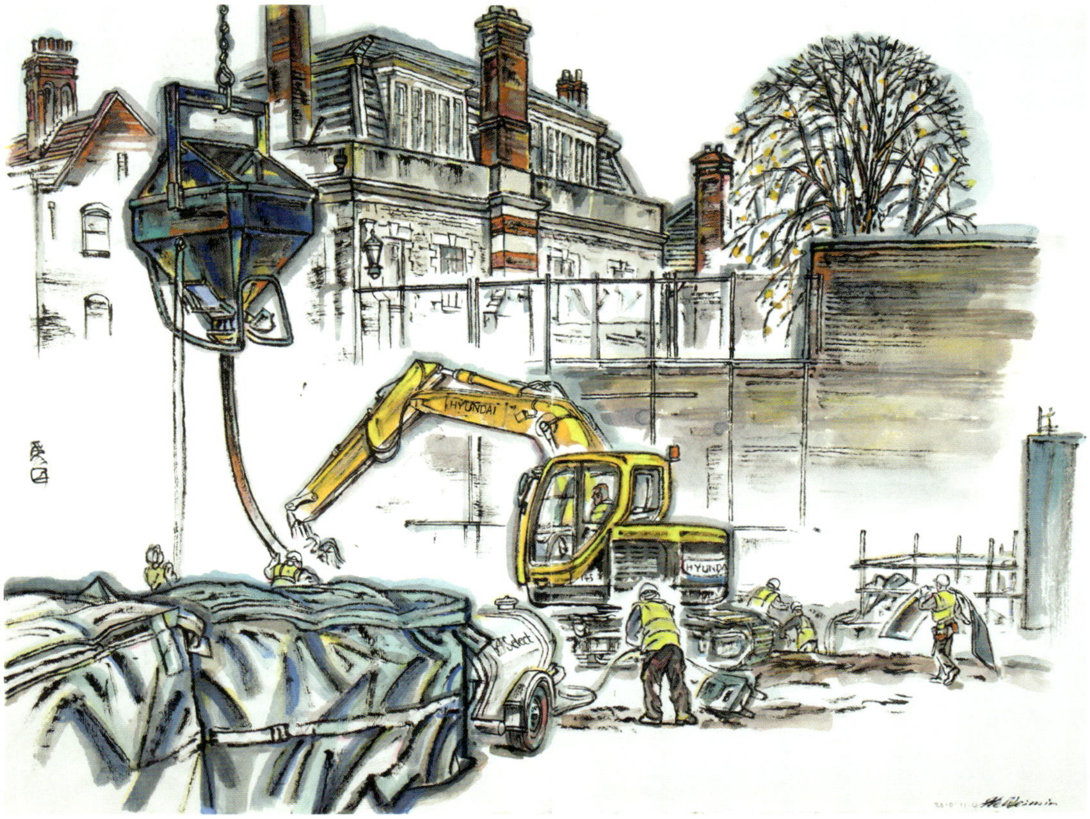

CAT.91
On a drip – Somerville College student accommodation.
4 November 2010. Brush, ink and watercolour on album leaves.
Paper size: 41.6 × 55.6 cm

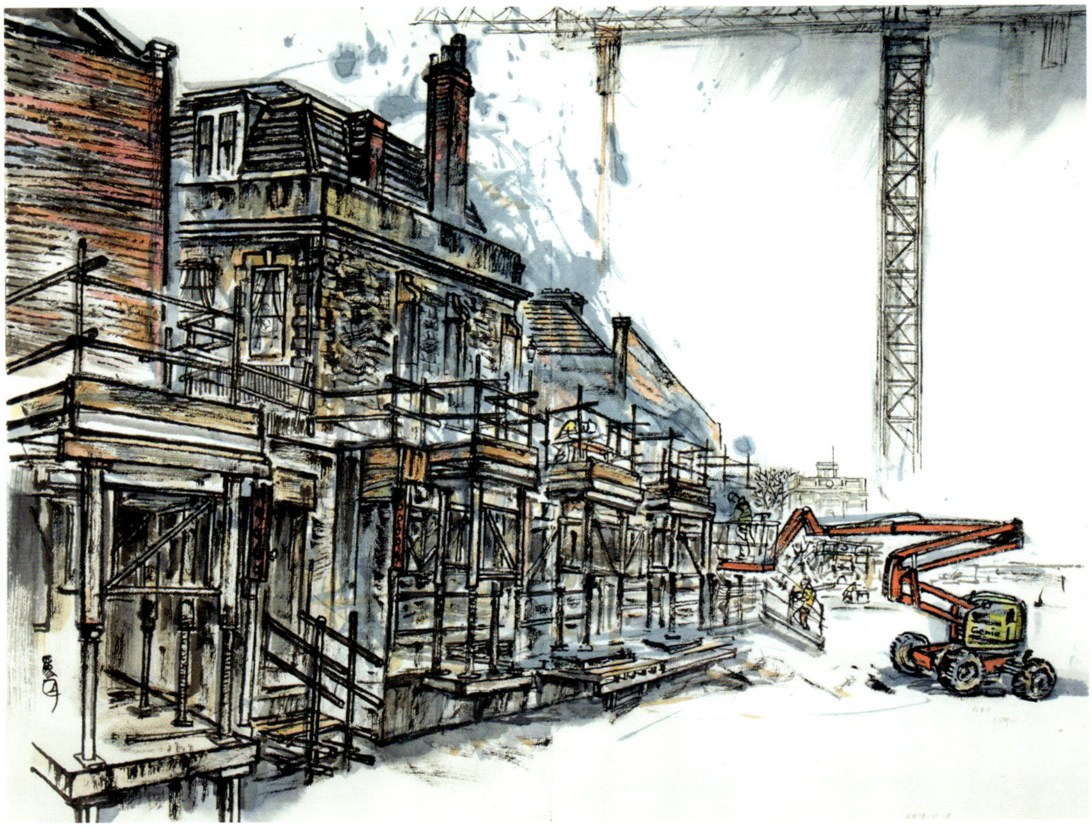

CAT.92
Installation – Somerville College student accommodation.
18 November 2010. Brush, ink and watercolour on album leaves.
Paper size: 41.6 × 55.6 cm

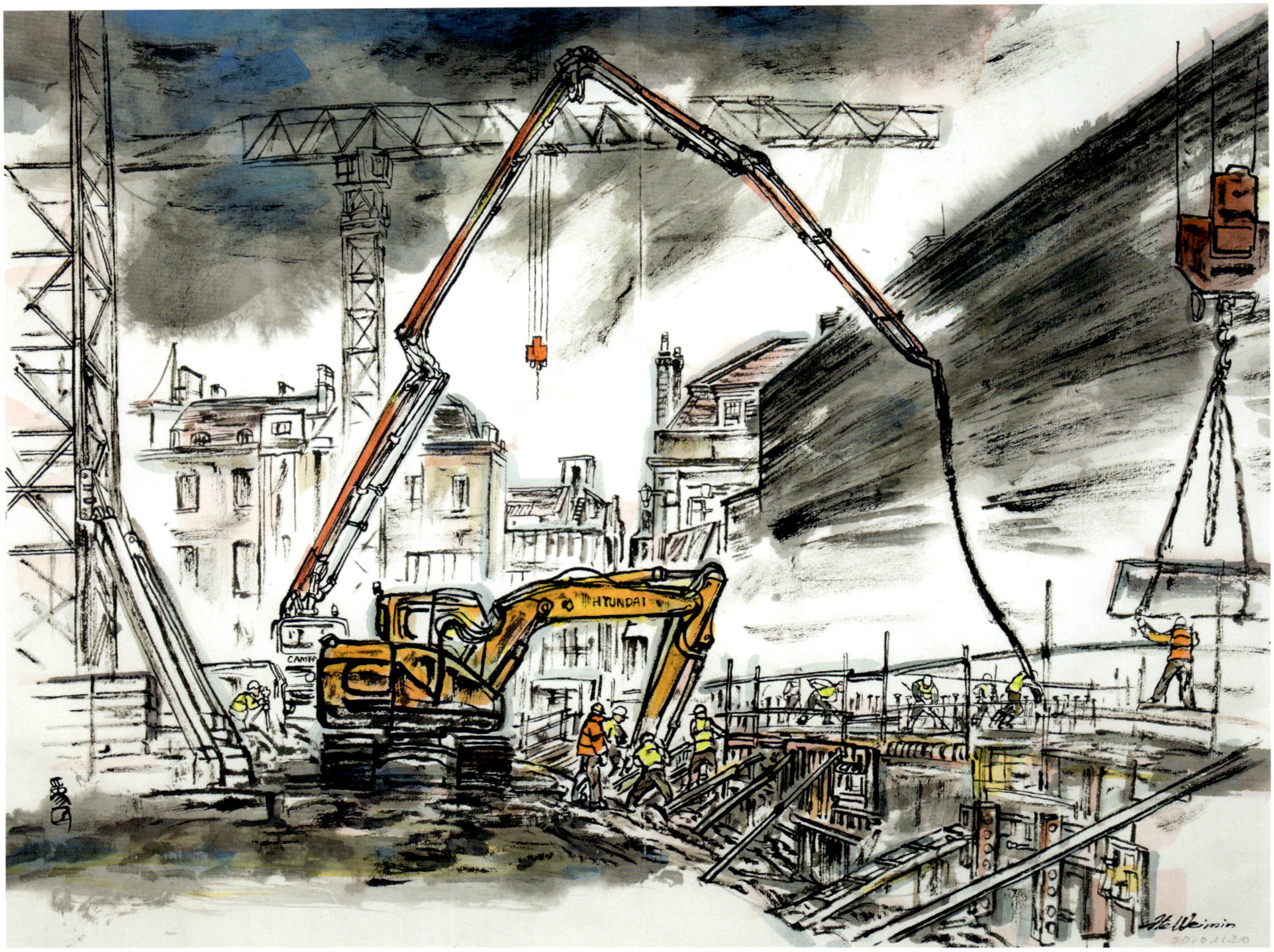

CAT.93
Concrete pumping – Somerville College student accommodation. 20 November 2010.
Brush, ink and watercolour on album leaves.
Paper size: 41.6 × 55.6 cm

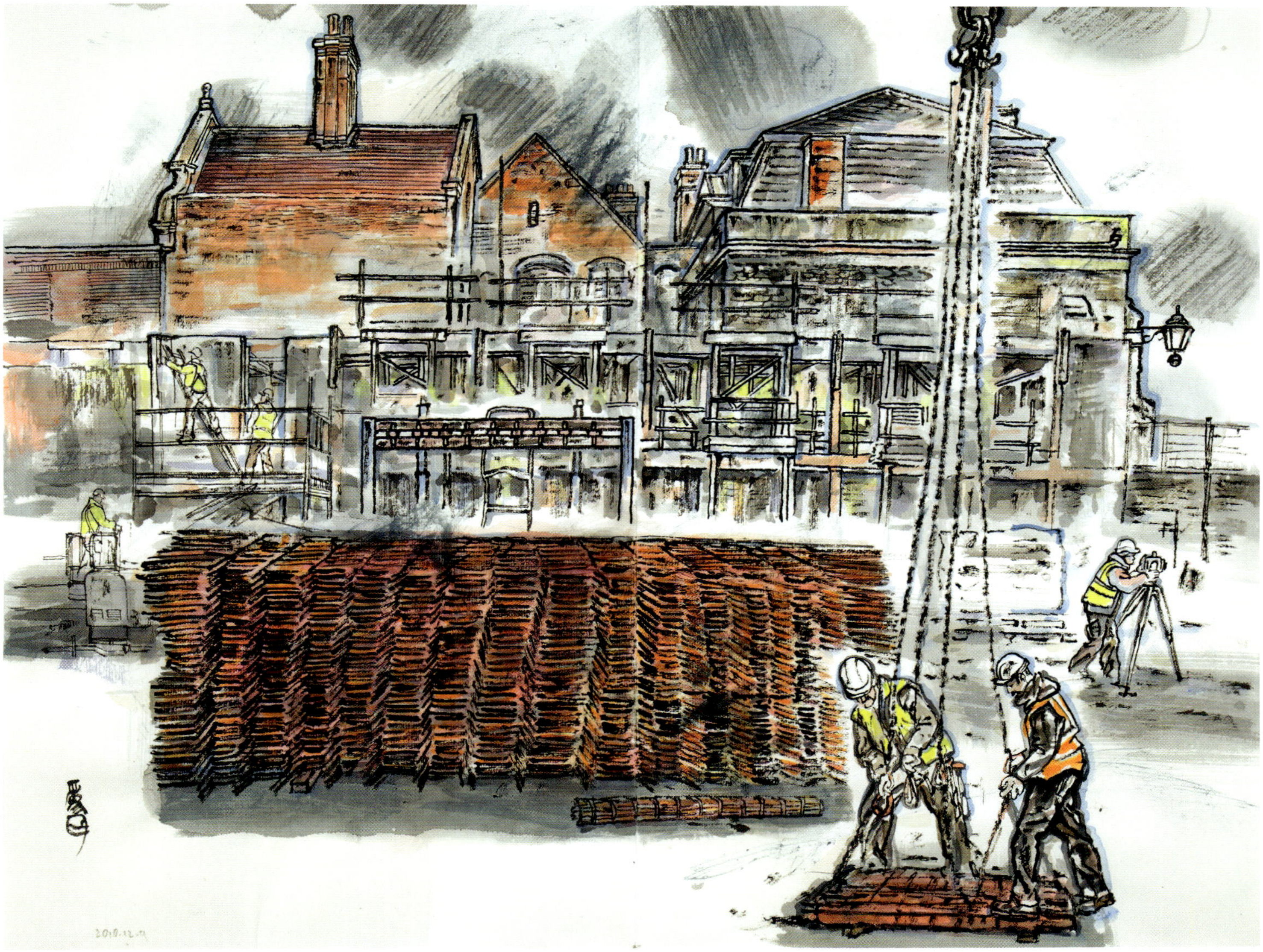

CAT.94

Red matrix – Somerville College student accommodation. 9 December 2010. Brush, ink and watercolour on album leaves. Paper size: 41.6 × 55.6 cm

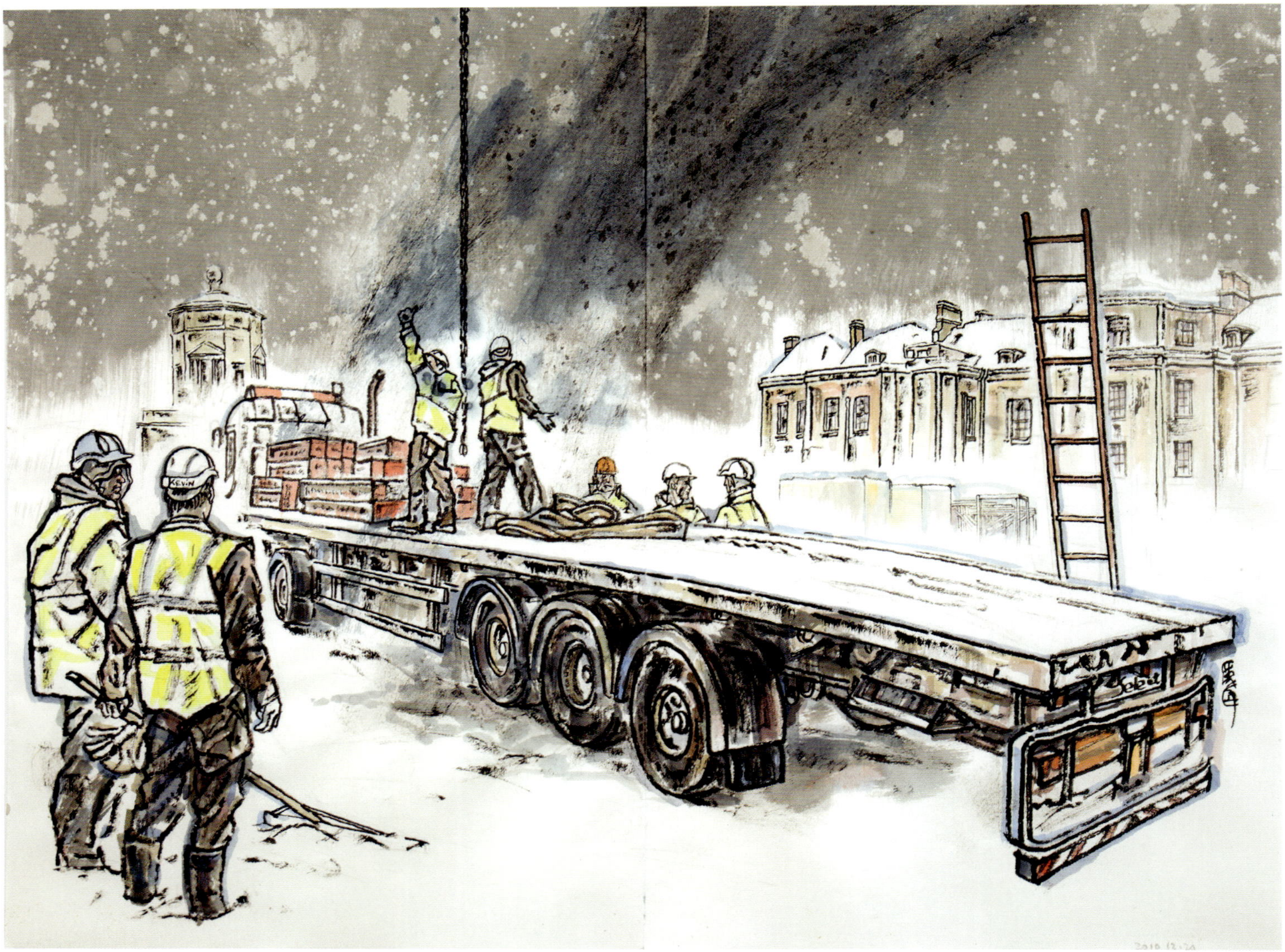

CAT.95
Floating snowflakes – Somerville College student accommodation. 20 December 2010.
Brush, ink and watercolour on album leaves.
Paper size: 41.6 × 55.6 cm

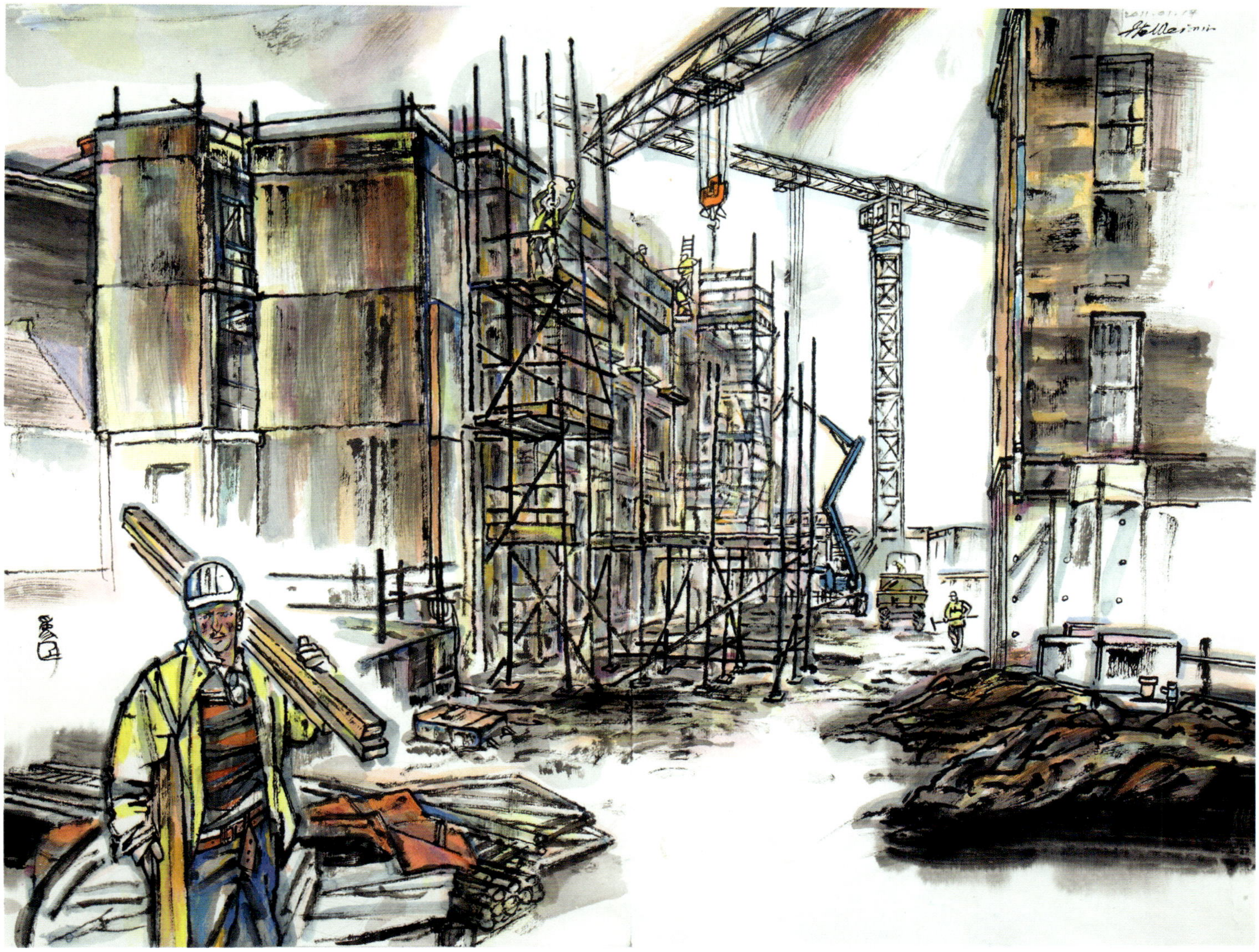

CAT.96

Encounter – Somerville College student accommodation. 14 January 2011. Brush, ink and watercolour on album leaves. Paper size: 41.6 × 55.6 cm

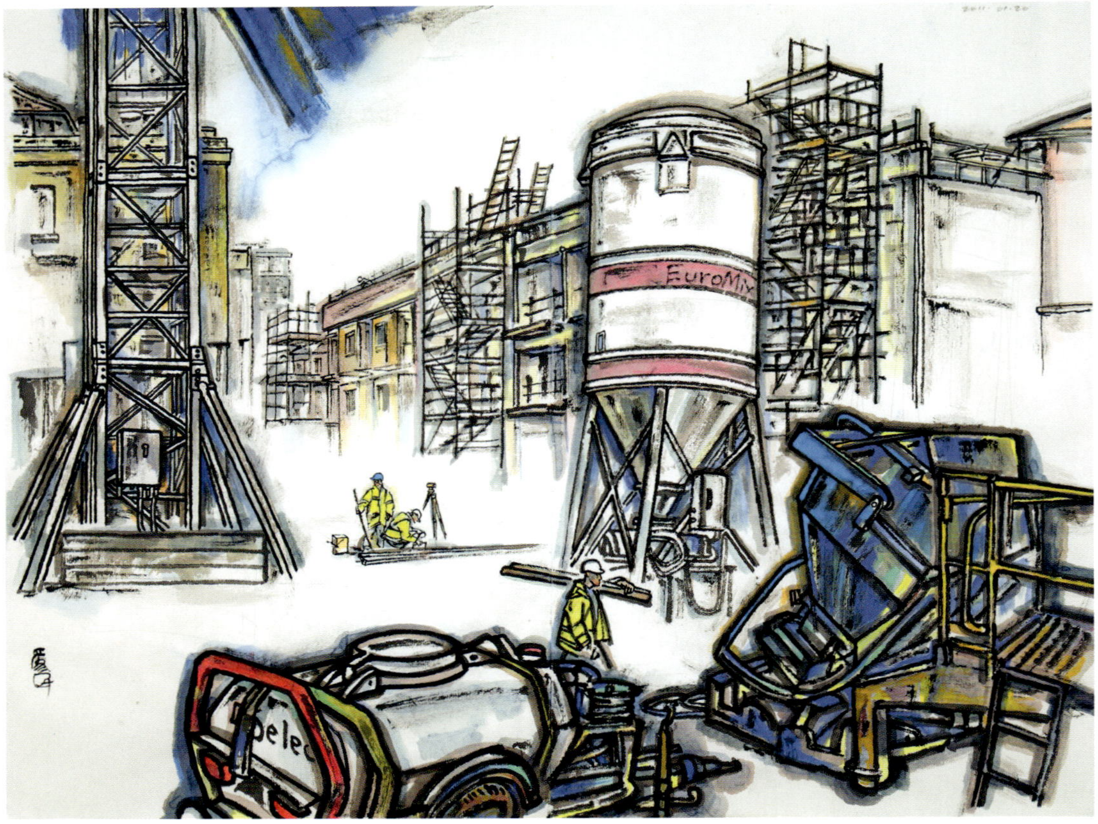

CAT.97
Yellow jackets and blue sky – Somerville College student accommodation. 20 January 2011.Brush, ink and watercolour on album leaves. Paper size: 41.6 × 55.6 cm

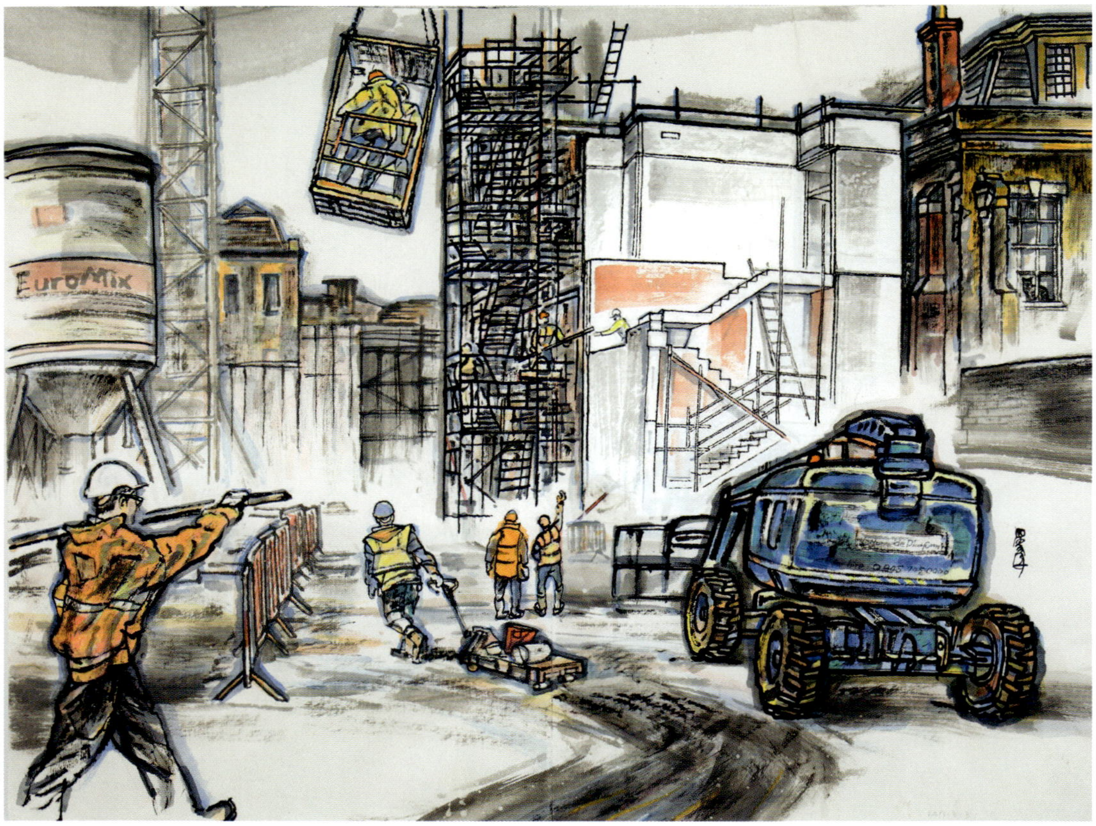

CAT.98
Suspended in motion – Somerville College student accommodation. 3 February 2011. Brush, ink, watercolour and collage on album leaves. Paper size: 41.6 × 55.6 cm

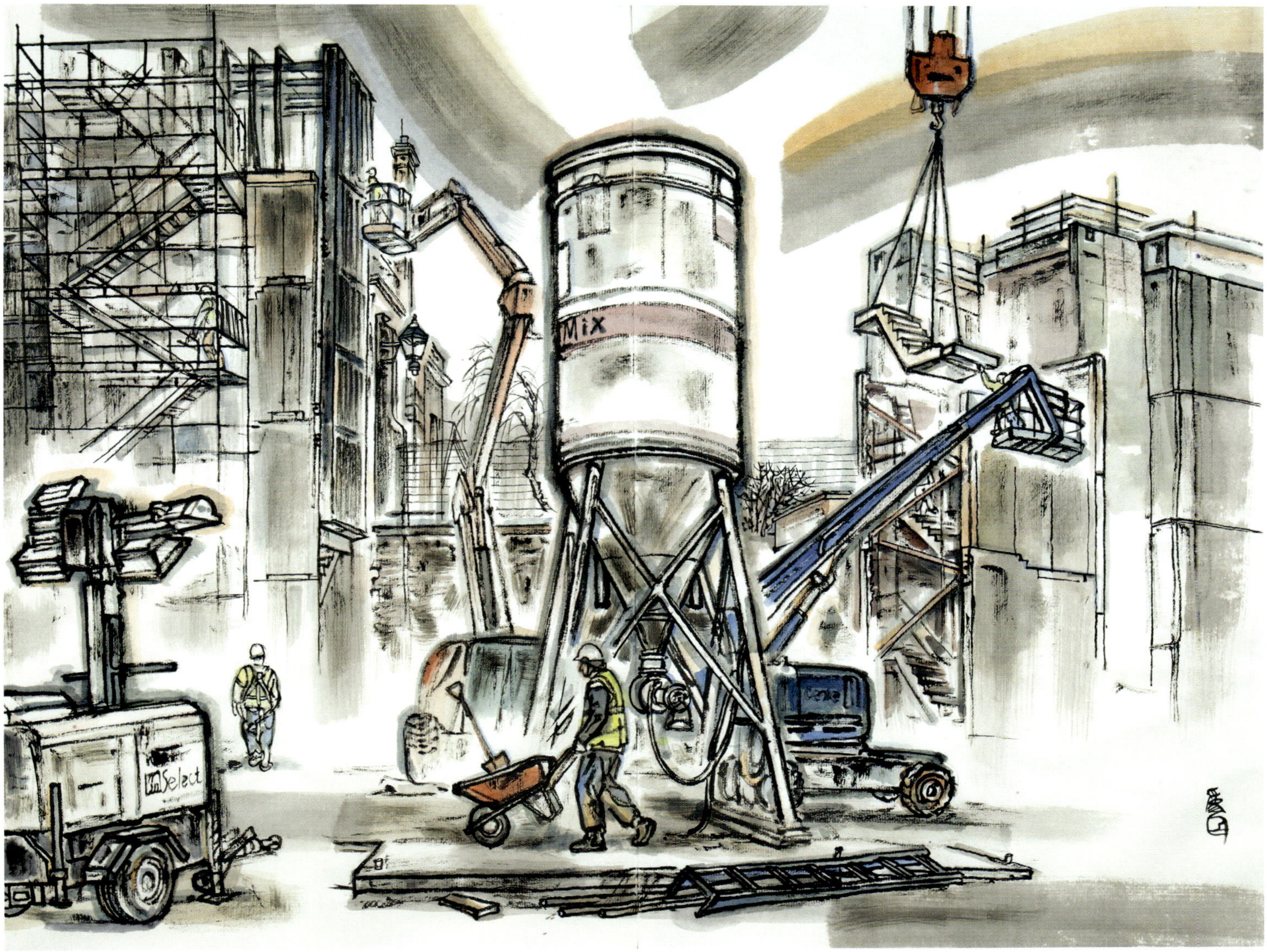

CAT.99

Cement mixing – Somerville College student accommodation. 16 February 2011.
Brush, ink and watercolour on album leaves.
Paper size: 41.6 × 55.6 cm

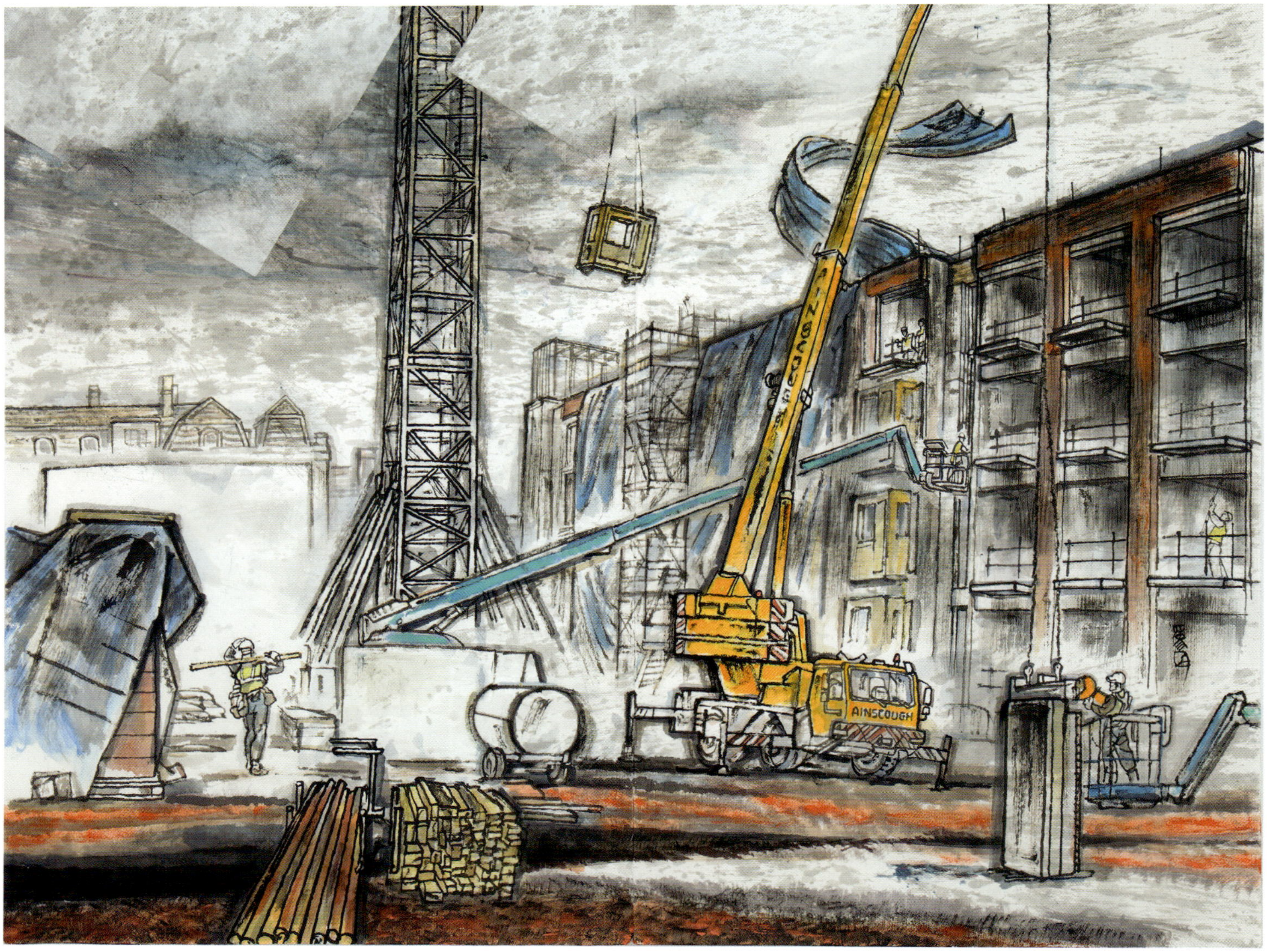

CAT.100

Defying the winds – Somerville College student accommodation. 24 February 2011. Brush, ink, watercolour and collage on album leaves. Paper size: 41.6 × 55.6 cm

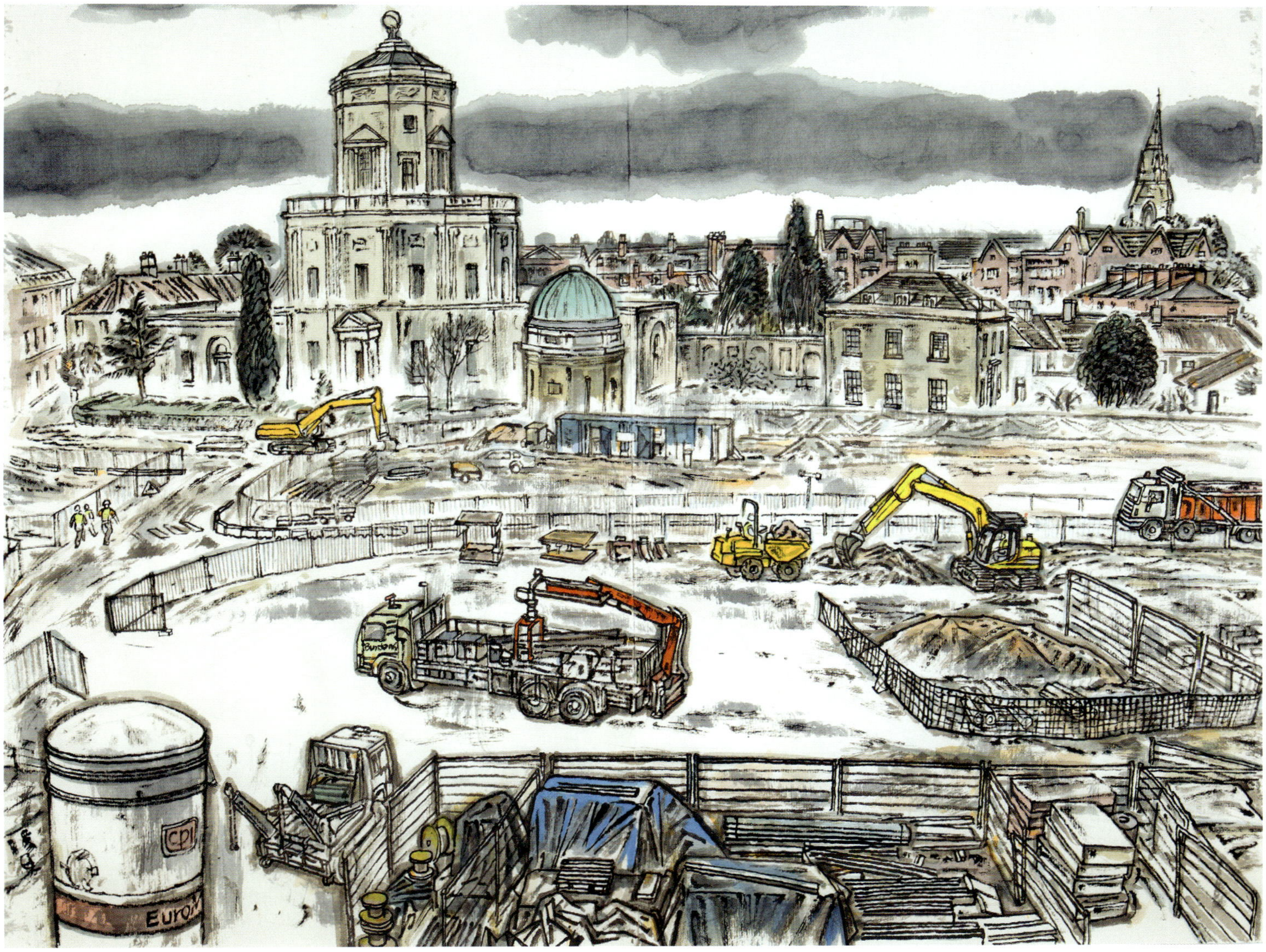

CAT.101
Observing the Observatory. 9 March 2011.
Brush, ink and watercolour on album leaves.
Paper size: 41.6 × 55.6 cm

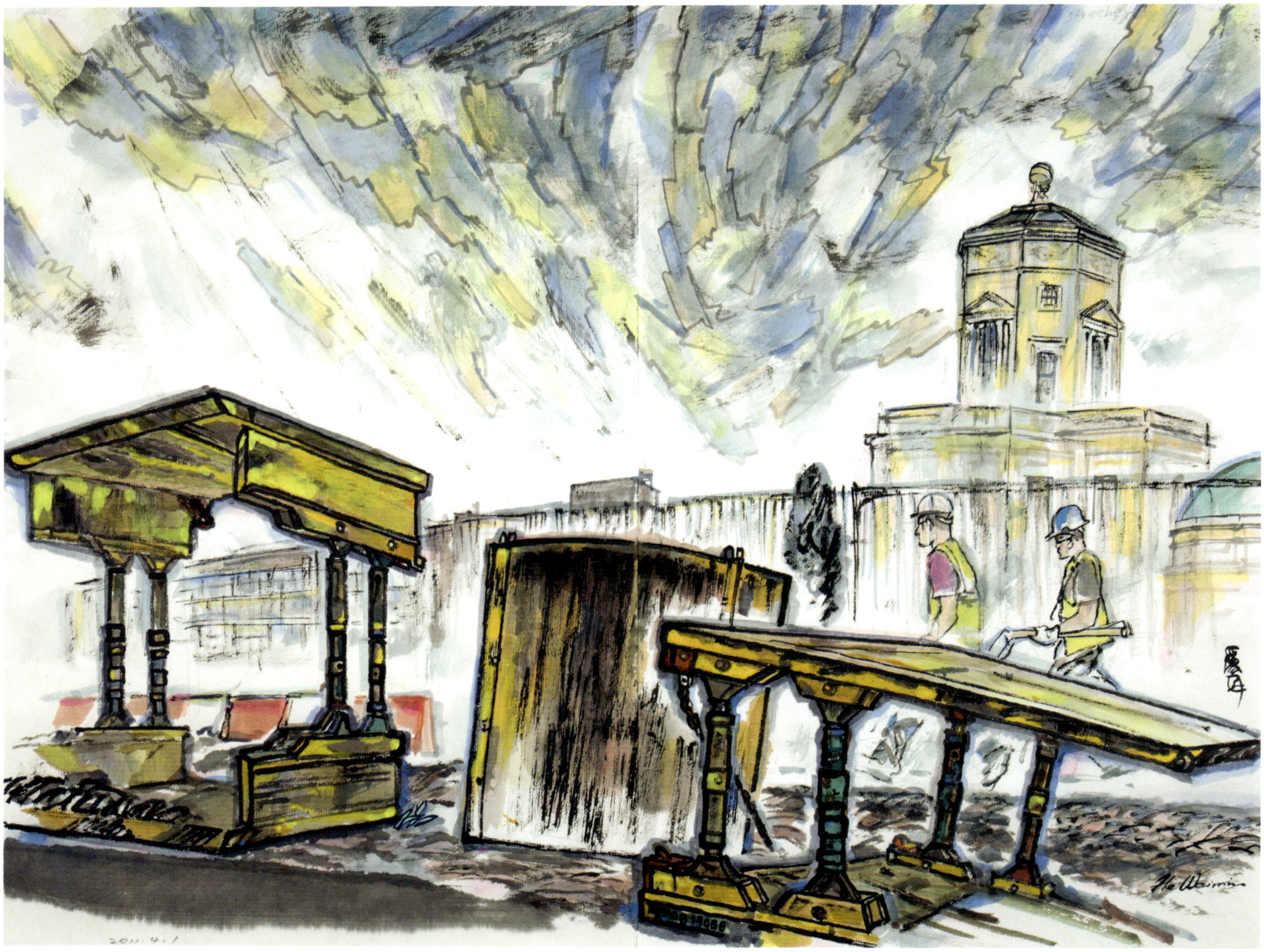

CAT.102
Start of a new day. 1 April 2011. Brush, ink and watercolour on album leaves. Paper size: 41.6 × 55.6 cm

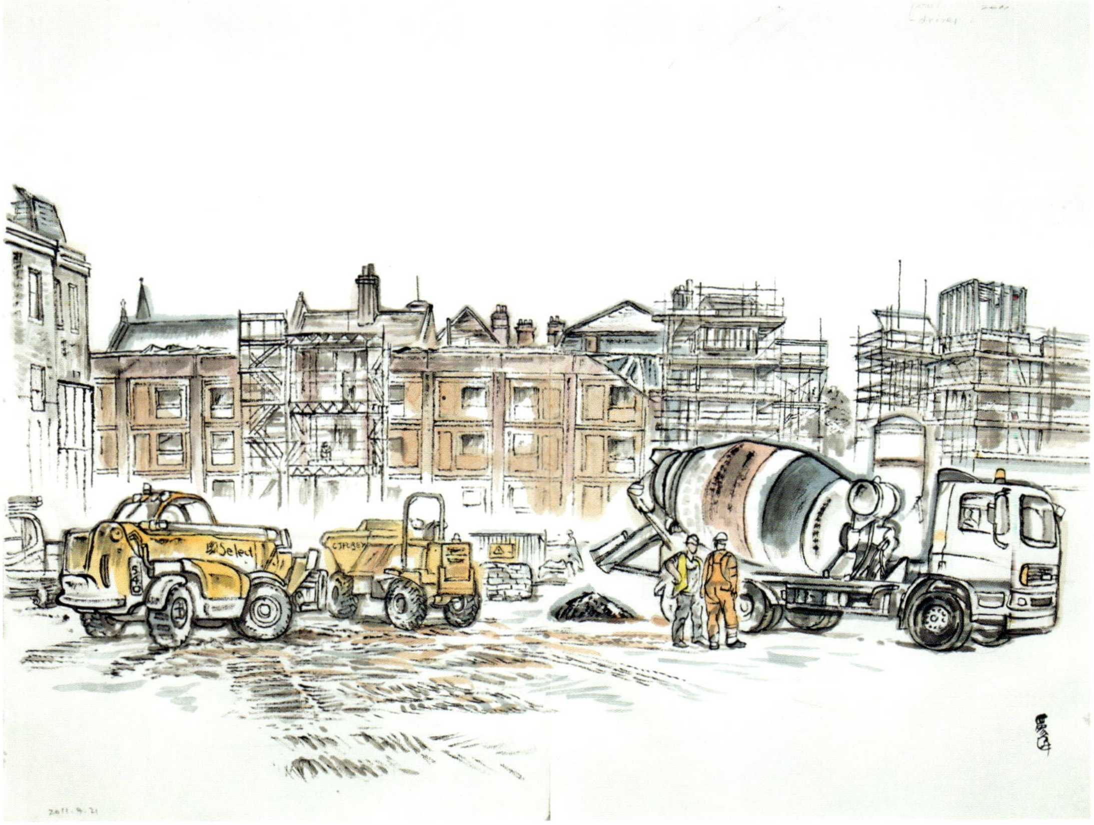

CAT.103
Calm at the end of the day – Somerville College student accommodation. 21 April 2011. Brush, ink and watercolour on album leaves. Paper size: 41.6 × 55.6 cm

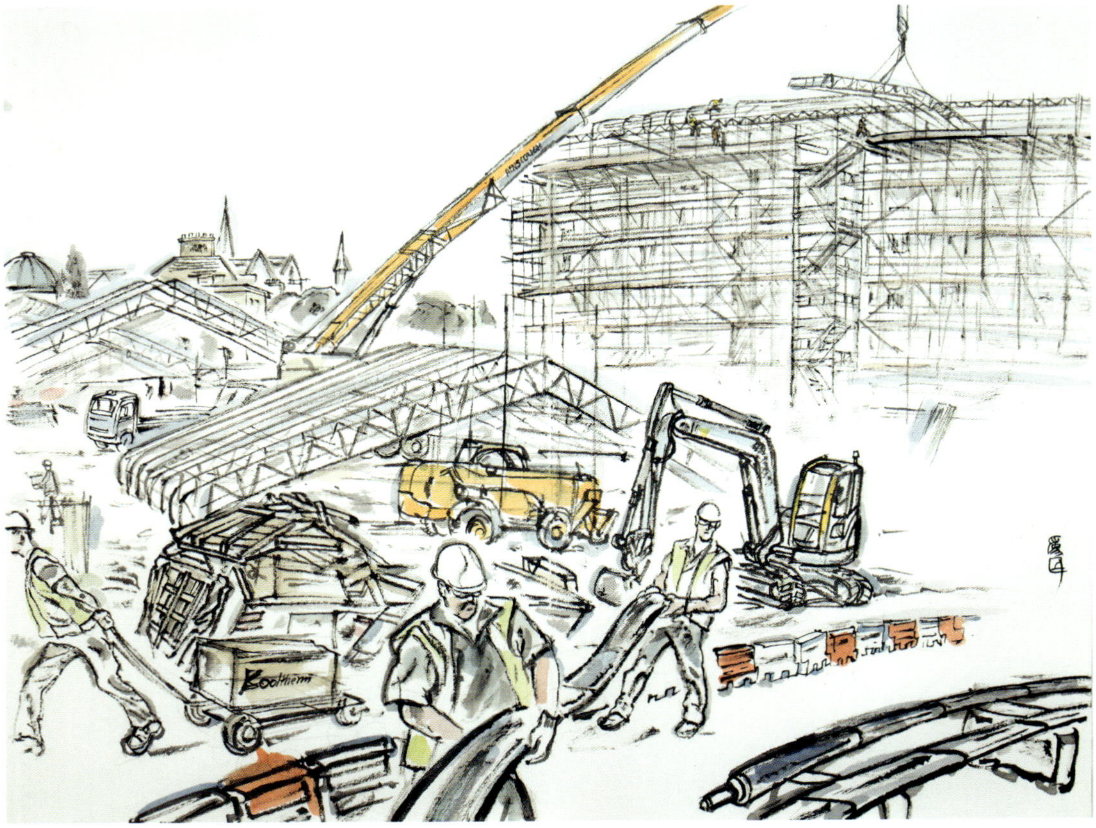

CAT.104
Raising the roof – Radcliffe Infirmary building. 2 June 2011. Brush, ink and watercolour on album leaves. Paper size: 41.6 × 55.6 cm

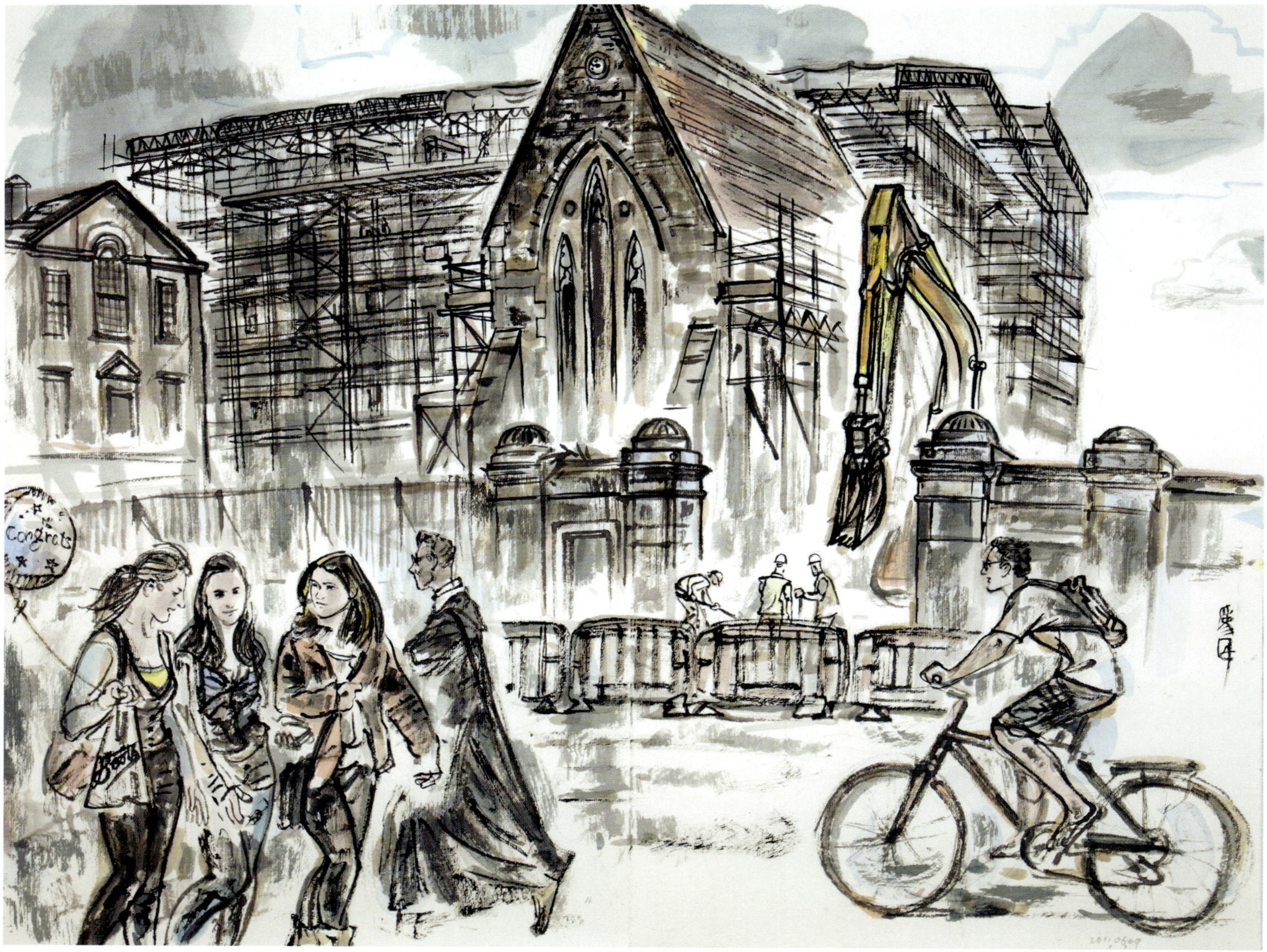

CAT.105
Town and gown – the Radcliffe Infirmary building under refurbishment. 9 June 2011.
Brush, ink and watercolour on album leaves.
Paper size: 41.6 × 55.6 cm

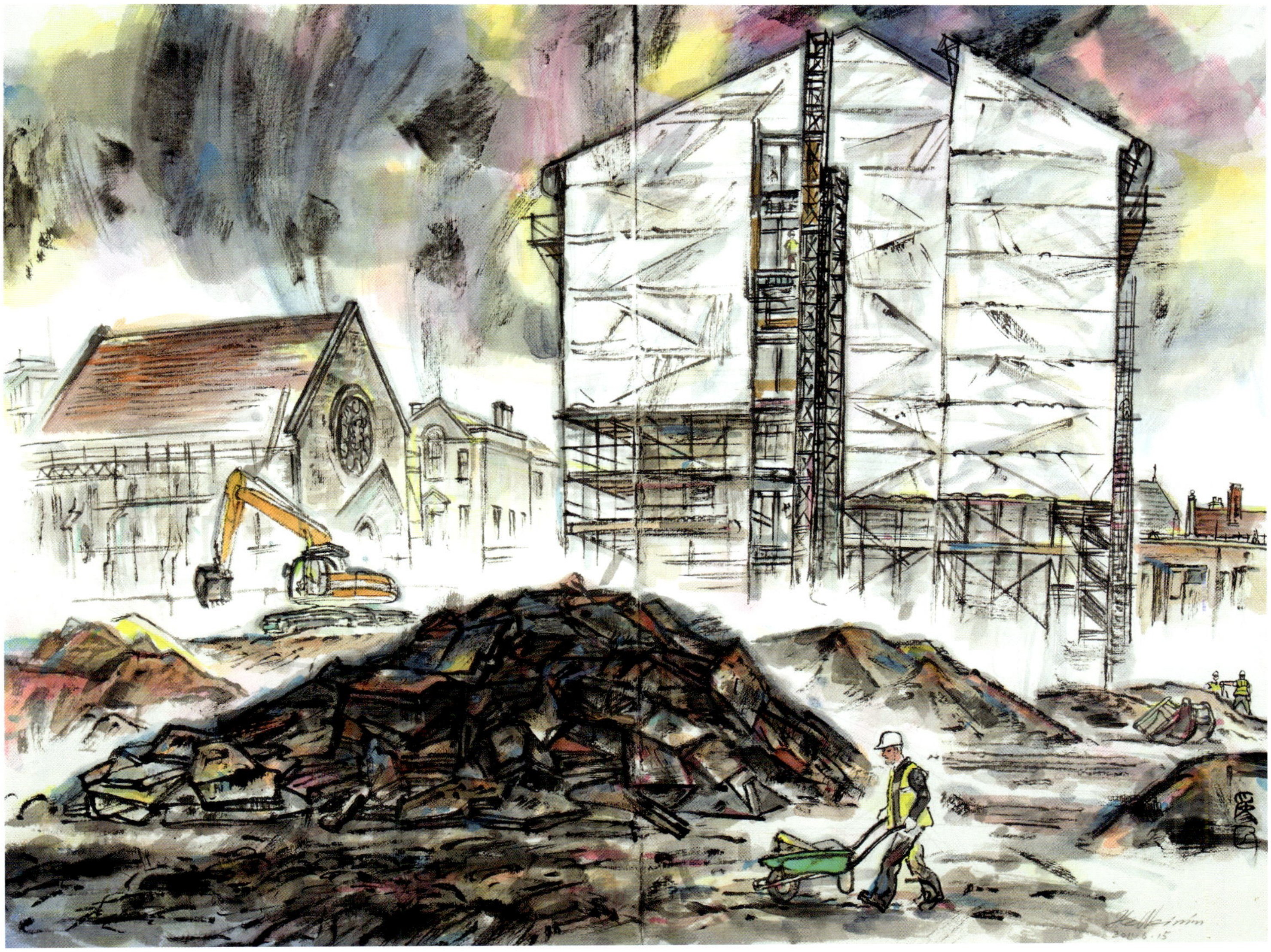

CAT.106
Green barrow – The Radcliffe Infirmary building under refurbishment. 15 June 2011.
Brush, ink and watercolour on album leaves.
Paper size: 41.6 × 55.6 cm

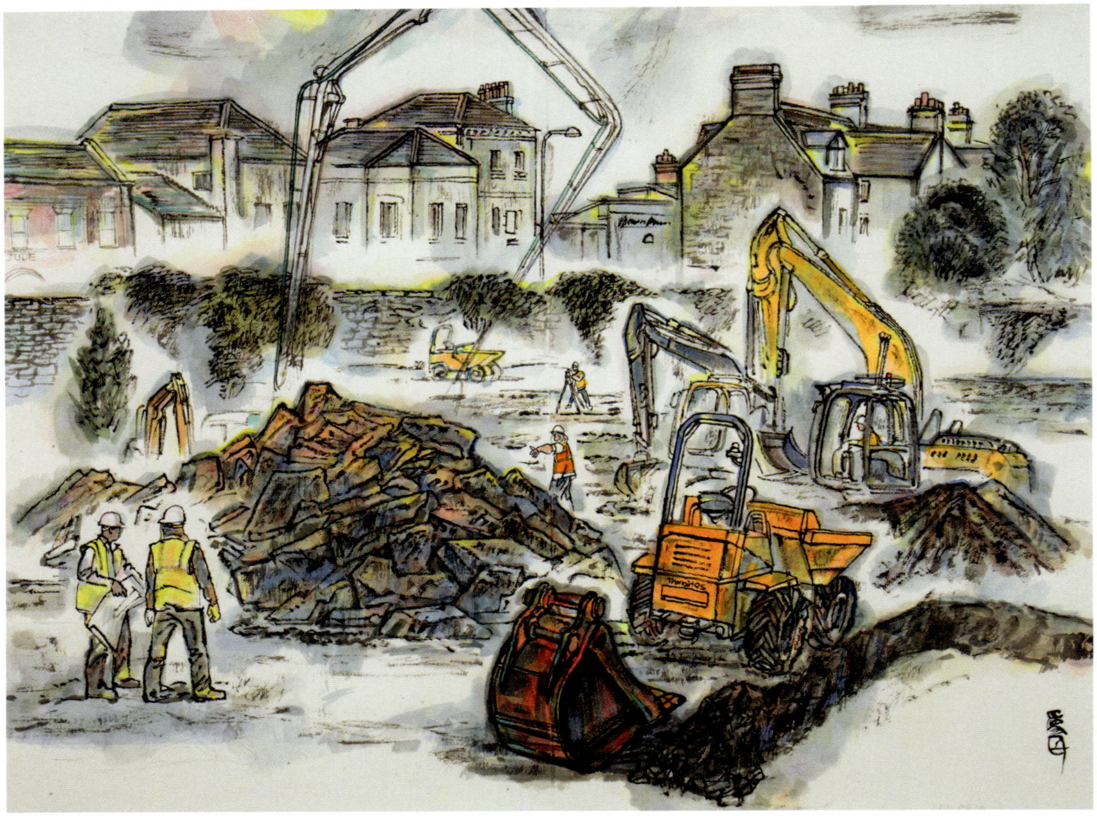

CAT.107
Rise of Jericho – Jericho Health Centre site. 16 June 2011. Brush, ink and watercolour on album leaves. Paper size: 41.6 × 55.6 cm

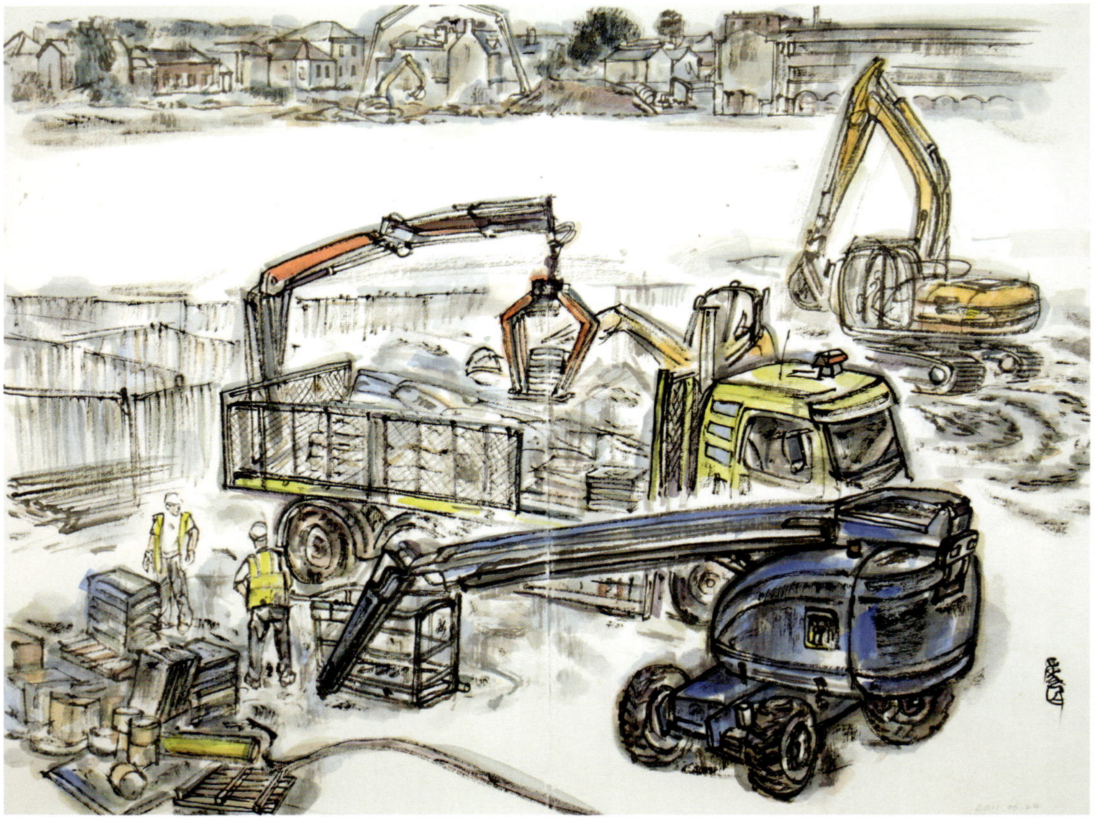

CAT.108
Loading concrete blocks. 20 June 2011. Brush, ink and watercolour on album leaves. Paper size: 41.6 × 55.6 cm

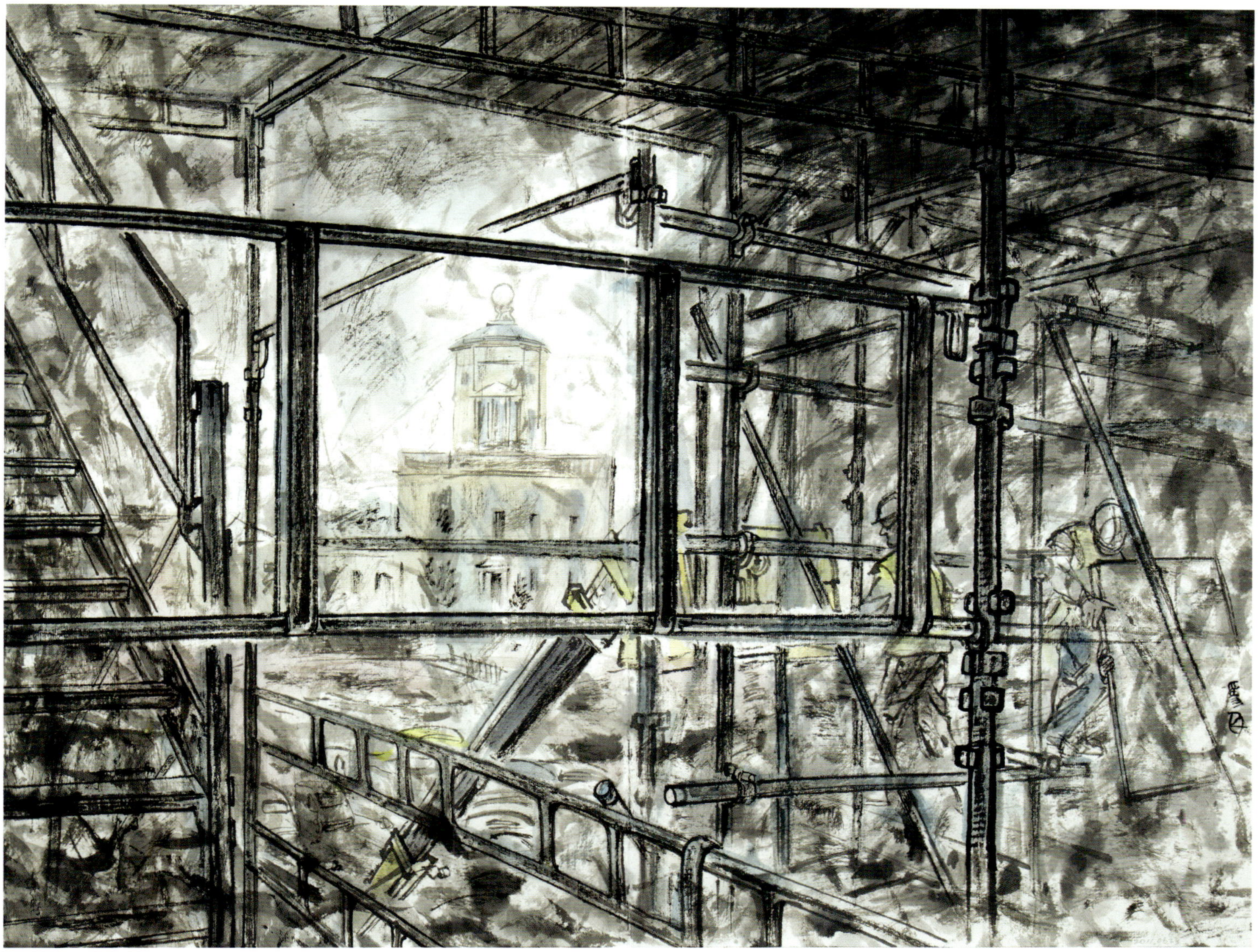

CAT.109
The gathering storm. 23 June 2011. Brush, ink and watercolour on album leaves. Paper size: 41.6 × 55.6 cm

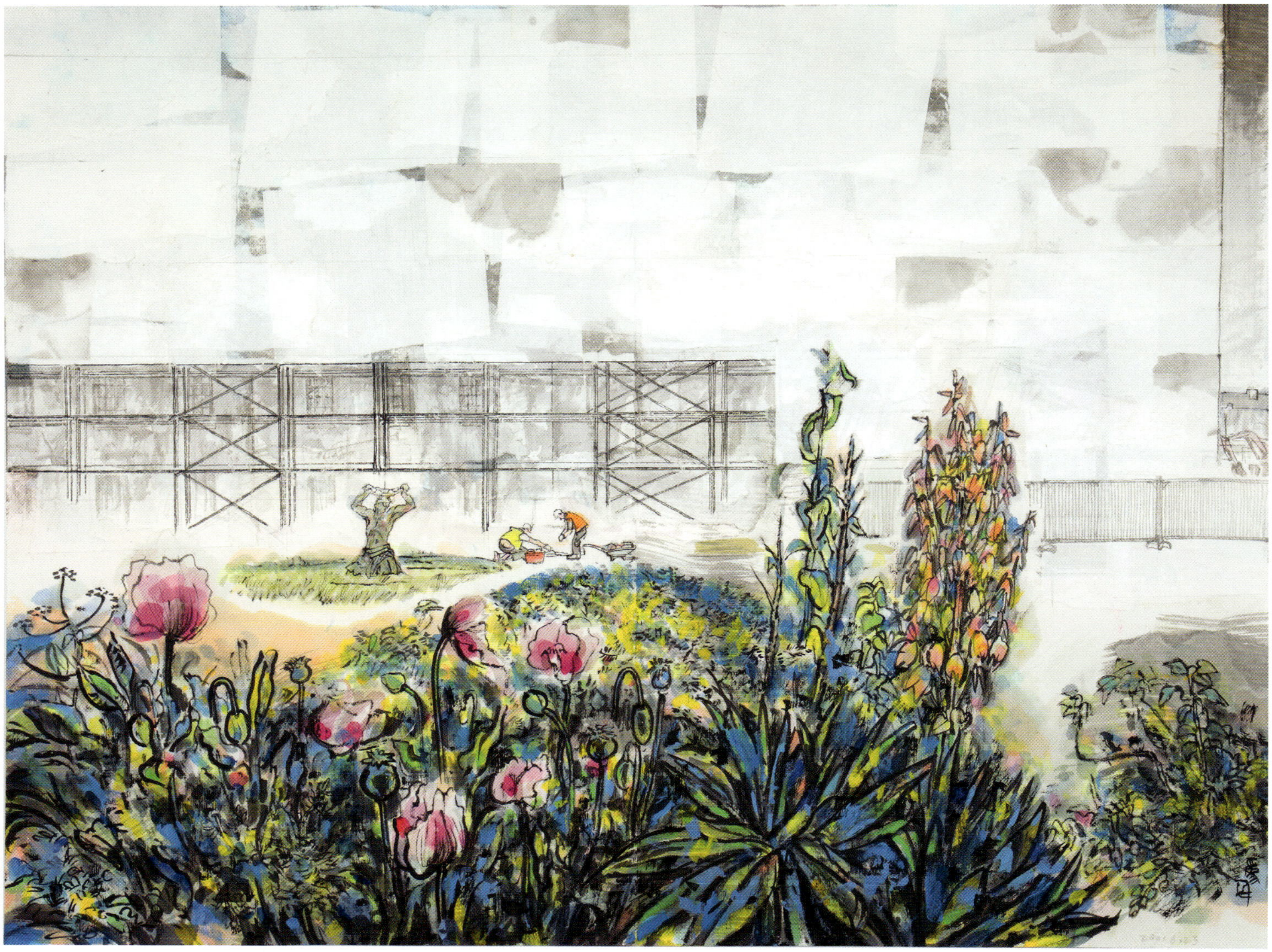

CAT.110
Thirsty Triton – the Radcliffe Infirmary.
23 June 2011. Brush, ink and watercolour on album leaves. Paper size: 41.6 × 55.6 cm

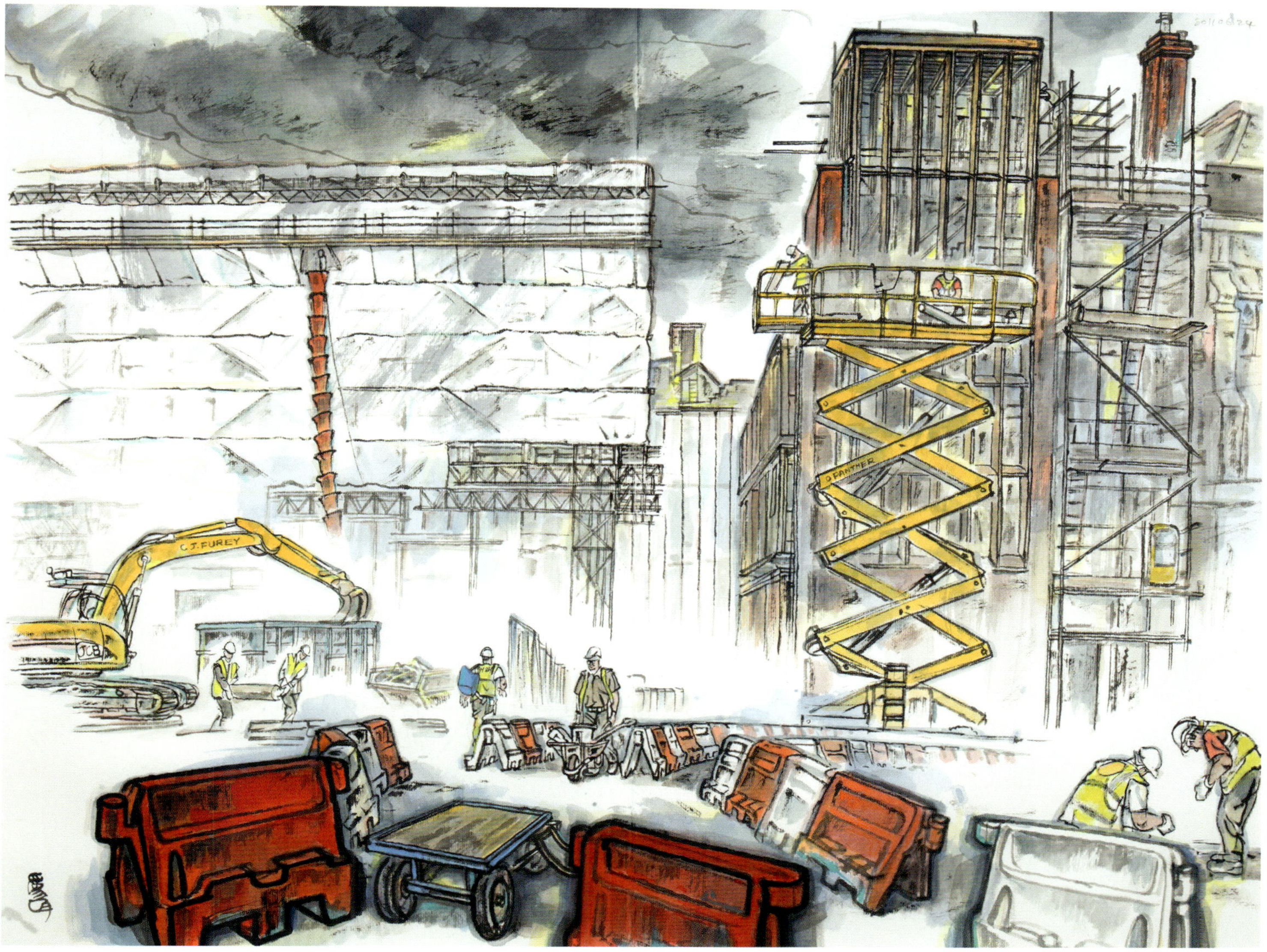

CAT.111

Clouds come and go – Somerville College student accommodation. 24 June 2011.
Brush, ink and watercolour on album leaves.
Paper size: 41.6 × 55.6 cm

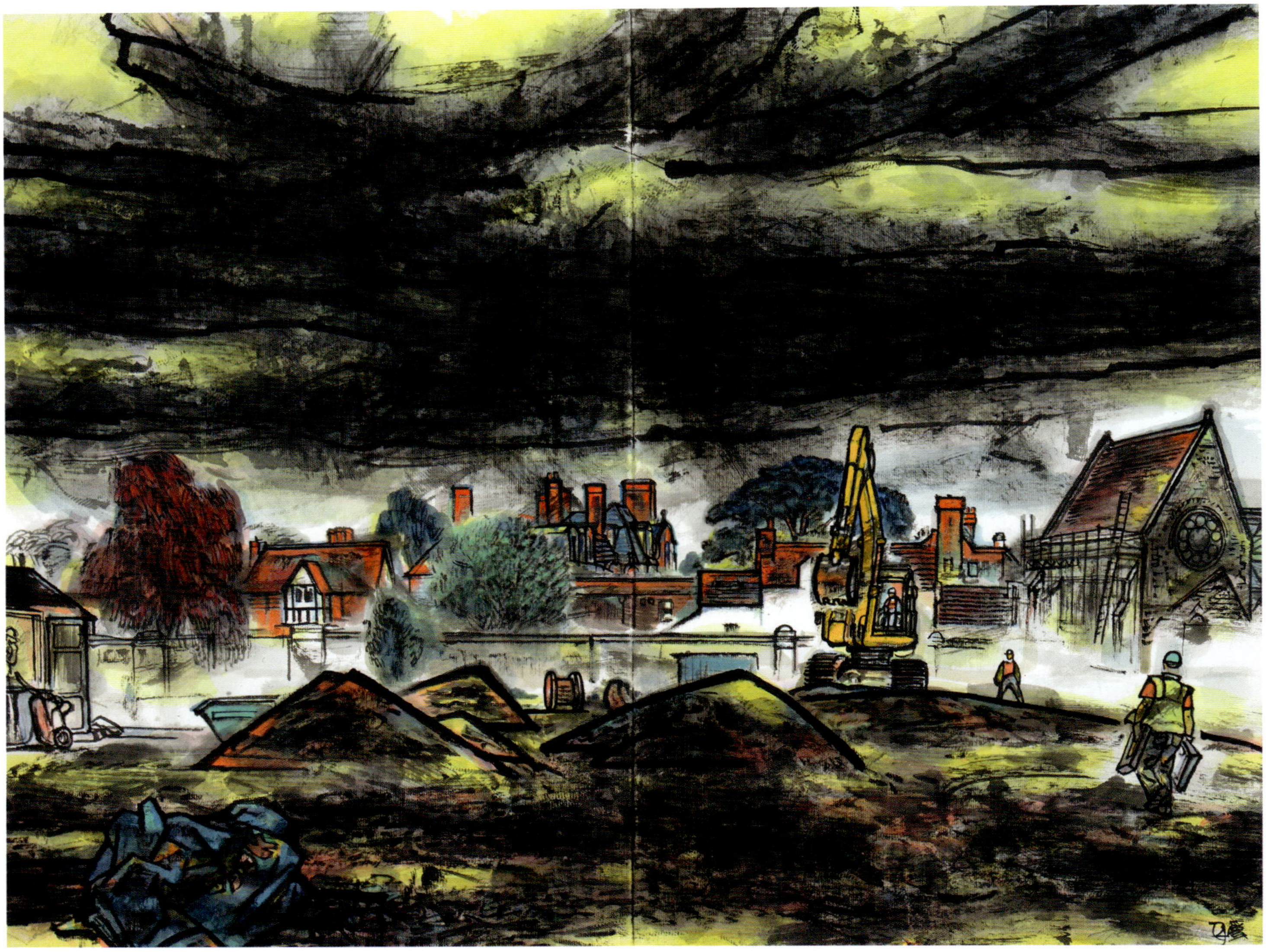

CAT.112
Dark matters. 29 June 2011. Brush, ink and watercolour on album leaves. Paper size: 41.6 × 55.6 cm

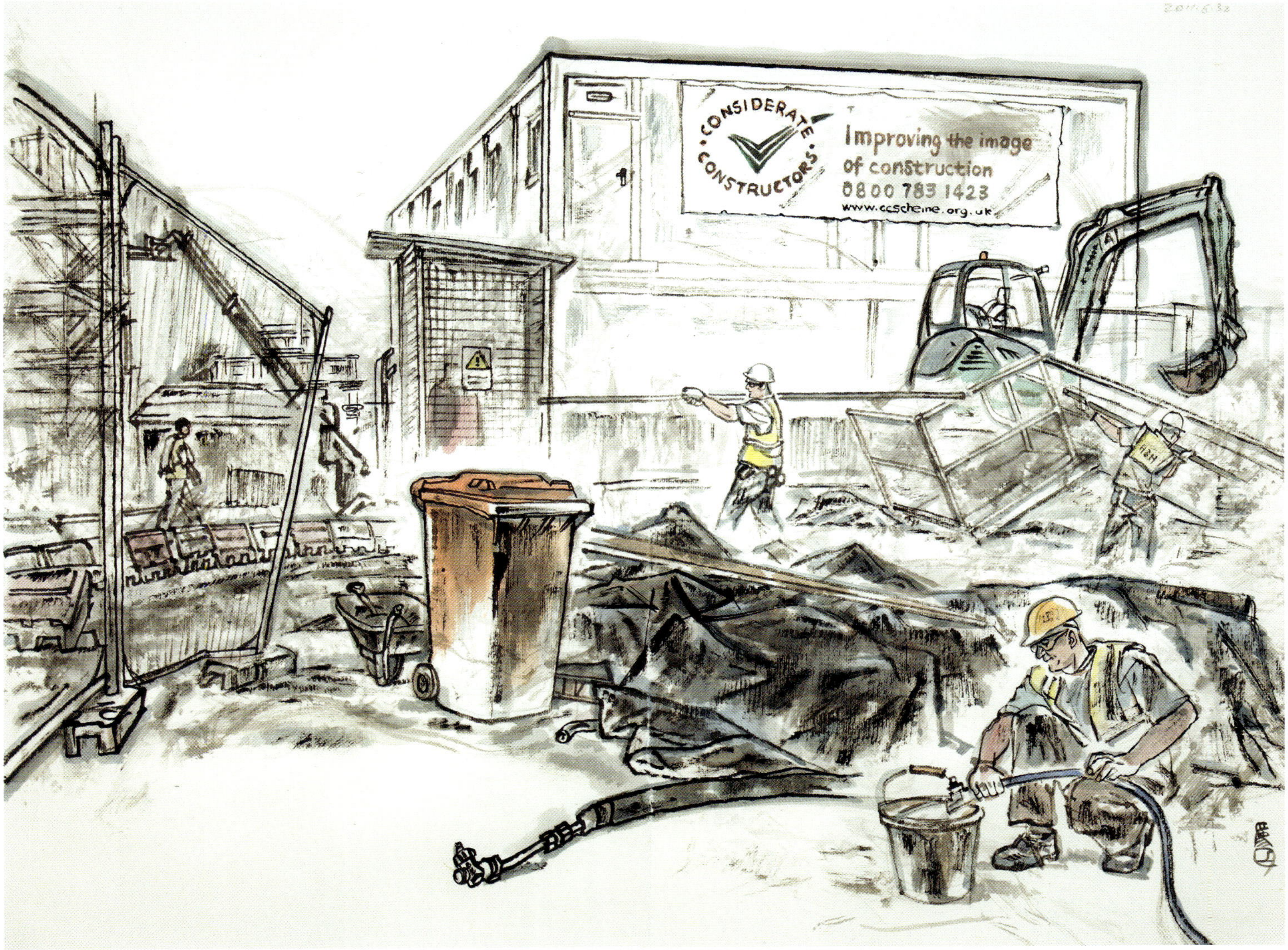

CAT.113
Considerate constructors – Laing O'Rourke office. 30 June 2011. Brush, ink and watercolour on album leaves. Paper size: 41.6 × 55.6 cm

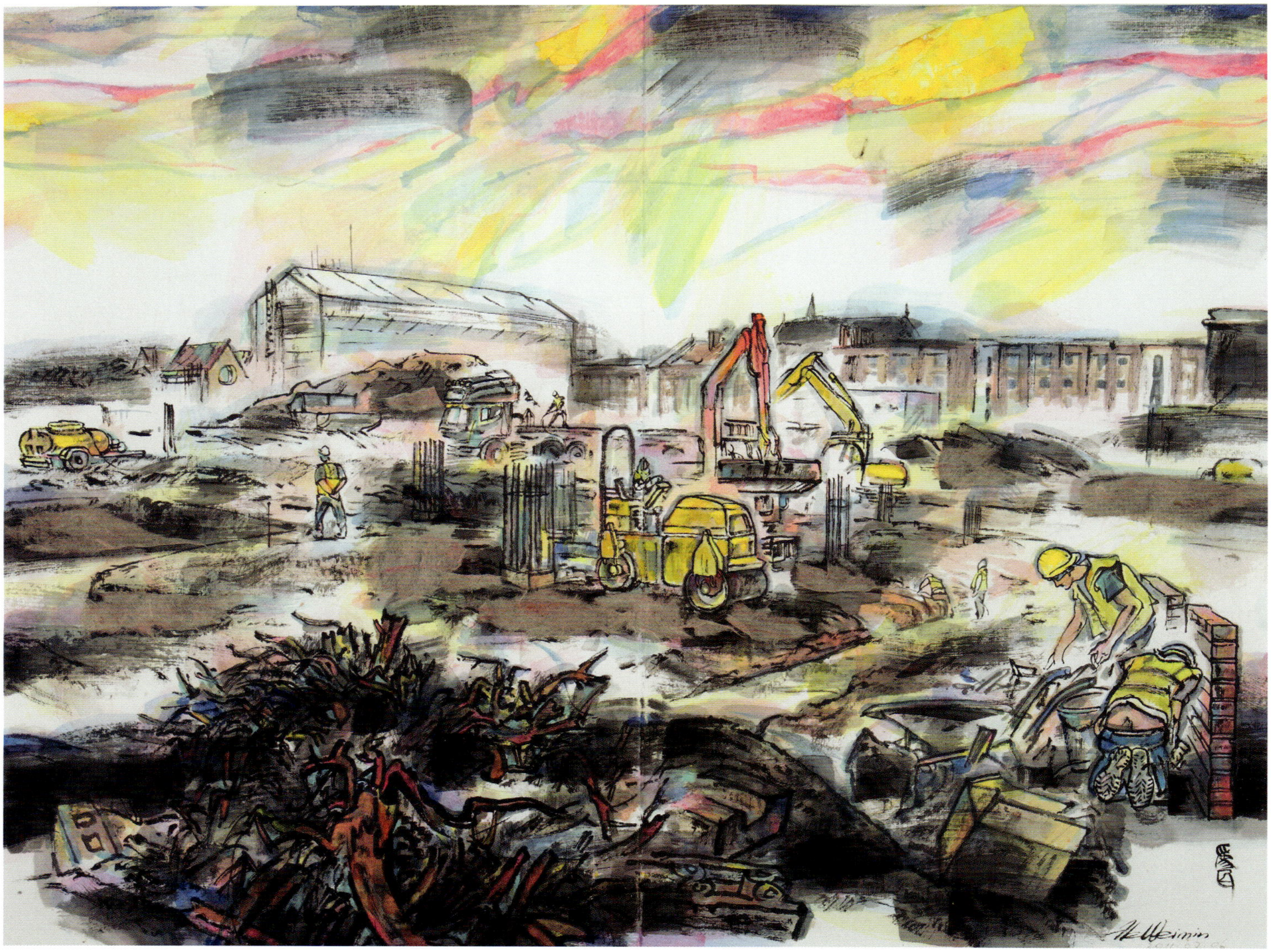

CAT.114
Old tree roots – Jericho Health Centre. 6 July 2011. Brush, ink and watercolour on album leaves. Paper size: 41.6 × 55.6 cm

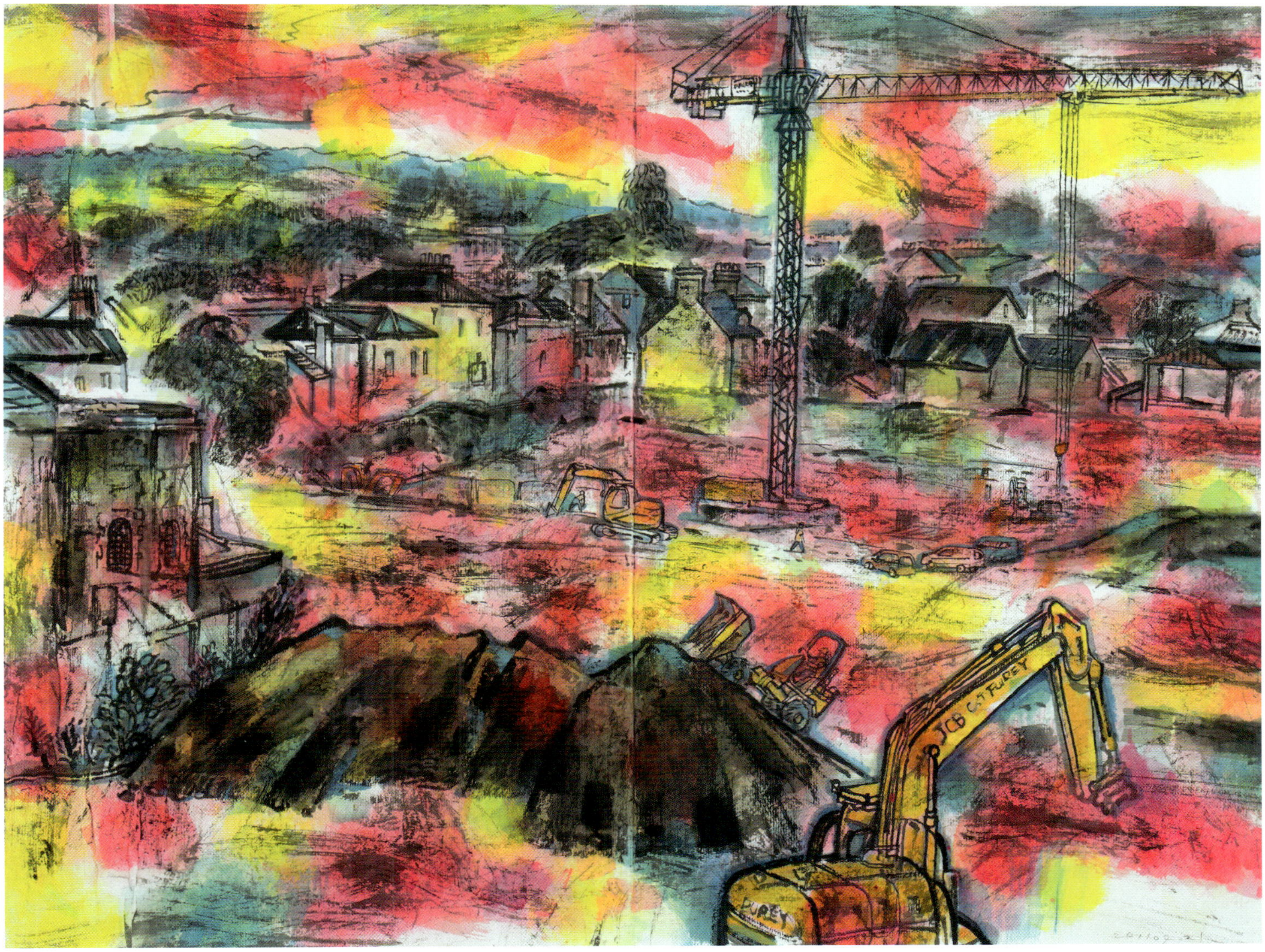

CAT.115
Melody of pink and yellow. 21 July 2011.
Brush, ink and watercolour on album leaves.
Paper size: 41.6 × 55.6 cm

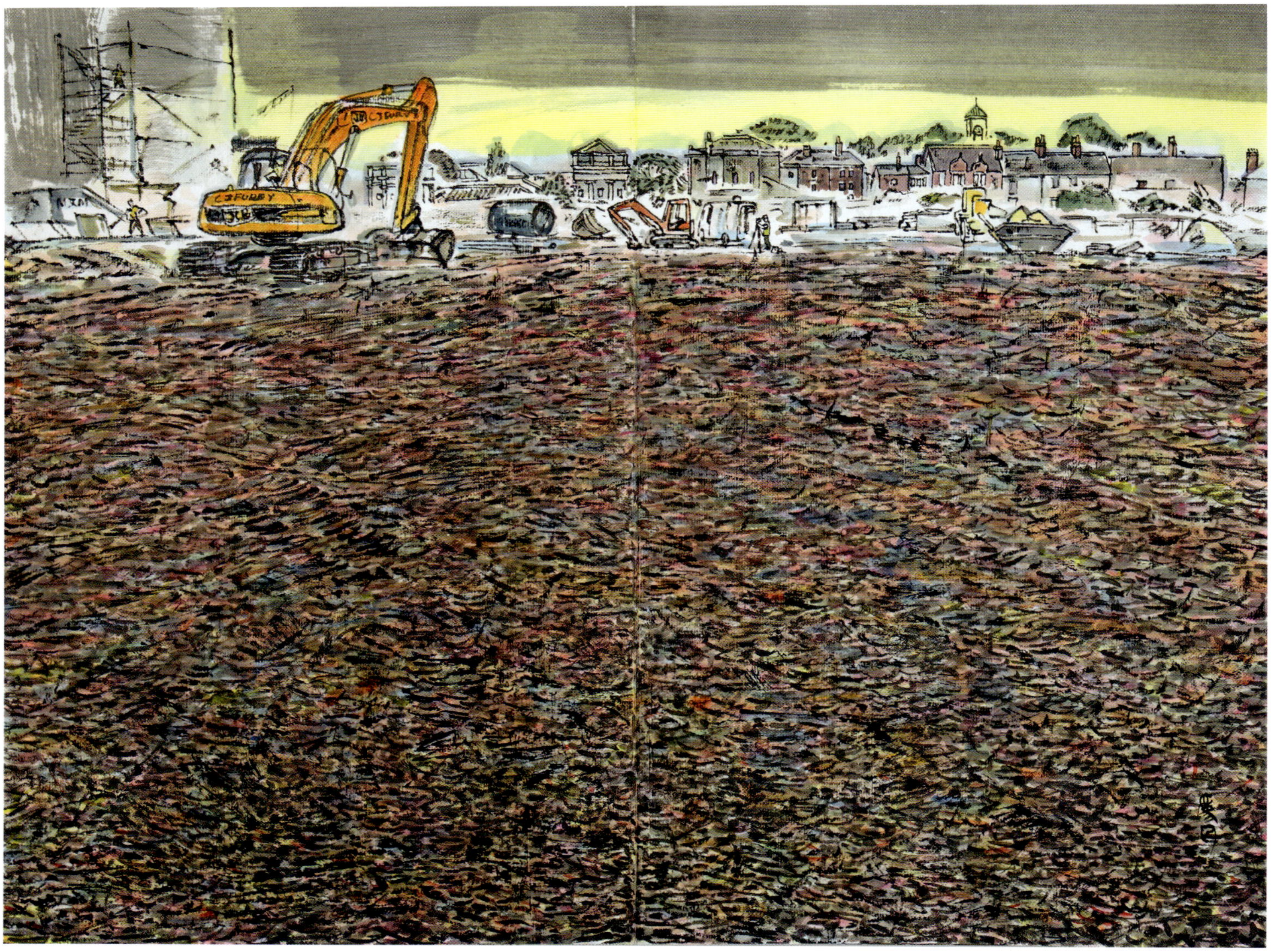

CAT.116
The land may never be the same again – first day of construction of the Mathematical Institute. 25 July 2011. Brush, ink and watercolour on album leaves. Paper size: 41.6 × 55.6 cm

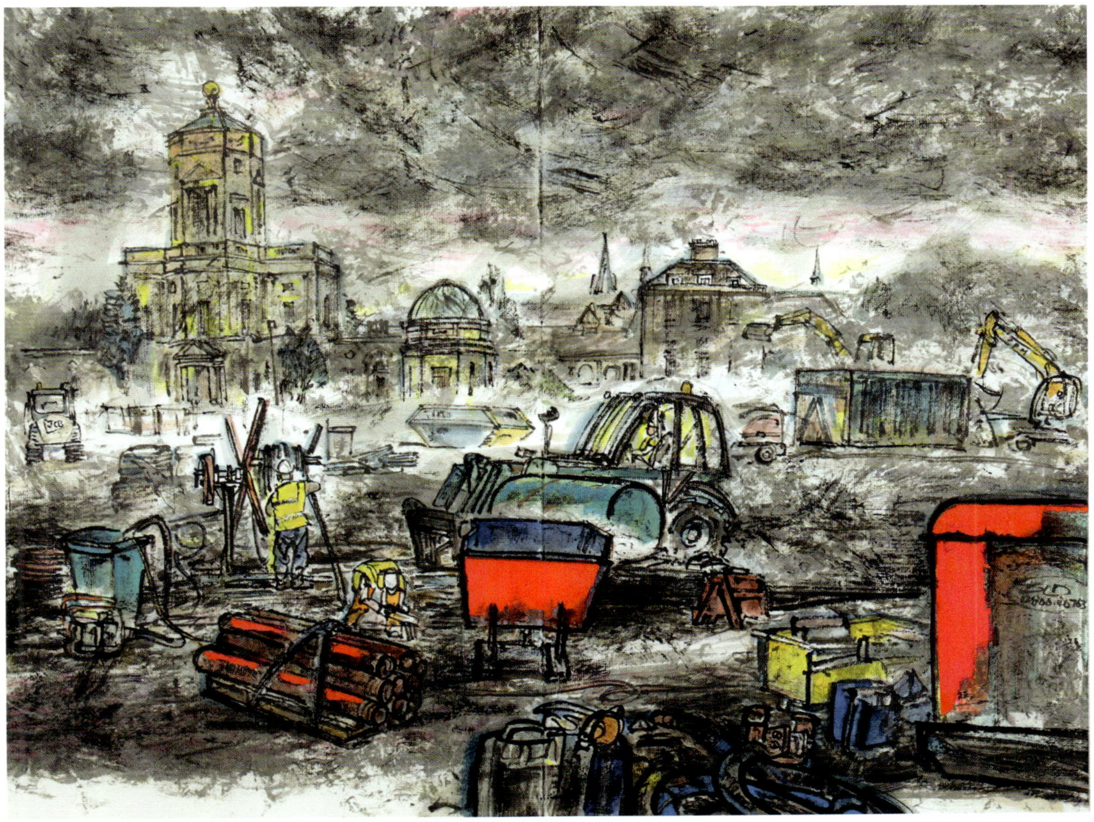

CAT.117
Overcast – Mathematical Institute. 28 July 2011. Brush, ink, watercolour and collage on album leaves. Paper size: 41.6 × 55.6 cm

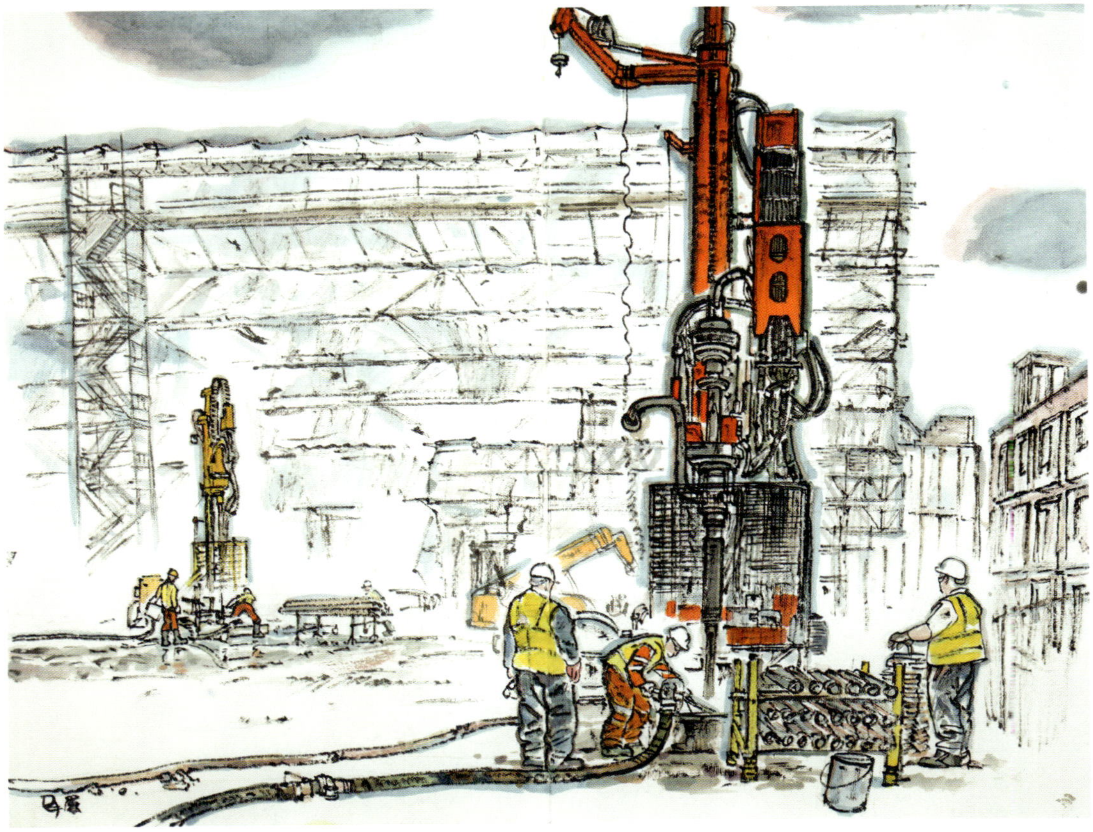

CAT.118
Drilling down – Somerville College student accommodation. 29 July 2011. Brush, ink and watercolour on album leaves. Paper size: 41.6 × 55.6 cm

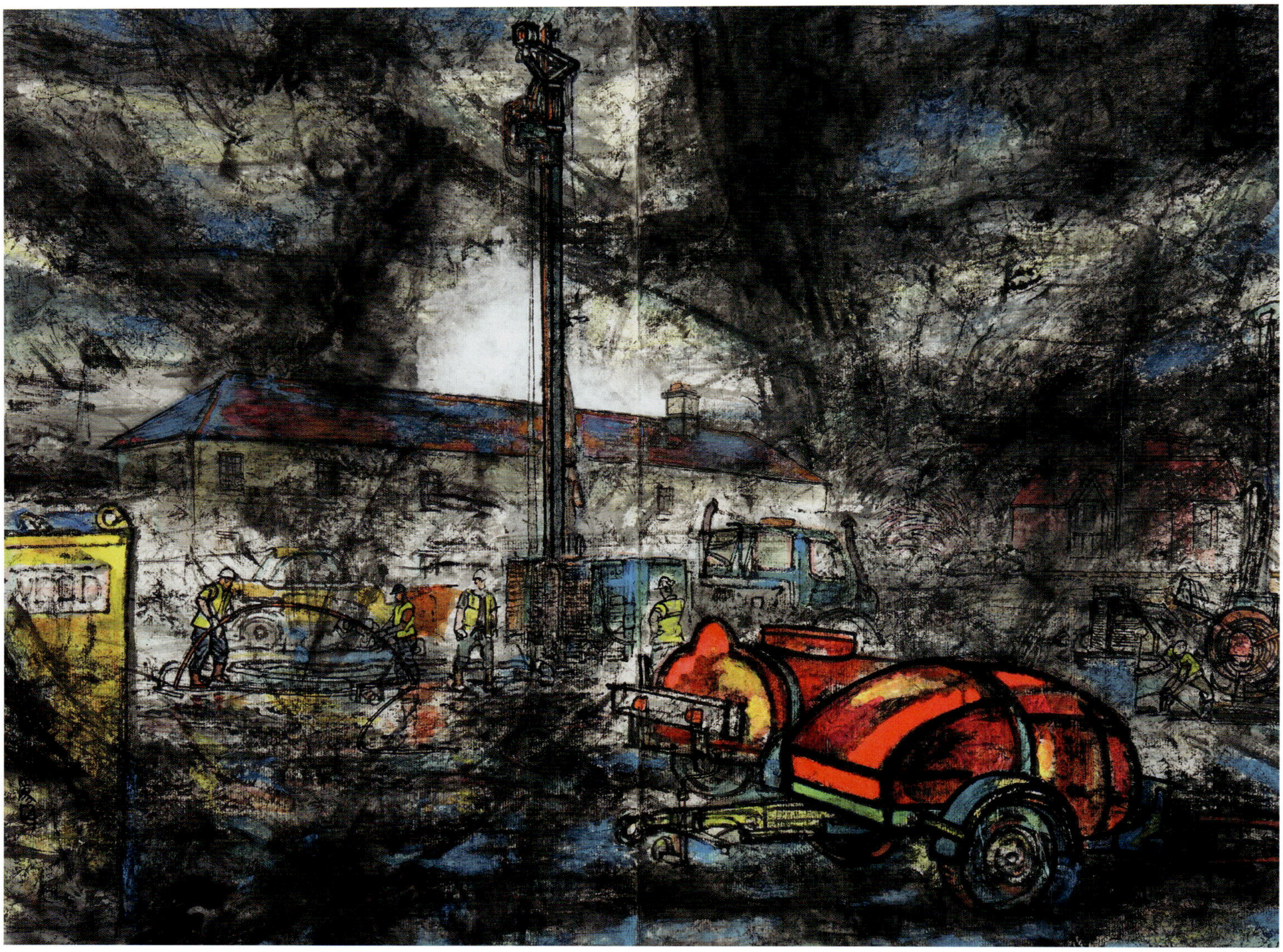

CAT.119

Machines, workmen and dancing strokes – Mathematical Institute. 1 August 2011. Brush, ink, watercolour and collage on album leaves. Paper size: 41.6 × 55.6 cm

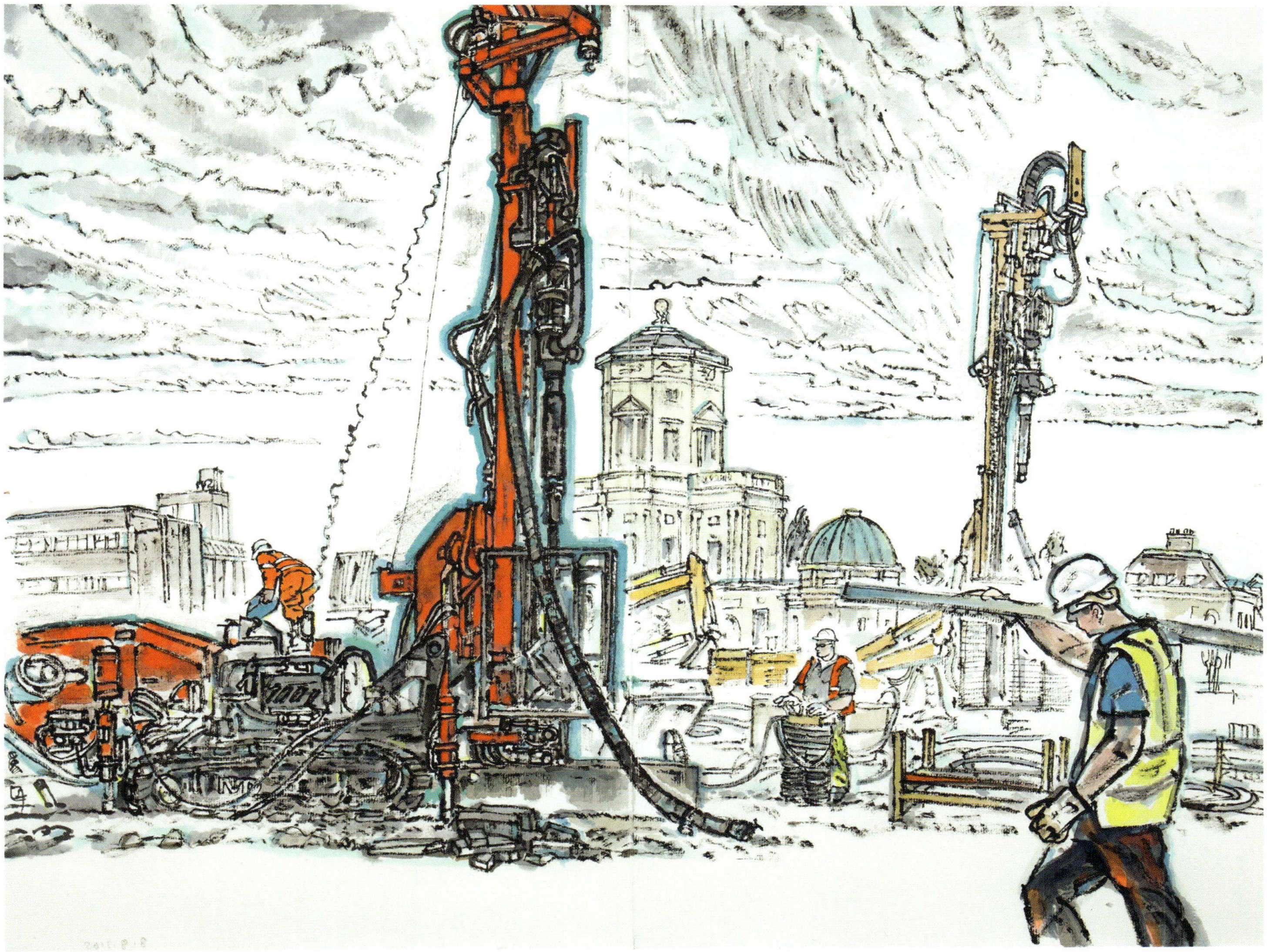

CAT.120
Operation starts – Mathematical Institute.
8 August 2011. Brush, ink and watercolour on album leaves. Paper size: 41.6 × 55.6 cm

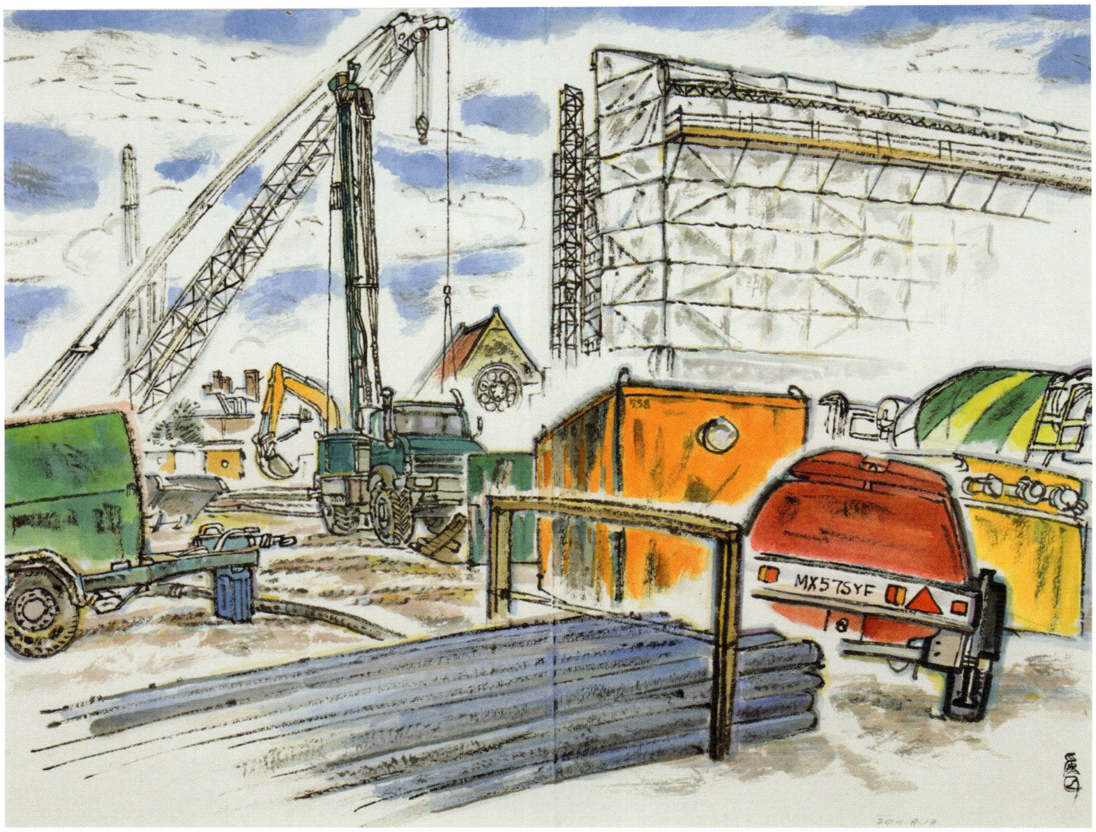

CAT.121
The eye of St Luke – Mathematical Institute.
17 August 2011. Brush, ink and watercolour on album leaves. Paper size: 41.6 × 55.6 cm

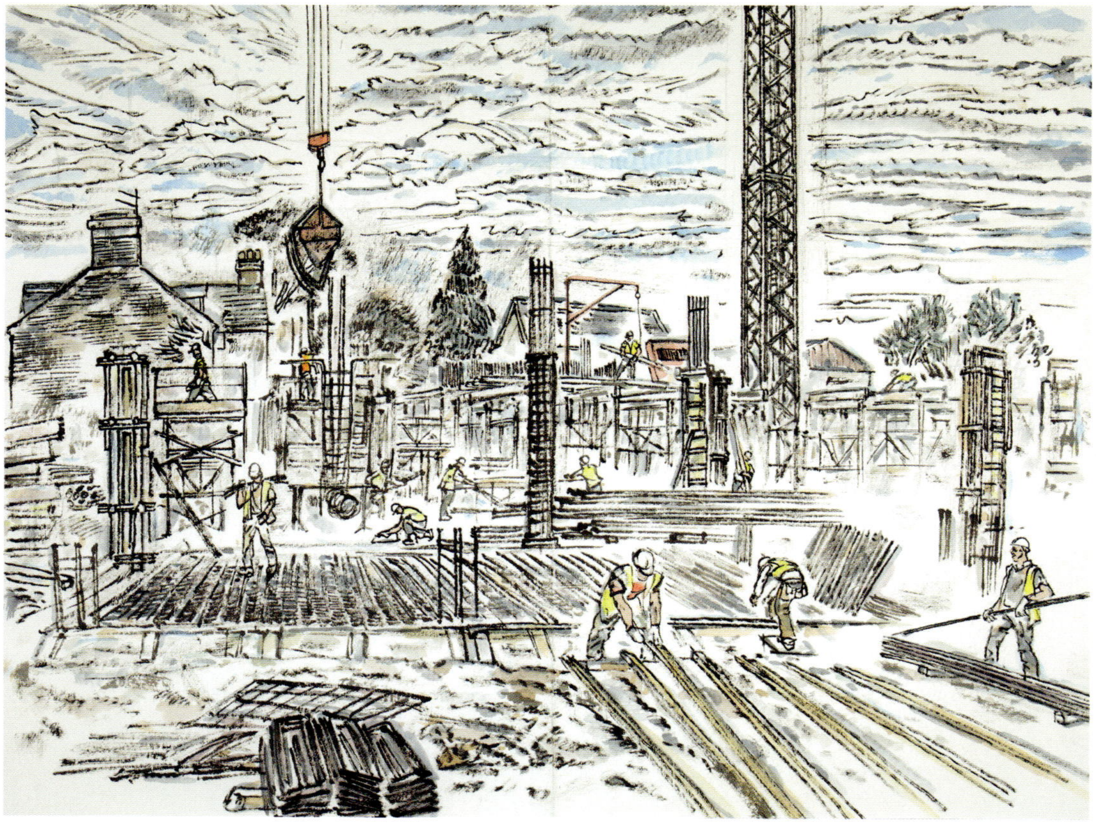

CAT.122
Grid irons – Jericho Health Centre. 20 August 2011. Brush, ink and watercolour on album leaves. Paper size: 41.6 × 55.6 cm

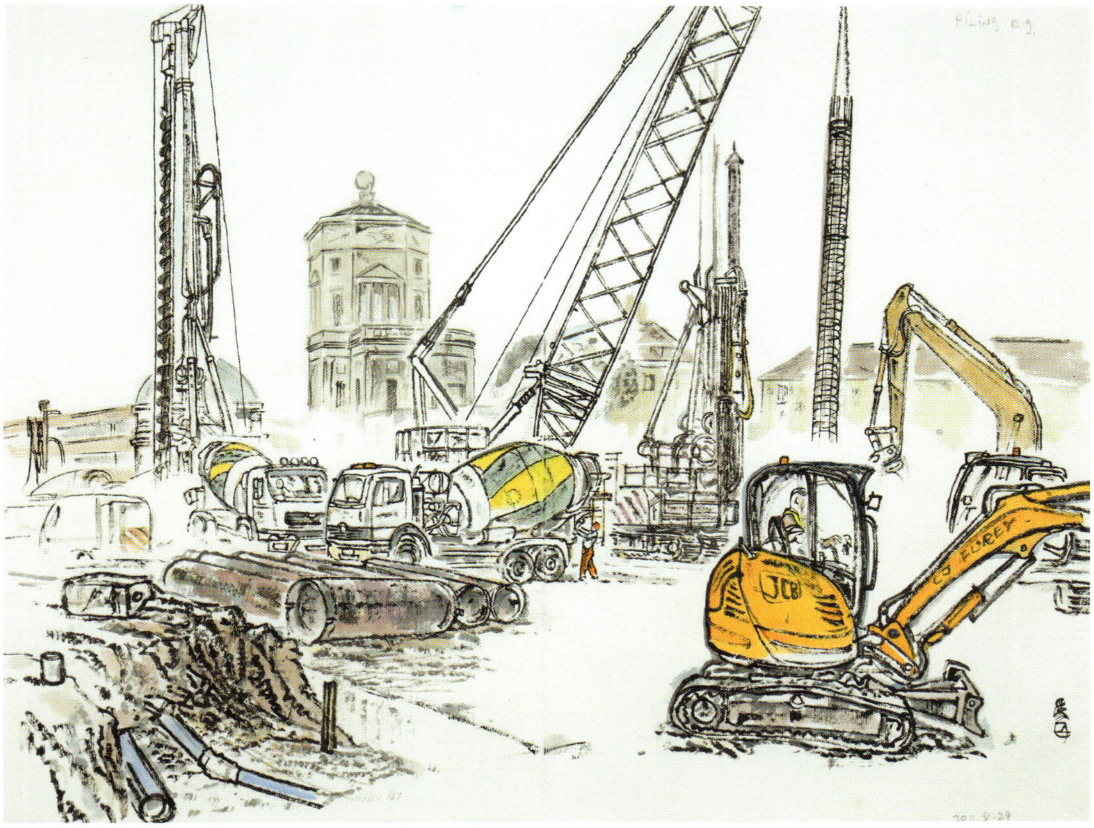

CAT.123
Piling rig in action – Mathematical Institute. 24 August 2011. Brush, ink and watercolour on album leaves. Paper size: 41.6 × 55.6 cm

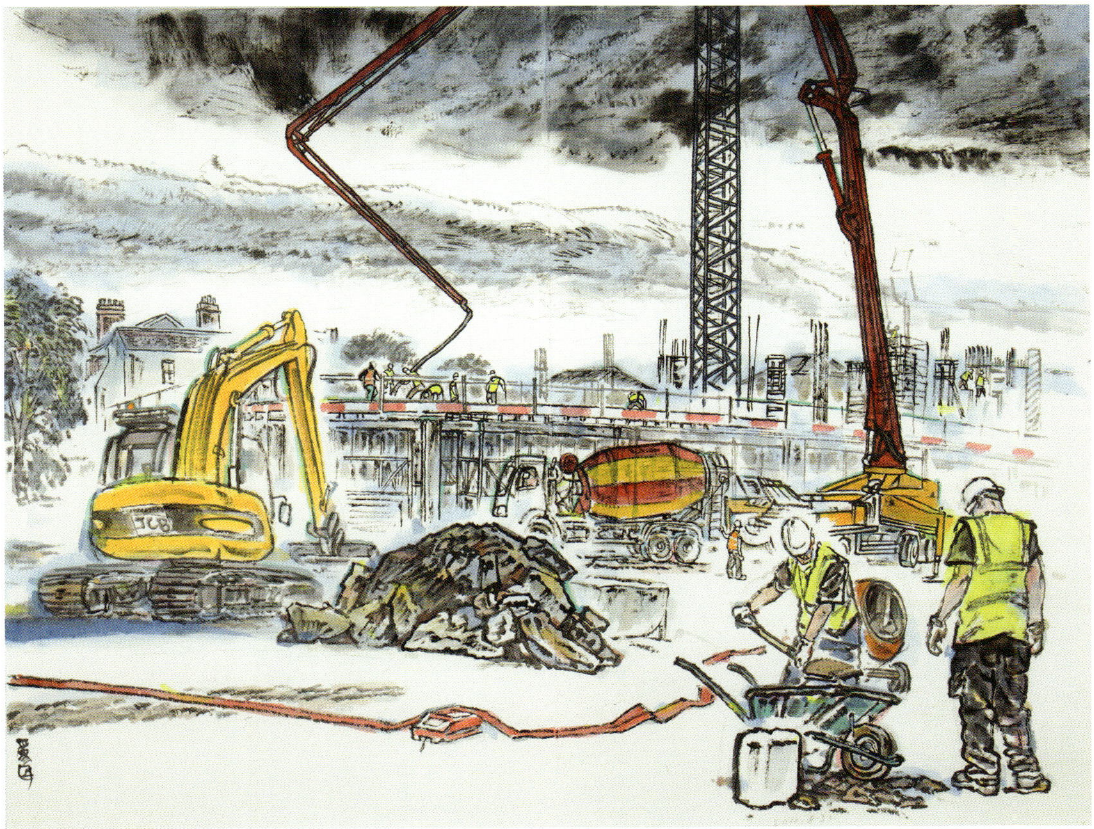

CAT.124
Lifelines – Jericho Health Centre. 31 August 2011. Brush, ink and watercolour on album leaves. Paper size: 41.6 × 55.6 cm

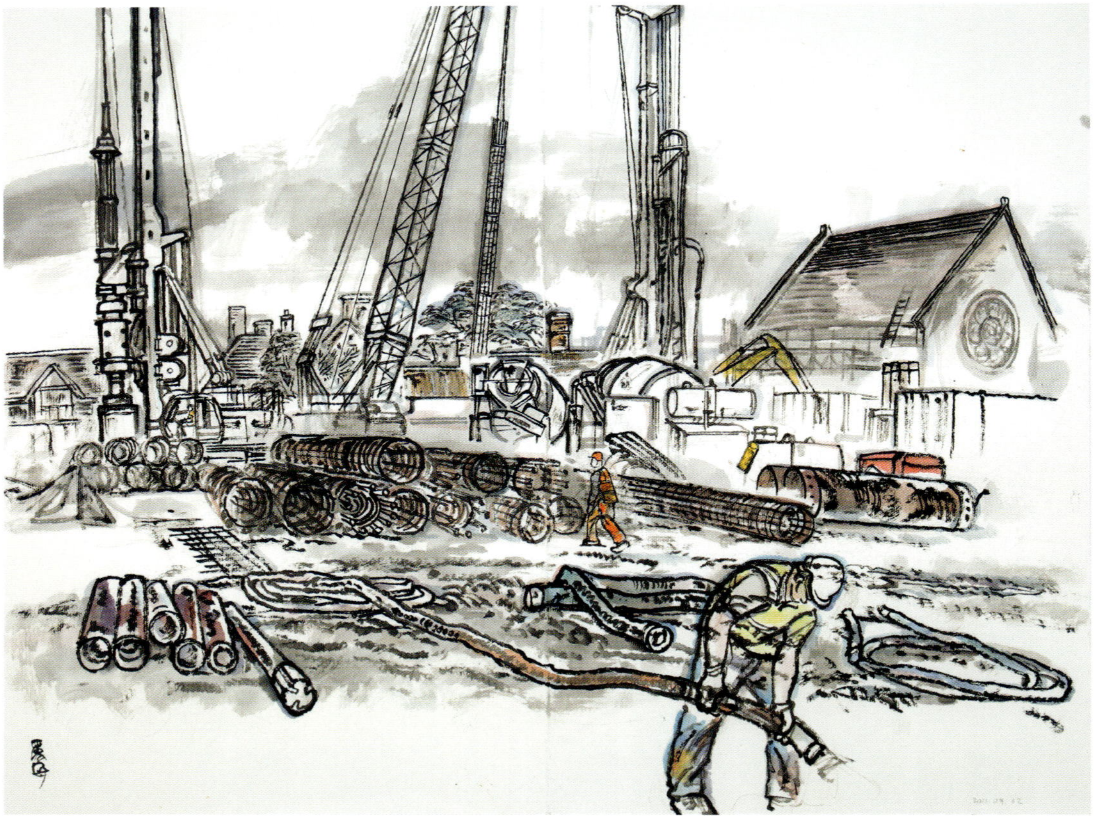

CAT.125
Builder with pipes – Mathematical Institute.
2 September 2011. Brush, ink and watercolour on album leaves. Paper size: 41.6 × 55.6 cm

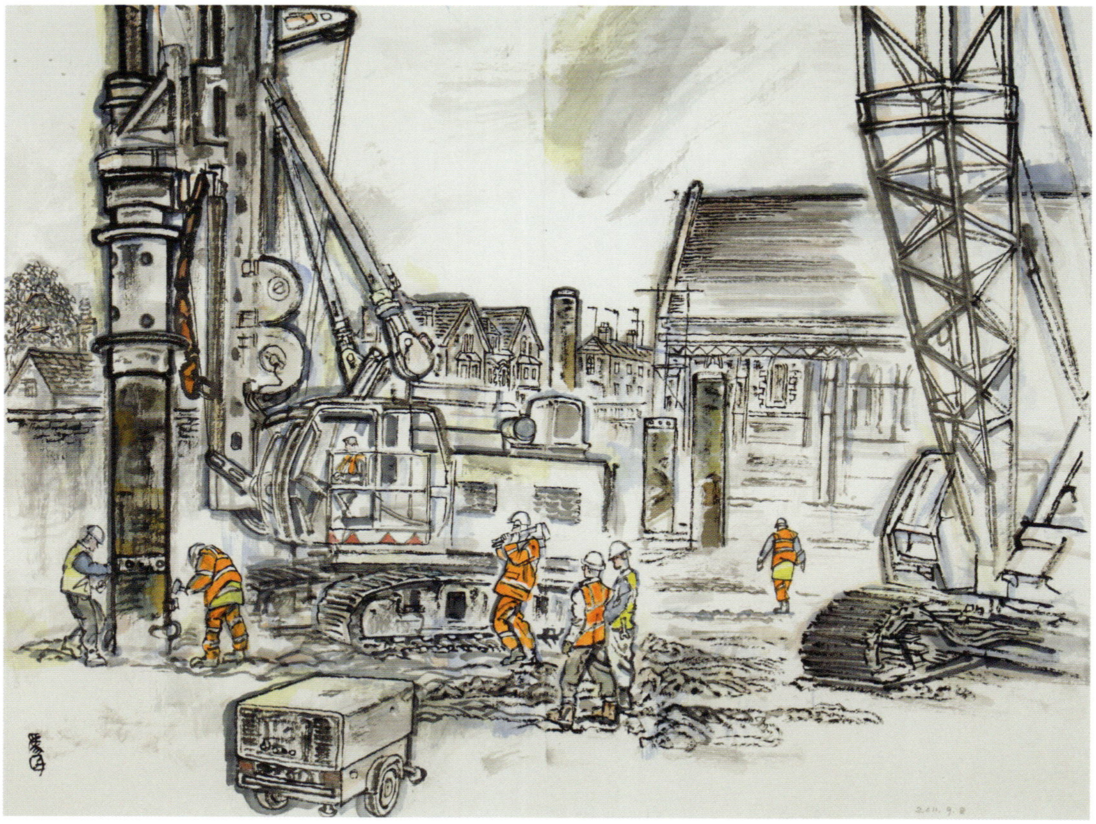

CAT.126
The first pillar – Mathematical Institute. 8 September 2011. Brush, ink and watercolour on album leaves. Paper size: 41.6 × 55.6 cm

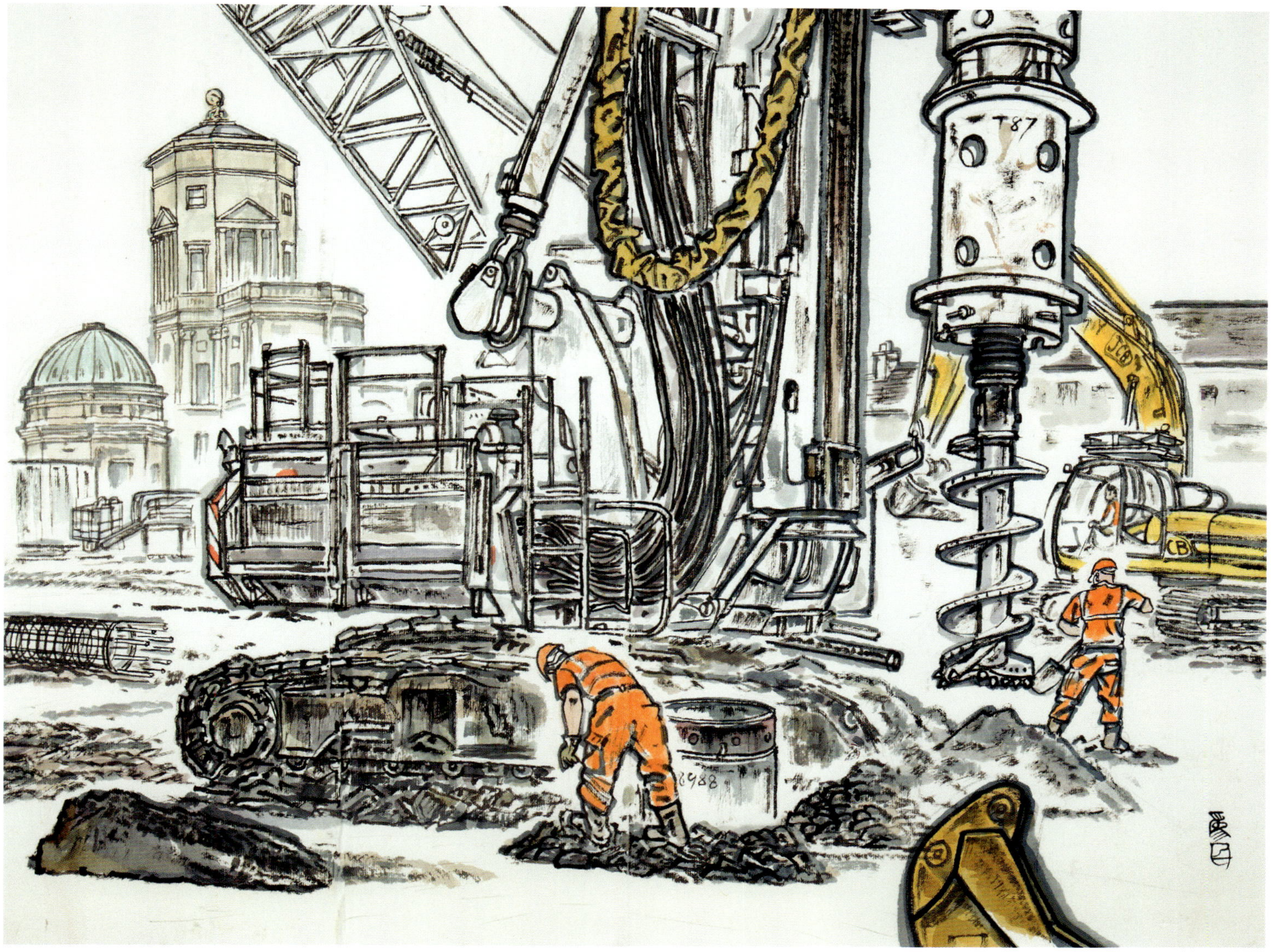

CAT.127
Breaking ground – Mathematical Institute. 15 September 2011. Brush, ink and watercolour on album leaves. Paper size: 41.6 × 55.6 cm

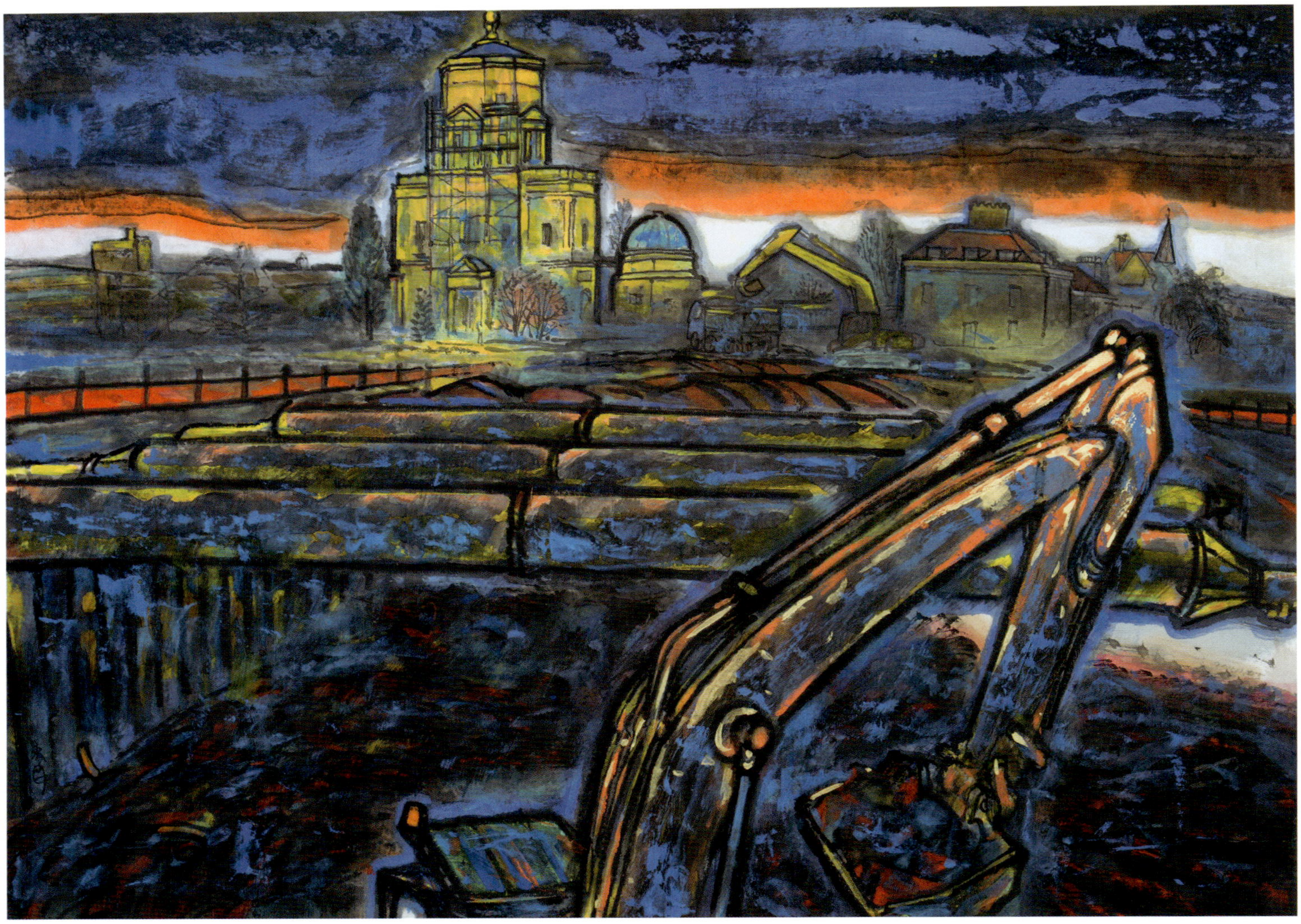

CAT.128
Dusk descends –Mathematical Institute. 5 November 2011. Brush, ink, watercolour and gouache on *xuan* paper. Paper size: 43.5 × 59.5 cm

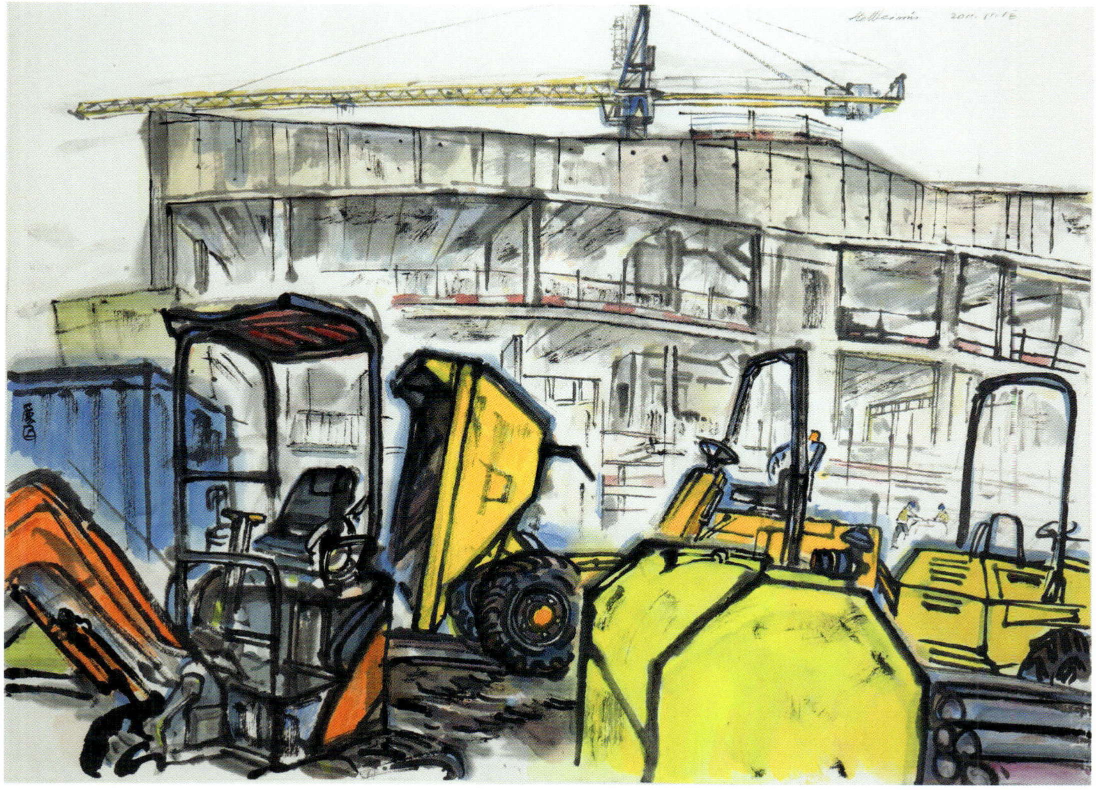

CAT.129
Builders' installation – Jericho Health Centre.
16 November 2011. Brush, ink and watercolour on *xuan* paper. Paper size: 43.5 × 59.5 cm

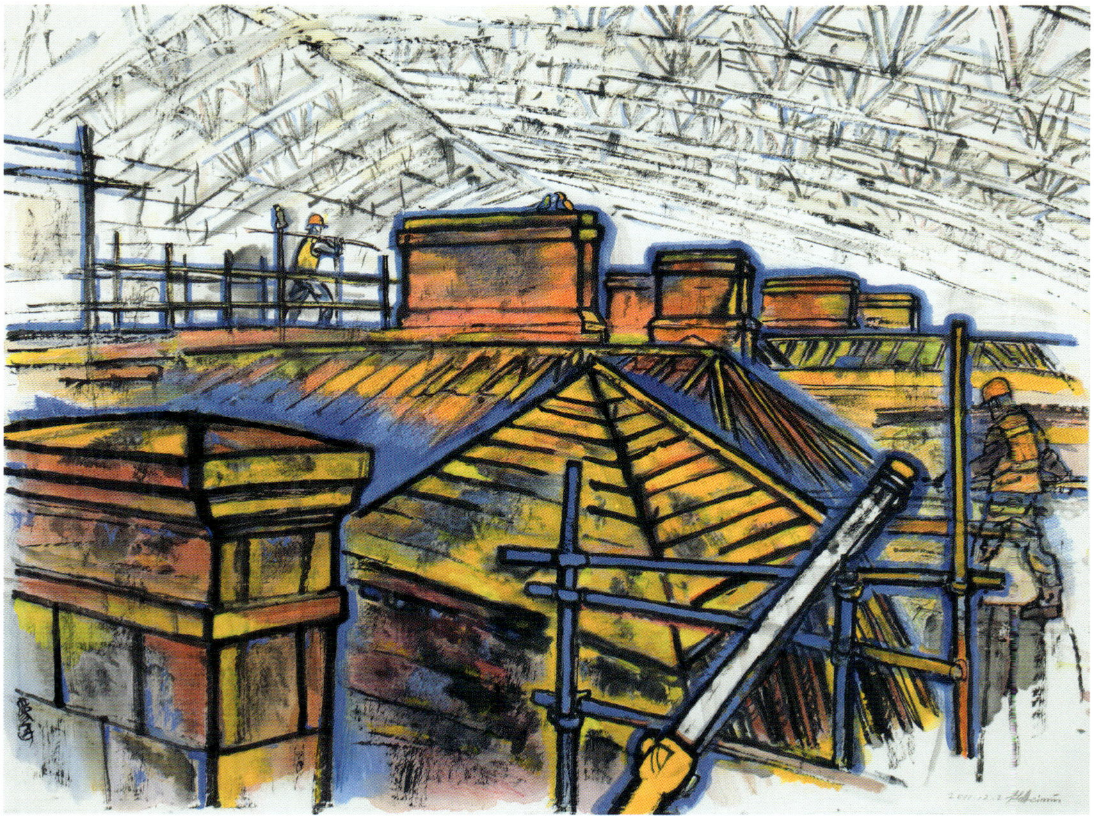

CAT.130
Roof above roof – the Radcliffe Infirmary building.
2 December 2011. Brush, ink and watercolour on *xuan* paper. Paper size: 43.5 × 59.5 cm

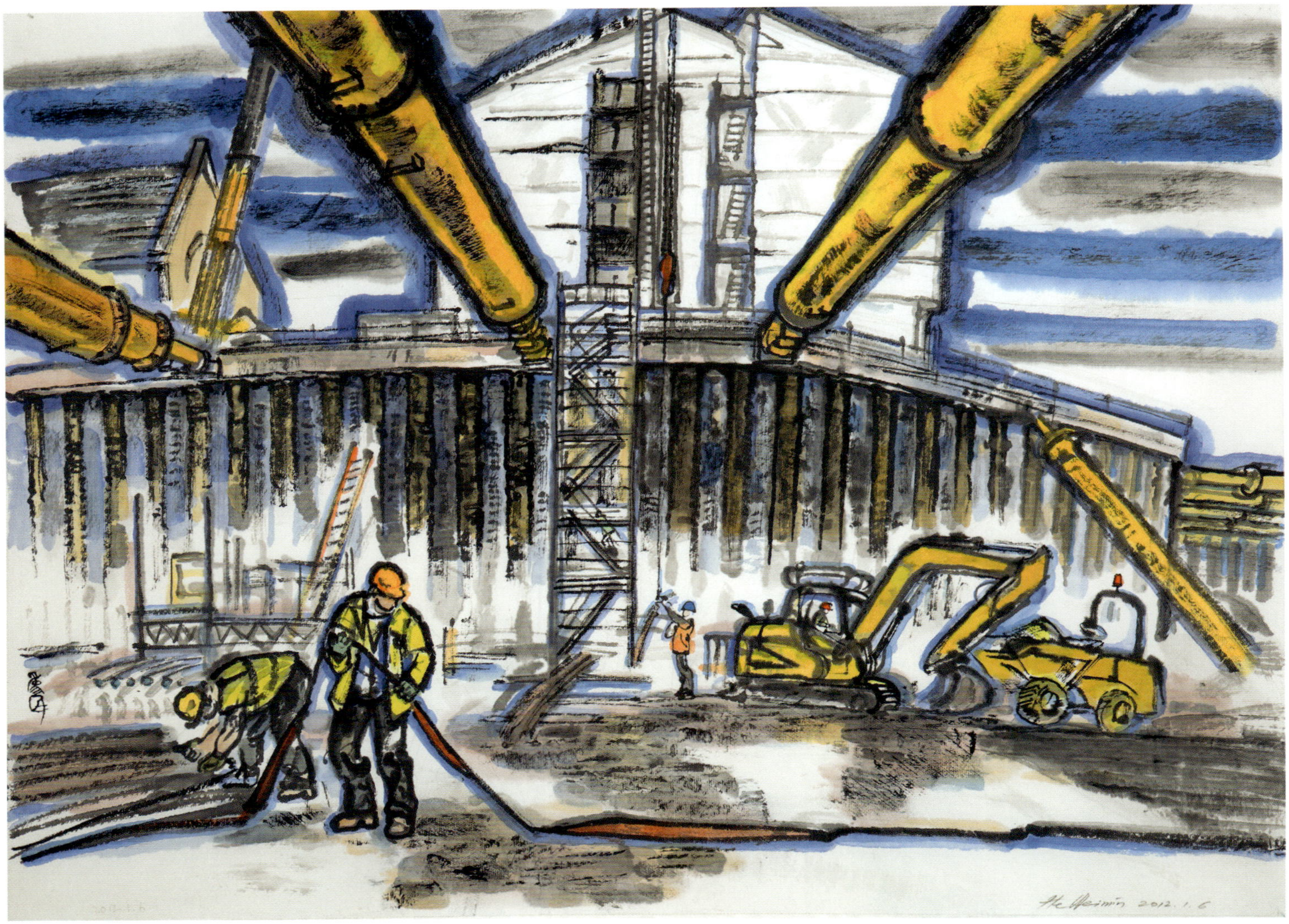

CAT.131
Building from below – Mathematical Institute. 6 January 2012. Brush, ink and watercolour on *xuan* paper. Paper size: 43.5 × 59.5 cm

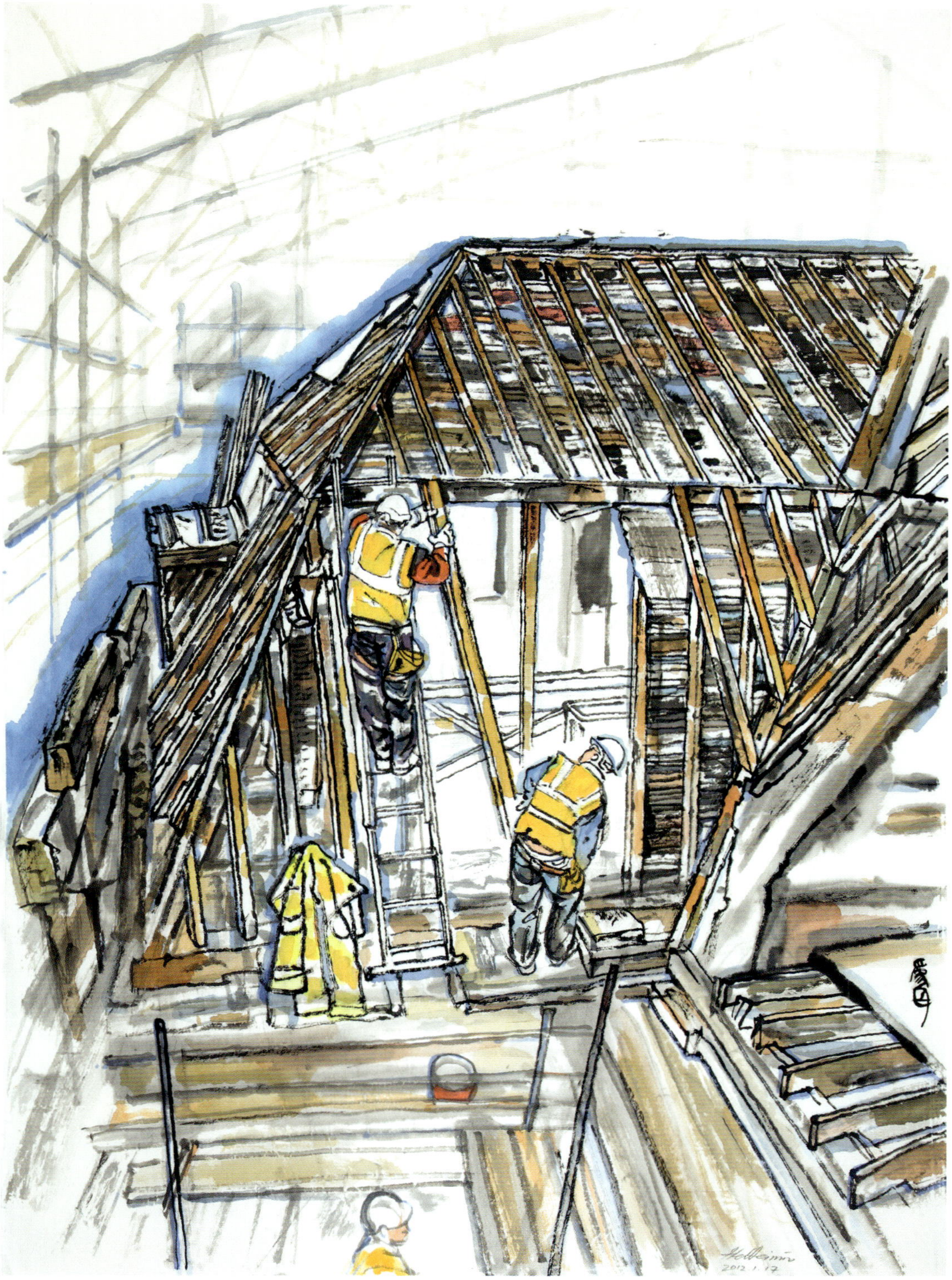

CAT.132
Old roof – Radcliffe Infirmary building. 17 January 2012. Brush, ink and watercolour on *xuan* paper. Paper size: 43.5 × 59.5 cm

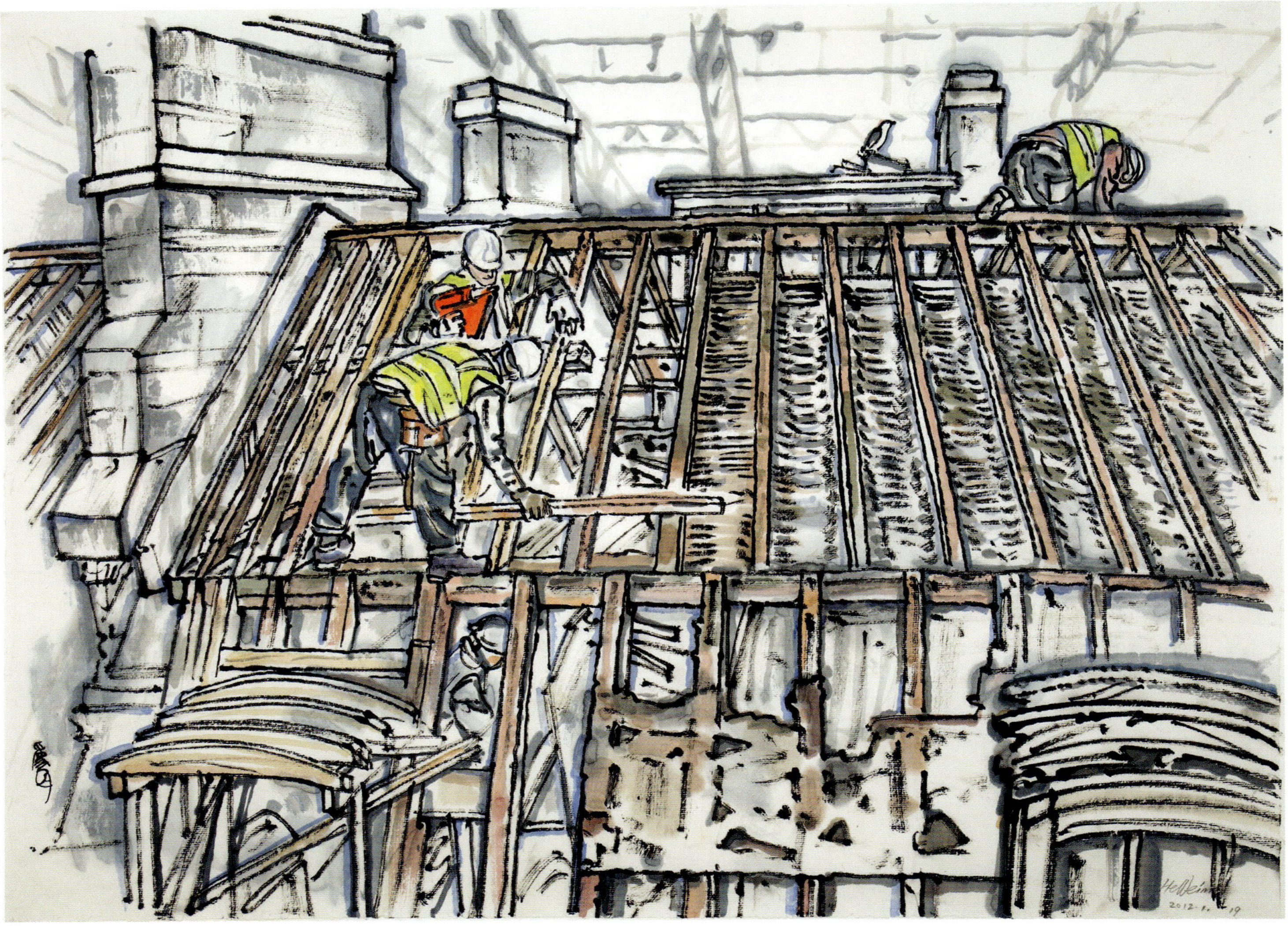

CAT.133
New timber – Radcliffe Infirmary building.
19 January 2012. Brush, ink and watercolour on *xuan* paper. Paper size: 43.5 × 59.5 cm

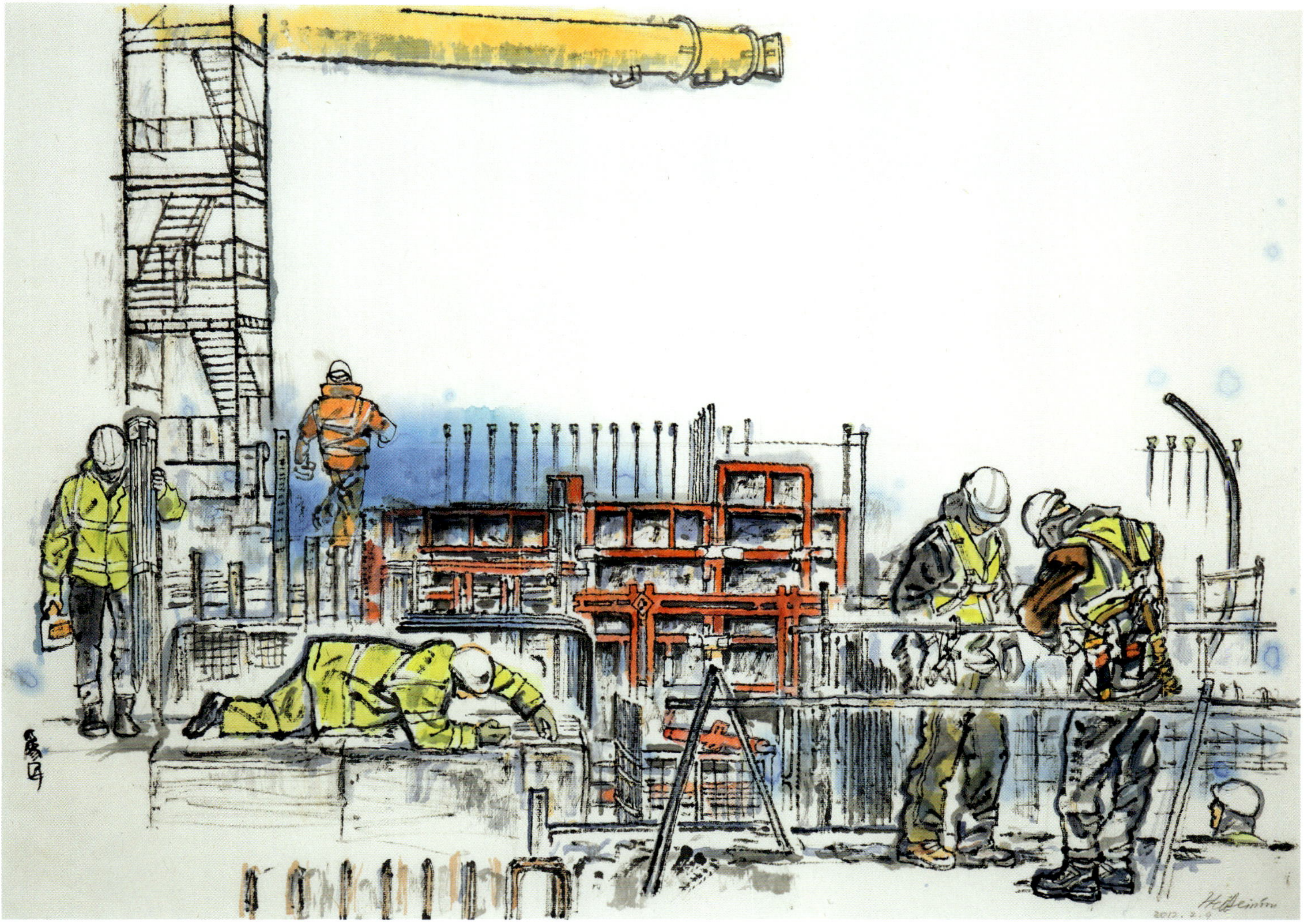

CAT.134

The yellow groundforce – Mathematical Institute.
4 February 2012. Brush, ink and watercolour on *xuan* paper. Paper size: 43.5 × 59.5 cm

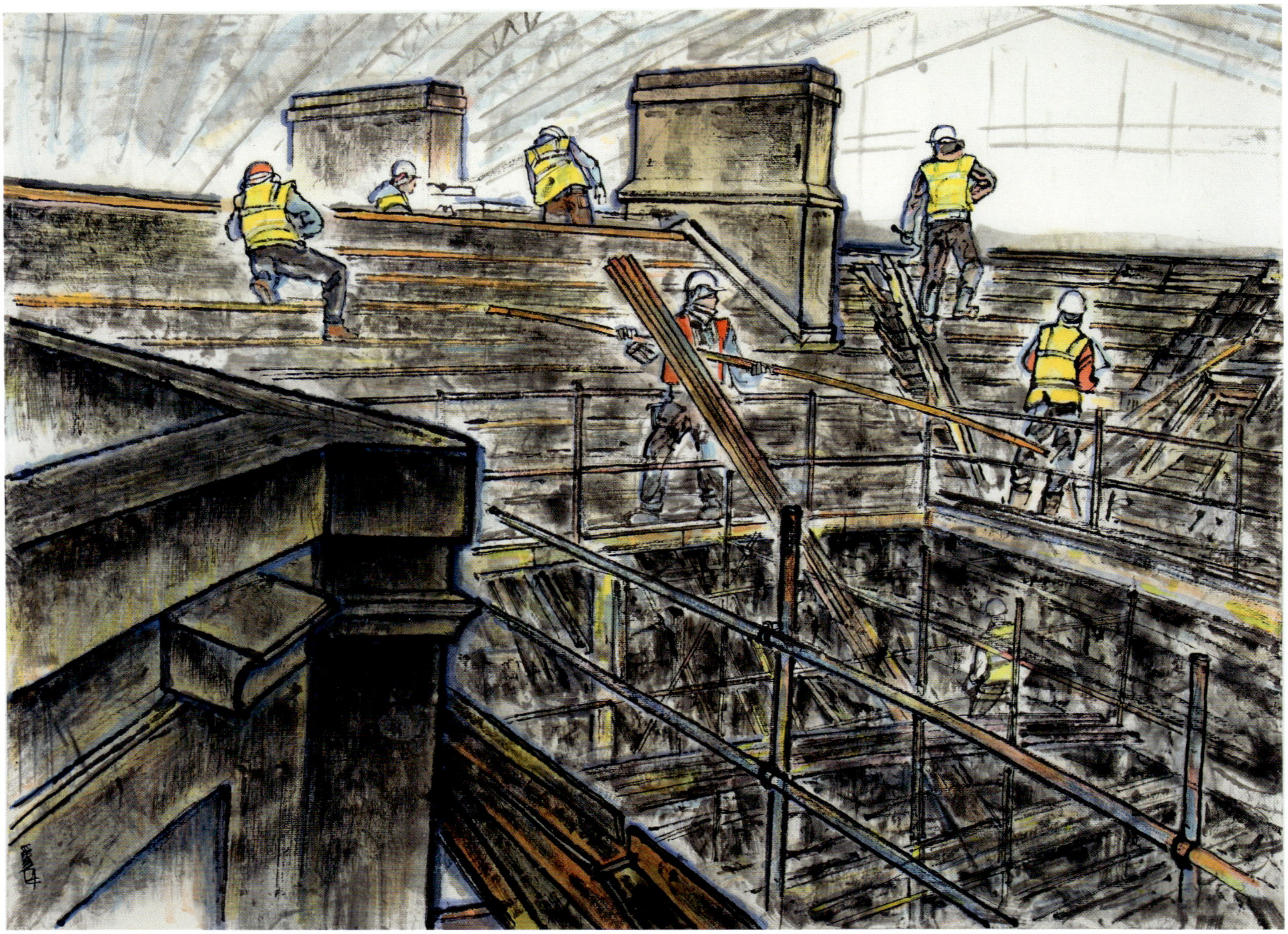

CAT.135
Caps on the roof – Radcliffe Infirmary building.
23 February 2012. Brush, ink and watercolour on
xuan paper. Paper size: 43.5 × 59.5 cm

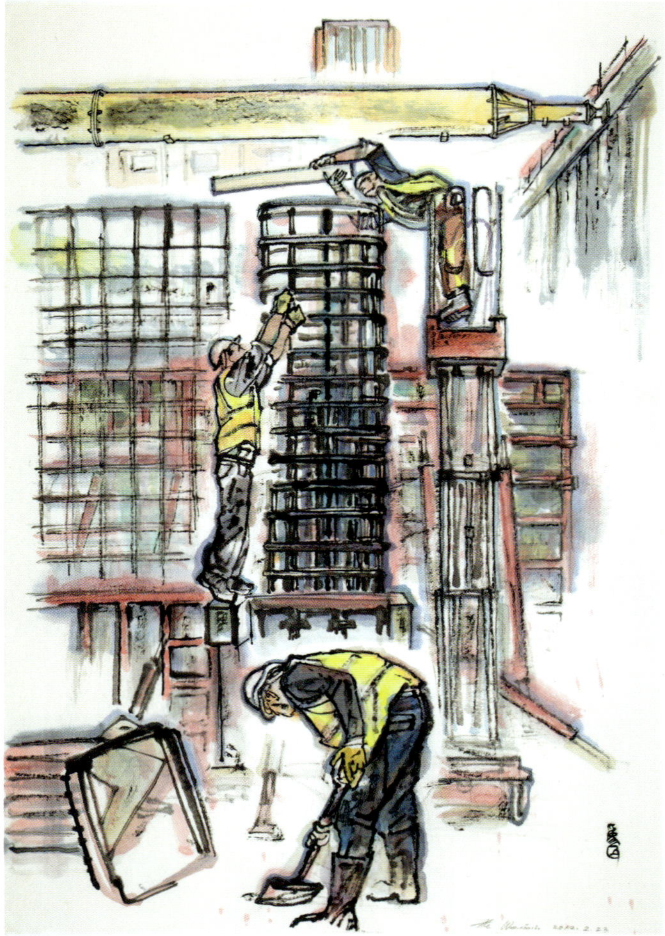

CAT.136
Foundation for the future – Mathematical Institute. 23 February 2012. Brush, ink and watercolour on *xuan* paper. Paper size: 59.5 × 43.5 cm

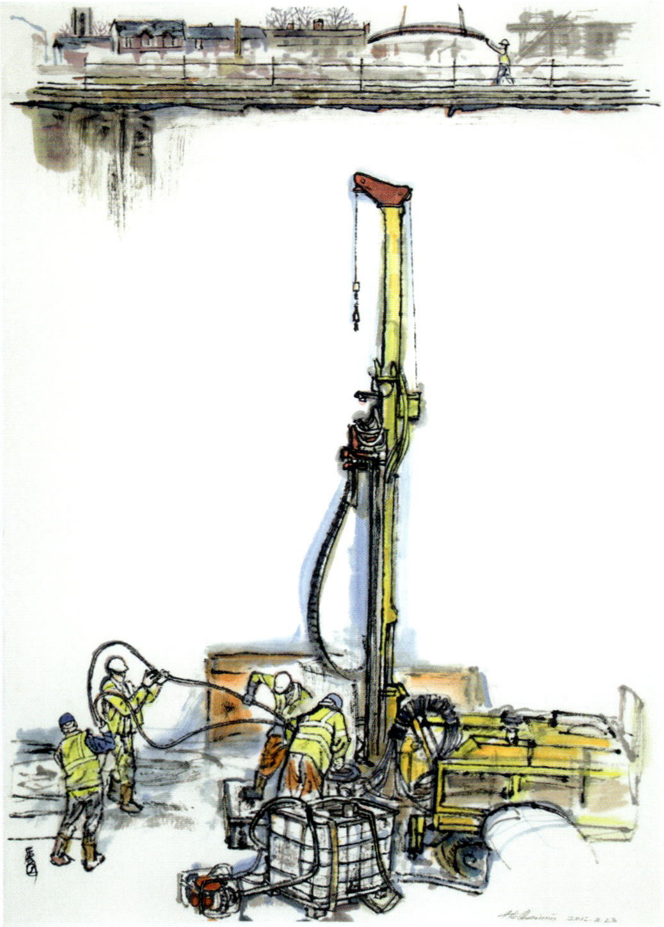

CAT.137
Under the city – Mathematical Institute. 23 February 2012. Brush, ink and watercolour on *xuan* paper. Paper size: 59.5 × 43.5 cm

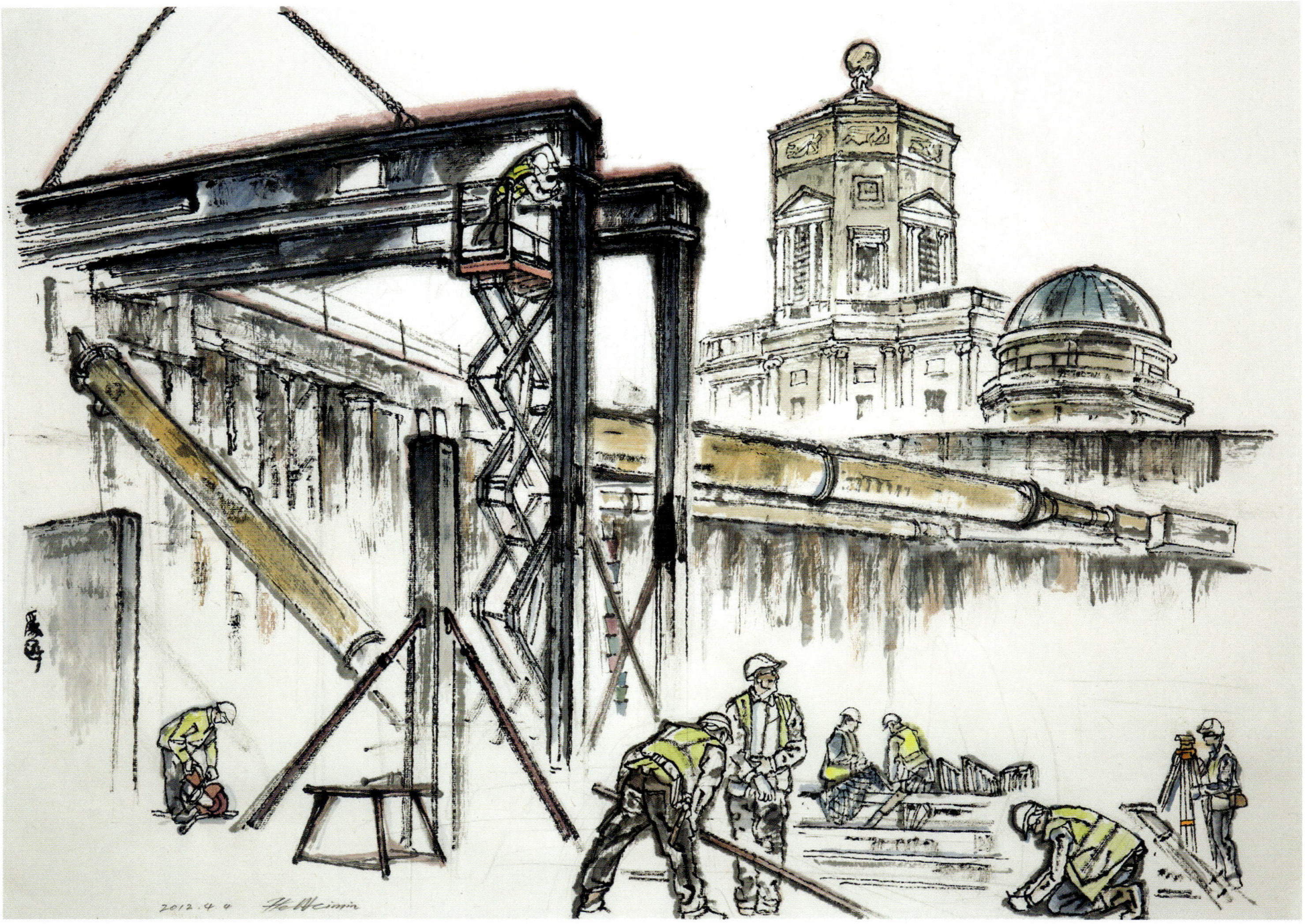

CAT.138

Arches of steel – Mathematical Institute.

4 April 2012. Brush, ink and watercolour on *xuan* paper. Paper size: 43.5 × 59.5 cm

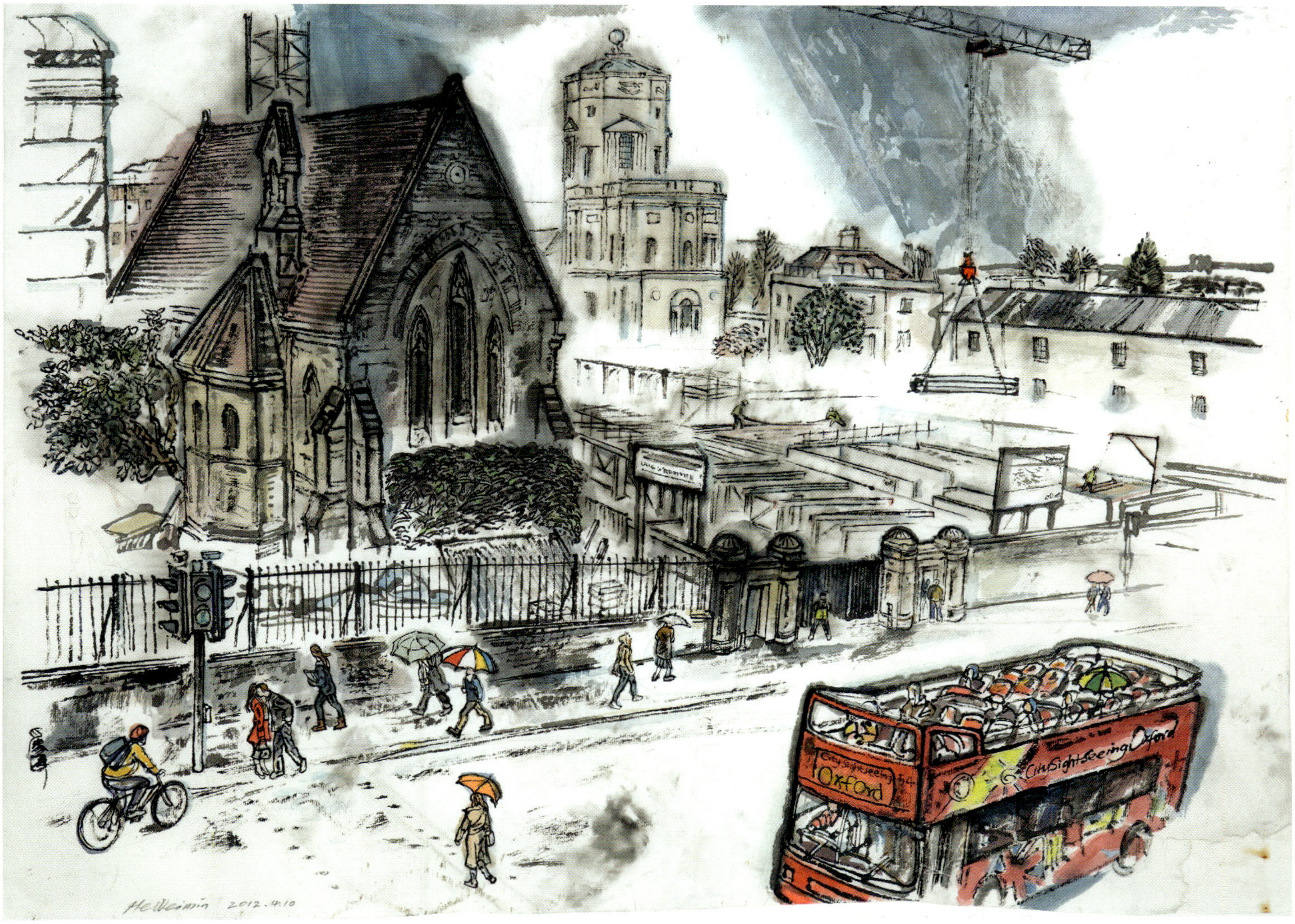

CAT.139

April shower – Mathematical Institute.
10 April 2012. Brush, ink and watercolour on *xuan* paper. Paper size: 43.5 × 59.5 cm

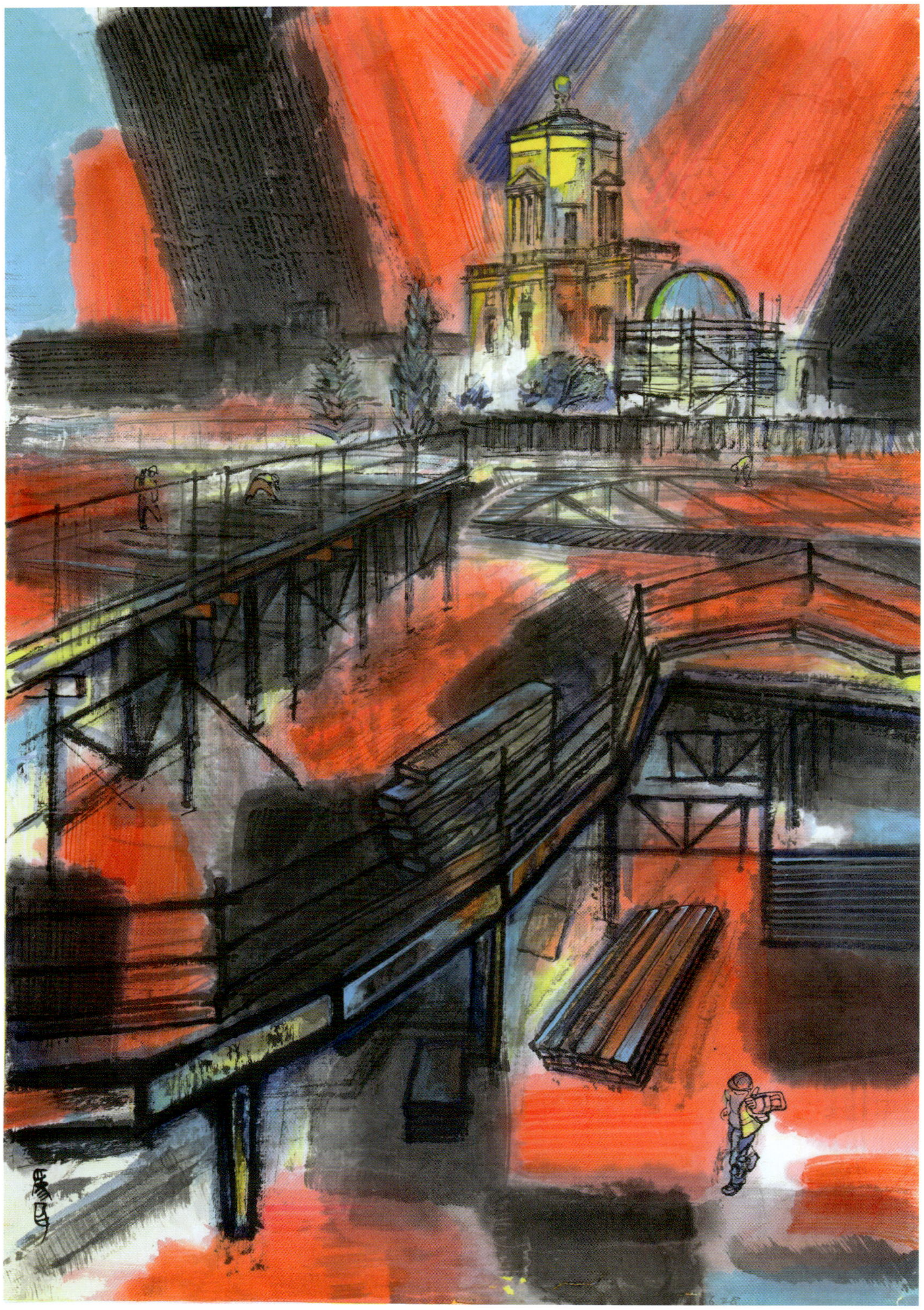

CAT.140
Beam of light over the Mathematical Institute. 28 June 2012. Brush, ink and watercolour on *xuan* paper. Paper size: 59.5 × 43.5 cm

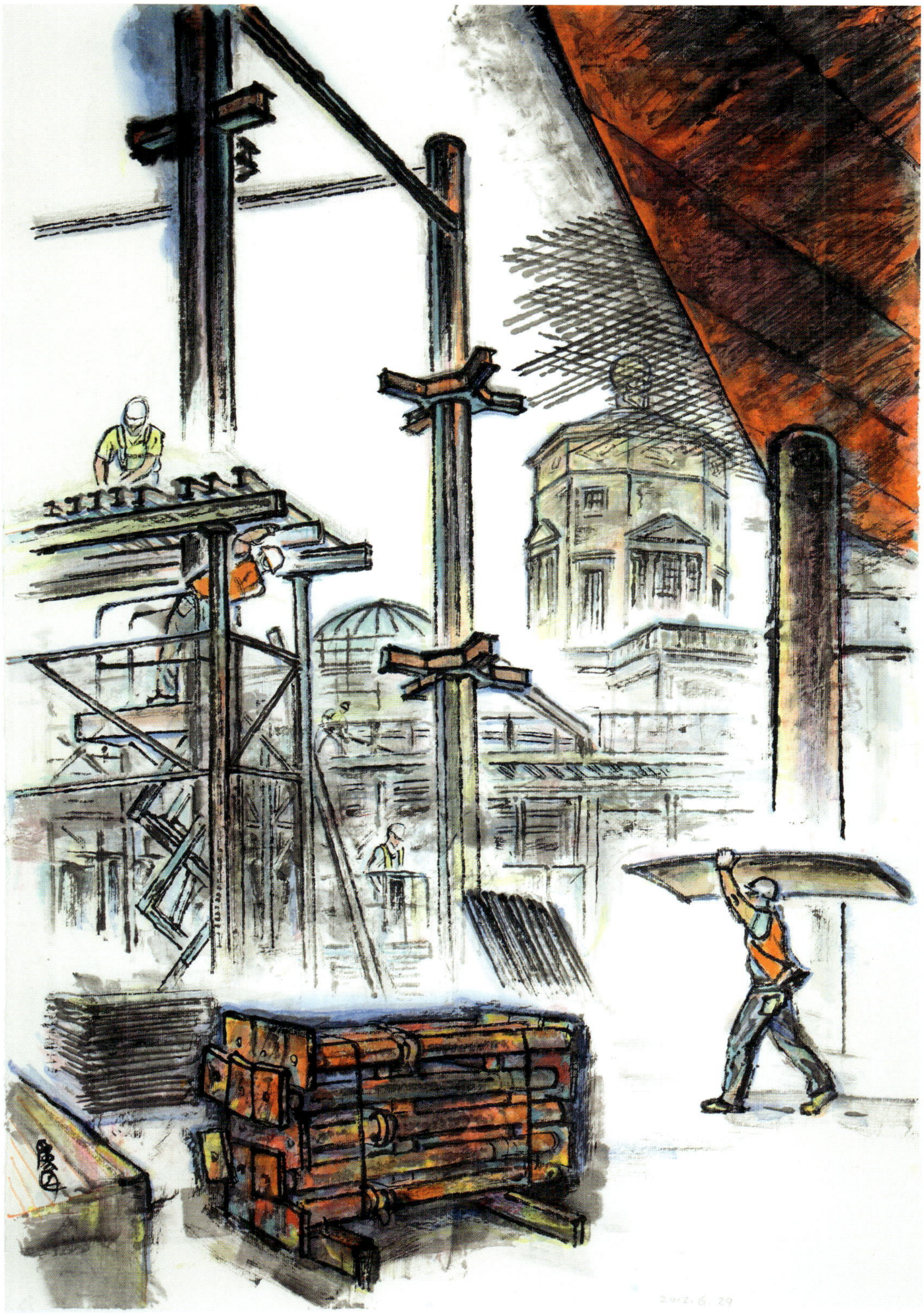

CAT.141
Bearing the load – Mathematical Institute. 29 June 2012. Brush, ink and watercolour on *xuan* paper. Paper size: 59.5 × 43.5 cm

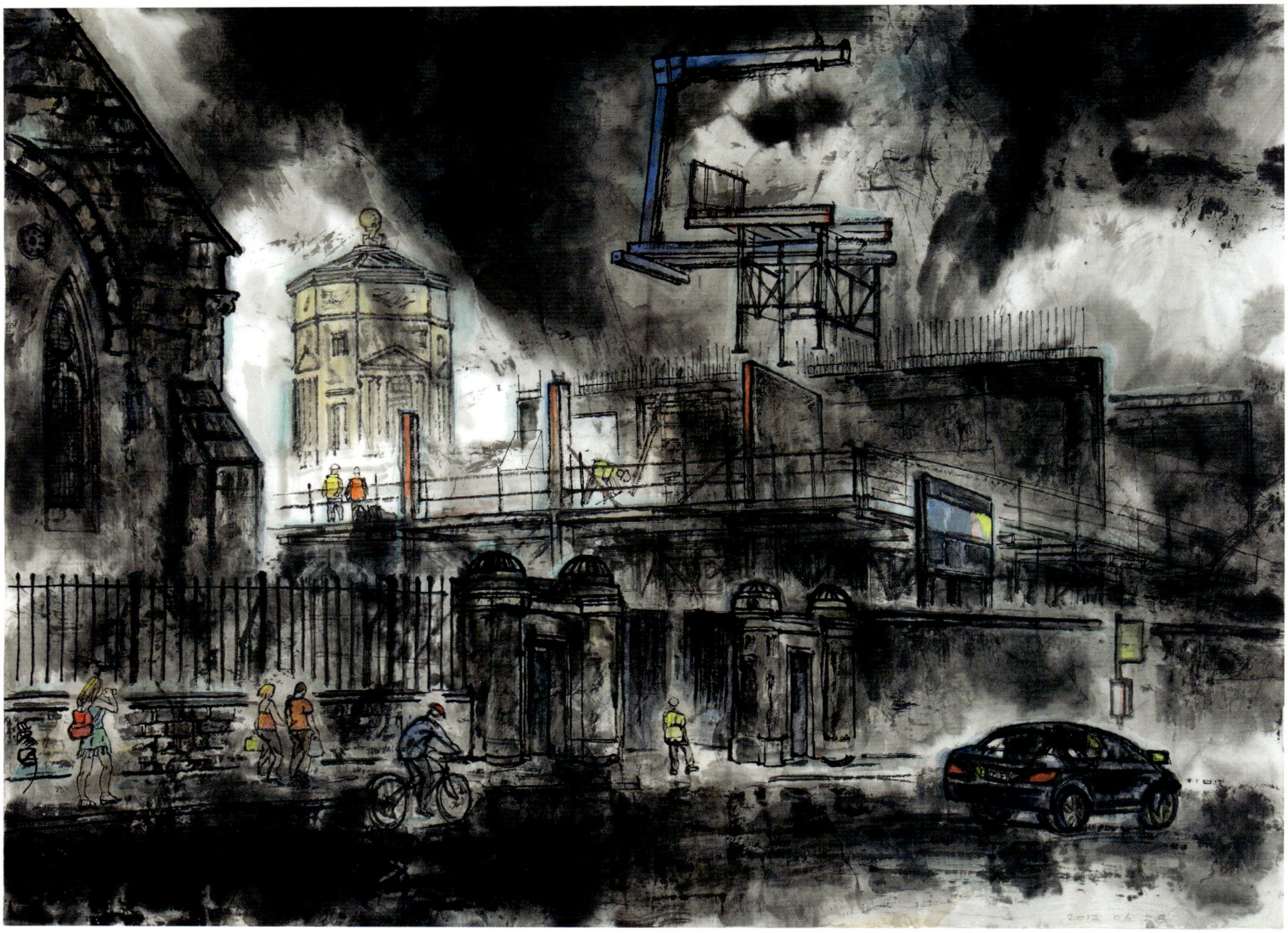

CAT.142

Sweeping darkness –Mathematical Institute.

28 June 2012. Brush, ink and watercolour on album leaves. Paper size: 43.5 × 59.5 cm

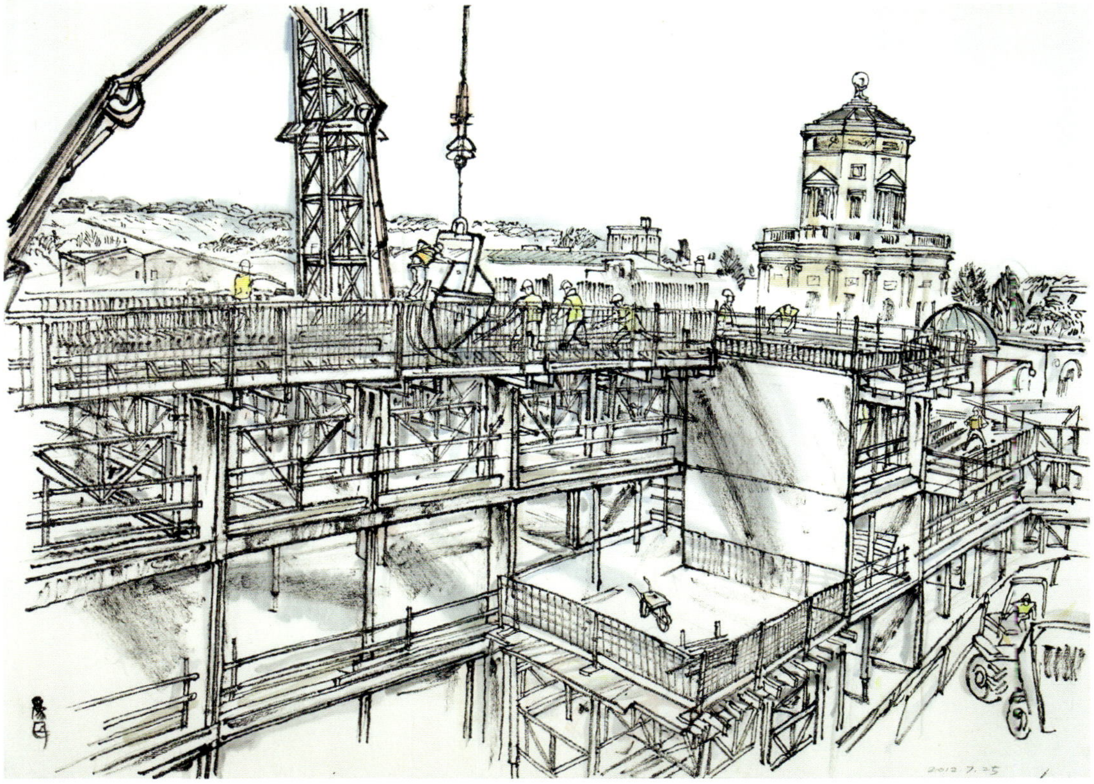

CAT.143
A clear day – Mathematical Institute. 25 July 2012. Brush, ink and watercolour on *xuan* paper. Paper size: 43.5 × 59.5 cm

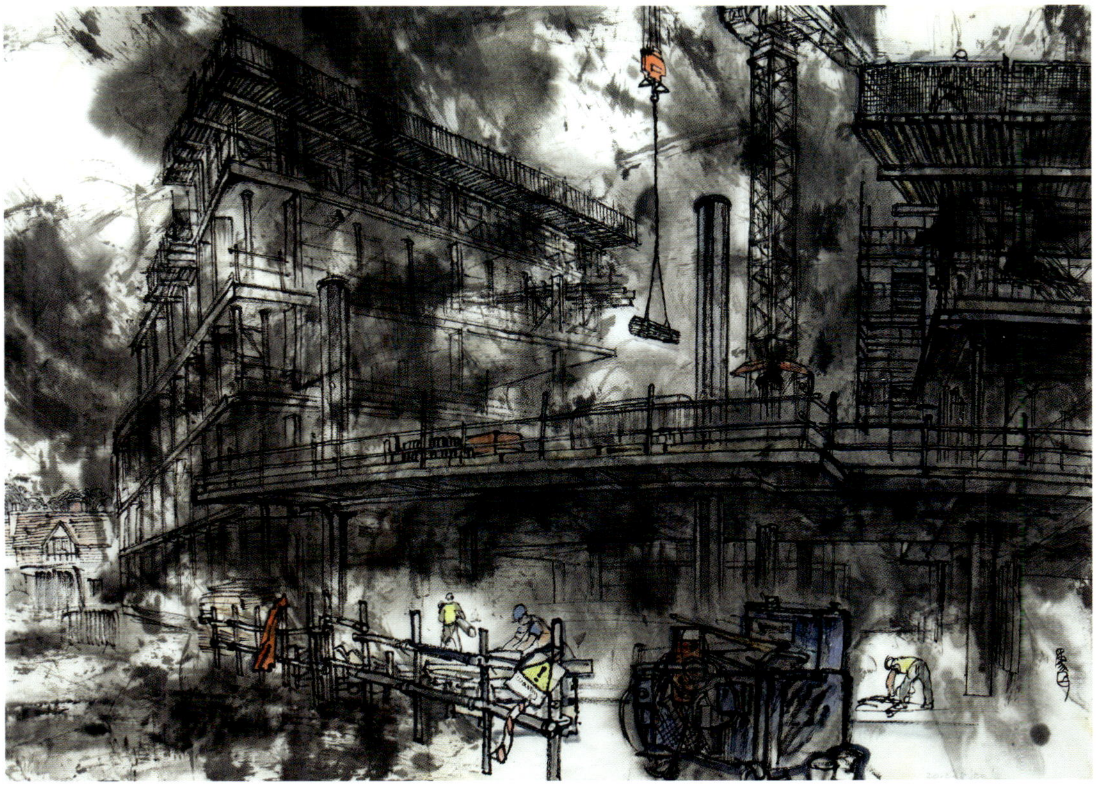

CAT.144
Silver lining – Mathematical Institute. 20 August 2012. Brush, ink and watercolour on *xuan* paper. Paper size: 43.5 × 59.5 cm

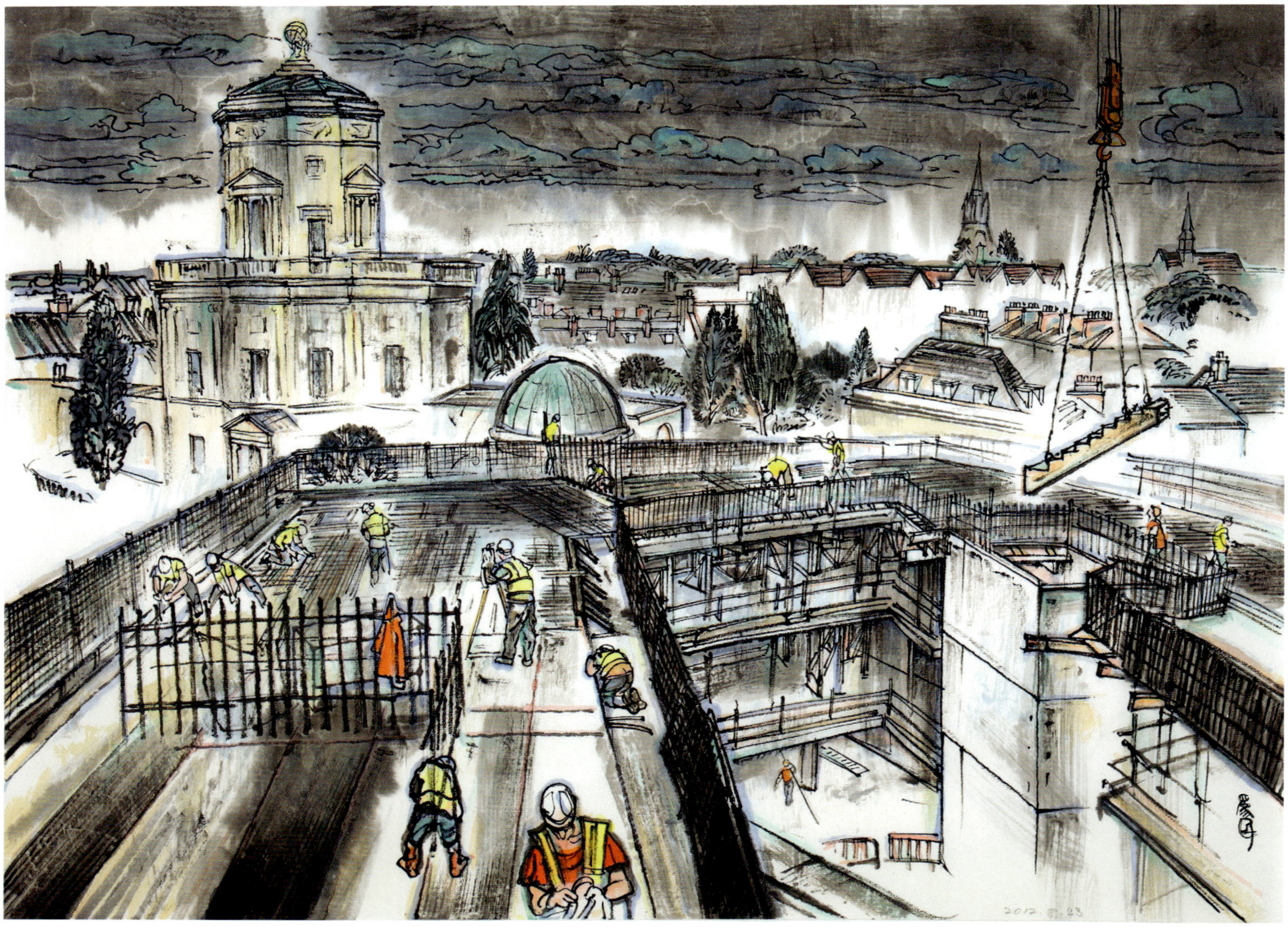

CAT.145
Building by numbers – Mathematical Institute.
23 August 2012. Brush, ink and watercolour on
xuan paper. Paper size: 43.5 × 59.5 cm

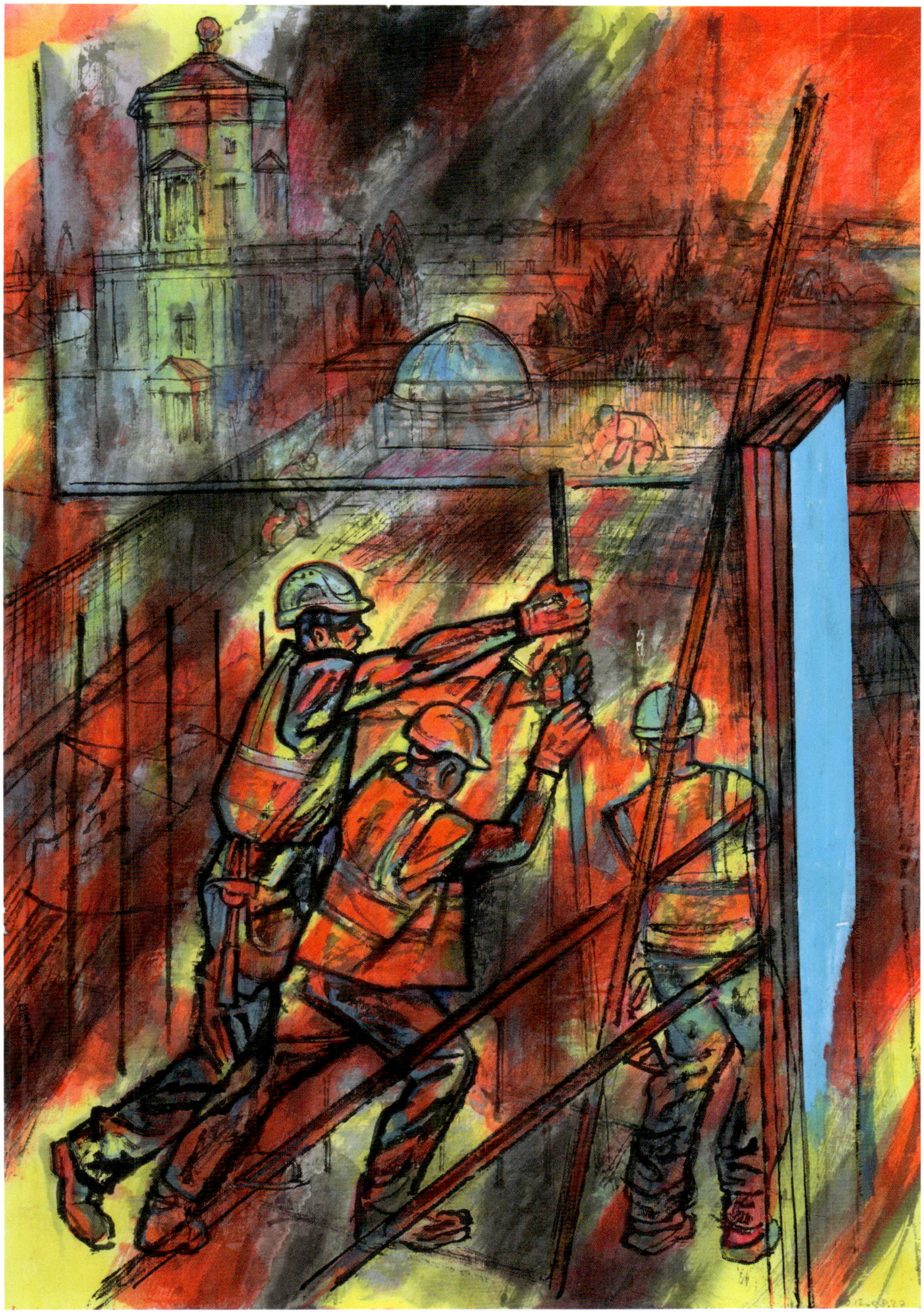

CAT.146
The ties that bind – Mathematical Institute.
27 August 2012. Brush, ink, watercolour and collage on *xuan* paper. Paper size: 59.5 × 43.5 cm

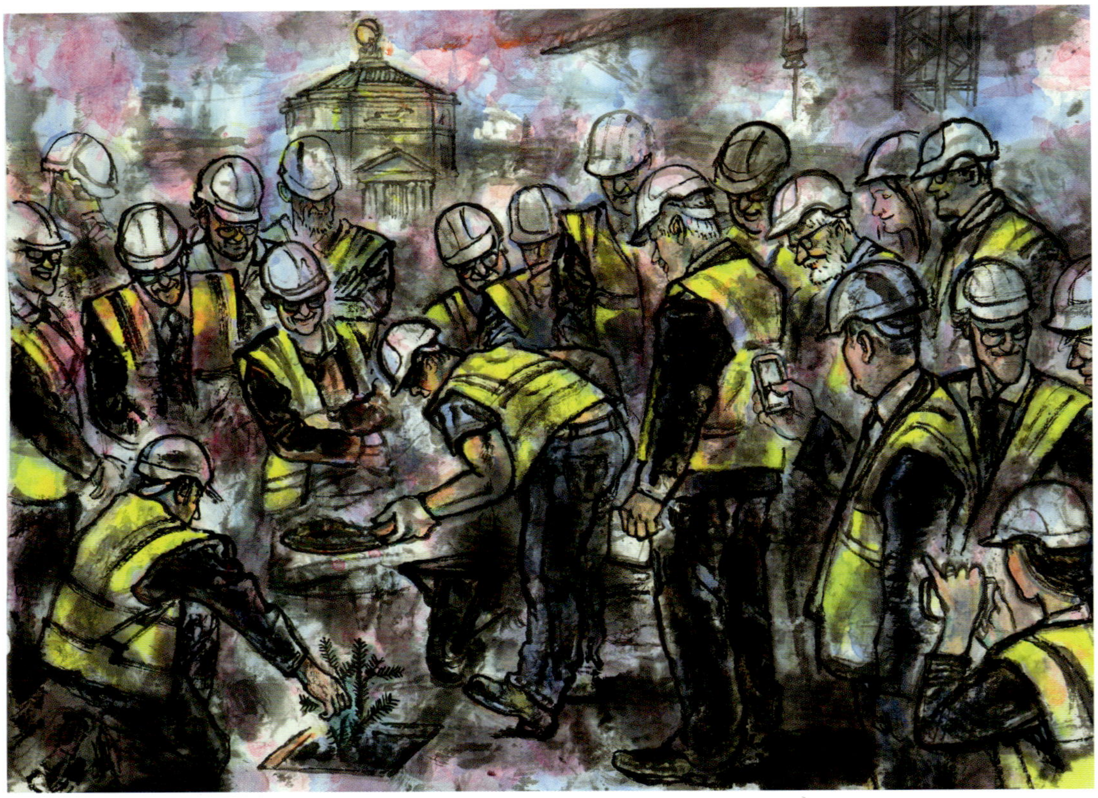

CAT.147
Topping out ceremony of the Mathematical Institute building. 31 August 2012. Brush, ink and watercolour on *xuan* paper. Paper size: 43.5 × 59.5 cm

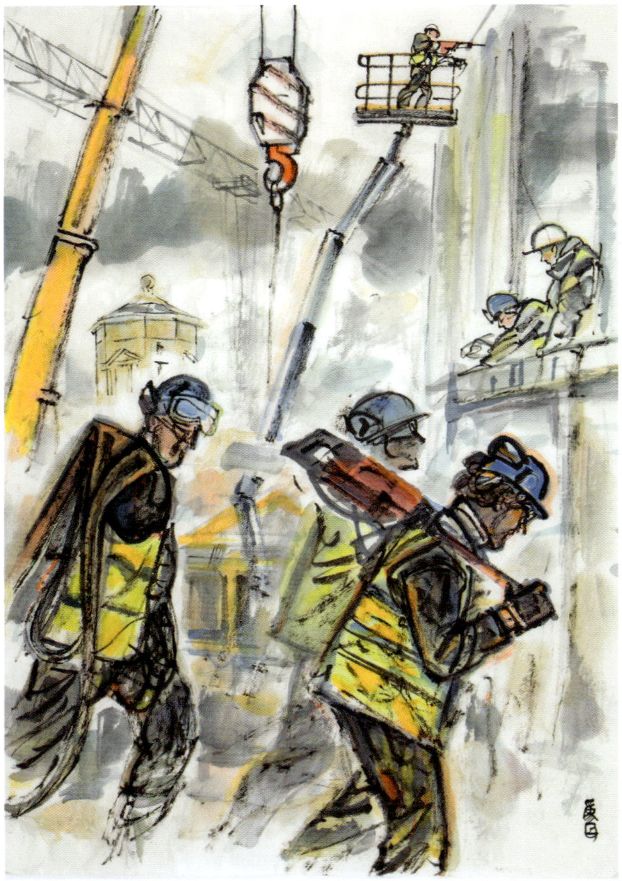

CAT.148
Daybreak – Mathematical Institute. 3 November 2012. Brush, ink and watercolour on *xuan* paper. Paper size: 59.5 × 43.5 cm

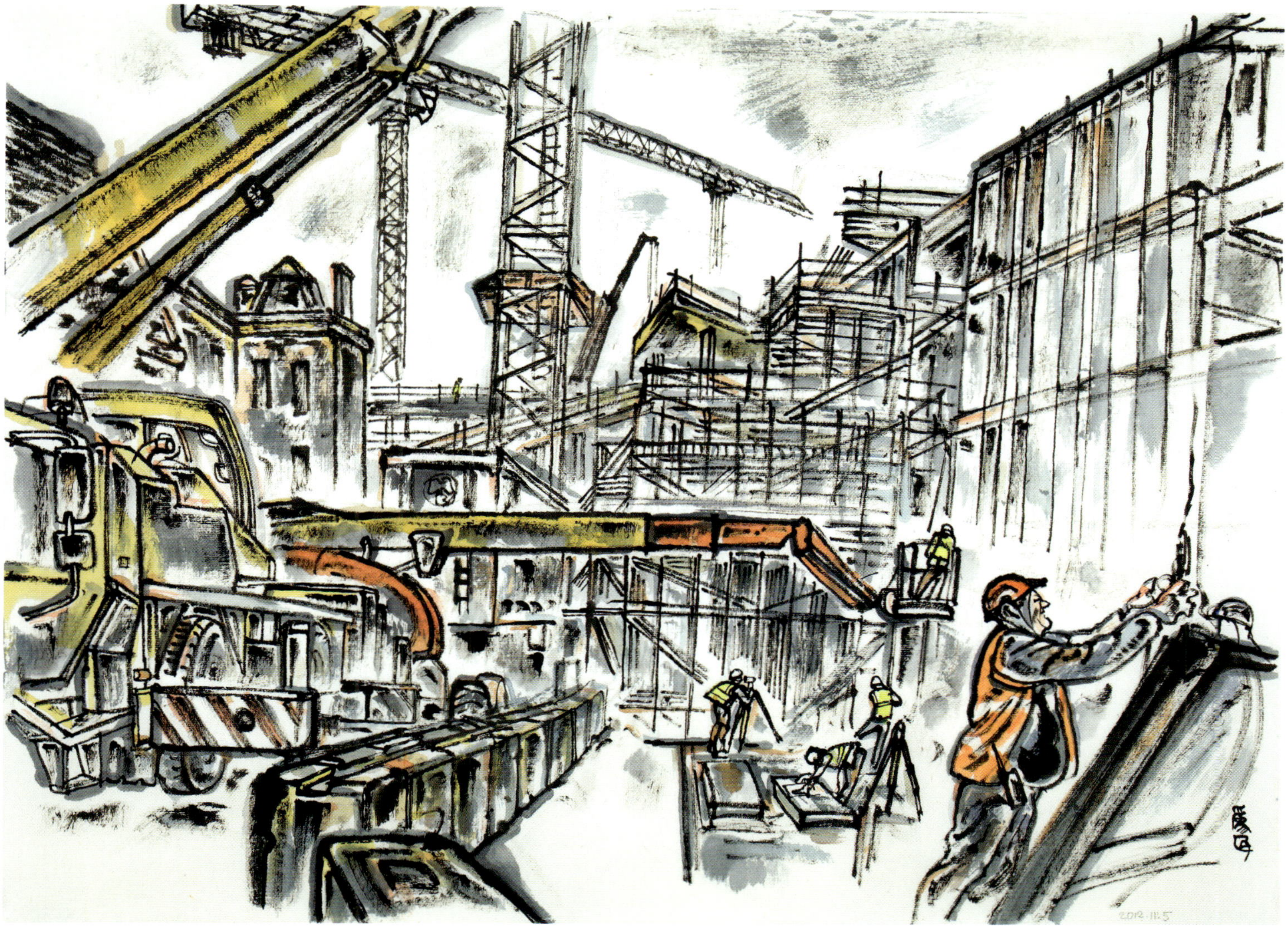

CAT.149
Matrix – Mathematical Institute. 5 November 2012. Brush, ink and watercolour on *xuan* paper. Paper size: 43.5 × 59.5 cm

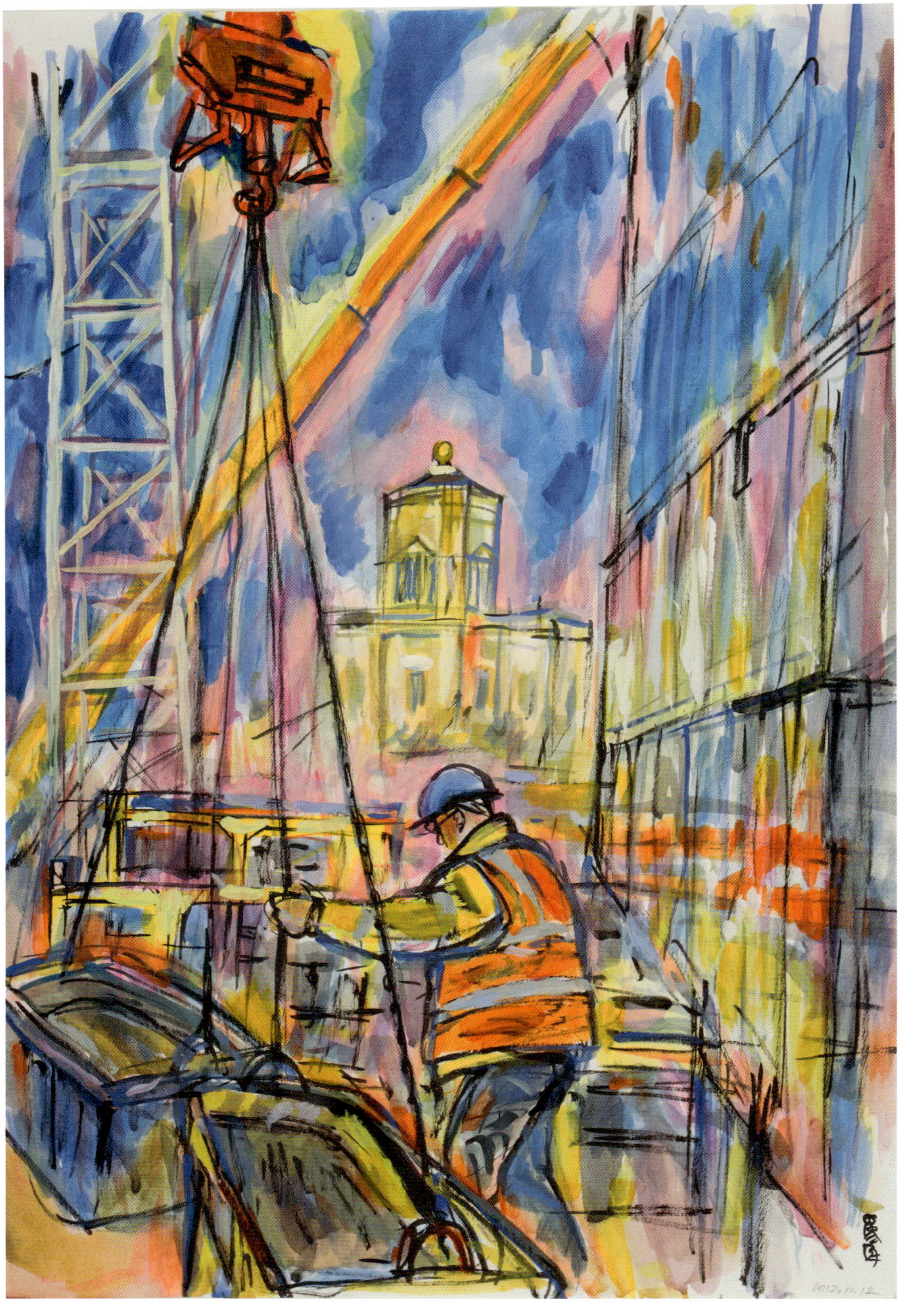

CAT.150
Reflections – Mathematical Institute. 12 November 2012. Brush, ink and watercolour on cartridge paper. Paper size: 59.4 × 42 cm

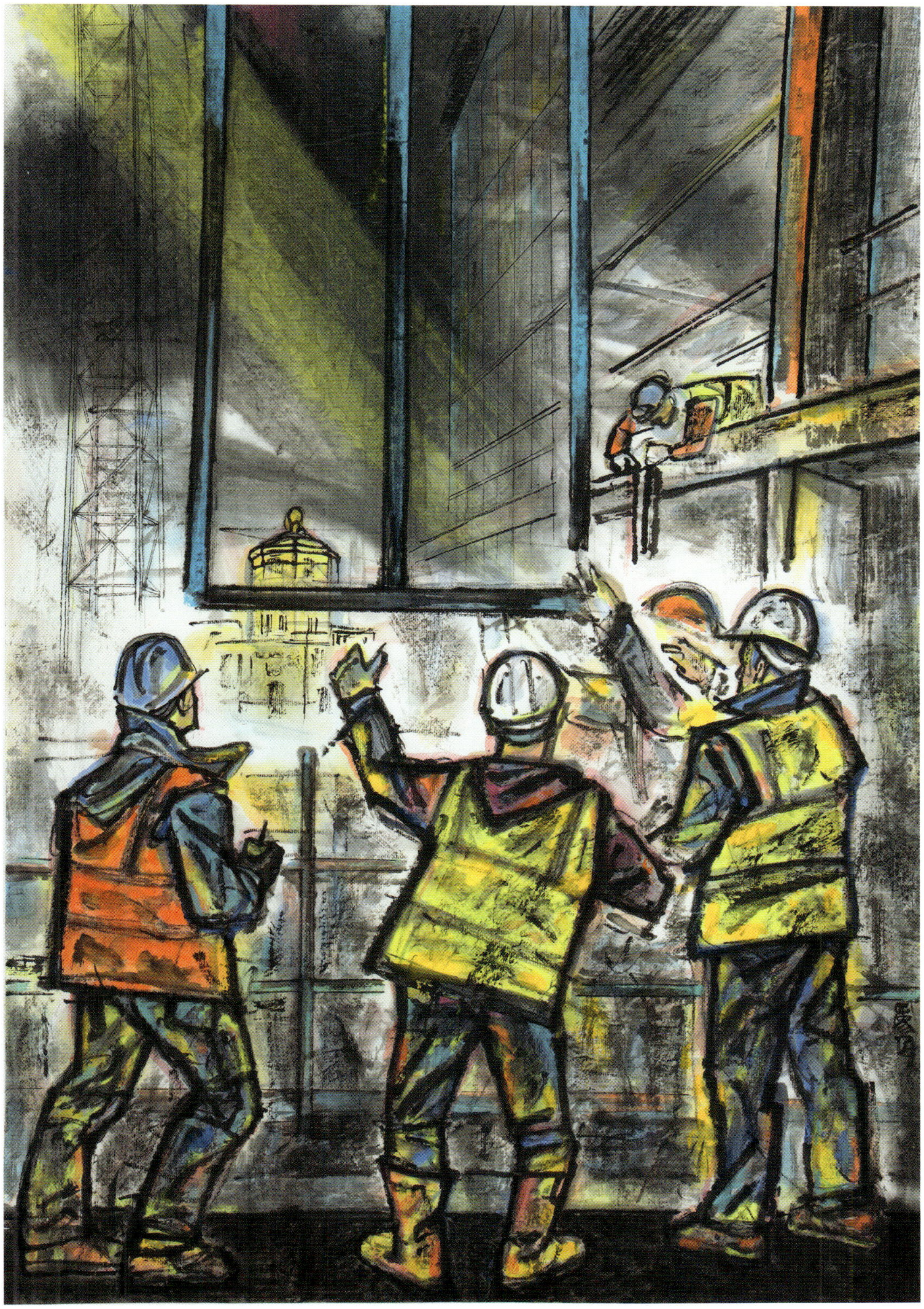

CAT.151
Shaft of golden light – Mathematical Institute.
14 November 2012. Brush, ink and watercolour on *xuan* paper. Paper size: 59.5 × 43.5 cm

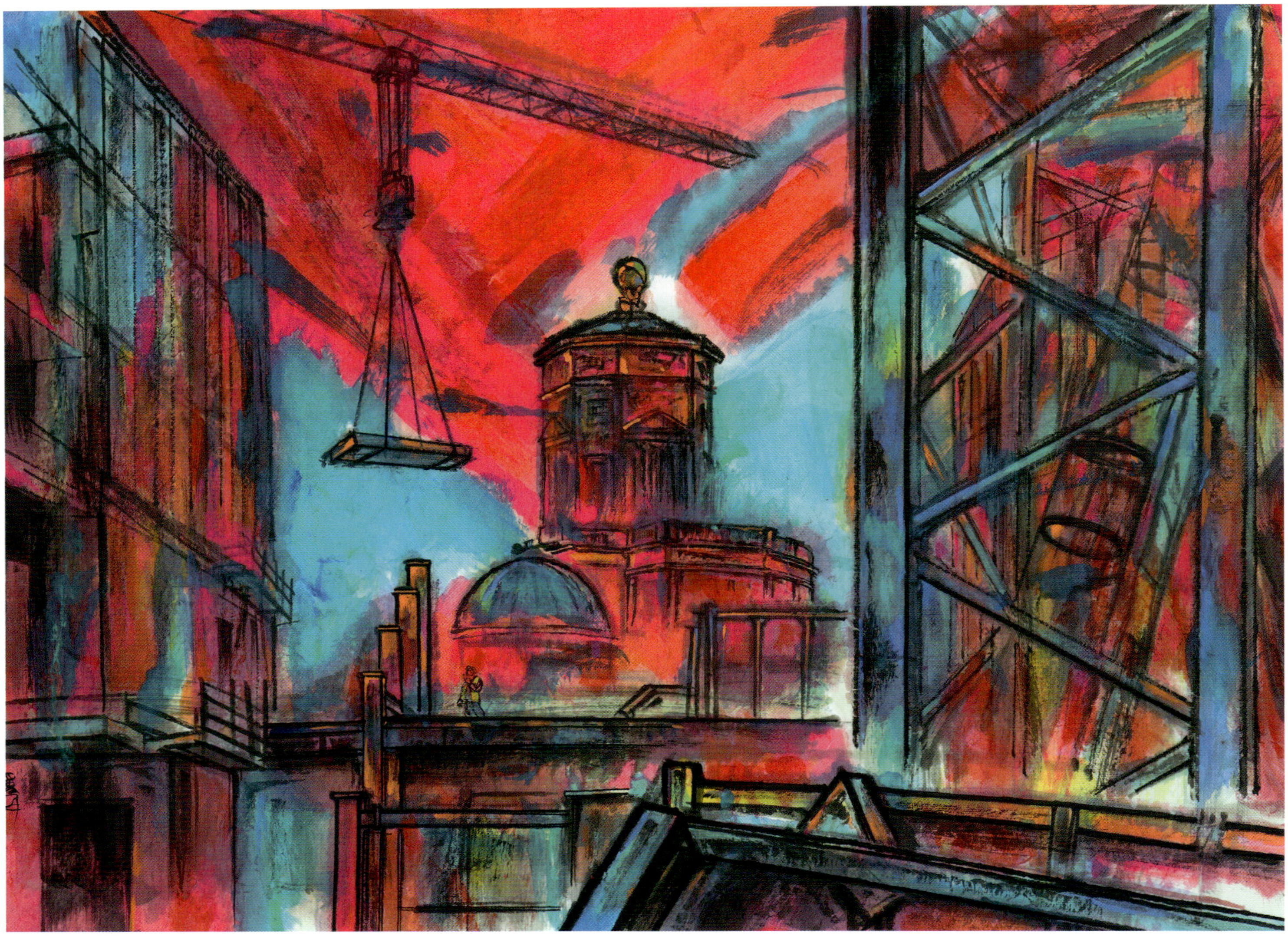

CAT.152

Breaking through – Mathematical Institute buildings. 9 January 2013. Brush, ink and watercolour on *xuan* paper. Paper size: 43.5 × 59.5 cm

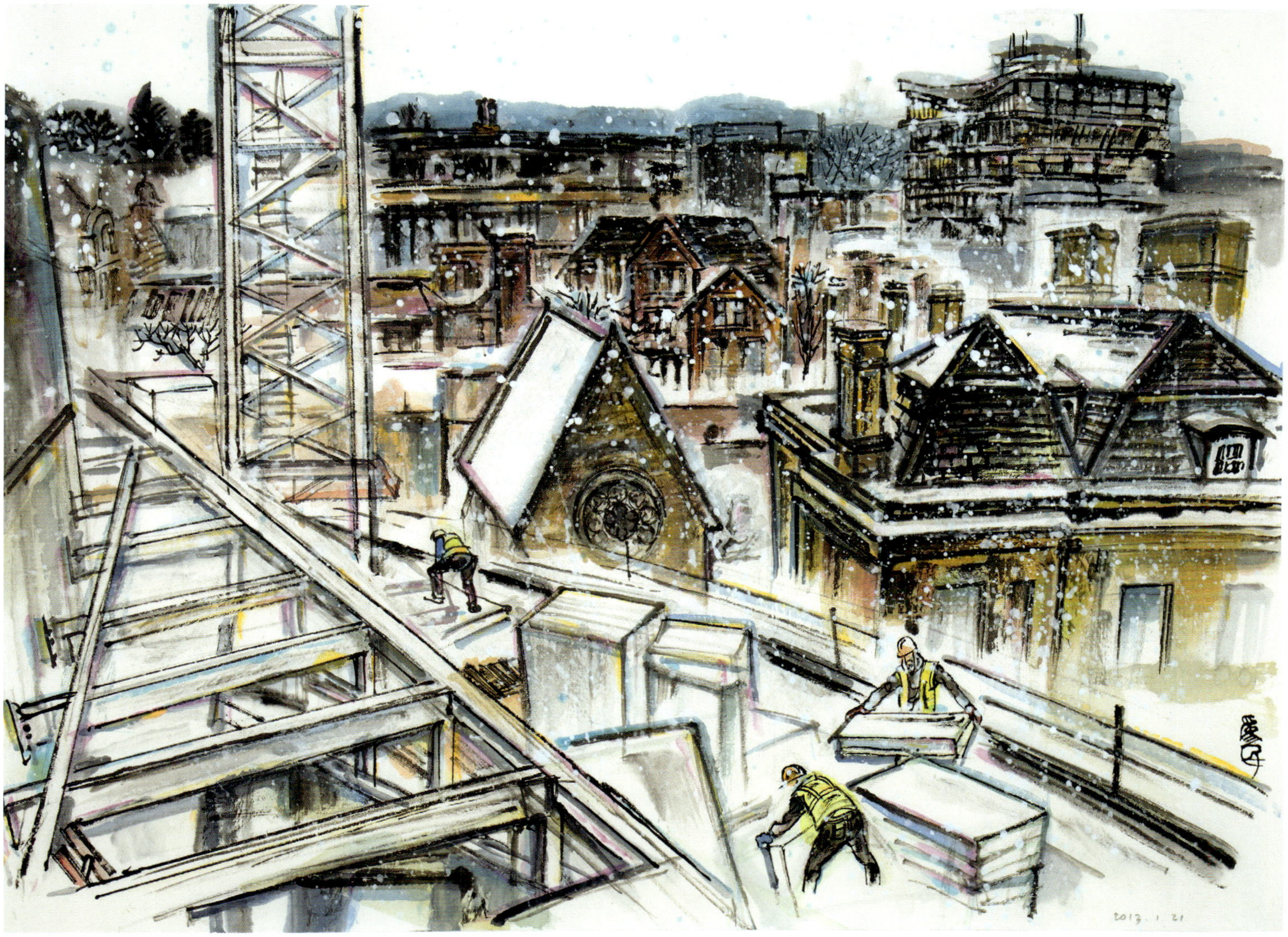

CAT.153
Under snow – Mathematical Institute. 21 January 2013. Brush, ink and watercolour on *xuan* paper. Paper size: 43.5 × 59.5 cm

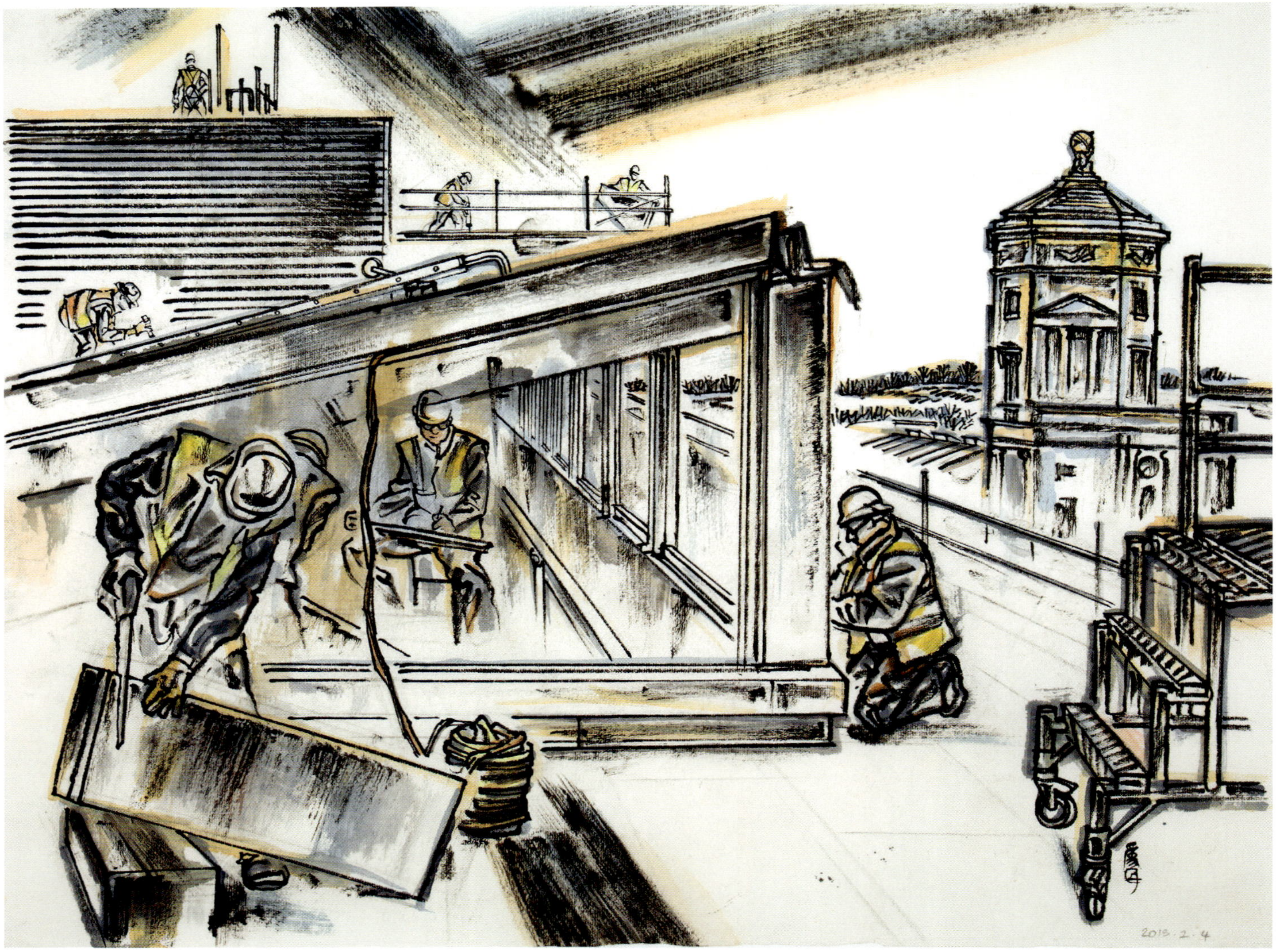

CAT.154
The artist observed – Mathematical Institute.
4 February 2013. Brush, ink and watercolour on *xuan* paper. Paper size: 43.5 × 59.5 cm

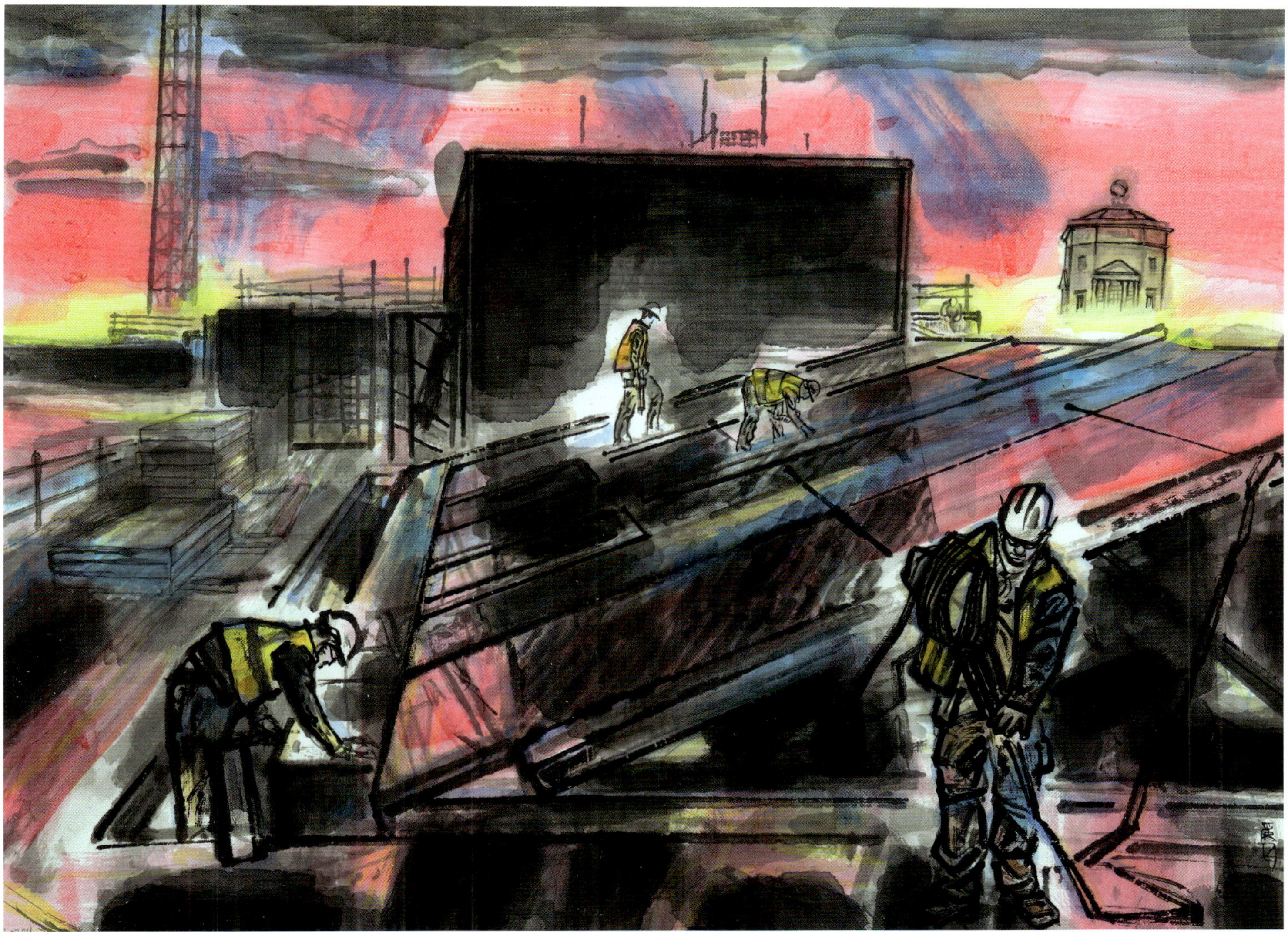

CAT.155
On the glass roof – Mathematical Institute.
4 February 2013. Brush, ink and watercolour
on *xuan* paper. Paper size: 43.5 × 59.5 cm

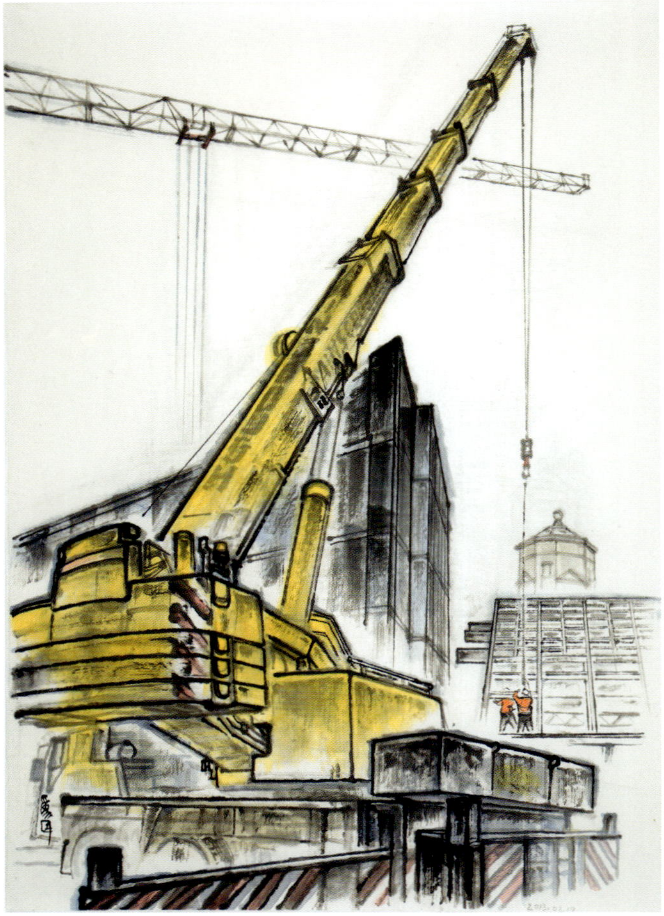

CAT.156
Yellow reaching arm – Mathematical Institute. 19 March 2013. Brush, ink and watercolour on *xuan* paper. Paper size: 59.5 × 43.5 cm

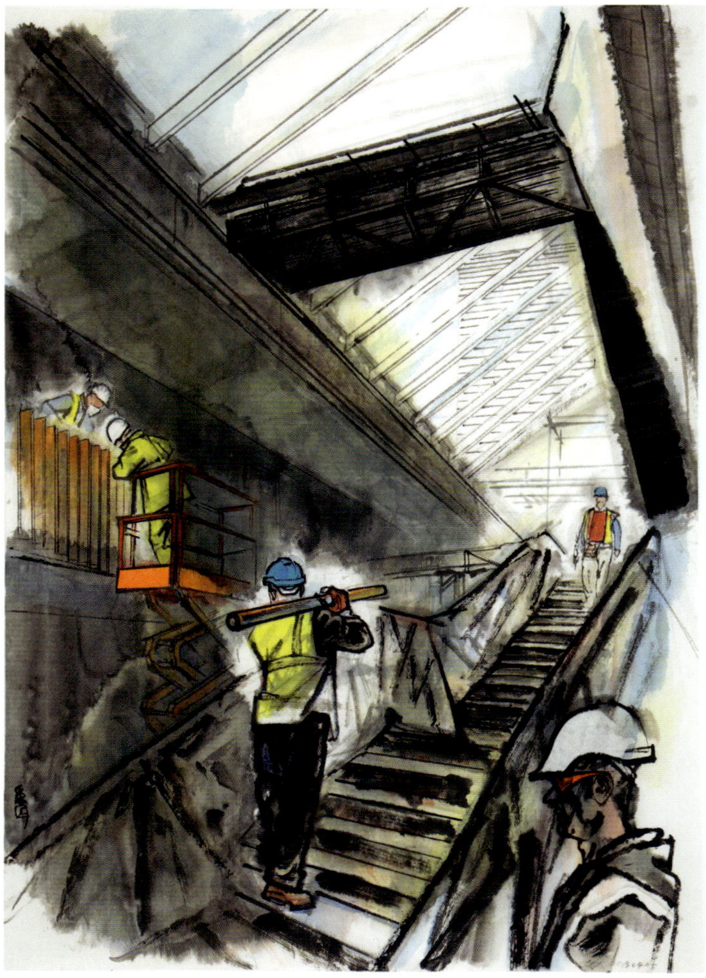

CAT.157
Stepping up and down – Mathematical Institute. 5 April 2013. Brush, ink, watercolur and collage on *xuan* paper. Paper size: 59.5 × 43.5 cm

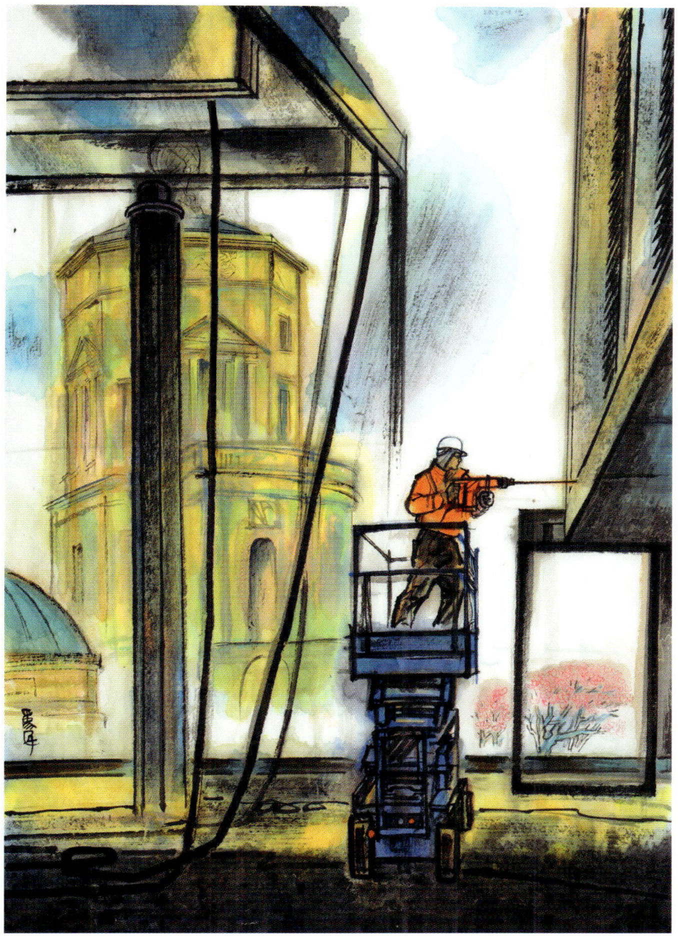

CAT.158
The power of the drill – Mathematical Institute. 14 April 2013. Brush, ink and watercolour on *xuan* paper. Paper size: 59.5 × 43.5 cm

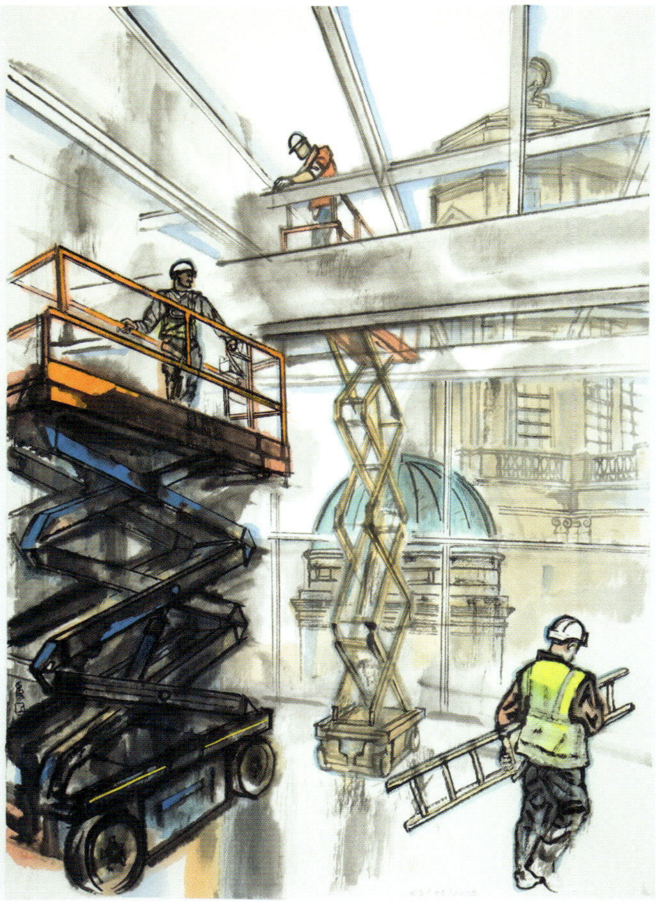

CAT.159
Retraction jack – Mathematical Institute. 3 May 2013. Brush, ink, watercolour and collage on *xuan* paper. Paper size: 59.5 × 43.5 cm

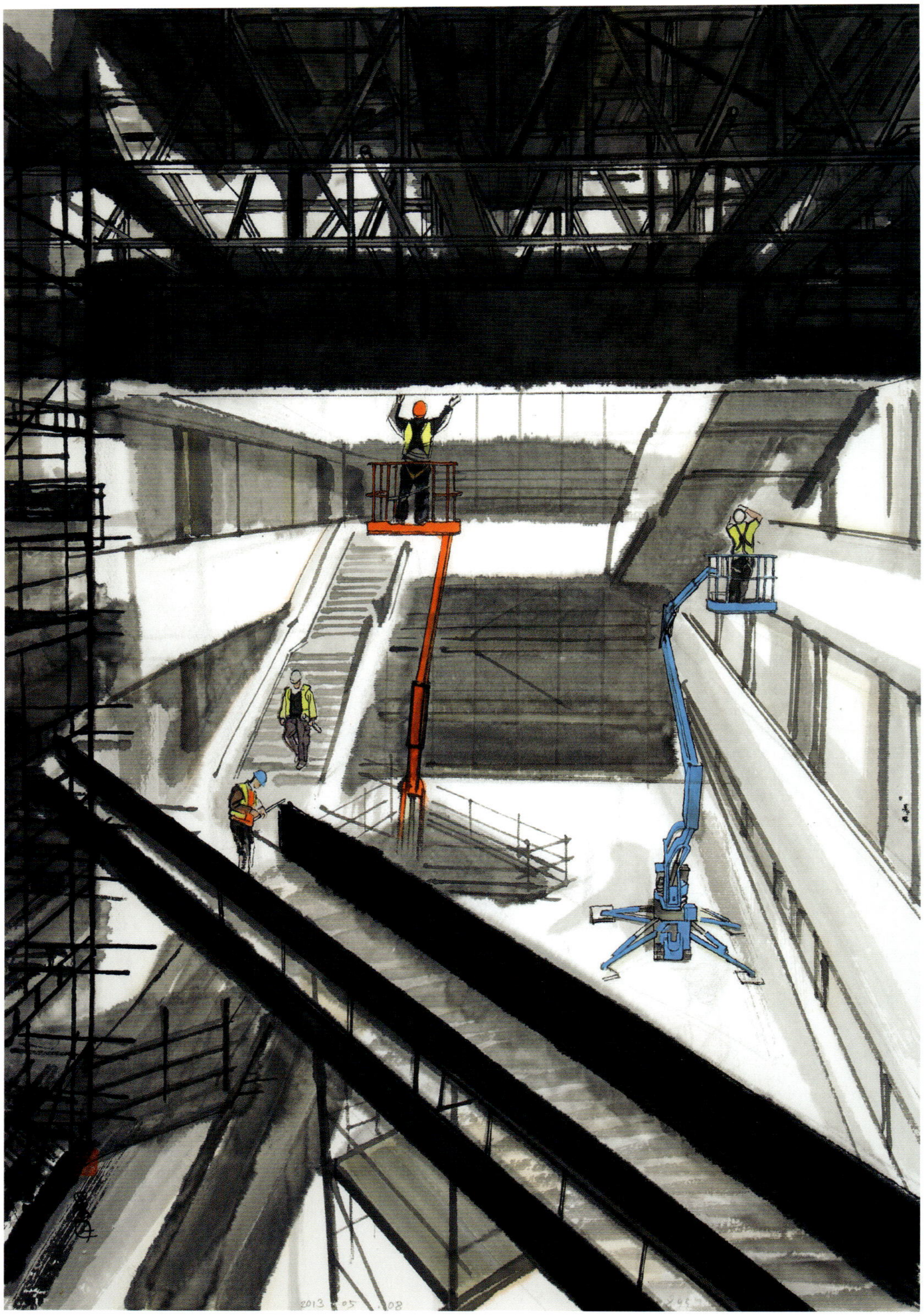

CAT.160
Red crane, blue crane – Mathematical Institute. 8 May 2013. Brush, ink and watercolour on *xuan* paper. Paper size: 59.5 × 43.5 cm

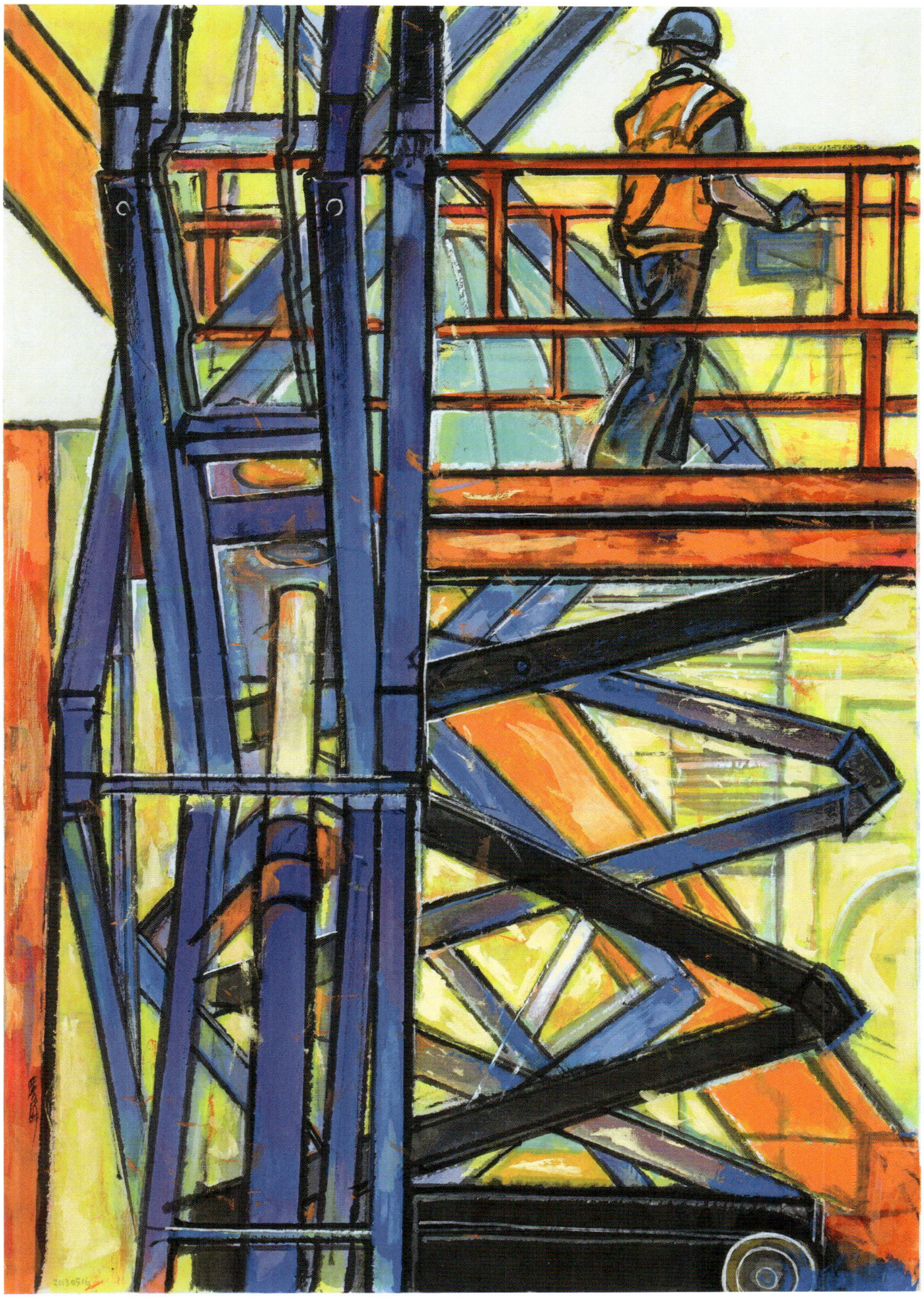

CAT.161

Elevating the lines – Mathematical Institute. 16 May 2013. Brush, ink, watercolour and collage on *xuan* paper. Paper size: 59.5 × 43.5 cm

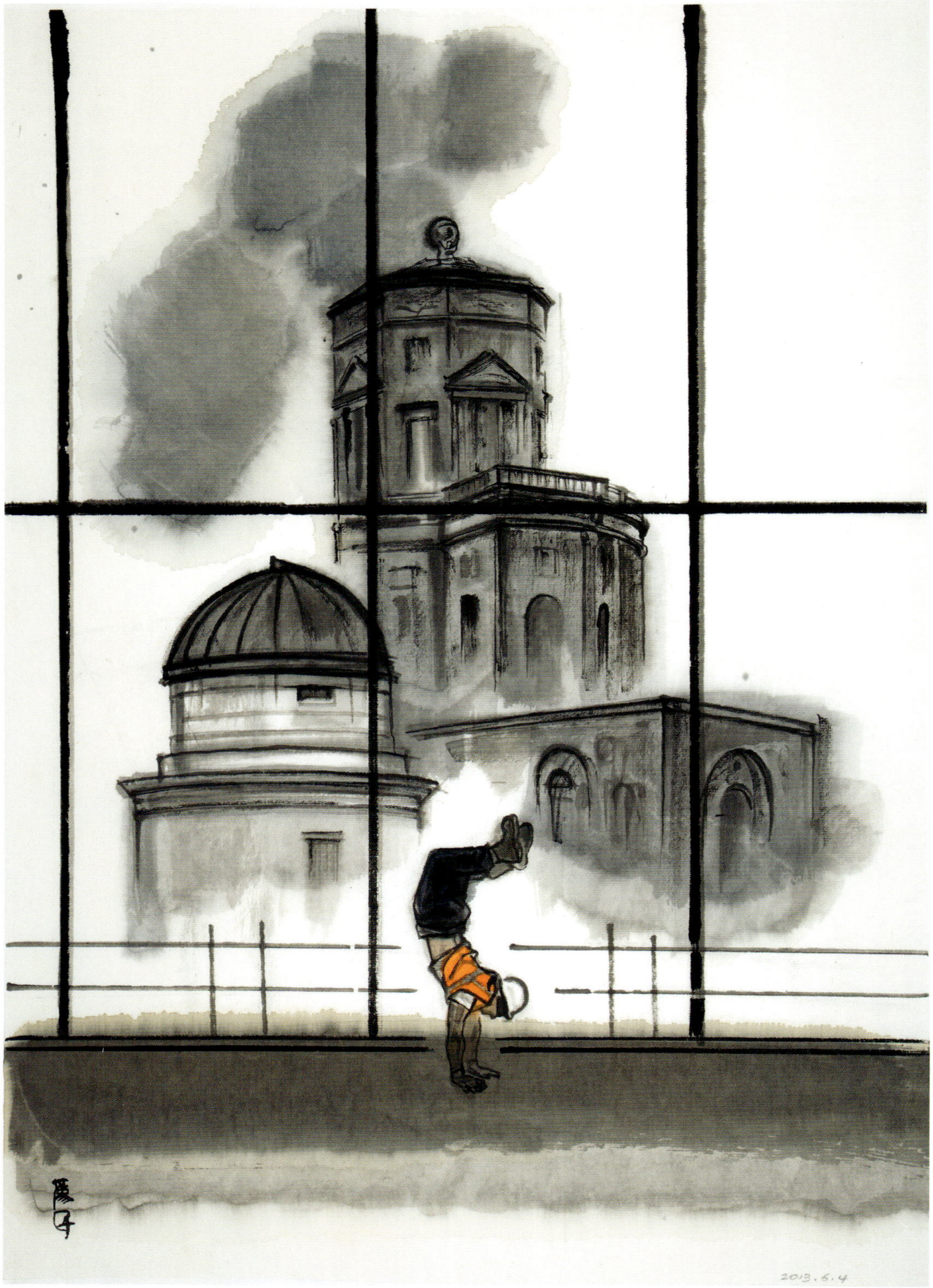

CAT.162
Job done – Mathematical Institute. 4 June 2013. Brush, ink and watercolour on *xuan* paper. Paper size: 59.5 × 43.5 cm

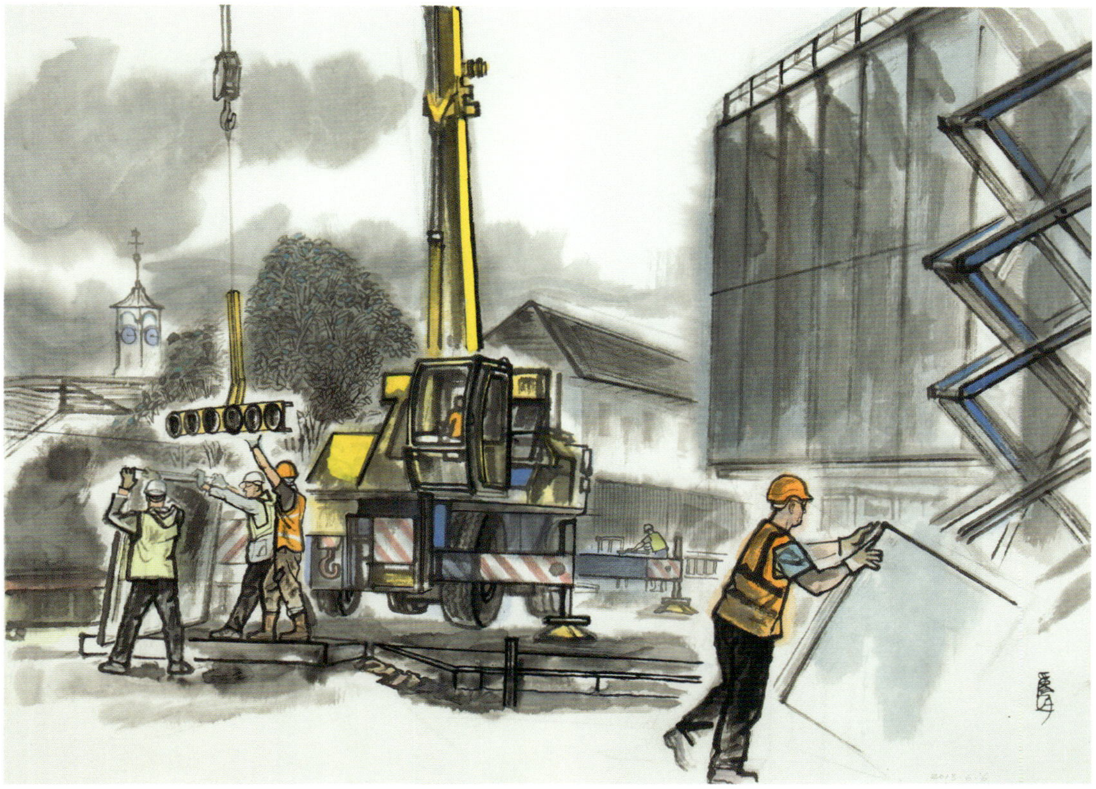

CAT.163
Keeping time – Mathematical Institute. 6 June 2013. Brush, ink and watercolour on *xuan* paper. Paper size: 43.5 × 59.5 cm

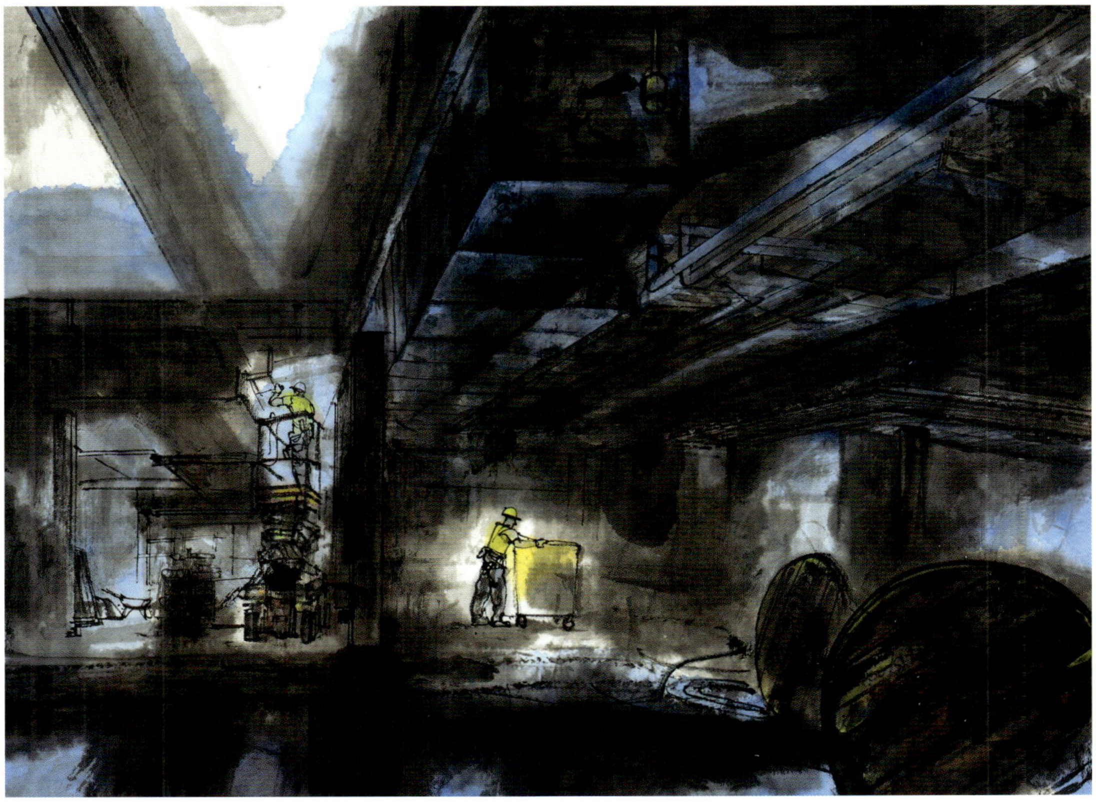

CAT.164
Electricians at work – Mathematical Institute. 6 June 2013. Brush, ink and watercolour on *xuan* paper. Paper size: 43.5 × 59.5 cm

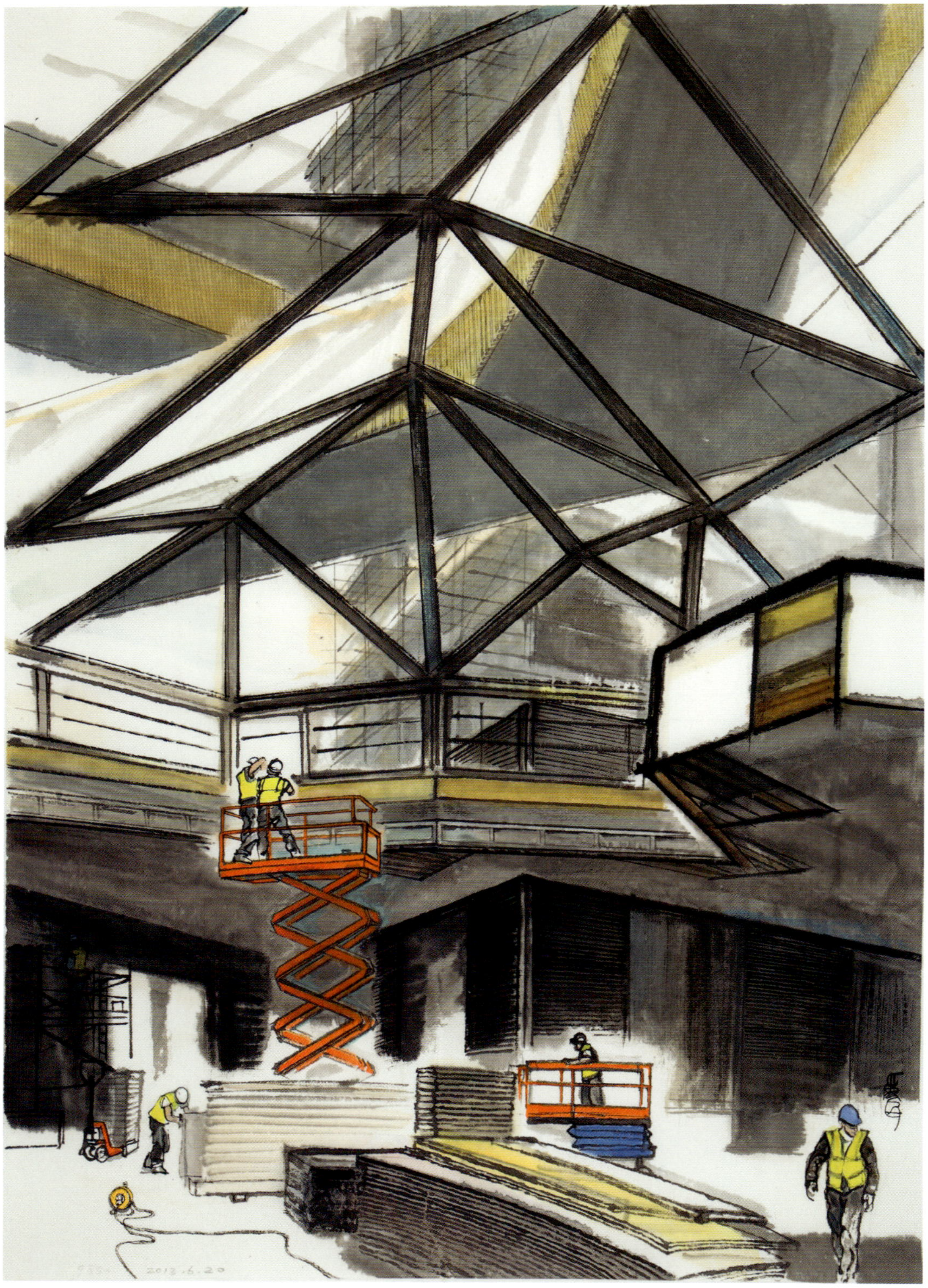

CAT.165
Crystal maze – Mathematical Institute. 20 June 2013. Brush, ink and watercolour on *xuan* paper. Paper size: 59.5 × 43.5 cm

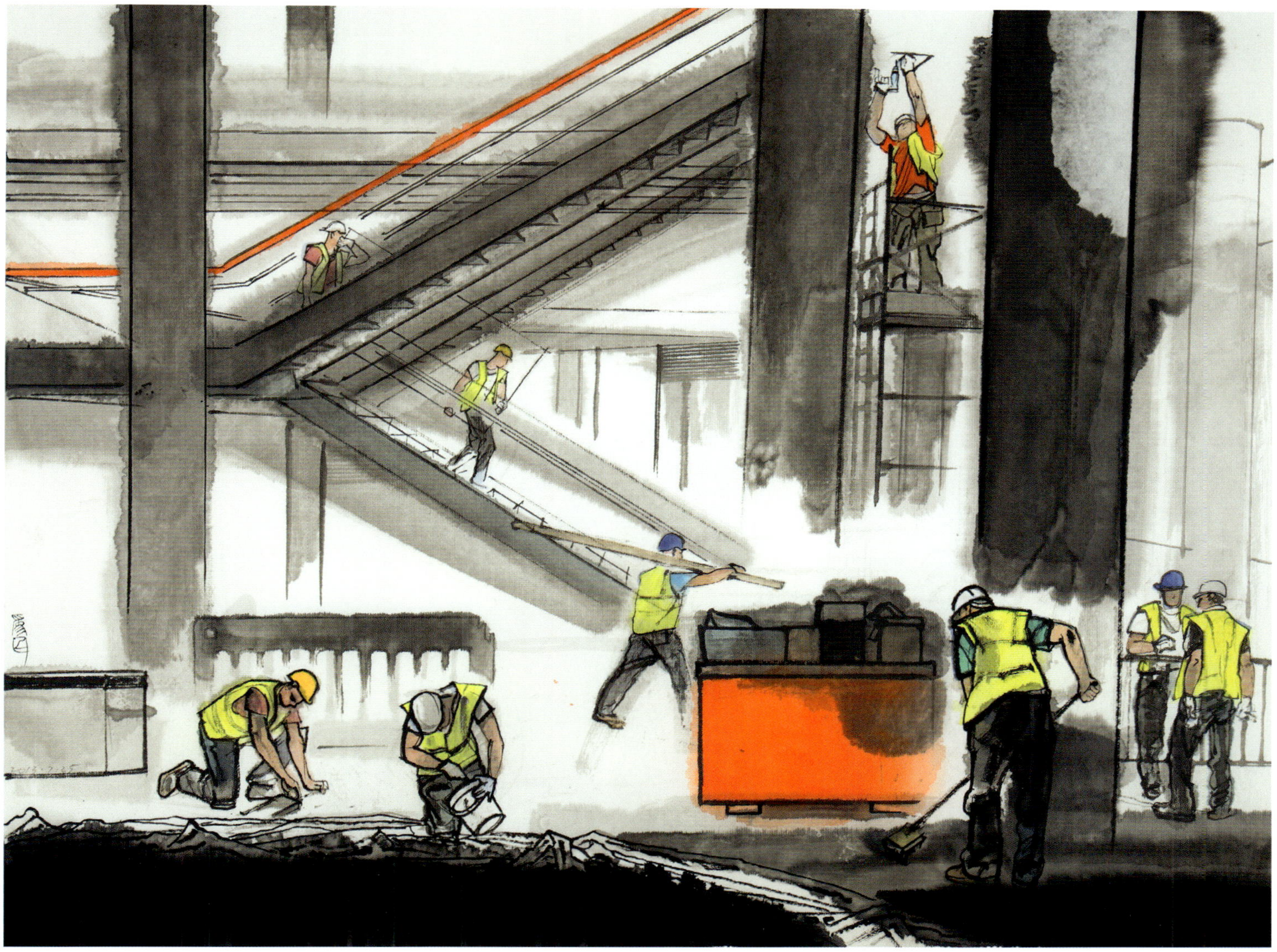

CAT.166
Final stages – Mathematical Institute.
25 July 2013. Brush, ink and watercolour on *xuan* paper. Paper size: 43.5 × 59.5 cm

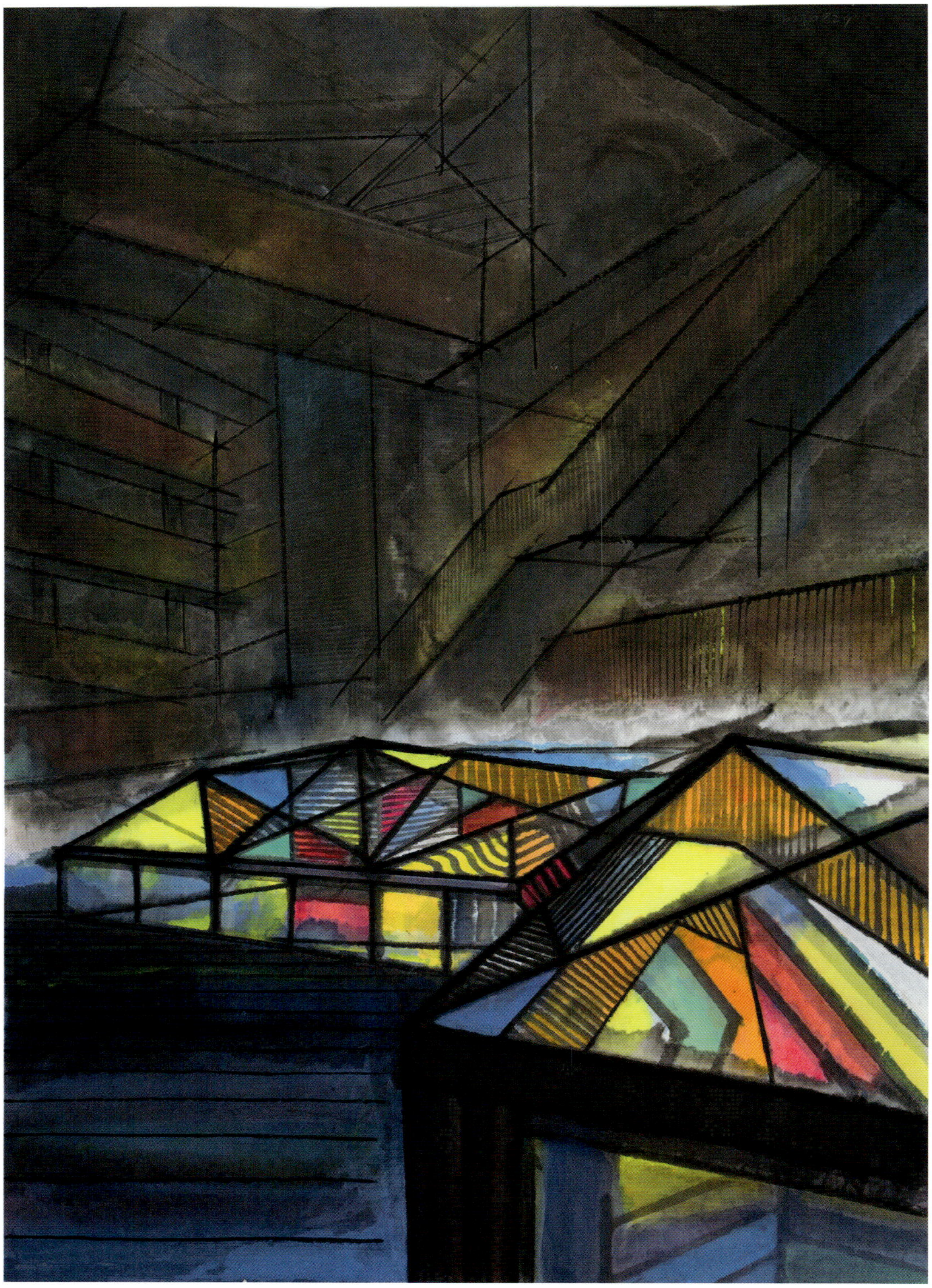

CAT.167
Shining lights – Mathematical Institute. 29 August 2013. Brush, ink and watercolour on *xuan* paper. Paper size: 59.5 × 43.5cm

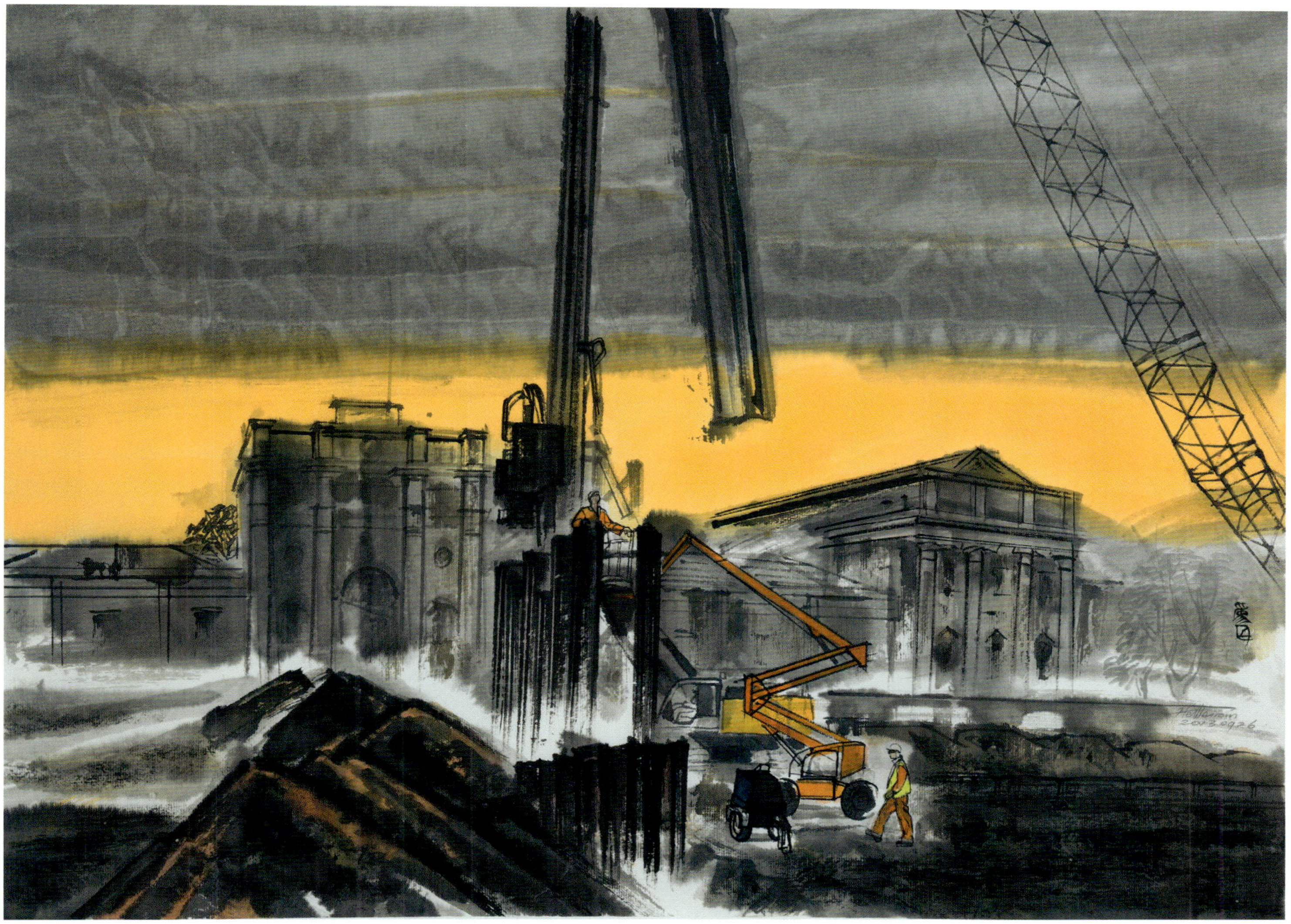

CAT.168
Golden sunset – Blavatnik School of Government. 26 September 2013. Brush, ink and watercolour on *xuan* paper. Paper size: 43.5 × 59.5 cm

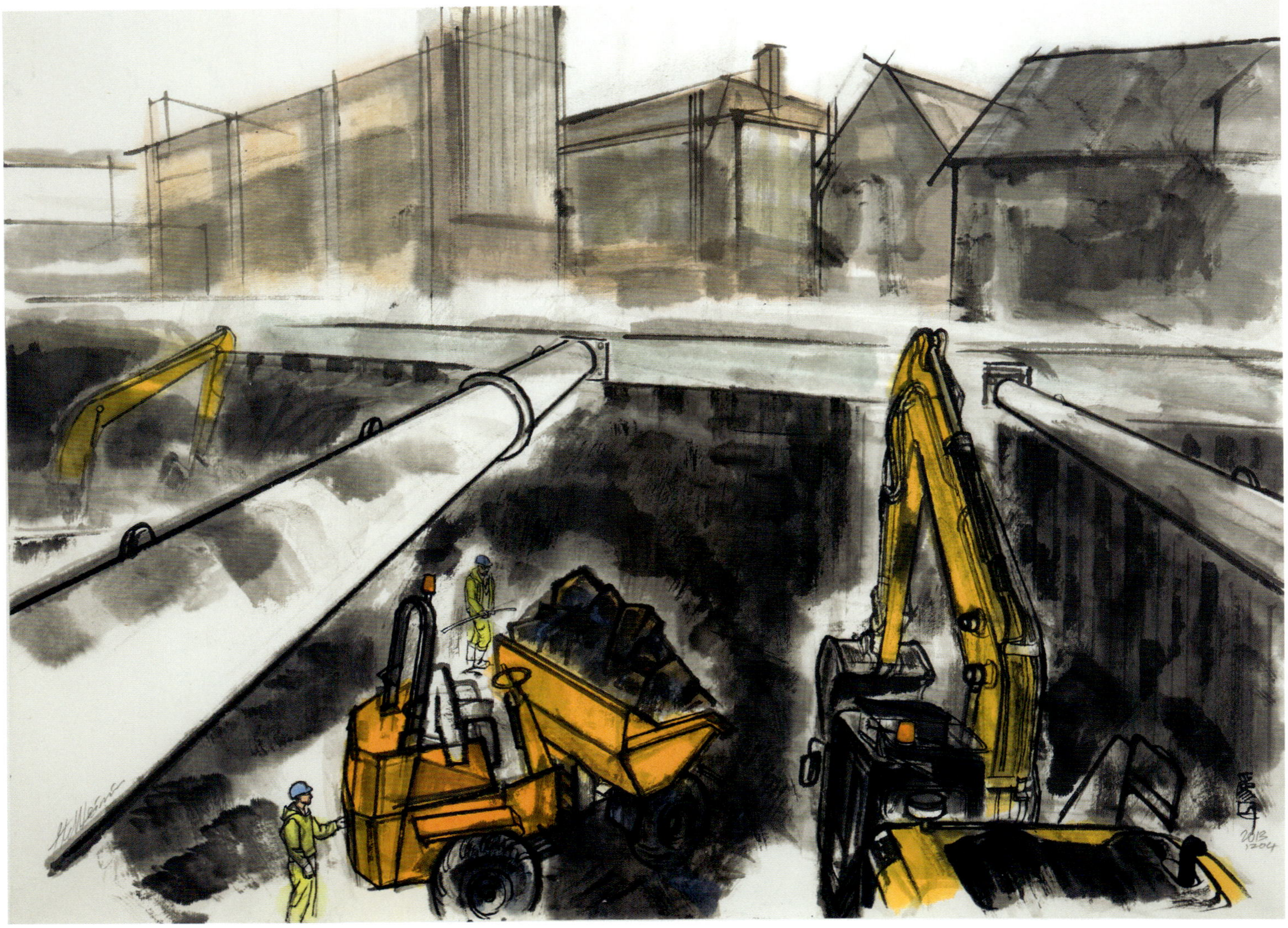

CAT.169

Under the props – Blavatnik School of Government. 4 December 2013. Brush, ink and watercolour on *xuan* paper. Paper size: 43.5 × 59.5 cm

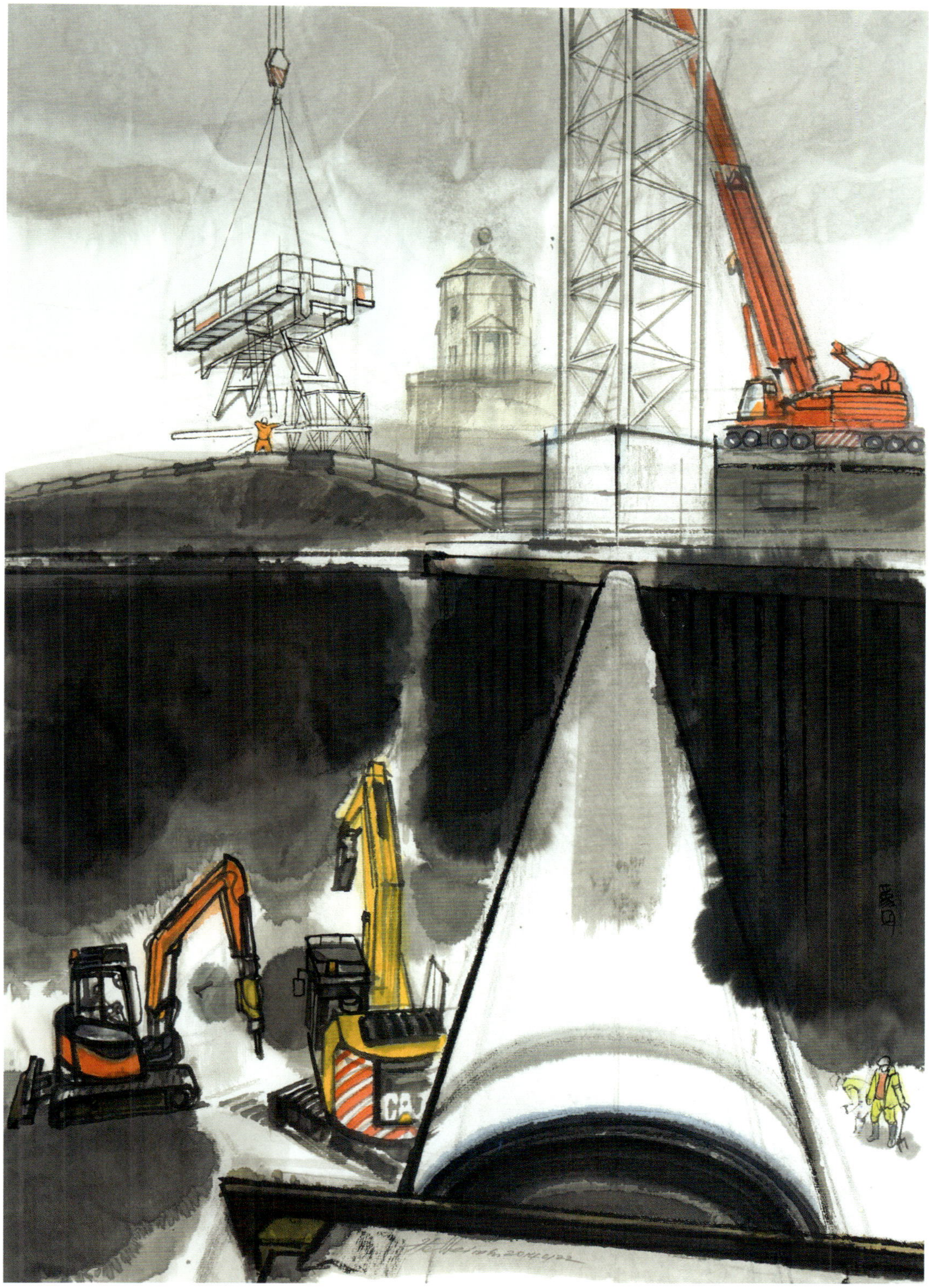

CAT.170
Day of drizzle – Blavatnik School of Government. 22 January 2014. Brush, ink and watercolour on *xuan* paper. Paper size: 59.5 × 43.5cm

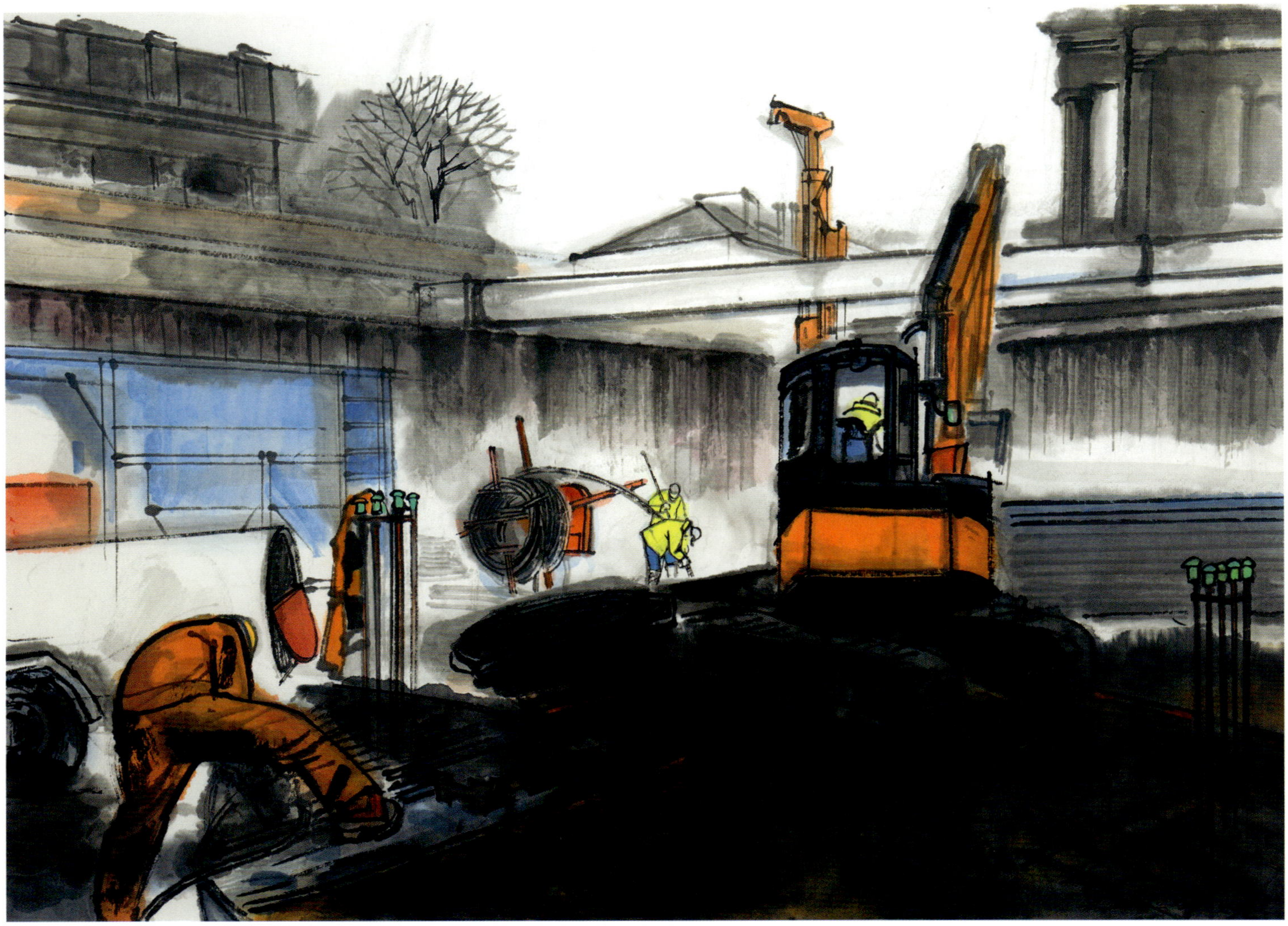

CAT.171
Down with the drill – Blavatnik School of Government. 30 January 2014. Brush, ink and watercolour on *xuan* paper. Paper size: 59.5 × 43.5 cm

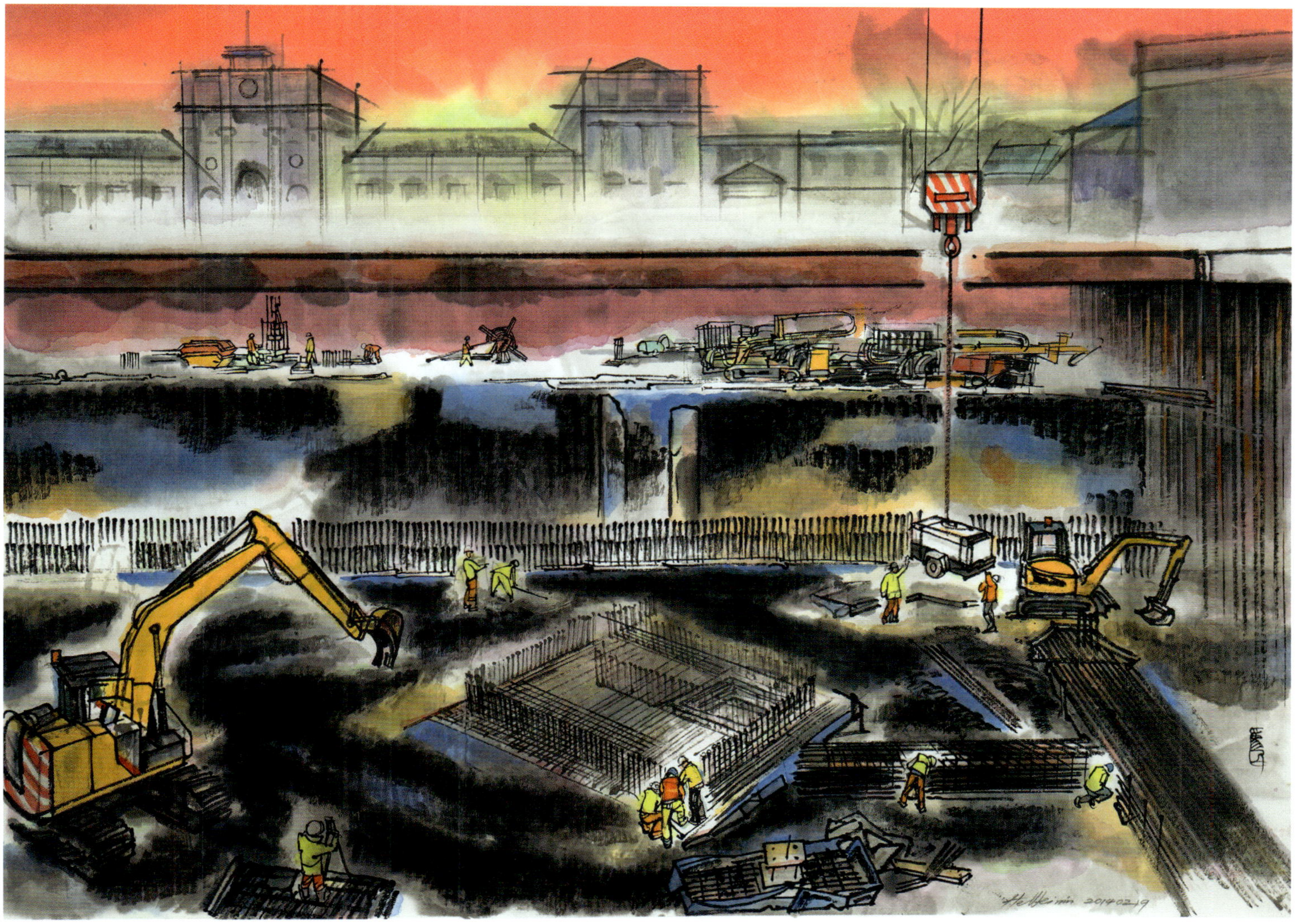

CAT.172
Red sky, black earth – Blavatnik School of Government. 19 February 2014.
Brush, ink and watercolour on *xuan* paper. Paper size: 43.5 × 59.5 cm

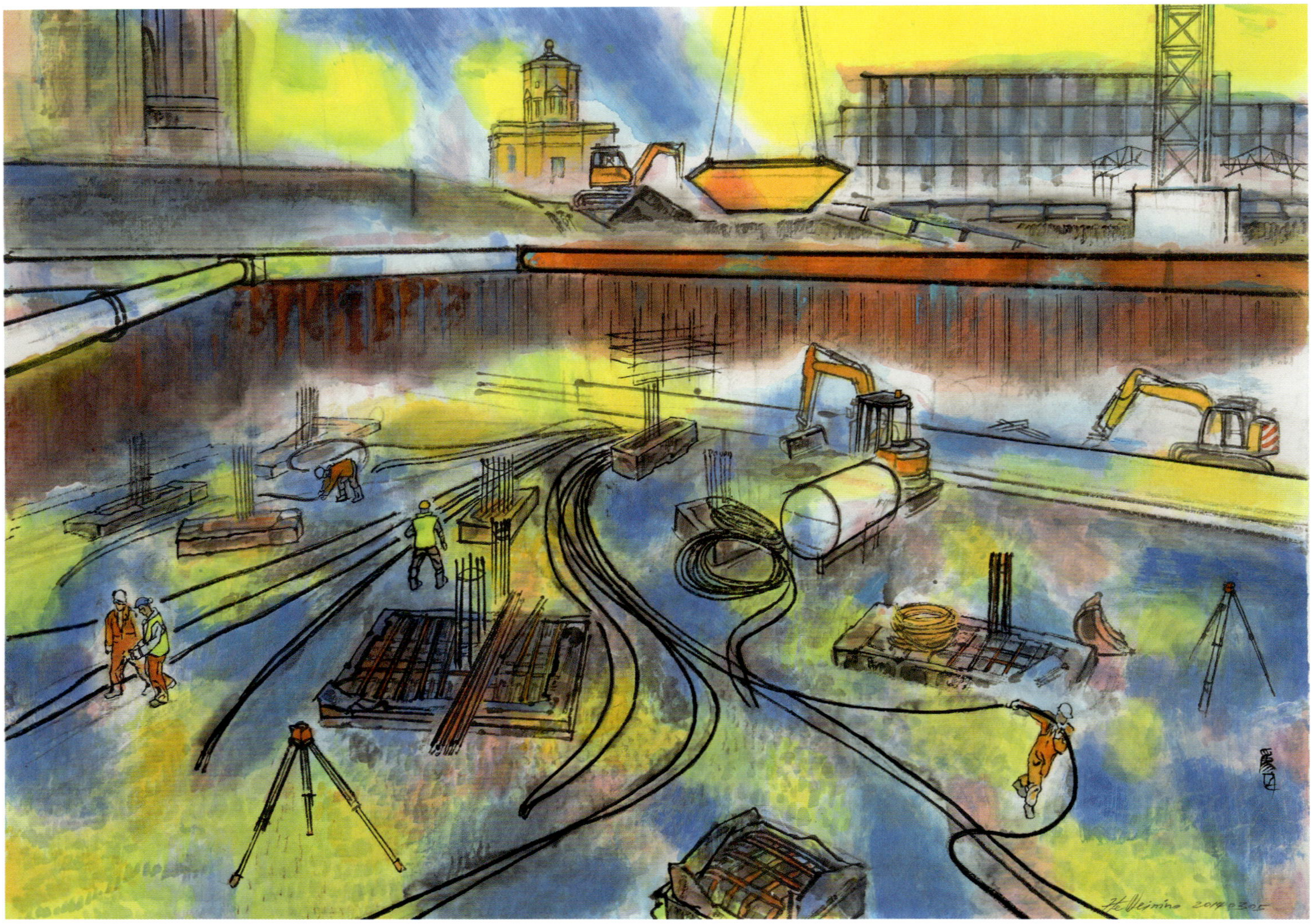

CAT.173
Arrival of spring – Blavatnik School of Government. 5 March 2014. Brush, ink and watercolour on *xuan* paper. Paper size: 43.5 × 59.5 cm

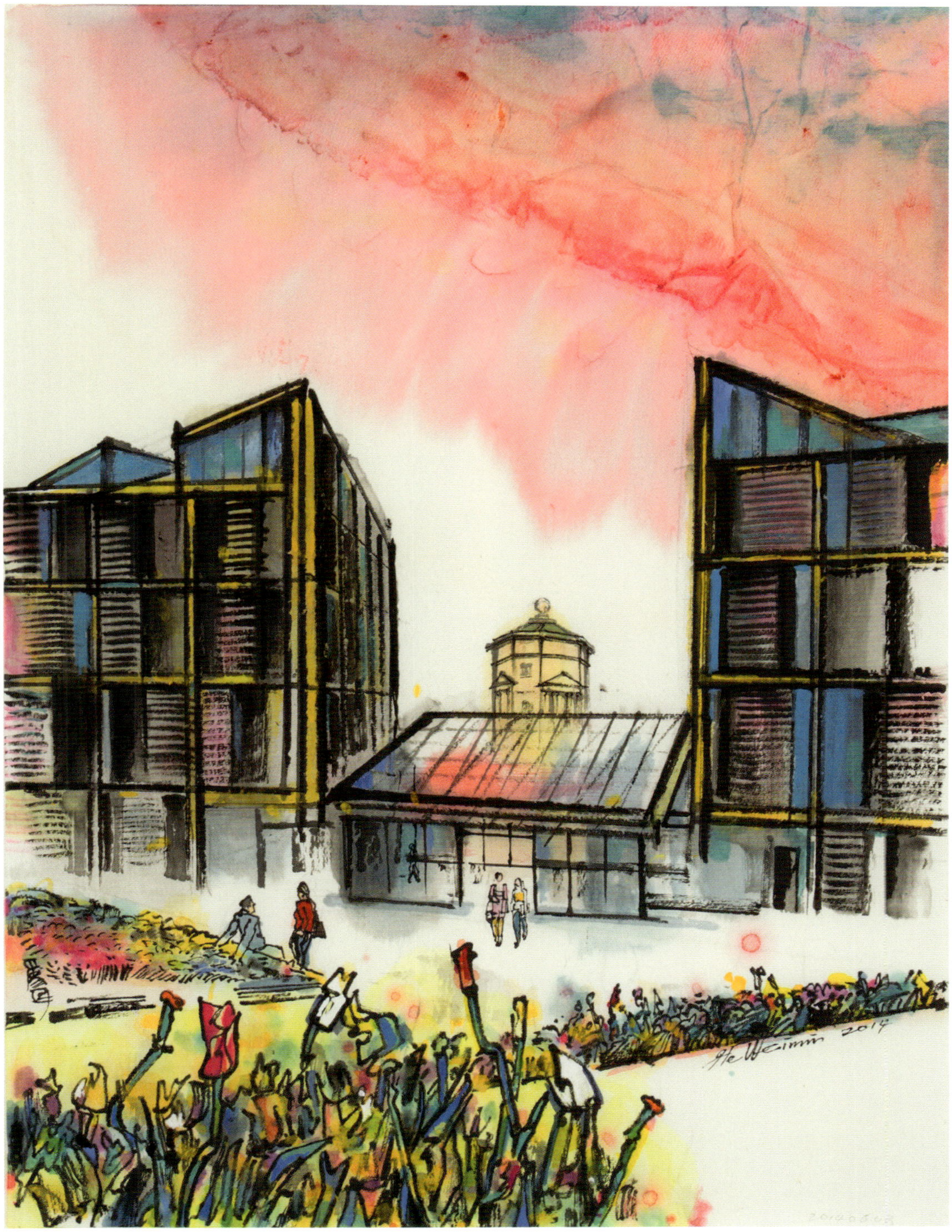

CAT.174
Pink sky, Mathematical Institute. 8 August 2014. Brush, ink and watercolour on *xuan* paper. Paper size: 50.5 × 34.5 cm

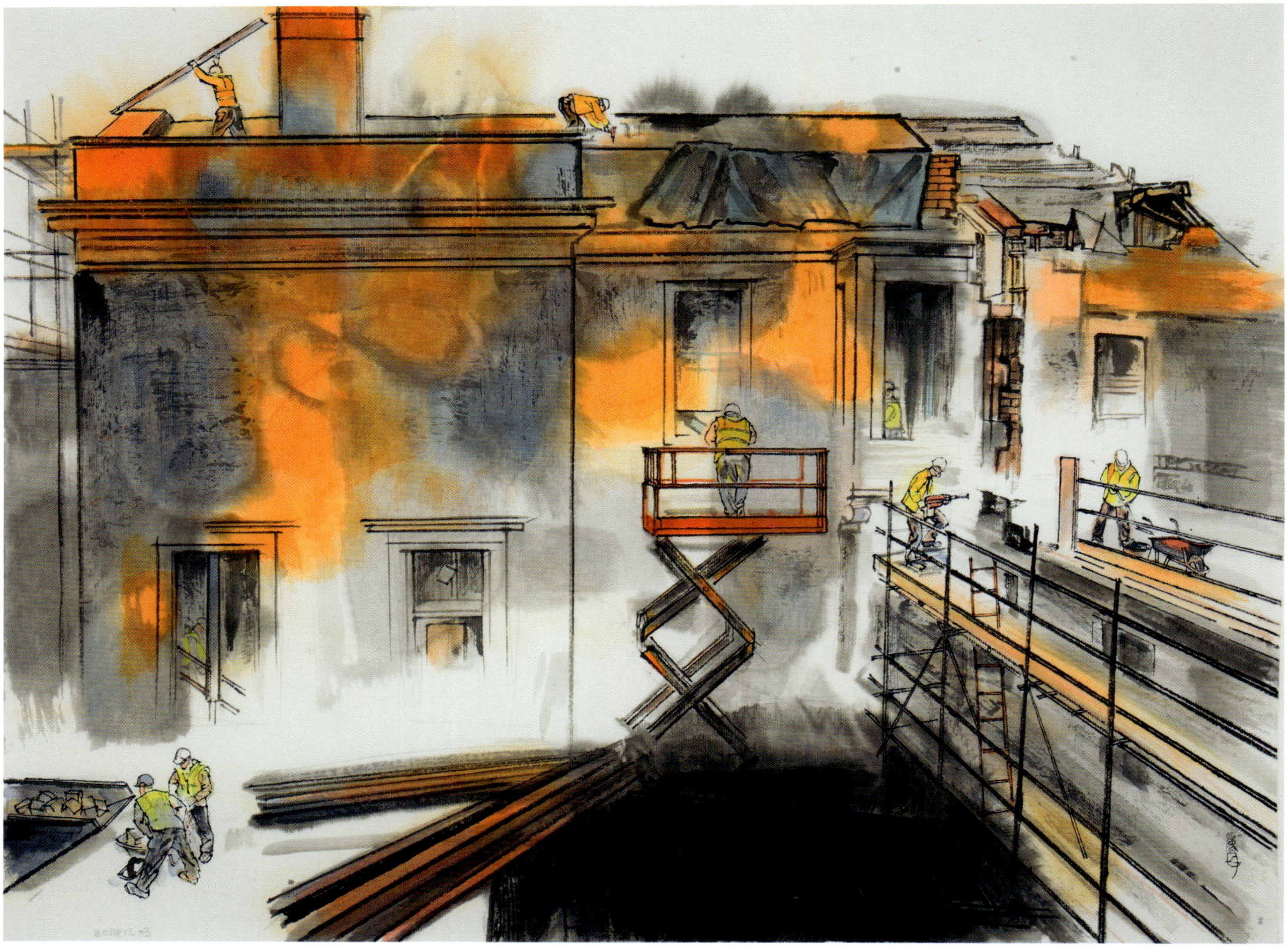

CAT.175
The setting sun – refurbishment of the Outpatients building. 3 December 2014.
Brush, ink and watercolour on *xuan* paper.
Paper size: 43.5 × 59.5 cm

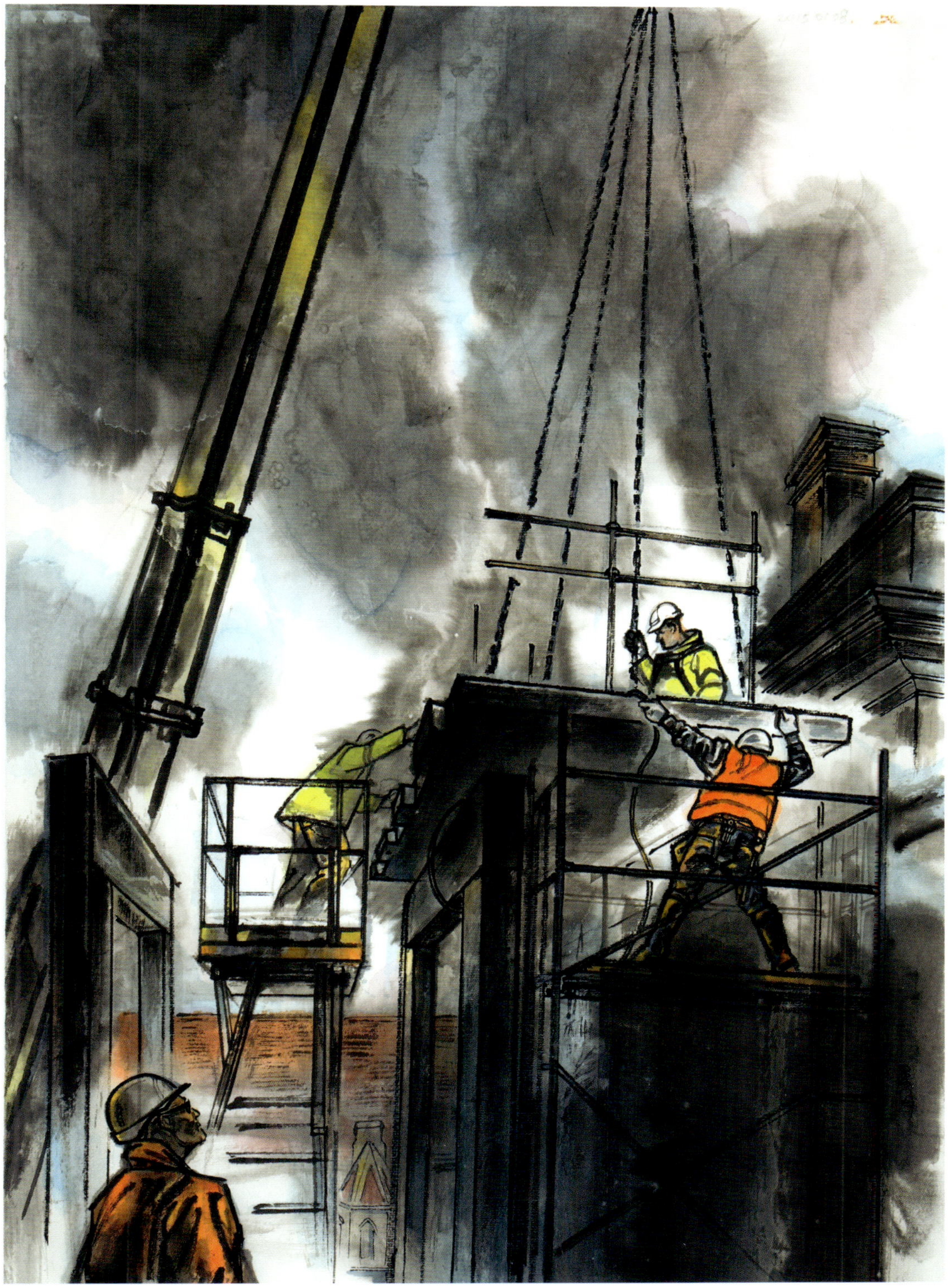

CAT.176
Lifting into place – Outpatients building under refurbishment.
9 January 2015. Brush, ink and watercolour on *xuan* paper.
Paper size: 59.5 × 43.5 cm

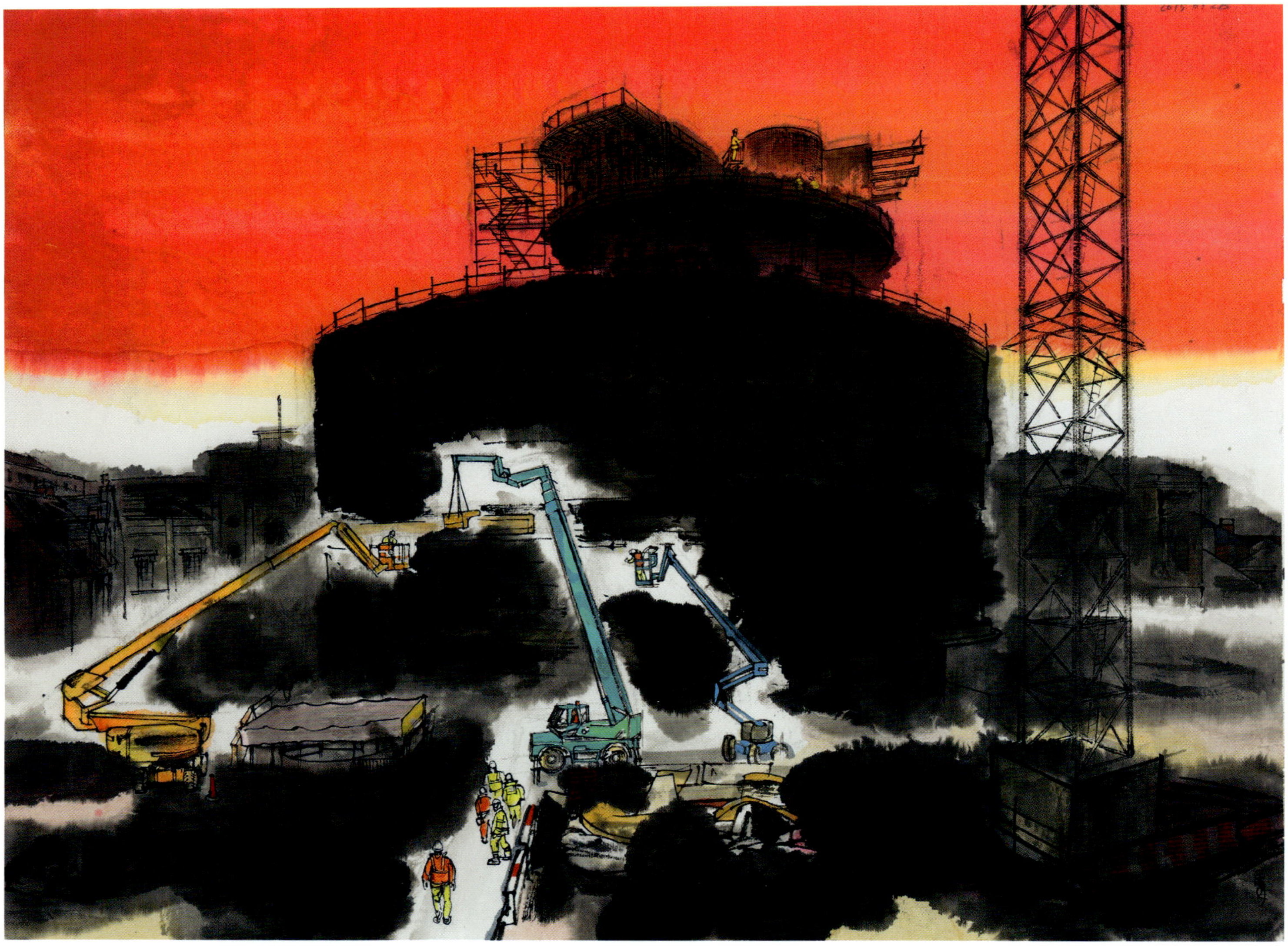

CAT.177
Blood red sunset– Blavatnik School of Government. 28 January 2015. Brush, ink and watercolour on *xuan* paper. Paper size: 43.5 × 59.5 cm

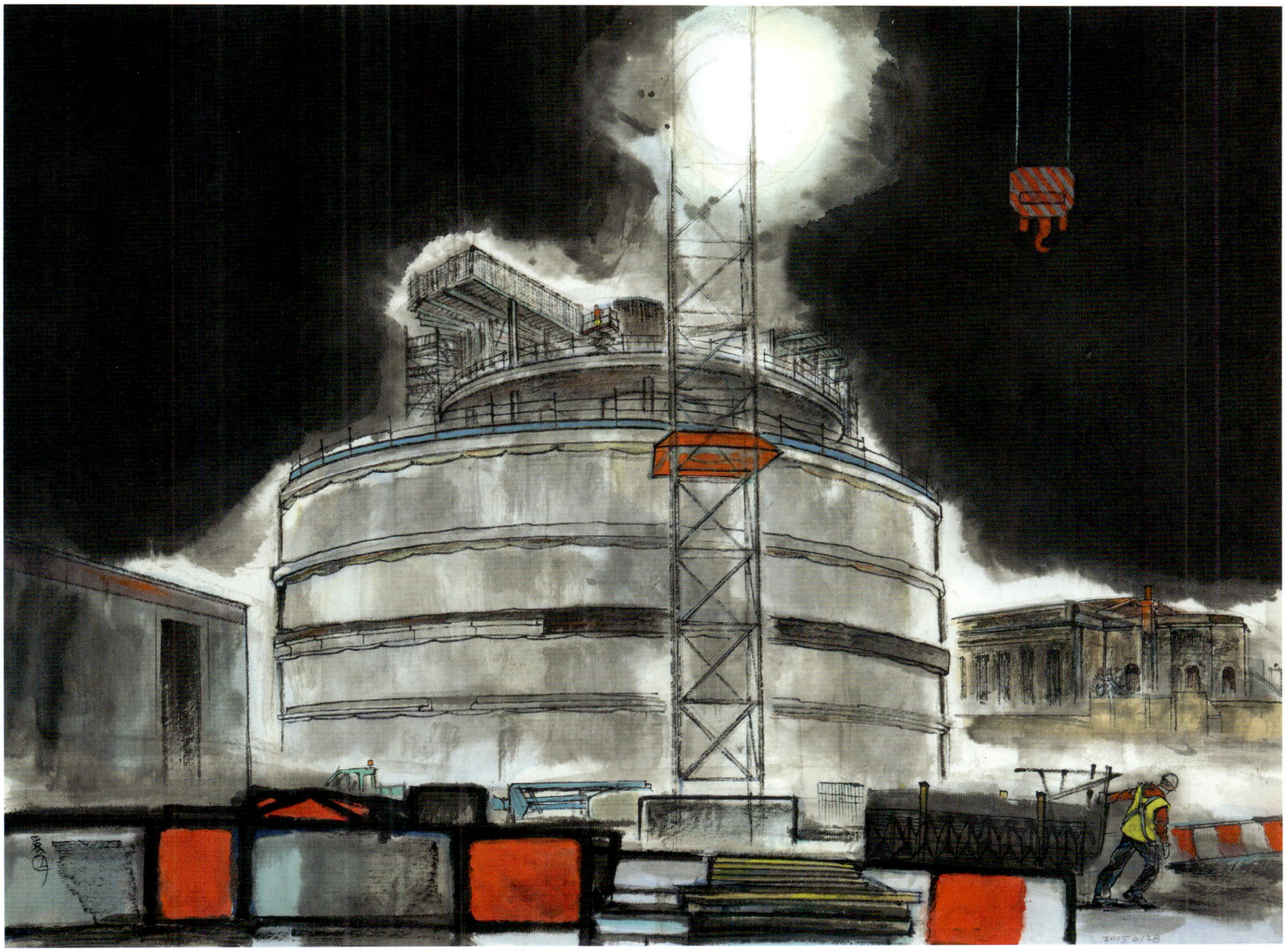

CAT.178
Dark sky – Blavatnik School of Government.
28 January 2015. Brush, ink, watercolour and collage on *xuan* paper. Paper size: 43.5 × 59.5 cm

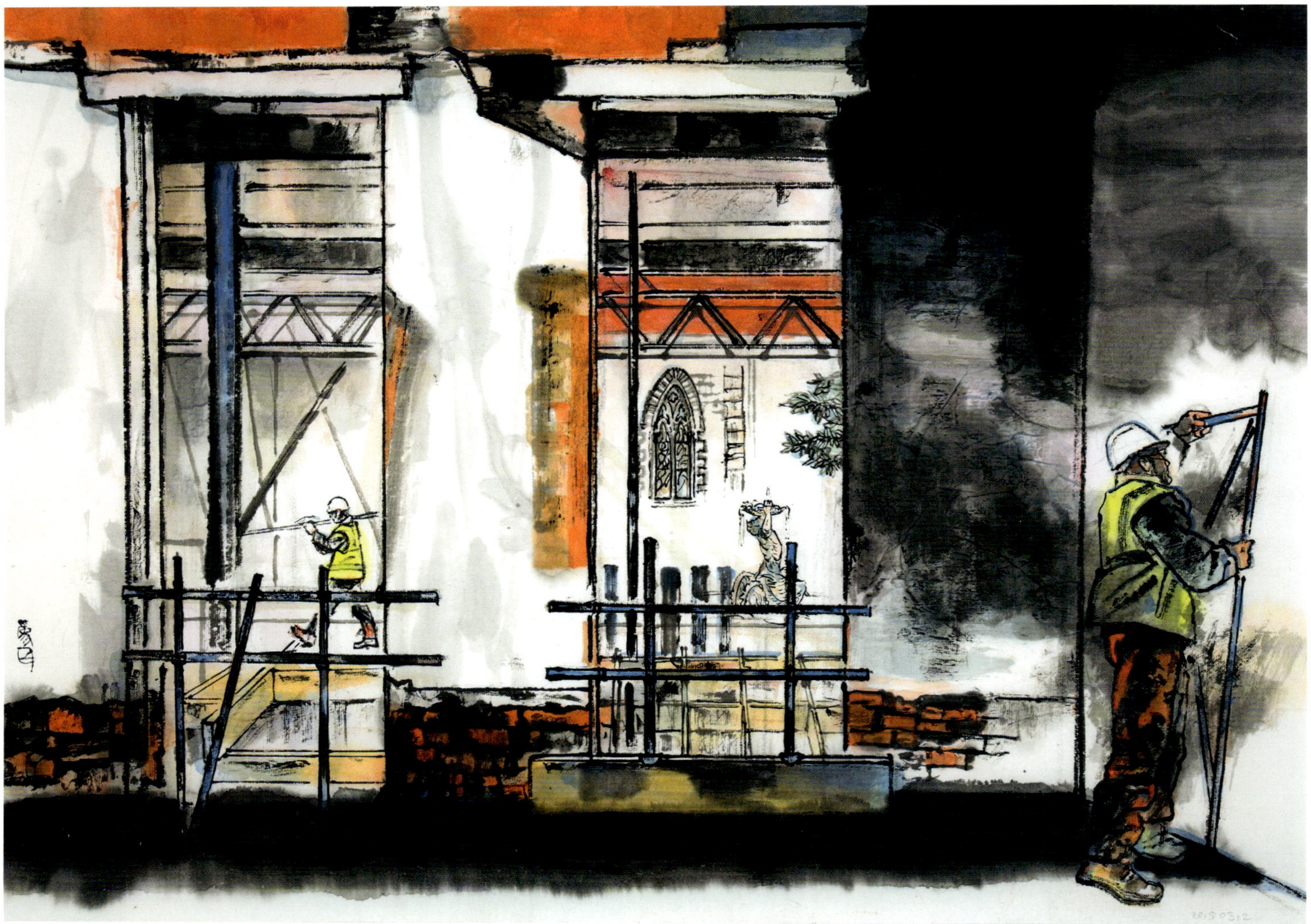

CAT.179
St Luke's chapel framed. 12 March 2015. Brush, ink and watercolour on *xuan* paper. Paper size: 43.5 × 59.5 cm

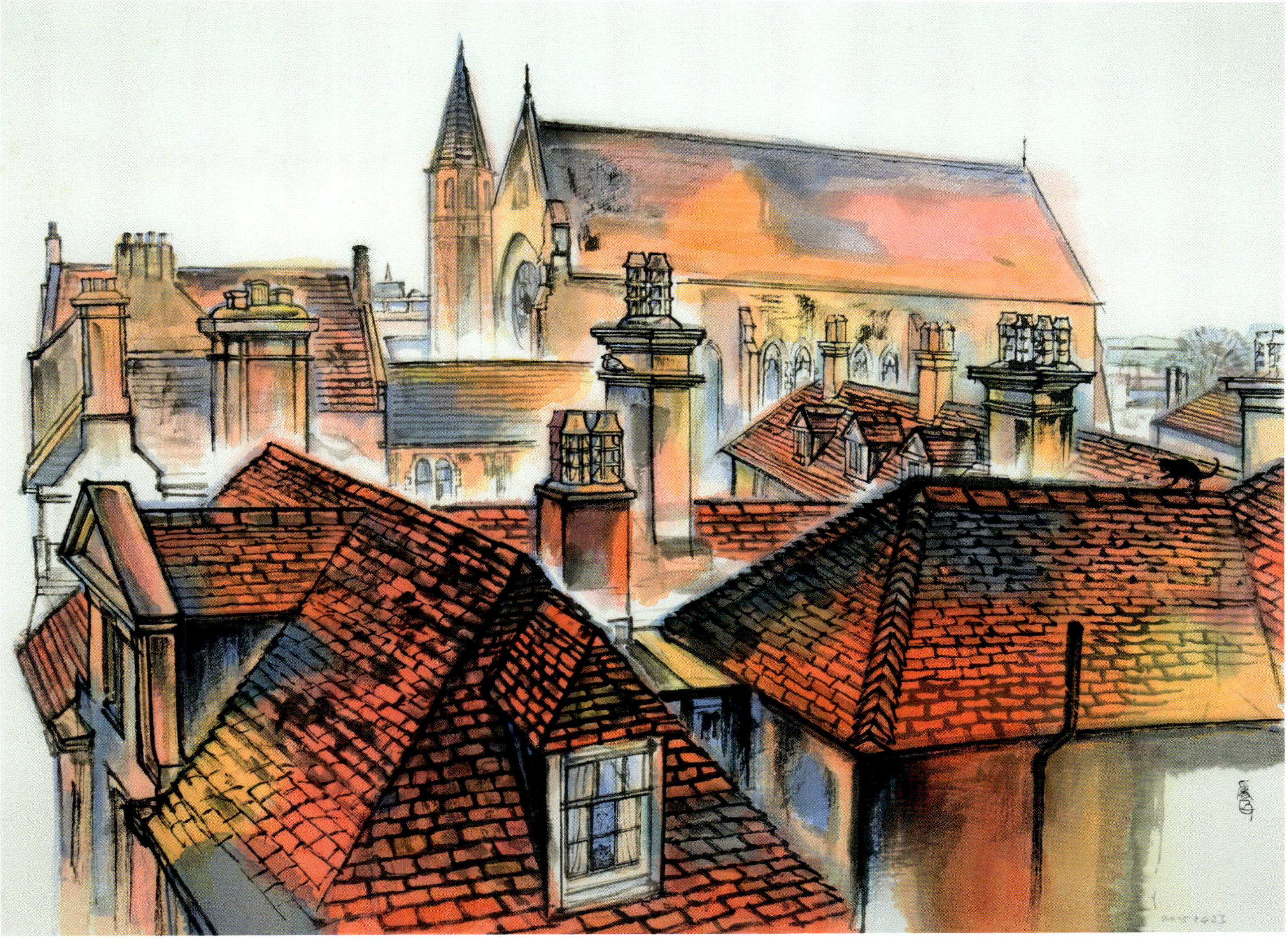

CAT.180
Roofs – Somerville College from the Outpatients building. 23 April 2015. Brush, ink, watercolour and collage on *xuan* paper. Paper size: 43.5 × 59.5 cm

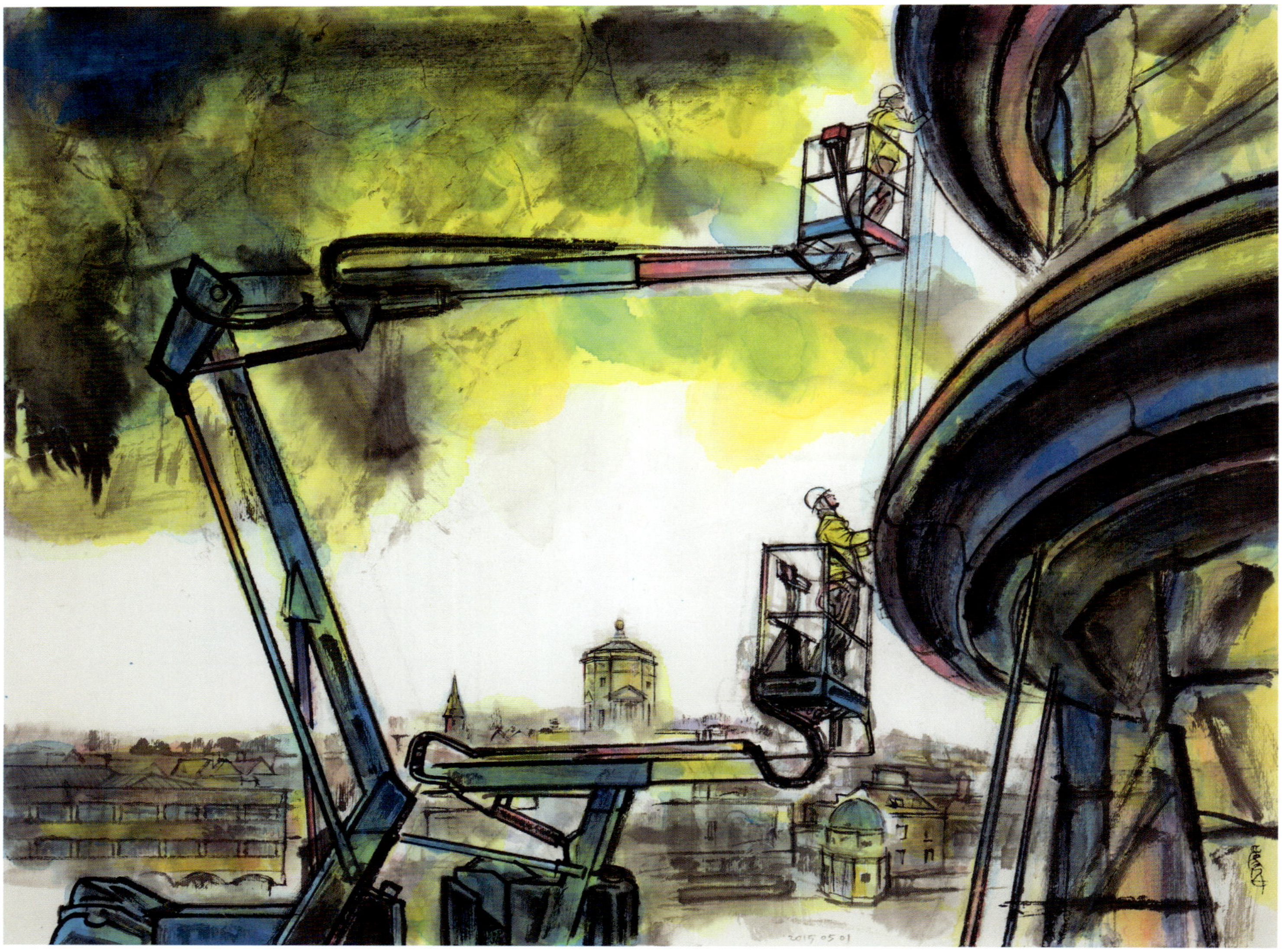

CAT.181
Aiming high – Blavatnik School of Government. 1 May 2015.Brush, ink and watercolour on *xuan* paper. Paper size: 43.5 × 59.5 cm

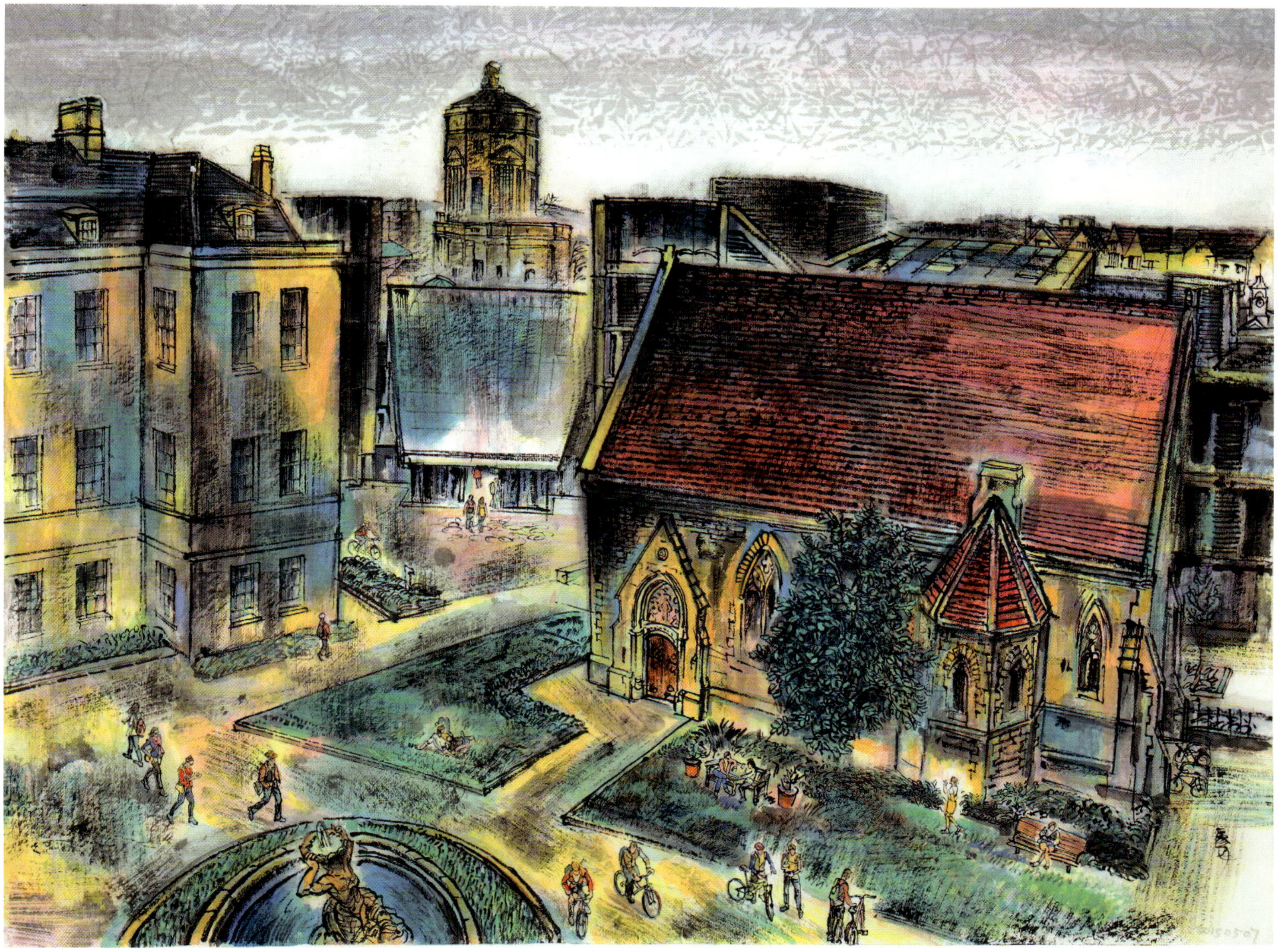

CAT.182
Transformation – Radcliffe Observatory Quarter. 7 May 2015. Brush, ink and watercolour on *xuan* paper. Paper size: 43.5 × 59.5 cm

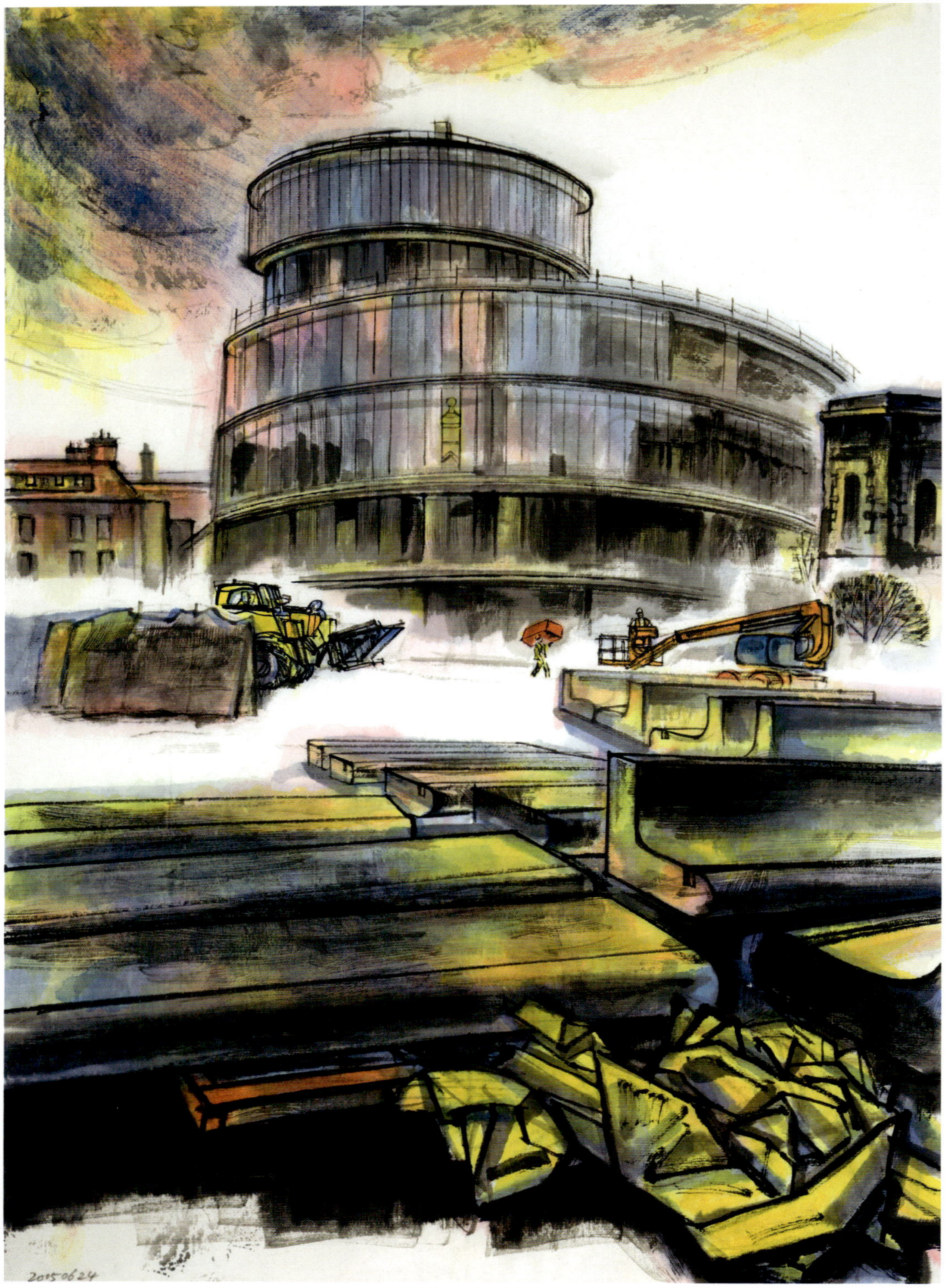

CAT.183
Circles in the sky – Blavatnik School of Government.
24 June 2015. Brush, ink and watercolour on *xuan* paper. Paper size: 59.5 × 43.5 cm

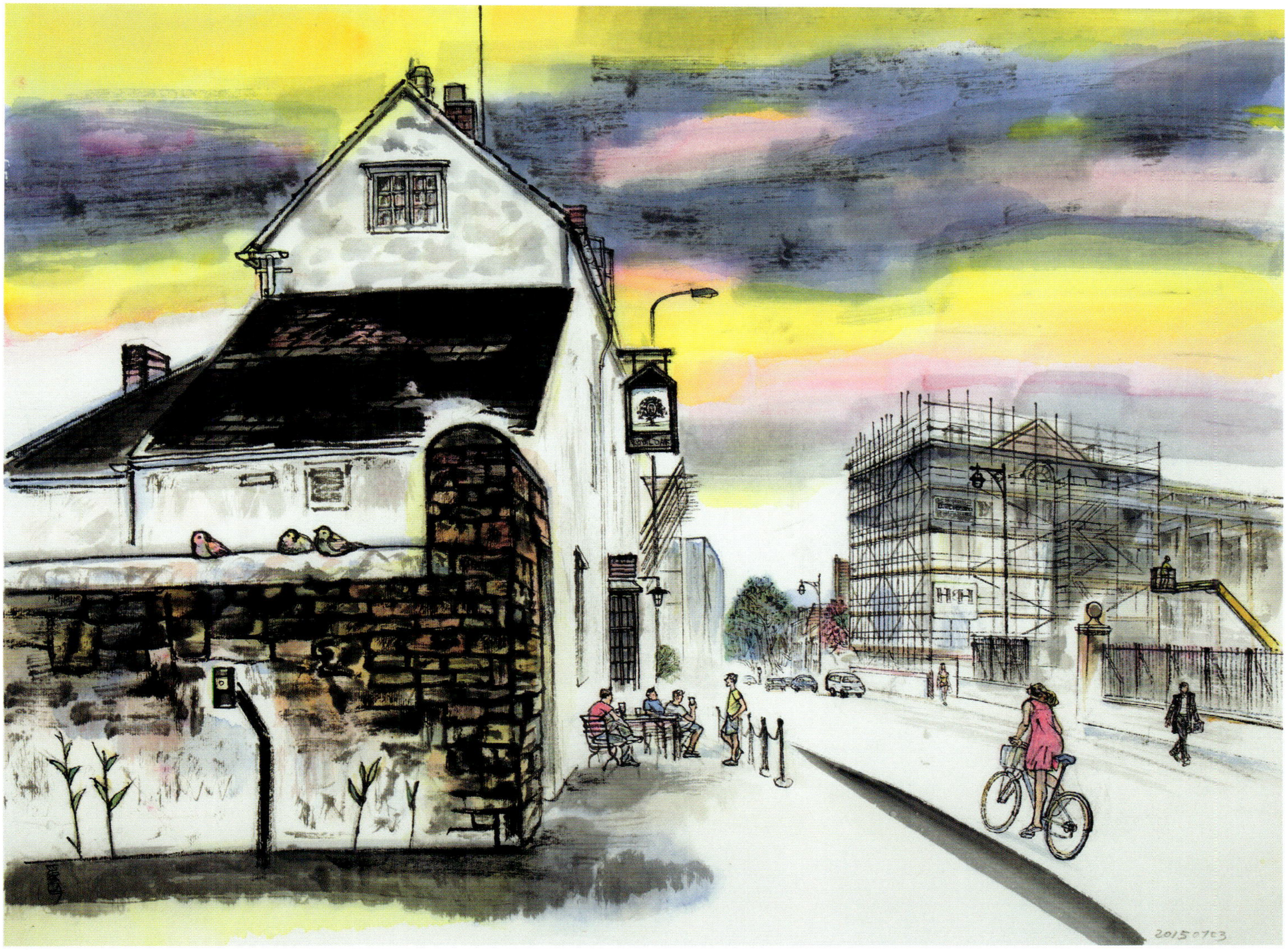

CAT.184
A beautiful end to a beautiful day – Refurbishment of the Outpatients building.
3 July 2015. Brush, ink and watercolour on *xuan* paper. Paper size: 43.5 × 59.5 cm

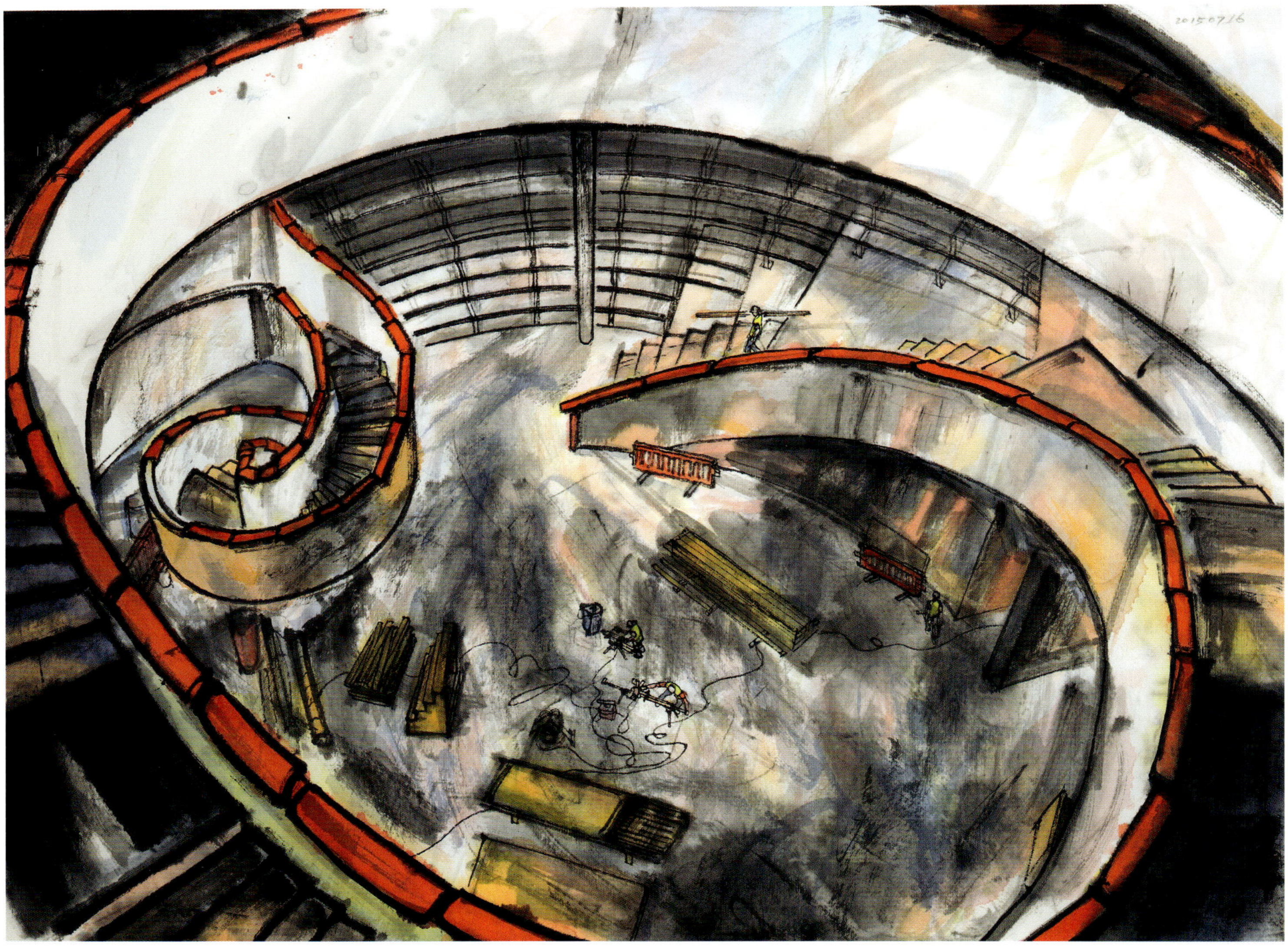

CAT.185
Upward spiral – Blavatnik School of Government building. 16 July 2015. Brush, ink and watercolour on *xuan* paper. Paper size: 43.5 × 59.5 cm

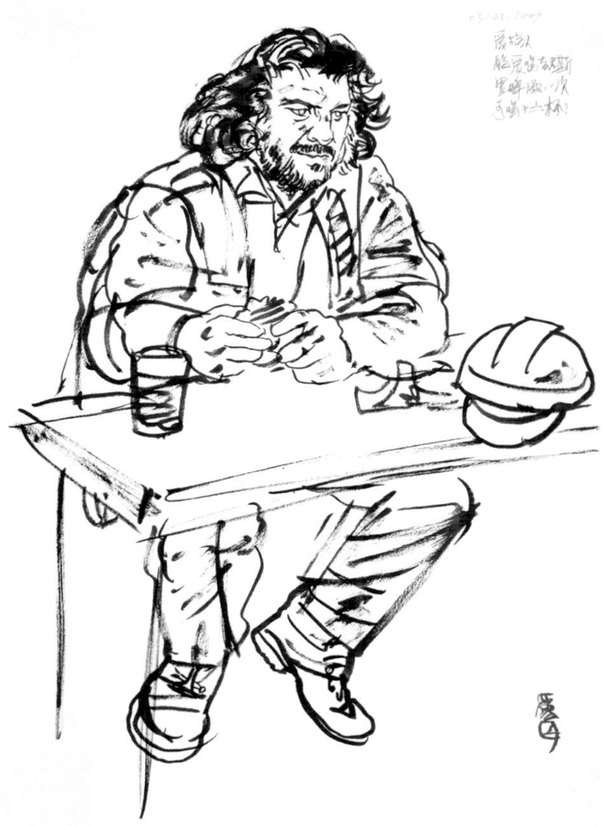

CAT.186 (left)
Anon. *Construction worker.* 3 March 2009. Brush and ink on cartridge paper. Paper size: 42 × 27.9 cm

CAT.187 (bottom right)
Parker *Construction worker.* 18 March 2009. Brush and ink on cartridge paper. Paper size: 59.4 × 42 cm

CAT.188 (bottom left)
Anon. *Construction worker.* March 2009. Brush and ink on cartridge paper. Paper size: 59.4 × 42 cm

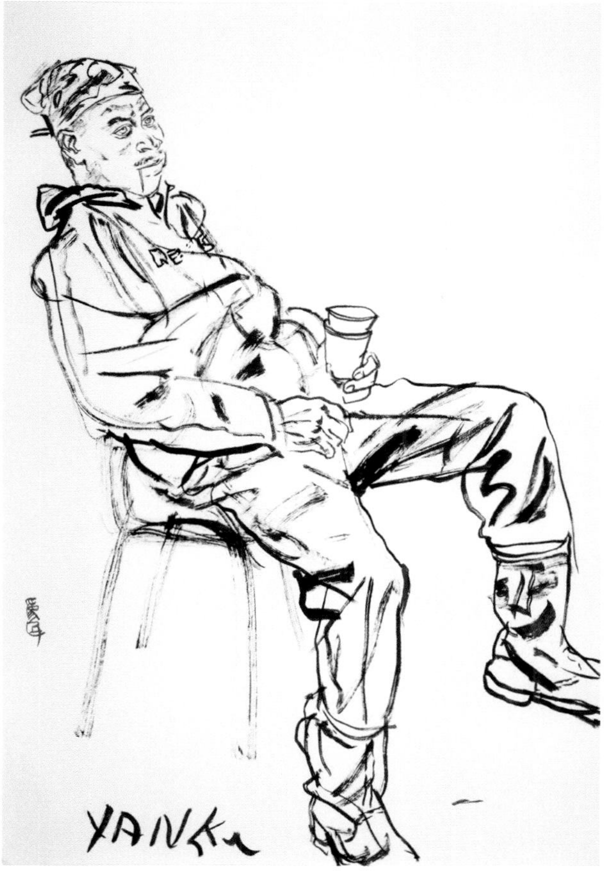

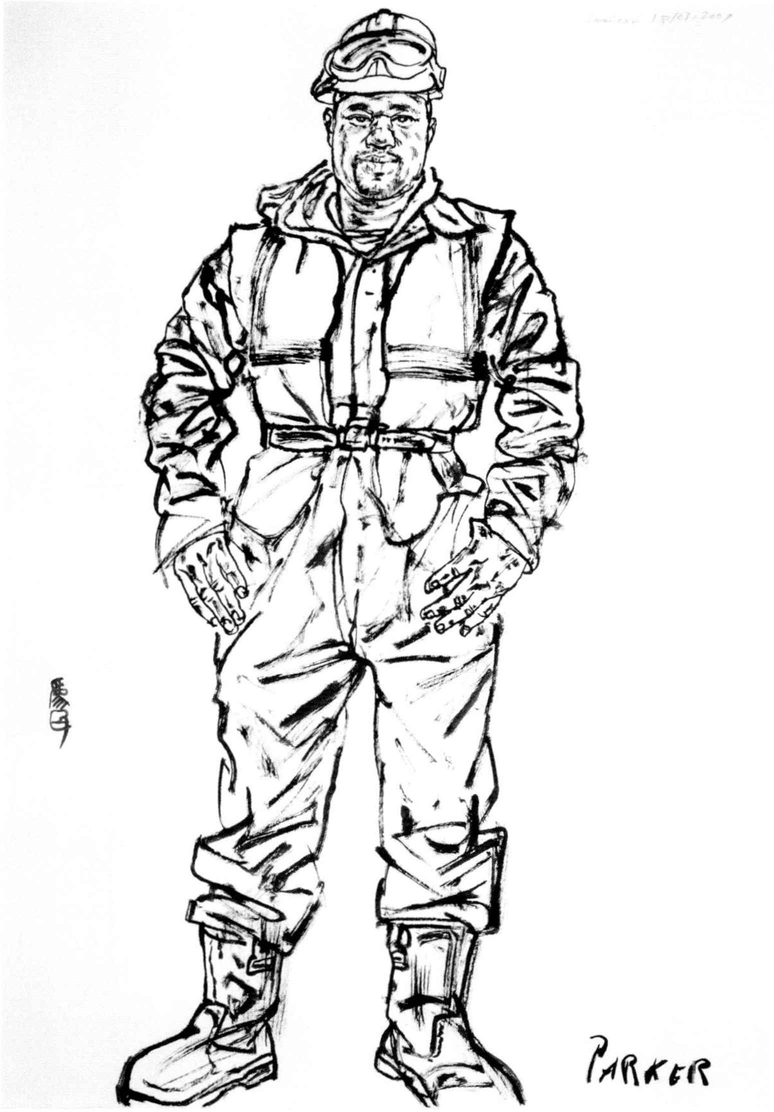

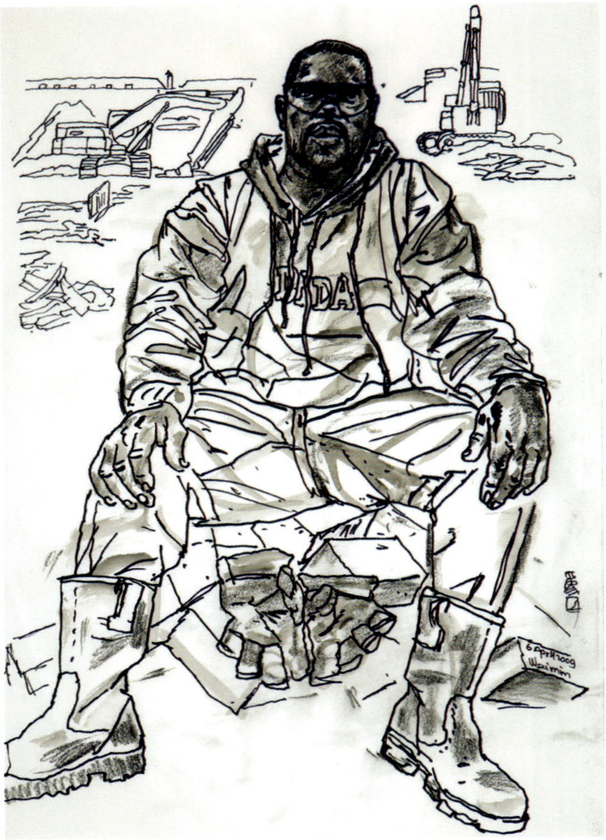

CAT.189 (left)
Anon. *Construction worker*
6 April 2009.
Felt-tip pen, charcoal and ink on cartridge paper. Paper size: 42 × 27.9 cm

CAT.190 (bottom right)
Anon. *Construction worker*
21 April 2009. Brush and ink on cartridge paper. Paper size: 59.4 × 42 cm

CAT.191 (bottom left)
Joe Excavator driver
21 August 2010.
Brush, ink and watercolour on album leaves. Paper size: 50 × 35cm

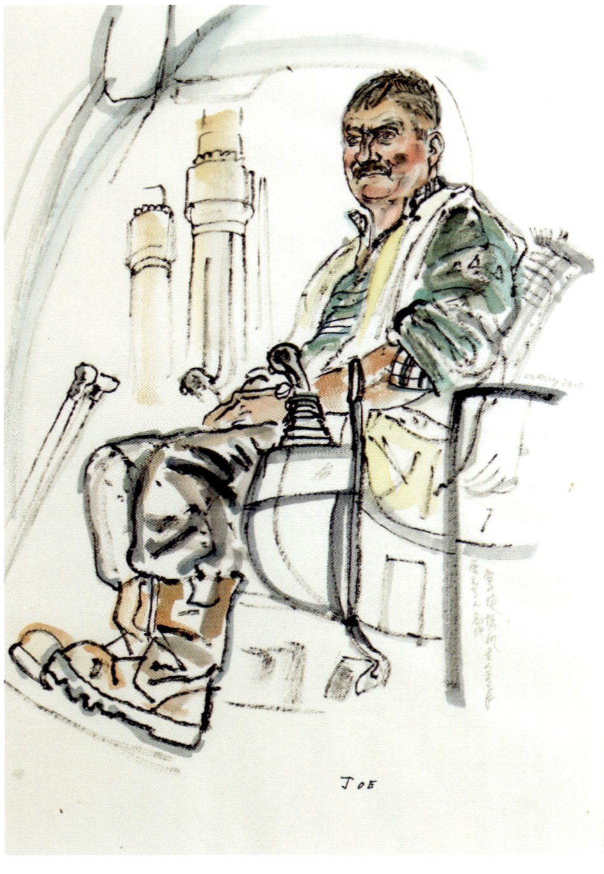

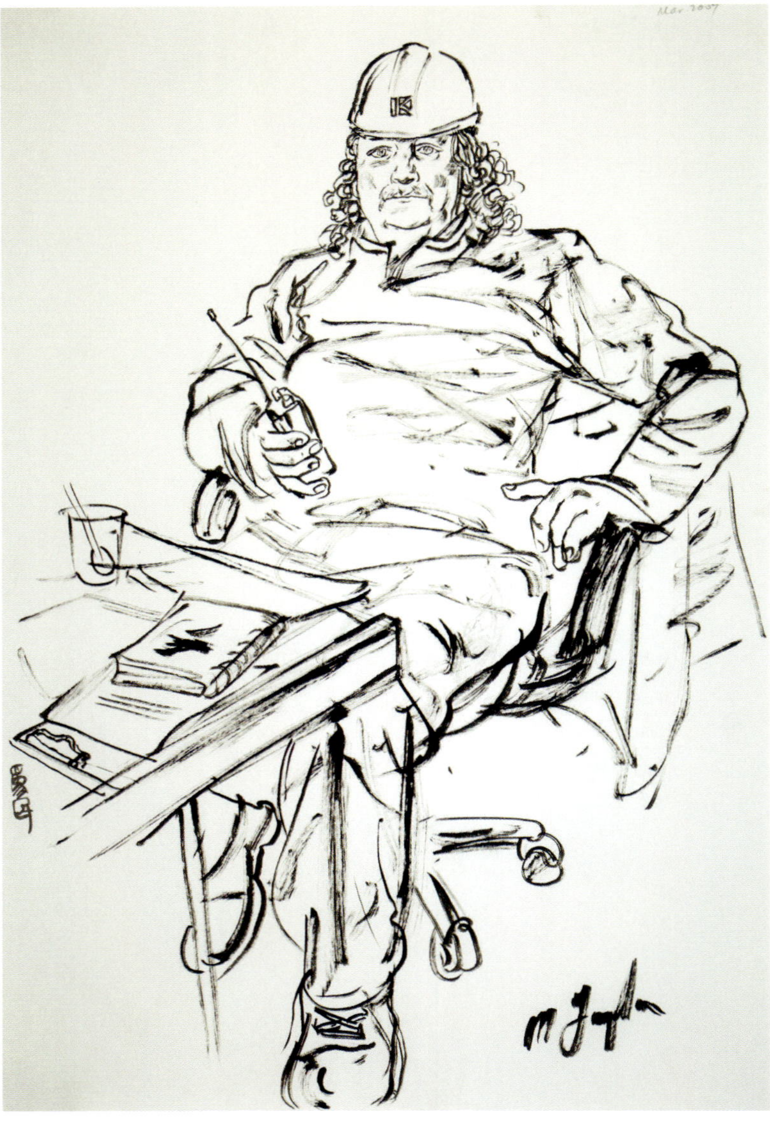

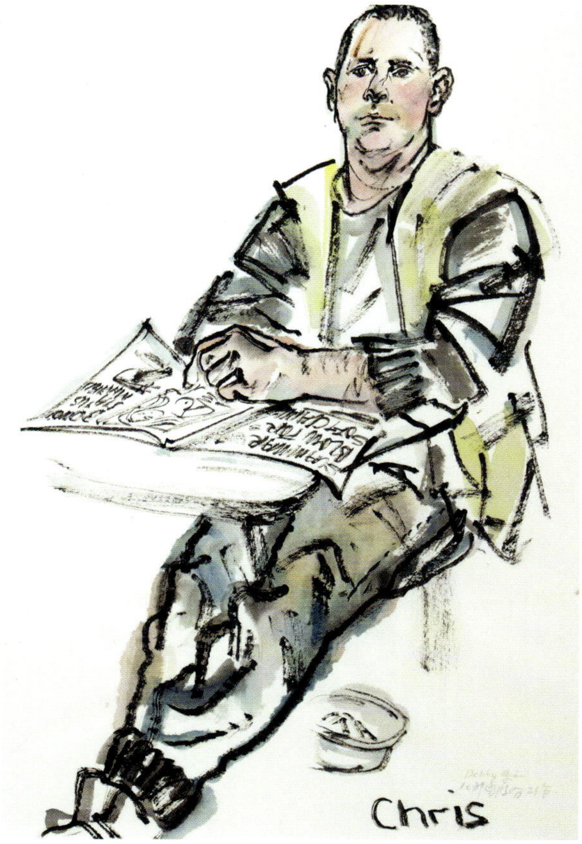

CAT.192 (left)
Chris Construction worker. 17 January 2011. Brush, ink and watercolour on album leaves. Paper size: 50 × 35cm

CAT.193 (bottom right)
Jason Whitelock *Expanded ground worker*
31 August 2011. Brush and ink on sketchbook made of cartridge paper. Paper size: 42 × 27.9 cm

CAT.194 (bottom left)
Gary Brown *Construction worker*
1 September 2009. Brush and ink on sketchbook made of cartridge paper. Paper size: 59.4 × 42 cm

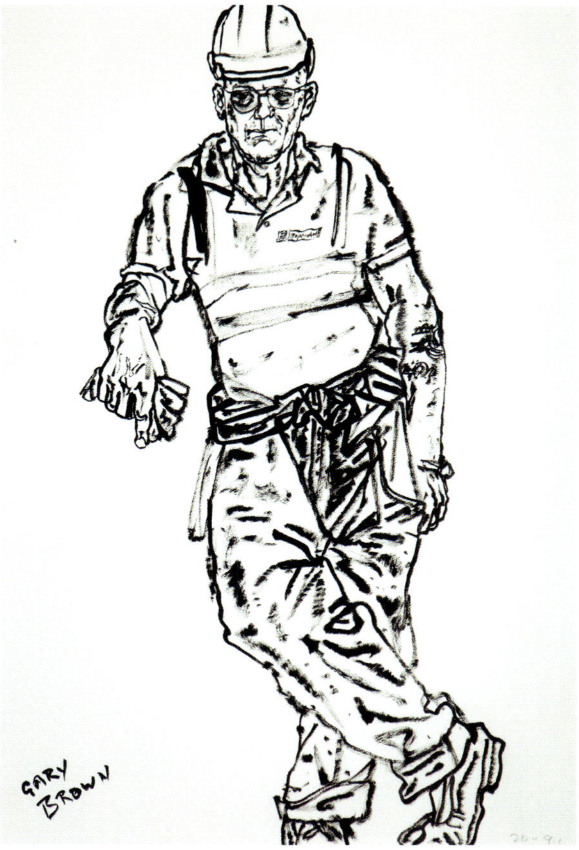

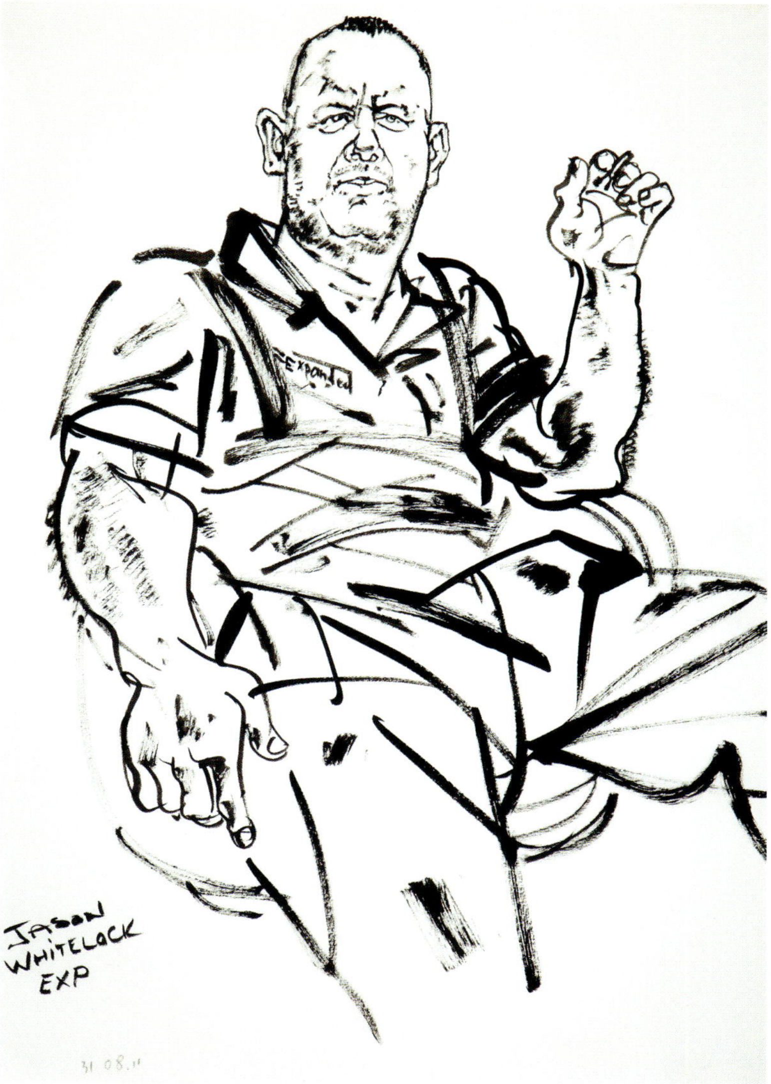

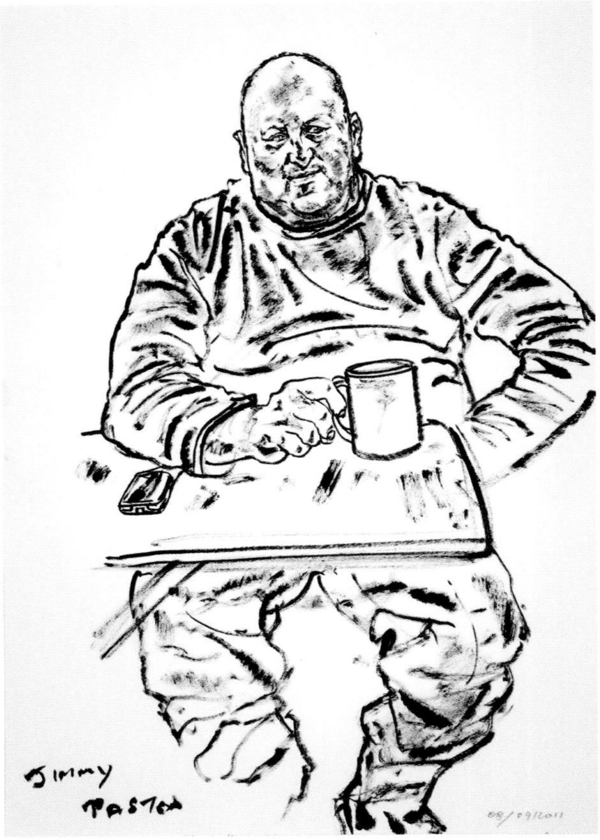

CAT.195 (left)
Jimmy Paston *Construction worker.*
8 September 2011. Brush and ink on sketchbook made of cartridge paper. Paper size: 42 × 27.9 cm

CAT.196 (bottom right)
Joe Odoi-Smith *Carpenter.*
11 November 2011. Brush and ink on *xuan* paper. Paper size: 59.5 × 43.5 cm

CAT.197 (bottom left)
Kevin Denley *Expanded ground worker.*
23 November 2011. Brush and ink on *xuan* paper. Paper size: 59.5 × 43.5 cm

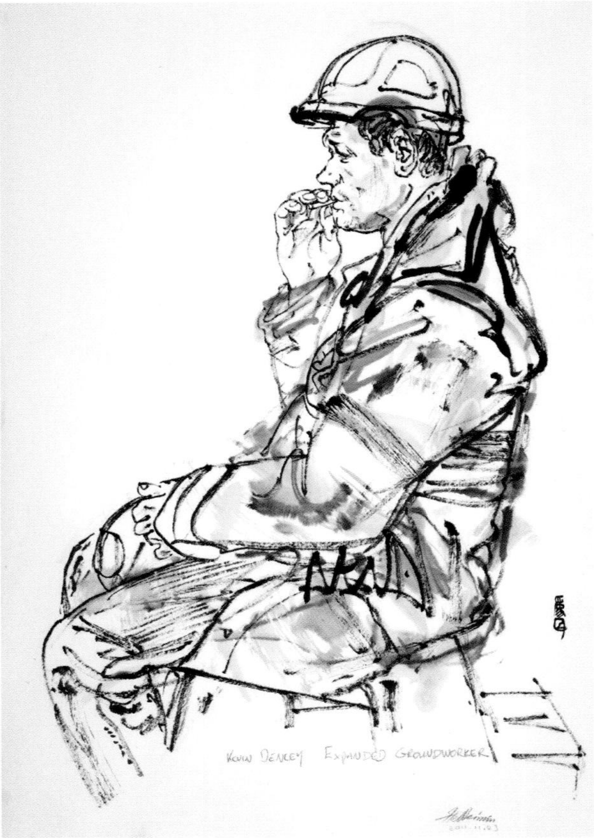

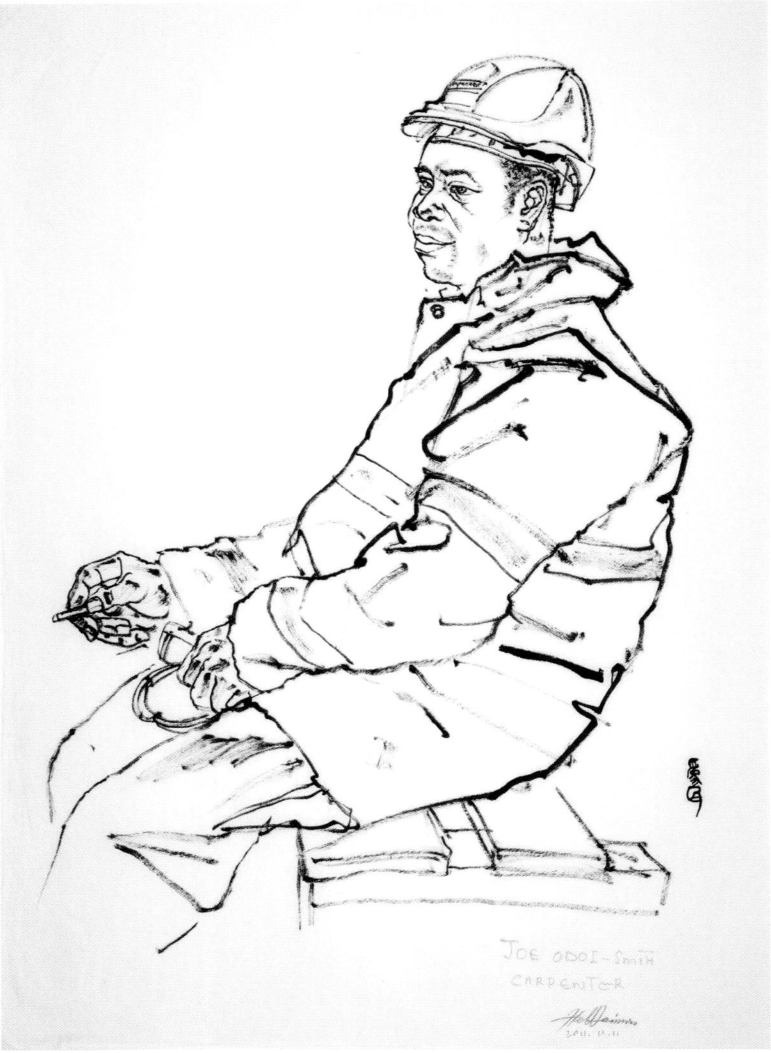

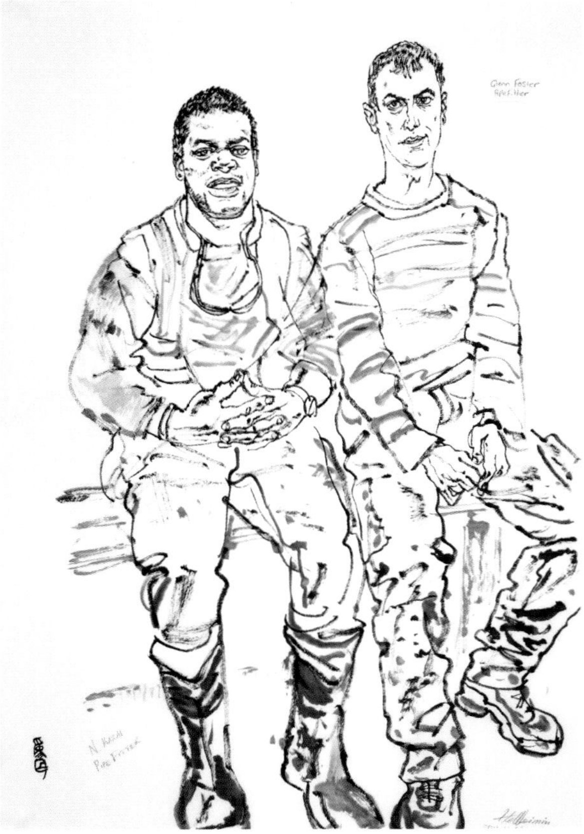

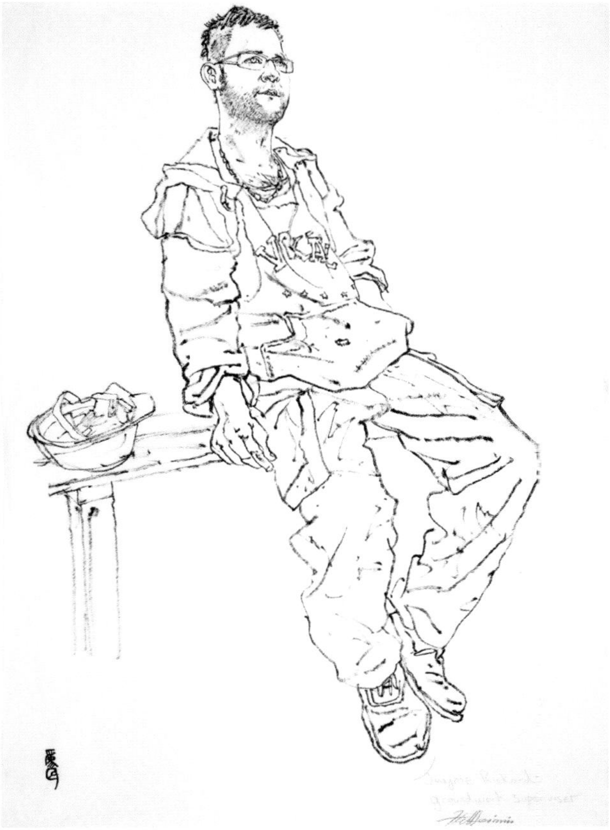

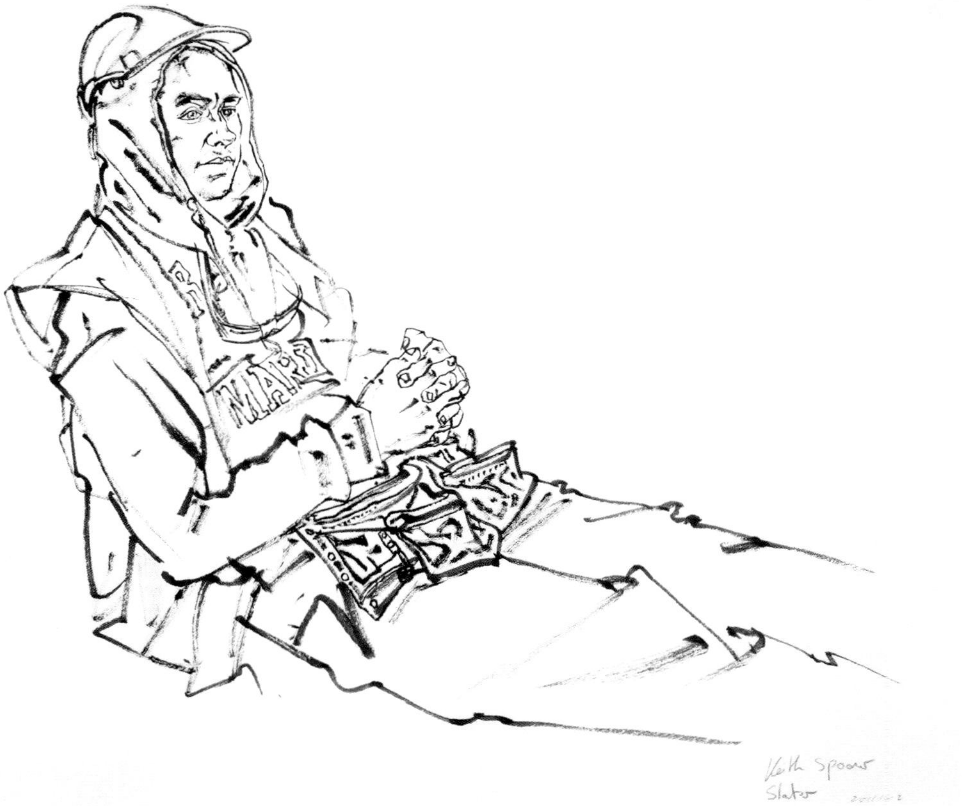

CAT.198 (top left)
N. Kazai and **Glenn Foster** *Pipe fitters*. 23 November 2011. Brush and ink on *xuan* paper. Paper size: 59.5 × 43.5 cm

CAT.199 (top right)
Jayme Rickard *Groundwork supervisor*. 23 November 2011. Brush and ink on *xuan* paper. Paper size: 59.5 × 43.5 cm

CAT.200 (right)
Keith Spoons *Slater*. 2 December 2011. Brush and ink on *xuan* paper. Paper size: 43.5 × 59.5 cm

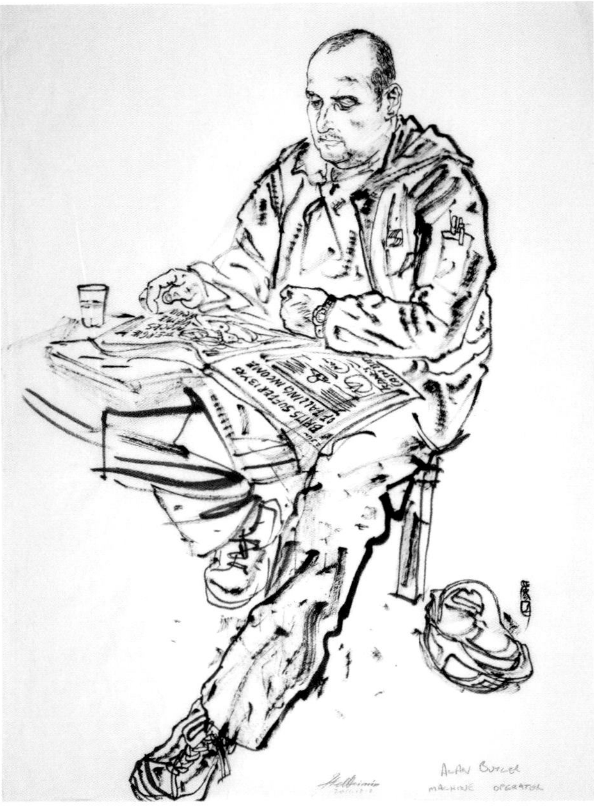

CAT.201 (left)
Alan Butler *Machine operator*. 2 December 2011. Brush and ink on *xuan* paper. Paper size: 59.5 × 43.5 cm

CAT.202 (bottom right)
R. Farfan *Gate man*. 8 December 2011. Brush and ink on *xuan* paper. Paper size: 59.5 × 43.5 cm

CAT.203 (bottom left)
D. Brock *Carpenter*. 8 December 2011. Brush and ink on *xuan* paper. Paper size: 59.5 × 43.5 cm

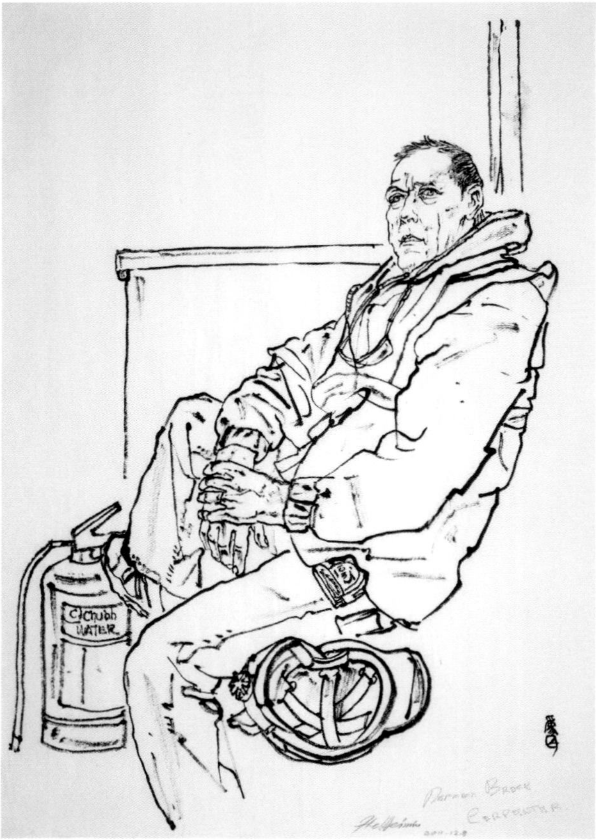

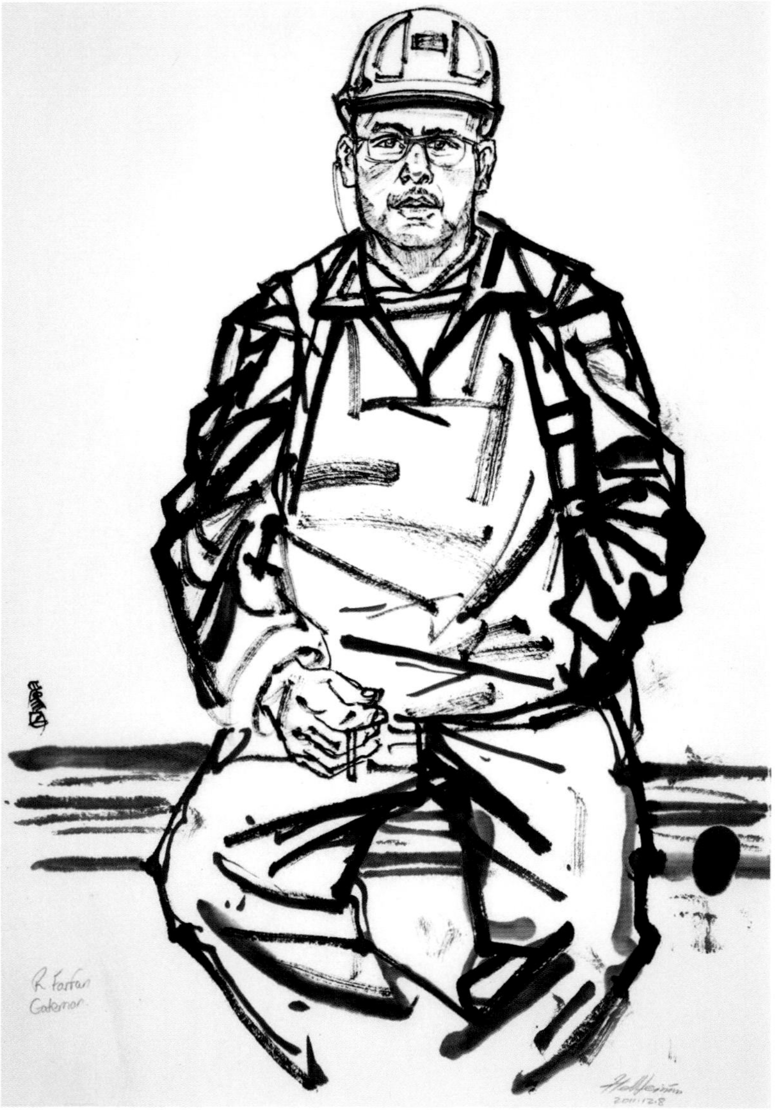

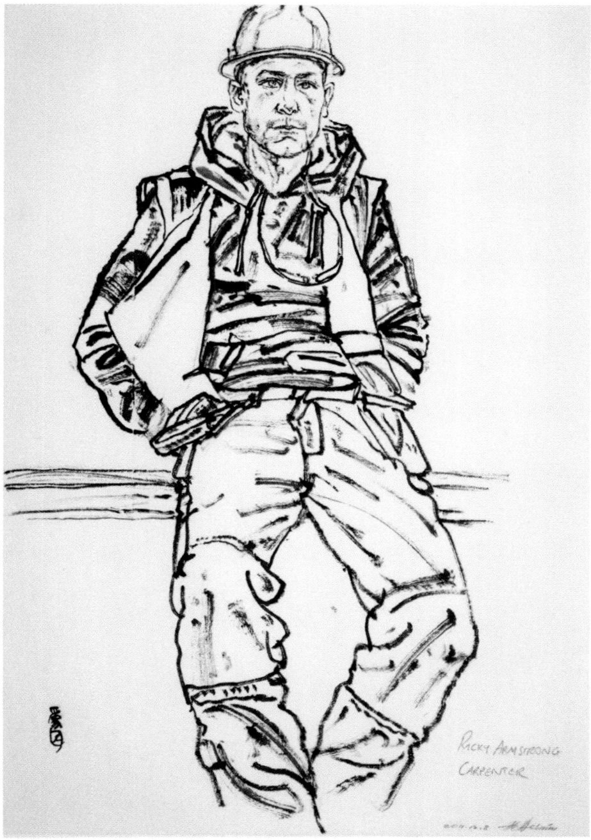

CAT.204 (left)
Ricky Armstrong *Carpenter*.
8 December 2011. Brush and ink on
xuan paper. Paper size: 59.5 × 43.5 cm

CAT.205 (bottom right)
M. Scarry *Bricklayer*. 8 December
2011. Brush and ink on *xuan* paper.
Paper size: 59.5 × 43.5 cm

CAT.206 (bottom left)
Mangawa Itimu *Steel fixer*.
26 January 2012. Brush and ink on
xuan paper. Paper size: 59.5 × 43.5 cm

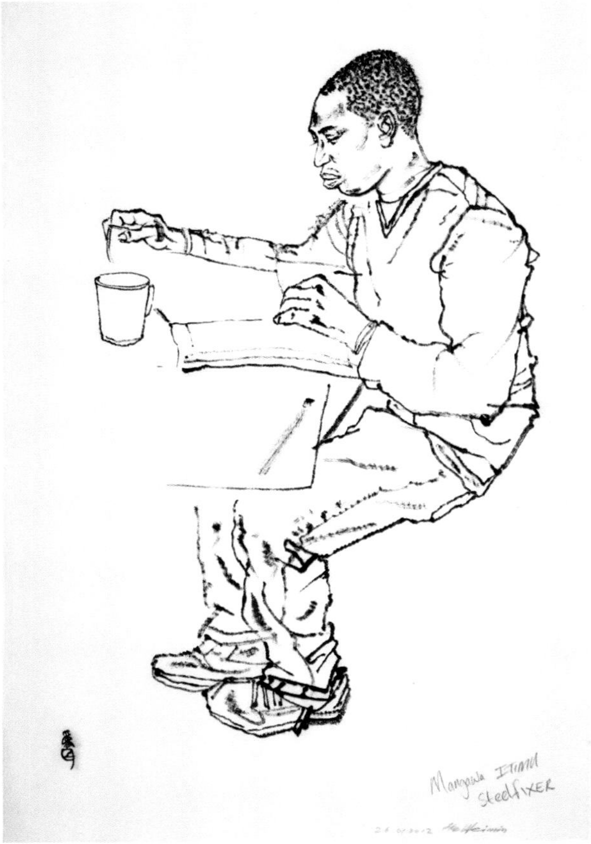

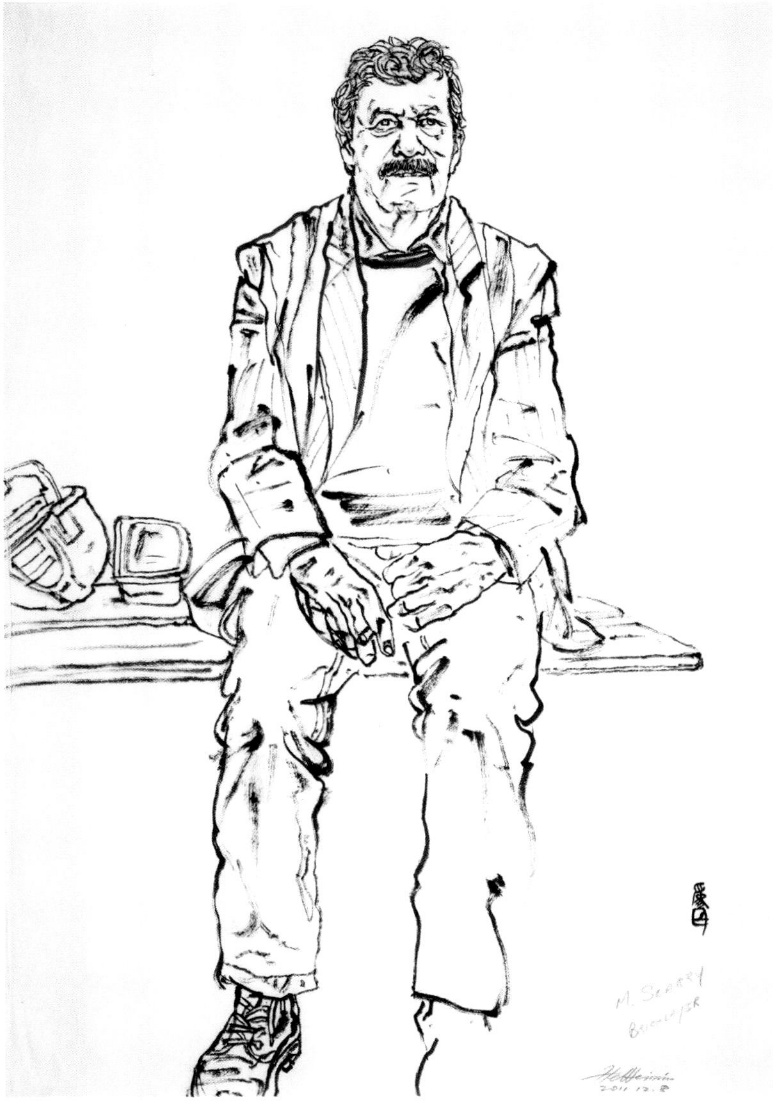

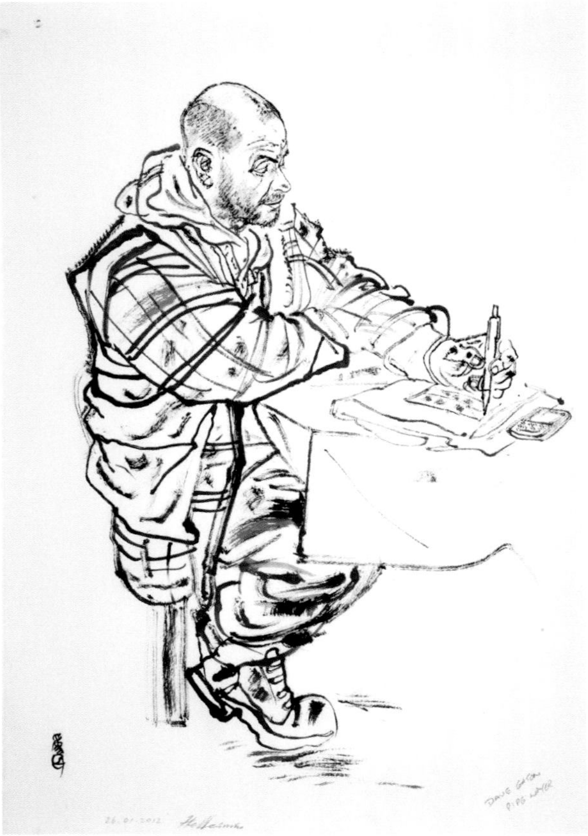

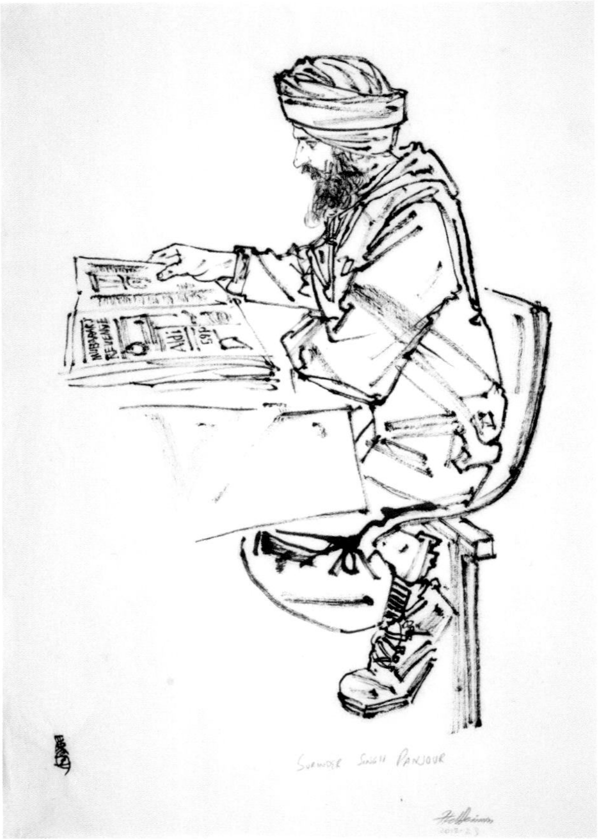

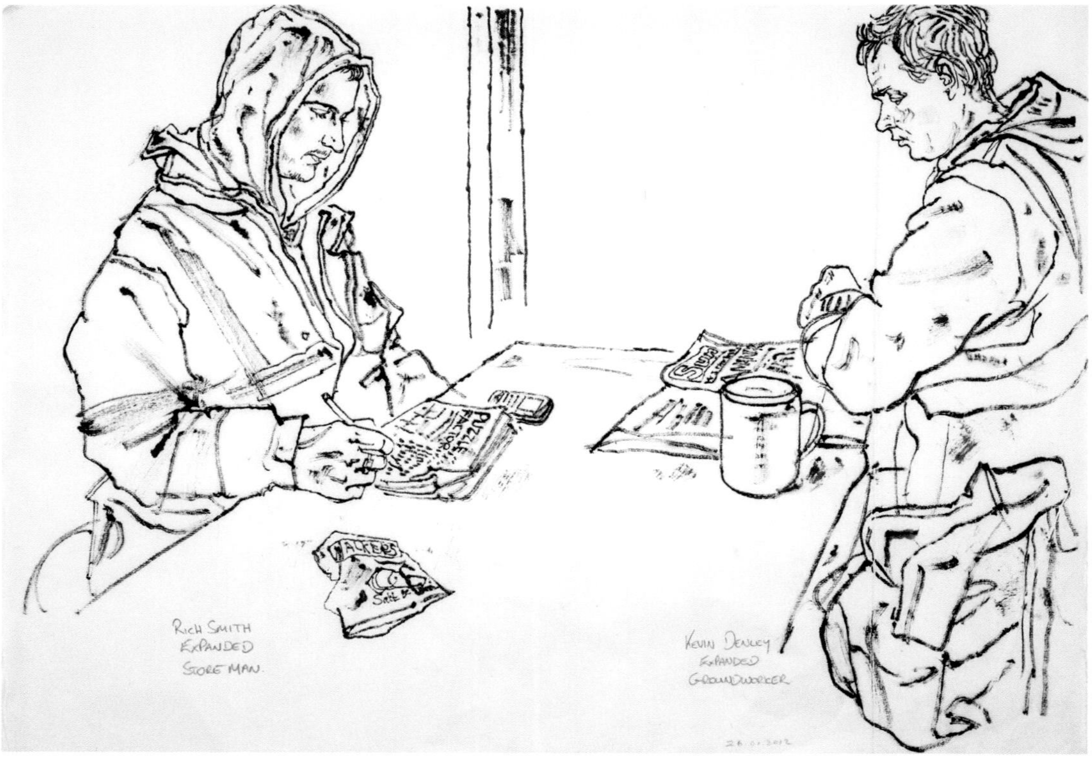

CAT.207 (top left)
Dave *Pipe layer*. 26 January 2012. Brush and ink on *xuan* paper. Paper size: 59.5 × 43.5 cm

CAT.208 (left)
Rich Smith *Expanded storeman* and **Kevin Denley** *Expanded ground worker*. 26 January 2012. Brush and ink on *xuan* paper. Paper size: 43.5 × 59.5 cm

CAT.209 (top right)
Surinder Singh Panjour *Construction worker*. 3 February 2012. Brush and ink on *xuan* paper. Paper size: 59.5 × 43.5 cm

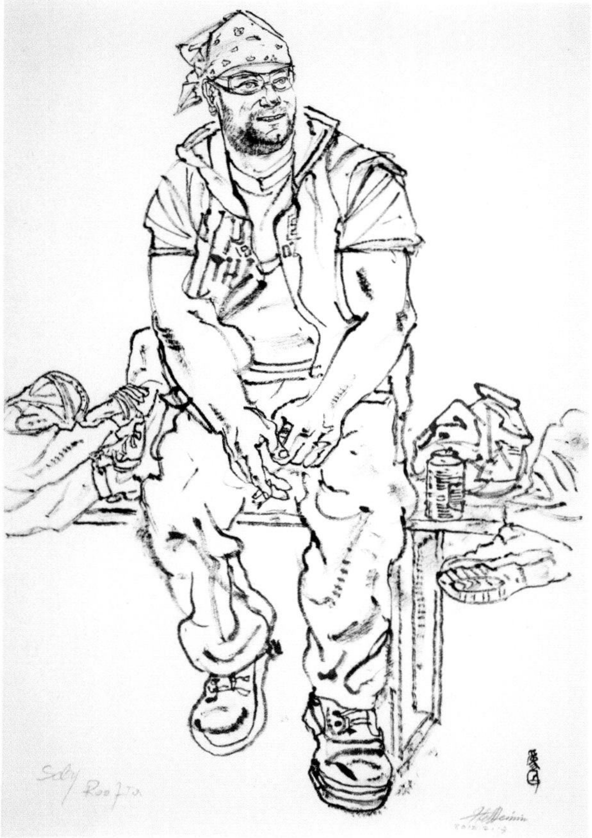

CAT.210 (left)
Anon. *Roofer*. 12 February 2012. Brush and ink on *xuan* paper. Paper size: 59.5 × 43.5 cm

CAT.211 (bottom right)
Rob *Stone mason*. 14 February 2012. Brush and ink on *xuan* paper. Paper size: 59.5 × 43.5 cm

CAT.212 (bottom left)
Richie More *Carpenter*. 16 February 2012. Brush and ink on *xuan* paper. Paper size: 59.5 × 43.5 cm

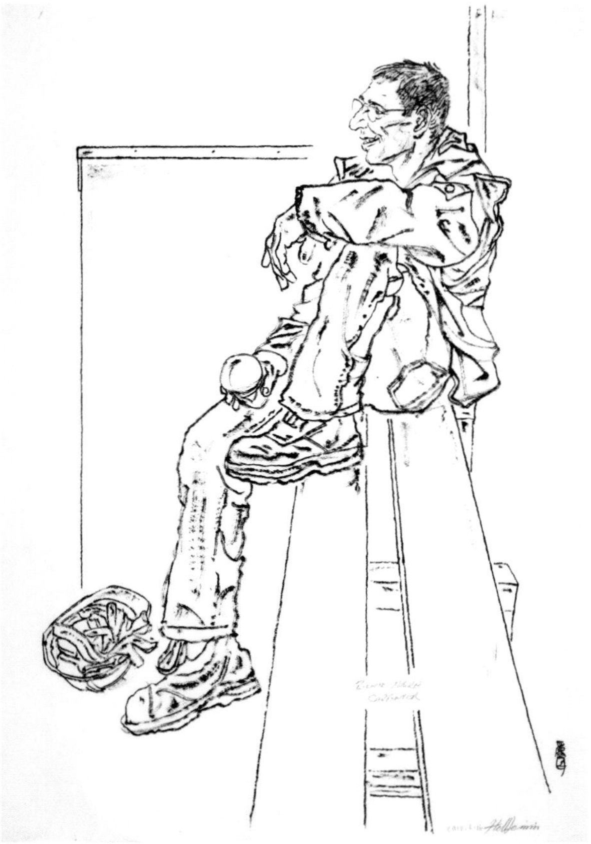

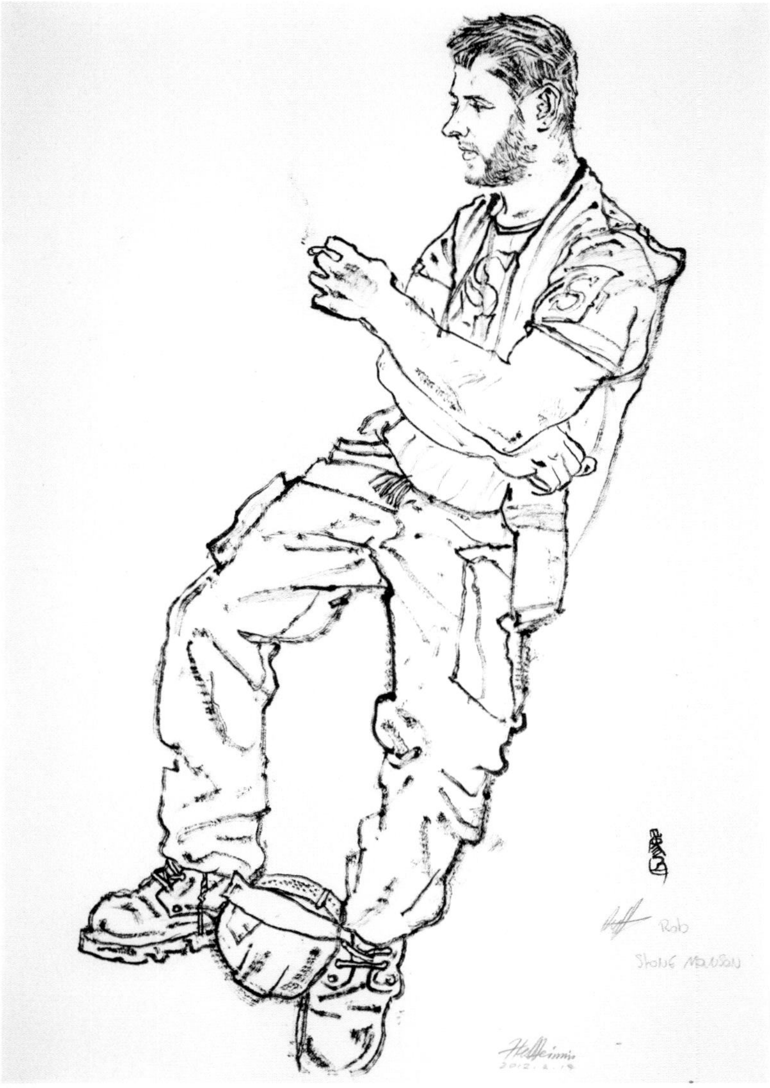

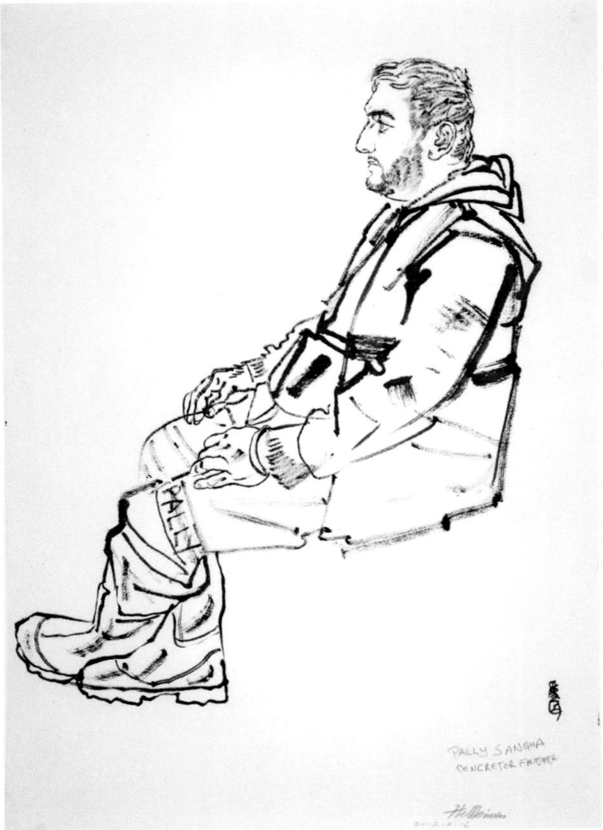

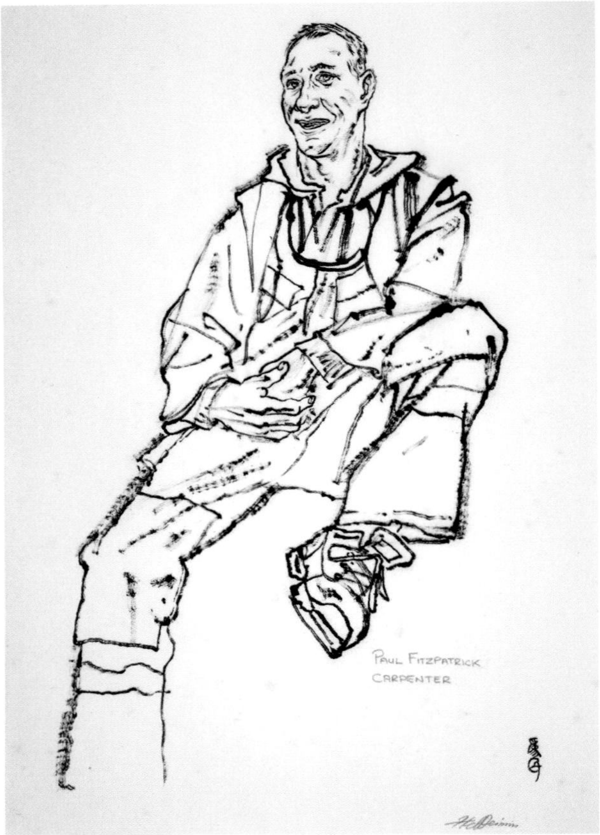

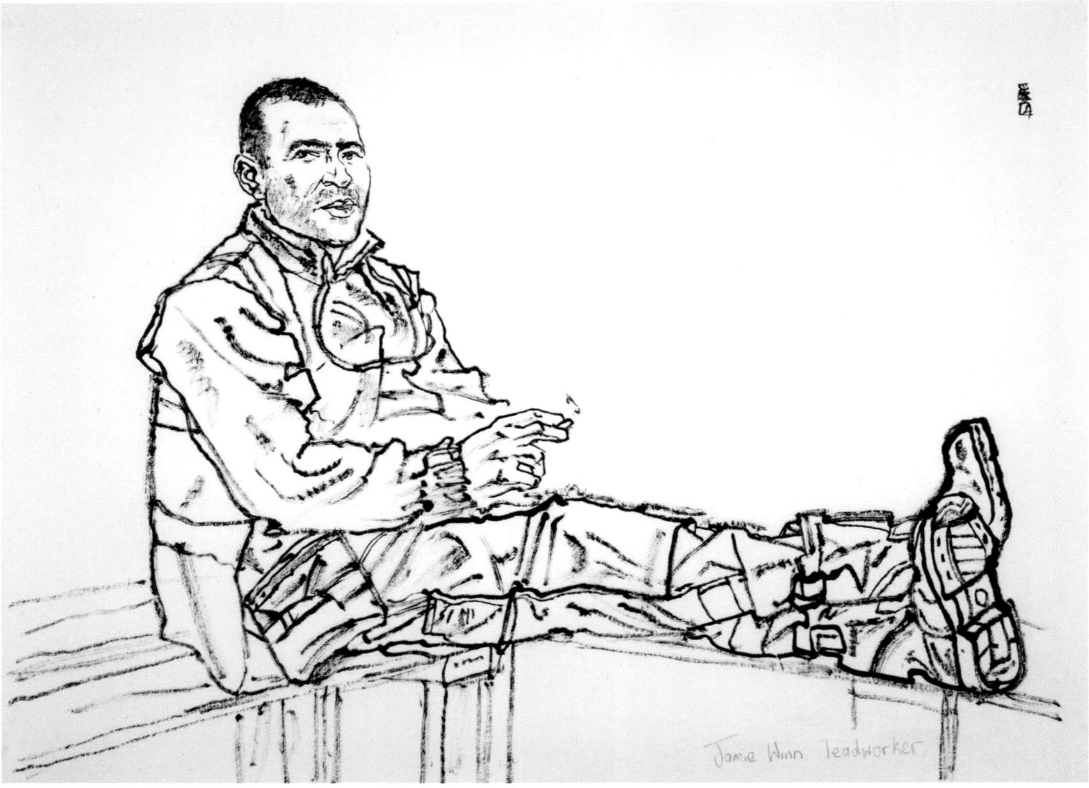

CAT.213 (top left)
Pally Sangha *Concrete finisher.*
16 February 2012. Brush and ink on *xuan* paper. Paper size: 59.5 × 43.5 cm

CAT.214 (left)
Jamie Winn *Lead worker.*
16 February 2012. Brush and ink on *xuan* paper. Paper size: 43.5 × 59.5 cm

CAT.215 (top right)
Paul Fitzpatrick *Carpenter.*
16 February 2012. Brush and ink on *xuan* paper. Paper size: 59.5 × 43.5 cm

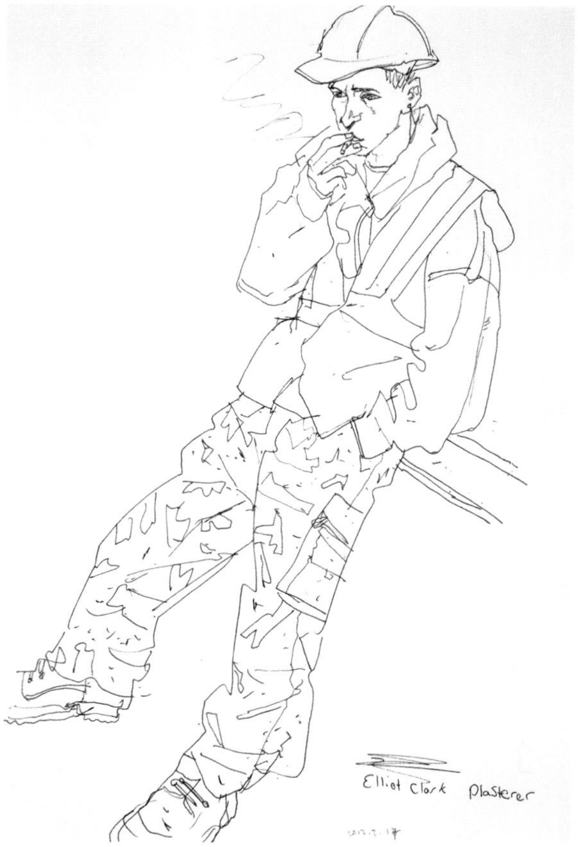

CAT.216 (left)
Elliot Clark *Plasterer*.
17 February 2012. Pen and ink on sketchbook made of cartridge paper. Paper size: 42 × 27.9 cm

CAT.217 (bottom right)
Peter Devenport *Leak sealer*
17 February 2012. Brush and ink on *xuan* paper. Paper size: 59.5 × 43.5 cm

CAT.218 (bottom left)
Christopher Burniston
Bricklayer. 23 February 2012. Brush and ink on *xuan* paper. Paper size: 59.5 × 43.5 cm

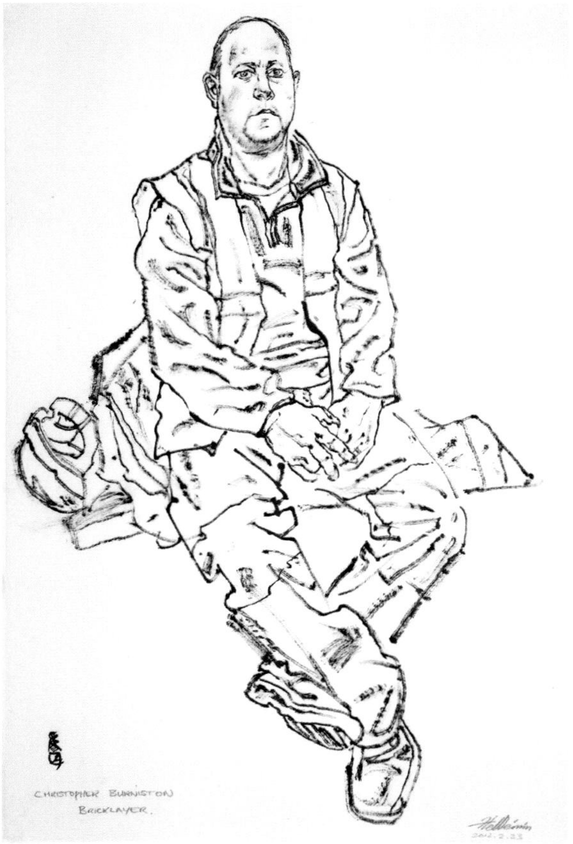

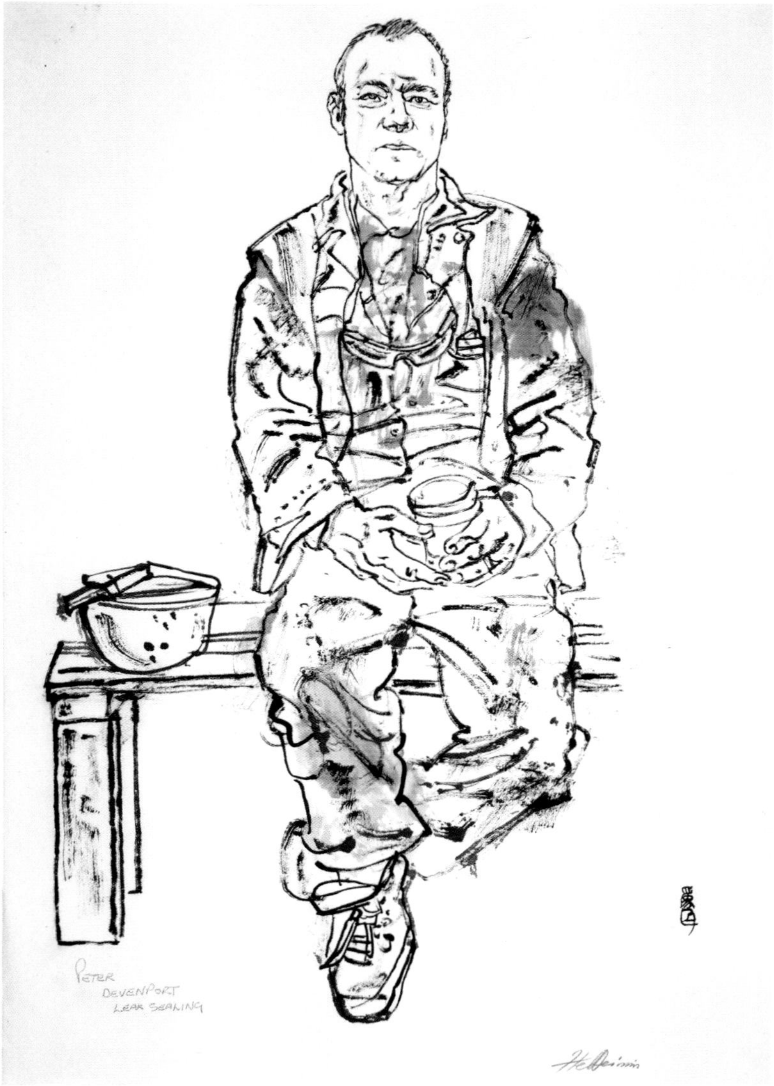

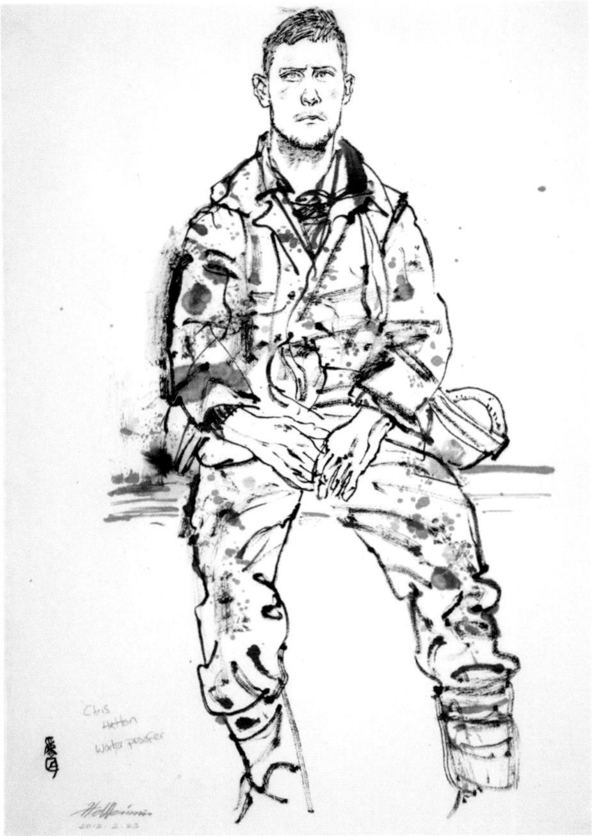

CAT.219 (left)
Chris Hatton *Water proofer*.
23 February 2012. Brush and ink on
xuan paper. Paper size: 59.5 × 43.5 cm

CAT.220 (bottom right)
David Pilcher *Carpenter*. 23 February
2012. Brush and ink on *xuan* paper.
Paper size: 59.5 × 43.5 cm

CAT.221 (bottom left)
Chippy Phil Richards *Construction
worker*. 8 March 2012. Brush and ink on
xuan paper. Paper size: 59.5 × 43.5 cm

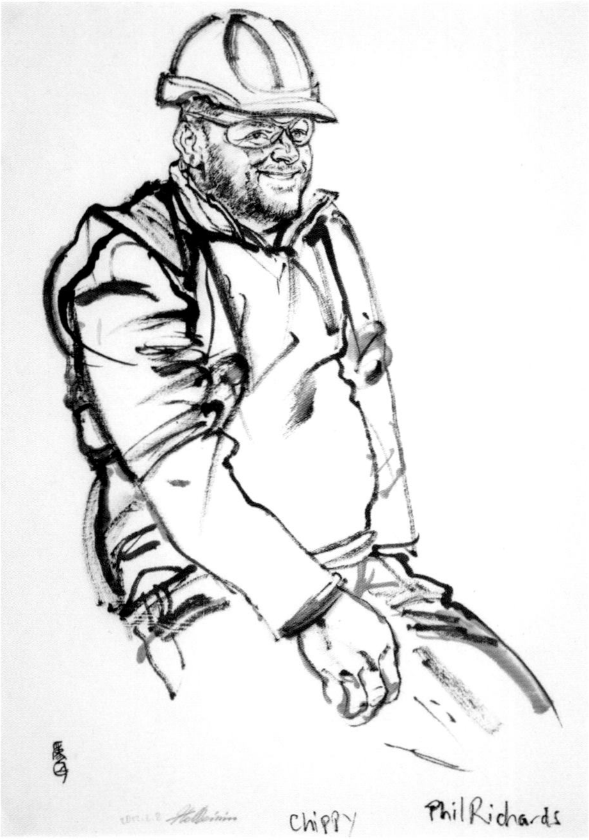

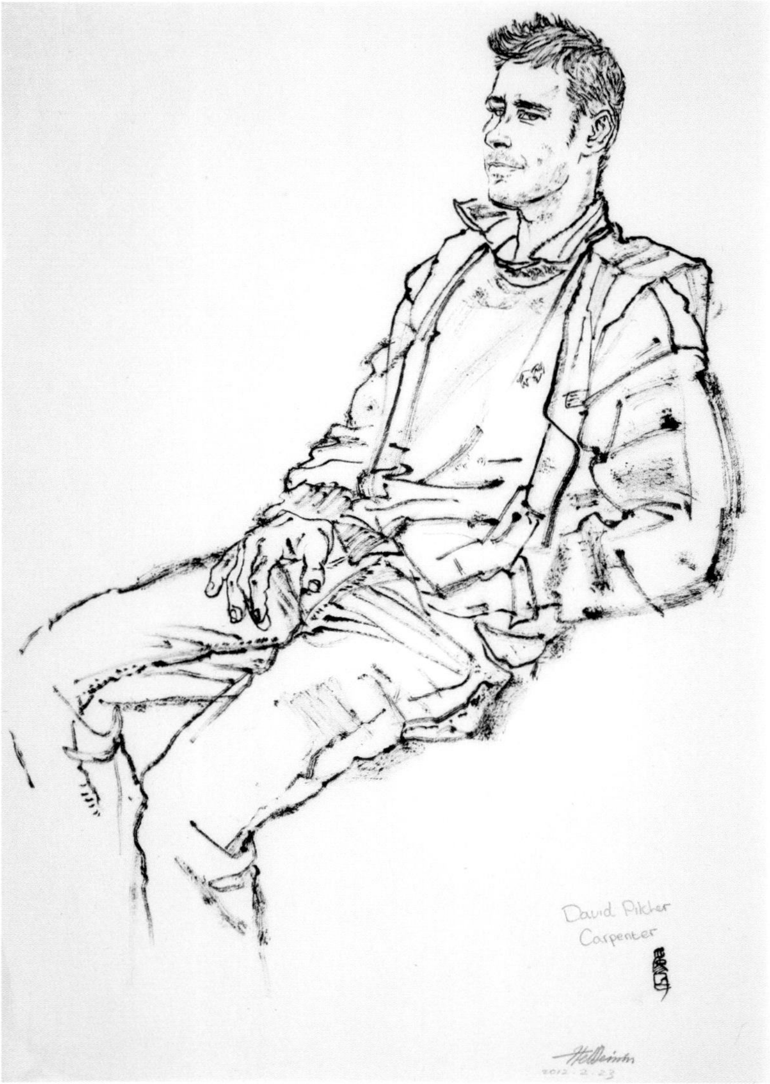

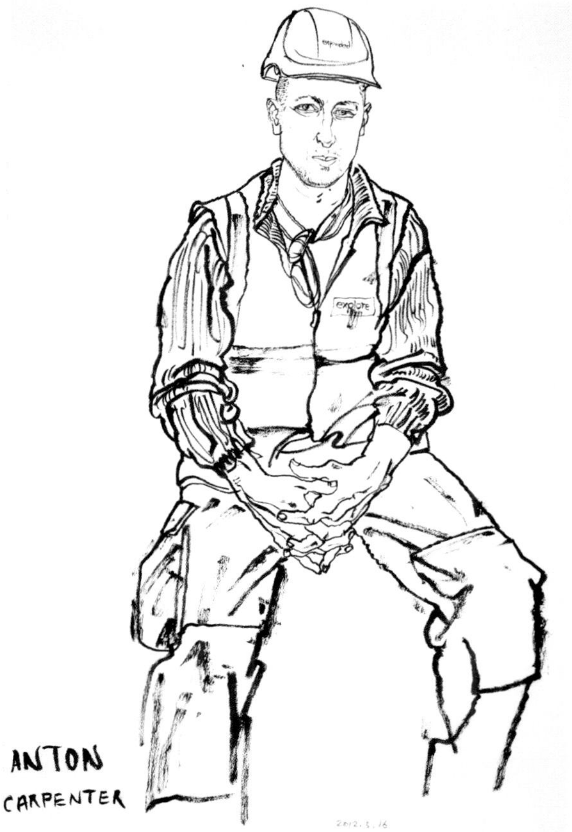

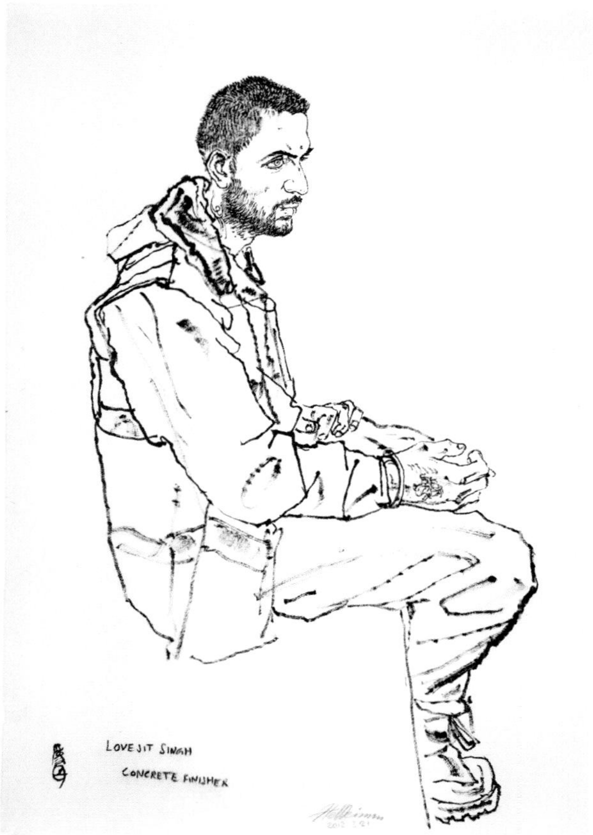

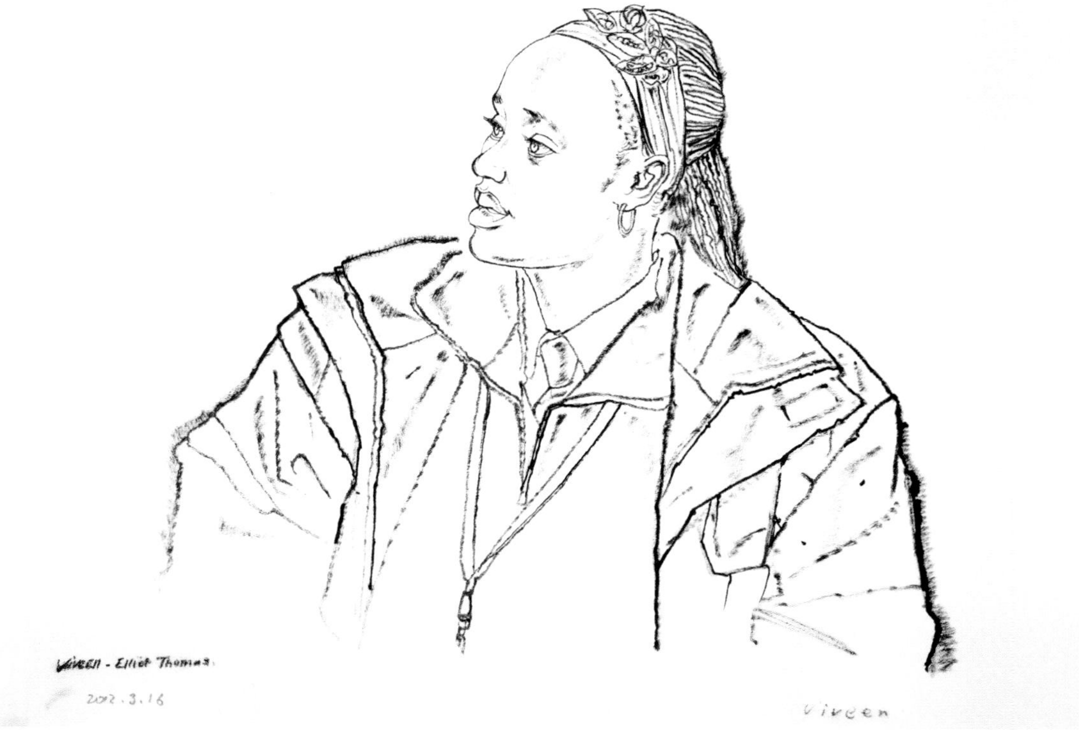

CAT.222 (top left)
Anton *Carpenter*. 16 March 2012. Brush and ink on sketchbook made of cartridge paper. Paper size: 42 × 27.9 cm

CAT.223 (right)
Viveen Elliot Thomas *Member of security staff*. 16 March 2012. Brush and ink on sketchbook made of cartridge paper. Paper size: 27.9 × 42 cm

CAT.224 (top right)
Love Sit Singh *Concrete finisher*. 21 March 2012. Brush and ink on *xuan* paper. Paper size: 59.5 × 43.5 cm

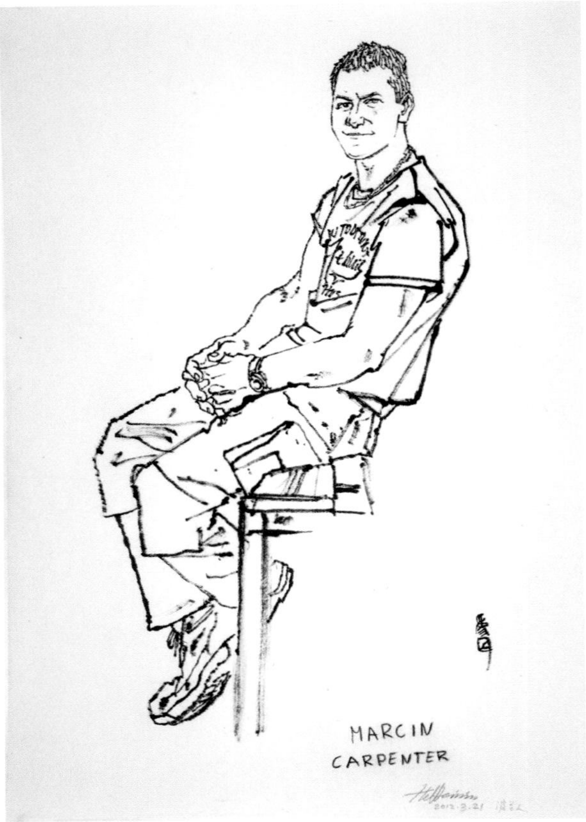

CAT.225 (left)
Marcin *Carpenter*. 21 March 2012. Brush and ink on *xuan* paper. Paper size: 59.5 × 43.5 cm

CAT.226 (bottom left)
Sohan Singh Sandhu *Concrete finisher*. 22 March 2012. Brush and ink on *xuan* paper. Paper size: 59.5 × 43.5 cm

CAT.227 (bottom right)
Paul Reeve *Steel fixer*. 13 June 2012. Brush and ink on *xuan* paper. Paper size: 59.5 × 43.5 cm

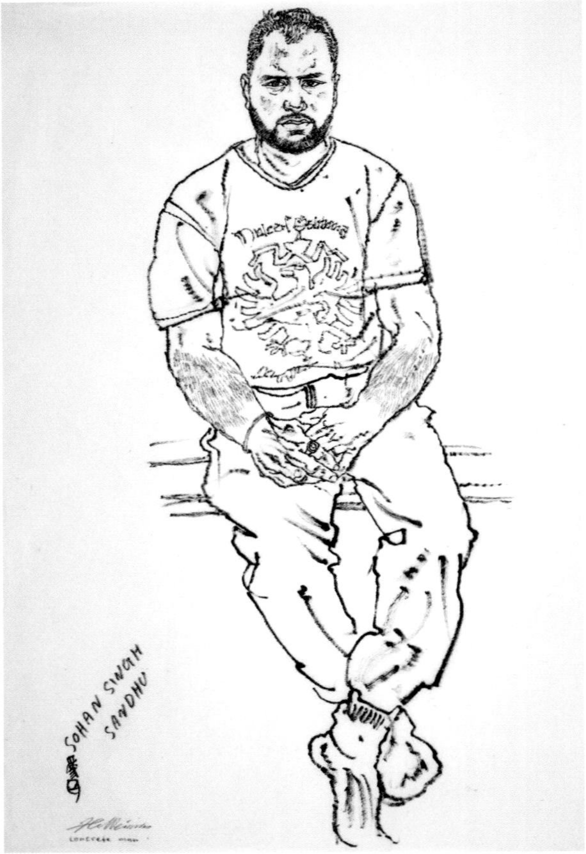

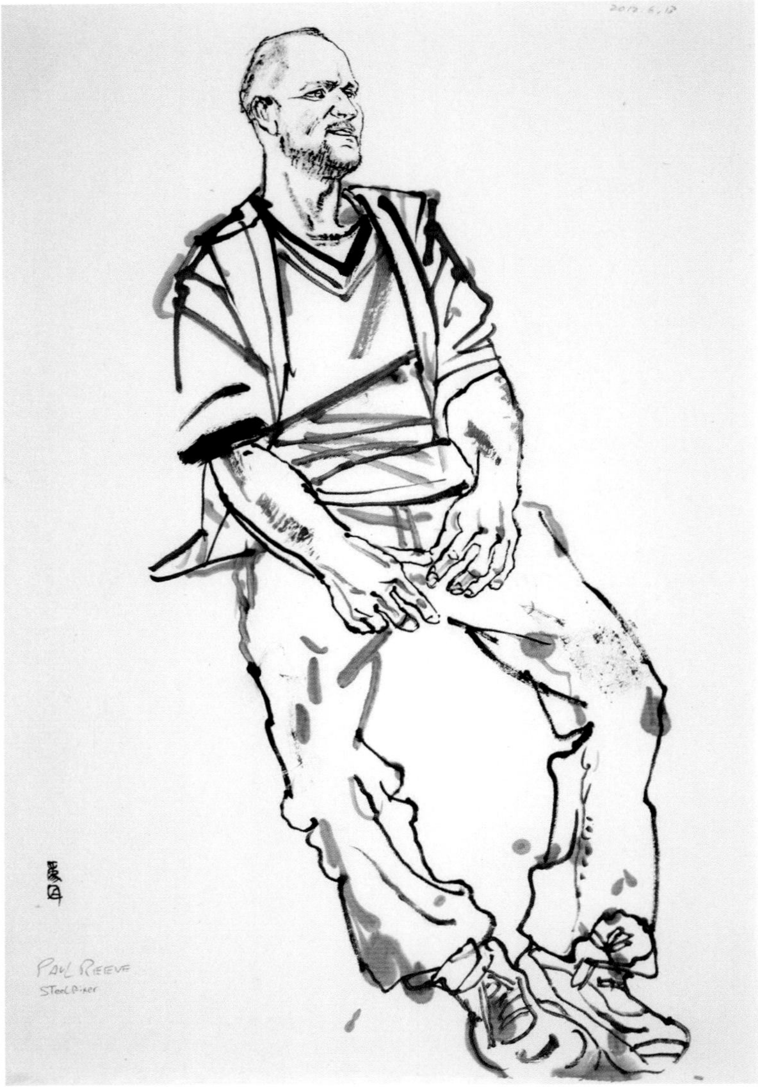

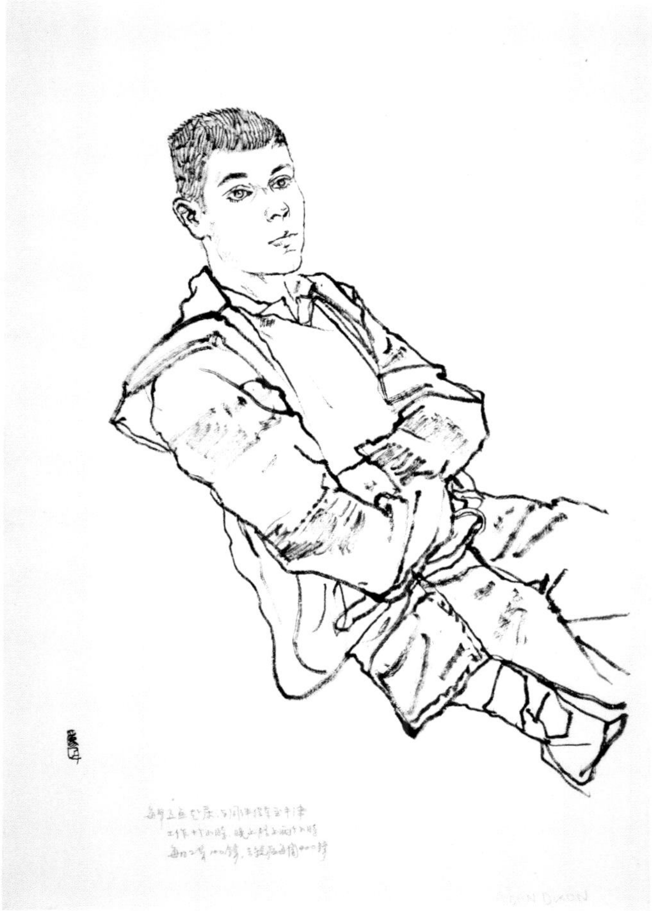

CAT.228
Aidan Dixon *Construction worker*. 14 January 2013. Brush and ink on *xuan* paper. Paper size: 59.5 × 43.5 cm

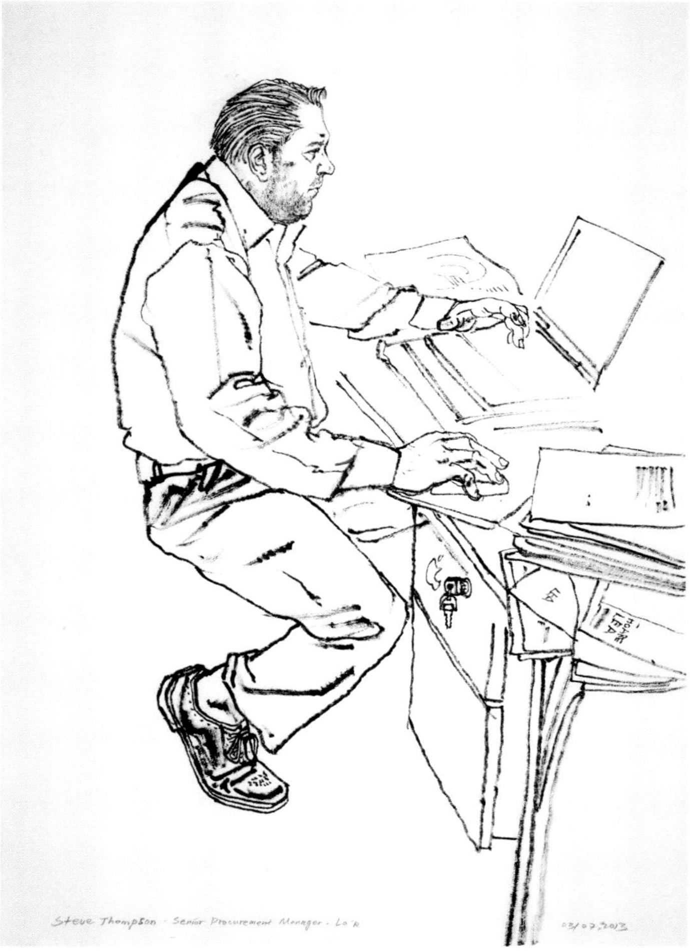

CAT.229
Steve Thompson *Senior procurement manager, Laing O'Rourke*. 3 July 2013. Brush and ink on *xuan* paper. Paper size: 59.5 × 43.5 cm

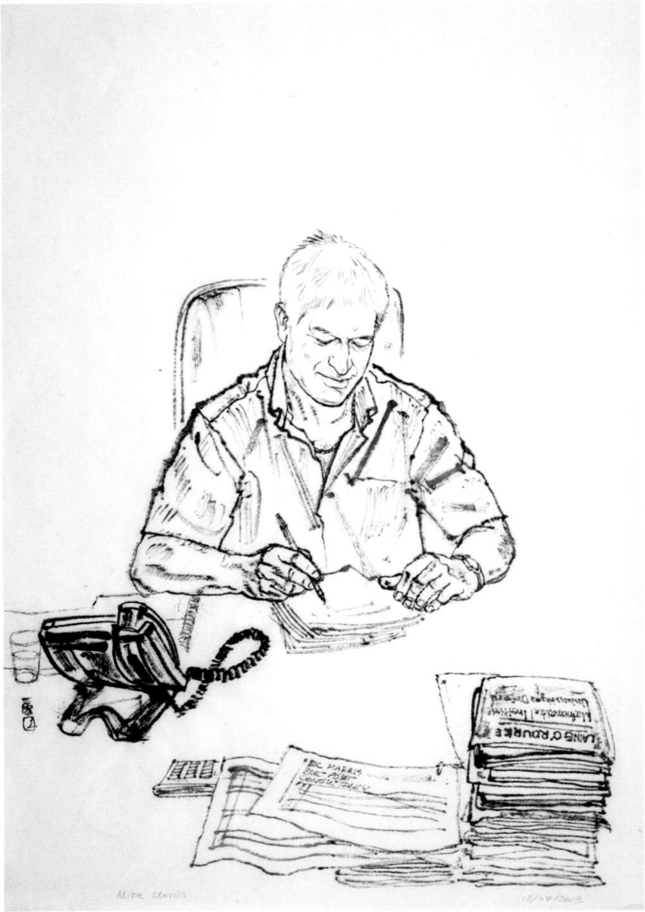

CAT.230
Mike Morris *Project director, Laing O'Rourke Construction Company*. 18 July 2013. Brush and ink on *xuan* paper. Paper size: 59.5 × 43.5 cm

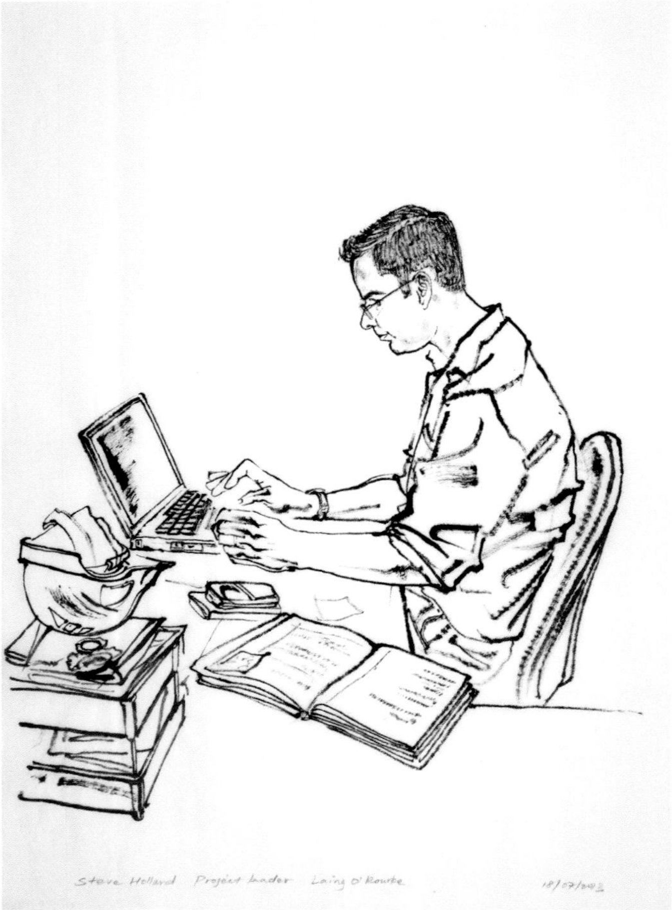

CAT.231
Steve Hollard *Project leader, Laing O'Rourke Construction Company*. 18 July 2013. Brush and ink on *xuan* paper. Paper size: 59.5 × 43.5 cm

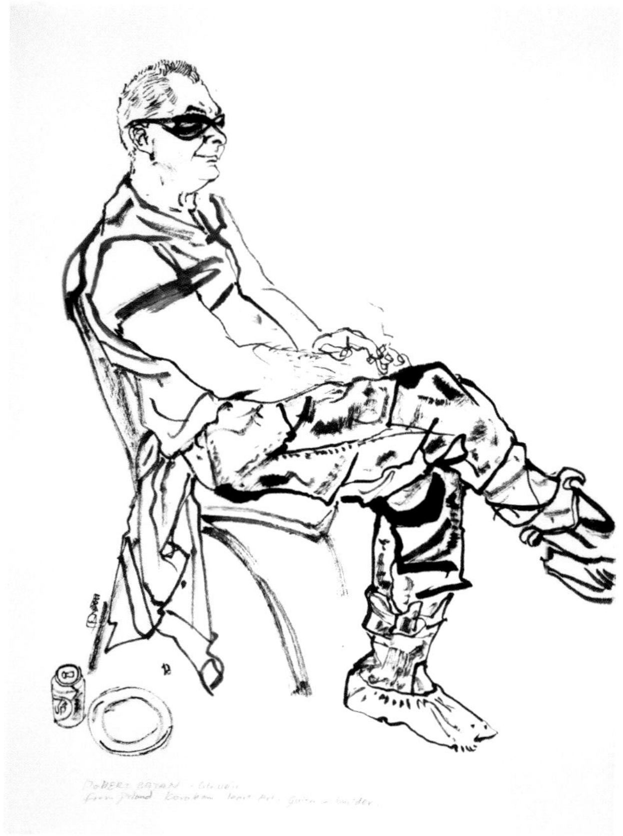

CAT.232
Robert Bajan *Construction worker*. 8 August 2013. Brush and ink on *xuan* paper. Paper size: 59.5 × 43.5 cm

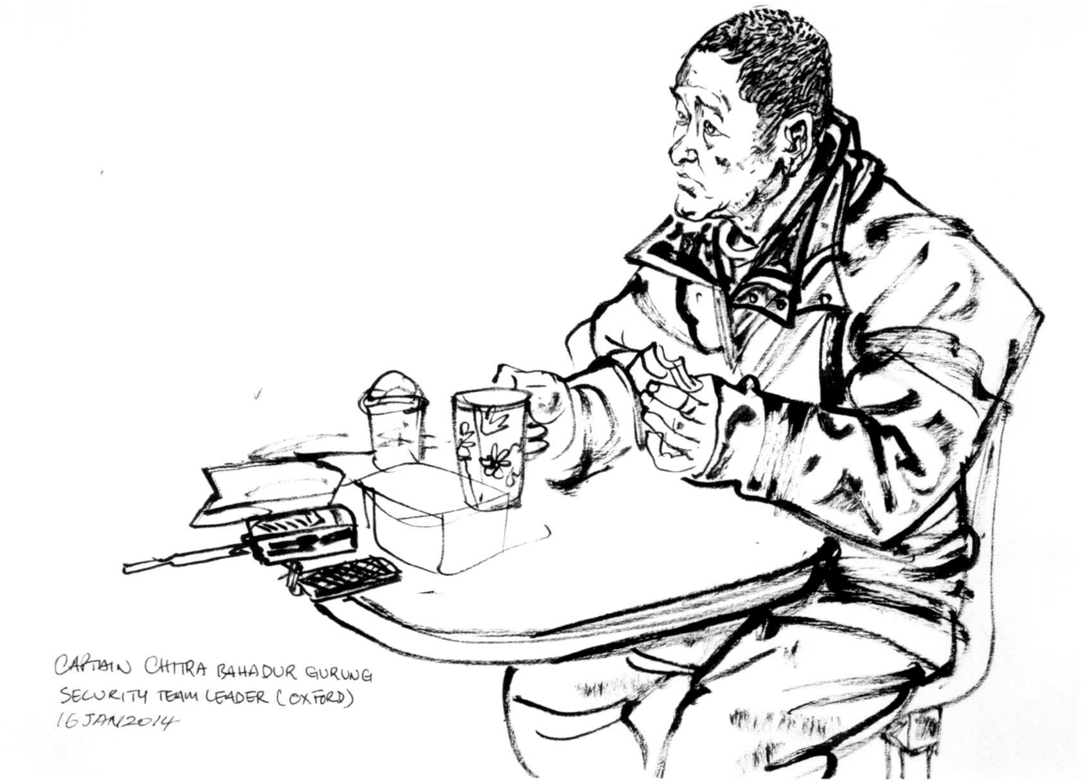

CAT.233
Captain Chitra Bahadur Gurung *Security team leader*. 16 January 2014. Brush and ink on sketchbook made of cartridge paper. Paper size: 27.9 × 42 cm

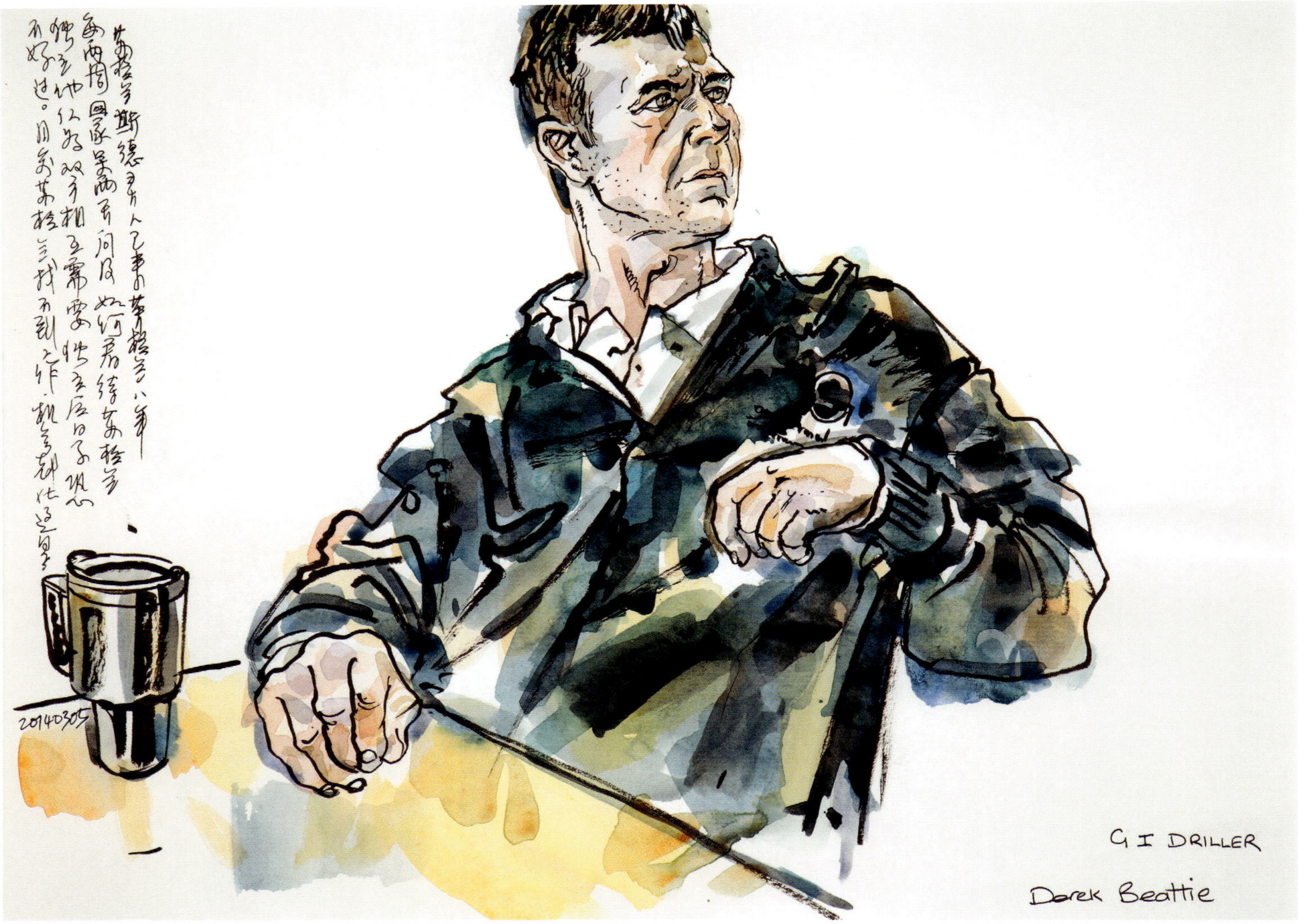

CAT.234 (right)
Derek Beattie *G I driller*. 5 March 2014. Brush and watercolour on sketchbook made of cartridge paper. Paper size: 27.9 × 42 cm

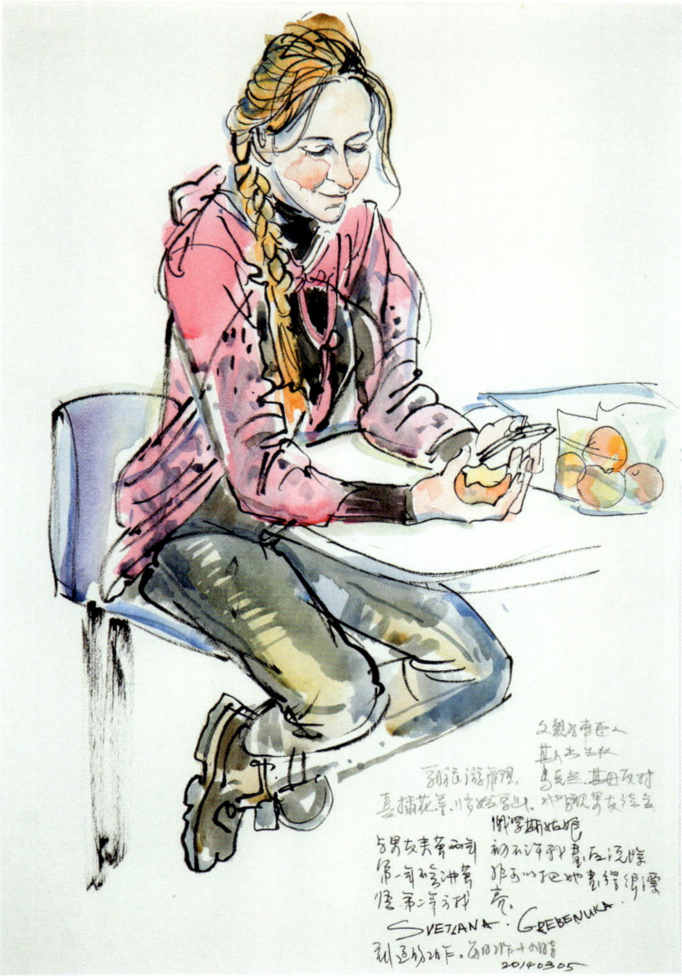

CAT.235 (bottom left)
Svetlana Grebenuka *Cleaner*. 5 March 2014. Brush and watercolour on sketchbook made of cartridge paper. Paper size: 42 × 27.9 cm

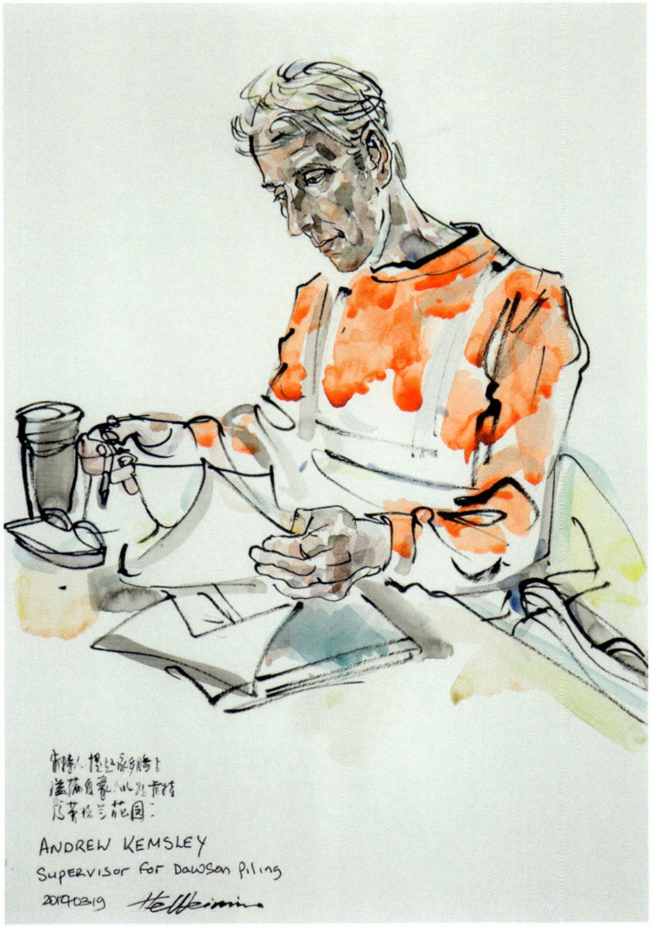

CAT.236 (bottom right)
Andrew Kemsley *Supervisor for Dawson Piling*. 19 March 2014. Brush and watercolour on sketchbook made of cartridge paper. Paper size: 42 × 27.9 cm

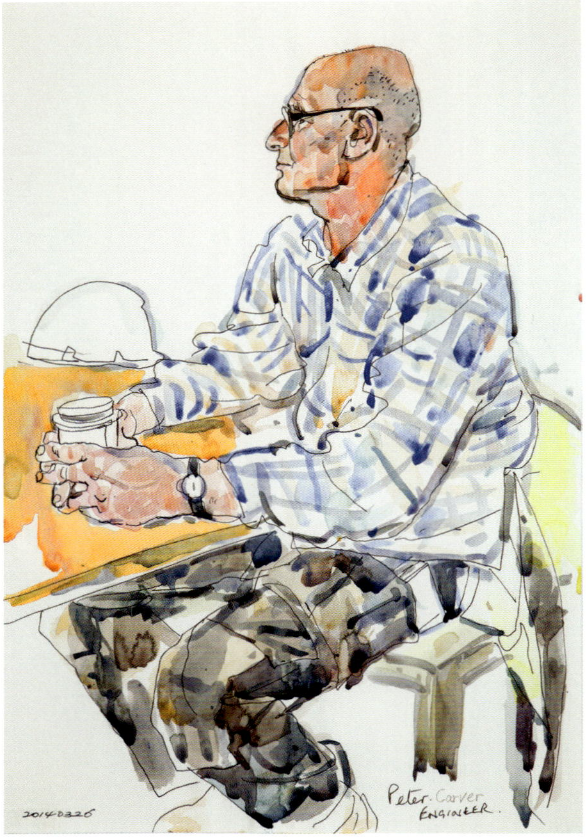

CAT.237 (left)
Peter Carver *Engineer*. 26 March 2014. Brush and watercolour on sketchbook made of cartridge paper. Paper size: 42 × 27.9 cm

CAT.238 (bottom right)
Lucky *Concrete finisher*. 9 April 2014. Brush and watercolour on sketchbook made of cartridge paper. Paper size: 42 × 27.9 cm

CAT.239 (bottom left)
Mohan Singh Badal *Steel fixer*. 9 April 2014. Brush and watercolour on sketchbook made of cartridge paper. Paper size: 42 × 27.9 cm

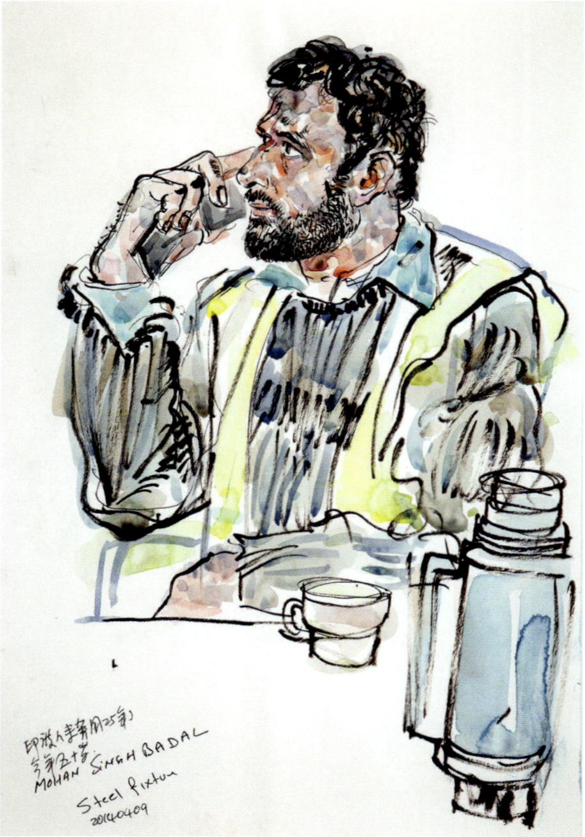

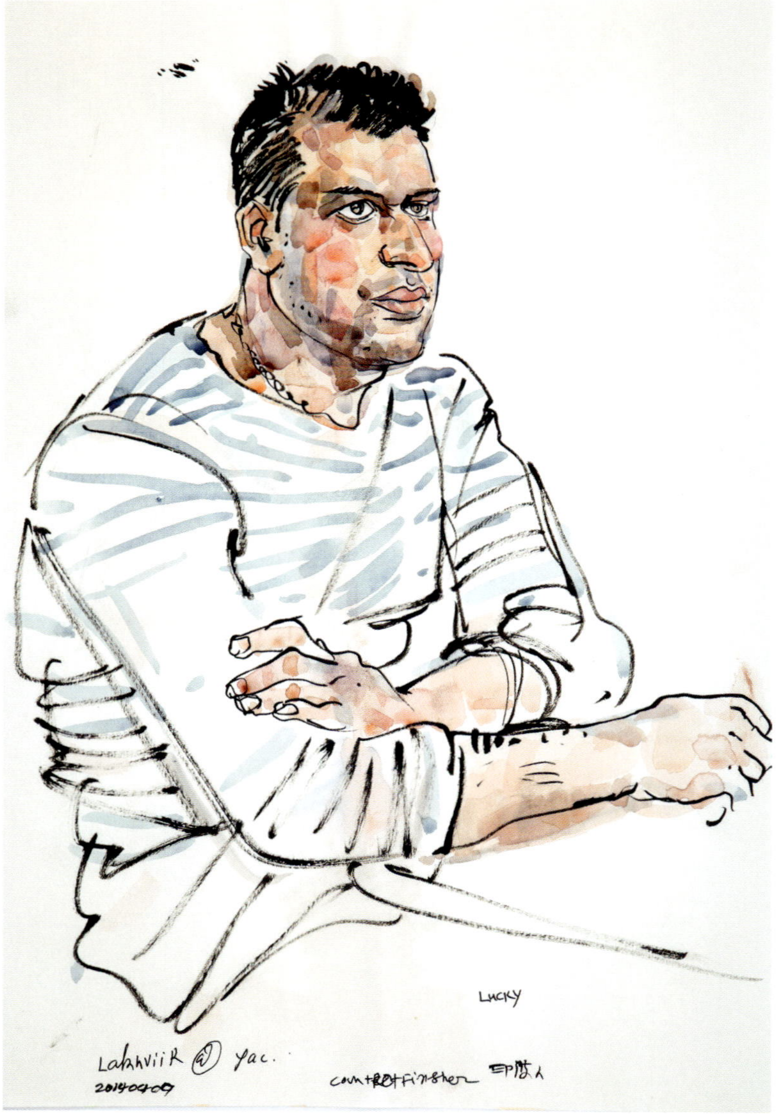

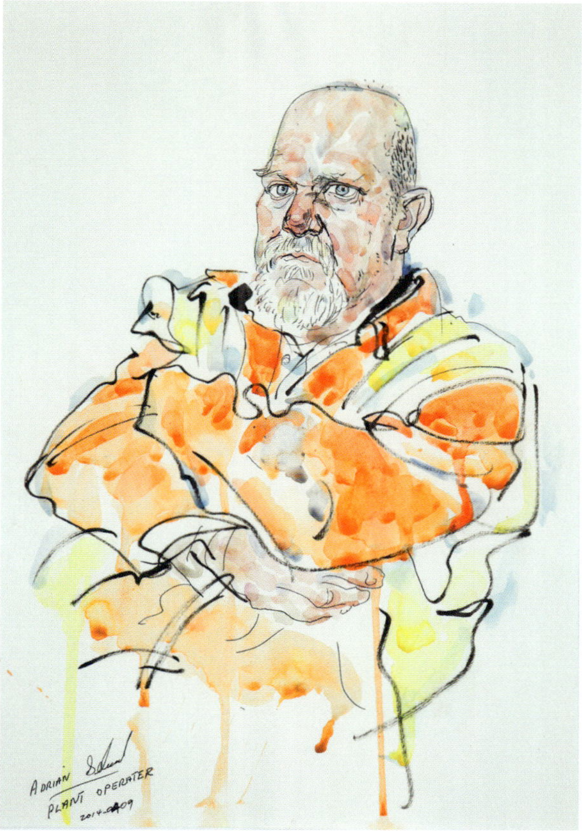

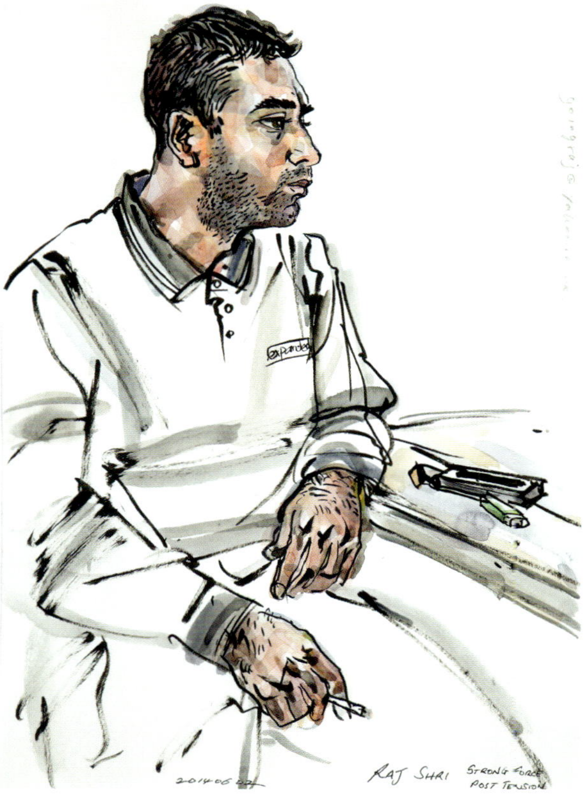

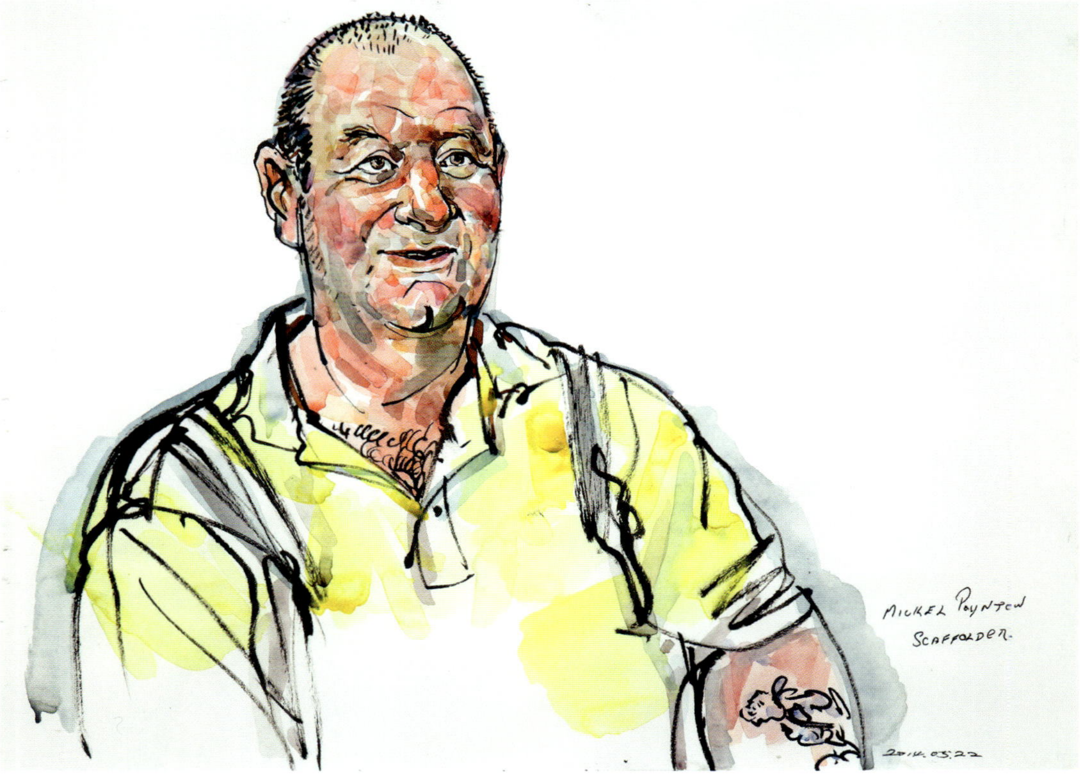

CAT.240 (top left)
Adrian *Plant operator*. 9 April 2014. Brush and watercolour on sketchbook made of cartridge paper. Paper size: 42 × 27.9 cm

CAT.241 (right)
Mickel Payntow *Scaffolder*. 22 May 2014. Brush and watercolour on sketchbook made of cartridge paper. Paper size: 27.9 × 42 cm

CAT.242 (top right)
Raj Shri *Post tension worker, Strong Force*. 2 June 2014. Brush and watercolour on sketchbook made of cartridge paper. Paper size: 42 × 27.9 cm

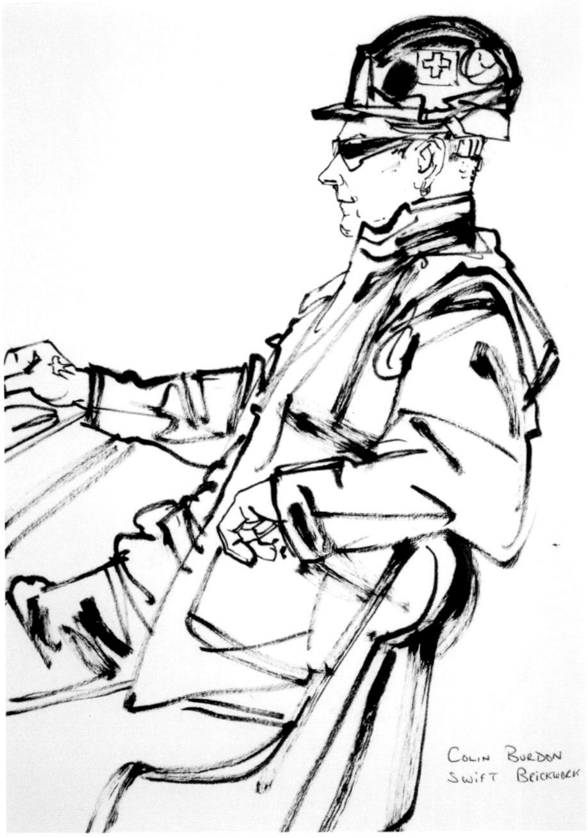

CAT.243 (left)
Colin Burdon *Bricklayer*.
June 2014. Brush and ink on sketchbook made of cartridge paper. Paper size: 42 × 27.9 cm

CAT.244 (bottom right)
Mel Banks *Expanded project manager, Laing O'Rourke*. 3 July 2014. Pen and ink on sketchbook made of cartridge paper. Paper size: 42 × 27.9 cm

CAT.245 (bottom left)
H. S. Randhawa *Concrete finisher*. 3 July 2014. Brush and ink on sketchbook made of cartridge paper. Paper size: 42 × 27.9 cm

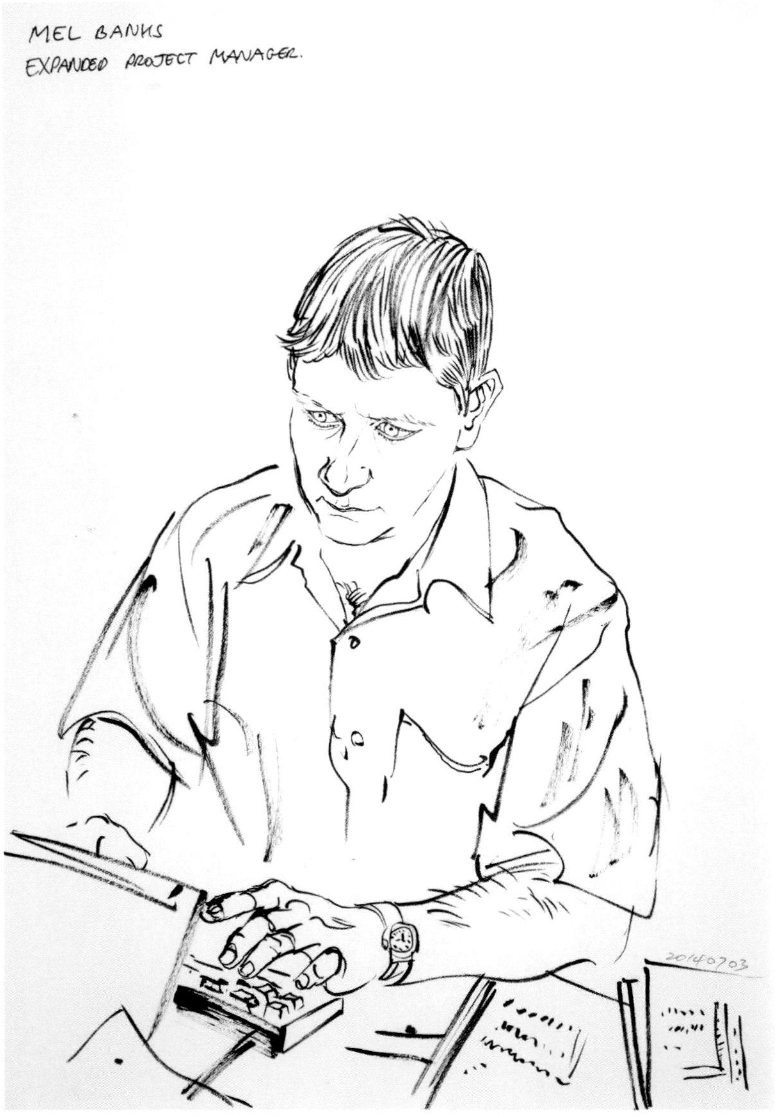

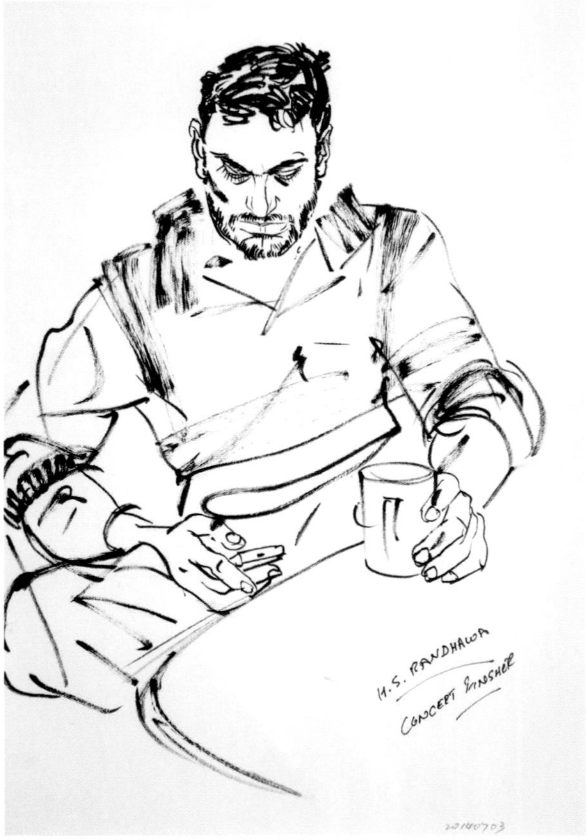

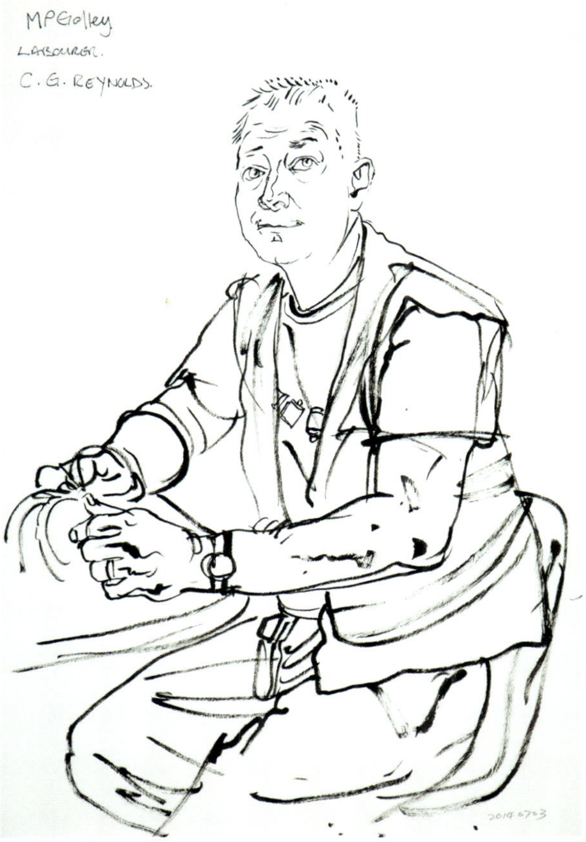

CAT.246 (left)
M. P. Galley *Construction worker, C. G. Reynolds*. 3 July 2014. Brush and ink on sketchbook made of cartridge paper. Paper size: 42 × 27.9 cm

CAT.247 (bottom right)
Pal Singh *Concrete finisher*. 3 July 2014. Brush and watercolour on sketchbook made of cartridge paper. Paper size: 42 × 27.9 cm

CAT.248 (bottom left)
Davy Donaghy *Joiner*. 3 July 2014. Brush and watercolour on sketchbook made of cartridge paper. Paper size: 42 × 27.9 cm

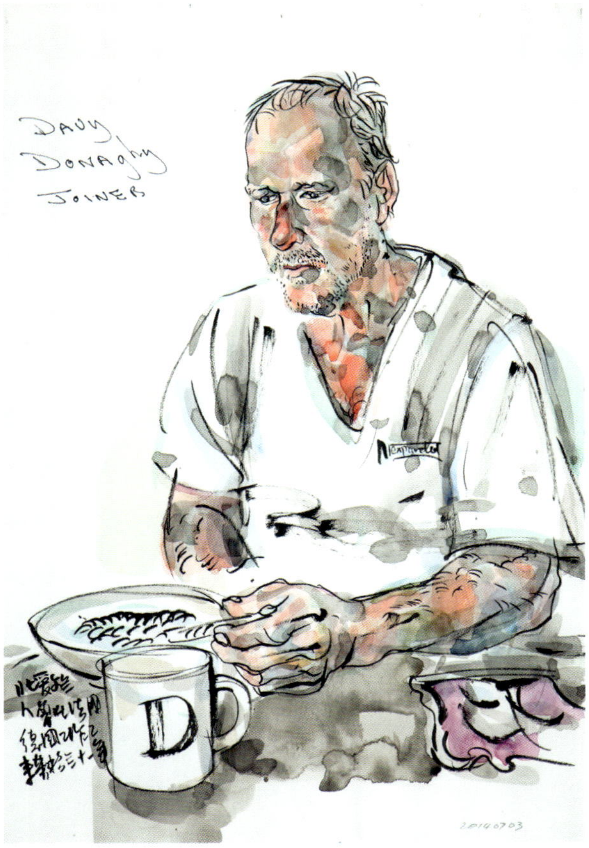

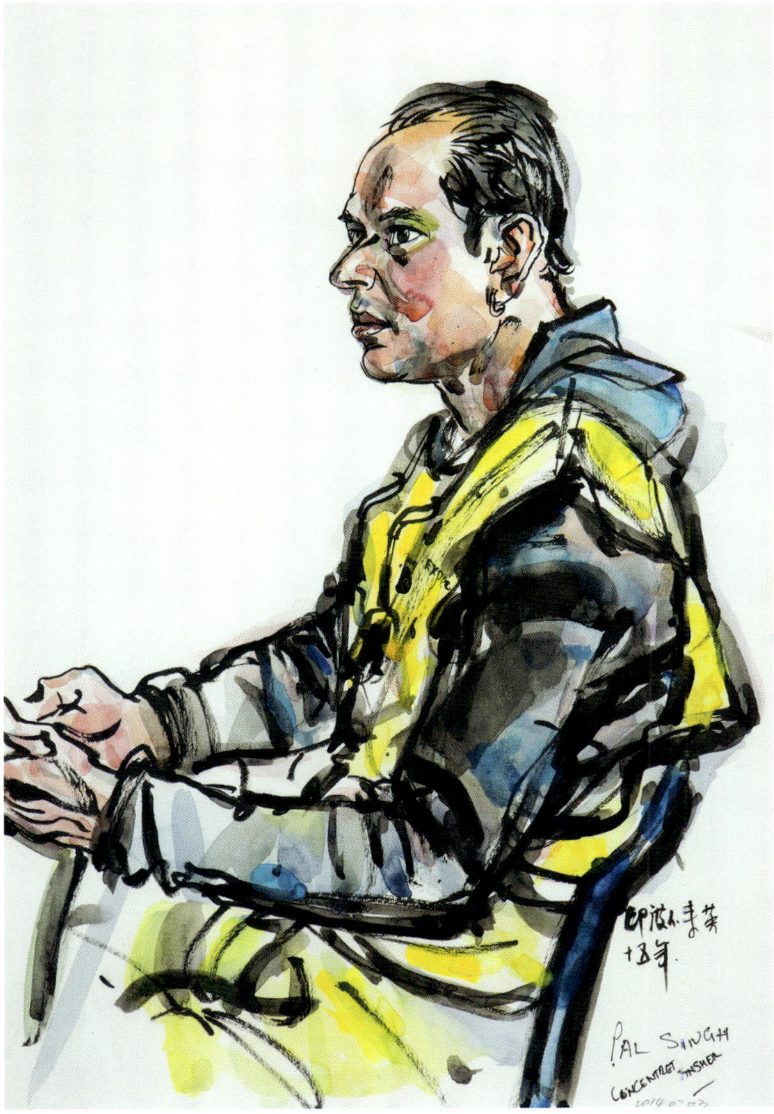

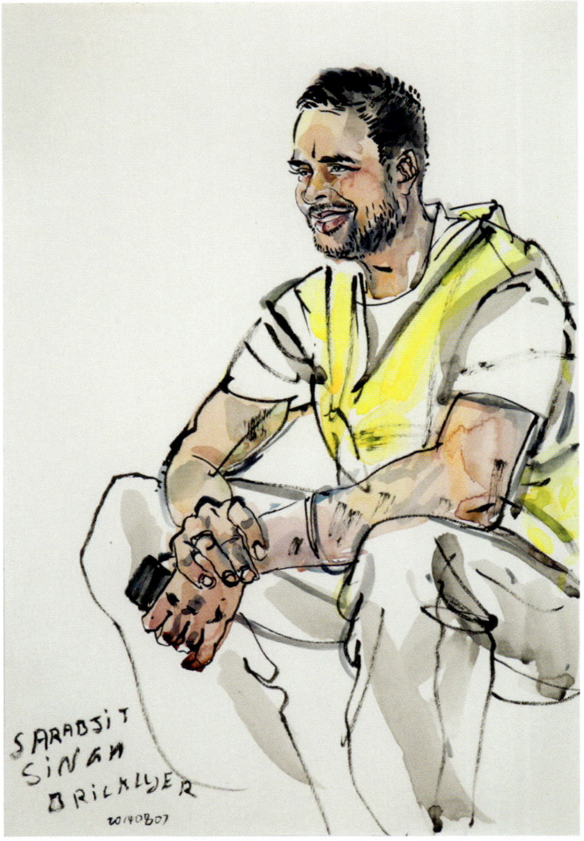

CAT.249 (left)
Sarabjit Singh *Bricklayer*. 7 August 2014. Brush and watercolour on sketchbook made of cartridge paper. Paper size: 42 × 27.9 cm

CAT.250 (bottom right)
Artoin Tafoi *Electrician*. 4 September 2014. Brush and ink on sketchbook made of cartridge paper. Paper size: 42 × 27.9 cm

CAT.251 (bottom left)
Tim Jay *Supervisor*. 2 October 2014. Project manager, Laing O'Rourke. Pen and ink on sketchbook made of cartridge paper. Paper size: 42 × 27.9 cm

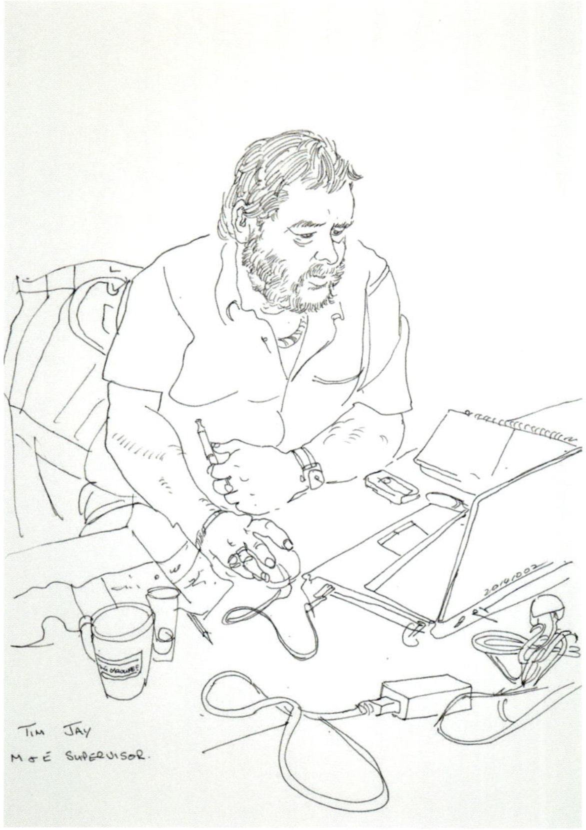

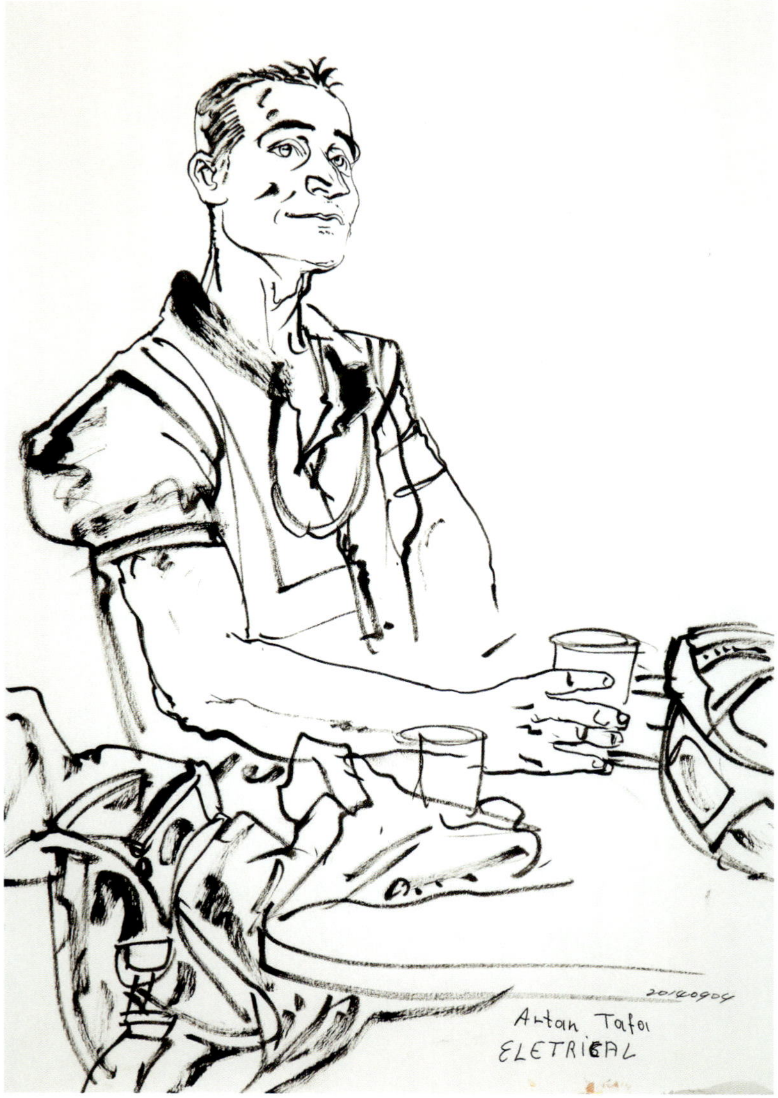

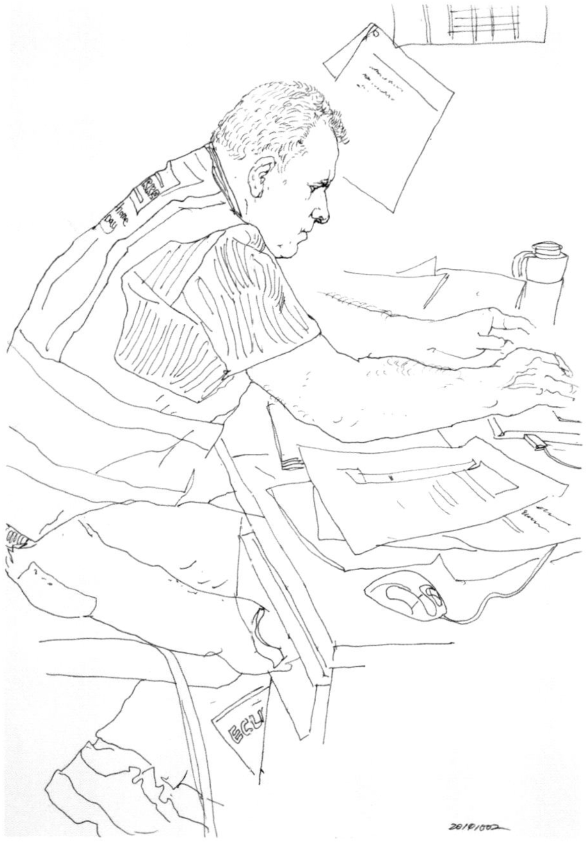

CAT.252 (left)
John Kenneally *Construction manager*. 2 October 2014. Pen and ink on sketchbook made of cartridge paper. Paper size: 42 × 27.9 cm

CAT.253 (bottom right)
Amrik Singh *Concrete finisher*. 2 October 2014. Brush and ink on sketchbook made of cartridge paper. Paper size: 42 × 27.9 cm

CAT.254 (bottom left)
Satnam Singh *Concrete finisher*. 20 November 2014. Brush and ink on sketchbook made of cartridge paper. Paper size: 42 × 27.9 cm

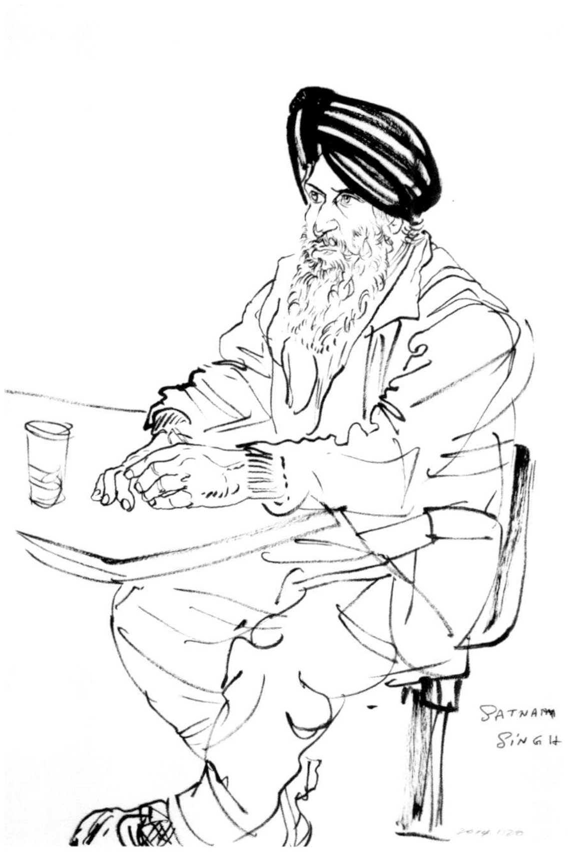

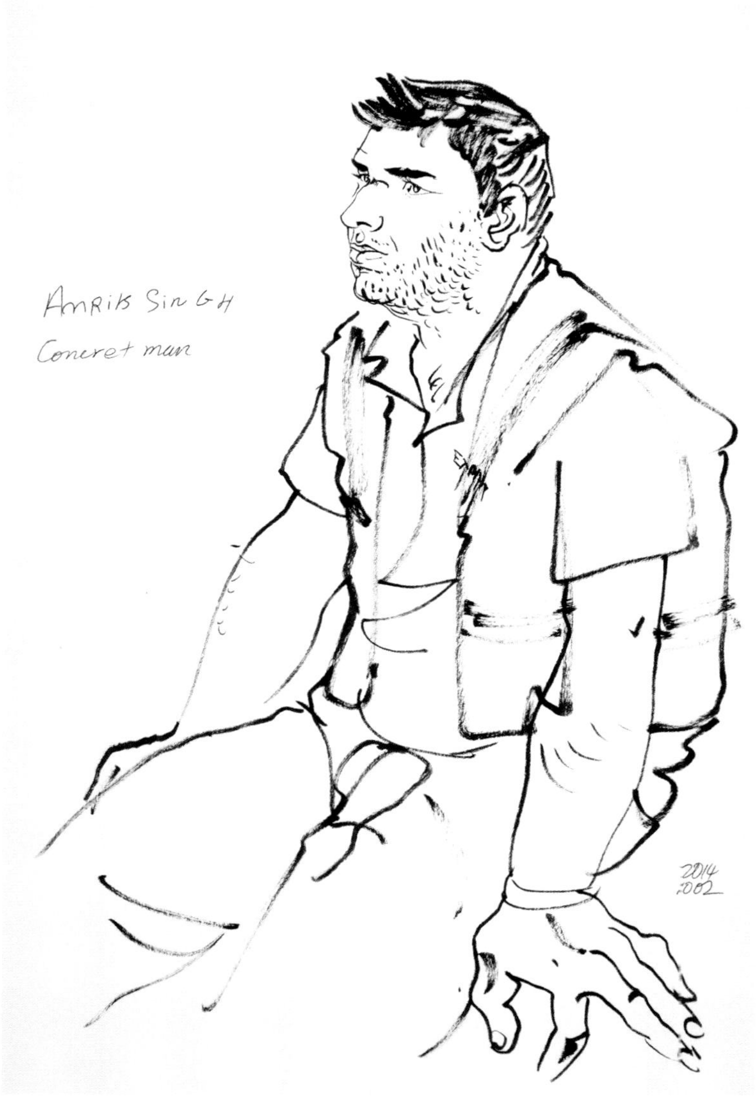

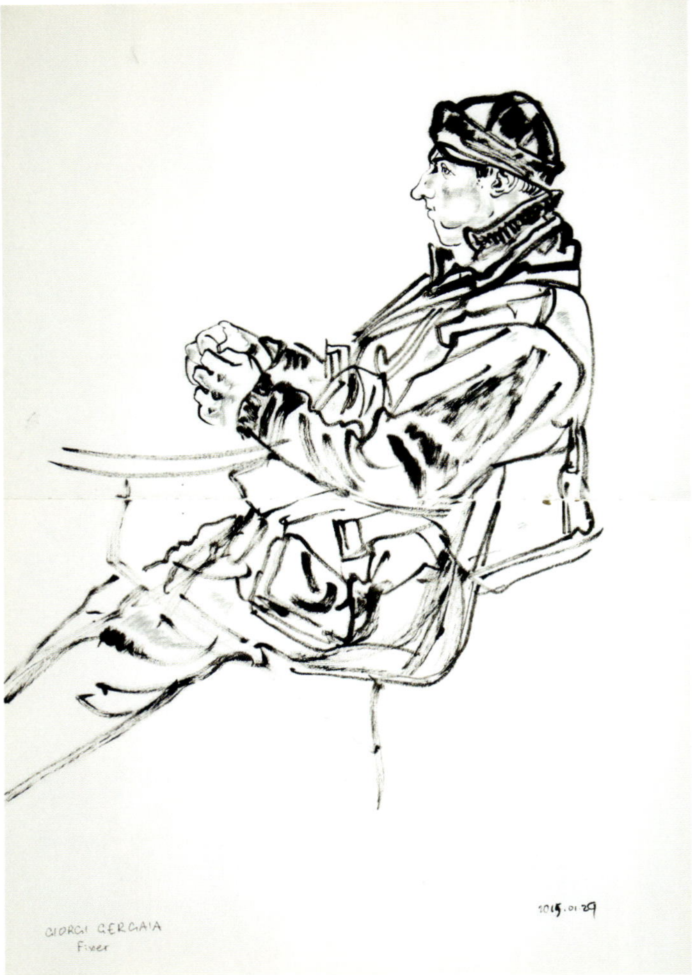

CAT.255
Giorgi Gergaia *Fixer*. 29 January 2015. Brush and ink on sketchbook made of cartridge paper. Paper size: 42 × 59.4 cm

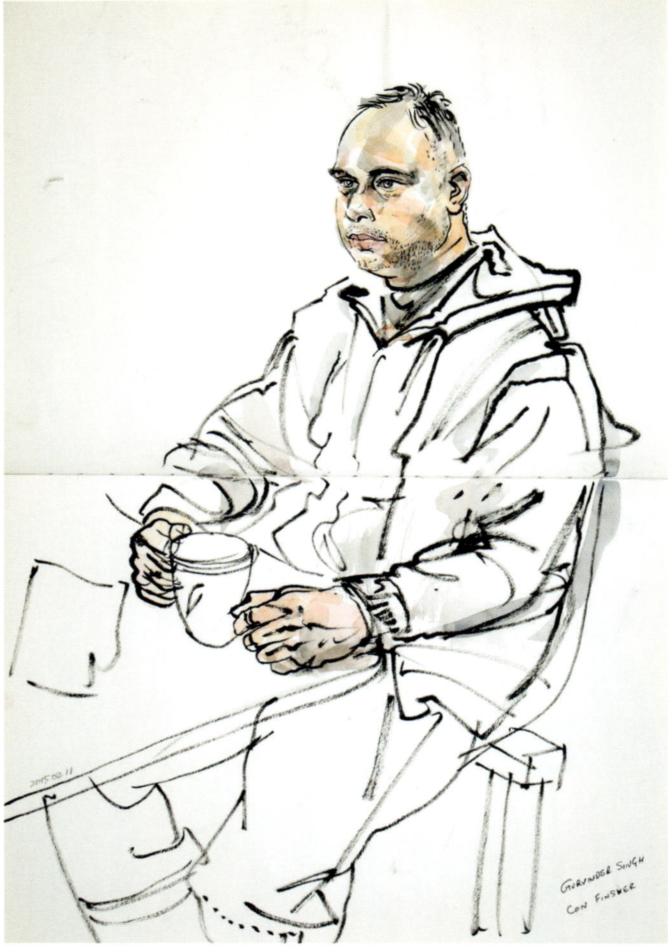

CAT.256
Gurvinder Singh *Concrete finisher*. 11 February 2015. Brush and watercolour on sketchbook made of cartridge paper. Paper size: 42 × 27.9 cm

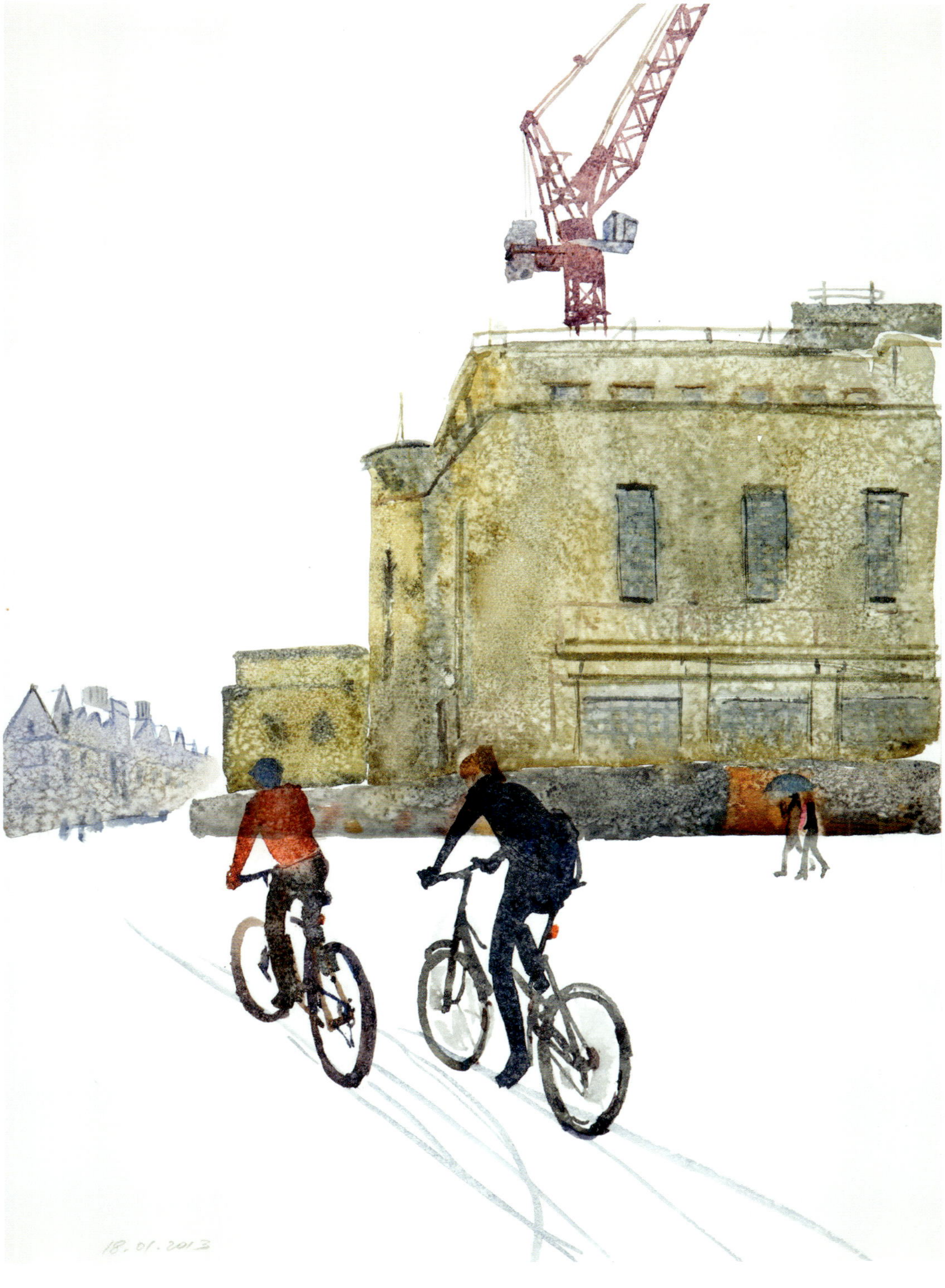

CAT.257
Snowy day. 18 January 2013. Watercolour on hot pressed watercolour paper. Paper size: 42 × 29.7 cm

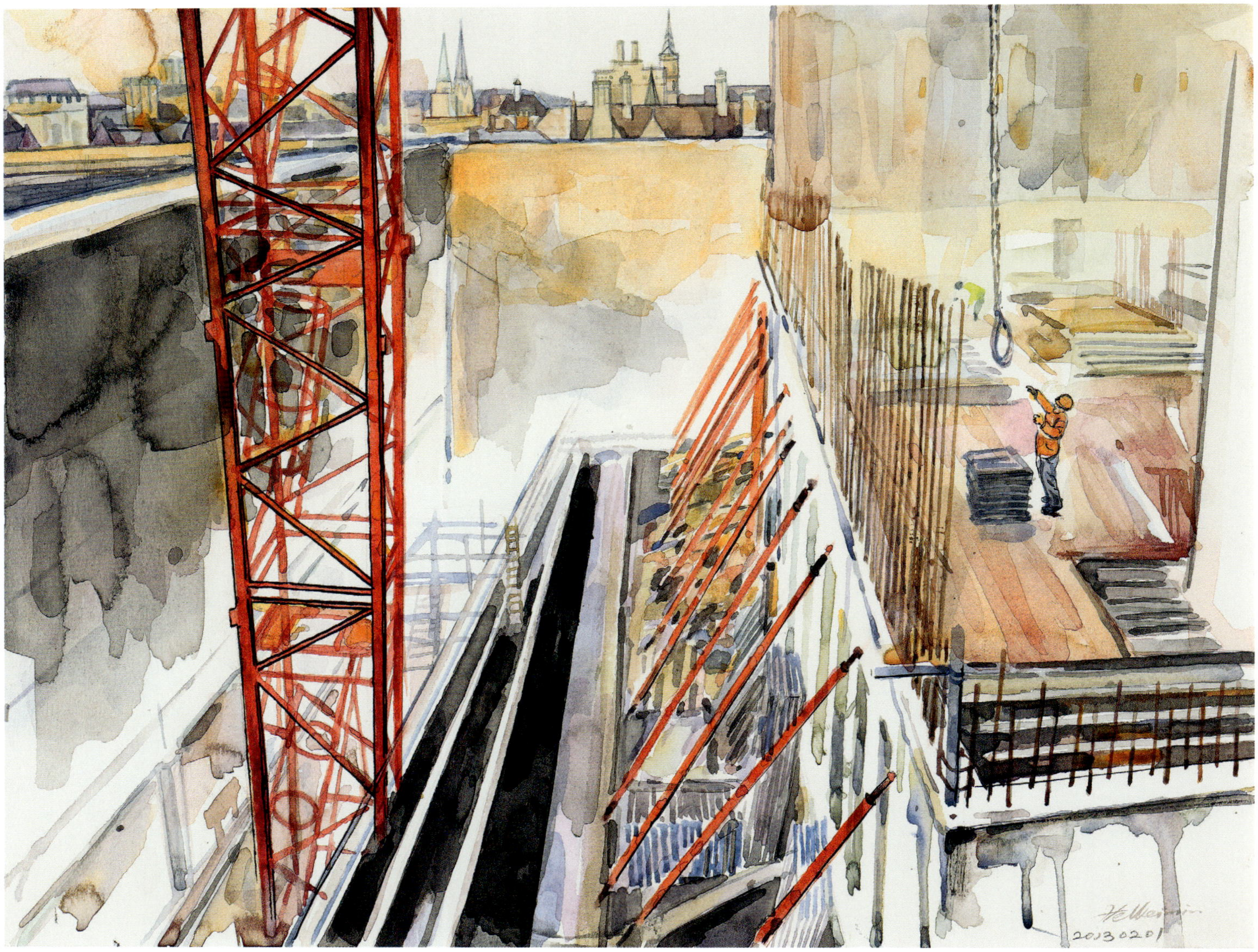

CAT.258
The red crane. 1 February 2013.
Watercolour on hot pressed watercolour paper. Paper size: 29.7 × 42 cm

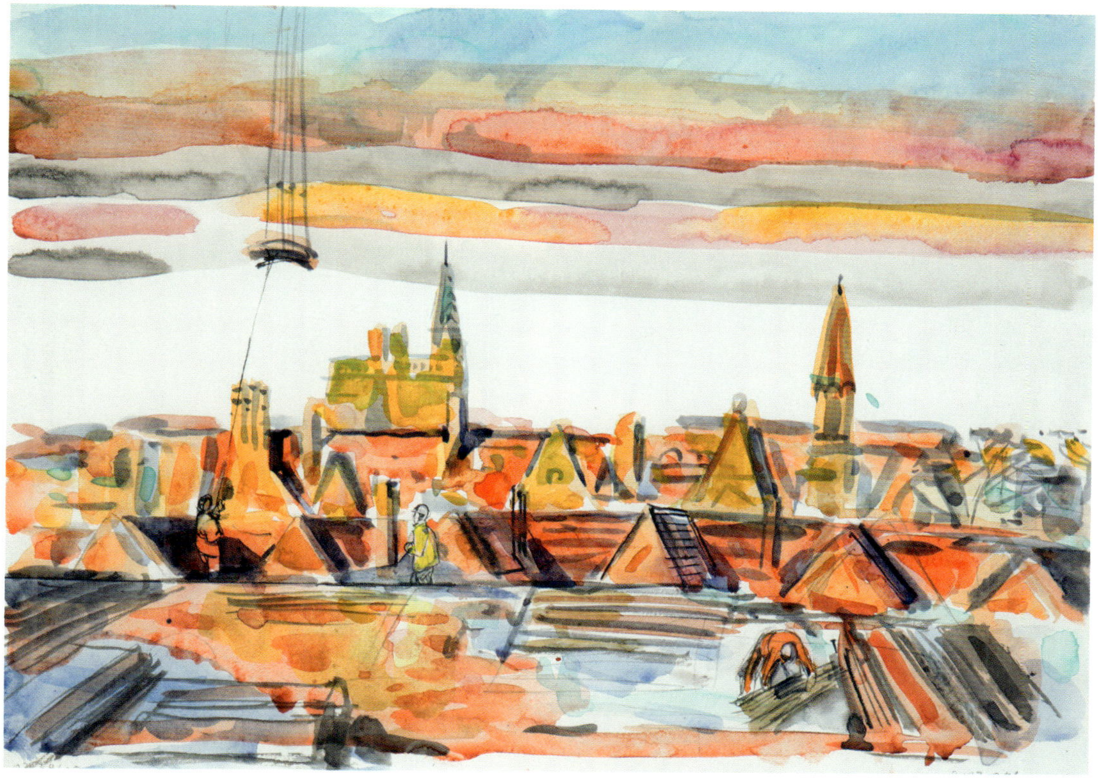

CAT.259
Through the clouds. February 2013. Watercolour on sketchbook made of cartridge paper. Paper size: 29.7 × 42 cm

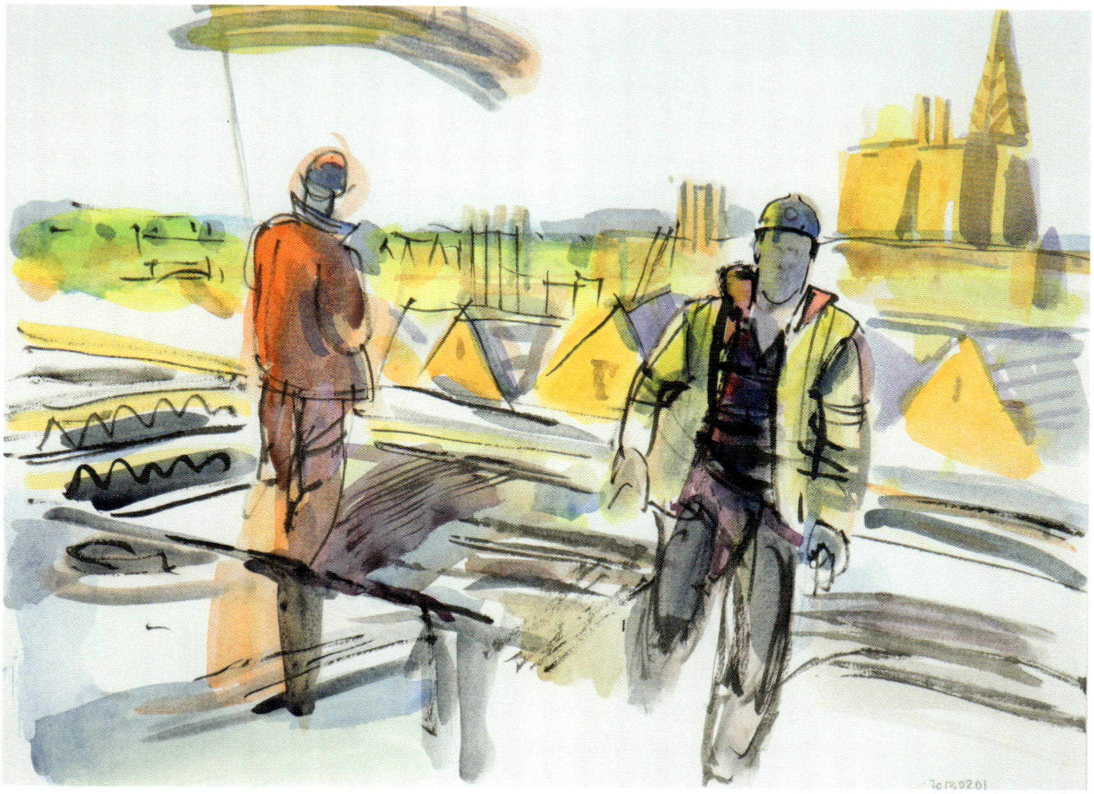

CAT.260
Unloading onto the Weston Library roof. 1 February 2013. Watercolour on sketchbook made of cartridge paper. Paper size: 29.7 × 42 cm

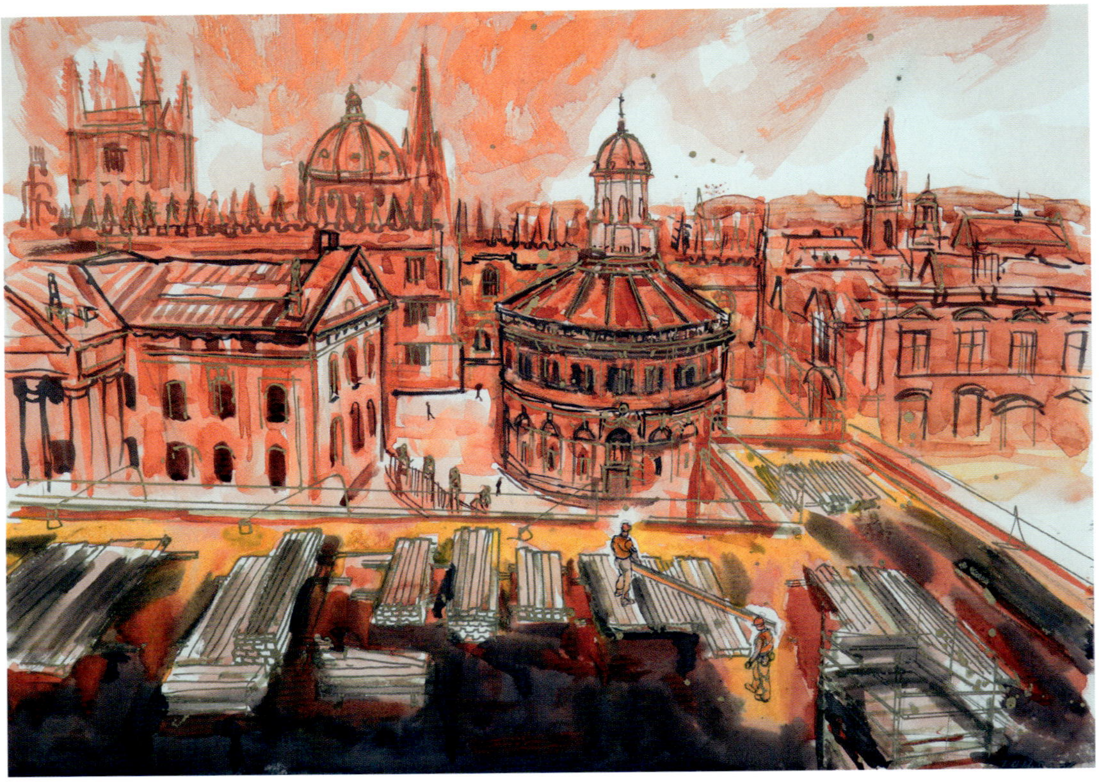

CAT.261
Red dreaming spires. 6 April 2013 (completed in 2016). Watercolour on sketchbook made of cartridge paper. Paper size: 29.7 × 42 cm

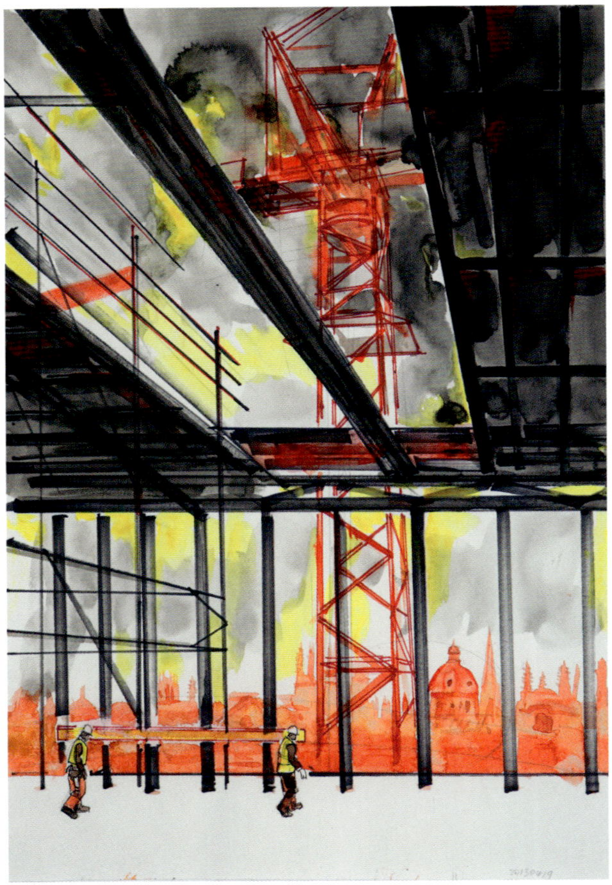

CAT.262
Crane tower over the Weston Library. 19 April 2013 (completed in 2016). Watercolour on sketchbook made of cartridge paper. Paper size: 42 × 29.7 cm

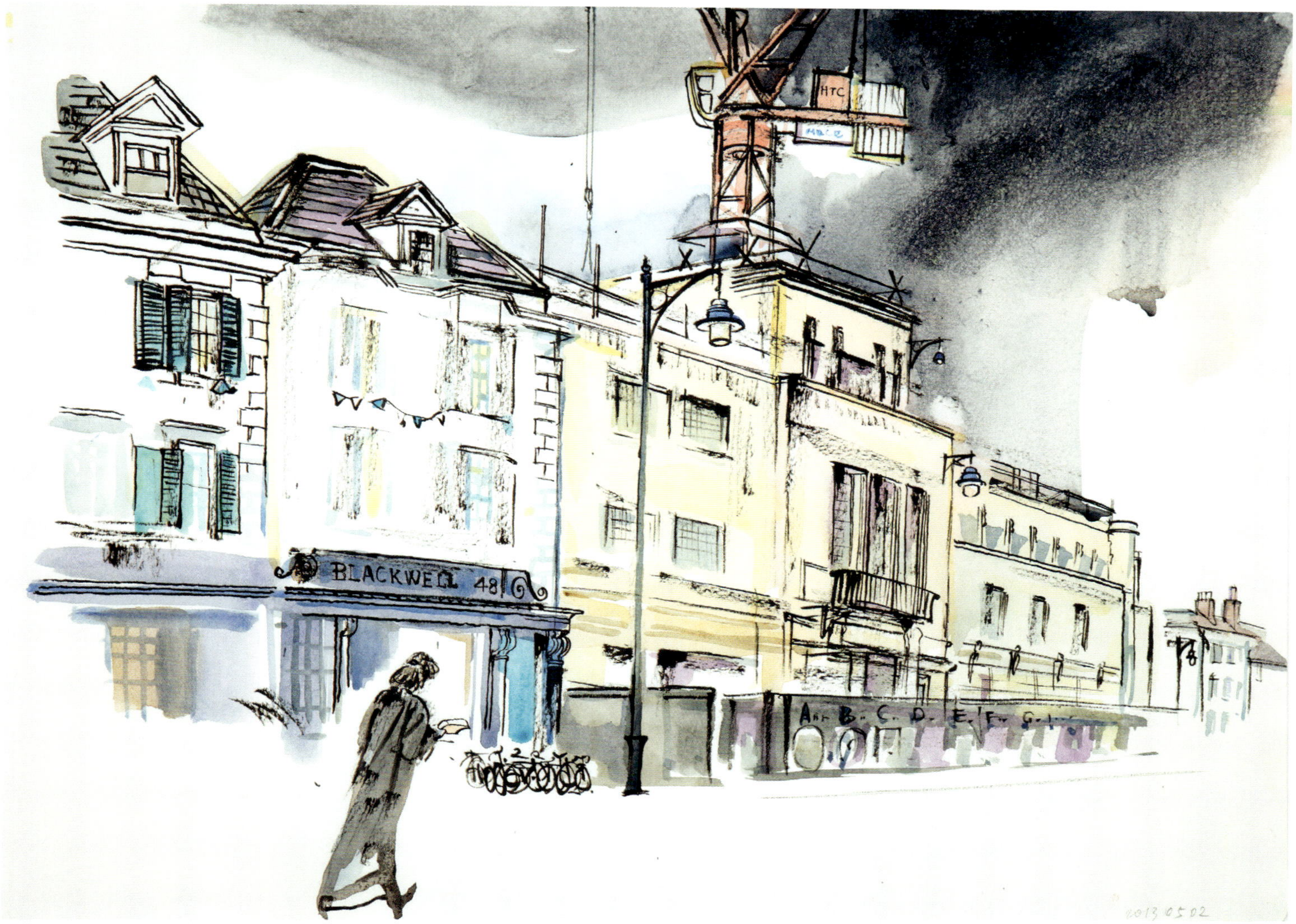

CAT.263
A book lover. 2 May 2013. Watercolour on hot pressed watercolour paper. Paper size: 29.7 × 42 cm

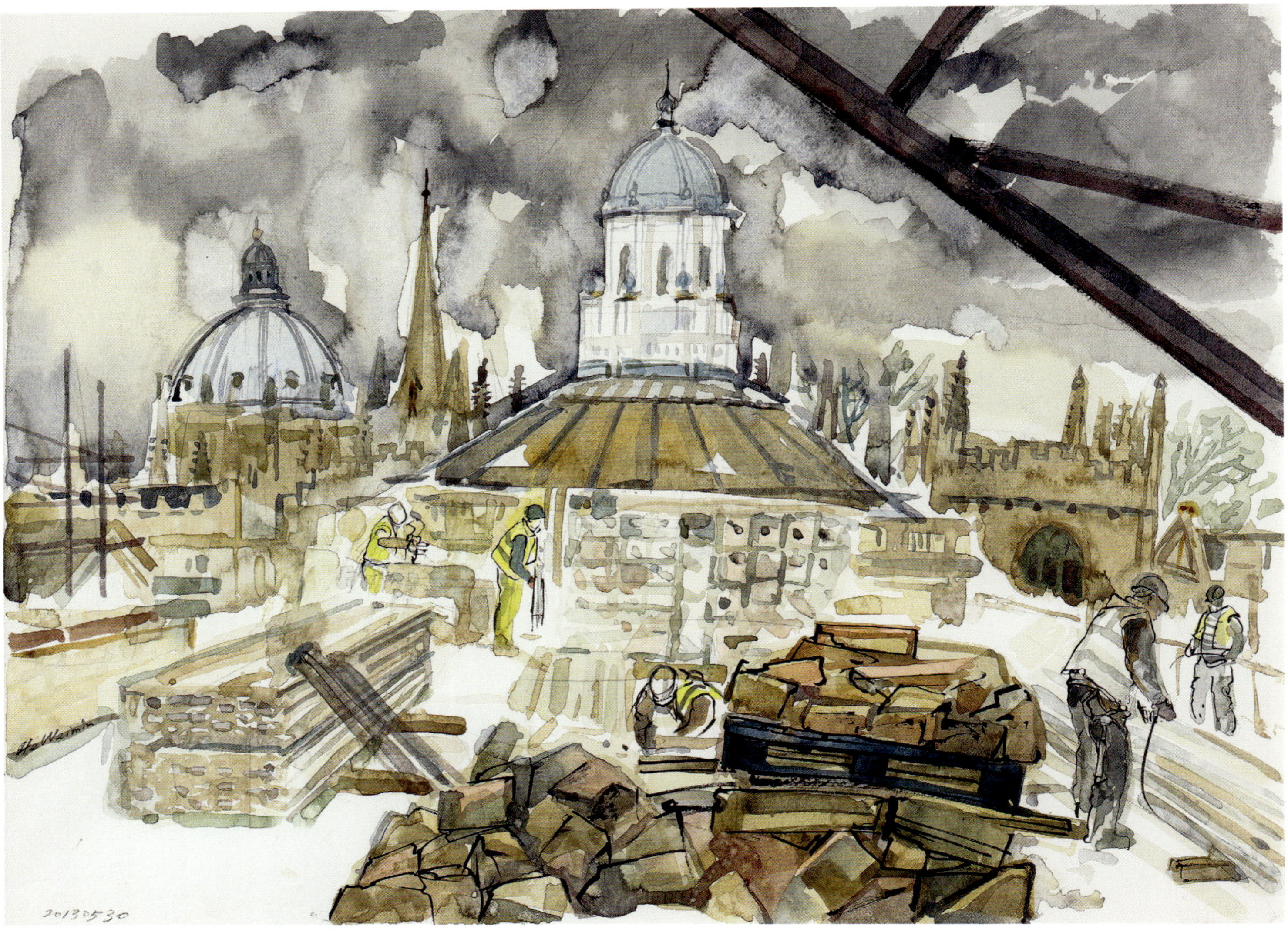

CAT.264
On the roof of the Weston Library.
30 May 2013. Watercolour on hot pressed watercolour paper. Paper size: 29.7 × 42 cm

CAT.265
Building a palace for books.
14 June 2013. Watercolour on hot pressed watercolour paper. Paper size: 29.7 × 42 cm

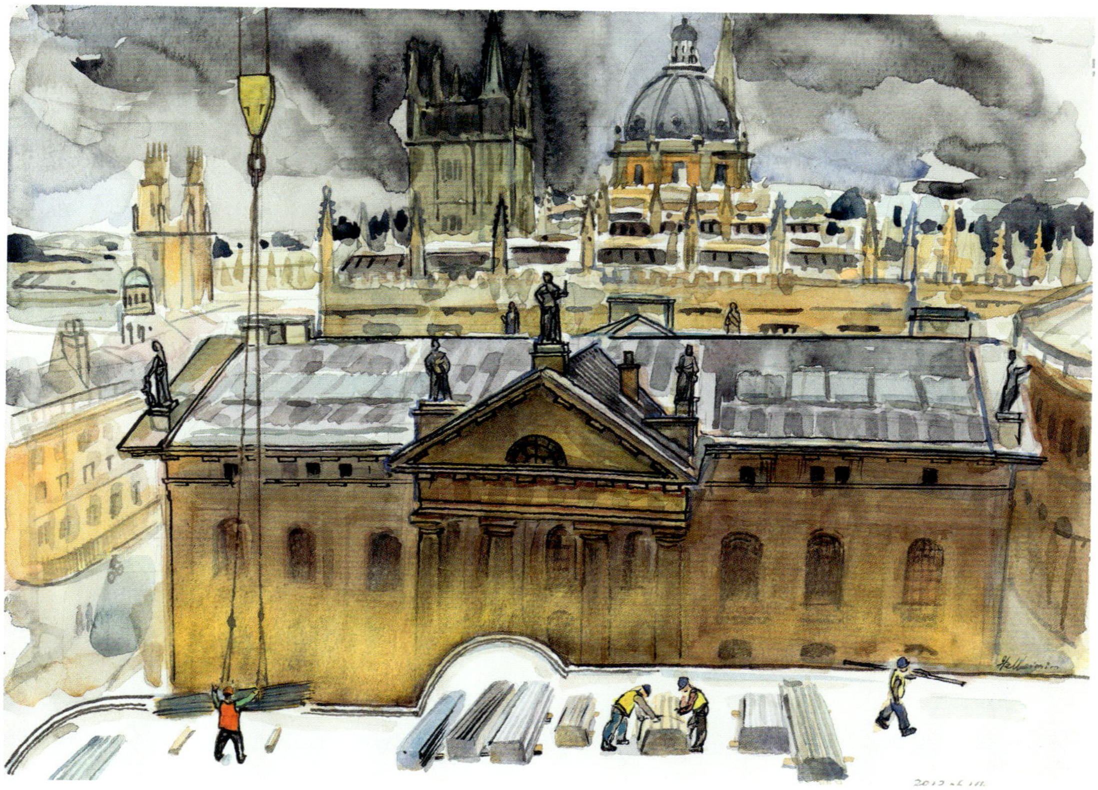

CAT.266
The season of blooms.
27 June 2013. Watercolour on hot pressed watercolour paper. Paper size: 29.7 × 42 cm

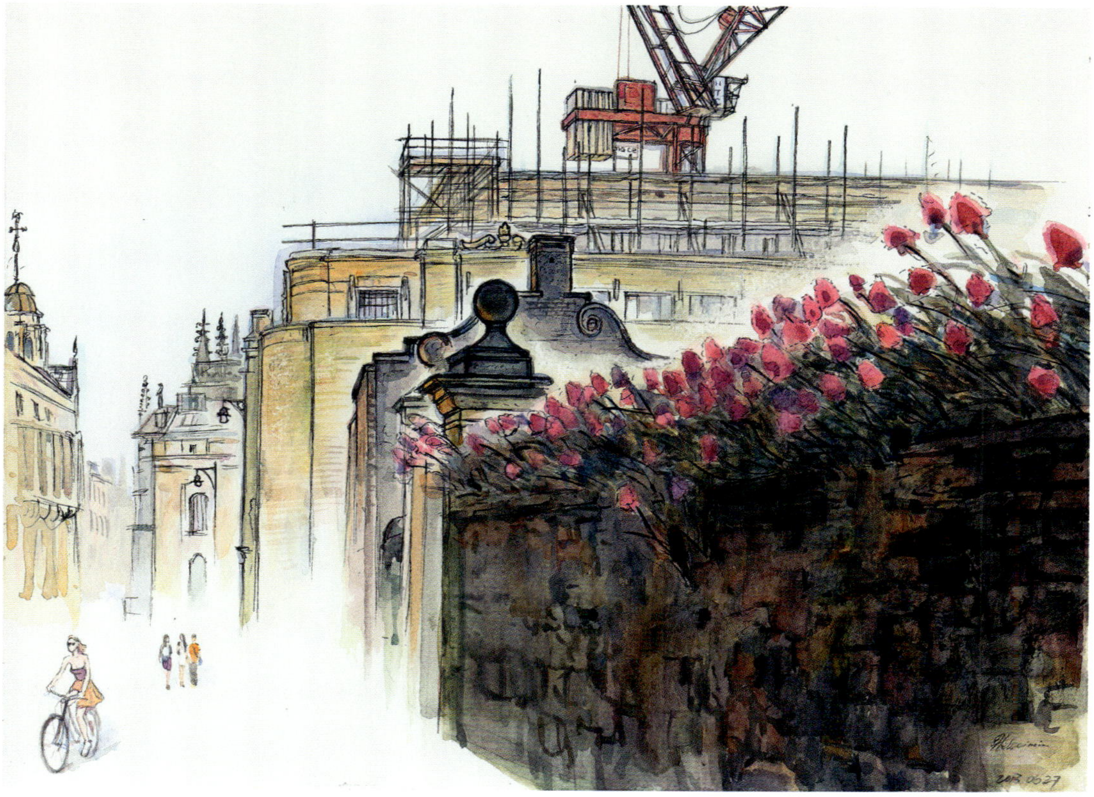

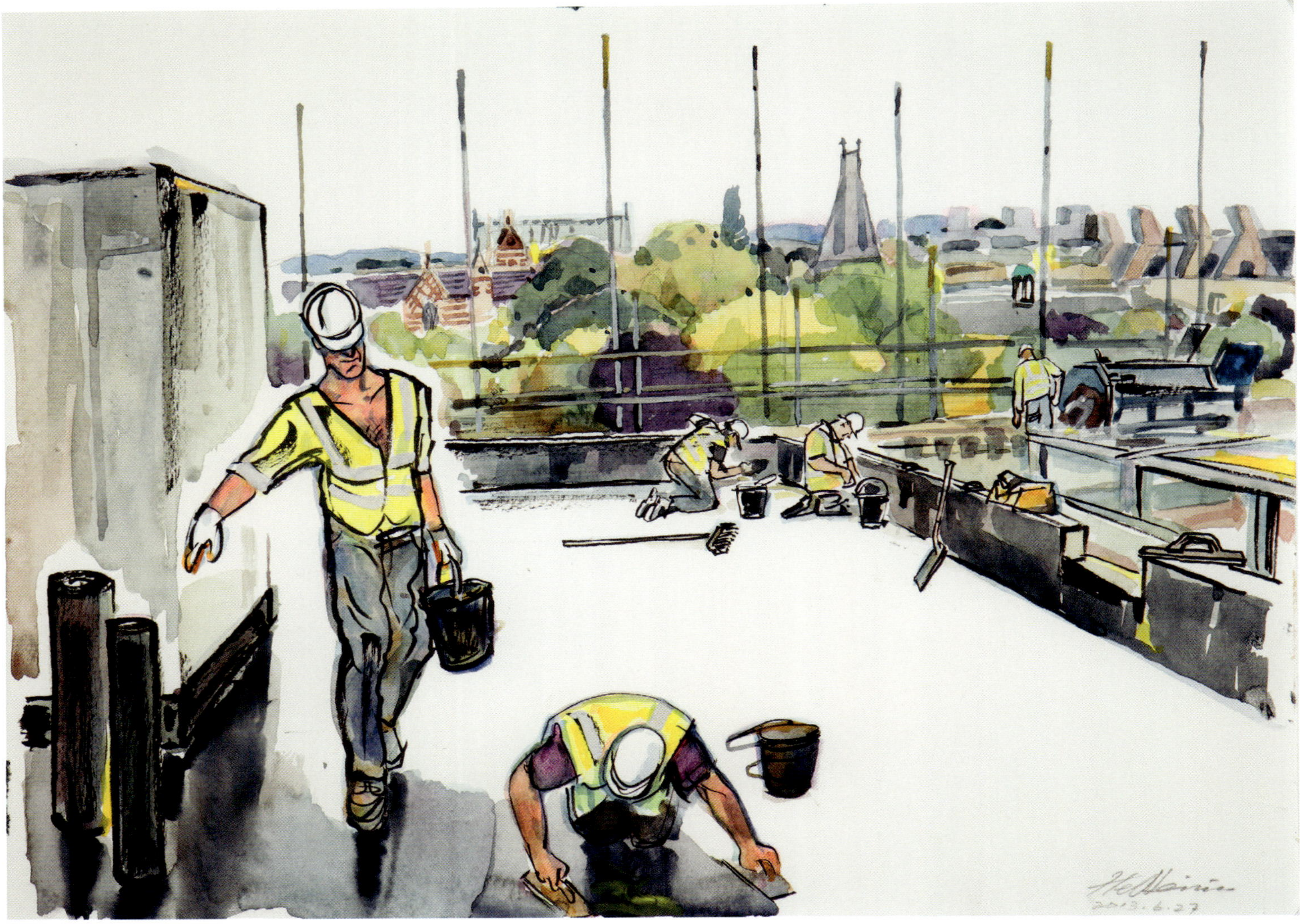

CAT.267
Roofing with asphalt. 27 June 2013.
Watercolour on hot pressed watercolour paper.
Paper size: 29.7 × 42 cm

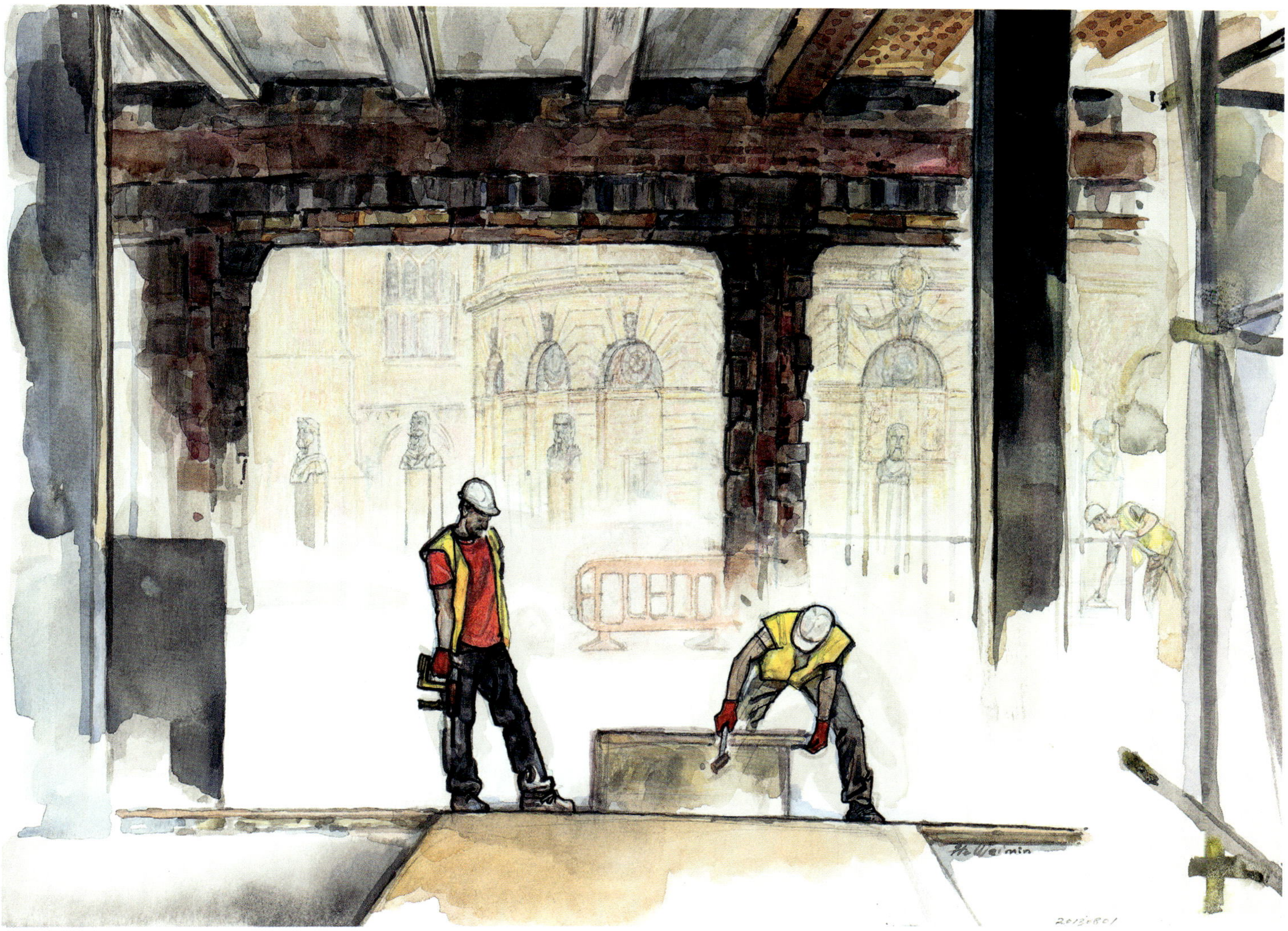

CAT.268

Sun on the Sheldonian. 1 August 2013.
Watercolour on hot pressed watercolour paper.
Paper size: 29.7 × 42 cm

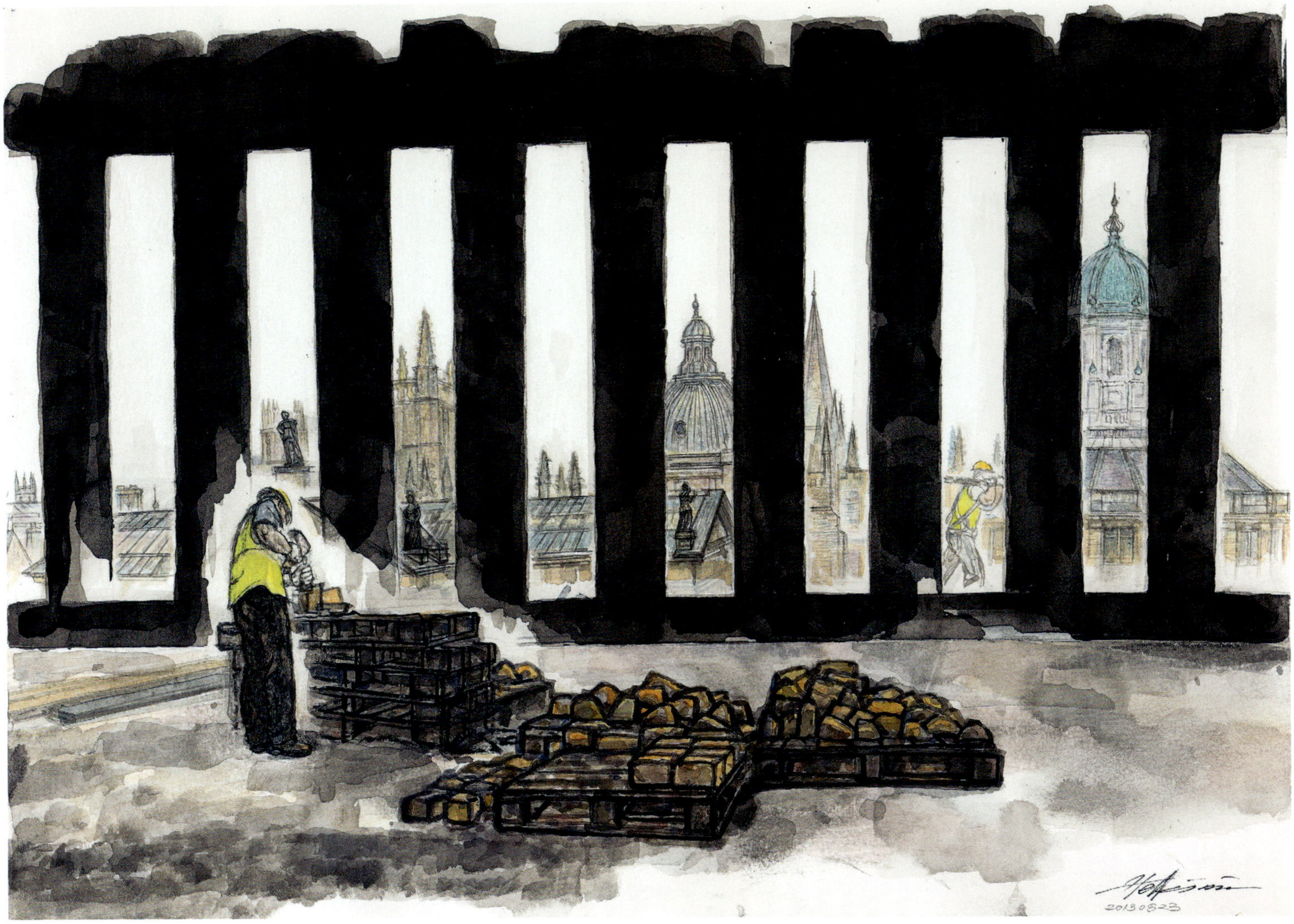

CAT.269
Through the windows of knowledge – the Charles Wendell David Reading Room. 23 August 2013. Watercolour on hot pressed watercolour paper. Paper size: 29.7 × 42 cm

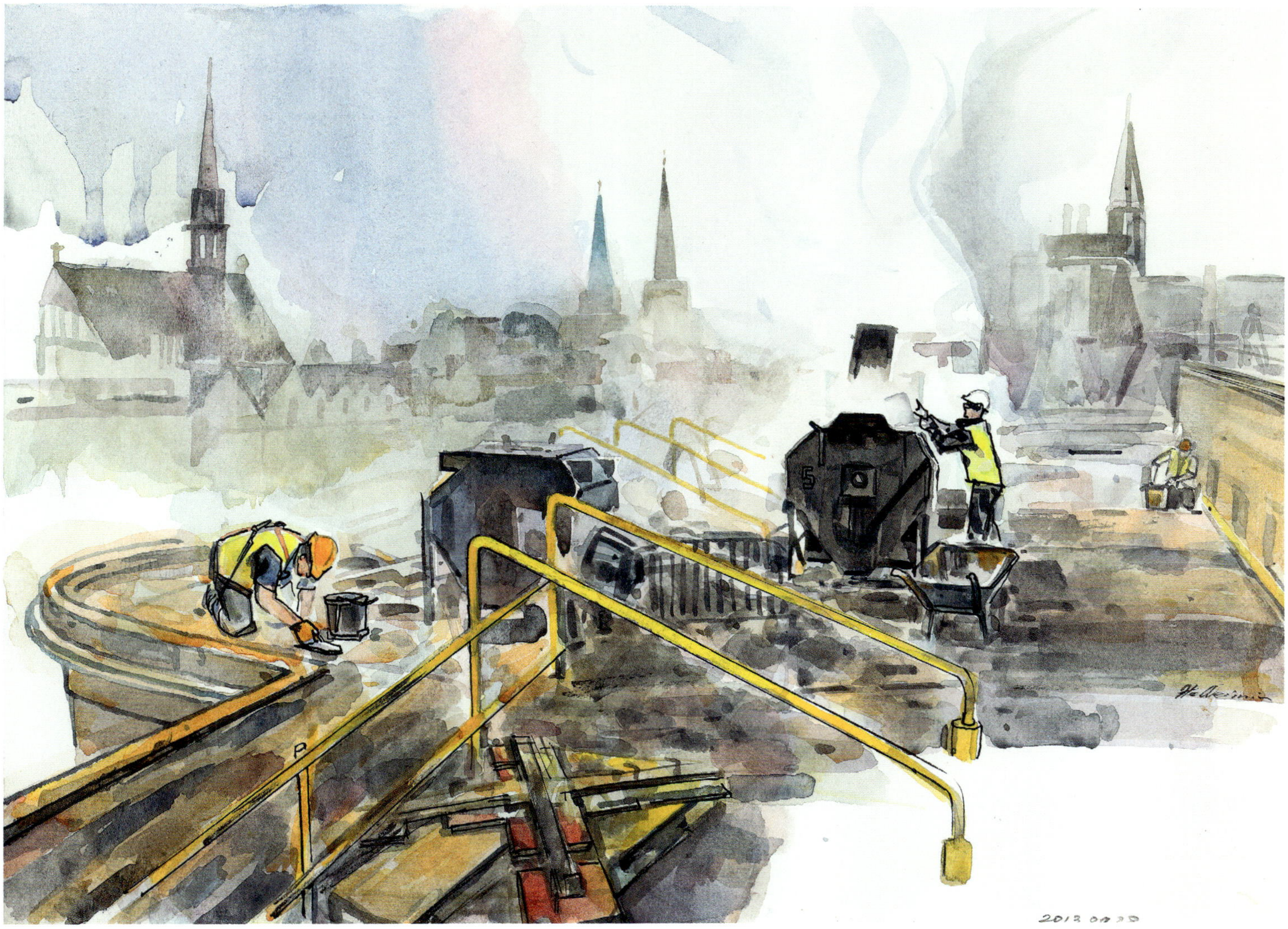

CAT.270
Steam over the spires. 28 September 2013.
Watercolour on hot pressed watercolour paper.
Paper size: 29.7 × 42 cm

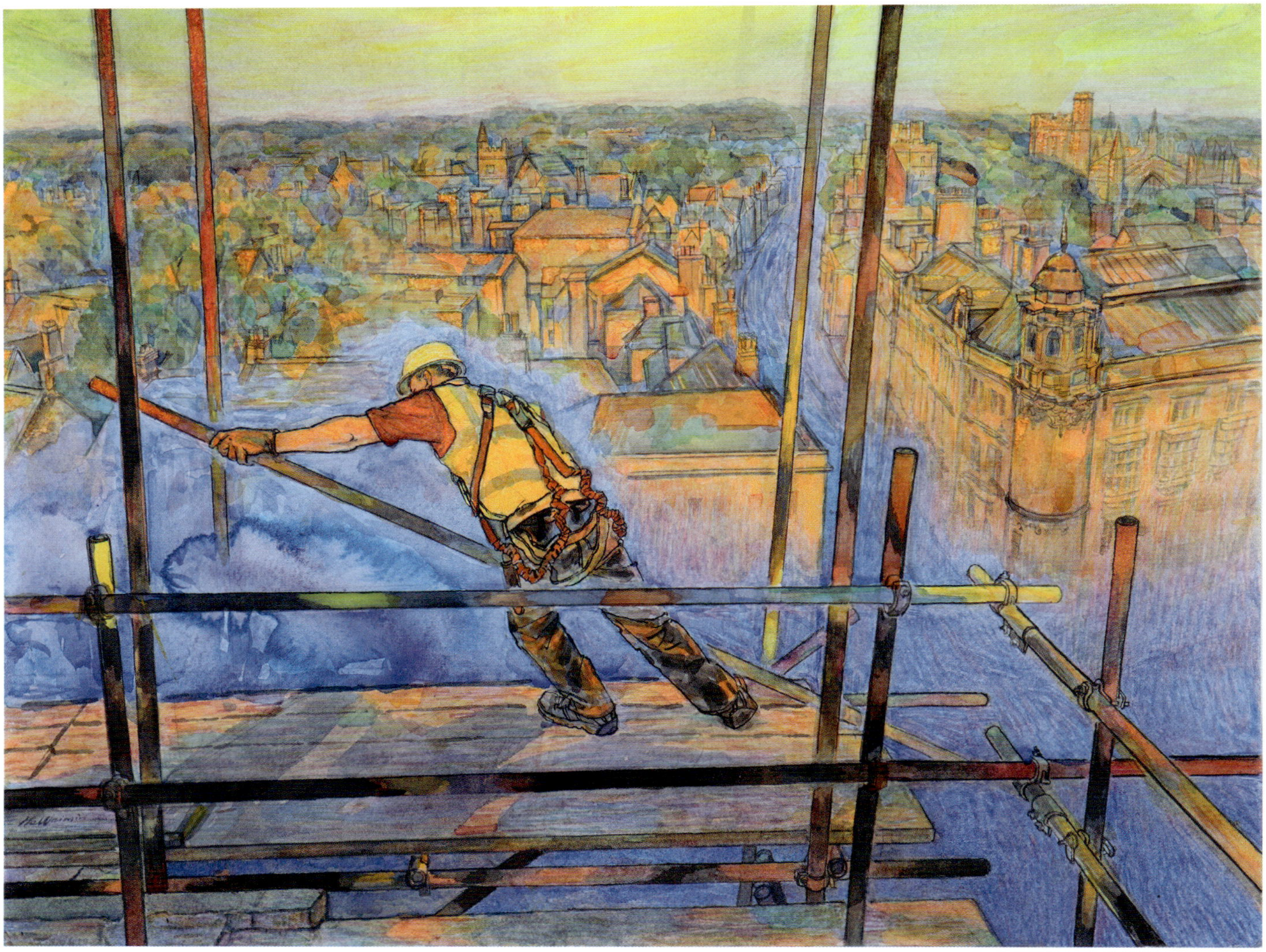

CAT.271
Blue mist. 30 September 2013 (completed in 2016). Watercolour on hot pressed watercolour paper. Paper size: 29.7 × 42 cm

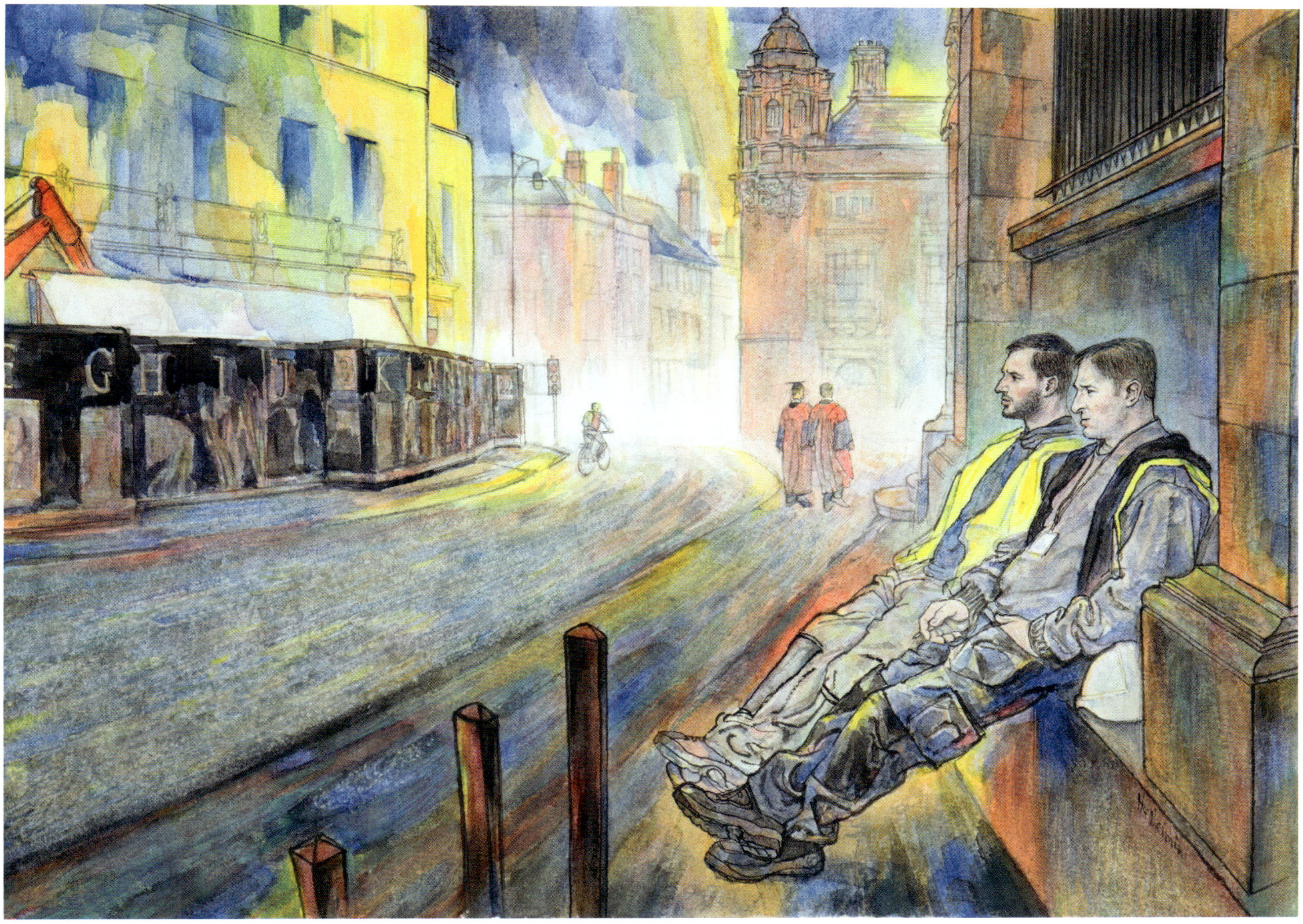

CAT.272

On the Broad. 7 March 2014 (completed in 2016). Watercolour on hot pressed watercolour paper. Paper size: 29.7 × 42 cm

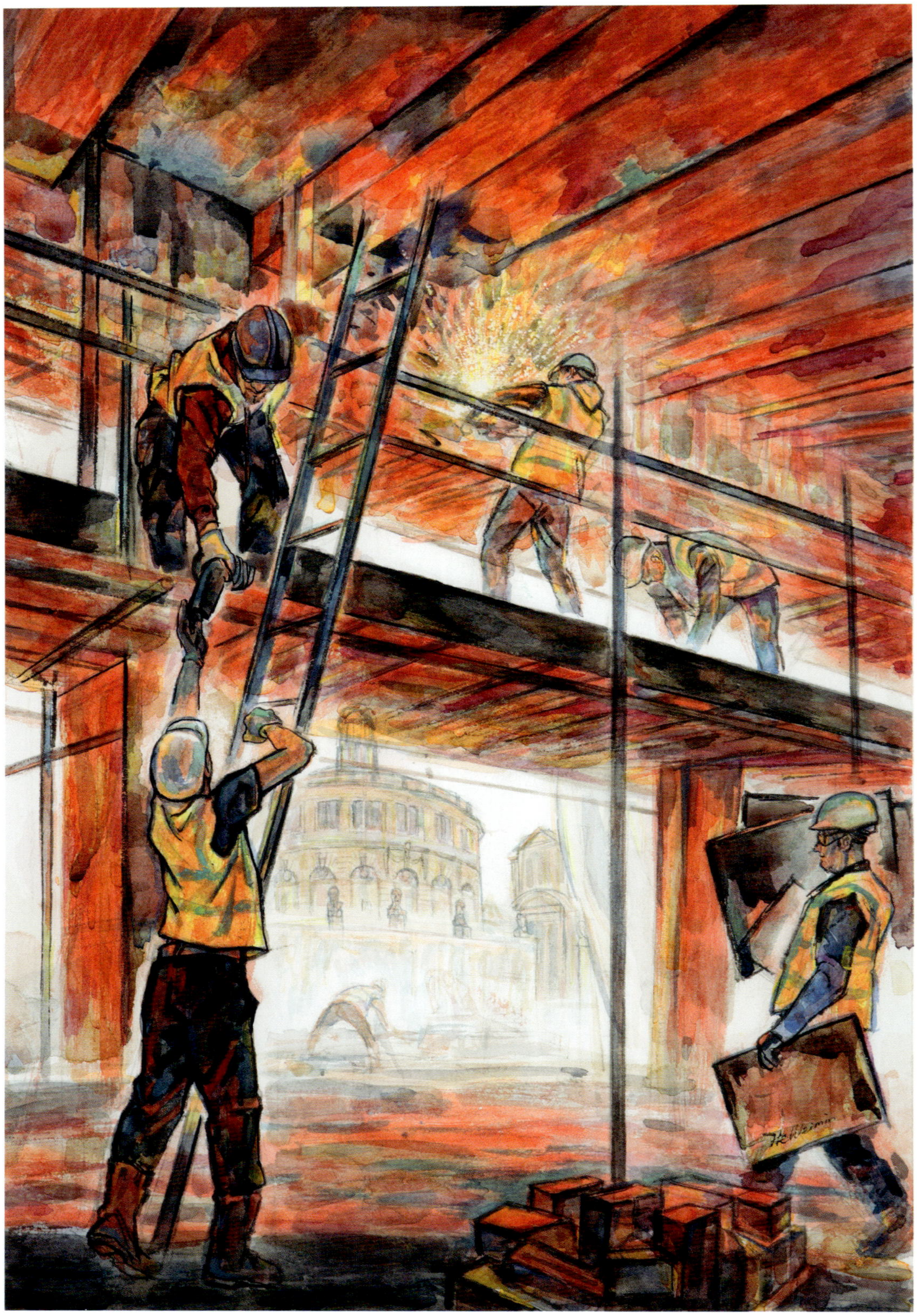

CAT.273

Slates and ladders – work on the roof of the Blackwell Hall.

7 March 2014. Watercolour on hot pressed watercolour paper. Paper size: 42 × 29.7 cm

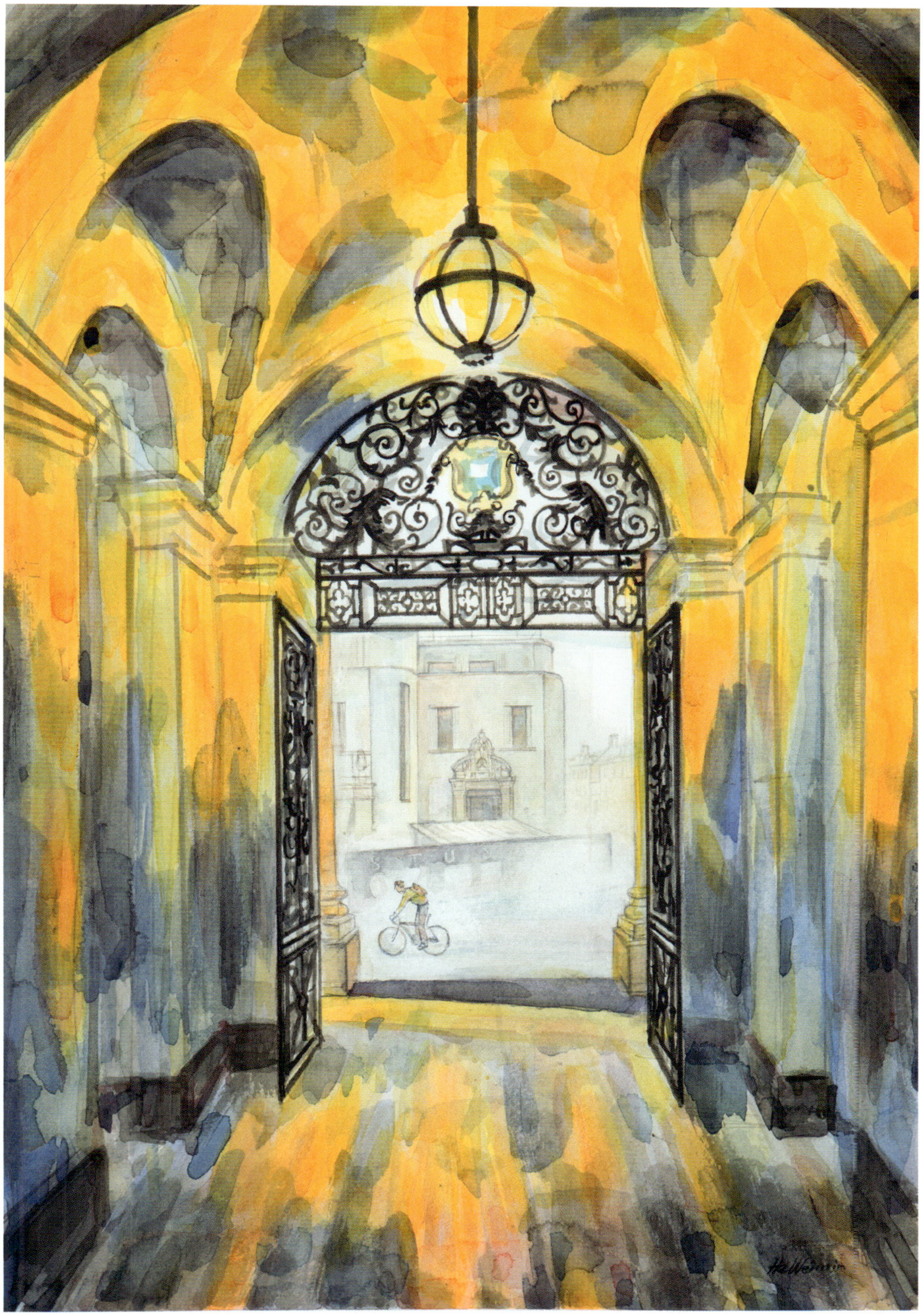

CAT.274
Passing by – the Weston Library, through the Clarendon Building. 24 April 2014. Watercolour on hot pressed watercolour paper (completed in 2016). Paper size: 42 × 29.7cm

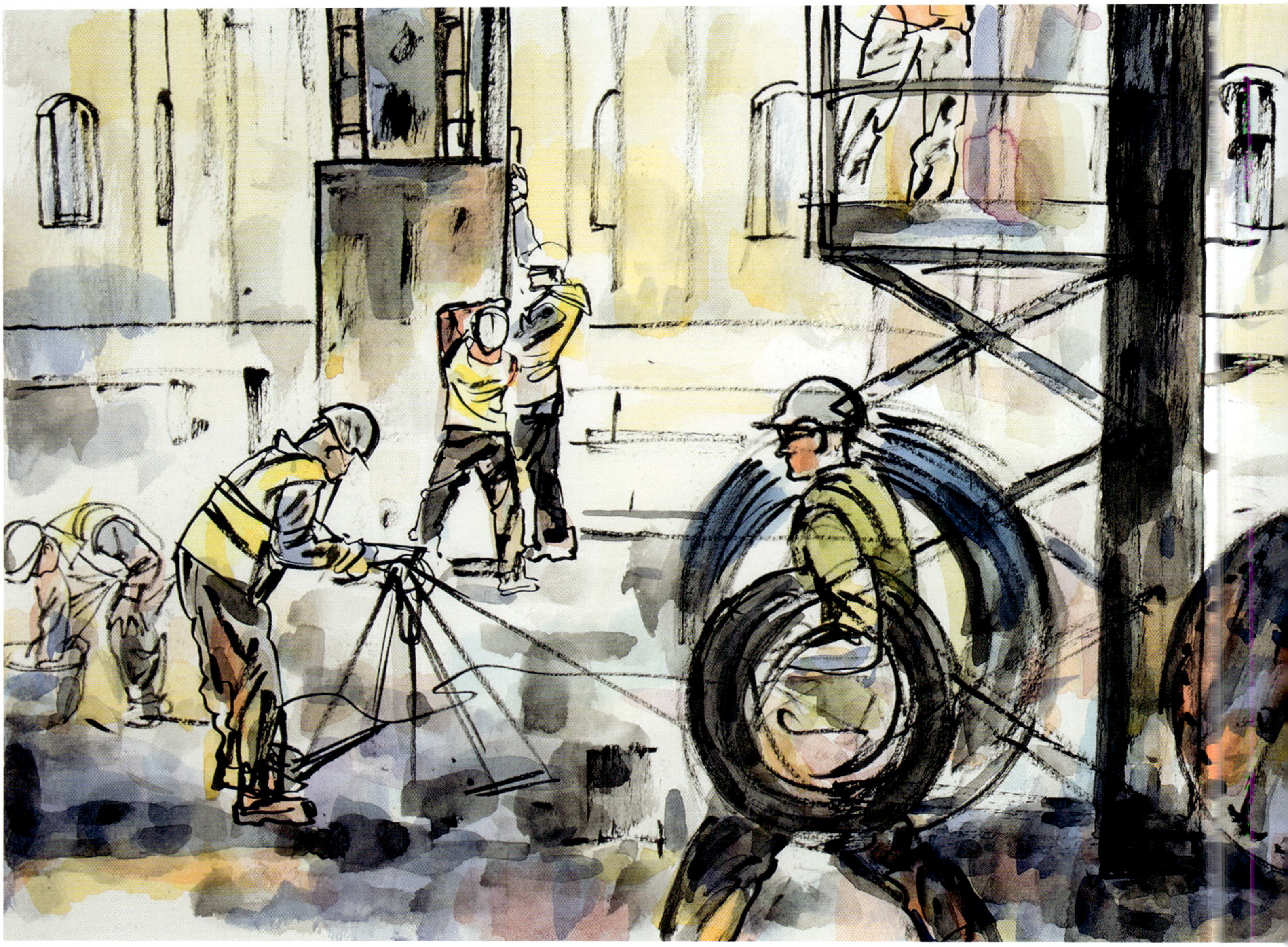

CAT.275
Many trades, one goal – Weston Library.
7 May 2014. Watercolour on sketchbook made of hot pressed watercolour paper. Paper size: 29.7 × 84 cm

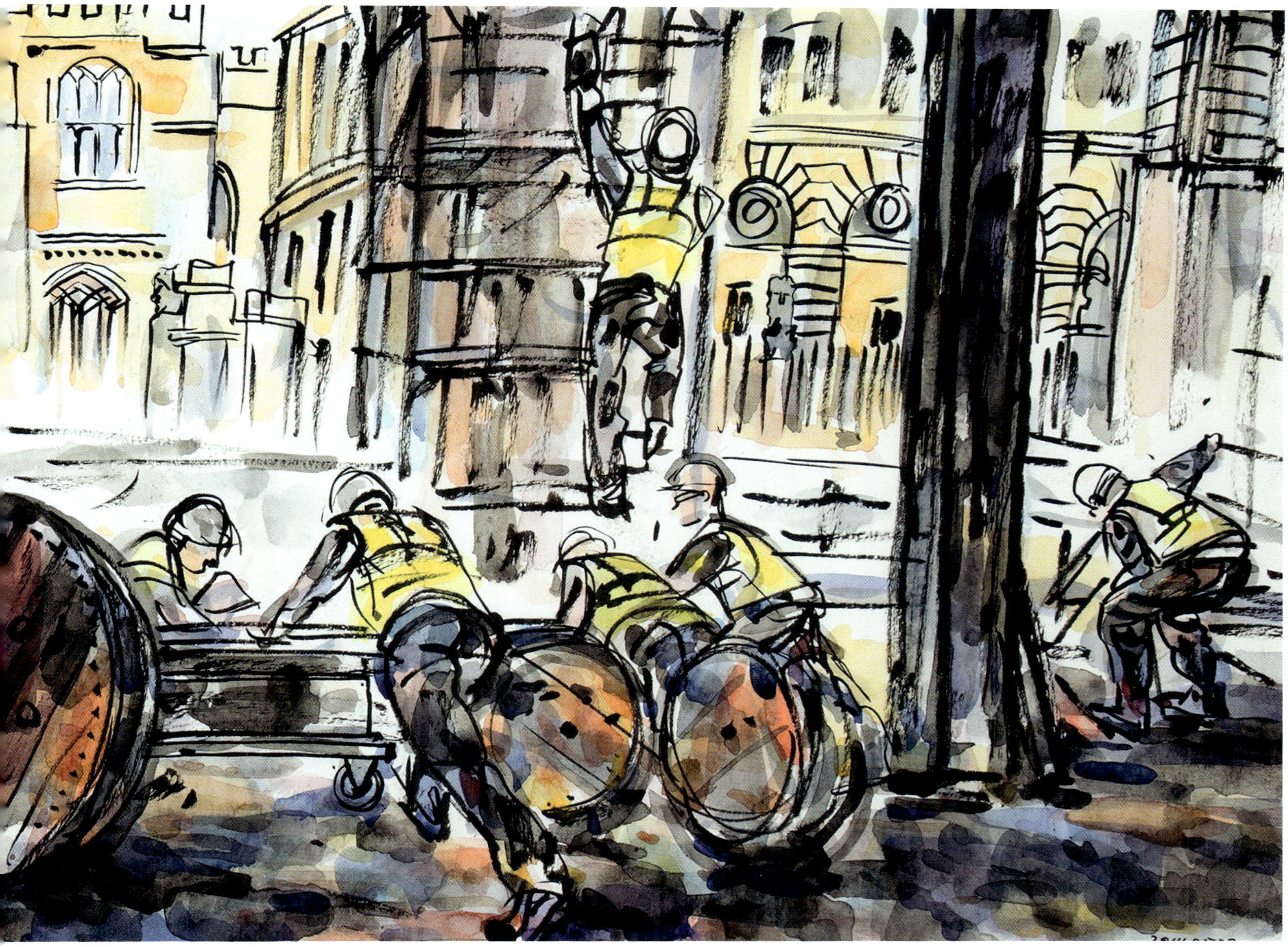

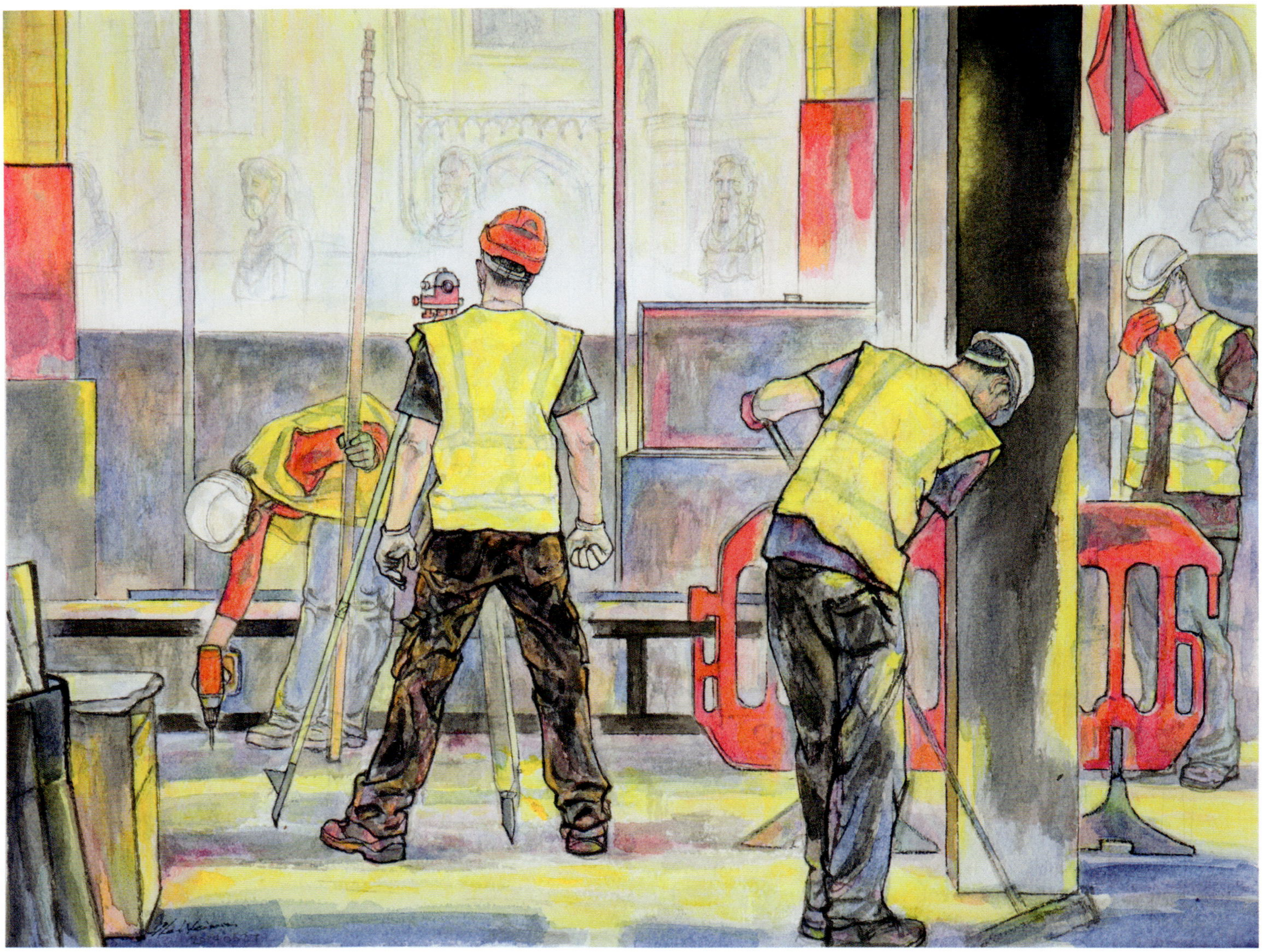

CAT.276
Builders take centre stage – Blackwell Hall of the Weston Library. 27 June 2014 (completed in 2016). Watercolour on hot pressed watercolour paper. Paper size: 29.7 × 42 cm

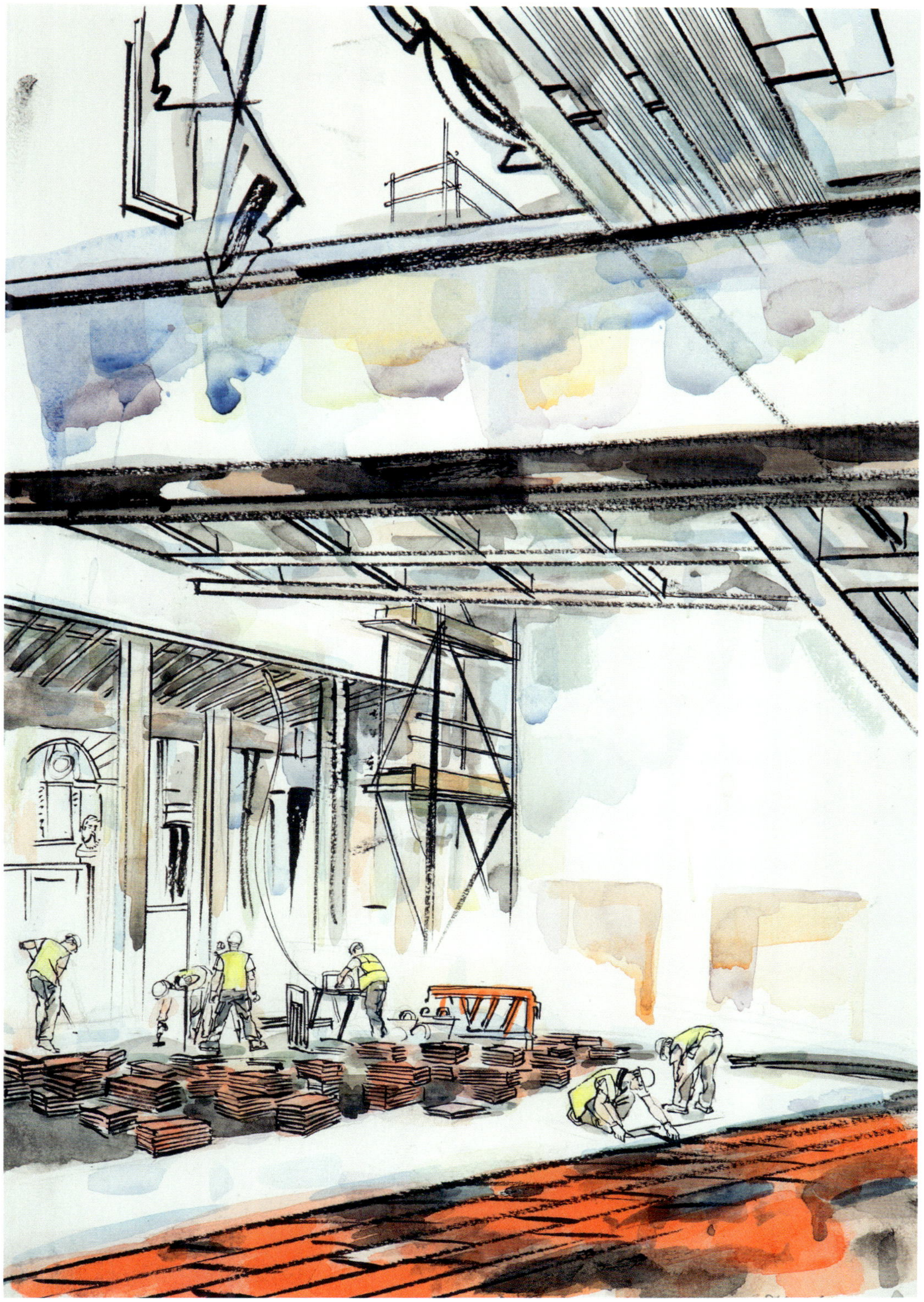

CAT.277
Red slabs of the Blackwell Hall. 27 June 2014. Watercolour on sketchbook made of hot pressed watercolour paper. Paper size: 42 × 29.7 cm

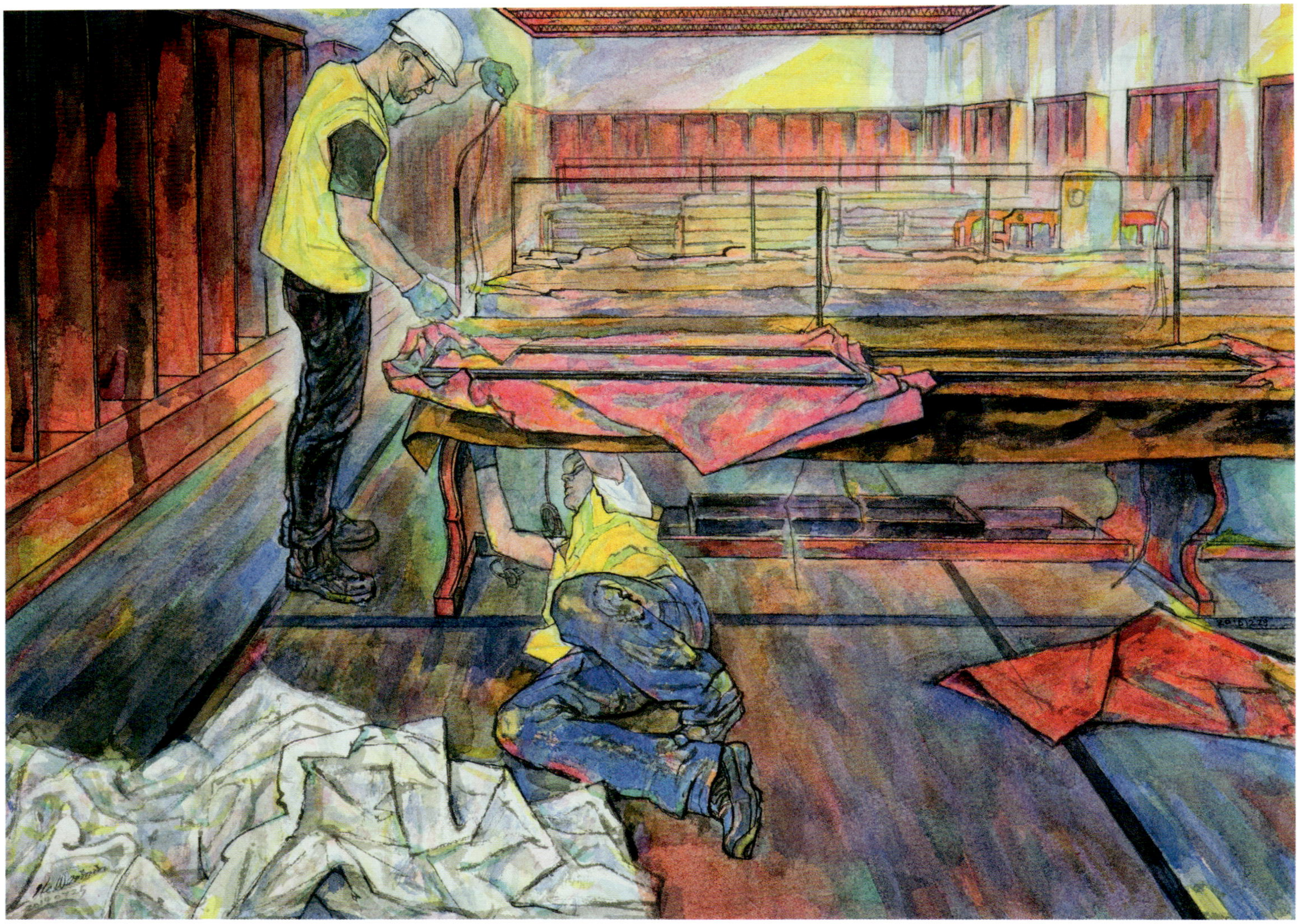

CAT.278

Yellow light in the reading room. 25 July 2014 (completed in 2016). Watercolour on hot pressed watercolour paper. Paper size: 29.7 × 42 cm

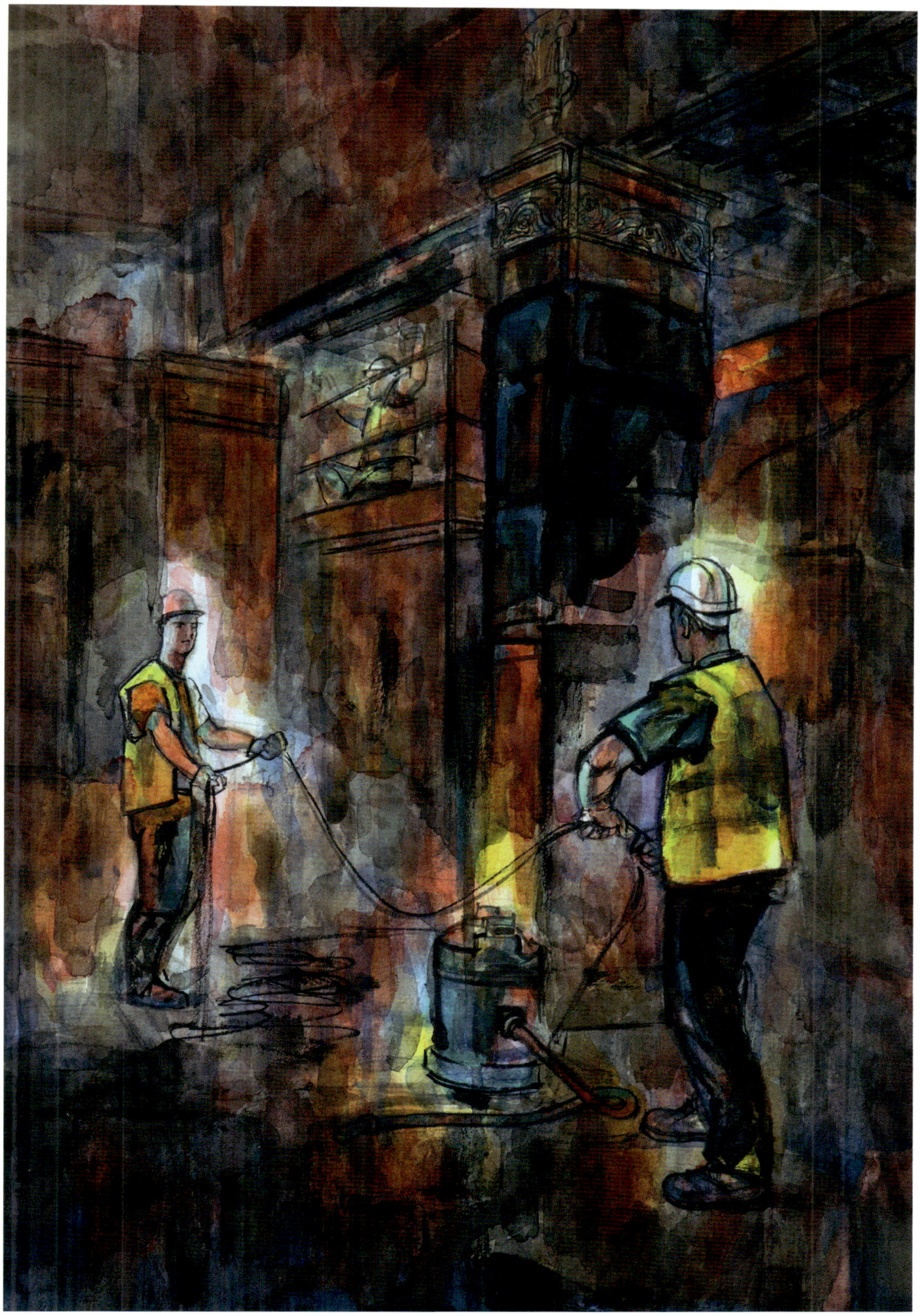

CAT.279
Wiring up the Weston Library.
25 July 2014. Watercolour on hot pressed watercolour paper. Paper size: 42 × 29.7 cm

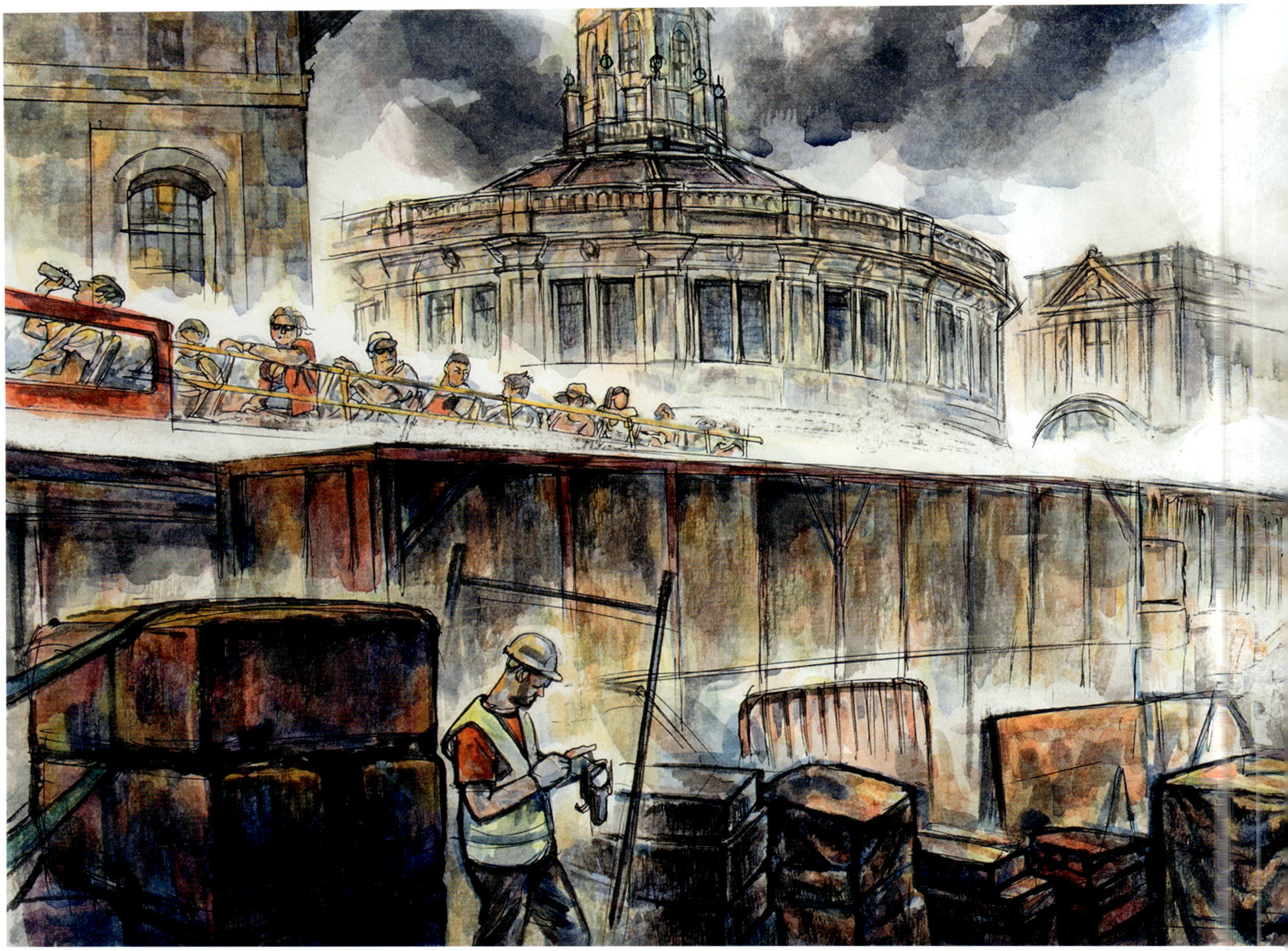

CAT.280
Site seeing – reconstruction of the Weston Library.
8 August 2014 (completed in 2016). Pen and watercolour on sketchbook made of hot pressed watercolour paper. Paper size: 29.7 × 84 cm

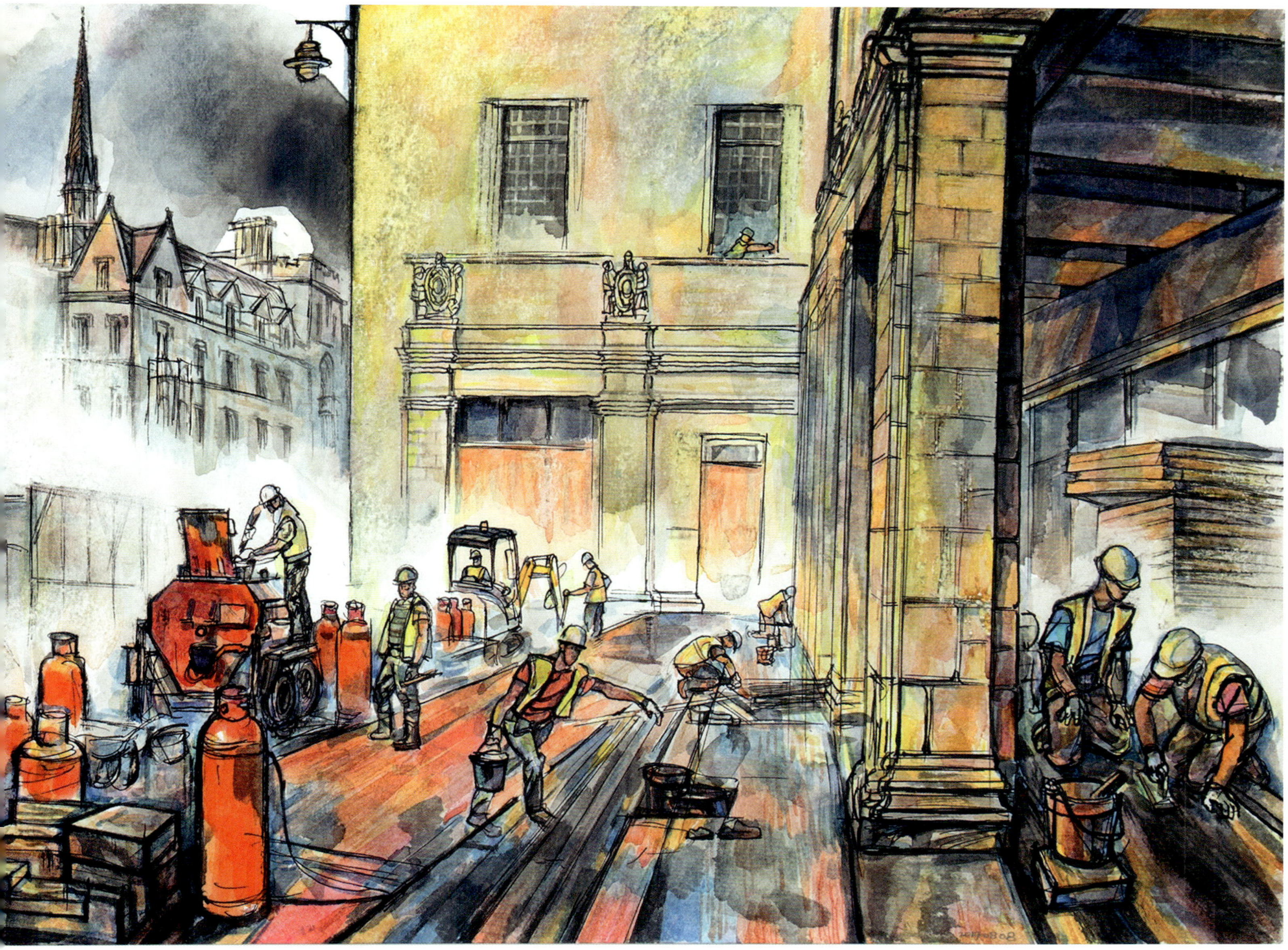

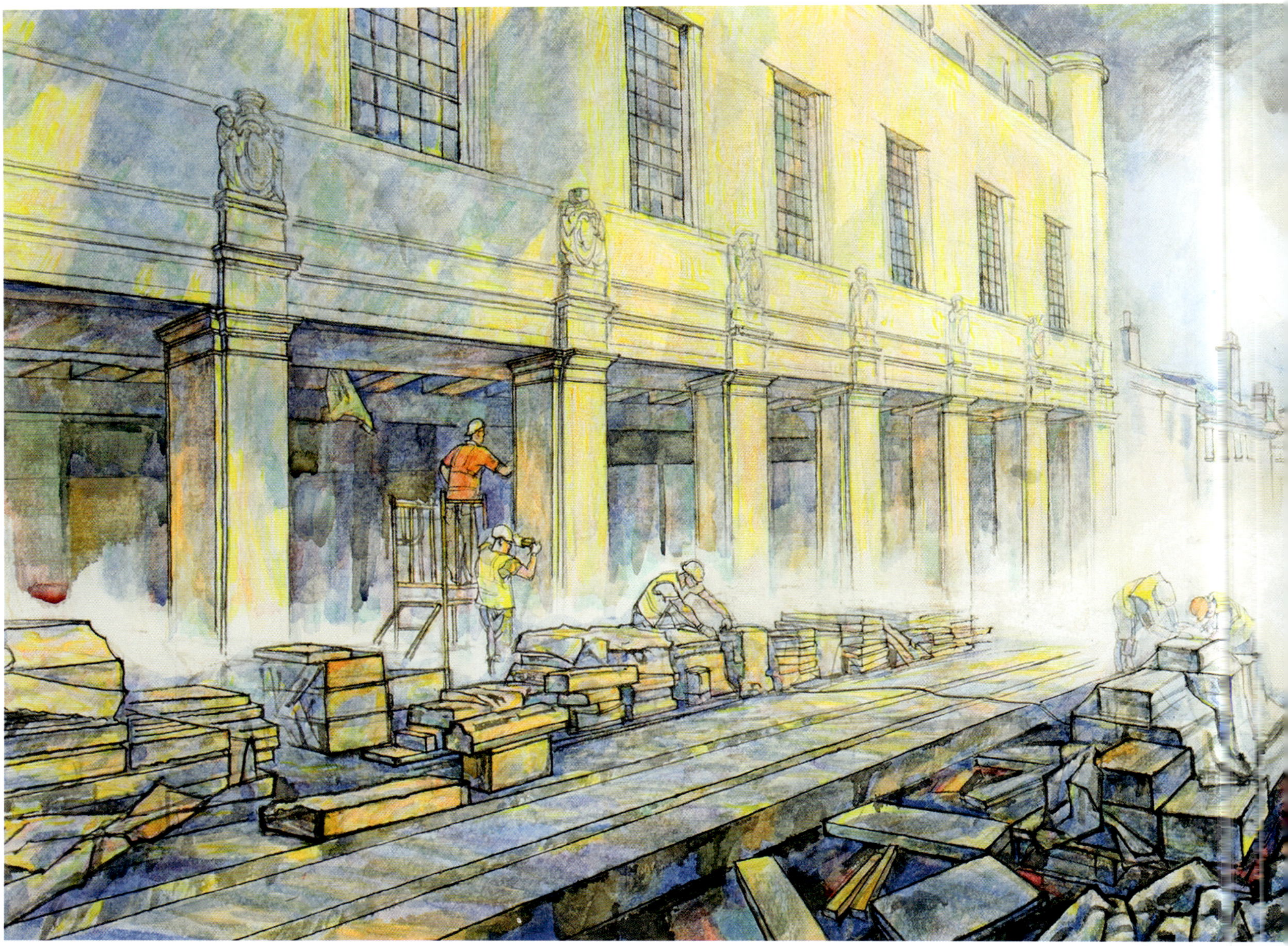

CAT.281
Dust, noise and sunshine – reconstruction of the Weston Library. 29 August 2014 (completed in 2016). Pen and watercolour on sketchbook made of hot pressed watercolour paper. Paper size: 29.7 × 84 cm

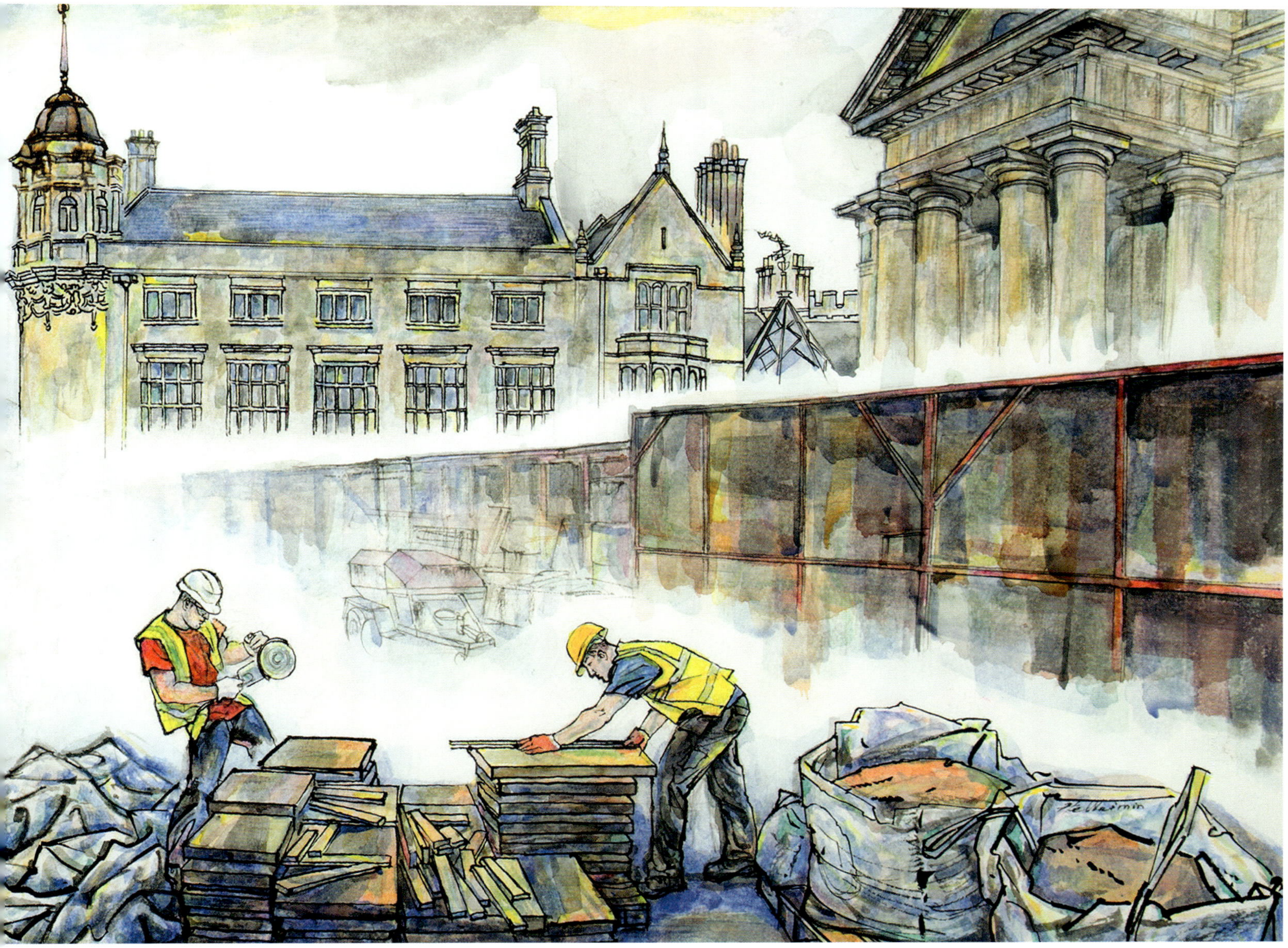

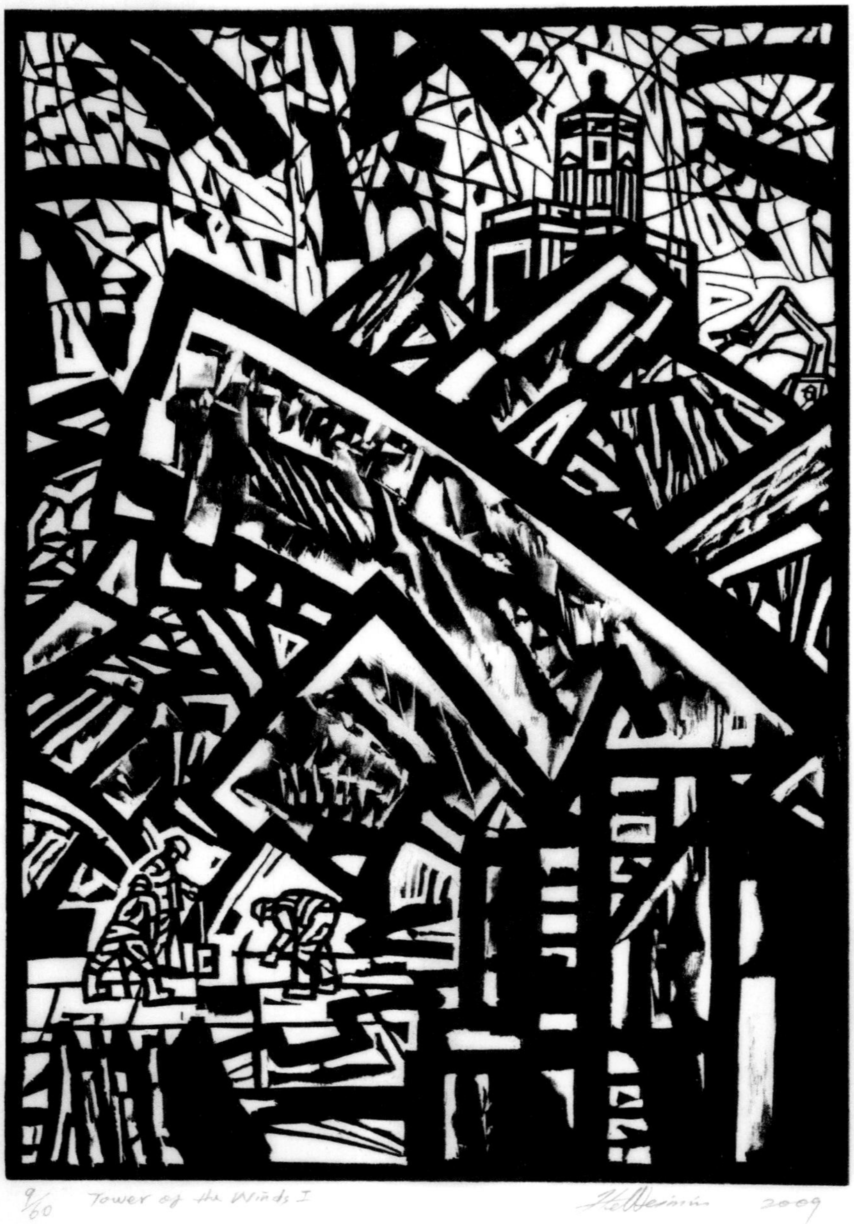

CAT.282
Tower of the winds I. 2009.
Woodcut. Image size: 36 × 26 cm.
Paper size: 46 × 36 cm

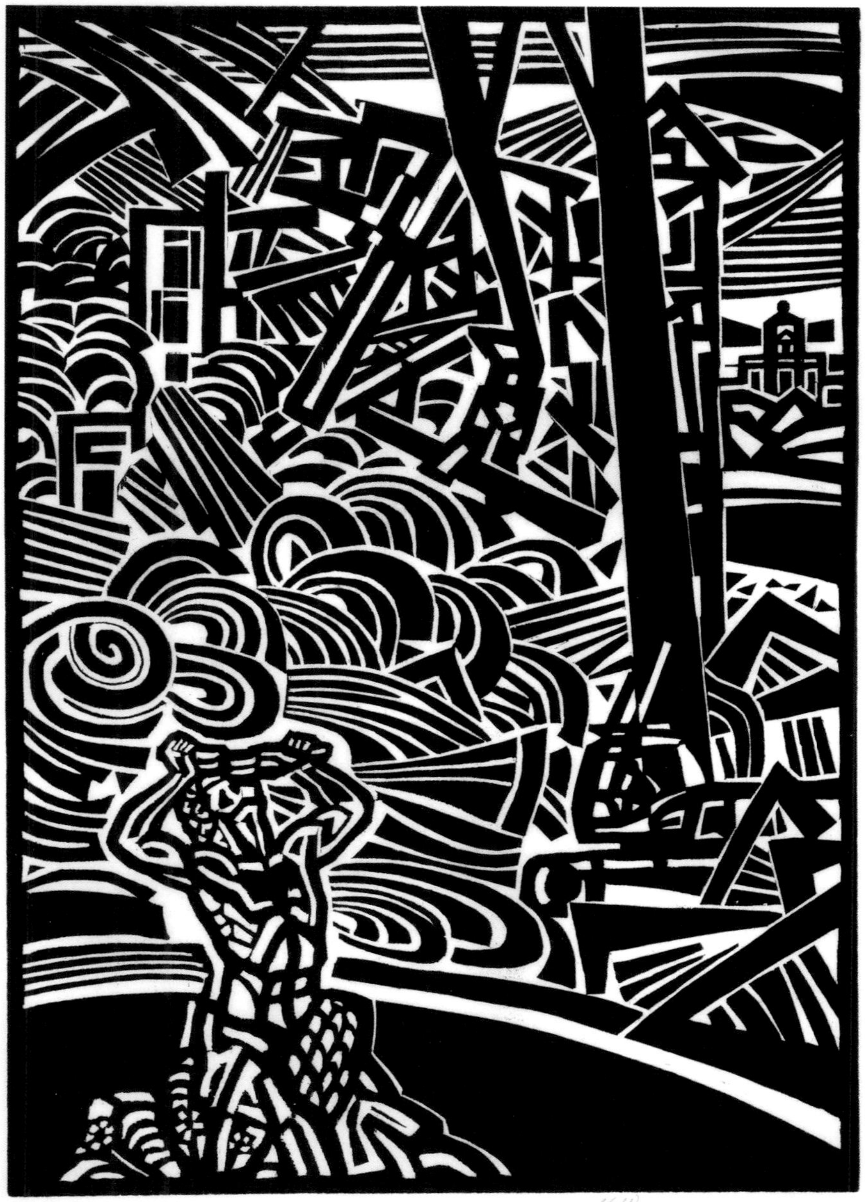

CAT.283
Tower of the winds II. 2009.
Woodcut. Image size: 36 × 26 cm.
Paper size: 46 × 36 cm

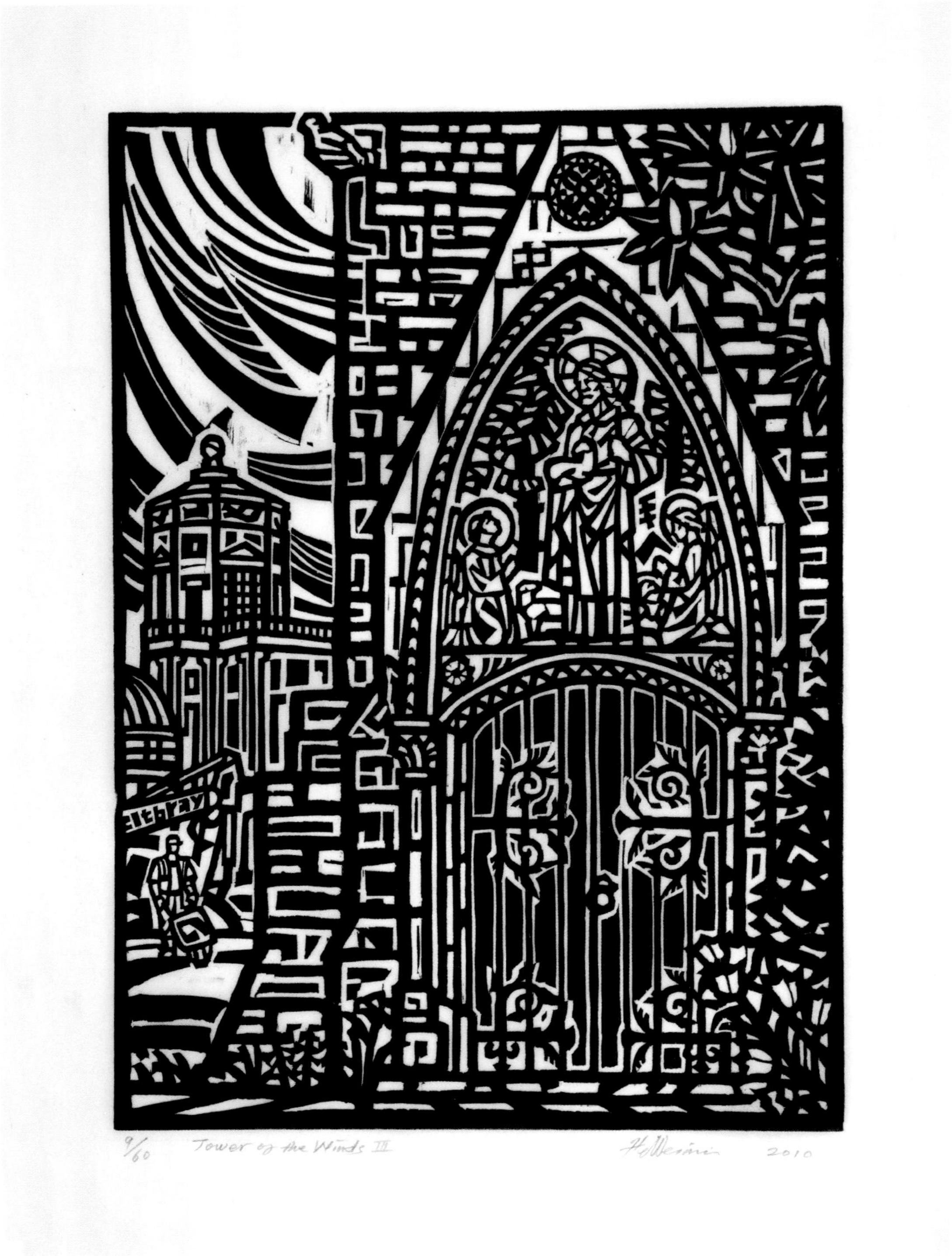

CAT.284
Tower of the winds III. 2010.
Woodcut. Image size: 36 × 26 cm.
Paper size: 46 × 36 cm

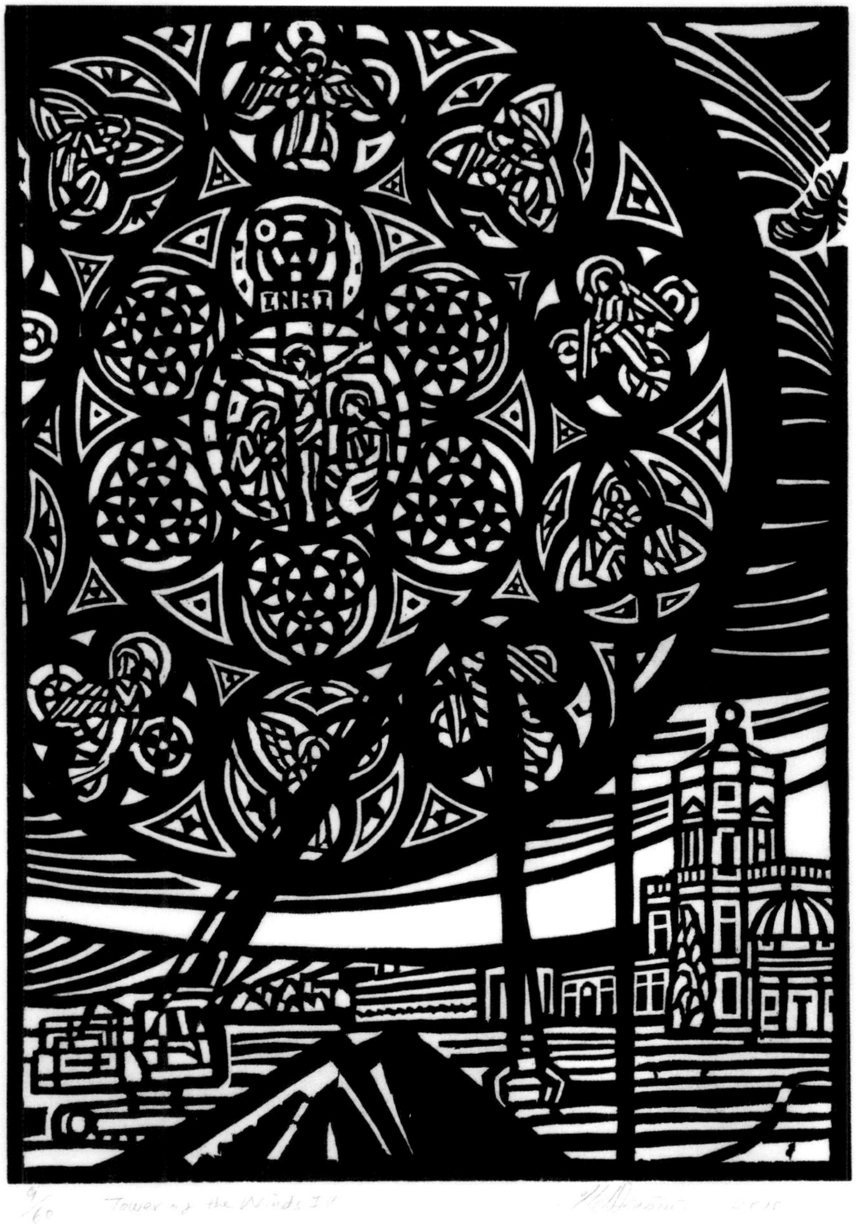

CAT.285
Tower of the winds IV. 2010.
Woodcut. Image size: 36 × 26 cm.
Paper size: 46 × 36 cm

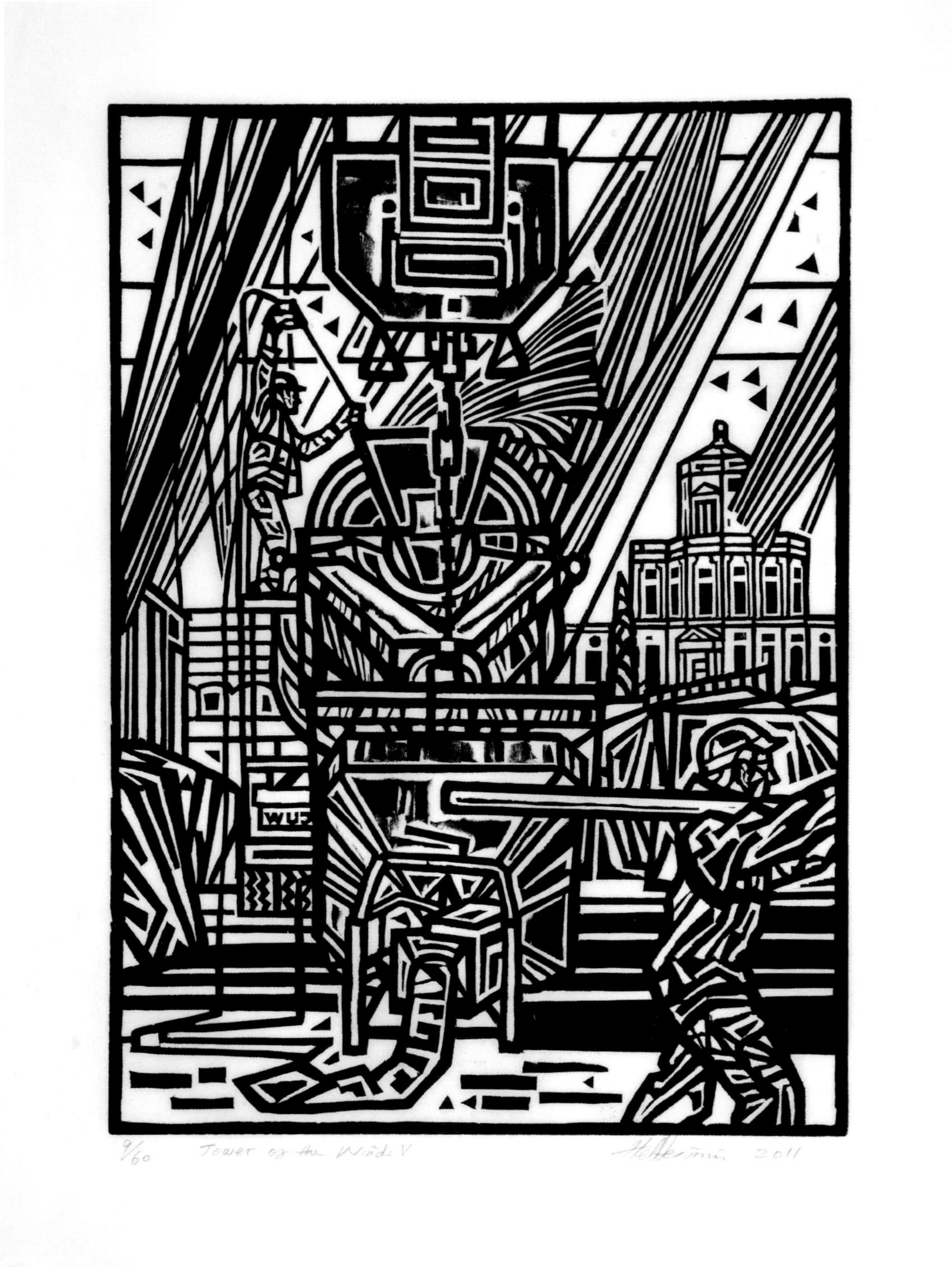

CAT.286
Tower of the winds V
2011. Woodcut.
Image size: 36 × 26 cm
Paper size: 46 × 36 cm

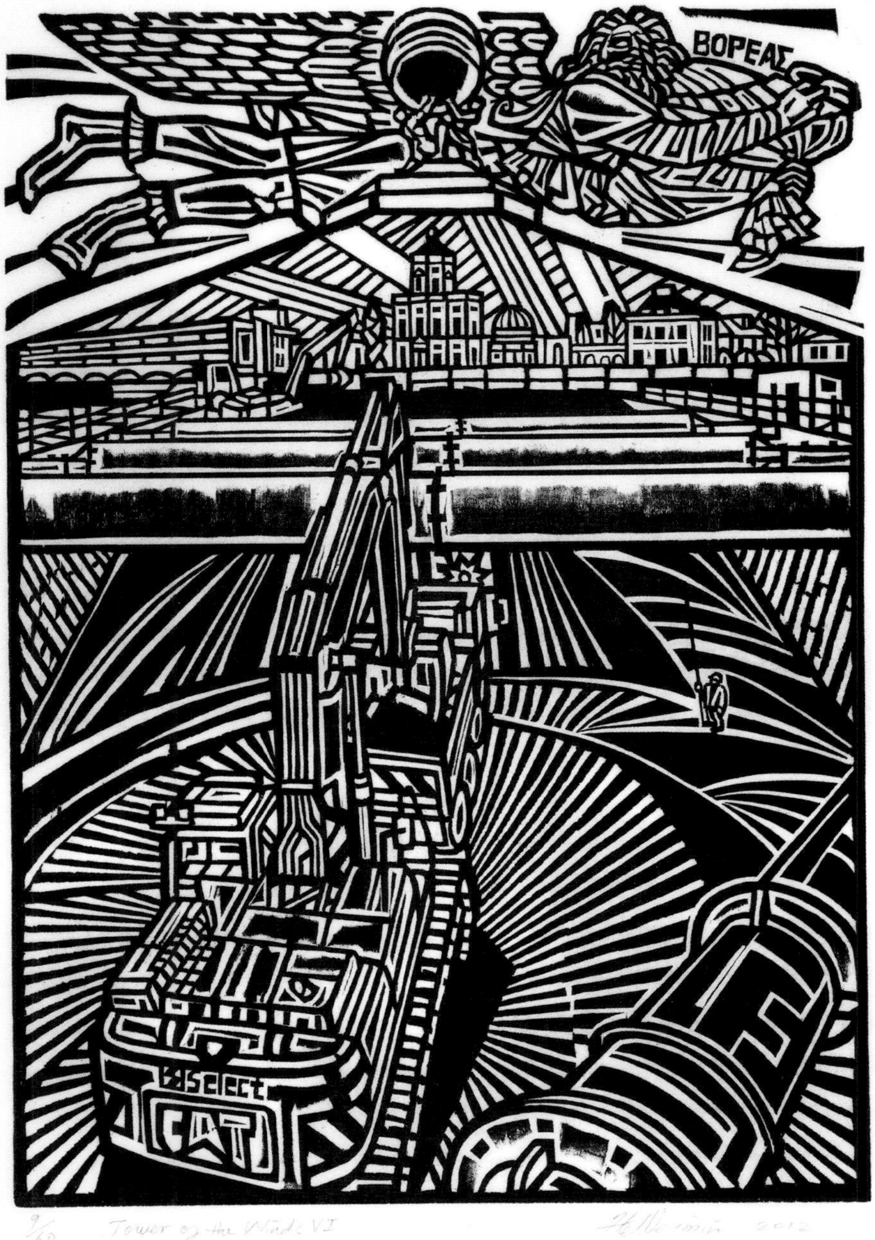

CAT.287
Tower of the winds VI
2012. Woodcut.
Image size: 36 × 26 cm
Paper size: 46 × 36 cm

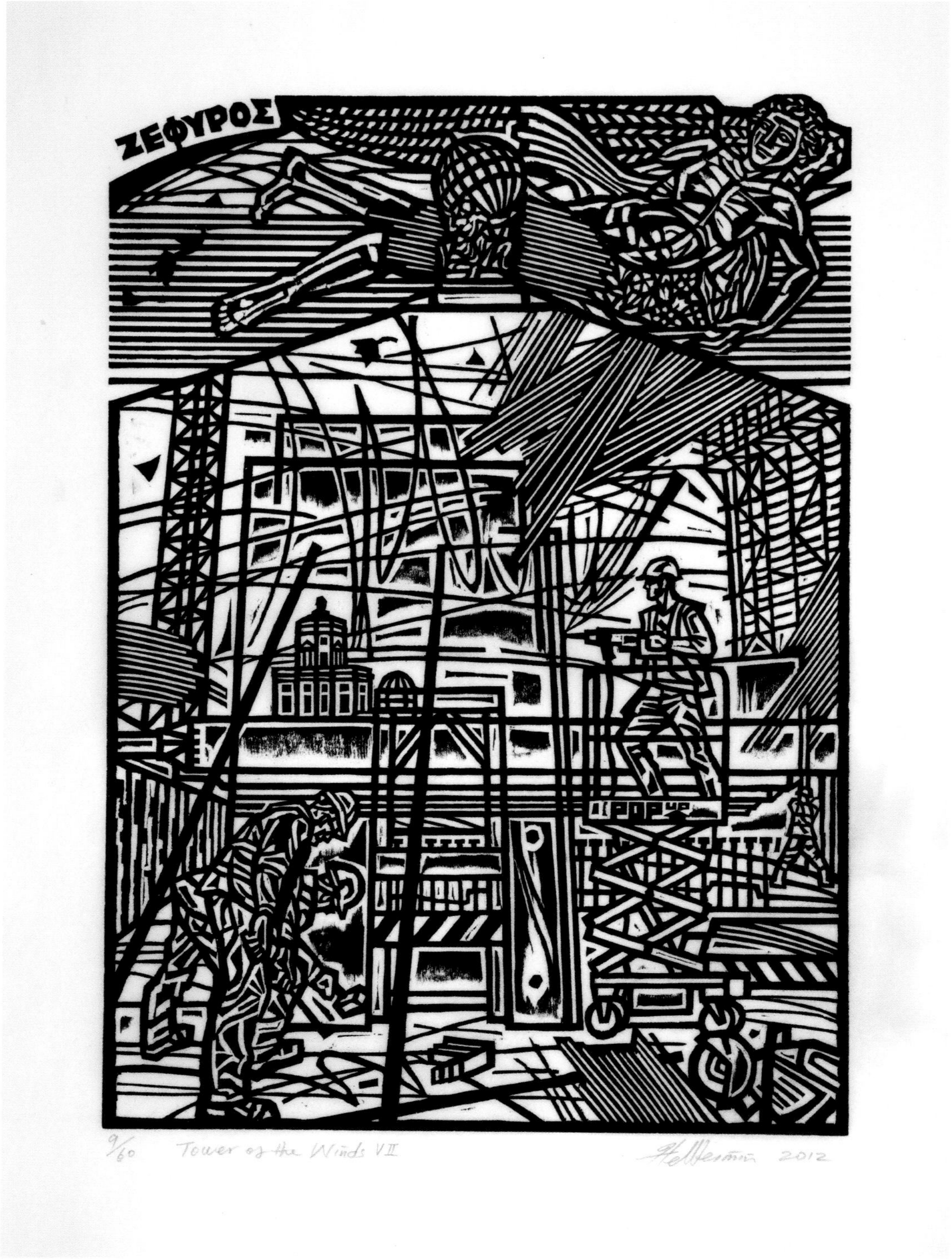

CAT.288
Tower of the winds VII. 2012.
Woodcut. Image size: 36 × 26 cm.
Paper size: 46 × 36 cm

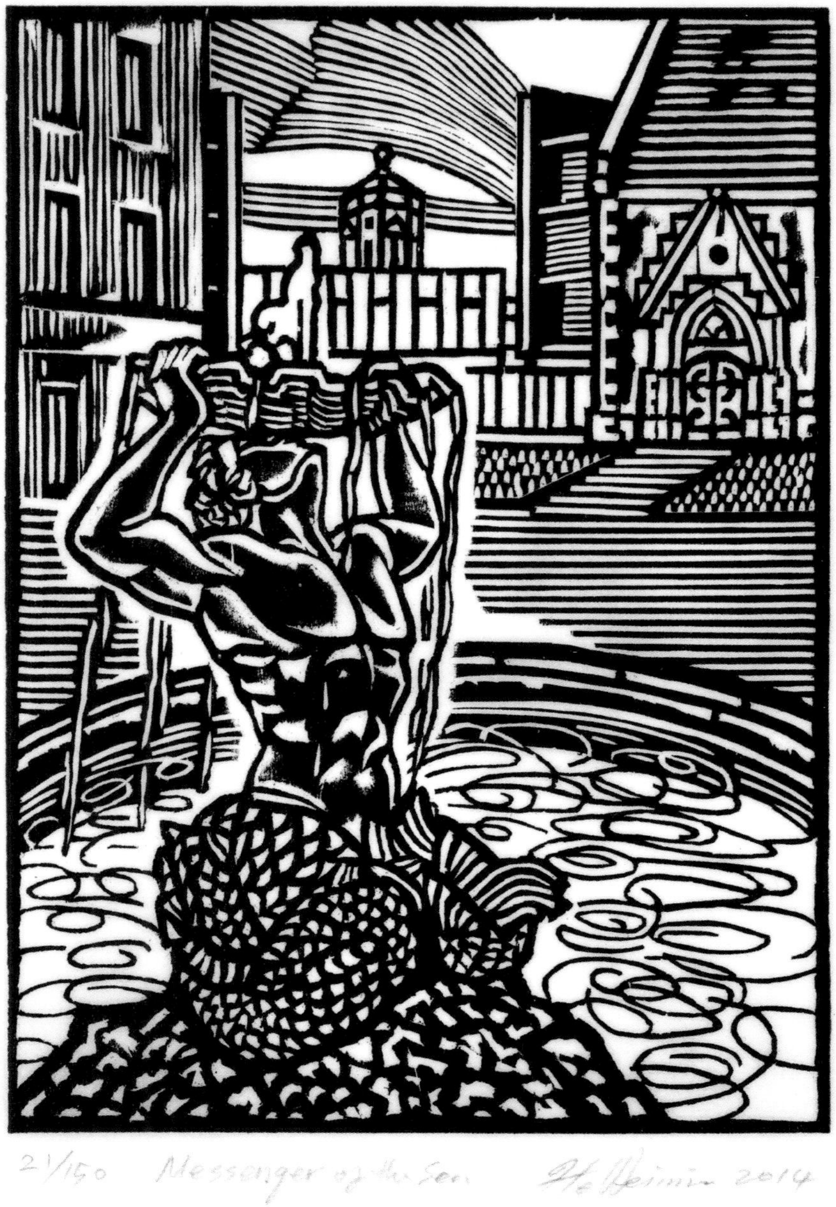

CAT.289
Messenger of the sea. 2014.
Woodcut. Image size: 19 × 14 cm.
Paper size: 31 × 24 cm

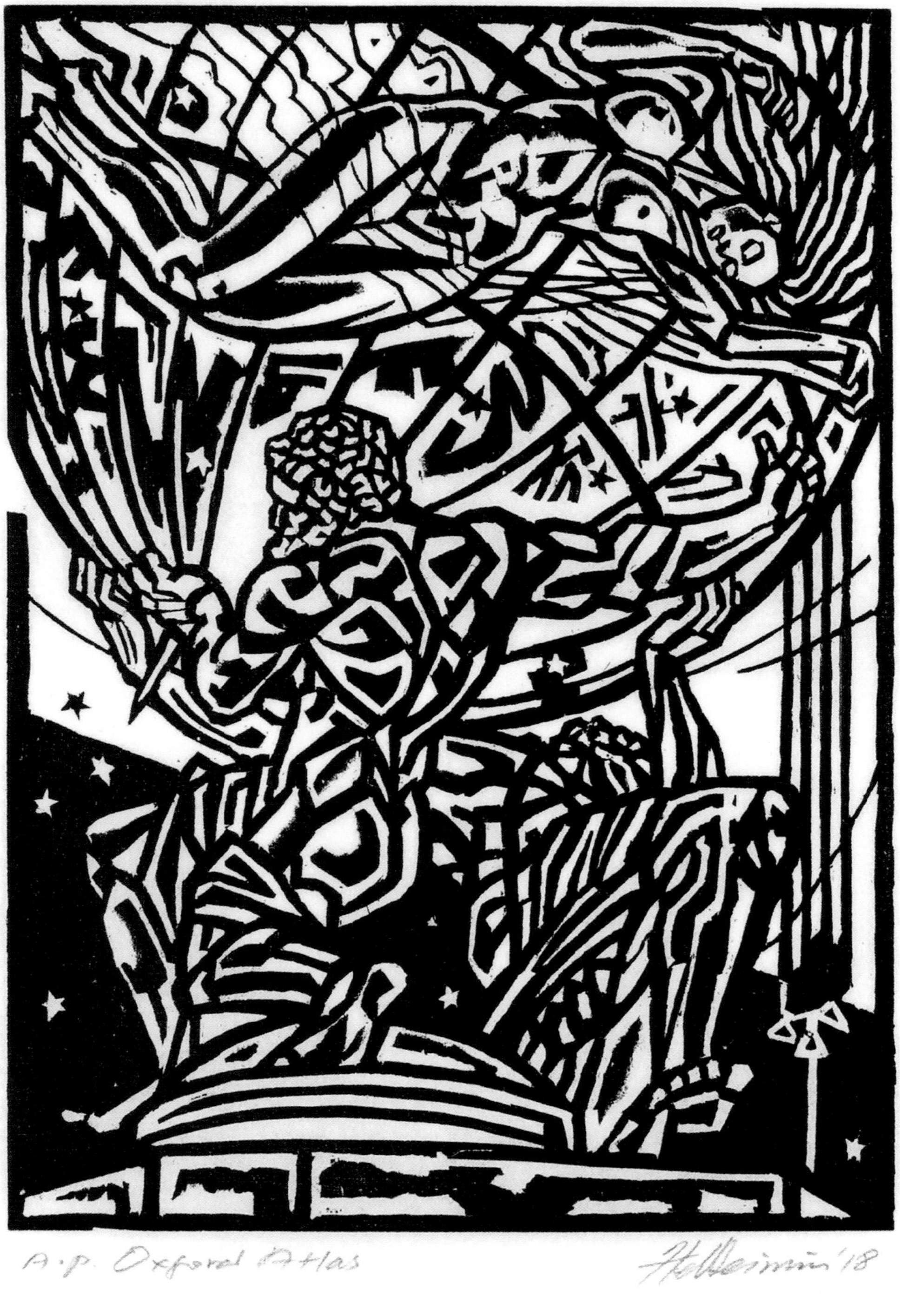

CAT.290
Oxford Atlas. 2018. Woodcut.
Image size: 19 × 14 cm. Paper size: 31 × 24 cm